Plan of the Book

Why do you need this new edition?

This edition of *The Little, Brown Handbook* differs from the previous edition in countless ways. Here are six that make the book indispensable:

1. Media-rich eText versions for *MyCompLab, MyWritingLab*, and the iPad ▪ **Video tutorials** illustrate key principles. ▪ **Podcasts** discuss common questions about grammar and usage. ▪ **Sample papers and documents** provide models of common writing assignments. ▪ **Exercises** from the handbook and additional exercises give opportunities for practice. ▪ **Checklists** from the handbook allow you to adapt key summaries for your own use ▪ *MyCompLab* and *MyWritingLab* include additional resources on grammar, writing, and research.

2. More help with academic writing ▪ An introduction on **joining the academic community** provides tips for succeeding in face-to-face and online classes. ▪ Discussions of **genre** help you get started on college writing assignments. ▪ Discussions of **academic integrity and writing responsibly** throughout help you write successfully in an academic setting.

3. More help with research writing and documentation ▪ A revised chapter on **plagiarism** helps you recognize and avoid plagiarism. ▪ Material on **evaluating online sources**—Web sites, social-networking sites, blogs, wikis, and multimedia—shows you how to distinguish between reliable and unreliable sources. ▪ Updated **annotated sample sources** illustrate how to find and format bibliographic information in articles and books and on Web sites.

4. More help with the writing process ▪ Coverage of **thesis** explains how to pose a thesis question and move from the question to a thesis statement. ▪ Coverage of **paragraphs** foregrounds relating paragraphs in an essay.

5. New help with visual and media literacy ▪ A new chapter on **presenting writing** helps you make choices when designing documents, using visuals and other media, writing for the Web, and making oral presentations. ▪ Chapters on **critical reading, reading arguments, and working with sources** show how to analyze ads, graphs, and other visuals.

6. More help with grammar and usage ▪ More than twenty **new and revised exercises** give hands-on practice. ▪ **New and revised** ⟨CULTURE LANGUAGE⟩ notes provide added help if you are using standard American English as a second language or dialect. ▪ **Revised chapters on effective words** discuss and illustrate online dictionaries and thesauruses and give tips for avoiding the shortcuts of online communication in academic writing.

ALWAYS LEARNING

MyCompLab®

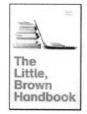

The Little, Brown Handbook

MYCOMPLAB STUDENT REGISTRATION

Before You Begin
To register for MyCompLab, you will need:
- ☑ **A MyCompLab student access code** (packaged with your new text, available standalone at your bookstore, or available for purchase with a credit card at www.pearsoncustom.com/co/ppccenglish
- ☑ **A valid email address that you check regularly.**

In addition, your instructor will provide you with:
- ☑ A **Course ID** needed to join your instructor's course. _____

REGISTRATION AND LOGIN
HOW TO GET A STUDENT ACCESS CODE: With your textbook.
Receive an access code card when you purchase a new Pearson English textbook or check with your bookstore to purchase a standalone access code card.
HOW TO REGISTER A STUDENT ACCESS CODE
- From www.pearsoncustom.com/co/ppccenglish
  - Click *Student* in the "Register" box
  - Enter your **Course ID**, which your instructor provided. If you **do not** know your Course ID, do not continue the registration process. Please contact your instructor.
  - **Sign in** with your Pearson account username and password. You have a Pearson account if you have used other Pearson online products. Enter your username and password, and click **Sign-In.**
  - If you don't have a Pearson account, click **"Create."**
  - Complete your account set up by entering your first and last name, email address, a username and password, your access code, and any other required information.

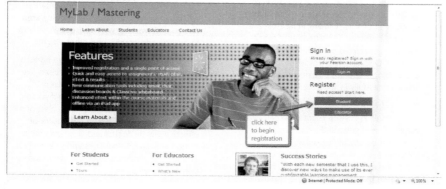

TIP! Be sure to take note of your login name and password—write them down in a place you will not forget.

HOW TO SIGN IN

- **From** www.pearsoncustom.com/co/ppccenglish
    - o Click *Sign in* at the "Sign In" box.
    - o Enter your username and password

HOW TO PURCHASE ACCESS ONLINE

- o Go to www.pearsoncustom.com/co/ppccenglish
- o Click **Student** in the "Register" box.
- o Enter your **Course ID**, which your instructor provided. If you **do not** know your Course ID, do not continue the registration process. Please contact your instructor
- o **Sign in** with your Pearson account username and password. You have a Pearson account if you have used other Pearson online products. Enter your username and password, and click **Sign-In**
- o If you don't have a Pearson account, click 'create'

TIP! Be sure to take note of your login name and password—write them down in a place you will not forget.

H. Ramsey Fowler • Jane E. Aaron

The Little, Brown Handbook

Custom Edition for Pikes Peak Community College

Taken from:
The Little, Brown Handbook, Twelfth Edition
by H. Ramsey Fowler and Jane E. Aaron

Pearson Learning Solutions, 501 Boylston Street, Suite 900, Boston, MA 02116
A Pearson Education Company
www.pearsoned.com

Printed in the United States of America

4 5 6 7 8 9 10 v092 17 16 15 14 13 12

000200010271653410

AD

ISBN 10: 1-256-70453-9
ISBN 13: 978-1-256-70453-9

Preface for Students: Using This Book

The Little, Brown Handbook is a basic resource that will answer almost any question you have about writing. Here you can find how to get ideas, develop paragraphs, punctuate quotations, find sources for research projects, cite sources, or write a résumé. The handbook can help you not only in writing courses but also in other courses and outside of school.

Don't let the size of the handbook put you off. You need not read the whole book to get something out of it, and no one expects you to know everything included. Primarily a reference tool, the handbook is written and arranged to help you find the answers you need when you need them, quickly and easily.

Using this book will not by itself make you a good writer; for that, you need to care about your work at every level, from finding a subject to spelling words. But learning how to use the handbook and its information can give you the means to write *what* you want in the *way* you want.

Reference aids

You have many ways to find what you need in the handbook:

- **Use the directory.** "Plan of the Book," inside the front cover, displays the book's entire contents.
- **Use a glossary.** "Glossary of Usage" (pp. 845–61) clarifies more than 275 words that are commonly confused and misused. "Glossary of Terms" (pp. 862–84) defines more than 350 words used in discussing writing.
- **Use the index.** Beginning on page 887, the extensive index includes every term, concept, and problem word or expression mentioned in the book.
- **Use a list.** Three helpful aids fall inside the book's back cover: (1) "⟨CULTURE LANGUAGE⟩ Guide" pulls together all the book's material for students who are using standard American English as a second language or a second dialect. (2) "Editing Symbols" explains abbreviations often used to comment on papers. And (3) "Useful Lists and Summaries" indexes topics that students frequently ask about.
- **Use the elements of the page.** As shown in the illustration on the next page, the handbook constantly tells you where you are and what you can find there.

vii

The handbook's page elements

Running head (header) showing the topic being discussed on this page

368 Pronoun reference

Principal causes of unclear pronoun reference

Icon for the eText linking to a video tutorial, podcast, sample document, student paper, exercise, or checklist

▪ More than one possible antecedent (below):

| Confusing | To keep birds from eating seeds, soak them in blue food coloring. |
| Clear | To keep birds from eating seeds, soak the seeds in blue food coloring. |

▪ Antecedent too far away (facing page):

| Confusing | Employees should consult with their supervisor who require personal time. |
| Clear | Employees who require personal time should consult with their supervisor. |

Summary or checklist box providing key information in accessible form

▪ Antecedent only implied (p. 370):

| Confusing | Many children begin reading on their own by watching television, but this should probably be discounted in government policy. |
| Clear | Many children begin reading on their own by watching television, but such self-instruction should probably be discounted in government policy. |

Section heading, a main convention or topic labeled with the section code, **19a:** chapter number (**19**) and section letter (**a**)

See also pages 371–72.

Page tab containing the section code (**19a**) and editing symbol (**ref**)

19a Make a pronoun refer clearly to one antecedent.

When either of two nouns can be a pronoun's antecedent, the reference will not be clear:

| Confusing | Emily Dickinson is sometimes compared with Jane Austen, but she was quite different. |

Examples, always indented, with underlining and annotations highlighting sentence elements and revisions

Revise such a sentence in one of two ways:

▪ Replace the pronoun with the appropriate noun:

| Clear | Emily Dickinson is sometimes compared with Jane Austen, but Dickinson [or Austen] was quite different. |

▪ Avoid repetition by rewriting the sentence. If you use the pronoun, make sure it has only one possible antecedent:

| Clear | Despite occasional comparison, Emily Dickinson and Jane Austen were quite different. |

Sentences that report what someone said, using verbs such as *said* or *told*, often require direct rather than indirect quotation.

Web box linking to the eText and *MyCompLab*

mycomplab

Visit *mycomplab.com* for the eText and for resources and more exercises on pronoun reference.

An English pronoun does need a clear antecedent nearby, but don't use both a pronoun and its antecedent as the subject of the same sentence or clause: *Jim* [not *Jim he*] *told Mark to go alone.* (See also pp. 391–92.)

Culture-language connection, a pointer for students using standard American English as a second language or a second dialect

Exercise 19.3 Revising: Pronoun reference

Revise the following paragraph so that each pronoun refers clearly to a single specific and appropriate antecedent.

In Charlotte Brontë's *Jane Eyre*, she is a shy young woman that takes a job as governess. Her employer is a rude, brooding man named Rochester. He lives in a mysterious mansion on the English moors, which contributes an eerie quality to Jane's experience. Eerier still are the fires, strange noises, and other unexplained happenings in the house; but Rochester refuses to discuss this. Eventually, they fall in love. On the day

Exercise providing opportunity for practice

Content and organization

An overview of the handbook's contents appears inside the front cover. Briefly, the book divides into the following sections:

- Introduction: Participating in the academic community, including getting the most from your classes and developing your integrity as a student and writer.
- Chapters 1–5: The writing process, writing and revising paragraphs, and presenting your writing in print, online, and orally.
- Chapters 6–11: Reading and writing in and out of college, with chapters on critical thinking and reading, academic writing, reading arguments, writing arguments, taking essay exams, and public writing.
- Chapters 12–26: Sentence basics, including the conventions of English grammar, errors that affect clarity, and techniques of effective sentences.
- Chapters 27–36: Punctuation and mechanics (capital letters, italics, and the like).
- Chapters 37–40: Words—how to use them appropriately and precisely, how to edit them for conciseness, how to spell them.
- Chapters 41–47: Research writing, from planning through revising, with detailed help on finding and evaluating electronic sources, a complete guide to citing sources, and two sample papers.
- Chapters 48–52: Writing in the academic disciplines, including concepts, tools, and source citations in literature, other humanities, the social sciences, and the natural and applied sciences.

Recommended usage

The conventions described and illustrated in this handbook are those of standard American English—the label given the dialect used in higher education, business, and the professions. (See also pp. 177–79.) The handbook stresses written standard English, which is more conservative than the spoken dialect in matters of grammar and usage. A great many words and constructions that are widely spoken remain unaccepted in careful writing.

When clear distinctions exist between the language of conversation and that of careful writing, the handbook provides examples of each and labels them *spoken* and *written*. When usage in writing itself varies with the level of formality intended, the handbook labels examples *formal* and *informal*. When usage is mixed or currently changing, the handbook recommends that you choose the more conservative usage because it will be accepted by all readers.

Print and eText versions

The Little, Brown Handbook is available as a print book and in several electronic versions:

■ A Pearson eText provides the complete handbook and the electronic resources described below. The eText is accessible through *MyCompLab* and *MyWritingLab*, both interactive learning environments with abundant resources for writing. You can gain access to *MyCompLab* and *MyWritingLab* through your course instructor, with the purchase of a new copy of the handbook, or through an independent purchase at *mycomplab.com* or *mywritinglab.com*.

■ A Pearson eText app for the iPad provides the complete handbook and the electronic resources described below.

■ A *CourseSmart* e-textbook provides all of the handbook's content in a format that enables you to search the text, bookmark passages, integrate your class notes, and print reading assignments that incorporate lecture notes. To subscribe, visit *coursesmart.com*.

eText resources

Icons in the handbook's margins link to a wealth of electronic resources:

■ 👁 Nearly two hundred video tutorials illustrate key concepts, offering tips and guidance on critical reading, evaluating sources, avoiding plagiarism, and many other topics.

■ (•• More than thirty audio podcasts discuss common questions about grammar, usage, punctuation, and mechanics.

■ 📰 More than seventy student papers and sample documents illustrate the range of writing you'll do in composition classes, your other courses, the workplace, and the community.

■ 🌟 Exercises from the handbook as well as additional exercises offer ample opportunities to sharpen your writing, grammar, and research skills.

■ ✓ More than twenty editable checklists from the handbook allow you to adapt key summaries for your own use.

Preface for Instructors

The Little, Brown Handbook always addresses both the current and the recurrent needs of writing students and teachers. This twelfth edition is no exception. Writing and its teaching change continuously, and the handbook has changed both in content and in format. At the same time, much about writing does not change, and the handbook remains a comprehensive, clear, and accessible guide to a host of writing situations and challenges.

The Little, Brown Handbook is actually many books in one, and each is stronger in this edition. The revisions—highlighted below with New—affect most pages.

A guide to academic writing

The handbook gives students a solid foundation in the goals and requirements of college writing.

- New An introduction, "Joining the Academic Community," provides tips for succeeding in face-to-face and online classes and for writing responsibly in academic situations.
- New Key chapters stress academic integrity and avoiding plagiarism—the new introduction, Chapter 7 on academic writing, and Chapter 44 on avoiding plagiarism—and other chapters throughout the handbook reinforce these important topics.
- New Common genres of academic writing receive emphasis in the context of the writing process, academic writing, and writing in the disciplines. Eighteen examples of academic genres appear throughout the handbook. (See p. 172 for a list.)
- New Fresh examples of academic writing—an informative essay, a literacy narrative, a proposal argument, and a literary argument—supplement the many sample papers and projects in the handbook.
- New Summarizing receives new emphasis in Chapter 7 on critical reading.
- Synthesis receives special emphasis wherever students might need help balancing their own and others' views, such as in responding to texts.
- Parts 9 and 10 give students a solid foundation in research writing and writing in the disciplines (literature, other humanities, social sciences, natural and applied sciences), along with extensive coverage of documentation in MLA, Chicago, APA, and CSE styles.

A guide to research writing and documentation

With detailed advice, the handbook always attends closely to research writing and source citation. The discussion stresses using the library as Web gateway, managing information, evaluating and synthesizing sources, integrating source material, and avoiding plagiarism. The extensive coverage of four documentation styles—MLA, Chicago, APA, and CSE—reflects each style's latest version.

- New To help students develop their own perspectives on their research subjects, the text stresses asking questions, entering into dialog with sources, and presenting multiple views fairly and responsibly.
- New Reflecting the varied ways that students may seek sources, the discussion of libraries' Web portals covers research guides and centralized search engines and also updates the material on databases.
- New An expanded discussion of evaluating Web sources—Web sites, social-networking sites, blogs, wikis, multimedia—helps students discern purposes and distinguish between reliable and unreliable sources.
- Case studies in source evaluation show the application of critical criteria to sample articles, Web documents, and a blog.
- New The revised chapter on avoiding plagiarism and documenting sources gives more examples of deliberate and accidental plagiarism, new examples of material that must be cited, updated advice about avoiding plagiarism with online sources, and a new exercise on revising sentences to avoid plagiarism.
- Two research papers illustrate MLA style. One of them is a paper-in-progress, following a student through the research process and culminating in an annotated essay on green consumerism.
- New Updated, annotated samples of key source types illustrate MLA and APA documentation, showing students how to find the bibliographical information needed to cite each type.
- For all styles, color highlighting makes authors, titles, dates, and other citation elements easy to grasp.
- New Updated source lists in Part 10 provide reliable starting points for research in every discipline.

A guide to writing as a process

The handbook takes a practical approach to assessing the writing situation, generating ideas, developing the thesis statement, revising, and other elements of the writing process.

- New Genre joins subject, purpose, and audience as a key element of every writing situation, affecting content, format, and readers' expectations.

- New Expanded coverage of thesis now includes a detailed discussion of developing a thesis question and moving from the question to a thesis statement.
- New A student's informative paper on college football shows techniques for achieving whole-essay unity and coherence. This essay is one of many student writing samples, including a work-in-progress on career prospects amid globalization and outsourcing.
- New Chapter 4 on paragraphs opens with a discussion of relating paragraphs in the essay, expands on the discussion of coherence, and includes many new examples.
- New A comprehensive chapter on presenting writing covers designing print and electronic documents, creating and using visuals and other media in multimodal writing projects, and giving oral presentations.

A guide to usage, grammar, and punctuation

The handbook's core reference material reliably and concisely explains basic concepts and common errors, provides hundreds of annotated examples from across the curriculum, and offers frequent exercises (including end-of-part exercises that combine several kinds of problems).

- New More than twenty new and revised exercises, all in connected discourse, provide hands-on practice.
- New Part 8 on effective words includes many fresh examples, discussion and samples of online dictionaries and thesauruses, and advice on avoiding abbreviations, fragments, and other features of online communication.
- Summary and checklist boxes provide quick-reference help, with color highlighting to distinguish sentence elements.

A guide to visual and media literacy

The handbook helps students process nonverbal information and use it effectively in their writing.

- New Chapter 5 on presenting writing and Chapter 42 on finding sources give practical suggestions for creating, selecting, and integrating visuals and multimedia into college writing projects.
- New Thorough discussions of critically reading advertisements, graphs, and other visuals appear in Chapter 6 on critical reading, Chapter 8 on reading arguments, and Chapter 43 on working with sources.
- Illustrations in many of the handbook's student papers show various ways to support written ideas with visual information.

A guide for culturally and linguistically diverse writers

At notes and sections labeled 〈CULTURE LANGUAGE〉, the handbook provides extensive rhetorical and grammatical help for writers whose first language or dialect is not standard American English.

- Fully integrated coverage, instead of a separate section, means that students can find what they need without having to know which problems they do and don't share with native SAE speakers.
- "〈CULTURE LANGUAGE〉 Guide," inside the back cover, orients students with advice on mastering SAE and pulls all the integrated coverage together in one place.
- **New** Many 〈CULTURE LANGUAGE〉 notes throughout the handbook use simpler language and add sentence-length examples. New notes cover oral presentations, plagiarism, and reading aloud.

An accessible reference guide

The handbook is designed to be easy to use.

- A clean, uncluttered page design uses color and type clearly to distinguish parts of the book and elements of the pages.
- Color highlighting in boxes and on documentation models distinguishes important elements.
- Annotations on both visual and verbal examples connect principles and illustrations.
- Dictionary-style headers in the index make it easy to find entries.
- Helpful endpapers offer several paths to the book's content.
- More than 160 boxes provide summaries and checklists of key information.
- A preface just for students outlines the book's contents, details reference aids, explains the page layout, and describes the print and e-textbook versions.

Print and electronic versions

The twelfth edition is available both in print and as an eText in the following formats:

- **New** A Pearson eText provides the complete handbook and electronic resources on the *MyCompLab* and *MyWritingLab* Web sites (see the facing page for more on the eText resources and on *MyCompLab* and *MyWritingLab*).
- **New** A Pearson eText app for the iPad provides the complete handbook and electronic resources (see the facing page for more on the eText resources).
- A *CourseSmart* e-textbook, which is available by subscription at *coursesmart.com*, gives students access to all of the book's con-

tent in a format that enables them to search the text, bookmark passages, integrate their notes, and print reading assignments that incorporate lecture notes.

eText resources for students and instructors

New Icons in the handbook's margins link to a wide array of electronic resources:

- ◉ Nearly two hundred video tutorials illustrate key concepts, offering tips and guidance on critical reading, evaluating sources, avoiding plagiarism, and many other topics.

- (●• More than thirty audio podcasts discuss common misconceptions about grammar, usage, punctuation, and mechanics.

- 📄 More than seventy student papers and sample documents illustrate the range of writing that students do in composition and other courses, the workplace, and the community.

- ✳ Exercises from the handbook as well as additional exercises offer students ample opportunities to sharpen their writing, grammar, and research skills.

- ✓ More than twenty editable checklists from the handbook allow students to adapt key summaries for their own use.

Supplements

Pearson offers a variety of support materials to make teaching easier and to help students improve as writers. The following resources are geared specifically to *The Little, Brown Handbook*. For more information on these and scores of additional supplements, visit *pearsonhighered.com* or contact your local Pearson sales representative.

- The Web site *MyCompLab* (*mycomplab.com*) integrates instruction, multimedia tutorials, and exercises for writing, grammar, and research with an online composing space and assessment tools. This seamless, flexible environment comes from extensive research in partnership with composition faculty and students across the country. It provides help for writers in the context of their writing, with functions for instructors' and peers' commentary. Special features include an e-portfolio, a bibliography tool, tutoring services, an assignment builder, and a gradebook and course-management organization created specifically for writing classes. In addition, *MyCompLab* includes the eText version of *The Little, Brown Handbook* (see opposite).
- The Web site *MyWritingLab* (*mywritinglab.com*) is a complete online-learning system with more than nine thousand exercises

to help students become better writers. The exercises are progressive: within each skill module, students move from literal comprehension to critical application to use of skills in their own writing. The exercises cover grammar extensively and also extend to the writing process, paragraph development, essay development, and research. A thorough diagnostic test reveals students' individual needs, and an easy-to-use tracking system enables students and instructors to monitor all work done on the site. In addition, *MyWritingLab* includes the eText version of *The Little, Brown Handbook* (see p. xiv).

- The *Instructor's Annotated Edition of The Little, Brown Handbook* has been thoroughly revised by Cynthia Marshall, Wright State University. It provides a complete teaching system in one book. Integrated with the student text are essays on teaching, updated reading suggestions, specific tips for class discussions and activities, and answers to the handbook's exercises.

- The *Instructor's Resource Manual* includes all the teaching material and exercise answers from the *Instructor's Annotated Edition*.

- *The Little, Brown Handbook Answer Key* provides answers to the handbook's exercises.

- *The Little, Brown Workbook,* by Donna Gorrell, parallels the handbook's organization but provides many more exercises and briefer instructional text. A separate answer key is available.

- *Diagnostic and Editing Tests and Exercises* are cross-referenced to *The Little, Brown Handbook* and are available both in print and online.

- *VangoNotes* are study guides in MP3 format that enable students to download handbook information onto their own players and then listen to it whenever and wherever they wish. The notes include "need to know" tips for each handbook chapter, practice tests, audio flash cards for learning key concepts and terms, and a rapid review for exams. For more information, visit *VangoNotes.com*.

Acknowledgments

The Little, Brown Handbook stays fresh and useful because instructors talk with Pearson's sales representatives and editors, answer questionnaires, write detailed reviews, and send us personal notes. For the twelfth edition, we are especially grateful to the many instructors who communicated with us directly or through reviews. The improvements in this new edition respond to the experiences and insights of the following instructors: Paula Berggren, Baruch College, the City University of New York; Clair Berry, Southwest Tennessee Community College; Yvonne Goodrich Cassidy, Alfred State College; Sandra Cooper, College of Central Florida; Dawn

Copeland, Motlow State Community College; Howard Cox, Angelina College; Maureen Groome, Brevard Community College; Holly French Hart, Bossier Parish Community College; Sue Henderson, East Central College; David Hennessy, Broward College; Melissa M. Joarder, Delaware County Community College; Christopher Morelock, Walters State Community College; Guy Moyer, University of Maryland University College; Dixie Shaw-Tillmon, the University of Texas, San Antonio; Ann C. Spurlock, Mississippi State University; and Nancy M. Staub, Lamar University.

In responding to the ideas of these thoughtful critics, we had the help of several creative people. Aaron McCullough, University of Michigan, guided us through the labyrinth of the contemporary library. Marilyn Hochman suggested improvements in the notes for students whose first language or dialect is not standard English. Sylvan Barnet, Tufts University, continued to lend his expertise in the chapter "Reading and Writing about Literature," which is adapted from his *Short Guide to Writing about Literature* and *Introduction to Literature* (with William Burto and William E. Cain). Ellen Kuhl provided creative, meticulous, and invaluable help with the material on research writing. And Carol Hollar-Zwick, sine qua non, served brilliantly as originator, sounding board, critic, coordinator, researcher, producer, and friend.

A superb publishing team helped us make this book. Our editors at Longman—Suzanne Phelps Chambers, Anne Brunell Ehrenworth, and Erin Reilly—offered perceptive insights into instructors' and students' needs, while Laney Whitt responded to our many requests with efficiency and cheer. The production editor, Bob Ginsberg, helped us resolve sometimes competing production goals in favor of quality and accuracy. Vernon Nahrgang copyedited the manuscript with unique precision and care. At Nesbitt Graphics, Jerilyn Bockorick made the book a pleasure to use, and Susan McIntyre performed her usual calm (and calming) miracles of scheduling and management to produce the book. We are grateful to all these collaborators.

Contents

INTRODUCTION

Joining the Academic Community

When you take college courses, you enter a community of teachers and students whose basic goal is to share and build knowledge about a subject, whether it is English, history, engineering, or something else. You participate in this community first by studying each subject, acquiring its vocabulary, and learning to express yourself in its ways. As you learn more about the subject, you contribute to the community and to its knowledge by asking questions and communicating your answers in writing. This active contribution to knowledge building is the core of academic work, and it depends on the integrity of everyone involved.

As you try to grasp the content of assigned reading and understand new concepts, academic knowledge building may at first seem out of reach. But developing the skills will be easier if you follow the advice in this chapter for engaging with course material, becoming an academic writer, developing academic integrity, and communicating with your instructor, your classmates, and other people at your school.

I1 Getting the most from college courses

You will enjoy each course and learn more from it if you are an active, engaged member of the class. Follow the guidelines below to prepare for and contribute to your classes.

- **Participate in class.** Whether your class meets face to face or online, push aside other concerns so that you can listen attentively, ask questions, take notes, and add your voice to discussions. (See the box on the next page for special advice on taking courses online.)

- **Take notes.** Use the notes you take in class to integrate all the components of the course—your instructor's views and approach to the material, your own thoughts, and the assigned reading,

1

Taking online courses

I1

Video
tutorial

The advice in this introduction and this entire handbook applies to courses taught face to face or online. But with online courses you'll work usually alone and often at your own pace. The following tips can help you succeed.

- **Study the syllabus.** The course outline will tell you the course goals, reading assignments, and writing assignments. Generally it will be your only reminder of what's expected.
- **Be disciplined.** Plan and stick to a regular study schedule so that you don't fall behind. When doing coursework, turn off distractions such as the cell phone, TV, and music player.
- **Participate.** If the course involves work with other students, take an active role. If you have questions or comments on the course material or wonder how you're doing in the course, ask the instructor.
- **Back up your work.** With all work and communication online, a computer crash could be disastrous. Routinely copy notes, drafts, and completed assignments to a flash drive, external hard drive, or online storage service such as Carbonite (*carbonite.com*).

even if you've already read it. When you're in class, record in your own words what you hear as completely as possible. Also try to sort out the main ideas from the secondary and supporting ones. If you miss something, leave space to insert it later. Review your notes shortly after class to reinforce learning.

- **Do assigned reading.** The assigned reading you do for college courses—such as textbooks, journal articles, essays, and works of literature—requires a greater focus on understanding and retention than does the reading you do for entertainment or for practical information. This book describes an active process that will help you become an efficient and effective reader. See pages 145–60.
- **Be open to new perspectives.** College classes should not only add to what you know but also provoke reflection. You will get more out of the college experience if you are curious about new ideas and open to thinking about them.
- **Work with integrity.** All of your college work represents you to your instructor, your classmates, and the entire college community. Whether participating in class, taking an exam, or writing a paper, always show respect for others and for yourself with careful, honest work. See the facing page for more on academic integrity.
- **Get help when you need it.** Most instructors hold weekly office hours, and many hold online office hours. In addition, most schools provide writing centers, tutoring centers, library tours, and other services.

12 Becoming an academic writer

As a college student you will probably do quite a lot of writing. Academic writing assignments vary, of course, depending on the discipline, the course, and the instructor. However, even within this variety you can orient yourself to each assignment by focusing on the key goals listed below. Each goal is discussed in more detail elsewhere in this book.

- **Know what the assignment requires.** Most assignments at least suggest a possible subject; they imply a purpose, audience, and genre (or type of writing); and they specify a length and a deadline. In that context, you refine your subject, your purpose, and your sense of audience as you proceed through the writing process, discussed in detail in Chapters 1–3.
- **Develop and organize your writing.** Most academic papers center on a main point, or thesis, and support the thesis with evidence. For more on developing a thesis and organizing a paper, see pages 36–52.
- **Synthesize your own and others' ideas.** College writing often involves researching and interacting with the works of other writers—being open to their ideas, responding to them, questioning them, comparing them, and using them to answer questions. Such interaction requires you to read critically (the subject of Chapter 6) and to synthesize, or integrate, others' ideas into your own. For an explanation of synthesis, see pages 173–75.
- **Use academic language.** Unless your instructor specifies otherwise, use formal, standard English, always avoiding the informalities of texting and online communication such as abbreviations and incomplete sentences. Academic language is discussed in detail on pages 177–79 and 524–32.
- **Revise and edit your writing.** College writing assignments require careful writing. Allow yourself enough time to revise and edit so that readers can see your main ideas, follow your train of thought, and make sense of your sentences. Consult this book's discussion of revision and editing on pages 58–61 and 67–69.
- **Acknowledge your sources.** As discussed in the following section, academic writers build on the work of others by fully crediting borrowed ideas and information. Always record the publication information of any source you consult so that you can cite it if you use it in your writing.

13 Developing academic integrity

Academic integrity is the foundation of academic knowledge building. Trusting in one another's honesty allows students and scholars to examine and extend the work of other scholars, and it allows teachers to guide and assess the progress of their students.

As a student, you'll have opportunities to develop and demonstrate your integrity in class preparation and participation, in exams, and especially in writing. Many writing assignments will require you to consult sources such as journal articles, Web sites, and books. These works belong to their creators; you are free to borrow from them *if* you do so with integrity. That means representing the sources accurately, not misinterpreting or distorting what they say. It also means crediting the sources, not **plagiarizing**, or presenting sources' ideas and information as if you originated them. On most campuses, plagiarism is a punishable offense.

Plagiarism can be deliberate or accidental. Deliberate plagiarism is outright cheating: copying another writer's sentence and passing it off as your own, buying a paper from the Web, or getting someone else to write a paper for you. Accidental plagiarism is more common among students, often arising from careless or inexperienced handling of sources. For instance, you might cut and paste source information into your own ideas without clarifying who said what, or you might present a summary of a source without recognizing that parts of it are actually quoted. In these cases the plagiarism is unintentional, but it is still plagiarism.

You can build your integrity as a writer by working to develop your own ideas and by handling sources responsibly. The following tips can help. Note that Chapters 41–52 contain extensive discussions of researching and citing sources.

Gaining perspective

Consider your own knowledge and perspective on a subject before you start to research. This forethought will make it easier for you to recognize other authors' perspectives and to treat them fairly in your writing—whether or not you agree with them.

- Before you consult sources, gauge what you already know and think about your subject. Give yourself time to know your own mind before rushing to others for information. Then you'll be able to reflect on how the sources reinforce, contradict, or expand what you already know.
- Evaluate sources carefully. Authors generally write from particular perspectives, and some are more overt about their biases than others. You needn't reject a source because it is biased; indeed, often you'll want to consider multiple perspectives. But you do need to recognize and weigh the writer's position. See pages 612–25 for a discussion of evaluating sources.
- Treat sources fairly. Represent an author's ideas and perspectives as they were originally presented, without misunderstanding or distortion. Be careful in paraphrasing and summarizing not to

misrepresent the author's meaning. Be careful in editing quotations not to omit essential words.

Managing sources

You can avoid plagiarism by keeping close track of the sources you consult, the ideas that influence your thinking, and the words and sentences you borrow—and by carefully citing the sources in your writing. If these habits are unfamiliar to you, keep the following list handy.

- **Keep track of source information as you read.** Get in the habit of always recording publication information (author, title, date, and so on) of any source you read as well as any ideas you glean from it. The box on page 581 lists what to record.
- **Be careful with quotations.** If you cut and paste a portion of an article, Web site, or other source into your document, put quotation marks around it so that you don't mix your words and the source's words accidentally. Check any quotation that you use in your own writing against the original source. For a more detailed discussion of how to quote sources, see pages 637–39.
- **Use your own words in paraphrases and summaries.** A paraphrase or summary presents the ideas of a source but not in the exact words of the original and not in quotation marks. You will be less likely to use the source author's words (and thus plagiarize) if you look away from the source while you write down what you remember from it. Note, though, that you must still cite the source of a summary or paraphrase, just as you do with a quotation. For a more detailed discussion of how to summarize and paraphrase sources, see pages 633–37.
- **Cite your sources.** As you draft, be conscious of when you're using source information and be conscientious about clearly marking where the borrowed material came from. In your final draft you'll use a particular style of citation within your text to refer to a detailed list of sources at the end. This book presents four such styles: MLA style for English and some other humanities (pp. 667–713); Chicago style for history, philosophy, and some other humanities (785–96); APA style for the social sciences (804–23); and CSE style for the natural and applied sciences (834–41).

14 Communicating in an academic setting

As a member of an academic community, you will not only write papers and projects but also write directly to instructors, classmates, and other people at your school via e-mail, course blogs, or course-management systems such as *Blackboard*, *Desire2Learn*, and *Moodle*.

14

Though rarely as formal as assigned writing, this communication is also rarely as informal as what you might text a friend, post on *Twitter*, or comment on *Facebook*.

Even in a short e-mail, your message will receive a better hearing if you present yourself well and show respect for your reader(s). The message below illustrates an appropriate mix of formality and informality when addressing an instructor:

E-mail message

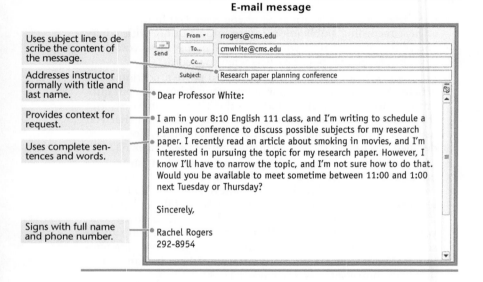

Uses subject line to describe the content of the message.

Addresses instructor formally with title and last name.

Provides context for request.

Uses complete sentences and words.

Signs with full name and phone number.

From ▾ rrogers@cms.edu
To... cmwhite@cms.edu
Cc...
Subject: Research paper planning conference

Dear Professor White:

I am in your 8:10 English 111 class, and I'm writing to schedule a planning conference to discuss possible subjects for my research paper. I recently read an article about smoking in movies, and I'm interested in pursuing the topic for my research paper. However, I know I'll have to narrow the topic, and I'm not sure how to do that. Would you be available to meet sometime between 11:00 and 1:00 next Tuesday or Thursday?

Sincerely,

Rachel Rogers
292-8954

Here are guidelines for such communication:

- **Use the medium your instructor prefers.** Don't text, tweet, or use a social-networking site unless you're invited to do so.
- **Use names.** In the body of your message, address your reader(s) by name if possible. Unless your teachers instruct otherwise, always address them formally, using *Professor, Dr., Ms.,* or *Mr.,* as appropriate, followed by the last name. Sign off with your own name and information on how to contact you.
- **Pay attention to tone.** Don't use all capital letters, which SHOUT. And use irony or sarcasm only cautiously: in the absence of facial expressions, either one can lead to misunderstanding.
- **Pay attention to correctness.** Especially when you write to instructors, avoid the shortcuts of texting and tweeting, such as incomplete sentences and abbreviations (*u* for *you, r* for *are,* and so on). (See also p. 526.) Proofread for errors in grammar, punctuation, and spelling.

■ **Send messages only to the people who need them.** As a general rule, avoid sending messages to many recipients at once—all the students in a course, say—unless what you have to say applies to all of them. Before you hit Reply All in response to a message, ensure that "all" want to see the response.

■ **Guard your own and others' privacy.** Online tools allow us to broadcast hurtful information about others—and allow others to do the same to us. Before you post a message about yourself or someone else, consider whether it's worthwhile and who will see it, not only now but in the future. When forwarding messages, make sure not to pass on previous private messages by mistake.

■ **Don't write anything that you wouldn't say face to face or wouldn't write in a printed letter.** Electronic messages can be saved and forwarded and can be retrieved in disputes over grades and other matters.

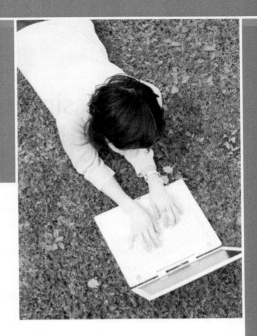

PART 1

The Process of Writing

1

Assessing the Writing Situation

"Writing is easy," snarled the late sportswriter Red Smith. "All you do is sit down at the typewriter and open a vein." Most writers would smile in agreement, and so might you. Like anything worthwhile, writing well takes hard work. This chapter and the next two will show you some techniques that writers have found helpful for starting, continuing, and completing college assignments.

1a Understanding how writing happens

Every time you sit down to write, you embark on a **writing process**—the term for all the activities, mental and physical, that go into creating what eventually becomes a finished piece of work. Even for experienced writers the process is usually messy, which is one reason that it is sometimes difficult. Though we may get a sense of ease and orderliness from a published magazine article, we can safely assume that the writer had to work hard to achieve those qualities, struggling to express half-formed thoughts, shaping and reshaping paragraphs to make a point convincingly.

There is no *one* writing process; no two writers proceed in the same way, and even an individual writer adapts his or her process to the task at hand. Still, most writers experience writing as a **recursive** process in which the following stages overlap and influence one another:

- **Analyzing the writing situation:** considering subject, purpose, audience, genre (type of writing), and other elements of the project (pp. 12–24).
- **Discovering or planning:** posing a question, gathering information, focusing on a central theme, and organizing material (pp. 25–52).
- **Drafting:** answering the question and expressing and connecting ideas (pp. 54–58).

mycomplab

Visit *mycomplab.com* for the eText and for resources and more exercises on assessing the writing situation.

10

The process of writing

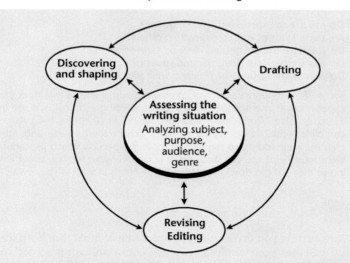

Writing is usually a recursive process: at each stage your work can affect and be affected by every other stage. Assessing the writing situation generally starts the process and then continues in the other stages.

- Revising: reconsidering the central question or idea, rethinking and improving content and organization, developing supporting ideas more thoroughly, and deleting tangents (pp. 58–61).
- Editing: improving sentences and checking grammar, punctuation, word choice, and presentation (pp. 67–69).

Note Like many others, you may believe that writing is only, or even mainly, a matter of correctness. True, any written message will find a more receptive audience if it is correct in grammar, spelling, and similar matters. But these concerns should come late in the writing process, after you've allowed yourself to discover what you want to say, freeing yourself to make mistakes along the way. As one writer put it, you need to get the clay on the potter's wheel before you can shape it into a bowl, and you need to shape the bowl before you can perfect it. So get your clay on the wheel, and work with it until it looks like a bowl. Then worry about correctness.

Exercise 1.1 Starting a writing journal

Recall several writing experiences that you have had—a letter you had difficulty composing, an essay you enjoyed writing, an all-nighter spent happily or miserably on a term paper, a posting to a blog that received a surprising response. What do these experiences reveal to you about writing, particularly your successes and problems with it? Consider the following questions:

Do you like to experiment with language?
Are some kinds of writing easier than others?
Do you have trouble getting ideas or expressing them?
Do you worry about grammar and spelling?
Do your readers usually understand what you mean?

Record your thoughts as part of continuing journal entries that track your experiences as a writer. (See pp. 28–30 on keeping a journal, and see the exercises titled "Considering your past work" in Chapters 1–4.) As you complete writing assignments for your composition course and other courses, keep adding to the journal, noting especially which procedures seem most helpful to you. Your aim is to discover your feelings about writing so that you can develop a dependable writing process of your own.

1b Analyzing the writing situation

Any writing you do for others occurs in a context that both limits and clarifies your choices. You are communicating something about a particular subject to a particular audience of readers for a specific reason. You may be required to write in a particular genre. You may need to conduct research. You'll be up against a length requirement and a deadline. And you may be expected to present your work in a certain format and medium.

Exercise

These are the elements of the **writing situation,** and analyzing them at the very start of a project can tell you much about how to proceed. (For more information about these elements, refer to the page numbers given in parentheses.)

Context

■ **What is your writing for?** A course in school? Work? Something else? What do you know of the requirements for writing in this context?

■ **What are the basic requirements of the writing task?** Consider requirements for length, deadline, subject, purpose, audience, and genre. What leeway do you have?

■ **What medium will you use to present your writing?** Will you deliver it on paper, online, or orally? What does the presentation method require in preparation time, special skills, and use of technology?

Subject (pp. 14–17)

■ **What does your writing assignment require you to write about?** If you don't have a specific assignment, what subjects might be appropriate for this situation?

■ **What interests you about the subject?** What do you already know about it? What questions do you have about it?

■ **What does the assignment require you to do with the subject?**

Purpose (pp. 17–19)

- **What aim does your assignment specify?** For instance, does it ask you to explain something or argue a point?
- **Why are you writing?**
- **What do you want your work to accomplish?** What effect do you intend it to have on readers?
- **How can you best achieve your purpose?**

Audience (pp. 19–22)

- **Who will read your writing?** Why will your readers be interested (or not) in your writing? How can you make your writing interesting to them?
- **What do your readers already know and think about your subject?** What characteristics—such as education or political views—might influence their response?
- **How should you project yourself in your writing?** What role should you play in relation to your readers, and what information should you provide? How informal or formal should your writing be?
- **What do you want readers to do or think after they read your writing?**

Genre (pp. 23–24)

- **What genre, or type of writing, does the assignment call for?** Are you to write an analysis, a report, a proposal, or some other type? Or are you free to choose the genre in which to write?
- **What are the conventions of the genre you are using?** For example, readers might expect a claim supported by evidence, a solution to a defined problem, clear description, or easy-to-find information.

Research (pp. 570–658)

- **What kinds of evidence will best suit your subject, purpose, audience, and genre?** What combination of facts, examples, and expert opinions will support your ideas?
- **Does your assignment require research?** Will you need to consult sources or conduct interviews, surveys, or experiments?
- **Even if research is not required, what information do you need to develop your subject?** How will you obtain it?
- **What documentation style should you use to cite your sources?** (See pp. 657–58 on source documentation in the academic disciplines.)

Deadline and length

- **When is the assignment due?** How will you apportion the work you have to do in the time available?
- **How long should your writing be?** If no length is assigned, what seems appropriate for your subject, purpose, and audience?

Presentation

- What format or method of presentation does the assignment specify or imply? (See pp. 117–34 on academic writing, pp. 135–42 on oral presentations, and pp. 235–50 on business and other public writing.)
  - How might you use headings, lists, illustrations, video, and other elements to achieve your purpose? (See pp. 120–30.)

Exercise 1.2 Analyzing a writing situation

The following assignment was given in a survey course in psychology. What does the assignment specify about the elements of the writing situation? What does it imply? Given this assignment, how would you answer the preceding questions about the writing situation?

When is psychotherapy most likely to work? That is, what combinations of client, therapist, and theory tend to achieve good results? In your paper, cite studies supporting your conclusions. Length: 1500 to 1800 words. Post your paper online to me and to your discussion group by March 30.

1c Discovering and limiting a subject

For most college writing, you will write in response to an assignment. The assignment may specify your subject, or it may leave the choice to you. (If you're stuck, use the discovery techniques on pp. 25–35 to think of subjects.) Whether the subject is assigned or not, it will probably need thought if it is to achieve these aims:

- The subject should be suitable for the assignment.
- It should be neither too general nor too limited for the length of the project and the deadline assigned.
- It should be something that interests you and that you are willing to learn more about.

1 Responding to a specific assignment

Many assignments will set boundaries for your subject. For instance, you might be asked to discuss what makes psychotherapy effective, to prepare a lab report on a physics experiment, or to analyze a character in a short story.

Such assignments may seem to leave little room for you to move around, but in fact you'll have several questions to answer:

- **What's wanted from you?** Writing assignments often contain words such as *discuss, describe, analyze, report, interpret, explain, define, argue,* and *evaluate.* These words specify your approach to your subject, the kind of thinking expected, your general purpose, and even the form your writing should take. (See pp. 17–19 for more on purpose.)

■ **For whom are you writing?** Many assignments will specify or imply your readers, but sometimes you will have to figure out for yourself who your audience is and what it expects from you. (For more on analyzing audience, see pp. 19–22.)

■ **What kind of research is required?** Sometimes an assignment specifies the kinds of sources you are expected to consult, and you can use such information to choose your subject. (If you are unsure whether research is required, check with your instructor.)

■ **How can you narrow the assigned subject to do it justice in the length and time required?** (See below.)

dev

1c

2 Responding to a general assignment

Some assignments specify features such as length and amount of research, but they leave the choice of subject entirely to you. Others are somewhat more focused—for instance, "Respond to a reading assigned in this course" or "Discuss a proposal for solving a local social problem"—but still give you much leeway in choosing a particular reading or a particular proposal. To find your approach, consider your own experiences, interests, or curiosities:

■ **What subject do you already know something about or have you been wondering about?** Athletic scholarships? Unemployment in your town?

■ **Have you recently disagreed with someone over a substantial issue?** The change in relations between men and women? The methods being used to fight terrorism?

■ **What have you read or seen lately?** A shocking book? A violent or funny movie? An effective television commercial?

■ **What topic in the reading or class discussion for a course has intrigued you?** An economic issue such as taxes? A psychological problem such as depression?

■ **What makes you especially happy or especially angry?** A hobby? The behavior of your neighbors?

■ **Which of your own or others' dislikes and preferences would you like to understand better?** The demand for hybrid cars? The decision to become a vegetarian?

Once you have a subject, you'll also need to answer the questions in the bulleted list on specific assignments (opposite and above).

3 Narrowing a subject to a question

Let's say you've decided to write about social-networking Web sites or about a character in a short story. You've got a subject, but it's still broad, worthy of a lengthy article if not a whole book. For a relatively brief paper, you'll need a narrow focus in order to provide the specific details that make writing significant and interesting—all within the required length and deadline.

Video
tutorial

One helpful technique for narrowing a subject is to ask focused questions about it, seeking one that seems appropriate for your assignment and that promises to sustain your interest through the writing process. The following examples illustrate how questioning can scale down broad subjects to specific subjects that are limited and manageable:

Broad subjects	Specific subjects
Social-networking sites	What draws people to these sites? How do the sites alter the ways people interact? What privacy protections should the sites provide for users?
Mrs. Mallard in Kate Chopin's "The Story of an Hour"	What changes does Mrs. Mallard undergo? Why does Mrs. Mallard respond as she does to news of her husband's death? What does the story's irony contribute to the character of Mrs. Mallard?
Lincoln's weaknesses as President	What was Lincoln's most significant error as commander-in-chief of the Union army? Why did Lincoln delay emancipating the slaves? Why did Lincoln have difficulties controlling his cabinet?
Federal aid to college students	Which students should be entitled to federal aid? How adequate are the kinds of federal aid available to college students? Why should the federal government aid college students?

As these examples illustrate, your questions should not lend themselves to yes-or-no answers but should require further thinking. Here are some guidelines for posing questions:

- **Reread the assignment.** Consider what it tells you about purpose, audience, genre, sources, length, and deadline.
- **Pursue your interests.** If questions don't come easily, try freewriting or brainstorming (pp. 30–32) or use a tree diagram (pp. 44–45).
- **Ask as many questions as you can think of.**
- **Test the question that seems most interesting and appropriate by roughly sketching out the main ideas.** Consider how many paragraphs or pages of specific facts, examples, and other details you would need to pin those ideas down. This thinking should give you at least a vague idea of how much work you'd have to do and how long the resulting paper might be.
- **Break a too-broad question down further, and repeat the previous step.**

The Internet can also help you limit a general subject. On the Web, browse a directory such as *ipl2* (*ipl.org*). As you pursue increasingly narrow categories, you may find a suitably limited topic.

Don't be discouraged if the perfect question does not come easily or early. You may find that you need to do some planning and writing, exploring different facets of the general subject and pursuing your specific interests, before you hit on the best question. And the question you select may require further narrowing or may shift subtly or even dramatically as you move through the writing process.

Exercise 1.3 Narrowing subjects

Following are some general writing assignments. Use the given information and your own interests to pose specific questions for three of these assignments.

Exercise

1. For a writing course, consider how Web sites such as *YouTube* are altering the experience of popular culture. Length: three pages. Deadline: one week.
2. For a course in sociology, research and analyze the dynamics of a particular group of people. Length: unspecified. Deadline: four weeks.
3. For a writing course, read and respond to an essay in a text you are using. Length: three pages. Deadline: two weeks.
4. For a government course, consider possible restrictions on legislators. Length: five pages. Deadline: two weeks.
5. For a letter to the editor of the town newspaper, describe the effects of immigration on your community. Length: two pages. Deadline: unspecified.

Exercise 1.4 Considering your past work: Discovering and limiting a subject

Think of something you've recently written—perhaps an application essay, a business report, or a term paper. How did your subject evolve from beginning to end? In retrospect, was it appropriate for your writing situation? How, if at all, might it have been modified?

Exercise

Exercise 1.5 Finding and narrowing a subject for your essay

As the first step in developing a three- to four-page essay for the instructor and the other students in your writing course, choose a subject and narrow it. Use the guidelines in the previous section to come up with a question that is suitably interesting, appropriate, and specific.

1d Defining a purpose

When you write, your **purpose** is your chief reason for communicating something about a topic to a particular audience. Purpose thus links both the specific situation in which you are working and the goal you hope to achieve. It is your answer to a potential reader's question, "So what?"

The general purposes for writing

- To entertain readers
- To express your feelings or ideas
- To explain something to readers (exposition)
- To persuade readers to accept or act on your opinion (argument)

Video
tutorial

1 Defining a general purpose

Your purpose may fall into one of four general categories: entertainment, self-expression, explanation, or persuasion. These purposes may overlap in a single piece of writing, but usually one predominates. And the dominant purpose will influence your particular slant on your topic, the supporting details you choose, even the words you use.

In college or public writing, by far the most common purposes are explanation and persuasion:

- **Writing that is mainly explanatory is often called** *exposition* (from a Latin word meaning "to explain or set forth"). Using examples, facts, and other evidence, you present an idea about your subject so that readers understand it as you do. Almost any subject is suitable for exposition: how to pitch a knuckleball, why you want to major in business, the implications of a new discovery in computer science, the interpretation of a short story, the causes of an economic slump. Exposition is the kind of writing encountered most often in newspapers, magazines, and textbooks.

- **Writing that is primarily persuasive is often called** *argument.* Using examples, facts, and other evidence, you support your position on a debatable subject so that readers will at least consider your view and perhaps agree with it or act on it. A newspaper editorial favoring city council reform, a business proposal for a new personnel policy, a student paper recommending more required courses or defending a theory about human psychological development—all these are arguments. (Chapters 8–9 discuss argument in some detail and provide examples.)

2 Defining a specific purpose

A writing assignment will often specify or imply both a general and a specific purpose. Say, for instance, that a psychology teacher assigns a review of the research on infants' perception of color. You know that the purpose is generally to explain, more specifically to summarize and analyze the established findings on the subject. You want readers to come away understanding the current state of the investigation into the subject. In addition, you want your instructor to see that you can competently read and write about others' work. (See pp. 170–71 for more on purpose in academic writing.)

Here are more examples of specific purposes:

> To explain the methods and results of an engineering experiment so that readers understand and accept your conclusions
>
> To analyze how Annie Dillard's "Total Eclipse" builds to its climax so that readers appreciate the author's skill
>
> To explain the reasons for a new policy on technology use in dorm rooms so that students understand why the guidelines are needed
>
> To persuade readers to support the college administration's plan for more required courses
>
> To argue against additional regulation of guns so that readers perceive the disadvantages for themselves
>
> To argue for additional gun licensing so that readers agree on its necessity

dev

1e

With any writing assignment, try to define your specific purpose as soon as you have formed a question about your subject. Don't worry, though, if you feel uncertain of your purpose at the start. Sometimes you may not discover your purpose until you begin drafting, or you may find that your initial sense of purpose changes as you move through the writing process.

Exercise 1.6 Finding purpose in assignments
For each of your questions from Exercise 1.3 (p. 17), suggest a likely general purpose (entertainment, self-expression, explanation, persuasion) and try to define a specific purpose as well.

Exercise 1.7 Considering your past work: Defining a purpose
Look over two or three things you've written in the past year or so. What was your specific purpose in each one? How did the purpose influence your writing? Did you achieve your purpose?

Exercise

Exercise 1.8 Defining a purpose for your essay
For your essay-in-progress, use your thinking so far about your subject (Exercise 1.5, p. 17) to define a general and specific purpose for your writing.

1e Considering the audience

- Who are my readers?
- Why will they read my writing?
- What will they expect from my writing?
- What can I do to interest them in my writing?
- How do I want them to perceive me?
- What do I want them to think or do after they read my writing?

The preceding questions are central to any writing project, and they will crop up again and again. Except in writing meant only for yourself, you are always trying to communicate with readers— something about a particular subject, for a particular purpose.

Your audience will often be specified or implied in a writing assignment. When you write an editorial for the student newspaper, your audience consists of other students at your school. When you write a report on a physics experiment, your audience consists of your physics instructor and perhaps other physicists or your classmates. Considering the needs and expectations of your readers can help you form or focus a question about your subject, gather answers to the question, and ultimately decide what to say and how to say it.

1 Knowing what readers expect

As a reader yourself, you know what readers expect from writing:

- **Context:** a link between what they read and their own knowledge and experiences.
- **Predictability:** an understanding of the writer's purpose and how it is being achieved.
- **Information:** the specific facts, examples, and other details that make the subject clear, interesting, and convincing.
- **Respect:** a sense that the writer respects their values and beliefs, their backgrounds, and their intelligence.
- **Voice:** a sense that the writer is a real person whose mind and values are expressed in the writing (see opposite).
- **Readability, clarity, and correctness:** writing that is organized, focused, and free of unnecessary stumbling blocks and mistakes.

For much academic and public writing, readers have definite needs and expectations. Thus Chapter 7 discusses academic writing in general, Chapters 48–52 discuss writing in various disciplines, and Chapter 11 discusses public writing. Even in these areas, you must make many choices based on audience. In other areas where the conventions of structure and presentation are less well defined, the choices are even more numerous. The following box contains questions that can help you define and make these choices.

Questions about audience

Checklist

Identity and expectations

- Who *are* my readers?
- What are my readers' expectations for the genre of my writing? Do readers expect features such as a particular organization and format, distinctive kinds of evidence, or a certain style of documenting sources?

- What do I want readers to know or do after reading my work? How should I make that clear to them?
- How should I project myself to readers? How formal or informal will they expect me to be? What role and tone should I assume?

Characteristics, knowledge, and attitudes

- What characteristics of readers are relevant for my subject and purpose? For instance:

Age and sex
Occupation: students, professional colleagues, etc.
Social or economic role: subject-matter experts, voters, car buyers, potential employers, etc.
Economic or educational background
Ethnic background
Political, religious, or moral beliefs and values
Hobbies or activities

- How will the characteristics of readers influence their attitudes toward my subject?
- What do readers already know and *not* know about my subject? How much do I have to tell them? What aspects of my subject will be interesting and relevant to them?
- How should I handle any specialized terms? Will readers know them? If not, should I define them or avoid them?
- What ideas, arguments, or information might surprise, excite, or offend readers? How should I handle these points?
- What misconceptions might readers have of my subject and/or my approach to it? How can I dispel these misconceptions?

Uses and format

- What will readers do with my writing? Should I expect them to read every word from the top, to scan for information, to look for conclusions? Can I help readers by providing a summary, headings, illustrations, or other aids? (See pp. 117–42 on presenting writing.)

dev

1e

2 Expressing your voice

Your sense of your audience will influence three key elements of what you write:

- The specific information you use to gain and keep the attention of readers and to guide them to accept your conclusions. This information may consist of concrete details, facts, examples, or other evidence that makes your ideas clear, supports your assertions, and suits your readers' needs. The evidence may come from your experience or from outside sources.
- The role you choose to play in relation to your readers. Depending on your purpose and your attitude toward your topic, you will want readers to perceive you in a certain way. The

possible roles are many and varied—for instance, scholar, storyteller, lecturer, guide, reporter, advocate, inspirer.

■ **The tone you use.** **Tone** in writing is like tone of voice in speaking: words and sentence structures on the page convey some of the same information as pitch and volume in the voice. Depending on your aims and what you think your readers will expect and respond to, your tone may be formal or informal. The attitude you convey may be serious or light, forceful or calm, irritated or cheerful.

These three elements contribute to what's often called **voice:** your projection of yourself into the writing. Your voice conveys your sense of the world as it applies to the particular writing situation: this subject, this purpose, this audience. Thus voice can vary quite a bit from one writing situation to another, as the following memos illustrate. Both were written by a student who worked part-time in a small company and wanted to get the company to recycle paper. But the two memos address different readers.

To coworkers	
Ever notice how much paper collects in your trash basket every day? Well, most of it can be recycled with little effort, I promise. Basically, all you need to do is set a bag or box near your desk and deposit wastepaper in it. I know, space is cramped in these little cubicles. But can't we all accept a little more crowding when the earth's at stake? . . .	**Voice:** a peer who is thoughtful, cheerful, and sympathetic

Information: how employees could handle recycling; no mention of costs

Role: colleague

Tone: informal, personal (*Ever notice*; *Well*; *you*; *I know, space is cramped*) |

To management	
In my four months here, I have observed that all of us throw out baskets of potentially recyclable paper every day. Considering the drain on our forest resources and the pressure on landfills that paper causes, we could make a valuable contribution to the environmental movement by helping to recycle the paper we use. At the company where I worked before, employees separate clean wastepaper from other trash at their desks. The maintenance staff collects trash in two receptacles, and the trash hauler (the same one we use here) makes separate pickups. I do not know what the hauler charges for handling recyclable material. . . .	**Voice:** a subordinate who is thoughtful, responsible, and serious

Information: specific reasons; view of company as a whole; reference to another company; problem of cost

Role: employee

Tone: formal, serious (*Considering the drain*; *forest resources*; *valuable contribution*; no *you*) |

Projecting your writing voice can be challenging when you are responding to another's work or drawing on multiple sources for evidence. Especially if you feel unconfident about your subject, you may be tempted to let the other writers do the talking for you. See pages 173–75 and 626–28 on maintaining your voice by using synthesis.

Exercise 1.9 Considering audience

Exercise

Choose one of the following subjects and, for each audience specified, ask the questions on pages 20–21. Decide on four points you would make, the role you would assume, and the tone you would adopt for each audience. Then write a paragraph for each based on your decisions.

1. The effects of smoking: for elementary school students and for adult smokers
2. Your opposition to a proposed law requiring adult bicyclists to wear helmets: for cyclists who oppose the law and for people who favor it
3. Why your neighbors should remove the wrecked truck from their front yard: for your neighbors and for your town zoning board

Exercise 1.10 Considering your past work: Writing for a specific audience

Exercise

How did audience figure in a piece of writing you've done in the recent past—perhaps an essay for an application or a paper for a course? Who were your readers? How did your awareness of them influence your voice? At what point in the writing process did you find it most productive to consider your readers consciously?

Exercise 1.11 Analyzing the audience for your essay

Use the questions on pages 20–21 to determine as much as you can about the probable readers of your essay-in-progress (see Exercises 1.5 and 1.8). What might be an appropriate voice for your writing? What specific information will your readers need? What role do you want to assume? What tone will best convey your attitude toward your topic?

1f   Using genres

Writers use familiar **genres**, or types of writing, to express their ideas. You can recognize many genres: the poems and novels of literature, the résumé in business writing, the news article about a sporting event. In college you will be asked to write in a wide range of genres, such as analyses, lab reports, reviews, proposals, oral presentations, even blog posts.

Most simply, a genre is the conventional form that writing takes in a certain context. In academic writing, genre conventions help to further the aims of the disciplines; for instance, the features of a lab report emphasize the procedures, results, and conclusion that are important in scientific investigation. The conventions also help to improve communication because the writer knows what readers expect and readers can predict what they will encounter in the writing. Suppose your instructor assigns an argument essay and asks classmates to read one another's drafts. As you approach one paper titled "Animal Rights," you expect the essay to contain the conventional elements of argument: an introduction, a main claim or thesis about animal rights, paragraphs that develop that claim with evidence, and a conclusion. When the draft meets your expectations in these respects, you can settle into its substance. However, if instead of an argument you find a funny narrative about the writer's dog, your thwarted expectations will throw off your response. Searching for the argument, you might even miss the humor in the story.

When you receive a writing assignment, be sure to understand any requirements relating to genre:

1f

- **Is a particular genre being assigned?** An assignment that asks you to write an analysis, an argument, or a report has specified the genre for you to use. In contrast, an assignment that asks you to write for the purpose of recruiting new members to a club leaves the choice of genre up to you—perhaps a flyer to post on campus, a brochure to hand out in the cafeteria, an e-mail message, or a *Facebook* page.
- **What are the conventions of the genre?** Your instructor and/or your textbook will probably outline the requirements for you. You can also learn about a genre by reading samples of it. Consult page 172 for a list of the sample documents in this handbook.
- **What flexibility do you have?** Within their conventions, most genres still allow plenty of room for your own approach and voice. Again, reading samples will show you much about your options.

Exercise

Exercise 1.12 Thinking about genre

Following is a list of writing genres in no particular order. You should be familiar with most of them even if you haven't studied or written in them.

personal essay	posting on the college Web site
informative flyer	memoir
brochure	written report
oral report	informative Web site
letter to the editor	

For each of the following subject-audience pairs, suggest one of the above genres that might be appropriate and explain why you think its features would work.

1. Subject: your memories of learning to read. Audience: your writing class.
2. Subject: state laws against texting while driving. Audience: sixteen-year-olds.
3. Subject: a new cyberbullying policy on your campus. Audience: students on your campus.
4. Subject: the carbon footprint of dogs. Audience: people in your city.
5. Subject: results of a survey on dating behavior on your campus. Audience: a psychology class.

Exercise

Exercise 1.13 Considering your past work: Analyzing genre

Look over two or three things you've recently written, such as an application essay, a report, an essay for class, or a letter of complaint. Can you identify the genre of each piece? How does what you wrote meet your readers' expectations for the genre? How does your writing change from one genre to another?

Exercise 1.14 Determining the genre for your essay
For your essay-in-progress, use your thinking so far about your subject, purpose, and audience to determine the genre of your essay. List the expectations readers will have for an essay in that genre.

2

Discovering and Shaping Ideas

Once you have assessed your writing situation, or even while you're assessing it, you'll begin answering the question you posed about your subject (pp. 14–15). As you generate ideas and information, they in turn may cause you to rephrase your lead question, which will open up new areas to explore. Throughout this discovery process, you'll also be bringing order to your thoughts, focusing and organizing them so that readers will respond as you intend.

2a Discovering ideas

Video
tutorial

For some writing projects, you may have little difficulty finding what you have to say about your subject: possible answers to your starting question will tumble forth as ideas on paper or screen. But when you're stuck for what to say, you'll have to coax answers out. Instead of waiting around for inspiration to strike, use a technique to get your mind working. Anything is appropriate: if you like to make drawings or take pictures, for instance, then try that.

The following pages describe techniques for discovering ideas. These techniques are to be selected from, not followed in sequence: some may help you during early stages of the writing process, even before you're sure of your topic; others may help you later on; and one or two may not help at all. Give yourself ample time with the techniques, experimenting to discover which ones work best for you.

Note **Whatever techniques you use, do your work in writing, not just in your head.** Your work will be retrievable, and the act of

mycomplab
Visit *mycomplab.com* for the eText and for resources and more exercises on discovering and shaping Ideas.

dev
2a

Discovering and shaping ideas

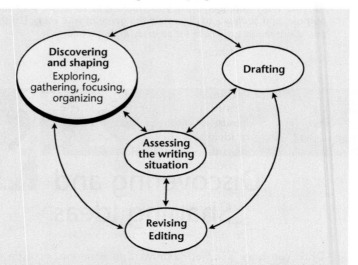

Discovering ideas and shaping them may occur at any point in the writing process, from the initial choice of subject through drafting and revision.

writing will help you concentrate and lead you to fresh, sometimes surprising, insights.

CULTURE LANGUAGE The discovery process encouraged here rewards rapid writing without a lot of thinking beforehand about what you will write or how. If your first language is not standard American English, you may find it helpful initially to do this exploratory writing in your native language or dialect and then to translate the worthwhile material for use in your drafts. This process can be productive, but it is extra work. Eventually, you'll want to move to composing in standard American English.

Techniques for discovering a subject

Video tutorial

- Read (opposite).
- Keep a journal (p. 28).
- Observe your surroundings (p. 30).
- Freewrite (p. 30).
- Brainstorm (p. 31).
- Draw (p. 32).
- Use the journalist's questions (p. 33).
- Use the patterns of development (p. 33).

1 Reading

Many assignments require you to respond to reading or to consult texts as sources for your writing. But even when reading is not required, it can help you locate or develop a subject by introducing you to ideas you didn't know or by expanding on what you already know.

For example, say you were writing in favor of amateur athletics, a subject to which you had given a lot of thought. You might be inclined to proceed entirely on your own, drawing on facts, examples, and opinions already in your head. But a little digging in sources might open up more ideas. For instance, an article in *Time* magazine could introduce you to an old rule for amateur status, or a comment on a blog could suggest an argument in favor of amateurism that hadn't occurred to you. *Remember: whenever you use the information or ideas of others in your writing, you must acknowledge your sources in order to avoid the serious offense of plagiarism.* (See Chapter 44.)

dev

2a

Often you will be given an assignment that asks you to use a text or texts in your writing. In a composition course, Katy Moreno's instructor distributed "It's a Flat World, after All," an essay by Thomas L. Friedman about globalization and the job market. The instructor then gave the following assignment, calling for a response to reading:

> In "It's a Flat World, after All," Thomas L. Friedman describes today's global job market, focusing not on manufacturing jobs that have been "outsourced" to overseas workers but on jobs that require a college degree and are no longer immune to outsourcing. Friedman argues that keeping jobs in the United States requires that US students, parents, and educators improve math and science education. As a college student, how do you respond to this analysis of the global market for jobs? What do you think today's college students should be learning?

To respond to Friedman's essay, Moreno had to digest its argument. On first reading the essay, she had found it convincing because Friedman's description of the job market matched her family's experience: her mother had lost her job when it was outsourced to India. After rereading the essay, however, Moreno was not persuaded that more math and science would necessarily improve students' opportunities and preserve their future jobs. She compared Friedman's advice with details she recalled from her mother's experience, and she began to develop a response by writing in her journal:

> Friedman is certainly right that more jobs than we realize are going overseas—that's what happened to Mom's job and we were shocked! But he gives only one way for students like me to compete—take more math and science. At first I thought he's totally right. But then I thought that what he said didn't really explain what happened to Mom—she had lots of math + science +

tons of experience, but it was her salary, not better training, that caused her job to be outsourced. An overseas worker would do her job for less money. So she lost her job because of money + because she wasn't a manager. Caught in the middle. I want to major in computer science, but I don't think it's smart to try for the kind of job Mom had—at least not as long as it's so much cheaper for companies to hire workers overseas.

dev
2a

When you read for ideas, you need to be active, probing the text and illustrations with your mind, nurturing any sparks they set off. Always write while you read, taking notes on content and—just as important—on what the content makes you *think*. If you read passively, absorbing content like a sponge and not interacting with it, you won't have much to say about it. (See pp. 146–47 for specific tips on active reading.)

2 Keeping a journal

Video
tutorial

A **journal** is a place to record your responses, thoughts, and observations about what you read, see, hear, or experience. It can also be a good source of ideas for writing. It is a kind of diary, but one more concerned with ideas than with day-to-day events. *Journal* comes from the Latin for "daily," and many journal keepers do write faithfully every day; others make entries less regularly, when the mood strikes or an insight occurs or they have a problem to work out.

Advantages of a journal

Writing in a journal, you are writing to yourself. That means you don't have to worry about main ideas, organization, correct grammar and spelling, or any of the other requirements of writing for others. You can work out your ideas and feelings without the pressure of an audience "out there" who will evaluate your thinking and expression. The freedom and flexibility of a journal can be liberating. Like many others, you may find writing easier, more fun, and more rewarding than you thought possible.

You can keep a journal either on paper (such as a notebook) or on a computer. If you write in the journal every day, or almost, even just for a few minutes, the routine will loosen up your writing muscles and improve your confidence. Indeed, journal keepers often become dependent on the process for the writing practice it gives them, the concentrated thought it encourages, and the connection it fosters between personal, private experience and public information and events.

Usually for the same reasons, teachers of writing and other subjects sometimes require students to keep journals. The teachers may even collect students' journals to monitor progress, but they read the journals with an understanding of purpose (in other words, they do not evaluate work that was not written to be evaluated), and they usually just credit rather than grade the work.

CULTURE · LANGUAGE — A journal can be especially helpful if your first language is not standard American English. You can practice writing to improve your fluency, try out sentence patterns, and experiment with vocabulary words. Equally important, you can experiment with applying what you know from experience to what you read and observe.

Uses of a journal

Two uses of a journal are discussed elsewhere in this book: a reading journal, in which you think critically (in writing) about what you read (pp. 146, 758–59); and a research journal, in which you record your activities and ideas while you pursue a research project (p. 571). But you can use a journal for other purposes as well. Here are just a few:

- Prepare for or respond to a course you're taking by puzzling over a reading or a class discussion.
- Build ideas for specific writing assignments.
- Sketch possible designs for a Web composition.
- Explore your reactions to events, trends, or the media.
- Confide your hopes.
- Write about your own history: an event in your family's past, a troubling incident in your life, a change you've seen.
- Analyze a relationship that disturbs you.
- Practice various forms or styles of writing—for instance, poems or songs, reviews of movies, or reports for TV news.

dev 2a

The writing you produce in your journal will help you learn and grow, and even the personal and seemingly nonacademic entries can supply ideas when you are seeking a subject to write about or are developing an essay. A thought you recorded months ago about a chemistry lab may provide direction for a research paper on the history of science. Two entries about arguments with your brother may suggest what you need to anchor a psychology paper on sibling relations. If you keep your journal on a computer, you can even copy passages from it directly into your drafts.

On pages 27–28 we saw Katy Moreno's journal response to an essay she read. The next two student samples give a taste of journal writing for different purposes. In the first, Charlie Gabnes tries to work out a personal problem with his child:

> Will's tantrums are getting worse—more often, more intense. Beginning to realize it's affecting my feelings for him. I feel resentment sometimes, and it's not as easy for me to cool off afterward as for him. Also I'm afraid of him sometimes for fear a tantrum will start, so treat him with kid gloves. How do we break this cycle?

In the second example Megan Polanyis ponders something she learned from her biology textbook:

Ecology and *economics* have the same root—Greek word for house. Economy = managing the house. Ecology = studying the house. In ecology the house is all of nature, ourselves, the other animals, the plants, the earth, the air, the whole environment. Ecology has a lot to do with economy: study the house in order to manage it.

3 Observing your surroundings

Sometimes you can find a good subject or good ideas by looking around you, not in the half-conscious way most of us move from place to place in our daily lives but deliberately, all senses alert. On a bus, for instance, are there certain types of passengers? What seems to be on the driver's mind? On campus, which buildings stand out? Are bicyclists and pedestrians at peace with each other?

To get the most from observation, you should have a mobile device or a notepad and pen handy for taking notes and making sketches. If you have a camera, you may find that the lens sees things your unaided eyes do not notice. (When observing or photographing people, though, keep some distance, take photographs quickly, and avoid staring. Otherwise your subjects will feel uneasy.) Back at your desk, study your notes, sketches, or photographs for oddities or patterns that you'd like to explore further.

In some academic writing, you'll be expected to formalize observation and perhaps combine it with surveys, interviews, or experiments. See pages 608–10.

4 Freewriting

Writing into a subject

Many writers find subjects or discover ideas by **freewriting:** writing without stopping for a certain amount of time (say, ten minutes) or to a certain length (say, one page). The goal of freewriting is to generate ideas and information from *within* yourself by going around the part of your mind that doesn't want to write or can't think of anything to write. You let words themselves suggest other words. *What* you write is not important; that you *keep* writing is. Don't stop, even if that means repeating the same words until new words come. Don't go back to reread, don't censor ideas that seem off-track or repetitious, and above all don't stop to edit: grammar, punctuation, vocabulary, spelling, and the like are irrelevant at this stage.

The physical act of freewriting may give you access to ideas you were unaware of. For example, the following freewriting by a student, Robert Benday, drew him into the subject of writing as a disguise:

Write to write. Seems pretty obvious, also weird. What to gain by writing? never anything before. Writing seems always—always—Getting corrected for trying too hard to please the teacher, getting corrected for not trying hard enuf. Frustration, nail biting, sometimes getting carried away making sentences to tell stories, not even true stories, *esp.* not true stories, *that* feels like creating something. Writing just pulls the story out of me. The story lets me be someone else, gives me a disguise.

(A later phase of Benday's writing appears on p. 33.)

If you can dim or turn off your computer monitor, you can try **invisible writing** to keep moving forward while freewriting. As you type to a dark screen, the computer will record what you type but keep it from you and thus prevent you from tinkering with your prose. Invisible writing may feel uncomfortable at first, but it can free the mind for very creative results. When you've finished freewriting, simply turn the monitor on or turn up the brightness control to read what you've written, and then save or revise it as appropriate. Later you may be able to transfer some of your freewriting directly into your draft.

dev

2a

Invisible writing can be especially helpful if you are uneasy writing in standard American English and you tend to worry about errors while writing. The blank computer screen leaves you no choice but to explore ideas without giving attention to the way you are expressing them. If you choose to write with the monitor on, concentrate on *what* you want to say, not *how* you are saying it.

Focused freewriting

Focused freewriting is more concentrated: you start with your question about your subject and answer it without stopping for, say, fifteen minutes or one full page. As in all freewriting, you push to bypass mental blocks and self-consciousness, not debating what to say or editing what you've written. With focused freewriting, though, you let the physical act of writing take you into and around your subject.

An example of focused freewriting can be found in Katy Moreno's journal response to Thomas L. Friedman's "It's a Flat World, after All" (pp. 27–28). Since she already had an idea about Friedman's essay, Moreno was able to start there and expand on the idea.

5 Brainstorming

In **brainstorming,** you focus intently on your subject for a fixed amount of time (say, fifteen minutes), pushing yourself to list every idea and detail that comes to mind. Like freewriting, brainstorming requires turning off your internal editor so that you keep moving ahead instead of looping back over what you have already written to correct it. It makes no difference whether the ideas and details are expressed in phrases or complete sentences. It makes no difference if they seem silly or irrelevant. Just keep pushing. If you are working on a computer, the technique of invisible writing, described above, can help you move forward.

Here is an example of brainstorming by a student, Johanna Abrams, responding to the question *What can a summer job teach?*

> summer work teaches—
>
> > how to look busy while doing nothing
> > how to avoid the sun in summer
> > seriously: discipline, budgeting money, value of money
>
> which job? Burger King cashier? baby-sitter? mail-room clerk?
> mail room: how to sort mail into boxes: this is learning??
> how to survive getting fired—humiliation, outrage
> Mrs. King! the mail-room queen as learning experience
> the shock of getting fired: what to tell parents, friends?
> Mrs. K was so rigid—dumb procedures
> Mrs. K's anger, resentment: the disadvantages of being smarter than your boss
> The odd thing about working in an office: a world with its own rules for how
> > to act
> what Mr. D said about the pecking order—big chick (Mrs. K) pecks on little
> > chick (me)
> probably lots of Mrs. Ks in offices all over—offices are all barnyards
> Mrs. K a sad person, really—just trying to hold on to her job, preserve her
> > self-esteem
> a job can beat you down—destroy self-esteem, make you desperate enough to
> > be mean to other people
> how to preserve/gain self-esteem from work??
> if I'd known about the pecking order, I would have been less arrogant

dev

2a

(A later phase of Abrams's writing appears on p. 44.)

When you think you've exhausted the ideas on your topic, you can edit and shape the list into a preliminary outline of your paper (see pp. 43–44). Working on a computer makes this step fairly easy: you can delete weak ideas, expand strong ones, and rearrange items with a few keystrokes. You can also freewrite from the list if you think some items are especially promising and deserve more exploration.

6 Drawing

Like freewriting and list making, the technique of **clustering** or **idea mapping** uses free association to produce rapid, unedited work. But it also emphasizes the *relations* between ideas by combining writing and nonlinear drawing. Start with your topic at a center point and then radiate outward with ideas. Pursue related ideas in a branching structure until they seem exhausted. Then do the same with other ideas, staying open to connections, continuously branching out or drawing arrows.

The following example shows how Robert Benday used the technique for ten minutes to expand on the topic of creative writing as a means of disguise, an idea he arrived at through freewriting (see pp. 30–31). Though he ventured into one dead end, Benday also circled into the interesting possibility (at the bottom) that the fiction writer is like a god who forgives himself by creating characters that represent his good and bad qualities.

Clustering or idea mapping

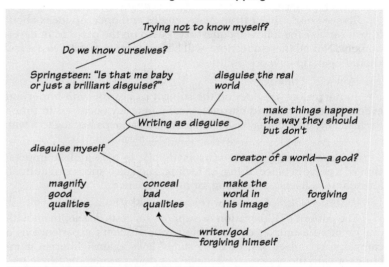

7 Using the journalist's questions

Asking yourself a set of questions about your subject—and writing out the answers—can help you look at the subject objectively and see fresh possibilities in it. Asking questions can also provide some structure to the development of ideas.

One such set of questions is that posed by a journalist with a story to report:

- Who was involved?
- What happened and what were the results?
- When did it happen?
- Where did it happen?
- Why did it happen?
- How did it happen?

These questions can also be useful in probing an essay subject, especially if you are telling a story or examining causes and effects.

8 Using the patterns of development

The **patterns of development**—such as narration, definition, comparison and contrast, and classification—are ways we think about and understand a vast range of subjects, from our own daily experiences to the most complex scientific theories. They also serve as strategies and patterns for writing about these subjects, as illustrated by the discussions and paragraph-length examples on pages

98–108. You may want to refer to those pages for more information about each pattern.

To see your subject from many angles and open up ideas about it, you can ask the following questions based on the patterns of development. Not all these questions will be productive, but at least a few should open up new possibilities.

How did it happen?

In **narration** you develop the subject as a story, with important events usually arranged chronologically (as they occurred in time): for instance, an exciting basketball game or the steps leading to a war.

How does it look, sound, feel, smell, taste?

In **description** you use sensory details to give a clear impression of a person, place, thing, or feeling, such as a species of animal, a machine, a friend, a building, or an experience.

What are examples of it or reasons for it?

The pattern of **illustration** or **support** suggests development with one or more examples of the subject (one student's experience as a campaign volunteer, say, or three states' laws against Internet gambling) or with the reasons for believing or doing something (three reasons for majoring in English, four reasons for increasing federal aid to college students).

What is it? What does it encompass, and what does it exclude?

These questions lead to **definition:** specifying what the subject is and is not to give a precise sense of its meaning. Abstract terms—such as *justice*, *friendship*, and *art*—especially need defining (see p. 190).

What are its parts or characteristics?

Using the pattern of **division** or **analysis,** you separate a subject such as a bicycle or a short story into its elements and examine the relations between elements. The first step in critical thinking, analysis is also discussed on pages 155–56.

What groups or categories can it be sorted into?

Classification involves separating a large group (such as cars) into smaller groups (conventional gas, hybrid, plug-in electric) based on the characteristics of the individual items (the kinds of engines). Another example: academic, business, personal, literary, and other types of writing.

How is it like, or different from, other things?

With **comparison and contrast** you point out the similarities and differences between ideas, objects, people, places, and so on: the differences between two similar computer systems, for instance, or the similarities between two opposing political candidates.

Is it comparable to something that is in a different class but more familiar to readers?

This question leads to **analogy,** an extended comparison of unlike subjects. Analogy is often used to explain a topic that may be unfamiliar to readers (for instance, the relation of atoms in a molecule) by reference to a familiar topic (two people dancing close together).

Why did it happen, or what results did it have?

With **cause-and-effect analysis,** you explain why something happened or what its consequences were or will be, or both: the causes of cerebral palsy, the effects of a Supreme Court decision, the causes and effects of a gradual change in the climate.

How do you do it, or how does it work?

In **process analysis** you explain how the subject happens (how a plant grows, how a robot works) or how to accomplish it (how to write an essay).

Exercise 2.1   Considering your past work: Discovering ideas

In the past how have you generated the ideas for writing? Have you used any of the techniques described on the preceding pages? Have you found the process especially enjoyable or difficult? If some writing tasks were easier than others, what do you think made the difference?

Exercise

Exercise 2.2   Keeping a journal

If you haven't already started a journal on your own or in response to Exercise 1.1 (pp. 11–12), try to do so now. Every day for at least a week, write for at least fifteen minutes about anything on your mind—or consult the list on page 29 for ideas of what to write about. At the end of the week, write about your experience. What did you like about journal writing? What didn't you like? What did you learn about yourself or the world from the writing? How can you use this knowledge?

Exercise 2.3   Using freewriting, brainstorming, or drawing

If you haven't tried any of them before, experiment with freewriting, brainstorming, or drawing. Continue with the subject you selected in Exercise 1.5 (p. 17), or begin with a new subject. Write or draw for at least ten minutes without stopping to reread and edit. (Try using invisible writing as described on p. 31 if you're freewriting or brainstorming on a computer.) When you finish your experiment, examine what you have written for ideas and relationships that could help you develop the subject. What do you think of the technique you tried? Did you have any difficulties with it? Did it help you loosen up and generate ideas?

Exercise 2.4   Sending an online query

When you have spent some time developing your subject, consider any doubts you may have or any information you still need. Send a message to your classmates posing your questions and asking for their advice and insights.

Exercise 2.5   Developing your subject

Use at least two of the discovery techniques discussed on the preceding pages to develop the subject you selected in Exercise 1.5 (p. 17). (If you completed Exercise 2.3 above, then use one additional technique.) Later exercises for your essay-in-progress will be based on the ideas you generate in this exercise.

**dev
2b**

2b Developing a thesis

Your readers will expect an essay you write to be focused on a central idea, or **thesis**, to which all the essay's paragraphs, all its general statements and specific information, relate. The thesis is the controlling idea, the main point, the conclusion you draw from your evidence. In answering your question about your subject, the thesis is the intellectual position you are taking.

Often the thesis is expressed in a one- or two-sentence **thesis statement** toward the beginning of an essay. As an expression of the thesis, the thesis statement serves four crucial functions and one optional one:

Functions of the thesis statement

Video
tutorial

- The thesis statement narrows your subject to a single, central idea that you want readers to gain from your essay.
- It claims something specific and significant about your subject, a claim that requires support.
- It conveys your purpose—usually explanation or argument in college writing.
- It establishes your voice, suggesting your attitude toward your subject and the role you assume with readers.
- It often concisely previews the arrangement of ideas, in which case it can also help you organize your essay.

1 Starting with a thesis question

A thesis statement probably will not leap fully formed into your head. Many writers begin the process of developing a thesis by turning the assignment into a **thesis question.** If you used questions to narrow your subject (pp. 15–17), the thesis question continues this approach but with a sharper focus. A thesis question can help you figure out your position, organize your ideas, start drafting, and stay on track.

Consider again Katy Moreno's assignment on page 27:

> . . . As a college student, how do you respond to [Friedman's] analysis of the global market for jobs? What do you think today's college students should be learning?

Responding to the assignment, Moreno first rephrased it as two questions:

> To what extent do I agree or disagree with Friedman's argument that students today need better technical training to compete in the global job market?

> What should college students be learning?

Then Moreno reread Friedman's essay to clarify the disagreement she first expressed in her journal writing (pp. 27–28) and to begin applying this response to her own experience of her mother's job loss. The result was a single question that would guide her thinking:

> How does my mother's job loss contradict Friedman's argument about technical training as key to success in the global job market?

dev

2b

2 Moving from thesis question to thesis statement

Drafting a thesis statement can occur at almost any time in the process of writing. Some instructors suggest that students develop a thesis statement when they have a good stock of ideas, to give a definite sense of direction. Other instructors suggest that students work with their thesis question at least through drafting, to keep options open. And no matter when it's drafted, a thesis statement can change during the writing process, as the writer discovers ideas and expresses them in sentences.

Katy Moreno chose to try writing her thesis statement before drafting. Working from her thesis question (above), she wrote a sentence that named a topic and made a claim about it:

> The outsourcing of my mother's job proves that Thomas L. Friedman's advice to improve students' technical training is too narrow.

Moreno's topic is the outsourcing of her mother's job, and her claim is that Friedman's advice is too narrow. Although Moreno later revised her thesis statement (pp. 38–39), this draft statement gave her direction, and she used it in the first draft of her paper.

Following are more examples of thesis questions and answering thesis statements. Each statement consists of a topic and a claim. Notice how each statement also expresses purpose. Statements 1–3 are **explanatory:** the writers mainly want to explain something to readers, such as how a company survived a scandal. Statements 4–6 are **argumentative:** the authors mainly want to convince readers of something, such as that drivers' use of cell phones should be outlawed. Most of the thesis statements you write in college papers will be either explanatory or argumentative.

Thesis question	Explanatory thesis statement
1. How did Home Inc. survive the scandal over its hiring practices?	After Home Inc.'s hiring practices were exposed in the media, the company's survival depended on policy changes and a well-publicized outreach to employees and consumers. [**Topic:** the company's survival. **Claim:** depended on two actions.]
2. Why did Abraham Lincoln delay in emancipating the slaves?	Lincoln delayed emancipating any slaves until 1863 because his primary goal was to restore and preserve the Union, with or without slavery. [**Topic:** Lincoln's delay. **Claim:** was caused by his goal of preserving the Union.]

Thesis question	Explanatory thesis statement
3. What steps can prevent juvenile crime?	Juveniles can be diverted from crime by active learning programs, full-time sports, and intervention by mentors and role models. [**Topic:** juvenile crime. **Claim:** can be prevented in three ways.]

Thesis question	Argumentative thesis statement
4. Why should drivers' use of cell phones be banned?	Drivers' use of cell phones should be outlawed because people who talk and drive at the same time cause accidents. [**Topic:** drivers' use of cell phones. **Claim:** should be outlawed because it causes accidents.]
5. Which college students should be entitled to federal aid?	As an investment in its own economy, the federal government should provide a tuition grant to any college student who qualifies academically. [**Topic:** federal aid. **Claim:** should be provided to any college student who qualifies academically.]
6. Why should strip-mining be controlled?	Strip-mining should be tightly controlled in this region to reduce its pollution of water resources, its destruction of the land, and its devastating effects on people's lives. [**Topic:** strip-mining. **Claim:** should be tightly controlled for three reasons.]

Often the thesis statement predicts the organization of the essay that will follow, as statements 1, 3, and 6 do. For example, the essay that followed from statement 3 had three main points: active learning programs, full-time sports, and mentors and role models. Many students prefer this type of thesis statement because it helps them organize their writing and keep on track during drafting.

CULTURE LANGUAGE In some cultures it is considered rude or unnecessary for a writer to state his or her main idea outright or to state it near the beginning. When writing in American schools or workplaces, you can assume that your readers expect a clear and early idea of what you think.

3 Revising a thesis statement

You may have to write and rewrite a thesis statement before you come to a conclusion about your position. Katy Moreno used her draft thesis statement (previous page) in the first draft of her paper, but it didn't work well at that stage. She saw that it put too little emphasis on her actual topic (*technical training*) and overstated her disagreement with Friedman (*proves . . . is too narrow*). In addition, a reader's comment showed Moreno that her claim wasn't specific: Friedman's advice is *too narrow* for what? In her first revision, Moreno tried to emphasize her intended subject:

Technical training by itself . . .

Then she worked on her claim:

. . . can be too narrow to produce the communicators and problem solvers needed by contemporary businesses.

This statement clarified the claim (*can be too narrow to produce . . .*) and said why the subject was significant (. . . *communicators and problem solvers needed by contemporary businesses*). However, Moreno had dropped her mother's experience of losing her job to outsourcing, which was a key point in her response to Friedman's essay. Moreno tried again, adding her mother's experience:

dev

2b

My mother's experience of having her job outsourced showed that technical training by itself can be too narrow to produce the communicators and problem solvers needed by contemporary businesses.

For her final revision, Moreno responded to another reader's suggestion that she state her point of disagreement with Friedman more clearly:

My mother's experience of having her job outsourced taught a lesson that Thomas L. Friedman overlooks: technical training by itself can be too narrow to produce the communicators and problem solvers needed by contemporary businesses.

Often you must deliberately consider your audience as you draft a thesis statement. One student, Ben Nelson, was writing an argument for more student parking on campus. He arrived fairly easily at his initial claim:

Most students who commute to campus must drive to school, and they need more places to park.

However, to persuade school administrators to take action, Nelson realized that he needed to focus on them as his audience and strengthen his voice:

The school must provide enough parking spaces to accommodate the many students who drive to school and to protect all students from otherwise dangerous traffic congestion.

As you draft and revise your thesis statement over the course of the writing process, test it with the questions in the box on the next page. Here are other examples of thesis statements revised to meet the requirements given in the box:

Exercise

Original	Revised
Cell phones can be convenient, but they can also be dangerous. [Not unified: how do the two parts of the sentence relate?]	The convenience of cell phones does not justify the risks of driving while talking or texting.

Checklist for revising the thesis statement

- How well does the **subject** of your statement capture the subject of your paper?
- What **claim** does your statement make about your subject?
- What is the **significance** of the claim? How does it answer "So what?" and convey your purpose?
- How can the claim be **limited** or made more **specific**? Does it state a single idea and clarify the boundaries of the idea?
- How **unified** is the statement? How does each word and phrase contribute to a single idea?
- How well does the statement convey your **voice**?

Original	Revised
This new product brought in over $300,000 last year. [A statement of fact, not a claim about the product: what is significant about the product's success?]	This new product succeeded because of its innovative marketing campaign, including widespread press coverage, in-store entertainment, and a consumer newsletter.
People should not go on fad diets. [A vague statement that needs limiting with one or more reasons: what's wrong with fad diets?]	Fad diets can be dangerous when they deprive the body of essential nutrients or rely excessively on potentially harmful foods.
Televised sports are different from live sports. [A general statement: how are they different, and why is the difference significant?]	Although television cannot transmit all the excitement of a live game, its close-ups and slow-motion replays reveal much about the players and the strategy of the game.
Television viewing can reduce loneliness, cause laughter, and teach children. [Lacks voice: what is the writer's attitude toward the subject?]	Despite its many faults, television has at least one strong virtue: it provides replacement voices that can ease loneliness, spark healthful laughter, and even educate young children.

Note You may sometimes need more than one sentence for your thesis statement, particularly if it requires some buildup:

> Modern English, especially written English, is full of bad habits that interfere with clear thinking. Getting rid of these habits is a first step to political regeneration.
>
> —Adapted from George Orwell, "Politics and the English Language"

However, don't use this possibility to produce a wordy, general, or disunified statement. The two (or more) sentences must build on each other, and the final sentence must present the key assertion of your paper.

Exercise 2.6 Evaluating thesis statements

Exercise

Evaluate the following thesis statements, considering whether each one is sufficiently significant, specific, and unified. Also consider whether each conveys the writer's voice. Rewrite the statements as necessary to meet these goals.

dev

2c

1. Aggression usually leads to violence, injury, and even death, and we should use it constructively.
2. The religion of Islam is widely misunderstood in the United States.
3. Manners are a kind of social glue.
4. One episode of a radio talk show amply illustrates both the appeal of such shows and their silliness.
5. The poem is about motherhood.

Exercise 2.7 Considering your past work: Developing a thesis

Have you been aware in the past of focusing your essays on a central idea, or thesis? Have you found it more efficient to try to pin down your idea early or to let it evolve during drafting? To what extent has a thesis helped or hindered you in shaping your draft?

Exercise

Exercise 2.8 Drafting and revising your own thesis statement

Continuing from Exercise 2.5 (p. 35), write a thesis statement for your essay-in-progress. As much as possible at this point, your statement should be significant, specific, and unified, and it should convey your attitude toward your subject.

2c   Organizing ideas

An effective essay has a recognizable shape—an arrangement of parts that guides readers, helping them see how ideas and details relate to each other and contribute to the whole. You may sometimes let an effective organization emerge over one or more drafts. But many writers find that organizing ideas to some extent before drafting can provide a helpful sense of direction, as a map can help a driver negotiate a half-familiar system of roads. If you feel uncertain about the course your essay should follow or have a complicated topic with many parts, devising a shape for your material can clarify your options.

Before you begin organizing your material, look over all the writing you've done so far—freewriting, notes from reading, whatever. Either on paper or on a computer, pull together a master list of all the ideas and details that you think you might want to include. You can add to or subtract from the list as you think about shape.

1 Distinguishing the general and the specific

To organize material for an essay, you need to distinguish general and specific ideas and see the relations between ideas. **General** and **specific** refer to the number of instances or objects included in a group signified by a word. The "ladder" below illustrates a general-to-specific hierarchy.

dev
2c

Most general
↑ life form
| plant
| flowering plant
| rose
| American Beauty rose
↓ Uncle Dan's prize-winning American Beauty rose
Most specific

Here are some tips for arranging the ideas in your preliminary writing:

- **Underline, boldface, or circle the most general ideas.** These are the ideas that offer the main support for your thesis statement. They will be more general than the evidence that in turn supports them.

- **Make connections between each general idea and the more specific details that support it.** On paper, start with a fresh sheet, write each general idea down with space beneath it, and add specific information in the appropriate spaces. On a computer, re-arrange supporting information under more general points. You can use the Comment function to add notes about connections.

- **Respect the meanings of ideas.** Think through the implications of ideas as you sort them. Otherwise, your hierarchies could become jumbled, with *rose*, for instance, illogically subordinated to *animal*, or *life form* somehow subordinated to *rose*.

- **Remove information that doesn't fit.** If you worry about losing deleted information, transfer the notes to a separate sheet of paper or word-processing file.

- **Fill holes where support seems skimpy.** If you recognize a hole but don't know what to fill it with, try using a discovery technique such as freewriting or drawing, or go back to your research sources.

- **Experiment with various arrangements of general ideas and supporting information.** Seek an order that presents your material clearly and logically. On paper, you can cut the master list apart and paste or tape each general idea and its support on a separate piece of paper. Then try different orders for the pages. On a computer, first save the master list and duplicate it. To move material around, select a block of text and either copy and then paste it where you want it or (a little quicker) drag the selected text to where you want it.

2 Choosing an organizing tool

Some writers view outlines as chores and straitjackets, but they need not be dull or confining. There are different kinds of outlines, some more flexible than others. All of them can enlarge and clarify your thinking, showing you patterns of general and specific, suggesting proportions, and highlighting gaps or overlaps in coverage.

Many writers use outlines not only before but also after drafting— to check the underlying structure of the draft when revising it (see p. 60). No matter when it's made, though, an outline can be changed to reflect changes in your thinking. View any outline you make as a tentative sketch, not as a fixed paint-by-numbers diagram.

dev

2c

A scratch or informal outline

For many essays, especially those with a fairly straightforward structure, a simple listing of ideas and perhaps their support may provide adequate direction for your writing.

A **scratch outline** lists the key points of the paper in the order they will be covered. Here is Katy Moreno's scratch outline for her essay on the global job market:

Thesis statement

My mother's experience of having her job outsourced taught a lesson that Thomas L. Friedman overlooks: technical training by itself can be too narrow to produce the communicators and problem solvers needed by contemporary businesses.

Scratch outline

Mom's outsourcing experience
   Excellent tech skills
   Salary too high compared to overseas tech workers
   Lack of planning + communication skills, unlike managers who kept jobs
Well-rounded education to protect vs. outsourcing
   Tech training, as Friedman says
   Also, experience in communication, problem solving, other management skills

Moreno put more into this outline than its simplicity might imply, not only working out an order for her ideas but also sketching their implications.

An **informal outline** is usually more detailed than a scratch outline, including key general points and the specific evidence for them. A student's informal outline appears below.

Thesis statement

After Home Inc.'s hiring practices were exposed in the media, the company avoided a scandal with policy changes and a well-publicized outreach to employees and consumers.

Informal outline

Background on scandal
   Previous hiring practices
   Media exposure and public response (brief)

> Policy changes
>> Application forms
>> Interviewing procedures
>> Training of personnel
> Outreach to employees
>> Signs and letters
>> Meetings and workshops
> Outreach to consumers
>> Press conference
>> Store signs
>> Advertising—print and radio

A tree diagram

In a **tree diagram,** ideas and details branch out in increasing specificity. Like any outline, the diagram can warn of gaps, overlaps, and digressions. But unlike more linear outlines, it can be supplemented and extended indefinitely, so it is easy to alter for new ideas and arrangements discovered during drafting and revision.

Below is a tree diagram by Johanna Abrams, based on her earlier brainstorming about a summer job (p. 32) and the following thesis statement:

Thesis statement

Two months working in a large government agency taught me that an office's pecking order should be respected.

Tree diagram

Each main part of the four-part diagram represents a different general idea about the summer-job experience. Within each part, information grows more specific as it branches downward.

A tree diagram or other visual map can be especially useful for planning a project for the Web. The diagram can help you lay out the organization of your project and its links and later can serve as a site map for your readers. (For more on composing for the Web, see pp. 130–34.)

A formal outline

For complex topics requiring complex arrangements of ideas and support, you may want or be required to construct a **formal outline**. More rigidly arranged and more detailed than other outlines, a formal outline not only lays out main ideas and their support but also shows the relative importance of all the essay's elements and how they connect with one another.

dev

2c

Note Because of its structure, a formal outline can be an excellent tool for planning a revision. For instance, you might use an outline to check that your organization is logical or to see how a new section might fit in. Katy Moreno created the following formal outline to plan expansions and other changes that were suggested by readers of her first draft.

Video
tutorial

Thesis statement

My mother's experience of having her job outsourced taught a lesson that Thomas L. Friedman overlooks: technical training by itself can be too narrow to produce the communicators and problem solvers needed by contemporary businesses.

Formal outline

I. Summary of Friedman's article
  A. Reasons for outsourcing
    1. Improved technology and access
    2. Well-educated workers
    3. Productive workers
    4. Lower wages
  B. Need for improved technical training in US
II. Mother's experience
  A. Outsourcing of job
    1. Mother's education, experience, performance
    2. Employer's cost savings
  B. Retention of managers' jobs
    1. Planning skills
    2. Communication skills
III. Conclusions about ideal education
  A. Needs of US businesses
    1. Technical skills
    2. Management skills
      a. Communication
      b. Problem solving
      c. Versatility
  B. Personal goals
    1. Technical training
    2. English and history courses for management skills

Moreno's outline illustrates several principles of outlining that can help ensure completeness, balance, and clear relationships. (These principles largely depend on distinguishing between the general and the specific. See p. 42.)

See p. 42.

- **All the outline's parts are systematically indented and labeled.** Roman numerals (I, II) label primary divisions of the essay, followed by capital letters (A, B) for secondary divisions, Arabic numerals (1, 2) for principal supporting points, and small letters (a, b) for details. Each succeeding level contains more specific information than the one before it.

- **The outline divides the material into several groups.** A list like the one following needs tighter, more logical groups to show the relationships between A and B and between C and D. (Compare this example with part III of Moreno's actual outline.)

> III. Conclusions about ideal education
> A. Business needs for technical skills
> B. Needs for management skills such as communication and problem solving
> C. Personal goal of technical training
> D. Additional courses for management skills

- **Within each part of the outline, distinct topics of equal generality appear in parallel headings,** with the same indention and numbering or lettering. In the following example, points 3, 4, and 5 are more specific than point 2, not equally general, so they should appear as subheadings a, b, and c under it. (See section III.A of Moreno's outline.)

> A. Needs of US businesses
> 1. Technical skills
> 2. Management skills
> 3. Communication
> 4. Problem solving
> 5. Versatility

- **All subdivided headings in the outline break into at least two parts** because a topic cannot logically be divided into only one part. The following example violates this principle:

> B. Personal goals
> 1. Technical training along with other courses for management skills

Any single subdivision should be matched with another subdivision (as in section III.B of Moreno's actual outline), combined with the heading above it, or rechecked for its relevance to the heading above it.

- **All headings are expressed in parallel grammatical form** (see pp. 420–24 on parallelism). Moreno's is a **topic outline,** in which the headings consist of a noun (*summary, reasons, technology and access,* and the like) with modifiers (*of Friedman's essay, improved,*

Principles of the formal outline

- Labels and indentions indicate order and relative importance.
- Sections and subsections reflect logical relationships.
- Topics of equal generality appear in parallel headings.
- Each subdivision has at least two parts.
- Headings are expressed in parallel grammatical form.
- The introduction and conclusion may be omitted (though not, of course, from the essay).

Video tutorial

dev

2c

well-educated, and the like). In a **sentence outline** all headings are expressed as full sentences, as in the following rewrite of part III.A of Moreno's outline.

III. Friedman's article and my mother's experience lead me to conclusions about the ideal education.
   A. US businesses have dual needs for the jobs they keep here.
      1. They need employees with technical training.
      2. They need employees with management skills.

See pages 720–21 for a complete sentence outline.

- **The outline covers only the body of the essay, omitting the introduction and the conclusion.** The beginning and the ending are important in the essay itself, but you need not include them in the outline unless you are required to do so or you anticipate special problems with their organization.

3   Choosing a structure

Introduction, body, and conclusion

Structure is one of the features that distinguish genres of writing. For instance, a social science research report generally has distinct sections in an established order: abstract, introduction, method, results, and discussion. Many academic genres, particularly those in the humanities, do not come with such a detailed plan, but they still share a basic shape:

- The *introduction,* usually a paragraph or two, captures and focuses readers' attention. At a minimum, it announces and clarifies the topic. Often it ends with the thesis statement, making a commitment that the rest of the work delivers on. (See pp. 110–13 for more on introductions.)
- The *body* of the essay develops the thesis and thus fulfills the commitment of the introduction. The paragraphs in the body develop the general points that support the thesis—the items that would be labeled with Roman numerals and capital letters in a formal outline like the one on page 45. These general points are like the legs of a table supporting the top, the thesis. Each general point may take a paragraph or more, with the bulk of the content

providing the details, examples, and reasons (the wood of the table) to support the general point and thus the thesis.

■ The *conclusion* gives readers something to take away from the writing—a summary of ideas, for instance, or a suggested course of action. (See pp. 114–15 for more on conclusions.)

This basic shape applies mainly to traditional academic essays. Compositions for the Web generally have more flexible structures and lack formal conclusions. (See pages 130–34 for more on Web composition.) Other genres, such as proposals and other forms of public writing, are organized differently. (See pages 235–50 for more on public writing.)

CULTURE LANGUAGE If you are not used to reading and writing American academic prose, its pattern of introduction-body-conclusion and the particular organizations discussed below may seem unfamiliar. For instance, instead of introductions that focus quickly on the topic and thesis, you may be used to openings that establish personal connections with readers or that approach the thesis indirectly. And instead of body paragraphs that first emphasize general points and then support those points with specific evidence, you may be used to general statements without support (because writers can assume that readers will supply the evidence themselves) or to evidence without explanation (because writers can assume that readers will infer the general points themselves). When writing American academic prose, you need to take into account readers' expectations for directness and for the statement and support of general points.

Organizing the body by space or time

Video tutorial

Two organizational schemes—spatial and chronological—grow naturally out of the topic. A **spatial organization** is especially appropriate for essays that describe a place, an object, or a person. Following the way people normally survey something, you move through space from a chosen starting point to other features of the subject. Describing a building, for instance, you might begin with an impression of the whole, then scan exterior details from top to bottom, and then describe interior spaces.

Video tutorial

A **chronological organization** reports events as they occurred in time, usually from first to last. This pattern, like spatial organization, corresponds to readers' own experiences and expectations. It suits an essay in which you do one of the following:

■ Recount a sequence of events, such as a championship baseball game or the Battle of Gettysburg.

■ Explain a process from beginning to end—for instance, how to run a marathon or how a tree converts carbon dioxide to oxygen.

■ Explain the causes that led to an effect, such as the lobbying that helped to push a bill through the legislature. Alternatively, explain how a cause, such as a flood or a book, had multiple effects.

Schemes for organizing ideas in an essay

- Space
- Time
- Emphasis

General to specific	Increasing importance (climax)
Specific to general	Decreasing familiarity
Problem-solution	Increasing complexity

- Tell a story about yourself or someone else.
- Provide background—for instance, the making of a film you are analyzing or the procedure used in an experiment you are reporting.

Organizing the body for emphasis

Some organizational schemes must be imposed on ideas and information to aid readers' understanding and achieve a desired emphasis.

General to specific

Two ways of organizing essays depend on the distinction between the general and the specific, discussed on page 42. The **general-to-specific scheme** is common in expository and argumentative essays that start with a general discussion of the main points and then proceed to specific examples, facts, or other evidence. The following thesis statement forecasts a general-to-specific organization:

Video tutorial

> As an investment in its own economy, the United States should provide a tuition grant to any college student who qualifies academically.

The body of the essay might first elaborate on the basic argument and then provide the supporting data.

Specific to general

Sometimes you may anticipate that readers will not appreciate or agree with your general ideas before they see the support for them—for instance, in an expository essay that presents a unique way of looking at common experience, or in an argumentative essay that takes an unpopular view. In these cases a **specific-to-general scheme** can arouse readers' interest in specific examples or other evidence, and you can let the evidence build to statements of more general ideas. The following thesis statement could be developed in this way:

Video tutorial

> Although most of us are unaware of the public relations campaigns directed at us, they can significantly affect the way we think and live.

The writer might devote most of the essay to a single specific example of a public relations campaign and then explain more generally how the example typifies public relations campaigns.

Problem-solution

Many arguments use a **problem-solution scheme:** first outline a problem that needs solving; then propose a solution. (If the solution involves steps toward a goal, it may be arranged chronologically.) The following thesis statement announces a problem-solution paper:

> To protect users' privacy, social-networking sites such as *Facebook* should make removing photographs, videos, and other links a transparent and simple process.

Climax

Video
tutorial

A common scheme in both explanations and arguments is the **climactic organization,** in which ideas unfold in order of increasing drama or importance to reach a climax. For example, the following thesis statement lists three effects of strip-mining in order of their increasing severity, and the essay would cover them in the same order:

> Strip-mining should be tightly controlled in this region to reduce its pollution of water resources, its destruction of the land, and its devastating effects on people's lives.

As this example suggests, the climactic organization works well in arguments because it leaves readers with the most important point freshest in their minds. In exposition such an arrangement can create suspense and thus hold readers' attention.

Familiarity or complexity

Expository essays can also be arranged to take account of readers' knowledge of the subject. An essay on the effects of air pollution might proceed from **most familiar to least familiar**—from effects readers are likely to know to ones they may not know. Similarly, an explanation of animals' nervous systems might proceed from **simplest to most complex,** so that the explanation of each nervous system provides a basis for readers to understand the more difficult one following.

4 Checking for unity and coherence

In conceiving your organization and writing your essay, you should be aware of two qualities of effective writing that relate to organization: unity and coherence. When you perceive that someone's writing "flows well," you are probably appreciating these two qualities. An essay has **unity** if all its parts relate to and support the thesis statement. Check for unity with these questions:

- Is each main section relevant to the main idea (thesis) of the essay?
- Within main sections, does each example or detail support the principal idea of that section?

An essay has **coherence** if readers can see the relations among parts and move easily from one thought to the next. Check for coherence with these questions:

- Do the ideas follow in a clear sequence?
- Are the parts of the essay logically connected?
- Are the connections clear and smooth?

A unified and coherent outline will not necessarily guide you to a unified and coherent essay because so much can change during drafting. Thus you shouldn't be too hard on your outline, in case a seemingly wayward idea proves useful. But do cut obvious digressions and rearrange material that clearly needs moving.

dev

2c

Sample essay

The following essay illustrates some ways of achieving unity and coherence (highlighted in the annotations).

Who Benefits from the Money in College Football?

Anyone who follows Division 1-A college football cannot fail to notice the money that pours into every aspect of the sport—the lavish stadiums, corporate sponsorships, televised games, and long post-season bowl series. The influx of money may seem to benefit the players, but in reality the institutions that promote college football, not the players, have gotten rich. College football is a multimillion-dollar industry not for the players but for the colleges and universities, conferences, and television networks.

Colleges and universities are major players in the for-profit football industry. A vibrant football program attracts not only skilled coaches and talented players but also wealthy, sports-minded donors who give money for state-of-the art stadiums and facilities. These great facilities in turn attract fans, some of whom are willing to pay high ticket prices to watch games in luxurious sky boxes and thus generate more profits for the schools' athletic departments.

The athletic conferences to which the schools belong—such as the Big Ten, the Atlantic Coast Conference, and the PAC-10—reap financial rewards from college football. Each conference maintains a Web site to post schedules and scores, sell tickets and merchandise, and promote interest in its teams. However, the proceeds from ticket and merchandise sales surely pale in comparison to the money generated by the annual Bowl Championship Series—the three-week-long post-season football extravaganza. Each game is not only televised but also carries the name of a corporate sponsor that pays for the privilege of having its name attached to a bowl game.

Annotations (right margin):

Introduction establishing subject of essay

Thesis statement

Paragraph idea, linked to thesis statement

Paragraph developed with evidence supporting its idea

Paragraph idea, linked to thesis statement

Paragraph developed with evidence supporting its idea

Paragraph idea, linked to thesis statement

⌐ Like the schools and athletic conferences, the television networks profit from football. Networks sell advertising slots to the highest bidders for every televised game during the regular season and the Bowl Championship Series, and they work to sustain fans' interest in football by culti-

Paragraph developed with evidence supporting its idea

vating viewers on the Web. For instance, one network generates interest in up-and-coming high school players through *Scout.com*, a Web site that posts profiles of boys being recruited by colleges and universities and that is supported, at least in part, through advertising and paid subscriptions.

Transition and new paragraph idea, linked to thesis statement

⌐ Amid these money-making players are the actual football players, the young men who are bound by NCAA rules to play as amateurs and to receive no direct compensation for their hours of practice and field time.

Paragraph developed with evidence supporting its idea

True, their generous athletic scholarships cover tuition, room and board, and expenses such as uniforms, medical care, and travel. Yet compared to the millions of dollars spent on promoting football, the scholarships seem rather quaint and old-fashioned.

Conclusion echoing thesis statement and summarizing

Many critics have pointed out the disparity between players' rewards and the profits made by the industry and have called for allowing players to receive compensation in one form or another. But so far the schools, conferences, and networks have ignored these calls for change and have perpetuated a system that benefits everyone except the players.

—Terrence MacDonald (student)

Unity and coherence within paragraphs

The unity and coherence of writing begin in its paragraphs, so the two concepts are treated in greater detail in Chapter 4. You may want to consult two sections in particular before you begin drafting:

- The topic sentence and unity (pp. 82–85)
- Transitions and coherence (pp. 86–96, 115–16)

Unity and coherence on the Web

Unity and coherence may seem unimportant in compositions for the Web, in which entire documents are linked to each other so that it's easy to move among them. However, precisely because the Web is such a fluid medium, you risk losing or confusing your readers if you don't consider unity and coherence. Your project should have a clear purpose and clear ideas relating to that purpose, and the connections between ideas should be spelled out to orient readers. (For more on composing for the Web, see pp. 130–34.)

Exercise 2.9 Organizing ideas

Exercise

The following list of ideas was extracted by a student from freewriting he did for a brief paper on soccer in the United States. Using his thesis statement as a guide, pick out the general ideas and arrange the relevant specific points under them. In some cases you may have to infer general ideas to cover specific points in the list.

Thesis statement

Although its growth in the United States has been slow and halting, professional soccer may finally be poised to become a major American sport.

List of ideas

In countries of South and Latin America, soccer is the favorite sport.

In the United States the success of a sport depends largely on its ability to attract huge TV audiences.

Soccer was not often presented on US television.

In 2007 and 2010, the World Cup final was broadcast on ABC and on Spanish-language Univision.

In the past, professional soccer could not get a foothold in the United States because of poor TV coverage and lack of financial backing.

The growing Hispanic population in the United States could help soccer grow as well.

Investors have poured hundreds of millions of dollars into the top US professional league.

Potential fans did not have a chance to see soccer games.

Failures of early start-up leagues made potential backers wary of new ventures.

Recently, the outlook for professional soccer has changed dramatically.

The US television audience for the 2010 World Cup US-Ghana match was larger than the average US television audience for baseball's World Series.

Exercise 2.10 Creating a formal outline

Use your arrangement of general ideas and specific points from Exercise 2.9 as the basis for a formal topic or sentence outline. Follow the principles given on pages 45–47.

Exercise 2.11 Considering your past work: Organizing ideas

What has been your experience with organizing your writing? Many writers find it difficult. If you do, too, can you say why? What kinds of outlines or other organizing tools have you used? Which have been helpful and which have not?

Exercise

Exercise 2.12 Organizing your own essay

Continuing from Exercise 2.8 (p. 41), choose an appropriate organization for your essay-in-progress. Then experiment with organizing tools by preparing a tree diagram or other visual map or a scratch, informal, or formal outline.

3

Drafting, Revising, and Editing

The separation of drafting, revising, and editing from the planning and development discussed earlier is somewhat artificial because the stages almost always overlap during the writing process. Indeed, if you compose on a computer, you may not experience any boundaries between stages at all. Still, your primary goal during the writing process will usually shift from gathering and shaping information to forming connected sentences and paragraphs in a draft and then restructuring and rewriting the draft for presentation to an audience.

3a | Writing the first draft

Video tutorial

The only correct drafting style is the one that works for you. Generally, though, the freer and more fluid you are, the better. Some writers draft and revise at the same time, but most let themselves go during drafting and *especially* do not worry about errors. Drafting is the occasion to find and convey meaning through the act of writing. If you fear making mistakes while drafting, that fear will choke your ideas. You draft only for yourself, so errors do not matter. Write freely until you have worked out what you want to say; *then* focus on any mistakes you may have made.

Starting to draft sometimes takes courage, even for seasoned professionals. Students and pros alike find easy ways to procrastinate—checking messages, meeting for coffee, napping, tweeting about procrastinating. Such delays may actually help you if you let ideas for writing simmer at the same time. At some point, though, enough is enough: the deadline looms; you've got to get started. If the blankness still stares back at you, then try one of the techniques for unblocking listed in the box on the facing page.

Drafting

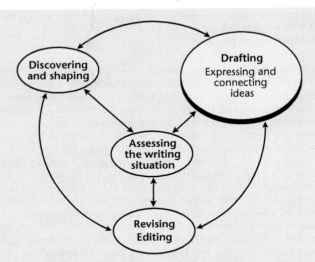

When you draft an essay, you work toward expressing and connecting the ideas you've developed. If you change direction or run out of ideas during drafting, you can always circle back to renew your purpose, discover new ideas, or rethink your thesis.

Ways to start drafting

- Read over what you've already written—notes, outlines, and so on. Immediately start your draft with whatever comes to mind.
- Freewrite (see pp. 30–31).
- Write scribbles or type nonsense until words you can use start coming.
- Pretend you're writing to a friend about your subject.
- Describe an image that represents your subject—a physical object, a facial expression, two people arguing over something, a giant machine gouging the earth for a mine, whatever.
- Write a paragraph. Explain what you think your essay will be about when you finish it.
- Skip the opening and start in the middle. Or write the conclusion.
- Start writing the part that you understand best or feel most strongly about. Using your outline, divide your work into chunks— say, one for the introduction, another for the first point, and so on. One of these chunks may call out to be written.

Video tutorial

You should find some momentum once you've started writing. If not, however, or if your energy flags, try one or more of the following techniques to keep moving ahead.

Video
tutorial

rev
3a

Ways to *keep* drafting

- **Set aside enough time.** For a brief essay, a first draft is likely to take at least an hour or two.
- **Work in a quiet place.**
- **Make yourself comfortable.**
- **If you must stop working, write down what you expect to do next.** Then you can pick up where you stopped with minimal disruption.
- **Be as fluid as possible, and don't worry about mistakes.** Spontaneity will allow your attitudes toward your subject to surface naturally in your sentences, and it will also make you receptive to ideas and relations you haven't seen before. Mistakes will be easier to find and correct later, when you're not also trying to create.
- **Keep going.** Skip over sticky spots; leave a blank if you can't find the right word; put alternative ideas or phrasings in brackets so that you can consider them later. If an idea pops out of nowhere but doesn't seem to fit in, quickly write it into the draft and bracket or boldface it for later attention. Use an asterisk (*) or some other symbol to mark places where you feel blocked or uncertain.
- **Resist self-criticism.** Don't worry about your style, grammar, spelling, punctuation, and the like. Don't worry about what your readers will think. These are very important matters, but save them for revision. On a computer, turn off automatic spelling- or grammar-checking functions if they distract you, or try invisible writing (p. 31).
- **Use your thesis statement and outline** to remind you of your planned purpose, organization, and content.
- **But don't feel constrained by your thesis and outline.** If your writing leads you in a more interesting direction, follow.

Video
tutorial

If you write on a computer, frequently save the text you're drafting—at least every five or ten minutes and every time you leave the computer. See pages 62–63 for tips on saving documents.

Whether you compose on paper or on a computer, you may find it difficult to tell whether a first draft is finished. The distinction between drafts can be significant because creating text is different from rethinking it and because your instructor may ask you and your classmates to submit your drafts, either on paper or online, so that others can give you feedback on them. For your own revision or others' feedback, you might consider a draft finished for any number of reasons: perhaps you've run out of ideas; perhaps you find yourself writing the conclusion; perhaps you've stopped adding content and are just tinkering with words.

Sample first draft

Following is Katy Moreno's first-draft response to Thomas L. Friedman's "It's a Flat World, after All." (The first two paragraphs include the page numbers in Friedman's article that Moreno summarized material from.) As part of her assignment, Moreno showed

the draft to four classmates, whose suggestions for revision appear in the margin of this draft. They used the Comment function of *Microsoft Word*, which allows users to add comments without inserting words into the document's text. (Notice that the classmates ignore errors in grammar and punctuation, concentrating instead on larger issues such as thesis, clarity of ideas, and unity.)

Title?

In "It's a Flat World, after All," Thomas L. Friedman argues that, most US students are not preparing themselves as well as they should to compete in today's economy. Not like students in India, China, and other countries are (34-37). The outsourcing of my mother's job proves that Thomas L. Friedman's advice to improve students' technical training is too narrow.

> **Comment [Jared]:** Your mother's job being outsourced is interesting, but your introduction seems rushed.

> **Comment [Rabia]:** The end of your thesis statement is a little unclear—too narrow for what?

Friedman describes a "flat" world where recent technology like the Internet and wireless communication make it possible for college graduates all over the globe, in particular in India and China, to get jobs that once were gotten by graduates of US colleges and universities (37). He argues that US students need more math and science in order to compete (37).

> **Comment [Erin]:** Can you include the reasons Friedman gives for overseas students' success?

I came to college with first-hand knowledge of globalization and outsourcing. My mother, who worked for sixteen years in the field of information technology (IT), was laid off six months ago when the company she worked for decided to outsource much of its IT work to a company based in India. My mother majored in computer science, had sixteen years of experience, and her bosses always gave her good reviews. She never expected to be laid off and was surprised when she was. She wasn't laid off because of her background and performance. In fact, my mother had a very strong background in math and science and years of training and job experience. The reason was because her salary and benefits cost the company more than outsourcing her job did. Which hurt my family financially, as you can imagine.

> **Comment [Nathaniel]:** Tighten this paragraph to avoid repetition? Also, how does your mother's experience relate to Friedman and your thesis?

A number of well-paid people in the IT department where my mother worked, namely IT managers, were not laid off. As my mother explained at the time, they kept their jobs because they were better at planning and they communicated better, they were better writers and speakers than my mother.

> **Comment [Erin]:** What were the managers better at planning for?

Like my mother, I am more comfortable in front of a computer than I am in front of a group of people. I planned

to major in computer science. Since my mother lost her job, though, I have decided to take courses in English and history too, where the classes will require me to do different kinds of work. When I enter the job market, my well-rounded education will make me a more attractive job candidate, and, will help me to be a versatile, productive employee.

Comment [Nathaniel]: Can you be more specific about the kinds of work you'll need to do?

Comment [Rabia]: Can you work this point into your thesis?

We know from our history that Americans have been innovative, hard-working people. We students have educational opportunities to compete in the global economy, but we must use our time in college wisely. As Thomas L. Friedman says, my classmates and I need to be ready for a rapidly changing future. We will have to work hard each day, which means being prepared for class, getting the best grades we can, and making the most of each class. Our futures depend on the decisions we make today.

Comment [Jared]: Conclusion seems to go off in a new direction. Friedman mentions hard work, but it hasn't been your focus before.

Comment [Rabia]: Don't forget your works cited.

Exercise

Exercise 3.1 Analyzing a first draft

Compare Moreno's draft with the previous step in her planning (her scratch outline) on page 43. List the places in the draft where the act of drafting led Moreno to rearrange her information, add or delete material, or explore new ideas. Mark Moreno's thesis statement and each key idea developing the thesis. Note places where you think the ideas could be clearer or better supported.

Exercise

Exercise 3.2 Considering your past work: Drafting

Think back over a recent writing experience. At what point in the writing process did you begin drafting? How did drafting go—smoothly, haltingly, painfully, painlessly? If you had difficulties, what were they? If you didn't, why do you think not?

Exercise 3.3 Drafting your essay

Prepare a draft of the essay you began in Chapters 1 and 2. Use your thesis statement and your outline as guides, but don't be unduly constrained by them. Concentrate on opening up options, not on closing them down. Do not, above all, worry about mistakes.

Exercise

3b Revising the first draft

Exercise

Revision literally means "re-seeing"—looking anew at ideas and details, their relationships and arrangement, the degree to which they work or don't work for the thesis. While drafting, you focus inwardly, concentrating on pulling your topic out of yourself. In revising, you look out to your readers, trying to anticipate how they will see your work. You adopt a critical perspective toward your work, examining it as a pole-vaulter or dancer would examine a video of his or her

Revising and editing

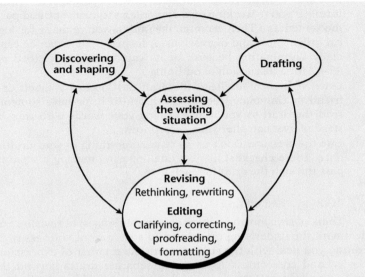

Often the process of revising requires you to rethink your purpose, clarify your thesis statement, develop more ideas, or reorganize. Save editing and proofreading until you are satisfied with the overall focus, development, and shape of your draft.

performance. (Writing teachers often ask students to read each other's drafts partly to develop this critical perspective. See pp. 75–76 for more on such collaboration.)

1 Gaining distance from your work

Reading your own work critically can be difficult. Changing or even deleting material that you've worked hard to express can be still more difficult. The key is to gain some objectivity toward your writing. The following techniques may help:

Video
tutorial

- Take a break after finishing your draft. A few hours may be enough; a whole night or day is preferable. The break will clear your mind, relax you, and give you some objectivity.
- Ask someone to read and react to your draft. Many writing instructors ask their students to submit their first drafts so that the instructor and, often, the other members of the class can serve as an audience to help guide revision. (See also pp. 77–78 on receiving and benefiting from comments.)
- Read your draft in a new medium. Typing a handwritten draft or printing out a word-processed draft can reveal weaknesses that you didn't see in the original.

rev
3b

■ **Outline your draft.** Highlight the main points supporting the thesis, and write these sentences down separately in outline form. (If you're working on a computer, you can copy and paste the sentences.) Then examine the outline you've made for logical order, gaps, and digressions. A formal outline can be especially illuminating because of its careful structure. (See pp. 43–47 for a discussion of outlining.)

■ **Listen to your draft.** Read the draft out loud to yourself or a friend or classmate, record and listen to it, or have someone read the draft to you. Experiencing your words with ears instead of eyes can alter your perceptions.

■ **Ease the pressure.** Don't try to re-see everything in your draft at once. Use a checklist like the one opposite, making a separate pass through the draft for each item.

2 Revising, then editing

Think of revision and editing as separate stages: in revision you deal with the underlying meaning and structure of your essay; in editing you deal with the surface, with the manner of expression, clarity, and correctness. By making separate drafts beyond the first—a revised one and then an edited one—you'll be less likely to waste time tinkering with sentences that you end up cutting, and you'll avoid the temptation to substitute editing for more substantial revision.

The temptation to edit while revising can be especially attractive on a computer because it's easy to alter copy. Indeed, writers sometimes find themselves editing compulsively, spinning their wheels with changes that cease to have any marked effect on meaning or clarity and that may in fact sap the writing of energy. Planning to revise and then to edit encourages you to look beyond the confines of the screen so that deeper issues of meaning and structure aren't lost to surface matters such as word choice and sentence arrangement.

3 Using a revision checklist

Set aside at least as much time to revise your essay as you took to draft it. Plan on going through the draft several times to answer the questions in the checklist opposite and to resolve any problems. (If you need additional information on any of the topics in the checklist, refer to the page numbers given in parentheses.) Note that the checklist can also help you if you have been asked to comment on another writer's draft (see pp. 76–77).

4 Titling your essay

The revision stage is a good time to consider a title. After drafting, you have a clearer sense of your direction, and the attempt to

Video
tutorial

Checklist for revision

See also specific revision checklists for arguments (p. 225), research papers (pp. 664–65), and literary analyses (p. 771).

Checklist

Assignment

How have you responded to the assignment for this writing? Verify that your genre, subject, and purpose are appropriate for the assignment.

rev
3b

Purpose

What is the purpose of your writing? Is it consistent throughout the paper? (See pp. 17–19.)

Audience and voice

How does the writing address the intended audience? How clearly can readers hear your writer's voice? What role will they see you as playing? What tone will they hear? (See pp. 19–22.)

Genre

How does your writing fit the conventions of the genre you're using—features such as organization, evidence, and format? (See pp. 23–24.)

Thesis

What is the thesis of your writing? Where does it become clear? Does any part of the paper stray from the thesis? Does the paper fulfill the commitment of the thesis? (See pp. 36–40.)

Organization

What are the main points of the paper? (List them.) How well does each support the thesis? How effective is their arrangement for the paper's purpose? (See pp. 42, 47–50.)

Development

How well do details, examples, and other evidence support each main point? Where, if at all, might readers find support skimpy or have trouble understanding the content? (See pp. 23–35, 98–99.)

Unity

What does each sentence and paragraph contribute to the thesis? Where, if at all, do digressions occur? Should they be cut, or can they be rewritten to support the thesis? (See pp. 50–52, 82–85.)

Coherence

How clearly and smoothly does the paper flow? Where does it seem rough or awkward? Can any transitions be improved? (See pp. 50–52, 86–88.)

Title, introduction, conclusion

How accurately and interestingly does the title reflect the essay's content? (See opposite and the next page.)

How well does the introduction engage and focus readers' attention? (See pp. 110–13.)

How effective is the conclusion in providing a sense of completion? (See pp. 114–15.)

sum up your essay in a title phrase can help you focus sharply on your topic, purpose, and audience.

Here are suggestions for titling an essay:

- A *descriptive title* is almost always appropriate and is often expected for academic writing. It announces the topic clearly, accurately, and as briefly as possible. The final title of Katy Moreno's essay is an example: "Can We Compete? College Education for the Global Economy." Other examples include "Images of Lost Identity in *North by Northwest,*" "An Experiment in Small-Group Dynamics," "Why Lincoln Delayed Emancipating the Slaves," and "Food Poisoning Involving *E. coli* Bacteria: A Review of the Literature."

- A *suggestive title*—the kind often found in popular magazines—may be appropriate for more informal writing. Examples include "Making Peace" (for an essay on the Peace Corps) and Thomas L. Friedman's "It's a Flat World, after All" (on the global job market). For a more suggestive title, Moreno might have chosen "Training for the New World" or "Education for a Flat World" (echoing Friedman's title). A suggestive title conveys the writer's attitude and main concerns but not the precise topic, thereby pulling readers into the essay to learn more. A source for such a title may be a familiar phrase, a fresh image, or a significant expression from the essay itself.

- A title tells readers how big the topic is. For Moreno's essay, the title "Globalization and Jobs" or "Competing in Today's Job Market" would have been too broad, whereas "Outsourcing Our Jobs" or "The Importance of a Broad Education" would have been too narrow because each deals with only part of the paper's content.

- A title should not restate the assignment or the thesis statement, as in "The Trouble with Thomas L. Friedman's View of the Global Job Market" or "What I Think about Technical Training and Today's Job Market."

For more information on essay titles, see pages 371–72 (avoiding reference to the title in the opening of the paper), 505 (capitalizing words in a title), and 715 (formatting a title in the final paper).

5 Revising on a computer

Video tutorial

Word processors have removed the mechanical drudgery of revising by hand or on a typewriter, but they have also complicated the process: you must conscientiously save your changes and manage the files you create, both discussed below. At the same time, like the more cumbersome revision methods, word processors allow you to display changes as you make them.

Saving changes

Computers malfunction frequently. You can avoid losing your work by taking two precautions:

■ **Save your work every five to ten minutes.** Most word processors have an Auto Save function that will save your work automatically as you type, at the interval you specify. Still, get in the habit of saving manually whenever you make major changes.

■ **After doing any major work on a project, create a backup version of the file.** Use a removable flash drive, or save files to the Internet with a storage service such as *Dropbox* (*dropbox.com*) or *Carbonite* (*carbonite.com*).

Managing files

You can organize your work for a course or the drafts of a paper by giving each file a name that indicates the content, the date, and (if you're sharing work with others) the author. The following screen shot shows Katy Moreno saving a document she named *Friedman_response_D1_2-7.doc* in a new folder titled *English110*. In addition to the date, the file name includes an identifier for the paper (*Friedman_response*) and the draft number (*D1*).

Save As screen

Save As copies an existing document.

Select New Folder if the document doesn't fit in existing folders—for instance, the first draft of a paper or the first paper in a course.

Displaying changes

You can keep track of the revisions you make in a document with an option often called Track Changes. The function highlights additions and deletions so they're easy to spot (see Katy Moreno's revised draft below). Tracking changes may encourage you to revise more freely because you can always revert to your original text. You can weigh the original and revised versions as you view them side by side. You can also evaluate the kinds of changes you are making. For instance, if during revision you see only minor surface alterations (word substitutions, added punctuation, and the like), then you might consider whether and where to read more deeply for more fundamental changes.

rev
3c

3c Examining a sample revision

Katy Moreno was satisfied with her first draft: she had her ideas down, and the arrangement seemed logical. Still, from the revision checklist she knew the draft needed work, and her classmates' comments (pp. 57–58) highlighted what she needed to focus on. The following revised draft shows Moreno's changes in response to these comments. Moreno used the Track Changes function on her word processor, so that deletions are crossed out and additions are in blue.

Descriptive title names topic and forecasts approach.	Can We Compete? College Education for the Global Economy ~~Title?~~
Expanded introduction draws readers into Moreno's topic, clarifies her point of agreement with Friedman, and states her revised thesis.	Today's students cannot miss news stories about globalization of the economy and outsourcing of jobs, but are students aware of how these trends are affecting the job market? In "It's a Flat World, after All," Thomas L. Friedman argues that most US students are not preparing themselves as well as ~~they should to compete in today's economy. Not like~~ students in India, China, and other countries ~~are~~ to compete in today's economy, which requires hard-working, productive scientists and engineers (34-37). Friedman's argument speaks to me because my mother recently lost her job when it was outsourced to India. But her experience taught a lesson that Friedman overlooks: technical training by itself can be too narrow to produce the communicators and problem solvers needed by contemporary businesses. ~~The outsourcing of my mother's job proves that Thomas L. Friedman's advice to improve students' technical training is too narrow.~~
Expanded summary of Friedman's article specifies qualities of overseas workers.	Friedman describes a "flat" world where recent technology like the Internet and wireless communication makes it possible for college graduates all over the globe, ~~in particular~~ to compete for high paying jobs that once belonged to graduates of US colleges and universities (34). He

focuses on workers **in India and China**~~,~~ who graduate from college with excellent educations in math and science, who are eager for new opportunities, and who are willing to work exceptionally hard, often harder than their American counterparts and, for less money ~~to get jobs that once were gotten by graduates of US colleges and universities~~ (37). ~~He~~ Friedman **argues that US students** must be better prepared academically, especially in ~~need more~~ **math and science**, so that they can get and keep jobs that will otherwise go overseas ~~in order to compete~~ (37).

~~I came to college with first hand knowledge of globalization and outsourcing. My mother, who worked for sixteen years in the field of information technology (IT), was laid off six months ago when the company she worked for decided to outsource much of its IT work to a company based in India. My mother~~ At first glance, my mother's experience of losing her job might seem to support the argument of Friedman that better training in math and science is the key to competing in the global job market. Her experience, however, adds dimensions to the globalization story, which Friedman misses. First my mother had the kind of strong background in math and science that Friedman says, today's workers need. She **majored in computer science,** rose within the information technology (IT) department of a large company, ~~had sixteen years of experience,~~ **and her bosses always gave her good** performance **reviews.** Still, when her employer decided to outsource most of its IT work, my mother lost her job. ~~She never expected to be laid off and was surprised when she was. She wasn't laid off because of her background and performance. In fact, my mother had a very strong background in math and science and years of training and job experience.~~ **The reason wasn't** because her technical skills were inadequate. Instead, **her salary and benefits cost the company more than outsourcing her job did.** Until wages rise around the globe, jobs like my mother's will be vulnerable. No matter how well you are trained. ~~Which hurt my family financially, as you can imagine.~~

The second dimension that Friedman misses is that ~~Aa~~ **number of well-paid people in** ~~the~~ my mother's **IT department** ~~where my mother worked~~**,** namely IT managers, were **not laid off. As my mother explained at the time, they kept their jobs because they** were experienced at figuring out the company's IT needs, planning for changes and, researching and proposing solutions. They also communicated better and were better at writing and speaking than my mother was. ~~were better at planning and, they communicated better, they were better writers and speakers than my mother.~~ Friedman misses these skills by focusing only on technical training. Without the ability to solve problems creatively and to communicate,

rev

3c

New opening sentences connect to introduction and thesis statement, restating points of agreement and disagreement with Friedman.

Revisions condense long example of mother's experience.

Concluding sentences reinforce the point of the paragraph and connect to thesis statement.

Numbered point (*second*) connects this paragraph to the previous one.

New examples support general point.

Concluding sentences connect paragraph to thesis.

people with technical expertise alone may not have enough to save their jobs. It wasn't enough to save my mother's.

Like my mother, I am more comfortable in front of a computer than I am in front of a group of people, and I had planned to major in computer science. Since my mother lost her job, ~~though~~ however, I have decided to take courses in English and history too, where the classes will require me to ~~do different kinds of work~~ read broadly, think critically, research, and communicate ideas in writing—skills that make managers. When I enter the job market, my well-rounded education will make me a more attractive job candidate, and, will help me ~~be a versatile, productive employee~~ become the kind of forward-thinking manager that US companies will always need to employ here in the US.

~~We know from our history that Americans have been innovative, hard working people. We students have educational opportunities to compete in the global economy, but we must use our time in college wisely. As Thomas L. Friedman says,~~ Many jobs that require a college degree are indeed going overseas, as Thomas L. Friedman says, and my classmates and I need to be ready for a rapidly changing future. But rather than focus only on math and science, we need to broaden our academic experiences so that the skills we develop make us not only employable, but also indispensable. ~~We will have to work hard each day, which means being prepared for class, getting the best grades we can, and making the most of each class. Our futures depend on the decisions we make today.~~

Margin notes:

New examples add specificity.

Expanded sentence connects to thesis statement.

New conclusion recaps Friedman's points and Moreno's thesis and points to the future.

New work-cited entry. (See p. 676 on MLA style.)

Work Cited

Friedman, Thomas L. "It's a Flat World, after All." *New York Times Magazine* 3 Apr. 2005: 32-37. Print.

Exercise

Exercise 3.4 Analyzing a revised draft

Can you see the reasons for most of the changes Moreno made in her revised draft? Where would you suggest further revisions, and why?

Exercise

Exercise 3.5 Considering your past work: Revising

In the past, have you usually revised your drafts extensively? Do you think your writing would benefit from more revision of the sort described in this chapter? Why or why not? Many students who don't revise much explain that they lack the time. Is time a problem for you? Can you think of ways to resolve the problem?

Exercise 3.6 Revising your own draft

Revise your own first draft from Exercise 3.3 (p. 58). Use the checklist for revision on page 61 as a guide. Concentrate on purpose, content, and organization, leaving smaller problems such as sentence structure, word choice, and grammar for the next draft.

3d Editing the revised draft

Editing for style, clarity, and correctness may come second to more fundamental revision, but it is still very important. A carefully developed essay will fall flat with readers if you overlook awkwardness and errors. In the following example of editing, Katy Moreno tightens wording, improves parallelism (with *consistently received*), corrects several comma errors, and repairs the final sentence fragment.

At first glance, my mother's experience of losing her job might seem to support the Friedman's argument of Friedman that better training in math and science is the key to competing in the global job market. However, Hher experience, however, adds dimensions to the globalization story, which that Friedman misses. First, my mother had the kind of strong background in math and science that Friedman says, today's workers need. She majored in computer science, rose within the information technology (IT) department of a large company, and consistently received her bosses always gave her good performance reviews. Still, when her employer decided to outsource most of its IT work, my mother lost her job. The reason wasn't because that her technical skills were inadequate. Instead, her salary and benefits cost the company more than outsourcing her job did. Until wages rise around the globe, jobs like my mother's will be vulnerable, Nno matter how well you are a person is trained.

1 Discovering what needs editing

After you've read and reread a draft to revise it, finding awkwardness and errors can be difficult. Try the following approaches to spot possible flaws in your revised draft:

Exercise

- Take a break, even fifteen or twenty minutes, to clear your head.
- Read the draft *slowly,* and read what you *actually see.* Otherwise, you're likely to read what you intended to write but didn't. (If you have trouble slowing down, try reading your draft from back to front, sentence by sentence.)
- Read as if you are encountering the draft for the first time. Put yourself in the reader's place.
- Have a classmate, friend, or relative read your work. Make sure you understand and consider the reader's suggestions, even if eventually you decide not to take them.
- Read the draft aloud or, even better, record it. Listen for awkward rhythms, repetitive sentence patterns, and missing or clumsy transitions.

■ **Learn from your own experience.** Keep a record of the problems that others have pointed out in your writing. (See p. 70 for a suggested format.) When editing, check your work against this record.

■ **Don't rely on a spelling or grammar/style checker to find what needs editing.** See the discussion of these checkers on pages 71–72.

rev
3d

2 Using an editing checklist

The following checklist emphasizes students' most common editing challenges. In your editing, work first for clear and effective sentences that flow smoothly from one to the next. Then check your sentences for correct spelling, grammar, and punctuation. Use the checklist's questions to guide your editing, making several passes through your draft. Refer to the page numbers in parentheses as needed.

Checklist for editing

Checklist

Are my sentences clear?

Do my words and sentences mean what I intend them to mean? Is anything confusing? Check especially for these:

Exact language (pp. 533-45)
Parallelism (pp. 420–25)
Clear modifiers (pp. 381–89)
Clear reference of pronouns (pp. 367–73)
Complete sentences (pp. 352–59)
Sentences separated correctly (pp. 360–66)

Are my sentences effective?

How well do words and sentences engage and hold readers' attention? How appropriate and effective is the voice created by words and sentences? Where does the writing seem wordy, choppy, or dull? Check especially for these:

Expression of voice (pp. 21–22)
Emphasis of main ideas (pp. 400–08)
Smooth and informative transitions (pp. 93–95, 115–16)
Variety in sentence length and structure (pp. 427–33)
Appropriate language (pp. 524–32)
Concise sentences (pp. 545–51)

Do my sentences contain errors?

Where do surface errors interfere with the clarity and effectiveness of my sentences? Check especially for these:

■ Spelling errors (pp. 553–56)
■ Sentence fragments (pp. 352–59)

■ Comma splices (pp. 360–65)
■ Verb errors

Verb forms, especially *-s* and *-ed* endings, correct forms of irregular verbs, and appropriate helping verbs (pp. 294–310)

Verb tenses, especially consistency (pp. 311–17, 377)

Agreement between subjects and verbs, especially when words come between them or the subject is *each, everyone,* or a similar word (pp. 323–30)

rev

3d

■ Pronoun errors

Pronoun forms, especially subjective (*he, she, they, who*) vs. objective (*him, her, them, whom*) (pp. 286–93)

Agreement between pronouns and antecedents, especially when the antecedent contains *or* or the antecedent is *each, everyone, person,* or a similar word (pp. 331–35)

■ Punctuation errors

Commas, especially with comma splices (pp. 360–65), with *and* or *but* (444–46), with introductory elements (447–48), with nonessential elements (449–53), and with series (455)

Apostrophes in possessives but not plural nouns (*Dave's/witches*) and in contractions but not possessive personal pronouns (*it's/its*) (pp. 473–78)

Note No writer needs every item on this list. As you receive feedback on your writing and grow more experienced with editing, you'll learn which items you need to focus on. To create an individualized editing checklist, see below.

3 Tracking your errors

You won't make all the errors described in this book; instead, you may make the same three or four kinds of errors in each essay you write. The key to correcting such errors is recognizing them, keeping track of them, and checking for them each time you edit your writing.

To track your errors, try making a chart like the one on the next page, with a vertical column for each assignment (or draft) and a horizontal row for each error or weakness that you or others have noted in your writing. Check marks indicate how often the problem occurs in every essay. The chart also provides a convenient place to keep track of words you misspell so that you can master their spellings. When you edit, check your work against the list so that you learn to see—and correct—the errors that you typically make.

4 Editing on a computer

When you write on a word processor, consider the additional approaches to editing given in the list on the next page.

rev

3d

Record of errors

	Assignment		
Weaknesses	*1*	*2*	*3*
not enough details for readers	✓	✓	✓
unity—wanders away from thesis	✓		
subject-verb agreement	✓		✓
comma splice	✓✓	✓	✓
misspellings	among deceive	rebel seize	omission cruelty

- ▪ **Don't rely on a spelling or grammar/style checker to find what needs editing.** See the discussion of these checkers below.
- ▪ **If possible, edit a double-spaced paper copy.** Many people find it much harder to spot errors on a computer screen than on paper.
- ▪ **Use the Find command to locate and correct your common problems**—certain misspellings, wordy phrases such as *the fact that,* overuse of *there is,* and so on.
- ▪ **Resist overediting.** The ease of editing on a computer can lead to rewriting sentences over and over, stealing the life from your prose. If your grammar/style checker contributes to the temptation, consider turning it off.
- ▪ **Take special care with additions and omissions.** Make sure you haven't omitted needed words or left in unneeded words.

Video
tutorial

5 Working with spelling and grammar/style checkers

A spelling checker and a grammar/style checker can be helpful *if* you work within their limitations. The programs miss many problems and may even flag items that are actually correct. Further, they know nothing of your purpose and your audience, so they cannot make important decisions about your writing. Always use these tools critically:

- ▪ **Read your work yourself** to ensure that it's clear and error-free.
- ▪ **Consider a checker's suggestions carefully,** weighing each one against your intentions. If you aren't sure whether to accept a checker's suggestion, consult a dictionary, writing handbook, or other source. Your version may be fine.

Using a spelling checker

Your word processor's spelling checker can be a great ally: it will flag words that are spelled incorrectly and will usually suggest alternative spellings that resemble what you've typed. However, this ally also has the potential to undermine you because of its limitations:

- **The checker may flag a word that you've spelled correctly** just because the word does not appear in its dictionary.
- **The checker may suggest incorrect alternatives.** In providing a list of alternative spellings for your word, the checker may highlight the one it considers most likely to be correct. For example, if you misspell *definitely* by typing *definately*, your checker may highlight *defiantly* as the correct option. You need to verify that the alternative suggested by the checker is actually what you intend before selecting it. Consult an online or printed dictionary when you aren't sure about the checker's recommendations.
- **Most important, a spelling checker will not flag words that appear in its dictionary but you have misused.** The jingle in the following screen shot has circulated widely as a warning about spelling checkers (we found it in the *Bulletin of the Missouri Council of Teachers of Mathematics*).

Spelling checker

I have a spelling checker,
It came with my PC;
It plainly marks four my revue
Mistakes I cannot sea.
I've run this poem threw it,
I'm sure your please too no.
Its letter perfect in it's weigh,
My checker tolled me sew.

A spelling checker failed to catch any of the thirteen errors in this jingle. Can you spot them?

Using a grammar/style checker

Grammar/style checkers can flag incorrect grammar or punctuation and wordy or awkward sentences. However, these programs can call your attention only to passages that *may* be faulty. They miss many errors because they are not capable of analyzing language in all its complexity. (For instance, they can't accurately distinguish a word's part of speech when there are different possibilities, as *light* can be a noun, a verb, or an adjective.) The checkers can't detect problems involving relationships between ideas, so they usually miss errors such as faulty parallelism, inconsistent verb tenses, and problems with adjectives or adverbs. And they often question passages that don't need editing, such as an appropriate passive verb or a deliberate and emphatic use of repetition. The screen shot on the next page illustrates the limitations.

Grammar/style checker

The checker flagged only one repetition of *light*, not the other three.

> Though there was only a light light breeze, I could not light the match so there was no way to light the light.

The checker flagged this sentence because it is long, but it is actually clear and correct.

> These programs are not yet capable of analyzing the language in all its complexity (for instance, they can't accurately distinguish a word's part of speech when there are different possibilities, as *light* can be a noun, a verb, or an adjective).

You can customize a grammar and style checker to suit your needs and habits as a writer. Most checkers allow you to specify whether to check grammar only or grammar and style. Some style checkers can be set to the level of writing you intend, such as formal, standard, and informal. (For academic writing choose formal.) You can also instruct the checker to flag specific grammar and style problems that tend to occur in your writing, such as mismatched subjects and verbs, apostrophes in plural nouns, overused passive voice, or a confusion between *its* and *it's*.

Exercise

Exercise 3.7   Considering your past work: Editing

How do you find what needs editing in your drafts? What kinds of changes do you make most often? Have you tried focusing on particular kinds of changes, such as correcting mistakes you made in previous writing? If your readers often comment on editing concerns in your work, what can you do to reduce such comments?

Exercise 3.8   Editing your own draft

Use the checklist for editing (pp. 68–69) and your own sense of your essay's needs to edit the revised draft of your essay-in-progress.

3e   Preparing and proofreading the final draft

After editing your essay, format and proofread it before you submit it to your instructor. Follow any required document format, such as MLA (pp. 714–16), Chicago (pp. 797–98), APA (pp. 823–26), or CSE (p. 841). If no format is specified, consult the document-design guidelines in Chapter 5. If you've composed on a word processor and are required to submit a printed paper, use the Print Preview function to check for formatting problems that may not otherwise show up on your screen.

Be sure to proofread the final essay several times to spot and correct errors. To increase the accuracy of your proofreading, you may need to find ways to keep yourself from relaxing into the rhythm and the content of your prose. The following box gives a few tricks, including some used by professional proofreaders:

Techniques for proofreading

Video
tutorial

- **Read printed copy,** even if you will eventually submit the paper electronically. Most people proofread more accurately when reading type on paper than when reading it on a computer screen. (At the same time, don't view the printed copy as necessarily error-free just because it's clean. Clean-looking copy may still harbor errors.)
- **Read the paper aloud.** Slowly and distinctly pronounce exactly what you see.
- **Place a ruler under each line as you read it.**
- **Read "against copy."** Compare your final draft one sentence at a time against the edited draft you copied it from.
- **Ignore content.** To keep the content of your writing from distracting you while you proofread, read the essay backward, end to beginning, examining each sentence as a separate unit. Or, taking advantage of a computer, isolate each paragraph from its context by printing it on a separate page. (Of course, reassemble the paragraphs before submitting the paper.)

rev
3f

3f Examining a final draft

Katy Moreno's final essay begins below, presented in MLA format except for page breaks and numbers. Comments in the margins point out key features of the essay's content.

Katy Moreno

Professor Lacourse

English 110

14 February 2011

Can We Compete?

College Education for the Global Economy

Today's students cannot miss news stories about globalization of the economy and outsourcing of jobs, but are students aware of how these trends are affecting the job market? In "It's a Flat World, after All," Thomas L. Friedman argues that most US students are not preparing themselves as well as students in India, China, and other countries to compete in today's economy, which requires hard-working, productive scientists and engineers (34-37). Friedman's argument speaks to me because my mother lost her job when it was outsourced to India. But her experience taught a lesson that Friedman overlooks: technical training by itself can be too narrow to produce the communicators and problem solvers needed by contemporary businesses.

Descriptive title

Introduction

Summaries of Friedman cited with parenthetical page numbers using MLA style (p. 667)

Thesis statement: basic disagreement with Friedman

Summary of Friedman's article

Friedman describes a "flat" world where recent technology like the Internet and wireless communication makes it possible for college graduates all over the globe to compete for high-paying jobs that once belonged to graduates of US colleges and universities (34). He focuses on workers in India and China who graduate from college with excellent educations in math and science, who are eager for new opportunities, and who are willing to work exceptionally hard, often harder than their American counterparts, and for less money (37). Friedman argues that US students must be better prepared academically, especially in math and science, so that they can get and keep jobs that will otherwise go overseas (37).

Transition to disagreements with Friedman

First disagreement with Friedman

Examples to support first disagreement

Example to qualify first disagreement

Clarification of first disagreement

At first glance, my mother's experience of losing her job might seem to support Friedman's argument that better training in math and science is the key to competing in the global job market. However, her experience adds dimensions to the globalization story that Friedman misses. First, my mother had the kind of strong background in math and science that Friedman says today's workers need. She majored in computer science, rose within the information technology (IT) department of a large company, and consistently received good performance reviews. Still, when her employer decided to outsource most of its IT work, my mother lost her job. The reason wasn't that her technical skills were inadequate; instead, her salary and benefits cost the company more than outsourcing her job did. Until wages rise around the globe, jobs like my mother's will be vulnerable, no matter how well a person is trained.

Second disagreement with Friedman

Explanation of second disagreement

Conclusion summarizing both disagreements with Friedman

The second dimension that Friedman misses is that a number of well-paid people in my mother's IT department, namely IT managers, were not laid off. As my mother explained at the time, they kept their jobs because they were experienced at figuring out the company's IT needs, planning for changes, researching and proposing solutions, and communicating in writing and speech—skills that her more narrow training and experience had missed. Friedman misses these skills by focusing only on technical training. Without the ability to solve problems creatively and to communicate, people with technical expertise alone may not have enough to save their jobs, as my mother learned.

Final point: business needs and author's personal goals

Like my mother, I am more comfortable in front of a computer than I am in front of a group of people, and I had planned to major in computer science. Since my mother lost her job, however, I have decided to take courses in English and history as well. Classes in these subjects will require me to read broadly, think critically, research, and communicate ideas in writing—in short, to develop skills that make managers. When I enter the job market, my well-rounded education will make me a more attractive job candidate and will help me to become the kind of forward-thinking manager that US companies will always need to employ here in the US.

Many jobs that require a college degree are indeed going overseas, as Thomas L. Friedman says, and my classmates and I need to be ready for a rapidly changing future. But rather than focus only on math and science, we need to broaden our academic experiences so that the skills we develop make us not only employable but also indispensable.

| Explanation of final point |
| Conclusion re-capping points of agreement and disagreement with Friedman and summarizing essay |

Work Cited

Friedman, Thomas L. "It's a Flat World, after All." *New York Times Magazine* 3 Apr. 2005: 32–37. Print.

Work cited in MLA style (see p. 676)

Exercise 3.9 Proofreading

Proofread the following passage, using any of the techniques listed on page 73 to bring errors into the foreground. There are thirteen errors in the passage: missing and misspelled words, typographical errors, and the like. If you are in doubt about any spellings, consult a dictionary.

Exercise

> An envirnmental group, Natural Resources Defense Council, has estimated that 5500 to 6200 children who are preschool today may contract cancer durng there lives becuase of the pesticides they consume in there food In addition, these children will be at greater risk for kidney damage, problems with immunity, and other serious imparments. The government bases it's pesticide-safety standards on adults, but childen consume many more the fruits and fruit products likely too contain pestcides.

Exercise 3.10 Preparing your final draft

Prepare the final draft of the essay you have been working on throughout Chapters 1–3. Proofread carefully and correct all errors before submitting your essay for review.

3g Giving and receiving comments

1 Working collaboratively

Almost all the writing you do in college will generate responses from an instructor. In courses that stress writing, you may submit early drafts as well as your final paper, and your readers may include your classmates as well as your instructor. Like Katy Moreno's, such courses may feature **collaborative learning**, in which students work together on writing, from completing exercises to commenting on each other's work to producing whole papers. Often such work occurs online through a course-management system such as *Blackboard*, *Desire2Learn*, or *Moodle* or through a class blog, e-mail list, or wiki.

Video tutorial

Whether you participate as a writer or as an online or face-to-face peer reviewer, collaboration can give you experience in reading written work and in reaching readers through writing. You may at first be anxious about criticizing others' work or sharing your own rough drafts, but you'll soon grow to appreciate the interaction and the confidence it gives you in your own reading and writing.

CULTURE LANGUAGE In some cultures writers do not expect criticism from readers, or readers do not expect to think critically about what they read. For example, readers may not question an unclear thesis or evaluate the evidence in an argument. If critical responses are uncommon in your native culture, collaboration may at first be uncomfortable for you. As a writer, consider that readers are responding to your draft or even your final paper more as an exploration of ideas than as the last word on your subject; then you may be more receptive to readers' suggestions. As a reader, allow yourself to approach a text skeptically—that is, with questions about the focus, content, and organization, such as *How does this general statement support the thesis?* or *How does this example support the general statement?* Know that your tactful questions and suggestions will usually be considered appropriate.

2 Responding to the writing of others

When you are the reader of someone else's writing, keep the following principles in mind:

Commenting on others' writing

Video tutorial

- Be sure you know what the writer is saying. If necessary, summarize the paper to understand its content. (See pp. 134–35.)
- Address only your most significant concerns with the work. Focus on the deep issues in other writers' drafts, especially early drafts: thesis, purpose, audience, organization, and support for the thesis. Use the revision checklist on p. 61 as a guide to what is significant. Unless you have other instructions, ignore mistakes in grammar, punctuation, spelling, and the like. (The temptation to focus on such errors may be especially strong if the writer is less experienced than you are with standard American English.) Emphasizing mistakes will contribute little to the writer's revision.
- Remember that you are the reader, not the writer. Don't edit sentences, add details, or otherwise assume responsibility for the paper.
- Phrase your comments carefully. Avoid misunderstandings by making sure comments are both clear and respectful. If you are responding on paper or online, not face to face with the writer, remember that the writer has nothing but your written words to go on. He or she can't ask you for immediate clarification and can't infer your attitudes from gestures, facial expressions, and tone of voice.

- **Be specific.** If something confuses you, say *why*. If you disagree with a conclusion, say *why*.
- **Be supportive as well as honest.** Tell the writer what you like about the paper. Word comments positively: instead of *This paragraph doesn't interest me,* say *You have an interesting detail here that I almost missed.* Comment in a way that emphasizes the effect of the work on you, the reader: *This paragraph confuses me because. . . .* And avoid measuring the work against a set of external standards: *This essay is poorly organized. Your thesis statement is inadequate.*
- **While reading, make your comments in writing.** Even if you will be delivering your comments in person later on, the written record will help you recall what you thought.
- **Link comments to specific parts of a paper.** Especially if you are reading the paper on a computer, be clear about what part of the paper each comment relates to. You can embed your comments directly into the paper, distinguishing them with highlighting or color. Or you can use the Comment function of a word processor (see below).

rev
3g

If you are reviewing others' drafts on a word processor, use the Comment function to add your responses without inserting words into the document's text. Usually found on the Insert menu, the function creates marginal annotations (such as those on Katy Moreno's first draft, pp. 57–58) or creates pop-ups that appear when readers move their cursors across words you have highlighted.

Video
tutorial

3 Responding to comments on your own writing

When you *receive* comments from others, whether your classmates or your instructor, you will get more out of the process if you follow the guidelines below.

Benefiting from comments on your writing

- **Think of your readers as counselors or coaches.** They can help you see the virtues and flaws in your work and sharpen your awareness of readers' needs.
- **Read or listen to comments closely.**
- **Know what the critic is saying.** If you need more information, ask for it, or consult the appropriate section of this handbook.
- **Don't become defensive.** Letting comments offend you will only erect a barrier to improvement in your writing. As one writing teacher advises, "Leave your ego at the door."
- **Revise your work in response to appropriate comments.** Whether or not you are required to act on comments, you will learn more from actually revising than from just thinking about it.

Video
tutorial

(continued)

Benefiting from comments on your writing
(continued)

- Remember that you are the final authority on your work. You should be open to suggestions, but you are free to decline advice when you think it is inappropriate.
- Keep track of both the strengths and the weaknesses others identify. Then in later assignments you can build on your successes and give special attention to problem areas.

rev
3h

As the last item in the preceding box indicates, you'll gain the most from collaboration if you carry your learning from one assignment into the next. To keep track of things to work on, try a chart like the one on page 70.

3h Preparing a writing portfolio

Your writing teacher may ask you to assemble samples of your writing into a portfolio, or folder, once or more during the course. Such a portfolio gives you a chance to consider all your writing over a period and to showcase your best work.

Teachers' requirements for portfolios vary. For instance, some teachers ask students to choose their five or so best papers and to submit final drafts only. Others ask for final papers illustrating certain kinds of writing—say, one narrative, one critique, one argument, one research paper, and so on. Still others ask for notes and drafts along with selected papers in order to see students' writing processes. If your class is using online writing tools, your work may be archived as part of the course site and you may be asked to submit your portfolio electronically.

Just as teachers' requirements differ, so do their purposes. But most are looking for a range of writing that demonstrates your progress and strengths as a writer. You, in turn, see how you have advanced from one assignment to the next, as you've had time for new knowledge to sink in and time for practice. Teachers often allow students to revise papers before placing them in the portfolio, even if the papers were submitted earlier. In that case, every paper in the portfolio can benefit from all your learning.

An assignment to assemble a writing portfolio will probably also provide guidelines for what to include, how the portfolio will be evaluated, and how (or whether) it will be weighted for a grade. Be sure you understand the purpose of the portfolio and who will read it. For instance, if your composition teacher will be the only reader and her guidelines urge you to show evidence of progress, you might include a paper that took big risks but never entirely succeeded. In contrast, if a committee of teachers will read your work and the guidelines urge you to demonstrate your competence as a writer, you might include only papers that did succeed.

Unless the guidelines specify otherwise, provide error-free copies of your final drafts, label all your samples with your name, and assemble them all in a folder. Add a cover letter or memo that lists the samples, explains why you've included each one, and evaluates your progress as a writer. The self-evaluation involved should be a learning experience for you and will help your teacher assess your development as a writer.

Sample
document

4
Writing and Revising Paragraphs

Most written texts consist of **paragraphs:** groups of sentences set off by beginning indentions or sometimes by extra space. Paragraphs develop the main ideas that support the central idea, or thesis, of a piece of writing, and they break these supporting ideas into manageable chunks. For readers, paragraphs signal the movement between ideas and provide breathers from long stretches of text.

In the body of an essay, you may use paragraphs for any of these purposes:

- To introduce and give evidence for a main point that supports your essay's central idea (its thesis). See pages 36–40 for a discussion of an essay's thesis.
- Within a group of paragraphs centering on one main point, to develop a key example or other important evidence.
- To shift approach—for instance, from pros to cons, from problem to solution, from questions to answers.
- To mark movement in a sequence, such as from one reason or step to another.

mycomplab

Visit *mycomplab.com* for the eText and for resources and more exercises on writing and revising paragraphs.

In addition, you will use paragraphs for special purposes:

- To introduce or to conclude an essay. See pages 110 and 114.
- To emphasize an important point or to mark a significant transition between points. See pages 115–16.
- In dialog, to indicate that a new person has begun speaking. See page 116.

Note On the Web the paragraphing conventions described in this chapter do not always apply. Web readers often skim text instead of reading word for word, and they are used to links that take them from the paragraph to another page. Writing for the Web, you may want to use shorter paragraphs than you would in print and save links for the ends of paragraphs lest readers miss important information. (For more on Web composition, see pp. 130–34.)

CULTURE LANGUAGE Not all cultures share the paragraphing conventions of American academic writing. The conventions are not universal even among users of standard American English: for instance, US newspaper writers compose very short paragraphs for the purpose of breaking up text in narrow columns. In some other languages, writing moves differently from English on the page—not from left to right, but from right to left or down rows from top to bottom. Even in languages that move as English does on the page, writers may not use paragraphs at all. Or they may use paragraphs but not state the central ideas or provide transitional expressions to show readers how sentences relate. If your native language is not English and you have difficulty writing paragraphs, don't worry about paragraphing during drafting. Instead, during a separate step of revision, divide your text into parts that develop your main points, and mark those parts with indentions. During the next step, you can revise your paragraphs to be sure that each has a clear central idea supported by evidence such as facts and examples.

Checklist for revising paragraphs

Checklist

- Does each paragraph contribute to the essay as a whole? Does each support the essay's central idea, or thesis? Does each relate to the paragraphs that come before and after it? (See opposite.)
- Is each paragraph unified? Does it adhere to one general idea that is either stated in a topic sentence or otherwise apparent? (See p. 82.)
- Is each paragraph coherent? Do the sentences follow a clear sequence? Are the sentences linked as needed by parallelism, repetition or restatement, pronouns, consistency, and transitional expressions? (See p. 86.)
- Is each paragraph developed? Is the general idea of each paragraph well supported with specific evidence such as details, facts, examples, and reasons? (See p. 98.)

4a Relating paragraphs in the essay

Paragraphs do not stand alone: they are key units of a larger piece of writing. Even if you draft a paragraph separately, it needs to connect to your central idea, or thesis—explaining it and deepening it. Together, paragraphs need to flow from one to the other so that readers easily grasp the points you are making and how each point contributes to the whole essay.

¶
4a

To see how effective body paragraphs work to help both writer and reader, look at the third and fourth paragraphs of Katy Moreno's essay "Can We Compete?" from the previous chapter. Responding to an article by Thomas L. Friedman, Moreno is supporting her thesis that Friedman overlooks the need for technical employees to be good communicators and problem solvers.

At first glance, my mother's experience of losing her job might seem to support Friedman's argument that better training in math and science is the key to competing in the global job market. — *Link to previous paragraph and to thesis*

However, her experience adds dimensions to the globalization story that Friedman misses. First, my mother had the kind of strong background in math and science that Friedman says today's workers need. — *New main point connected to thesis*

She majored in computer science, rose within the information technology (IT) department of a large company, and consistently received good performance reviews. Still, when her employer decided to outsource most of its IT work, my mother lost her job. The — *Details to support new point*

reason wasn't that her technical skills were inadequate; instead, her salary and benefits cost the company more than outsourcing her job did. Until wages rise around the globe, jobs like my mother's will be vulnerable, no matter how well a person is trained. — *Concluding sentences summing up paragraph and linking to thesis*

The second dimension that Friedman misses is that a number of well-paid people in my mother's IT department, namely IT managers, were not laid off. As my mother explained at the — *New main point linking to previous paragraph and to thesis*

time, they kept their jobs because they were experienced at figuring out the company's IT needs, planning for changes, researching and proposing solutions, and communicating in writing and speech—skills that her more narrow training and experience had missed. Friedman — *Details to support new point*

misses these skills by focusing only on technical training. Without the ability to solve problems creatively and to communicate, people with technical expertise alone may not have enough to save their jobs, as my mother learned. — *Concluding sentence summing up paragraph and linking to previous paragraph and to thesis*

Exercise

Exercise 4.1 Analyzing paragraphs in an essay

Analyze the fifth paragraph in Katy Moreno's essay in Chapter 3, pages 74–75. How does she relate the paragraph to the thesis statement and to other paragraphs?

Exercise 4.2 Considering your past work: Paragraphs in the essay

¶ un

4b

Examine the final draft of the essay you wrote throughout Chapters 1–3. Do all the paragraphs relate to your thesis? Are they arranged clearly and logically so that your main ideas flow from one paragraph to the next? What improvements can you make?

4b Maintaining paragraph unity

Video tutorial

Just as readers expect paragraphs to relate clearly to an essay's central idea, they also generally expect each paragraph to explore a single idea. They will be alert for that idea and will patiently follow its development. In other words, they will seek and appreciate paragraph **unity:** clear identification and clear elaboration of one idea and of that idea only.

Exercise

In an essay the thesis statement often asserts the main idea as a commitment to readers (see p. 36). In a paragraph a **topic sentence** often alerts readers to the essence of the paragraph by asserting the central idea and expressing the writer's attitude toward it. In a brief essay each body paragraph will likely treat one main point supporting the essay's thesis statement; the topic sentences simply elaborate on parts of the thesis. In longer essays paragraphs tend to work in groups, each group treating one main point. Then the topic sentences will tie into that main point, and all the points together will support the thesis.

1 Focusing on the central idea

Like the thesis sentence, the topic sentence is a commitment to readers, and the rest of the paragraph delivers on that commitment. Look again at the second paragraph by Katy Moreno on the previous page: the opening statement conveys Moreno's promise that she will explain something lacking in Friedman's argument, and the following sentences keep the promise. But what if Moreno had written this paragraph instead?

The second dimension that Friedman misses is that a number of well-paid people in my mother's IT department, namely IT managers, were not laid off. As my mother explained at the time, they kept their jobs because they were experienced at figuring out the company's IT needs, planning for changes, researching and proposing solutions, and communicating in writing. Like my	Topic sentence: general statement Details supporting topic sentence

mother, these managers had families to support, ⌉
so they were lucky to keep their jobs. Our family ⎬ Digression
still struggles with the financial and emotional |
effects of my mother's unemployment. ⌋

By wandering from the topic of why some managers kept their jobs, the paragraph fails to deliver on the commitment of its topic sentence.

You should expect digressions while you are drafting: if you allow yourself to explore ideas, as you should, then of course every paragraph will not be tightly woven, perfectly unified. But spare your readers the challenge and frustration of repeatedly shifting focus to follow your rough explorations: revise each paragraph so that it develops a single idea.

¶ un

4b

While revising your paragraphs for unity, you may want to highlight the central idea of each paragraph to be sure it's stated and then focus on it. On paper you can bracket or circle the idea. On a computer you can format the idea in color or highlight it with a color background. Just be sure to remove the color or highlighting before printing the final draft.

2 Placing the topic sentence

The topic sentence of a paragraph and its supporting details may be arranged variously, depending on how you want to direct readers' attention and how complex your central idea is. In the most common arrangements, the topic sentence comes at the beginning of the paragraph, comes at the end, or is not stated at all but is nonetheless apparent. The advantages of each approach are described here, with examples. If you write on a computer, you can easily experiment with the position of the topic sentence by moving the sentence around (or deleting it) to see the effect. (The sentence will probably take some editing to work smoothly into various positions.)

Topic sentence at the beginning

When you place the topic sentence first in a paragraph, it can help you select the details that follow. For readers, the topic-first model establishes an initial context in which all the supporting details can be understood. Reading Moreno's second paragraph on page 81, we easily relate all the content back to the point made in the first sentence.

The topic-first model is common in explanatory writing as well as in argument, as shown in the following paragraph:

It is a misunderstanding of the American ⌉ Topic sentence: state-
retail store to think we go there necessarily to ⎬ ment of misconception
buy. Some of us shop. There's a difference. Shop-
ping has many purposes, the least interesting ⌉
of which is to acquire new articles. We shop to |

cheer ourselves up. We shop to practice decision-making. We shop to be useful and productive members of our class and society. We shop to remind ourselves how much is available to us. We shop to remind ourselves how much is to be striven for. We shop to assert our superiority to the material objects that spread themselves before us.

Correction of misconception

—Phyllis Rose, "Shopping and Other Spiritual Adventures"

¶ un

4b

Topic sentence at the end

In some paragraphs the central idea may be stated at the end, after supporting sentences have made a case for the general statement. Since this model leads the reader to a conclusion by presenting all the evidence first, it can prove effective in argument. And because the point of the paragraph is withheld until the end, this model can be dramatic in exposition, too, as illustrated by the following example from an essay about William Tecumseh Sherman, a Union general during the US Civil War:

Sherman is considered by some to be the inventor of "total war": the first general in human history to carry the logic of war to its ultimate extreme, the first to scorch the earth, the first to consciously demoralize the hostile civilian population in order to subdue its army, the first to wreck an economy in order to starve its soldiers. He has been called our first "merchant of terror" and seen as the spiritual father of our Vietnam War concepts of "search and destroy," "pacification," "strategic hamlets," and "free-fire zones." As such, he remains a cardboard figure of our history: a monstrous arch-villain to unreconstructed Southerners, and an embarrassment to Northerners.

Information supporting and building to topic sentence

Topic sentence

—Adapted from James Reston, Jr., "You Cannot Refine It"

Expressing the central idea at the end of the paragraph does not eliminate the need to unify the paragraph. The idea in the topic sentence must still govern the selection of all the preceding details.

Central idea not stated

Occasionally, a paragraph's central idea will be stated in the previous paragraph or will be so obvious that it need not be stated at all. The following is from an essay on the actor Humphrey Bogart:

Usually he wore the trench coat unbuttoned, just tied with the belt, and a slouch hat, rarely tilted. Sometimes it was a captain's cap and a yachting jacket. Almost always his trousers were held up by a cowboy belt. You know the kind: one an Easterner waiting for a plane out of Phoenix buys just as a joke and then takes a liking to. Occasionally, he'd hitch up his slacks with it, and he often jabbed his thumbs behind it, his hands ready for a fight or a dame.

> Details adding up to the unstated idea that Bogart's character could be seen in his clothing

—Peter Bogdanovich,
"Bogie in Excelsis"

¶ un

4b

Paragraphs in descriptive writing (like the one above) and in narrative writing (relating a sequence of events) often lack stated topic sentences. But a paragraph without a topic sentence still should have a central idea, and its details should develop that idea.

Exercise 4.3   Finding the central idea

What is the central idea of each of the following paragraphs? In what sentence or sentences is it expressed?

Exercise

1.   At each step, with every graduation from one level of education to the next, the refrain from bystanders was strangely the same: "Your parents must be so proud of you." I suppose that my parents were proud, although I suspect, too, that they felt more than pride alone as they watched me advance through my education. They seemed to know that my education was separating us from one another, making it difficult to resume familiar intimacies. Mixed with the instincts of parental pride, a certain hurt also communicated itself—too private ever to be adequately expressed in words, but real nonetheless.

—Richard Rodriguez "Going Home Again"

2.   Though they do not know why the humpback whale sings, scientists do know something about the song itself. They have measured the length of a whale's song: from a few minutes to over half an hour. They have recorded and studied the variety and complex arrangements of low moans, high squeaks, and sliding squeals that make up the song. And they have learned that each whale sings in its own unique pattern.

—Janet Lieber (student), "Whales' Songs"

Exercise 4.4   Revising a paragraph for unity

The following paragraph contains ideas or details that do not support its central idea. Identify the topic sentence in the paragraph and delete the unrelated material.

Exercise

In the southern part of the state, some people still live much as they did a century ago. They use coal- or wood-burning stoves for heating and cooking. Their homes do not have electricity or indoor bathrooms or running water. The towns they live in don't receive adequate funding from the state and federal governments, so the schools are poor and in bad shape. Beside most homes there is a garden where fresh vegetables are gathered for canning. Small pastures nearby support livestock, including cattle, pigs, horses, and chickens. Most of the people have cars or trucks, but the vehicles are old and beat-up from traveling on unpaved roads.

Exercise 4.5   Considering your past work: Paragraph unity

For a continuing exercise in this chapter, choose a paper you've written in the past year. Examine the body paragraphs for unity. Do they have clear topic sentences? If not, are the paragraphs' central ideas still clear? Are the paragraphs unified around their central ideas? Should any details be deleted for unity? Should other, more relevant details be added in their stead?

¶ coh

4c

Exercise

Exercise 4.6   Writing a unified paragraph

Develop the following topic sentence into a unified paragraph by using the relevant information in the supporting statements. Delete each statement that does not relate directly to the topic, and then rewrite and combine sentences as appropriate. Place the topic sentence in the position that seems most effective to you.

Topic sentence

Mozart's accomplishments in music seem remarkable even today.

Supporting information

Wolfgang Amadeus Mozart was born in 1756 in Salzburg, Austria.
He began composing music at the age of five.
He lived most of his life in Salzburg and Vienna.
His first concert tour of Europe was at the age of six.
On his first tour he played harpsichord, organ, and violin.
He published numerous compositions before reaching adolescence.
He married in 1782.
Mozart and his wife were both poor managers of money.
They were plagued by debts.
Mozart composed over six hundred musical compositions.
His most notable works are his operas, symphonies, quartets, and piano concertos.
He died at the age of thirty-five.

Exercise

Exercise 4.7   Turning topic sentences into unified paragraphs

Develop three of the following topic sentences into detailed and unified paragraphs.

1. Men and women are different in at least one important respect.
2. The best Web search engine is [name].
3. Fans of _____ music [country, classical, rock, rap, jazz, or another kind] come in [number] varieties.
4. Professional sports have [or have not] been helped by extending the regular season with championship playoffs.
5. Working for good grades can interfere with learning.

4c   Achieving paragraph coherence

A paragraph is unified if it holds together—if all its details and examples support the central idea. A paragraph is **coherent** if readers

Ways to achieve paragraph coherence

- Organize effectively (p. 88).
- Repeat or restate key words and word groups (p. 91).
- Use parallel structures (p. 92).
- Use pronouns (p. 92).
- Be consistent in nouns, pronouns, and verbs (p. 93).
- Use transitional expressions (p. 93).

Video
tutorial

¶ coh

4c

can see *how* the paragraph holds together—how the sentences relate to each other—without having to stop and reread.

Incoherence gives readers the feeling of being yanked around, as the following example shows.

> The ancient Egyptians were masters of preserving dead people's bodies by making mummies of them. Mummies several thousand years old have been discovered nearly intact. — **Topic sentence**
>
> The skin, hair, teeth, finger- and toenails, and facial features of the mummies were evident. One can diagnose the diseases they suffered in life, such as smallpox, arthritis, and nutritional deficiencies. The process was remarkably effective. Sometimes apparent were the fatal afflictions of the dead people: a middle-aged king died from a blow on the head, and polio killed a child king. Mummification consisted of removing the internal organs, applying natural preservatives inside and out, and then wrapping the body in layers of bandages. — **Sentences related to topic sentence but disconnected from each other**

The paragraph as it was actually written appears below. It is much clearer because the writer arranged information differently and also built links into his sentences so that they would flow smoothly:

- After stating the central idea in a topic sentence, the writer moves to two more specific explanations and illustrates the second with four sentences of examples.
- Words in green repeat or restate key terms or concepts.
- Words in orange link sentences and clarify relationships.
- Underlined phrases are in parallel grammatical form to reflect their parallel content.

> The ancient Egyptians were masters of preserving dead people's bodies by making mummies of them. — **Topic sentence**
>
> Basically, mummification consisted of removing the internal organs, applying natural preservatives inside and out, and then wrapping the body in layers of bandages. — **Explanation 1: What mummification is**
>
> And the process was remarkably effective. Indeed, mummies several thousand years old have been discovered nearly — **Explanation 2: Why the Egyptians were masters**

intact. Their skin, hair, teeth, finger- and toenails, and facial features are still evident. Their diseases in life, such as smallpox, arthritis, and nutritional deficiencies, are still diagnosable. Even their fatal afflictions are still apparent: a middle-aged king died from a blow on the head; a child king died from polio.

> Specific examples of explanation 2

—Mitchell Rosenbaum (student),
"Lost Arts of the Egyptians"

¶ coh

4c

Though some of the connections in this paragraph were added in revision, the writer attended to them while drafting as well. Not only superficial coherence but also an underlying clarity of relationships can be achieved by tying each sentence to the one before—generalizing from it, clarifying it, qualifying it, adding to it, illustrating it. Each sentence in a paragraph creates an expectation of some sort in the mind of the reader, a question such as "How was a mummy made?" or "How intact are the mummies?" or "What's another example?" When you recognize these expectations and try to fulfill them, readers are likely to understand relationships without struggle.

1 Organizing the paragraph

Video tutorial

The paragraphs on mummies illustrate an essential element of coherence: information must be arranged in an order that readers can follow easily and that corresponds to their expectations. The common organizations for paragraphs correspond to those for entire essays: by space, by time, and for emphasis. (In addition, the patterns of development also suggest certain arrangements. See pp. 98–108.)

Note On a computer you can experiment with different paragraph organizations and emphases. Copy a paragraph, paste the copy into your document, and then try moving sentences around. To evaluate the versions, you'll need to edit each one so that sentences flow smoothly, attending to repetition, parallelism, transitions, and the other techniques for achieving coherence.

Organizing by space or time

A paragraph organized **spatially** focuses readers' attention on one point and scans a person, object, or scene from that point. The movement usually parallels the way people look at things, from top to bottom, from side to side, from near to far. Virginia Woolf follows the last pattern in the following paragraph:

Spatial organization

The sun struck straight upon the house, making the white walls glare between the dark windows. Their panes, woven thickly with green branches, held circles of impenetrable darkness.

> Description moving from outside (closer) to inside (farther)

Sharp-edged wedges of light lay upon the window-sill and showed inside the room plates with blue rings, cups with curved handles, the bulge of a great bowl, the criss-cross pattern in the rug, and the formidable corners and lines of cabinets and bookcases. Behind their conglomeration hung a zone of shadow in which might be a further shape to be disencumbered of shadow or still denser depths of darkness.

— Virginia Woolf, *The Waves*

> Unstated central idea: Sunlight barely penetrated the house's secrets.

¶ coh
4c

Student paper

Another familiar way of organizing the elements of a paragraph is **chronologically**—that is, in order of their occurrence in time. In a chronological paragraph, as in experience, the earliest events come first, followed by more recent ones.

Chronological organization

In early spring, millions of monarch butterflies that have spent the winter months in Mexico begin an annual migration north to the monarch's summer habitats. After covering about fifty miles a day, most make their first stop in Texas, where they lay their eggs on milkweed and die soon after. Their offspring continue the flight to the northern United States and Canada, laying the eggs of the next generation of monarchs along the way. By late spring, these offspring or their offspring reach their summer homes. In August, the third or fourth generation of the original monarchs begins the long return migration south. They do not reproduce in the north but return to where their ancestors wintered and hibernate there. The following spring they start the cycle over by flying north to Texas.

— Ben Kampe (student), "The Monarch Trail"

> Topic sentence

> Details in order of their occurrence

Organizing for emphasis

Some organizational schemes are imposed on paragraphs to achieve a certain emphasis. The most common is the **general-to-specific** scheme, in which the topic sentence often comes first and then the following sentences become increasingly specific. The paragraph on mummies (pp. 87–88) illustrates this organization: each sentence is either more specific than the one before it or at the same level of generality. Here is another illustration:

Student paper

General-to-specific organization

Perhaps the simplest fact about sleep is that individual needs for it vary widely. Most adults sleep between seven and nine hours, but occasionally people turn up who need twelve hours or so, while some rare types can get by on three or four. Rarest of all are those legendary types

> Topic sentence

> Supporting examples, increasingly specific

who require almost no sleep at all; respected researchers have recently studied three such people. One of them—a healthy, happy woman in her seventies—sleeps about an hour every two or three days. The other two are men in early middle age, who get by on a few minutes a night. One of them complains about the daily fifteen minutes or so he's forced to "waste" in sleeping.

—Lawrence A. Mayer,
"The Confounding Enemy of Sleep"

¶ coh

4c

In the less common **specific-to-general** organization, the elements of the paragraph build to a general conclusion:

Specific-to-general organization

It's disconcerting that so many college women, when asked how their children will be cared for if they themselves work, refer with vague confidence to "the day care center" as though there were some great amorphous kiddie watcher out there that the state provides. But such places, adequately funded, well run, and available to all, are still scarce in this country, particularly for middle-class women. And figures show that when she takes time off for family-connected reasons (births, child care), a woman's chances for career advancement plummet. In a job market that's steadily tightening and getting more competitive, these obstacles bode the kind of danger ahead that can shatter not only professions, but egos. A hard reality is that there's not much more support for our daughters who have family-plus-career goals than there was for us; there's simply a great deal more self and societal pressure.

— Common belief

— Actual situation

General conclusion:
topic sentence

—Judith Wax,
Starting in the Middle

As its name implies, the **problem-solution** arrangement introduces a problem and then proposes or explains a solution. The next paragraph argues that the legal drinking age causes problems that a lower age would help to solve.

Student
paper

Problem-solution organization

Although designed to keep young adults away from alcohol, the drinking age of twenty-one actually does the opposite. It attracts youths by making the behavior illegal, and it pushes alcohol consumption underground, thus removing it from the reach of law enforcement and school administrators. The drinking age should be lowered to eighteen. The lower age would not stop drinking on college campuses, but it would weaken the appeal of drinking and help the

Topic sentence and
clarification: statement
of the problem

Solution to the problem

police and colleges control the behavior and its effects.

—Yvonne St. Pierre (student),
"Drinking and the Law"

When your details vary in significance, you can arrange them in a **climactic** order, from least to most important or dramatic:

Climactic organization

Nature has put many strange tongues into the heads of her creatures. — Topic sentence
There is the frog's tongue, rooted at the front of the mouth so it can be protruded an extra distance for nabbing prey. — Least dramatic example
There is the gecko lizard's tongue, so long and agile that the lizard uses it to wash its eyes. But the ultimate lingual whopper has been achieved in the anteater. The anteater's head, long as it is, is not long enough to contain the tremendous tongue which licks deep into ant-hills. Its tongue is not rooted in the mouth or throat: it is fastened to the breastbone. — Most dramatic example

—Alan Devoe, "Nature's Utmost"

¶ coh

4c

Student paper

In other paragraph organizations, you can arrange details according to how you think readers are likely to understand them. In discussing the virtues of public television, for instance, you might proceed from **most familiar to least familiar,** from a well-known program to less well-known programs. Or in defending the right of government employees to strike, you might arrange your reasons from **simplest to most complex,** from the employees' need to be able to redress grievances to the more subtle consequences for relations between employers and employees.

2 Repeating or restating key words

Repeating or restating the important words in a paragraph binds the sentences together and keeps the paragraph's topic uppermost in readers' minds. In the next example, notice how the shaded words relate the sentences and stress the important ideas of the paragraph:

To the amazement of those who regard our culture as anti-intellectual, as lacking in any sense of the interior life, the United States has been the most receptive country in the world to psychotherapy. This apparent paradox has many explanations: we are a profoundly individualistic society, committed to the belief that people are responsible for their own lives; we are a success-oriented society, measuring people's value not so much by their family background as by their personal achievements; we are a pragmatic society, in which problems are by definition solvable. These characteristics combine to form a culture in which a sense of personal failure is widespread, but in which simple solutions seem immediately available.

—Ross Wetzsteon, "Psychochatter"

Note Though planned repetition can be effective, careless or excessive repetition weakens prose (see p. 549).

¶ coh

4c

3 Using parallel structures

Another way to achieve coherence is through **parallelism,** the use of similar grammatical structures for similar elements of meaning within a sentence or among sentences. (See Chapter 25 for a detailed discussion of parallelism.) Parallel structures help tie together the last three sentences in the paragraph on mummies (p. 88). In the following paragraph the underlined parallel structures link all sentences after the first one, and parallelism also appears within many of the sentences (as in *by supporting candidates and making speeches* in sentence 5 and *He served . . . , survived . . . , and earned* in sentence 8). The paragraph comes from a student's profile of President Ronald Reagan.

Ronald Reagan holds a particularly interesting place in American history, combining successful careers in show business and in politics. After graduating from college in 1932, he worked as a radio sports announcer with an affinity for describing game details. He then launched a successful film career, starring in dozens of movies. After a stint in the US Army, he assumed the role of host for *General Electric Theater*, a weekly TV program that ran from 1953 to 1962. He first entered politics by supporting candidates and making speeches in the 1950s and early 1960s. He became governor of California in 1966 and served for eight years. He ran unsuccessfully for the US presidency in 1976 and then won the job in 1980, when he became the fortieth President. He served two terms, survived an assassination attempt, and earned a popularity that most politicians can only envy.

—William Brooks (student), "Ronald Reagan, the Actor President"

4 Using pronouns

Pronouns such as *she, he, it, they,* and *who* refer to and function as nouns (see p. 257). Thus pronouns naturally help relate sentences to one another. In the following paragraph the pronouns and the nouns they refer to are shaded:

After dark, on the warrenlike streets of Brooklyn where I live, I often see women who fear the worst from me. They seem to have set their faces on neutral, and with their purse straps strung across their chests bandolier-style, they forge ahead as though bracing themselves against being tackled. I understand, of course, that the danger they perceive is not a hallucination. Women are particularly vulnerable to street violence, and young black males are drastically overrepresented among the perpetrators of that violence. Yet these truths are no solace against the kind of alienation that comes of being ever the suspect, a fearsome entity with whom pedestrians avoid making eye contact.

—Brent Staples, "Black Men and Public Space"

5 Being consistent

Being consistent is the most subtle way to achieve paragraph coherence because readers are aware of consistency only when it is absent. Consistency (or the lack of it) occurs primarily in the tense of verbs and in the number and person of nouns and pronouns (see Chapter 20). Although some shifts will be necessary to reflect your meaning, inappropriate shifts, as in the following passages, will interfere with a reader's ability to follow the development of ideas.

¶ coh

4c

Shifts in tense

In the Hopi religion, water is the driving force. Since the Hopi lived in the Arizona desert, they needed water urgently for drinking, cooking, and irrigating crops. Their complex beliefs are focused in part on gaining the assistance of supernatural forces in obtaining water. Many of the Hopi kachinas, or spirit essences, were directly concerned with clouds, rain, and snow.

Shifts in number

Kachinas represent the things and events of the real world, such as clouds, mischief, cornmeal, and even death. A kachina is not worshiped as a god but regarded as an interested friend. They visit the Hopi from December through July in the form of men who dress in kachina costumes and perform dances and other rituals.

Shifts in person

Unlike the man, the Hopi woman does not keep contact with kachinas through costumes and dancing. Instead, one receives a small likeness of a kachina, called a *tihu*, from the man impersonating the kachina. You are more likely to receive a tihu as a girl approaching marriage, though a child or older woman sometimes receives one, too.

Grammar checkers Grammar checkers cannot help you locate shifts in tense, number, or person among sentences. Shifts are sometimes necessary (as when tenses change to reflect actual differences in time). Furthermore, a passage with needless shifts may still consist of sentences that are grammatically correct, as all the sentences are in the preceding examples. The only way to achieve consistency in your writing is to review it yourself.

6 Using transitional expressions

Specific words and word groups, called **transitional expressions,** can connect sentences whose relationships may not be instantly clear to readers. Notice the difference in the following two versions of the same paragraph:

Video tutorial

Medical science has succeeded in identifying the hundreds of viruses that can cause the common cold. It has discovered the most effective means of prevention. One person transmits the cold viruses to another most often by hand.

Paragraph is choppy and hard to follow

An infected person covers his mouth to cough. He picks up the telephone. His daughter picks up the telephone. She rubs her eyes. She has a cold. It spreads. To avoid colds, people should wash their hands often and keep their hands away from their faces.

Medical science has **thus** succeeded in identifying the hundreds of viruses that can cause the common cold. It has **also** discovered the most effective means of prevention. One person transmits the cold viruses to another most often by hand. **For instance,** an infected person covers his mouth to cough. **Then** he picks up the telephone. **Half an hour later,** his daughter picks up the same telephone. **Immediately afterward,** she rubs her eyes. **Within a few days,** she, **too,** has a cold. **And thus** it spreads. To avoid colds, **therefore,** people should wash their hands often and keep their hands away from their faces.

Transitional expressions (shaded) remove choppiness and spell out relationships

—Kathleen LaFrank (student),
"Colds: Myth and Science"

There are scores of transitional expressions on which to draw. The following box shows many common ones, arranged according to the relationships they convey.

Transitional expressions

Podcast

To add or show sequence

again, also, and, and then, besides, equally important, finally, first, further, furthermore, in addition, in the first place, last, moreover, next, second, still, too

To compare

also, in the same way, likewise, similarly

To contrast

although, and yet, but, but at the same time, despite, even so, even though, for all that, however, in contrast, in spite of, nevertheless, notwithstanding, on the contrary, on the other hand, regardless, still, though, yet

To give examples or intensify

after all, an illustration of, even, for example, for instance, indeed, in fact, it is true, of course, specifically, that is, to illustrate, truly

To indicate place

above, adjacent to, below, elsewhere, farther on, here, near, nearby, on the other side, opposite to, there, to the east, to the left

To indicate time

after a while, afterward, as long as, as soon as, at last, at length, at that time, before, earlier, eventually, formerly, immediately, in the meantime, in the past, lately, later, meanwhile, now, presently, shortly, simultaneously, since, so far, soon, subsequently, suddenly, then, thereafter, until, when

To repeat, summarize, or conclude

all in all, altogether, as has been said, in brief, in conclusion, in other words, in particular, in short, in simpler terms, in summary, on the whole, that is, therefore, to put it differently, to summarize

To show cause or effect

accordingly, as a result, because, consequently, for this purpose, hence, otherwise, since, then, therefore, thereupon, thus, to this end, with this object

Note Draw carefully on the preceding lists because the expressions in each group are not interchangeable. For instance, *besides, finally,* and *second* may all be used to add information, but each has its own distinct meaning.

¶ coh

4c

To see where transitional expressions might be needed in your paragraphs, examine the movement from each sentence to the next. (On a computer or on paper, you can highlight the transitional expressions already present and then review the sentences that lack them.) Abrupt changes are most likely to need a transition: a shift from cause to effect, a contradiction, a contrast. You can smooth and clarify transitions *between* paragraphs, too. See pages 87, 96, and 115.

CULTURE LANGUAGE If transitional expressions are not common in your native language, you may be tempted to compensate when writing in English by adding them to the beginnings of most sentences. But such explicit transitions aren't needed everywhere, and in fact too many can be intrusive and awkward. When inserting transitional expressions, consider the reader's need for a signal: often the connection from sentence to sentence is already clear from the context, or it can be made clear by relating the content of sentences more closely (see pp. 91–92). When you do need transitional expressions, try varying their positions in your sentences, as shown in the sample paragraph on the facing page.

Punctuating transitional expressions

A transitional expression is usually set off by a comma or commas from the rest of the sentence:

Video tutorial

Immediately afterward, she rubs her eyes. Within a few days, she, too, has a cold.

See page 452 for more on this convention and its exceptions.

¶ coh

4c

7 Combining devices to achieve coherence within and among paragraphs

The devices for achieving coherence rarely appear in isolation in effective paragraphs. As any example in this chapter shows, writers usually combine sensible organization, parallelism, repetition, pronouns, consistency, and transitional expressions to help readers follow the development of ideas.

The following excerpts from Katy Moreno's essay on pages 73–75 illustrate how coherence techniques can bind sentences and paragraphs. The individual paragraphs are clearly organized and are closely linked by transitional sentences (noted in the annotations) and transitional words (shaded in orange). Verb tenses shift only to reflect changes in actual time between the past (*my mother had, She majored*) and the present (*better training . . . is, Friedman says, I am*). The pronouns *she* and *her* (underlined) make it clear when Moreno is discussing her mother. And Moreno uses repetition and restatement (shaded in green) to emphasize important words.

At first glance, my mother's experience of losing her job might seem to support Friedman's argument that better training in math and science is the key to competing in the global job market. However, her experience adds dimensions to the globalization story that Friedman misses. First, my mother had the kind of strong background in math and science that Friedman says today's workers need. She majored in computer science, rose within the information technology (IT) department of a large company, and consistently received good performance reviews. . . .

Transitional sentence connecting to previous paragraph and to thesis

The second dimension that Friedman misses is that a number of well-paid people in my mother's IT department, namely IT managers, were not laid off. . . .

Transitional sentence connecting to previous paragraph and to thesis

Like my mother, I am more comfortable in front of a computer than I am in front of a group of people, and I had planned to major in computer science. Since my mother lost her job, however, I have decided to take courses in English and history as well. . . .

Transitional sentence connecting to previous paragraph

Exercise 4.8 Analyzing paragraphs for coherence

Exercise

Study the paragraphs by Janet Lieber (p. 85), Hillary Begas (p. 100), and Freeman Dyson (pp. 101–02) for the authors' use of various devices to achieve coherence. Look especially for organization, parallel structures and ideas, repetition and restatement, pronouns, and transitional expressions.

Exercise 4.9 Arranging sentences coherently

After the topic sentence (sentence 1), the sentences in the student paragraph below have been deliberately scrambled to make the paragraph incoherent. Using the topic sentence and other clues as guides, rearrange the sentences in the paragraph to form a well-organized, coherent unit.

¶ coh

4c

We hear complaints about the Postal Service all the time, but we 1 should not forget what it does *right*. The total volume of mail delivered 2 by the Postal Service each year makes up almost half the total delivered in all the world. Its 70,000 employees handle 140,000,000,000 pieces of 3 mail each year. And when was the last time they failed to deliver yours? 4 In fact, on any given day the Postal Service delivers almost as much mail 5 as the rest of the world combined. That huge number means over 6 2,000,000 pieces per employee and over 560 pieces per man, woman, and child in the country.

Exercise 4.10 Eliminating inconsistencies

The following paragraph is incoherent because of inconsistencies in person, number, and tense. Identify the inconsistencies and revise the paragraph to give it coherence. For further exercises in eliminating inconsistencies, see pages 376, 378–79, and 379–80.

The Hopi tihu, or kachina likeness, is often called a "doll," but its owner, usually a girl or woman, does not regard them as a plaything. Instead, you treated them as a valued possession and hung them out of the way on a wall. For its owner the tihu represents a connection with the kachina's spirit. They are considered part of the kachina, carrying a portion of the kachina's power.

Exercise 4.11 Using transitional expressions

Transitional expressions have been removed from the following paragraph at the numbered blanks. Fill in each blank with an appropriate transitional expression (1) to contrast, (2) to intensify, and (3) to show effect. Consult the list on pages 94–95 if necessary.

All over the country, people are swimming, jogging, weightlifting, dancing, walking, playing tennis—doing anything to keep fit. ___(1)___ this school has consistently refused to construct and equip a fitness center. The school has ___(2)___ refused to open existing athletic facilities to all students, not just those playing organized sports. ___(3)___ students have no place to exercise except in their rooms and on dangerous public roads.

Exercise 4.12 Considering your past work: Paragraph coherence

Continuing from Exercise 4.5 (p. 86), examine the body paragraphs of your essay to see how coherent they are and how their coherence could be improved. Do the paragraphs have a clear organization? Do you use repetition and restatement, parallelism, pronouns, and transitional expressions to signal relationships? Are the paragraphs consistent in person, number, and tense? Revise two or three paragraphs in ways you think will improve their coherence.

Exercise 4.13   Writing a coherent paragraph

¶ dev

4d

Exercise

Write a coherent paragraph from the following information, combining and rewriting sentences as necessary. First, begin the paragraph with the topic sentence given and arrange the supporting sentences in a climactic order. Then combine and rewrite the supporting sentences, helping the reader see connections by introducing repetition and restatement, parallelism, pronouns, consistency, and transitional expressions.

Topic sentence
Hypnosis is far superior to drugs for relieving tension.

Supporting information
Hypnosis has none of the dangerous side effects of the drugs that relieve tension.
Tension-relieving drugs can cause weight loss or gain, illness, or even death.
Hypnosis is nonaddictive.
Most of the drugs that relieve tension do foster addiction.
Tension-relieving drugs are expensive.
Hypnosis is inexpensive even for people who have not mastered self-hypnosis.

Exercise 4.14   Turning topic sentences into coherent paragraphs

Exercise

Develop three of the following topic sentences into coherent paragraphs. Organize your information by space, by time, or for emphasis, as seems most appropriate. Use repetition and restatement, parallelism, pronouns, consistency, and transitional expressions to link sentences.

1. The most interesting character in the book [or movie] was _____.
2. Of all my courses, _____ is the one that I think will serve me best throughout life.
3. Although we in the United States face many problems, the one we should concentrate on solving first is _____.
4. The most dramatic building in town is the _____.
5. Children should not have to worry about the future.

4d   Developing the paragraph

In an essay that's understandable and interesting to readers, you will provide plenty of solid information to support your general statements. You work that information into the essay through the paragraph, as you build up each point relating to the thesis.

A paragraph may be unified and coherent but still be inadequate if you skimp on details. Take this example:

> Untruths can serve as a kind of social oil when they smooth connections between people. In preventing confrontation and injured feelings, they allow everyone to go on as before.

    General statements needing examples to be clear and convincing

This paragraph lacks **development,** completeness. It does not provide enough information for us to evaluate or even care about the writer's assertions.

¶ dev

4d

1 Using specific information

If they are sound, the general statements you make in any writing will be based on what you have experienced, observed, read, and thought. Readers will assume as much and will expect you to provide the evidence for your statements—sensory details, facts, statistics, examples, quotations, reasons. Whatever helps you form your views you need, in turn, to share with readers.

Here is the actual version of the preceding sample paragraph. With examples, the paragraph is more interesting and convincing.

> Untruths can serve as a kind of social oil when they smooth connections between people. Assuring a worried friend that his haircut is flattering, claiming an appointment to avoid an aunt's dinner invitation, pretending interest in an acquaintance's children—these lies may protect the liar, but they also protect the person lied to. In preventing confrontation and injured feelings, the lies allow everyone to go on as before.
> —Joan Lar (student), "The Truth of Lies"

    Examples specifying kinds of lies and consequences

If your readers often comment that your writing needs more specifics, you should focus on that improvement in your revisions. Try listing the general statements of each paragraph on lines by themselves with space underneath. Then use one of the discovery techniques discussed on pages 25–35 (freewriting, brainstorming, and so on) to find the details to support each sentence. Write these into your draft. If you write on a computer, you can do this revision directly on a copy of your draft by separating the sentences and exploring their support. Rewrite the supporting details into sentences, reassemble the paragraph, and edit it for coherence.

2 Using a pattern of development

If you have difficulty developing an idea or shaping your information, try asking yourself questions derived from the patterns of development. (The same patterns can help with essay development, too. See pp. 33–35.)

How did it happen? (Narration)

Video tutorial

Narration retells a significant sequence of events, usually in the order of their occurrence (that is, chronologically):

¶ dev
4d

Student paper

> Jill's story is typical for "recruits" to religious cults. She was very lonely in college and appreciated the attention of the nice young men and women who lived in a house near campus. They persuaded her to share their meals and then to move in with them. Between intense bombardments of "love," they deprived her of sleep and sometimes threatened to throw her out. Jill became increasingly confused and dependent, losing touch with any reality besides the one in the group. She dropped out of school and refused to see or communicate with her family. Before long she, too, was preying on lonely college students.
> —Hillary Begas (student), "The Love Bombers"

Important events in chronological order

As this paragraph illustrates, a narrator is concerned not just with the sequence of events but also with their consequence, their importance to the whole. Thus a narrative rarely corresponds to real time; instead, it collapses transitional or background events and focuses on events of particular interest. In addition, writers sometimes rearrange events, as when they simulate the workings of memory by flashing back to an earlier time.

How does it look, sound, feel, smell, taste? (Description)

Video tutorial

Description details the sensory qualities of a person, place, thing, or feeling. You use concrete and specific words to convey a dominant mood, to illustrate an idea, or to achieve some other purpose. Some description is **subjective**: the writer filters the subject through his or her biases and emotions. In the subjective description by Virginia Woolf on pages 88–89, the *glare* of the walls, the *impenetrable darkness*, the *bulge of a great bowl*, and the *formidable corners and lines* all indicate the feelings of the author about what she describes.

Student paper

In contrast to subjective description, journalists and scientists usually strive for description that is **objective**, conveying the subject without bias or emotion:

> The two toddlers, both boys, sat together for half an hour in a ten-foot-square room with yellow walls (one with a two-way mirror for observation) and a brown carpet. The room was unfurnished except for two small chairs and about two dozen toys. The boys' interaction was generally tense. They often struggled physically and verbally over several toys, especially a large red beach ball and a small wooden fire engine. The larger of the two boys often pushed the smaller away or pried his hands from the desired

Objective description: specific record of sensory data without interpretation object. This larger boy never spoke, but he did make grunting sounds when he was engaging the other. In turn, the smaller boy twice uttered piercing screams of "No!" and once shouted "Stop that!" When he was left alone, he hummed and muttered to himself.

—Ray Mattison (student),
"Case Study: Play Patterns of Toddlers"

What are examples of it or reasons for it? (Illustration or support)

¶ dev

4d

Video
tutorial

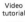

Student
paper

Some ideas can be developed simply by **illustration or support** —supplying detailed examples or reasons. The writer of the paragraph on lying (p. 99) developed her idea with several specific examples of her general statements. You can also supply a single extended example:

> The experience is a familiar one to many emergency-room medics. A patient who has been pronounced dead and unexpectedly recovers later describes what happened to him during those moments—sometimes hours—when his body exhibited no signs of life. According to one repeated account, the patient feels himself rushing through a long, dark tunnel while noise rings in his ears. Suddenly, he finds himself outside his own body looking down with curious detachment at a medical team's efforts to resuscitate him. He hears what is said, notes what is happening but cannot communicate with anyone. Soon his attention is drawn to other presences in the room—spirits of dead relatives or friends—who communicate with him nonverbally. Gradually he is drawn to a vague "being of light." This being invites him to evaluate his life and shows him highlights of his past in panoramic vision. The patient longs to stay with the being of light but is reluctantly drawn back into his physical body and recovers.
> —Kenneth L. Woodward, "Life after Death?"

Topic sentences

Single detailed example

Sometimes you can develop a paragraph by providing your reasons for stating a general idea:

> There are three reasons, quite apart from scientific considerations, that mankind needs to travel in space. The first reason is the need for garbage disposal: we need to transfer industrial processes into space, so that the earth may remain a green and pleasant place for our grandchildren to live in. The second reason is the need to escape material impoverishment: the resources of this planet are finite, and we shall not forgo

Topic sentence

Three reasons arranged in order of increasing drama and importance forever the abundant solar energy and minerals and living space that are spread out all around us. The third reason is our spiritual need for an open frontier: the ultimate purpose of space travel is to bring to humanity not only scientific discoveries and an occasional spectacular show on television but a real expansion of our spirit.

—Freeman Dyson, "Disturbing the Universe"

¶ dev

4d

What is it? What does it encompass, and what does it exclude? (Definition)

Video
tutorial

Student
paper

A **definition** says what something is and is not, specifying the characteristics that distinguish the subject from the other members of its class. You can easily define concrete, noncontroversial terms in a single sentence: *A knife is a cutting instrument* (its class) *with a sharp blade set in a handle* (the characteristics that set it off from, say, scissors or a razor blade). But defining a complicated or controversial topic often requires extended explanation, and you may need to devote a whole paragraph or even an essay to it. Such a definition may provide examples to identify the subject's characteristics. It may also involve other methods of development discussed here, such as classification or comparison and contrast.

The following definition of the word *quality* comes from an essay asserting that "quality in product and effort has become a vanishing element of current civilization":

In the hope of possibly reducing the hail of censure which is certain to greet this essay (I am thinking of going to Alaska or possibly Patagonia in the week it is published), let me say that quality, as I understand it, means investment of the best skill and effort possible to produce the finest and most admirable result possible. Its presence or absence in some degree characterizes every man-made object, service, skilled or unskilled labor— laying bricks, painting a picture, ironing shirts, practicing medicine, shoemaking, scholarship, writing a book. You do it well or you do it half-well. Materials are sound and durable or they are sleazy; method is painstaking or whatever is easiest. Quality is achieving or reaching for the highest standard as against being satisfied with the sloppy or fraudulent. It is honesty of purpose as against catering to cheap or sensational sentiment. It does not allow compromise with the second-rate.

— General definition

— Activities in which quality may figure

— Contrast between quality and nonquality

—Barbara Tuchman,
"The Decline of Quality"

What are its parts or characteristics? (Division or analysis)

Video
tutorial

Division and **analysis** both involve separating something into its elements, the better to understand it. Here is a simple example:

A typical daily newspaper compresses considerable information into the top of the first page, above the headlines. The most prominent feature of this space, the newspaper's name, is called the *logo* or *nameplate*. Under the logo and set off by rules is a line of small type called the *folio line*, which contains the date of the issue, the volume and issue numbers, copyright information, and the price. To the right of the logo is a block of small type called a *weather ear*, a summary of the day's forecast. And above the logo is a *skyline*, a kind of advertisement in which the paper's editors highlight a special feature of the issue.

> The subject being divided

> Elements of the subject, arranged spatially

¶ dev

4d

—Kansha Stone (student),
"Anatomy of a Paper"

Generally, analysis goes beyond simply identifying elements. Often used as a synonym for *critical thinking*, analysis also involves interpreting the elements' meaning, significance, and relationships. You identify and interpret elements according to your particular interest in the subject. (See pp. 154–60 for more on critical thinking and analysis.)

Student paper

The following paragraph comes from an essay about soap operas. The analytical focus of the whole essay is the way soap operas provide viewers with a sense of community missing from their own lives. The paragraph itself has a narrower focus related to the broader one.

The surface realism of the soap opera conjures up an illusion of "liveness." The domestic settings and easygoing rhythms encourage the viewer to believe that the drama, however ridiculous, is simply an extension of daily life. The conversation is so slow that some have called it "radio with pictures." (Advertisers have always assumed that busy housewives would listen, rather than watch.) Conversation is casual and colloquial, as though one were eavesdropping on neighbors. There is plenty of time to "read" the character's face; close-ups establish intimacy. The sets are comfortably familiar: well-lit interiors of living rooms, restaurants, offices, and hospitals. Daytime soaps have little of the glamour of their prime-time relations. The viewer easily imagines that the conversation is taking place in real time.

> Topic and focus: how "liveness" seems an extension of daily life

> Elements:
>   Slow conversation
>
>   Casual conversation
>
>   Intimate close-ups
>
>   Familiar sets
>
>   Absence of glamour
>   Appearance of real time

—Ruth Rosen, "Search for Yesterday"

What groups or categories can it be sorted into? (Classification)

Classification involves sorting many things into groups based on their similarities. Using the pattern, we scan a large group composed of many members that share at least one characteristic—workers, say—and we assign the members to smaller groups on the

Video tutorial

basis of some principle—salary, perhaps, or dependence on computers. Here is an example:

> In my experience, the parents who hire daytime sitters for their school-age children tend to fall into one of three groups. The first group includes parents who work and want someone to be at home when the children return from school. These parents are looking for an extension of themselves, someone who will give the care they would give if they were at home. The second group includes parents who may be home all day themselves but are too disorganized or too frazzled by their children's demands to handle child care alone. They are looking for an organizer and helpmate. The third and final group includes parents who do not want to be bothered by their children, whether they are home all day or not. Unlike the parents in the first two groups, who care for their children whenever and however they can, these parents are looking for a permanent substitute for themselves.
>
> —Nancy Whittle (student), "Modern Parenting"

Topic sentence

Three groups:
 Alike in one way (all hire sitters)
 No overlap in groups (each has a different attitude)

Classes arranged in order of increasing drama

¶ dev
4d

How is it like, or different from, other things? (Comparison and contrast)

Video tutorial

Asking about similarities and differences leads to **comparison and contrast:** comparison focuses on similarities, whereas contrast focuses on differences. The two may be used separately or together to develop an idea or to relate two or more things. Commonly, comparisons are organized in one of two ways. In the first, **subject by subject,** the two subjects are discussed separately, one at a time:

> Consider the differences also in the behavior of rock and classical music audiences. At a rock concert, the audience members yell, whistle, sing along, and stamp their feet. They may even stand during the entire performance. The better the music, the more active they'll be. At a classical concert, in contrast, the better the performance, the more *still* the audience is. Members of the classical audience are so highly disciplined that they refrain from even clearing their throats or coughing. No matter what effect the powerful music has on their intellects and feelings, they sit on their hands.
>
> —Tony Nahm (student), "Rock and Roll Is Here to Stay"

Subjects: rock and classical audiences

Rock audience

Classical audience

In the second comparative organization, **point by point,** the two subjects are discussed side by side and matched feature for feature:

Arguing is often equated with fighting, but there are key differences between the two. Participants in an argument approach the subject to find common ground, or points on which both sides agree, while people engaged in a fight usually approach the subject with an "us-versus-them" attitude. Participants in an argument are careful to use respectful, polite language, in contrast to the insults and worse that people in a fight use to get the better of their opponents. Finally, participants in an argument commonly have the goal of reaching a new understanding or larger truth about the subject they're debating, while those in a fight have winning as their only goal.

— Erica Ito (student),
"Is an Argument Always a Fight?"

Subjects: arguing and fighting	
Approach to subject: argument, fight	
Language: argument, fight	
Goal: argument, fight	

¶ dev
4d

The following examples show the two organizing schemes in outline form. The one on the left corresponds to the point-by-point paragraph about the differences between arguing and fighting. The one on the right uses the same information but reorganizes it to cover the two subjects separately: first one, then the other.

Point by Point

I. Approach to subject
 A. Argument
 B. Fight
II. Language
 A. Argument
 B. Fight
III. Goal
 A. Argument
 B. Fight

Subject by Subject

I. Argument
 A. Approach to subject
 B. Language
 C. Goal
II. Fight
 A. Approach to subject
 B. Language
 C. Goal

Is it comparable to something that is in a different class but more familiar to readers? (Analogy)

Whereas we draw comparisons and contrasts between elements in the same general class (audiences, disputes), we link elements in different classes with a special kind of comparison called **analogy.** Most often in analogy we illuminate or explain an unfamiliar, abstract class of things with a familiar and concrete class of things:

Student paper

We might eventually obtain some sort of bedrock understanding of cosmic structure, but we will never understand the universe in detail; it is just too big and varied for that. If we possessed an atlas of our galaxy that devoted but a single page to each star system in the Milky Way (so that the sun and all its planets were crammed on one page), that atlas would run to more than ten

Abstract subject: the universe, specifically the Milky Way
Concrete subject: an atlas

million volumes of ten thousand pages each. It would take a library the size of Harvard's to house the atlas, and merely to flip through it, at the rate of a page per second, would require over ten thousand years.

—Timothy Ferris,
Coming of Age in the Milky Way

¶ dev
4d

Video
tutorial

Student
paper

Why did it happen, or what results did it have? (Cause-and-effect analysis)

When you use analysis to explain why something happened or what is likely to happen, then you are determining causes and effects. **Cause-and-effect analysis** is especially useful in writing about social, economic, or political events or problems. In the next paragraph the author looks at the causes of Japanese collectivism, which he elsewhere contrasts with American individualism:

The *shinkansen* or "bullet train" speeds across the rural areas of Japan giving a quick view of cluster after cluster of farmhouses surrounded by rice paddies. This particular pattern did not develop purely by chance, but as a consequence of the technology peculiar to the growing of rice, the staple of the Japanese diet. The growing of rice requires the construction and maintenance of an irrigation system, something that takes many hands to build. More importantly, the planting and the harvesting of rice can only be done efficiently with the cooperation of twenty or more people. The "bottom line" is that a single family working alone cannot produce enough rice to survive, but a dozen families working together can produce a surplus. Thus the Japanese have had to develop the capacity to work together in harmony, no matter what the forces of disagreement or social disintegration, in order to survive.

—William Ouchi, *Theory Z*

> Effect: pattern of Japanese farming

> Causes: Japanese dependence on rice, which requires collective effort

> Effect: working in harmony

Cause-and-effect paragraphs tend to focus either on causes, as Ouchi's does, or on effects, as this paragraph does:

The consumerism of the postwar era [since World War II] has not been without its effects on the way we use our time. As people became accustomed to the material rewards of prosperity, desires for leisure time were eroded. They increasingly looked to consumption to give satisfaction, even meaning, to their lives. In both the workplace and the home, progress has repeatedly translated into more goods and services, rather than more free time. Employers channel productivity increases

> Cause: consumerism

> Effects:
> Erosion of leisure time
>
> Emphasis on goods and services

into additional income; housewives are led to use their labor-saving appliances to produce more goods and services. Consumerism traps us as we become habituated to the good life, emulate our neighbors, or just get caught up in the social pressures created by everyone else's choices. Work-and-spend has become a mutually reinforcing and powerful syndrome—a seamless web we somehow keep choosing, without even meaning to.
—Juliet B. Schor, *The Overworked American*

Higher income
Labor-saving devices

Habituation to the good life

Work-and-spend syndrome

¶ dev

4d

How does one do it, or how does it work? (Process analysis)

When you analyze how to do something or how something works, you explain the steps in a **process.** Paragraphs developed by process analysis are usually organized chronologically, as the steps in the process occur. Some process analyses tell the reader how to do a task:

Video tutorial

Student paper

As a car owner, you waste money when you pay a mechanic to change the engine oil. The job is not difficult, even if you know little about cars.

Process: changing oil

All you need is a wrench to remove the drain plug, a large, flat pan to collect the draining oil, plastic bottles to dispose of the used oil, and fresh oil.

Equipment needed

First, warm up the car's engine so that the oil will flow more easily. When the engine is warm, shut it off and remove its oil-filler cap (the owner's manual shows where this cap is). Then locate the drain plug under the engine (again consulting the owner's manual for its location) and place the flat pan under the plug. Remove the plug with the wrench, letting the oil flow into the pan. When the oil stops flowing, replace the plug and, at the engine's filler hole, add the amount and kind of fresh oil specified by the owner's manual. Pour the used oil into the plastic bottles and take it to a waste-oil collector, which any garage mechanic can recommend.
—Anthony Andreas (student), "Do-It-Yourself Car Care"

Steps in process

Other process analyses explain how processes are done or how they work in nature. The paragraph on monarch butterflies (p. 89) is one example. Here is another:

What used to be called "laying on of hands" is now practiced seriously by nurses and doctors.

Process: therapeutic touch

Studies have shown that therapeutic touch, as it is now known, can aid relaxation and ease pain, two effects that may in turn cause healing. A "healer"

Benefits

must first concentrate on helping the patient. Then, hands held a few inches from the patient's body, the healer moves from head to foot. Healers claim that they can detect energy disturbances in the patient that indicate tension, pain, or sickness. With further hand movements, the healer tries to redirect the energy. — Steps in process

Patients report feeling heat from the healer's hands, perhaps indicating an energy transfer between healer and patient. — How process works

— Lisa Kuklinski (student),
"Old Ways to Noninvasive Medicine"

Diagrams, photographs, and other visuals can do much to clarify process analyses. See pages 123–30 for guidelines on creating and clearly labeling visuals.

Combining patterns of development

Whatever pattern you choose as the basis for developing a paragraph, other patterns may also prove helpful. Combined patterns have appeared often in this section: Dyson analyzes causes and effects in presenting reasons (pp. 101–02); Tuchman uses contrast to define *quality* (p. 102); Nahm uses description to compare (p. 104); Ouchi uses process analysis to explain causes (p. 106).

3 Checking length

The average paragraph contains between 100 and 150 words, or between four and eight sentences. The appropriate length of a paragraph depends on the complexity of its topic, the role it plays in developing the thesis of the essay, and its position in the essay. Nevertheless, very short paragraphs often lack adequate development; they may leave readers with a sense of incompleteness. And very long paragraphs often contain irrelevant details or develop two or more topics; readers may have difficulty following, sorting out, or remembering ideas.

When you are revising your essay, reread the paragraphs that seem very long or very short, checking them especially for unity and adequate development. If the paragraph wanders, cut everything from it that does not support your main idea (such as sentences that you might begin with *By the way*). If it is underdeveloped, supply the specific details, examples, or reasons needed, or try one of the methods of development we have discussed here.

Exercise 4.15 Analyzing paragraph development

Examine the paragraphs by Richard Rodriguez (p. 85) and Judith Wax (p. 90) to discover how the authors achieve paragraph development. What pattern or patterns of development does each author use? Where does each author support general statements with specific evidence?

Exercise 4.16 Analyzing and revising skimpy paragraphs

The following paragraphs are not well developed. Analyze them, looking especially for general statements that lack support or leave questions in your mind. Then rewrite one into a well-developed paragraph, supplying your own concrete details or examples.

Exercise

¶ dev

4d

1. One big difference between successful and unsuccessful teachers is the quality of communication. A successful teacher is sensitive to students' needs and excited by the course subject. In contrast, an unsuccessful teacher seems uninterested in students and bored by the subject.

2. Gestures are one of our most important means of communication. We use them instead of speech. We use them to supplement the words we speak. And we use them to communicate some feelings or meanings that words cannot adequately express.

3. I've discovered that a computer can do much—but not every-thing—to help me improve my writing. I can easily make changes and try out different versions of a paper. But I still must do the hard work of revising.

Exercise 4.17 Considering your past work: Paragraph development

Continuing from Exercises 4.5 (p. 85) and 4.12 (p. 97), examine the de-velopment of the body paragraphs in your writing. Where does specific information seem adequate to support your general statements? Where does support seem skimpy? Revise the paragraphs as necessary to make your ideas clearer and more interesting. It may help you to pose the questions on pages 100–07.

Exercise 4.18 Writing with the patterns of development

Write at least three unified, coherent, and well-developed paragraphs, each one developed with a different pattern. Draw on the topics pro-vided here, or choose your own topics.

Exercise

1. **Narration**
   An experience of public speaking
   A disappointment
   Leaving home
   Waking up
2. **Description (objective or sub-jective)**
   Your room
   A crowded or deserted place
   A food
   An intimidating person
3. **Illustration or support**
   Why study
   Having a headache
   The best sports event
   Usefulness or uselessness of
   a self-help book

4. **Definition**
   Humor
   An adult
   Fear
   Authority
5. **Division or analysis**
   A television news show
   A barn
   A Web site
   A piece of music
6. **Classification**
   Factions in a dispute
   Styles of playing poker
   Types of Web sites
   Kinds of teachers
7. **Comparison and contrast**
   AM and FM radio DJs

Text messaging and tweeting

High school and college football

Movies on TV and in a theater

8. **Analogy**

Paying taxes and giving blood

The US Constitution and a building's foundation

Graduating from high school and being released from prison

9. **Cause-and-effect analysis**

Connection between tension and anger

Causes of failing or acing a course

Connection between credit cards and debt

Causes of a serious accident

10. **Process analysis**

Preparing for a job interview

Setting up a blog

Protecting your home from burglars

Making a jump shot

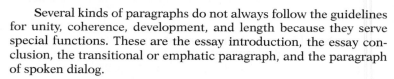

Writing special kinds of paragraphs

Exercise

Several kinds of paragraphs do not always follow the guidelines for unity, coherence, development, and length because they serve special functions. These are the essay introduction, the essay conclusion, the transitional or emphatic paragraph, and the paragraph of spoken dialog.

1 Opening an essay

Video tutorial

Most of your essays will open with a paragraph that draws readers from their world into your world. A good opening paragraph usually satisfies several requirements:

- It focuses readers' attention on your subject and arouses their curiosity about what you have to say.
- It specifies what your topic is and implies your attitude.
- Often it provides your thesis statement.
- It is concise and sincere.

The box below provides a range of options for achieving these goals.

Some strategies for opening paragraphs

Video tutorial

- Ask a question.
- Relate an incident.
- Use a vivid quotation.
- Offer a surprising statistic or other fact.
- State an opinion related to your thesis.
- Outline the argument your thesis refutes.
- Provide background.

- Create a visual image that represents your subject.
- Make a historical comparison or contrast.
- Outline a problem or dilemma.
- Define a word central to your subject.
- In some business or technical writing, summarize your paper.

Note If you are composing on the Web, you'll want to consider the expectations of Web readers. Your opening page may take the place of a conventional introduction, providing concise text indicating your site's subject and purpose, a menu of its contents, and links to other pages. (See pp. 130–34 for more on composing for the Web.)

CULTURE LANGUAGE The requirements and options for essay introductions may not be what you are used to if your native language is not English. In other cultures, readers may seek familiarity or reassurance from an author's introduction, or they may prefer an indirect approach to the subject. In academic and business English, however, writers and readers prefer concise, direct expression.

¶
4e

The funnel introduction

One reliably effective introduction forms a kind of funnel:

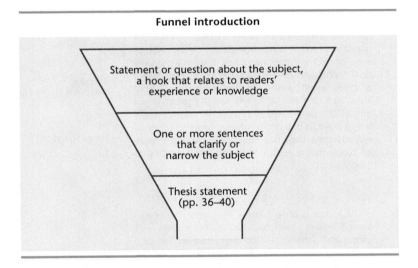

Funnel introduction

Statement or question about the subject, a hook that relates to readers' experience or knowledge

One or more sentences that clarify or narrow the subject

Thesis statement (pp. 36–40)

Here are two examples of the funnel introduction:

Can your home or office computer make you sterile? Can it strike you blind or dumb? The answer is: probably not. Nevertheless, reports of side effects relating to computer use should be examined, especially in the area of birth defects, eye complaints, and postural difficulties. Although little conclusive evidence exists to establish a causal link between computer use and problems of this sort, the circumstantial evidence can be disturbing.
—Thomas Hartmann,
"How Dangerous Is Your Computer?"

> Questions about subject

> Clarification of subject: bridge to thesis statement

> Thesis statement

The Declaration of Independence is so widely regarded as a statement of American

> Statement about subject

ideals that its origins in practical politics tend to
be forgotten. Thomas Jefferson's draft was intensely debated and then revised in the Conti-
nental Congress. Jefferson was disappointed with
the result. However, a close reading of both the
historical context and the revisions themselves indicates that the Congress improved the document for its intended purpose.

Clarification of subject: bridge to thesis statement

Thesis statement

          —Ann Weiss (student), "The Editing
          of the Declaration of Independence"

Other effective introductions

Several other types of introduction can be equally effective,
though they are sometimes harder to invent and control.

Quotation leading into the thesis statement

"It is difficult to speak adequately or justly of
London," wrote Henry James in 1881. "It is not a
pleasant place; it is not agreeable, or cheerful, or
easy, or exempt from reproach. It is only magnificent." Were he alive today, James, a connoisseur
of cities, might easily say the same thing about
New York or Paris or Tokyo, for the great city is
one of the paradoxes of history. In countless different ways, it has almost always been an unpleasant, disagreeable, cheerless, uneasy and reproach-
ful place; in the end, it can only be described as
magnificent.

Quotation

Bridge to thesis statement

Thesis statement

          —*Time*

Incident or image setting up the thesis statement

Canada is pink. I knew that from the map I
owned when I was six. On it, New York was
green and brown, which was true as far as I
could see, so there was no reason to distrust the
map maker's portrayal of Canada. When my parents took me across the border and we entered
the immigration booth, I looked excitedly for the
pink earth. Slowly it dawned on me: this foreign,
"different" place was not so different. I discovered that the world in my head and the world at
my feet were not the same.

Incident from writer's experience

Thesis statement

          —Robert Ornstein, *Human Nature*

Startling opinion or question

Caesar was right. Thin people need watching. I've been watching them for most of my
adult life, and I don't like what I see. When these
narrow fellows spring at me, I quiver to my toes.
Thin people come in all personalities, most of
them menacing. You've got your "together" thin

Opinion

person, your mechanical thin person, your condescending thin person, your tsk-tsk thin person. All of them are dangerous. — Thesis statement
—Suzanne Britt,
"That Lean and Hungry Look"

Background, such as a historical comparison

Throughout the first half of [the twentieth] century, the American Medical Association, the largest and most powerful medical organization in the world, battled relentlessly to rid the country of quack potions and cure-alls; and it is the AMA that is generally credited with being the single most powerful force behind the enactment of the early pure food and drug laws. — Historical background

Today, however, medicine's guardian seems to have done a complete about-face and become one of the pharmaceutical industry's staunchest allies—often at the public's peril and expense. — Thesis statement
—Mac Jeffery, "Does Rx Spell Rip-off?"

¶
4e

An effective introductory paragraph need not be long, as the following opener shows:

I've often wondered what goes into a hot dog. Now I know and I wish I didn't. —William Zinsser, *The Lunacy Boom*

Ineffective introductions

When writing and revising an introductory paragraph, avoid the following approaches that are likely to bore readers or make them question your sincerity or control:

Openings to avoid

■ **A vague generality or truth.** Don't extend your reach too wide with a line such as *Throughout human history . . .* or *In today's world. . . .* Readers can do without the warm-up.

Video tutorial

■ **A flat announcement.** Don't start with *The purpose of this essay is . . .*, *In this essay I will . . .*, or any similar presentation of your intention or topic.

■ **A reference to the essay's title.** Don't refer to the title of the essay in the first sentence—for example, *This is a big problem* or *This book is about the history of the guitar.*

■ *According to Webster. . . .* Don't start by citing a dictionary definition. A definition can be an effective springboard to an essay, but this kind of lead-in has become dull with overuse.

■ **An apology.** Don't fault your opinion or your knowledge with *I'm not sure if I'm right, but . . . ; I don't know much about this, but . . . ;* or a similar line.

¶
4e

2 Closing an essay

Most of your compositions will end with a closing statement or conclusion, a signal to readers that you have not simply stopped writing but have actually finished. The conclusion completes an essay, bringing it to a climax while assuring readers that they have understood your intention.

Note Compositions for the Web usually do not provide the kind of closure featured in essays. In fact, you'll need to ensure that your Web pages don't dead-end, leaving the reader stranded without options for moving backward or forward through your material. (For more on Web composition, see pp. 130–34.)

Effective conclusions

An essay conclusion may consist of a single sentence or a group of sentences, usually set off in a separate paragraph. The conclusion may take one or more of the following approaches:

Some strategies for closing paragraphs

- Recommend a course of action.
- Summarize the paper.
- Echo the approach of the introduction.
- Restate your thesis and reflect on its implications.
- Strike a note of hope or despair.
- Give a symbolic or powerful fact or other detail.
- Give an especially compelling example.
- Create an image that represents your subject.
- Use a quotation.

The following paragraph concludes the essay on the Declaration of Independence (the introduction appears on pp. 111–12):

> The Declaration of Independence has come to be a statement of this nation's political philosophy, but that was not its purpose in 1776. Jefferson's passionate expression had to bow to the goals of the Congress as a whole to forge unity among the colonies and to win the support of foreign nations.
>
> —Ann Weiss (student), "The Editing of the Declaration of Independence"

Echo of introduction: contrast between past and present

Restatement and elaboration of thesis

The next author uses a different technique—a vivid image—to conclude an essay about an aunt who committed suicide by drowning:

> My aunt haunts me—her ghost drawn to me because now, after fifty years of neglect, I alone devote pages of paper to her, though not origamied into houses and clothes. I do not think she always means me well. I am telling on her, and she was a spite suicide, drowning herself in

Summary

Video tutorial

Video tutorial

the drinking water. The Chinese are always very frightened of the drowned one, whose weeping ghost, wet hair hanging and skin bloated, waits silently by the water to pull down a substitute.

— Maxine Hong Kingston, "No Name Woman"

— Image

In the following paragraph the author concludes an essay on environmental protection with a call for action:

¶
4e

Until we get the answers, I think we had better keep on building power plants and growing food with the help of fertilizers and such insect-controlling chemicals as we now have. The risks are well known, thanks to the environmentalists. If they had not created a widespread public awareness of the ecological crisis, we wouldn't stand a chance. But such awareness by itself is not enough.

— Summary and opinion

Flaming manifestos and prophecies of doom are no longer much help, and a search for scapegoats can only make matters worse. The time for sensations and manifestos is about over. Now we need rigorous analysis, united effort and very hard work.

— Call for action

— Peter F. Drucker, "How Best to Protect the Environment"

Ineffective conclusions

The preceding examples illustrate ways of avoiding several pitfalls of conclusions:

Closings to avoid

- A repeat of the introduction. Don't simply replay your introduction. The conclusion should capture what the paragraphs of the body have added to the introduction.

- A new direction. Don't introduce a subject different from the one your essay has been about. If you arrive at a new idea, this may be a signal to start fresh with that idea as your thesis.

- A sweeping generalization. Don't conclude more than you reasonably can from the evidence you have given. If your essay is about your frustrating experience trying to clear a parking ticket, you cannot reasonably conclude that *all* local police forces are tied up in red tape.

- An apology. Don't cast doubt on your essay. Don't say, *Even though I'm no expert* or *This may not be convincing, but I believe it's true* or anything similar. Rather, to win your readers' confidence, display confidence.

Video tutorial

3 Using short emphatic or transitional paragraphs

A short emphatic paragraph can give unusual stress to an important idea, in effect asking the reader to pause and consider before moving on.

> In short, all those who might have taken responsibility ducked it, and catastrophe was inevitable.

A transitional paragraph, because it is set off by itself, moves a discussion from one point to another more slowly or more completely than does a single transitional expression or even a transitional sentence attached to a larger paragraph.

> These, then, are the causes of the current contraction in hospital facilities. But how does this contraction affect the medical costs of the government, private insurers, and individuals?

> So the debates were noisy and emotion-packed. But what did they accomplish? Historians have identified at least three direct results.

Use transitional paragraphs only to shift readers' attention when your essay makes a significant turn. A paragraph like the following one betrays a writer who is stalling:

> Now that we have examined these facts, we can look at some others that are equally central to an examination of this important issue.

4 Writing dialog

When recording a conversation between two or more people, start a new paragraph for each person's speech. The paragraphing establishes for the reader the point at which one speaker stops talking and another begins.

> The dark shape was indistinguishable. But once I'd flooded him with light, there he stood, blinking.
> "Well," he said eventually, "you're a sight for sore eyes. Should I stand here or are you going to let me in?"
> "Come in," I said. And in he came.
> —Louise Erdrich, *The Beet Queen*

Though dialog appears most often in fiction writing (the source of the preceding example), it may occasionally freshen or enliven narrative or expository essays. (For the use of quotation marks and other punctuation in passages of dialog, see pp. 458–60 and 484.)

Exercise

Exercise 4.19   Analyzing an introduction and conclusion

Analyze the introductory and concluding paragraphs in the first and final drafts of the student essay in Chapter 3, pages 57–58 and 73–75. What is wrong with the first-draft paragraphs? Why are the final-draft paragraphs better? Could they be improved still further?

Exercise 4.20   Considering your past work: Introductions and conclusions

Examine the opening and closing paragraphs of the essay you've been analyzing in Exercises 4.5, 4.12, and 4.17. Do the paragraphs fulfill the requirements and avoid the pitfalls outlined on pages 110–15? Revise them as needed for clarity, conciseness, focus, and interest.

5

Presenting Writing

Presenting your writing gives you a chance to display your hard work in the best possible light. Most of the time, this opportunity comes with challenges as well: to fulfill the requirements of the assignment, the conventions of the genre, and the expectations of your audience. This chapter will help you make decisions about designing papers effectively (below), incorporating visuals and other media (p. 123), designing Web compositions (130) and contributions to blogs and wikis (133), and making oral presentations (135).

5a   Designing academic writing

Many of the assignments you receive in college will require you to submit a written text either on paper or electronically—for instance, attached to an e-mail or uploaded to a course Web site. For such papers, the guidelines in this section will help you put your writing in an attractive, readable format. In addition, many academic style guides recommend specific formats. This book details four such formats:

- MLA, used in English, foreign languages, and some other humanities (pp. 714–16).
- Chicago, used in history, art history, religion, and some other humanities (pp. 797–98).
- APA, used in the social sciences (pp. 823–26).
- CSE, used in some natural and applied sciences (p. 841).

Other academic formats can be found in the style guides listed on pages 785, 804, and 835. Be sure to check with your instructor if you have any questions about the format he or she requires.

Some academic writing assignments will be purely digital—for instance, an autobiographical blog post, a Web site providing information about a service on your campus, or *PowerPoint* slides for an oral presentation. Many of the following design guidelines apply to such projects as well, but they receive separate attention on pages 130–42.

mycomplab

Visit *mycomplab.com* for the eText and for resources and exercises on presenting writing.

117

Note When you write outside your college courses, your audience will have certain expectations for how your writing should look and read. Guidelines for such writing appear in Chapter 11.

1 Using principles of design

Most of the principles of design respond to the ways we read. White space, for instance, relieves our eyes and helps to lead us through a document. Groupings or lists help to show relationships. Type sizes, images, and color add variety and help to emphasize important elements.

The sample document below shows the opening of a report for a marketing course. The page makes good use of white space, groups

5a

Sample marketing report

Provides adequate margins.

Emphasizes paragraph breaks with indentions.

Lists major sections in a bulleted list and uses parallel wording for parallel information.

Introduces photograph to indicate its meaning and purpose.

Captions the photograph so that it can be read independently from the text.

Creating the Next Generation of Smokers

Parents warn their children not to smoke. Schools teach kids and teens about the dangers of smoking. States across the country have enacted smoking bans, making it illegal for adults to smoke in restaurants, bars, workplaces, and public buildings. Yet despite these efforts, smoking among teens and young adults continues, and it does so in part because the film industry creates movies that promote smoking.

According to the organization Smoke Free Movies (2010), a group based in the School of Medicine at the University of California, San Francisco, tobacco companies and film makers collaborate to promote smoking in the following ways:

- Celebrities smoke in movies, giving the illusion that smoking is something they endorse.
- Movies portray smoking as glamorous, healthful, and socially respectable.
- Tobacco companies pay filmmakers to show their products.

This report examines these three aspects of smoking in movies in detail, and it concludes with a recommendation for reducing younger viewers' exposure to images of smoking in movies.

Smoking Celebrities

Despite proof that showing smoking in movies encourages young people to start smoking, more than half of movies feature well-known stars smoking (Fox, 2010). As Figure 1 shows, cigarettes often figure prominently, with the cigarette held close to the celebrity's head so that it is an integral part of the shot.

Figure 1. The actress Scarlett Johansson in *Black Dahlia* (2006), one of many movies released each year in which characters smoke. From *Daily Mail*, Associated Newspapers, 9 Mar. 2010.

similar elements, uses bullets and fonts for emphasis, and successfully integrates and explains the photograph.

As you design your own documents, follow the requirements of your assignment and think about your purpose, the expectations of your readers, and how readers will move through each document, on screen or on paper. Also consider the following general principles of design, noting how they overlap and support one another.

Exercise

Flow

5a

Many of the other design principles discussed here work toward the larger goal of conducting the reader through a document by establishing flow, a pattern for the eye to follow. In text-heavy documents like that on the facing page, flow may be achieved mainly with headings, lists, and illustrations. In more visual documents, flow will come as well from the arrangement and spacing of information.

Spacing

The blank space (called "white space") on a page or screen eases crowding and focuses readers' attention. On an otherwise full page of type, just the space indicating paragraphs (an indention or a line of extra space) gives readers a break and reassures them that ideas are divided into manageable chunks. In papers, reports, and other formal documents, spacing appears mainly in paragraph breaks, in margins, and around headings and lists. On a screen, space between heads and columns helps readers distinguish different types of content.

Grouping

Grouping information shows relationships visually, reinforcing the sense of the text itself. Here in this discussion, we treat the principles of design under visually identical headings to emphasize them and their similar importance. In the sample document on the previous page, the bulleted list details three ways that movies promote smoking. The list uses similar wording for all three items to reinforce their similarities. Thinking of likely groups as you write

---

Principles of design

- Create flow to conduct the reader through the document.
- Space elements to give the reader's eyes a rest and to focus the reader's attention.
- Group related elements in lists or under similar headings.
- Standardize elements to match appearance with content and to minimize variations.
- Emphasize important elements.

Video
tutorial

can help you organize your material so that it makes sense to you and your readers.

Standardizing

The design of a print or electronic document creates expectations in readers. For instance, headings in the same size and color signal information of the same importance, and a list signals items of parallel content. Just as the design creates expectations, so it should fulfill them, treating similar elements similarly. Anticipating design standards can help you as a writer as well, leading you toward consistency in your writing and emphasis of important elements.

Standardizing also creates clear, uncluttered documents. Too many variations in type fonts and sizes, colors, bullets, and the like overwhelm readers as they try to determine the organization of a text. For most academic papers, use a single type font for text and headings. Use type size and highlighting (such as CAPITAL LETTERS, **boldface**, or *italics*) to distinguish levels of headings.

Emphasizing

A document's design can help the audience read by stressing what's important. Type fonts and sizes, headings, indentions, color, boxes, white space—all these elements establish hierarchies of information, so that the reader almost instinctively grasps what is crucial and what is supplementary. In this book, for example, boxes like the one opposite set off summaries and other key information.

2 Using elements of design in academic writing

Applying the preceding principles involves margins, line spacing, and type fonts and may involve highlighting, headings, lists, color, and illustrations. Many assignments will prescribe the format you should use. If you are addressing readers who have vision loss, consider as well the points in the box opposite.

Note Your word processor may provide wizards or templates for many kinds of documents, such as letters, memos, reports, agendas, résumés, and brochures. **Wizards** guide you through setting up and writing complicated documents. **Templates** are preset forms to which you add your own text, headings, and other elements. Wizards and templates can be helpful, but not if they lead you to create cookie-cutter documents no matter what the writing situation. Always keep in mind that a document should be appropriate for your specific assignment, subject, audience, and purpose.

Margins

Use margins at the top, bottom, and sides of a printed page to prevent pages from overwhelming readers with unpleasant crowding. Most academic documents use a one-inch margin on all sides.

Line spacing

Most text-heavy academic documents are double-spaced, with an initial indention for paragraphs, while most documents designed to be read on screen are single-spaced, with an extra line of space between paragraphs. Double or triple spacing sets off headings in both.

Type fonts and sizes

The readability of text derives partly from the type fonts (or faces) and their sizes. For academic and business documents, generally choose a standard font, as in these samples:

5a

10-point Cambria   10-point Arial

12-point Cambria   **12-point Arial**

Fonts like Cambria and the one you're reading have **serifs**—the small lines finishing the letters, such as the downward strokes on the top of this T. Serif fonts are appropriate for formal writing and are easier for most people to read on paper. **Sans serif** fonts (*sans* means "without" in French), such as Arial above, are usually easier to read on a screen and are clearer on paper for readers with some vision loss (see the box below). Generally avoid decorative fonts such as Comic Sans, *Freestyle Script*, and **Impact** in academic writing.

The point size of a type font is not always a reliable guide to its actual size, but most standard fonts are readable in 10 or 12 points. If you are presenting your writing orally using *PowerPoint* slides, you will need to use a larger font. See pages 140–41 for tips on slide design.

Considering readers with vision loss

If your audience may include readers who have low vision, problems with color perception, or difficulties processing visual information, adapt your design to meet these readers' needs:

Video tutorial

- Use large type fonts. Most guidelines call for 14 points or larger.
- Use standard type fonts. Many people with low vision find it easier to read sans serif fonts such as Arial than serif fonts. Avoid decorative fonts with unusual flourishes, even in headings.
- Avoid words in all-capital letters.
- Avoid relying on color alone to distinguish elements. Label elements, and distinguish them by position or size.
- Use red and green selectively. To readers who are red-green color-blind, these colors will appear in shades of gray, yellow, or blue.
- Use contrasting colors. To make colors distinct, choose them from opposite sides of the color spectrum—violet and yellow, for instance, or orange and blue.
- Use only light colors for tints behind type. Make the type itself black or a very dark color.

5a

Highlighting

Within a document's text, underlined, *italic*, and **boldface** can emphasize key words or sentences. In a printed paper, you may sometimes use boldface to give strong emphasis—for instance, to a term being defined. In Web documents, boldface and underlining are common to indicate links to media and other sites.

As a general rule, use highlighting selectively to complement your meaning, not merely to decorate your work. Many readers find type embellishments distracting.

Headings

Headings are signposts: they direct the reader's attention by focusing the eye on a document's most significant content. In digital projects, headings may be decorative as well as functional, capturing the reader's attention with large sizes, lots of white space, and unconventional fonts. In academic writing, however, headings are more purely functional. They break the text of a long document into discrete parts, create emphasis, and orient the reader.

When you use headings in academic writing, follow these guidelines:

- **Use one, two, or three levels of headings** depending on the needs of your material and the length of your document. Some level of heading every two or so pages will help keep readers on track. (A three-page paper probably will not need headings.)
- **Create an outline of your document to plan where headings should go.** Reserve the first level of heading for the main points (and sections). Use a second and perhaps a third level of heading to mark subsections of supporting information.
- **Keep headings as short as possible** while making them specific about the material that follows.
- **Word headings consistently**—for instance, all questions (*What Is the Scientific Method?*), all phrases with *-ing* words (*Understanding the Scientific Method*), or all phrases with nouns (*The Scientific Method*).
- **Indicate the relative importance of headings** with type size, positioning, and highlighting, such as capital letters or boldface.

First-Level Heading
Second-Level Heading
Third-Level Heading

Generally, you can use the same type font and size for headings as for the text.

- **Don't break a page immediately after a heading.** Push the heading to the next page.

Note Document format in psychology and some social sciences requires a particular treatment of headings. See pages 825–26.

Lists

Lists give visual reinforcement to the relations between like items—for example, the steps in a process or the elements of a proposal. A list is easier to read than a paragraph, and it adds white space.

When wording a list, work for parallelism among items—for instance, all complete sentences or all phrases (see also pp. 423–24). Set the list with space above and below. Number the items, or mark them with bullets: centered dots or other devices, such as the squares used in the list below about color. On most word processors you can use the Format menu to create a list automatically.

Color

Unlike Web documents and other digital projects, which almost always use color, conventional academic writing rarely uses color for anything other than illustrations. (Ask your instructor for his or her preferences.) If you do use color in an academic document, follow these guidelines:

- Print text in black, not red, blue, or another color.
- Make sure that color headings are dark enough to be readable.
- Stick to the same color for all headings at the same level—for instance, red for primary headings, black for secondary headings.
- Use color for bullets, lines, and other nontext elements. But use no more than a few colors to keep pages clean.
- Use color to distinguish the parts of illustrations. Use only as many colors as you need to make your illustration clear.

See also page 121 on the use of color for readers who have vision loss.

5b   Using visuals and other media in multimodal writing

Academic writing is often **multimodal**—that is, it includes more than one medium, whether text, charts, photographs, video, or audio. A simple multimodal paper involves just two media—mainly text with some illustrations embedded in the text. A paper submitted online might add links to audio or video files as well. This section provides guidelines for selecting and using such media in your writing. The next sections treat media in Web compositions and in blogs and wikis.

Video
tutorial

Exercise

Caution Any visual or media file you include or link to in your writing requires the same detailed citation as a written source. See pages 652–58 for more on acknowledging sources.

1   Selecting visuals and other media

You can wait until you've drafted a paper before concentrating on what visuals and other media to include. This approach keeps your focus on the research and writing needed to craft what you want to say. But you can also begin thinking visually at the beginning of a project, as you might if your initial interest in the subject was sparked by a compelling image.

Depending on your writing situation, you might use anything from a table to a bar chart to a video to support your writing. The following pages describe and illustrate the options.

Note The Web is an excellent resource for visuals, audio, and video (see pp. 606–08). Your computer may include a program for creating tables, graphs, and other illustrations, or you can work with specialized software such as *Excel* (for graphs and charts) or *Adobe Illustrator* (for diagrams, maps, and the like). Use *PowerPoint* or a similar program for visuals in oral presentations (see pp. 140–41).

Tables

Tables usually present raw data, making complex information accessible to readers. The data may show how variables relate to one another or how two or more groups contrast, as in the example below. Some tables use rows and columns to present related textual information rather than data. See page 231 for an example.

Table

Descriptive title falls above the table.	The layout of rows and columns is clear: headings align with their data, and numbers align vertically down columns.
Headings label horizontal rows and vertical columns.	

Table 1

Public- and private-school enrollment of US students age five and older, 2009

	Number of students	Percentage in public school	Percentage in private school
All students	74,603,000	85	15
Kindergarten through grade 8	39,179,000	88	12
Grades 9-12	16,332,000	92	8
College (undergraduate)	16,366,000	77	23
Graduate and professional school	2,737,000	50	50

Source: Data from *Digest of Education Statistics: 2009*; Natl. Center for Educ. Statistics, Apr. 2010; Web; 10 May 2011; table 2.

Pie charts

Pie charts show the relations among the parts of a whole. The whole totals 100 percent, and each pie slice is proportional in size to its share of the whole. Pie charts are appropriate when shares, not the underlying data, are the focus.

Pie chart

Married (57.3%)

Never married (26.0%)

Divorced (10.4%)

Widowed (6.3%)

Color distinguishes segments of the chart. Use distinct shades of gray, black, and white if your paper will not be read in color.

Segment percentages total 100.

Every segment is clearly labeled.

Fig. 1. Marital status in 2008 of adults age eighteen and over. Data from *2010 Statistical Abstract*; US Census Bureau, Jan. 2009; Web; 26 Feb. 2011.

Caption below the chart explains it and credits the source.

Bar charts

Bar charts compare groups or time periods on a measure such as quantity or frequency. A bar chart is appropriate when relative size is important. A bar chart always starts with a zero point in the lower left corner so that the values on the vertical axis are clear.

Bar chart

Vertical scale shows and clearly labels the values being measured. Zero point clarifies values.

Horizontal scale shows and clearly labels the groups being compared.

Fig. 2. Lifetime prevalence of use of alcohol and other drugs among twelfth graders in 2010. Data from *Monitoring the Future: A Continuing Study of American Youth*; U of Michigan, 14 Dec. 2010; Web; 10 Apr. 2011.

Caption below the chart explains it and credits the source.

Line graphs

Line graphs show change over time in one or more subjects. They are an economical and highly visual way to compare many points of data. A line graph always starts with a zero point in the lower left corner so that the values on the vertical axis are clear.

Line graph

Vertical scale shows and clearly labels the values being measured. Zero point clarifies values.

Color and labels distinguish the subjects being compared. Use dotted and dashed black lines if your paper will not be read in color.

Horizontal scale shows and clearly labels the range of dates.

Caption below the graph explains it and credits the source.

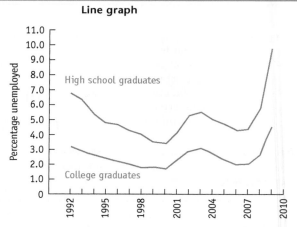

Fig. 3. Unemployment rates of high school graduates and college graduates, 1992-2010. Data from *Economics News Release*; US Dept. of Labor, Bureau of Labor Statistics, 7 Oct. 2010; Web; 6 June 2011.

Diagrams

Diagrams show concepts visually, such as the structure of an organization, the way something works or looks, or the relations among subjects. Often, diagrams show what can't be described economically in words. For other examples of diagrams, see pages 11, 111, and 132.

Diagram

Diagram makes concept comprehensible.

Caption below the diagram explains it and credits the source.

Fig. 4. RGB color theory, applied to televisions and computer monitors, in which all possible colors and white are created from red, green, and blue. From "Color Theory"; *Wikipedia*; Wikimedia, 15 Mar. 2005; Web; 13 May 2011.

Images: Photographs, fine art, advertisements, and cartoons

Sometimes you may focus an entire paper on critically analyzing an image such as a painting or an advertisement (see pp. 161–69 for an example). More often, you'll use images to support points you make in your papers or presentations. You might clarify an informative astronomy report with a photograph of Saturn (see below), sharpen an analysis of a graphic novel by reproducing a frame or illustration, offer an advertisement from the 1950s as evidence for an assertion about an attitude of the time, or capture the crux of a political debate with a cartoon.

5b

Photograph

Photograph shows subject more economically and dramatically than words could.

Fig. 5. View of Saturn from the *Cassini* spacecraft, showing the planet and its rings. From *Cassini-Huygens: Mission to Saturn and Titan*; US Natl. Atmospheric and Space Administration, Jet Propulsion Laboratory, 24 Feb. 2005; Web; 26 June 2011.

Caption below the image explains it and credits the source.

Video and audio

If you will present your writing digitally—for instance, as a Web page or blog—or orally with *PowerPoint* slides, you may choose to emphasize or illustrate points in your writing with embedded or linked video and audio files. For example, you might explain a process with a video of how something works, support an interpretation of a play with a video of a scene from a performance, or illustrate a profile of a person by linking to an interview. The screen shot on the next page shows a passage of text from an online paper that links to footage of the *I Have a Dream* speech delivered by Martin Luther King, Jr., in 1963.

2 Using visuals and other media effectively

An image or a video clip can attract readers' attention, but if it does no more it will amount to mere decoration or, worse, it will distract readers from the substance of your writing. Before using any visual or other media, consider whether it meets the requirements

Link to video file

King's speech uses inspirational techniques that are familiar in sermons. For example, in the final five minutes of the speech, King repeats "I have a dream" nine times and "let freedom ring" eleven times. In the video of the speech (http://www.youtube.com/watch?v=PbUtL_0vAJk), each repetition increases the power of the words and draws a stronger response from the audience.

5b

of your assignment, serves a purpose, and is appropriate for your audience.

Considering the requirements and limits of your writing situation

What do the type of writing you're doing and its format allow? Look through examples of similar writing to gauge the kinds of media, if any, that readers will expect. It matters, too, how you will present your work: a short animation sequence might be terrific in a *PowerPoint* presentation or on the Web, but a printed document requires photographs, drawings, and other static means of explanation.

Making visuals and other media support your writing

Ensure that any visual you use relates directly to a point in your writing, adds to that point, and gives your audience something to think about. In an evaluation of an advertisement, the ad itself would support the claim you make about it. In a paper arguing for earthquake preparedness, a photograph could provide a visual record of earthquake damage and a chart could show levels of current preparedness. The two images at the top of the next page supported a paper with this thesis: *By the mid-1960s, depictions of women in advertising reflected changing attitudes toward the traditional role of homemaker.*

Integrating visuals and other media into your writing

Readers should understand why you are including visuals or other media in your writing and how they relate to the overall project:

- In projects with embedded visuals, connect the visuals to your text. When you include visuals in your writing, refer to them at the point(s) where readers will benefit from consulting them—for instance, "See fig. 2" or "See table 1." Number figures and tables

Visuals as support

Visual examples support the thesis about changing attitudes toward women as homemakers.

Caption explains the visuals, tying them to the text of the paper and providing source information.

Fig. 1. An advertisement from 1945 (left) and a brochure illustration from 1965 (right) showing a change in the relationship between homemaking women and their appliances. Left: Hoover advertisement; 1945; print. Right: *Electric Ranges by Frigidaire*; 1965; print.

separately (Fig. 1, Fig. 2, and so on; Table 1, Table 2, and so on). And always include a caption that explicitly ties the image to your text—so that readers don't have to puzzle out your intentions—and provides source information.

■ In online projects using audio or video, work the files or links into your text. Your audience should know what you intend the media to show, whether you link to media from a mainly text document or you integrate text, sound, still images, and video into a complex Web project. For instance, in the *I Have a Dream* sample opposite, the embedded link to footage of the speech invites readers to see and hear King for themselves.

Using visuals and other media responsibly

Visuals and other media require special care to avoid distortion and to ensure honest use of others' material.

Video
tutorial

■ Create and evaluate tables, charts, and graphs carefully. Verify that the data you use are accurate and that the highlighted changes, relationships, or trends reflect reality. In a line graph, for instance,

(continued)

Using visuals and other media responsibly
(continued)

starting the vertical and horizontal axes at zero puts the lines in context. (See the sample on p. 126.) For a discussion of distortions and other misrepresentations in visuals, see pages 205–09.

▪ **Be skeptical of images you find on the Web.** Altered photographs are posted and circulated widely on the Web. If a photograph seems inauthentic, check into its source or don't use it.

▪ **Provide a source note.** You must credit the source whenever you use someone else's data to create a visual, embed someone else's visual in your document, or link to someone else's media file. Each discipline has a slightly different style for such source notes: those in the illustrations on pages 124–27 and 129 reflect MLA style. See also Chapters 46 and 50–52.

▪ **Obtain permission if it is required.** For projects that will reside on the Web, you may need to clear permission from the copyright holder of a visual or a media file. See pages 655–56 for a discussion of copyright and permission.

5c Presenting writing on the Web

You may already be experienced in creating Web-based writing projects—perhaps a *Facebook* page, a *Twitter* account, a blog, a movie, or a digital collage posted on *YouTube*. You know that the purposes and audiences for such multimodal Web writing vary widely, and so do readers' expectations for design.

Many creators of Web-based projects upload files into existing templates that make design fairly easy. Even if you choose to use such software, you will still have to make choices about elements such as fonts, colors, layout, headings, and so on. The design guidelines for academic writing on pages 117–23 can help you with such decisions, as can the following discussion of academic Web compositions such as a Web site or a multimodal project posted on a blog or wiki. For tips on using *PowerPoint* slides to support an oral presentation, see pages 140–41.

1 Conceiving a Web composition

Whether you are developing a Web site or preparing a digital composition to be posted on the Web, the following general guidelines will help you plan your project:

▪ **Consider how design can reflect your purpose for writing and your sense of audience.** Unlike a conventional academic paper, a Web composition often allows considerable design freedom. Think about how type fonts and sizes, headings, visuals and other media, background colors, and other design elements can connect with readers and further the purpose of your writing.

- **Anticipate how readers will move within your composition.** A digital document with links to other pages, posts, Web sites, and media can disorient readers as they scroll up and down and pursue various links. Page length, links, menus, and other cues should work to keep readers oriented.
- **Imagine what readers may see on their screens.** Each reader's screen frames and organizes the experience of a Web composition. Screen space is limited, and it varies widely. Text and visual elements should be managed for maximum clarity and effectiveness on a variety of screens.
- **Integrate visuals, audio, and video into the text.** Web compositions will likely include visuals such as charts and photographs as well as video (such as animation or film clips) and audio (such as music or excerpts from interviews). Any visual or sound element should add essential information that can't be provided otherwise, and it should be well integrated with the rest of your composition. Avoid using visuals and sound merely as attention grabbers. See pages 127–30 for tips on using media effectively and pages 606–08 for sources of images, audio, and video.
- **Acknowledge your sources.** It's easy to incorporate text, visuals, audio, and video from other sources into a Web composition, but you have the same obligation to cite your sources as you do in a printed document. (See pp. 648–54 on citing sources.) Your Web composition is a form of publication, like a magazine or a book. Unless the material you are using explicitly allows copying without permission, you may need to seek the copyright holder's permission, just as print publishers do. (See pp. 655–56 for more on copyright.)

5c

Note If you anticipate that some of your readers may have visual, hearing, or reading disabilities, you'll need to consider their needs while designing Web sites. Some of these considerations are covered on page 121, and others are fundamental to any effective Web-based design, as discussed in this section. In addition, avoid any content that relies exclusively on visuals or sound, instead supplementing such elements with text descriptions. At the same time, try to provide key concepts in words as well as in visuals and sound. For more on Web design for readers with disabilities, visit the American Council for the Blind at *acb.org/accessible-formats.html* and the World Wide Web Consortium at *www.w3.org/WAI*.

2 Creating a Web site

Traditional printed documents are intended to be read page by page in sequence. In contrast, Web sites are intended to be examined in whatever order readers choose as they follow links to pages within a site and to other sites. The diagram on the next page shows a schematic Web site, with pages at different levels (orange and then blue squares) interconnecting with the home page and with one another.

Sample document

Web site organization

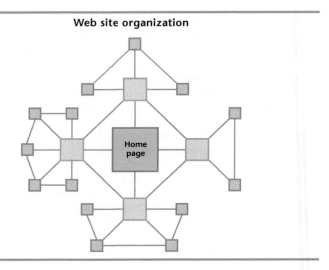

While reading Web sites, readers generally alternate between skimming pages for highlights and focusing intently on one section of text. To facilitate this kind of reading, you'll want to consider the guidelines on the previous two pages and also those following.

Structure and content

Sample
document

Organize your Web site so that it efficiently arranges your content and also orients readers:

- **Sketch possible site plans before getting started.** A diagram like the one above can help you develop the major components of your project and create a logical space for each component.
- **Consider how menus can provide overviews of the organization as well as direct access to the linked content.** The Web site on the facing page includes a menu near the top of the page.
- **Treat the first few sentences of any page as a get-acquainted space for you and your readers.** In the sample Web site, the text hooks readers with questions and orients them with general information.
- **Distill your text so that it includes only essential information.** Concise prose is essential in any writing situation, of course, but readers of Web sites expect to scan text quickly.

Flow

Take advantage of the Web's visual nature by thinking about how information will flow on each page:

- **Standardize elements of your design to create and fulfill expectations in readers.** For instance, develop a uniform style for the main headings of pages, for headings within pages, and for menus.

Web site home page

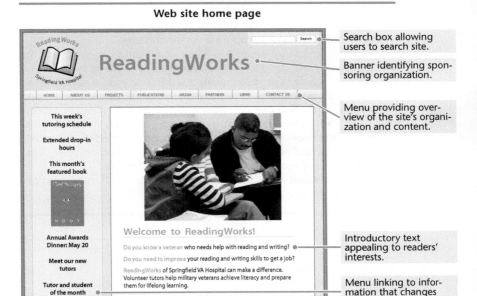

Search box allowing users to search site.

Banner identifying sponsoring organization.

Menu providing overview of the site's organization and content.

Introductory text appealing to readers' interests.

Menu linking to information that changes regularly.

■ **Make scanning easy for readers.** Focus readers on crucial text by adding space around it. Add headings to break up text and to highlight content. Use lists to reinforce the parallel importance of items. (See pp. 120–23 for more on all these design elements.)

Navigation

Provide a menu so that readers can navigate your Web site. Like the table of contents in a book, a menu lists the features of a site, giving its plan at a glance. By clicking on any item in the list, readers can go directly to a page that interests them.

Sample document

You can embed a menu at the top, side, or bottom of a page—or use more than one position. Menus at the top or side allow readers to move around the site without having to read the full home page. Menus at the bottom prevent readers from dead-ending—that is, reaching a point where they can't easily move forward or backward.

In designing a menu, keep it simple: many different type fonts and colors will overwhelm readers instead of orienting them. And make your menus look the same from one page to the next so that readers recognize them easily.

3 Posting to a blog or a wiki

Blogs and wikis are Web sites that allow users to post text and media such as images and video. Unlike other Web sites, which are generally designed to provide information, blogs and wikis encourage interaction: readers can comment on blog posts or, on a wiki, contribute to posts and collaborate on documents.

You may create a blog or a wiki as an academic assignment, in which case you will need to make decisions about the appearance of the site as a whole. For most academic blog or wiki writing, however, you will post drafts of your projects and comment on your classmates' work. You can compose and edit your text in your word processor and paste the text into the blog or wiki. At that point, you'll have the opportunity to write a descriptive title for your post, upload images and other media, and add links to other Web sites. You can also preview the post before making it public.

The illustration below shows a student's draft of a personal essay, which he posted to his class blog.

5c

Paper posted to a blog

Descriptive title providing context for the post.

Standard font for readability.

Illustration supporting a point in the post.

Embedded link to another Web site.

FRIDAY, FEBRUARY 18, 2011
Literacy narrative draft

Comics: Telling Stories in Words and Art

For my seventh birthday, I received a Calvin and Hobbes comic book. I devoured the book, reading it cover to cover countless times, and was instantly attracted to how drawings and words worked together to tell very funny stories about the characters. I didn't always understand the vocabulary, the jokes, and references to the 1980s, but I laughed at what I did get: the funny arguments, crazy games, and hilarious schemes.

The summer after my birthday I began drawing my own comics. I created two characters modeled on Calvin and Hobbes—a boy named Timmy and his dog Snuffy. Over the next five years, I drew hundreds of comics about Timmy, Snuffy, and Timmy's family and friends. I drew the strip shown here, about one of Timmy's many mishaps, when I was ten. I have this strip and some of my other favorites posted on my personal blog: johnsdoodles@blogger.com.

Timmy experienced much of what I did over the next several years. He went on vacation to places I visited with my family, like New York and San Francisco. He visited aunts, uncles, and grandparents. He exasperated his parents, annoyed his sister, learned to play an instrument, and dreamed of being a pilot. He also did things I had not experienced: he once trained for the school marathon and came in third, dreamed of going to the prom like his sister, and slid down what seemed like a mile-long hill on a sled. Through Timmy, I used language and drawing to explore ideas, dreams, experiences, and feelings, all the time trying to make them funny.

Although I still draw and write, I left Timmy behind the summer I turned twelve. However, occasionally I look back at my Timmy comics and find it interesting to see how I used words and images to develop and display my sense of place in the world.

Posted by John Heywood at 4:23 PM.

5d Making oral presentations

At some point during your college career, you will probably be called on to speak to a group. Oral presentation can be anxiety producing, even for those who are experienced at it. This section shows you how to present your writing to a listening audience, and it offers some techniques that are uniquely appropriate for effective oral presentations.

1 Writing and speaking

Writing and speechmaking have much in common: both require careful consideration of your subject, purpose, and audience. Thus the mental and physical activities that go into the writing process can also help you prepare and deliver a successful oral presentation.

Despite many similarities, however, writing for readers is not the same as speaking to listeners. Whereas a reader can go back and reread a written message, a listener cannot stop a speech to rehear a section. Several studies have reported that immediately after hearing a short talk, most listeners cannot recall half of what was said.

Effective speakers adapt to their audience's listening ability by reinforcing their ideas through repetition and restatement. They use simple words, short sentences, personal pronouns, contractions, and colloquial expressions. In formal writing, these strategies might seem redundant and too informal; but in speaking, they improve listeners' comprehension.

2 Considering purpose and audience

The most important step in developing an oral presentation is to identify your purpose: what do you want your audience to know or do as a result of your speech? Topic and purpose are *not* the same thing. Asking *What am I talking about?* is not the same as asking *Why am I speaking?*

An oral presentation may be anything from an informal report before a few peers to a formal address to your class. Whatever the situation, you're likely to be speaking for the same reasons that you write in school or at work: to explain something to listeners or to persuade listeners to accept your opinion or take an action. See pages 17–19 for more on these purposes.

Adapting to your audience is a critical task in public speaking as well as in writing. You'll want to consider the questions about audience on pages 20–21. But a listening audience requires additional considerations as well:

- ■ **Why is your audience assembled?** Listeners who attend because they want to hear you and your ideas may be easier to interest and motivate than listeners who are required to attend.

5d

Checklist

Checklist for an oral presentation

- **Purpose:** What do you want your audience to know or do as a result of your presentation? How can you achieve your purpose in the time and the setting you've been given? (See the previous page and below.)

- **Audience:** What do you know about the characteristics and opinions of your audience? How can this information help you adapt your presentation to your audience's interests, needs, and opinions? (See the previous page and below.)

- **Organization and content:** How are your ideas arranged? Where might listeners have difficulty following you? What functions do your introduction and conclusion perform? How relevant and interesting is your supporting material for your topic and your audience? (See the next page.)

- **Method of delivery:** What method of delivery do you plan: extemporaneous? reading from a text? memorized? a mixture? How does your method suit the purpose, setting, and occasion of your presentation? (See pp. 138–39.)

- **Vocal and physical delivery:** In rehearsing your presentation, what do you perceive as your strengths and weaknesses? Is your voice suitably loud for the setting? Are you speaking clearly? Are you able to move your eyes around the room so that you'll be making eye contact during the presentation? Is your posture straight but not stiff? Do your gestures reinforce your ideas? Do you use visual aids appropriately? (See pp. 139–41.)

- **Confidence and credibility:** What techniques will you use to overcome the inevitable anxiety about speaking? How will you project your confidence and competence? (See pp. 141–42.)

- **How large is your audience?** With a small group you can be informal. If you are speaking to a hundred or more people, you may need a public address system, a lectern, special lighting, and audiovisual equipment.

- **Where will you speak?** Your approach should match the setting—more casual for a small classroom, more formal for an auditorium.

- **How long are you scheduled to speak?** Whatever the time limit, stick to it. Audiences lose patience with someone who speaks longer than expected.

When speaking, unlike when writing, you can see and hear your audience's responses during your presentation. If you sense that an audience is bored, try to spice up your presentation. If an audience is restless, consult your watch to make sure you have not gone over your time. If you sense resistance, try to make midspeech adjustments to respond to that resistance.

3 Organizing the presentation

An effective oral presentation, like an effective essay, has a recognizable shape. The advice in Chapter 2 for organizing and outlining an essay serves the speechmaker as well as the writer (see pp. 41–52). Here are additional considerations for the introduction, conclusion, and supporting material.

The introduction

First impressions count. A strong beginning establishes an important relationship among three elements in an oral presentation: you, your topic, and your audience. More specifically, the beginning of an oral presentation should try to accomplish three goals:

5d

- Gain the audience's attention and interest. Begin with a question, an unusual example or statistic, or a relevant anecdote.
- Put yourself in the speech. If you demonstrate your expertise, experience, or concern, your audience will be more interested in what you say and more trusting of you.
- Introduce and preview your topic and purpose. By the time your introduction is over, listeners should know what your topic is and the direction you'll take them in as you develop your ideas.

In addition to these principles for beginning a speech, there are pitfalls to avoid:

- Don't try to cram too much into your introduction. Focus on engaging the audience and quickly previewing your talk.
- Don't begin with an apology. A statement such as *I wish I'd been given more time to get ready for this presentation* will only undermine your listeners' confidence in you.
- Don't begin with *My speech is about. . . .* The statement is dull, and it does little to clarify your purpose.

Supporting material

Just as you do when writing, you can and should support your main points with examples, facts, and other evidence. In addition, as a speaker you can draw on other kinds of supporting material:

- Use vivid description. Paint a mental image of a scene, a concept, an event, or a person.
- Use well-chosen quotations. They can add an emotional or humorous moment to your speech.
- Use true or fictional stories. A memorable narrative can rivet the audience's attention and illustrate your point.
- Use analogies. Comparisons between essentially unlike things, such as a politician and a tightrope walker, link concepts memorably. (For more on analogy, see p. 105.)

■ **Use visuals and other media.** A chart or graph can show data; audio or video can provide an effective example. See the discussion of media on pages 123–30 and tips for using presentation software such as *PowerPoint* on pages 140–41.

Use a variety of supporting materials in your speech. A presentation that consists of nothing but statistics can bore an audience. Nonstop storytelling may interest listeners but fail to achieve your purpose.

5d

The conclusion

Last impressions count as much as first impressions. You may hope that listeners will remember every detail of your speech, but they are more likely to leave with a general impression and a few ideas about you and your message. You want your conclusion to be clear, of course, but you also want it to be memorable. Remind listeners of how your topic and main idea connect to their needs and interests.

4 Delivering the presentation

Writing and speaking differ most obviously in the form of delivery: the writer is represented in print, the speaker is represented in person. This section describes the methods and techniques of oral presentation as well as some ways of coping with stage fright.

Methods of delivery

An oral presentation may be delivered impromptu, extemporaneously, from a text, or from memory. No one technique is best for all speeches; indeed, a single speech may include two or more forms or even all four—perhaps a memorized introduction, an extemporaneous body in which quotations are read from a text, and impromptu responses to audience questions during or after the speech.

■ **Speaking impromptu** is presenting with no planning or practice. You may be called on in a class to express your opinion or to summarize something you've written. An audience member may ask you a question at the end of an oral presentation. The only way to prepare for such occasions is to be well prepared in general—to be caught up on course reading, for instance, or to know the facts in a debate.

■ **Speaking extemporaneously,** which is typical of class lectures and many oral presentations, involves speaking from notes that guide you through the presentation. You prepare and practice, but you don't memorize the presentation or read it word for word from a text.

■ **Speaking from a text** involves writing the text out in advance and then reading aloud from it. With a text in front of you,

you're unlikely to lose your way, but you run the risk of being dull. To enliven reading from a text, write less formally so that the text sounds spoken: for instance, the sentence *Although costs rose, profits remained steady* reads well in writing but would sound stiff in speech. In addition, rehearse thoroughly so that you can read with expression and can look up frequently to make eye contact with listeners (see opposite).

- **Speaking from memory** offers the advantage of complete freedom from notes or a text, so that you can look at your audience every minute and can move away from a lectern and even into the audience. However, like most speakers you may seem less relaxed, not more relaxed, when presenting from memory, and you risk forgetting your place or a whole passage. At least reserve this method for just a part or two where you want to make a strong impression—perhaps the introduction and conclusion. And rehearse not only to memorize the words but to deliver the words fresh, as if for the first time.

5d

Vocal delivery

The sound of your voice will influence how your listeners receive you. When rehearsing, consider volume, speed, and articulation.

- **Speak loudly.** In a meeting with five other people, you can speak at normal volume. As your audience grows in size, so should your volume. Most speakers can project to as many as a hundred people, but a larger audience may require a microphone.
- **Speak slowly enough to be understandable.**
- **Speak clearly and correctly.** To avoid mumbling or slurring your words, practice articulating. Sometimes it helps to open your mouth a little wider than usual.

Physical delivery

You are more than your spoken words when you make an oral presentation. Your face and body also play a role in how your speech is received.

- **Stand up.** Always stand for a presentation, unless it takes place in a small room where standing would be inappropriate. You can see more audience members when you stand, and they in turn can hear your voice and see your gestures more clearly.
- **Stand straight and move around.** Turn your body toward one side of the room and then the other, step out from behind any lectern or desk, and gesture appropriately, as you would in conversation.
- **Make eye contact with listeners.** Move your gaze around the entire room, settle on someone, and establish direct eye contact; then move on to someone else.

Eye contact is customary in the United States, both in conversation and in oral presentation. Listeners expect it and may perceive a speaker who doesn't make eye contact as evasive or insincere.

Visual aids

5d

Sample
document

You can supplement an oral presentation with visual aids such as posters, models, slides, videos, or presentation software such as *PowerPoint*. Visual aids can emphasize key points, organize related concepts, and illustrate complex procedures. They can gain the attention of listeners and improve their understanding and memory.

The following guidelines can help you create effective and appropriate visual aids:

- **Use visual aids to underscore your points.** Short lists of key ideas, illustrations such as graphs or photographs, and objects such as models can make your presentation more interesting and memorable. But use visual aids judiciously: a constant flow of illustrations or objects will bury your message.

- **Match visual aids and setting.** An audience of five people may be able to see a photograph and share a chart; an audience of a hundred will need projected images.

- **Coordinate visual aids with your message.** Time each visual aid to reinforce a point you're making. Tell listeners what they're looking at—what they should be getting from the aid. Give them enough viewing time so that they don't mind turning their attention back to you.

- **Show visual aids only while they're needed.** To regain your audience's attention, remove or turn off any aid as soon as you have finished with it.

Many speakers use *PowerPoint* or other software to project main points, key images, video, or other elements. To use *PowerPoint* or other software effectively, follow the guidelines in the samples opposite and also these tips:

- **Don't put your whole presentation on screen.** Select key points and distill them to as few words as possible. Use slides as quick, easy-to-remember summaries or ways to present examples. For a twenty-minute presentation, plan to use approximately ten slides.

- **Use a simple design.** Avoid turning your presentation into a show about the software's many capabilities.

- **Make text readable.** The type should be easy to see for viewers in the back of the room, whether the lights are on or not.

- **Use a consistent design.** For optimal flow through the presentation, each slide should be formatted similarly.

PowerPoint slides

Making a Difference?

**A Service-Learning Project
at ReadingWorks**

Springfield Veterans
Administration Hospital

Jessica Cho
Nathan Hall
Alex Ramirez

SPRING 2011

First slide, introducing the
project and presentation.

Simple, consistent slide
design focusing viewers'
attention on information,
not *PowerPoint* features.

Semester goals

● Research adult literacy.

● Tutor military veterans.

● Keep a journal.

● Collaborate on documents
   for ReadingWorks.

● Report experiences and findings.

Later slide, including a title
and brief, bulleted points to
be explained by the speaker.

Photographs reinforcing the
project's activities.

▣ **Add relevant images and other media.** *PowerPoint* allows you to play images, audio, and video as part of your presentation. Before you add them, however, be sure each has a point so that you don't overload the presentation with bells and whistles. Use the guidelines on pages 123–30 for choosing and using visuals and other media.

▣ **Review all your slides before the presentation.** Using the Slide Sorter mode, go through the slides to be sure they are complete, consistent, and easy to read.

▣ **During the presentation don't talk to the computer or the projection.** Move away from both and face the audience.

Practice

Practicing an oral presentation is the equivalent of editing and proofreading a written text. You won't gain much by practicing silently in your head; instead, you need to rehearse out loud, with

5d

the notes you will be using. For your initial rehearsals, you can gauge your performance by making an audio- or videotape of yourself or by practicing in front of a mirror. A recording will let you hear mumbling, too-rapid delivery, grammatical errors, mispronounced words, and unclear concepts. A mirror or video will reveal your stance, your gestures, and your eye contact. Any of these practice techniques will tell you if your presentation is running too long or too short.

If you plan to use visual aids, you'll need to practice with them, too, preferably in the room where you'll make the presentation and certainly with the help of anyone who will be assisting you. Your goal is to eliminate hitches (upside-down slides, missing charts) and to weave the visuals seamlessly into your presentation.

Stage fright

Many people report that speaking in front of an audience is their number-one fear. Even many experienced and polished speakers have some anxiety about delivering an oral presentation, but they use this nervous energy to their advantage, letting it propel them into working hard on each presentation and rehearsing until they're satisfied with their delivery. They know that the symptoms of anxiety are usually imperceptible to listeners, who cannot see or hear a racing heart, an upset stomach, cold hands, and worried thoughts.

Several techniques can help you reduce your level of anxiety:

- **Use simple relaxation exercises.** Deep breathing or tensing and relaxing your stomach muscles can ease some of the physical symptoms of speech anxiety.
- **Think positively.** Instead of worrying about the mistakes you might make, concentrate on how well you've prepared and practiced your presentation and how significant your ideas are.
- **Don't avoid opportunities to speak in public.** Practice and experience build speaking skills and offer the best insurance for success.

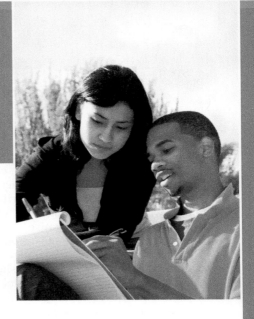

PART 2

Reading and Writing in and out of College

6

Forming a Critical Perspective

Throughout college and beyond, you will be expected to think, read, and write critically. **Critical** here means "skeptical," "exacting," "curious." When you operate critically, you question, test, and build on what others say and what you yourself think. The word *critical* does not mean "negative" in this context: you can think critically about something you like, don't like, or just view neutrally.

You already operate critically every day of your life, as when you probe a friendship ("What did she mean by that?"), discuss a movie you just saw ("Don't you think the bad guy was too obvious?"), or attempt to solve a problem ("How can I help my study group make progress on our project?"). Such questioning helps you figure out why things happen to you, what your experiences mean, and how you can create a needed change.

Video
tutorial

This chapter introduces more formal methods of critical thinking: preparing to read critically (next page), summarizing (p. 152), developing a critical response (p. 154), and viewing visuals critically (p. 161). Learning and applying these methods will both engage you in and prepare you for school courses, career, and life in a democratic society:

- Teachers and employers will expect you to think critically. In every field, you will need to assess what you read, see, and hear and to make a good case for your own ideas.
- Critical thinking helps you understand and express yourself. With it, you gain insight into your actions and ideas, can weigh them against opposing views, and can persuasively articulate your reasoning and motivations.
- Critical thinking improves your problem-solving skills. Seeing academic and real-life problems from multiple angles can open your mind to creative solutions.
- Your very independence and freedom depend on your ability to think, read, and write critically. An open democracy allows as much play for stupid and false claims as for sound ones, and

mycomplab

Visit *mycomplab.com* for the eText and for resources and more exercises on critical thinking and reading.

144

the claims that seem sound often conflict with each other. Critical thinking empowers you to decide rationally for yourself what's useful, fair, and wise—and what's not.

There's no denying that critical thinking, reading, and writing require discipline and hard work. Besides channeling your curiosity, paying attention, and probing, you will often need to consult experts, interpreting and evaluating their ideas. Such an approach also requires a healthy tolerance for doubt or uncertainty—that feeling you may have when the old rules don't seem to apply or when a change is frightening but still attractive. Out of uncertainty, though, comes creativity—the capacity to organize and generate knowledge, to explain, resolve, illuminate, play. Compared to passive, rote learning, creative work is more involving, more productive, and more enjoyable.

crit

6a

6a Using techniques of critical reading

In college much of your critical thinking will focus on written texts (a short story, a journal article, a blog) or on visual objects (a photograph, a chart, a film). Like all subjects worthy of critical consideration, such works operate on at least three levels: (1) what the creator actually says or shows, (2) what the creator does not say or show but builds into the work (intentionally or not), and (3) what you think. Discovering each level of the work involves a number of reading techniques that are discussed in this chapter and summarized in the following box.

Techniques of critical reading

For reading a work of literature, which requires a somewhat different approach, see pp. 758–65.

Video
tutorial

- **Writing:** making notes on your reading throughout the process (next page)
- **Previewing:** getting background; skimming (p. 147)
- **Reading:** interacting with and absorbing the text (pp. 149–51)
- **Summarizing:** distilling and understanding content (pp. 152–54)
- **Forming your critical response** (pp. 154–60):

   Analyzing: separating into parts
   Interpreting: inferring meaning and assumptions
   Synthesizing: reassembling parts; making connections
   Evaluating: judging quality and value

The techniques of critical reading are not steps in a firm sequence. You will not use all of them for all the reading you do. On some occasions, even when a close, critical reading is required, you may simply lack the time to preview, read, and reread. (But if your reading time is continually squeezed by your schedule, you may need to rethink your schedule.) On other occasions your reason for reading (your purpose) will determine which techniques you use.

Even a publication like *People* magazine is open to different methods of reading for different purposes:

Purpose	Learn some gossip while filling time in the dentist's office.
Kind of reading	Quick, uncritical
Purpose	Examine *People* as an artifact of our popular culture that reflects and perhaps even molds contemporary values.
Kind of reading	Close, critical

crit

6a

Course assignments, too, differ in their requirements. A book report may require writing, previewing, reading, and summarizing but not intense critical reading. An evaluation of a journal article, in contrast, requires all the techniques discussed here.

CULTURE LANGUAGE The idea of reading critically may require you to make some adjustments if readers in your native culture tend to seek understanding or agreement more than engagement from what they read. Readers of English use texts for all kinds of reasons, including pleasure, reinforcement, information, and many others. But they also read questioningly, to uncover the author's motives (*What are this author's biases?*), test their own ideas (*Can I support my point of view as well as this author supports hers?*), and arrive at new knowledge (*Why is the author's evidence so persuasive?*).

1 Writing while reading

You will write while you read to record information and ideas for use in a research paper. But writing while reading has another purpose as well: to help you get more from the work.

Critical reading is *active* reading. You interact with the work, bringing to it your experiences, knowledge, and questions. Making notes on what you read helps you construct the text for yourself as you come to understand how it works, why it works that way, and what you think about it.

If you own the material you're reading (a book, a photocopy, or a printout), you can make notes in the margins (see p. 143 for an example). If you don't own the material or if your notes won't fit in the margins, make notes separately using pen and paper or your computer. Many readers keep a **reading journal** in which they regularly work out questions and thoughts about what they read. One technique for keeping such a journal is to divide a page or computer screen into two vertical columns, the left side for the work itself, such as summary and questions, and the right side for what the work makes you think, such as agreements or doubts based on your own experiences, comparisons with other works, and ideas for writing. A two-column journal can encourage you to go beyond summarizing what you read to interacting critically with it because the blank right column will beckon you to respond. See page 151 for an example of this technique.

Note Whenever you photocopy or download a document or take notes separately from the text you're reading, be sure to record all necessary information about the text's location so that you can find it again and cite it fully if you use it. See page 581 for a list of information to record.

2 Previewing the material

When you're reading a work of literature, such as a story or a poem, it's often best to plunge right in (see pp. 758–59). But for critical reading of other works, it's worthwhile to **skim** before reading word for word, forming expectations and even preliminary questions. The preview will make your reading more informed and fruitful.

crit
6a

Use the questions in the following box as a guide to previewing a text.

Previewing a text

- **Gauge length and level.** Is the material brief and straightforward so that you can read it in one sitting, or does it require more time?

Video
tutorial

- **Check the facts of publication.** Does the date of publication suggest currency or datedness? Does the publisher or publication specialize in scholarly articles, popular books, or something else? For a Web publication, who or what sponsors the site—an individual? a non-profit organization? a government body? a college or university?

- **Look for content cues.** What do the title, introduction, headings, illustrations, conclusion, and other features tell you about the topic, the author's approach, and the main ideas?

- **Learn about the author.** Does a biography tell you about the author's publications, interests, biases, and reputation in the field? If there is no biography, what can you gather about the author from his or her words? Do a Web search to trace an unfamiliar author.

- **Consider your preliminary response.** What do you already know about the topic? What questions do you have about either the topic or the author's approach to it? What biases of your own—for instance, curiosity, boredom, or an outlook similar or opposed to the author's—might influence your reading of the work?

Exercise 6.1 Previewing an essay

Following is an essay on the US student-loan program by Thomas Sowell, an economist who writes on economics, politics, and education. The essay was first published in the 1990s, but the debate over student loans has hardly subsided. Since Sowell wrote, the number of college graduates with loan debt has increased by a third and the average amount they owe has almost tripled.

Exercise

Preview the essay using the preceding guidelines, and then read it once or twice, until you think you understand what the author is saying. Note your questions and reactions in writing.

Student Loans

1 The first lesson of economics is scarcity: There is never enough of anything to fully satisfy all those who want it.

2 The first lesson of politics is to disregard the first lesson of economics. When politicians discover some group that is being vocal about not having as much as they want, the "solution" is to give them more. Where do politicians get this "more"? They rob Peter to pay Paul.

3 After a while, of course, they discover that Peter doesn't have enough. Bursting with compassion, politicians rush to the rescue. Needless to say, they do not admit that robbing Peter to pay Paul was a dumb idea in the first place. On the contrary, they now rob Tom, Dick, and Harry to help Peter.

4 The latest chapter in this long-running saga is that politicians have now suddenly discovered that many college students graduate heavily in debt. To politicians it follows, as the night follows the day, that the government should come to their rescue with the taxpayers' money.

5 How big is this crushing burden of college students' debt that we hear so much about from politicians and media deep thinkers? For those students who graduate from public colleges owing money, the debt averages a little under $7,000. For those who graduate from private colleges owing money, the average debt is a little under $9,000.

6 Buying a very modestly priced automobile involves more debt than that. And a car loan has to be paid off faster than the ten years that college graduates get to repay their student loans. Moreover, you have to keep buying cars every several years, while one college education lasts a lifetime.

7 College graduates of course earn higher incomes than other people. Why, then, should we panic at the thought that they have to repay loans for the education which gave them their opportunities? Even graduates with relatively modest incomes pay less than 10 percent of their annual salary on the loan the first year—with declining percentages in future years, as their pay increases.

8 Political hysteria and media hype may focus on the low-income student with a huge debt. That is where you get your heart-rending stories—even if they are not at all typical. In reality, the soaring student loans of the past decade have resulted from allowing high-income people to borrow under government programs.

9 Before 1978, college loans were available through government programs only to students whose family income was below some cut-off level. That cut-off level was about double the national average income, but at least it kept out the Rockefellers and the Vanderbilts. But, in an era of "compassion," Congress took out even those limits.

10 That opened the floodgates. No matter how rich you were, it still paid to borrow money through the government at low interest rates. The money you had set aside for your children's education could be invested somewhere else, at higher interest rates. Then, when the student loan became due, parents could pay it off with the money they had set aside—pocketing the difference in interest rates.

crit

6a

To politicians and the media, however, the rapidly growing loans 11
showed what a great "need" there was. The fact that many students
welshed when time came to repay their loans showed how "crushing"
their burden of debt must be. In reality, those who welsh typically have
smaller loans, but have dropped out of college before finishing. People
who are irresponsible in one way are often irresponsible in other ways.

No small amount of the deterioration of college standards has been 12
due to the increasingly easy availability of college to people who are not
very serious about getting an education. College is not a bad place to
hang out for a few years, if you have nothing better to do, and if someone else is paying for it. Its costs are staggering, but the taxpayers carry
much of that burden, not only for state universities and city colleges, but
also to an increasing extent even for "private" institutions.

Numerous government subsidies and loan programs make it possi- 13
ble for many people to use vast amounts of society's resources at low
cost to themselves. Whether in money terms or in real terms, federal aid
to higher education has increased several hundred percent since 1970.
That has enabled colleges to raise their tuition by leaps and bounds and
enabled professors to be paid more and more for doing less and less
teaching.

Naturally all these beneficiaries are going to create hype and hys- 14
teria to keep more of the taxpayers' money coming in. But we would be
fools to keep on writing blank checks for them.

When you weigh the cost of things, in economics that's called 15
"trade-offs." In politics, it's called "mean-spirited." Apparently, if we just
took a different attitude, scarcity would go away.

—Thomas Sowell

3 Reading

After previewing a text, you can settle into it to learn what it
has to say.

First reading

The first time through new material, read as steadily as possible, trying to get the gist of what the author is saying.

- **Read in a place where you can concentrate.** Choose a quiet environment away from distractions such as music or talking.
- **Give yourself time.** Rushing yourself or worrying about something else you have to do will prevent you from grasping what
  you read.
- **Try to enjoy the work.** Seek connections between it and what
  you already know. Appreciate new information, interesting relationships, forceful writing, humor, good examples.
- **Make notes sparingly during this first reading.** Mark major stumbling blocks—such as a paragraph you don't understand—so
  that you can try to resolve them before rereading.

 If English is not your first language and you come
across unfamiliar words, don't stop and look up

every one. You will be distracted from an overall understanding of the text. Instead, try to guess the meanings of the unfamiliar words by using context clues, such as examples and synonyms of the words. Be sure to circle the words and look them up later. You may want to keep a vocabulary log of the words, their definitions, and the sentences in which they appeared.

Rereading

After the first reading, plan on at least one other. This time read *slowly*. Your main concern should be to grasp the content and how it is constructed. That means rereading a paragraph if you didn't get the point or using a dictionary to look up words you don't know.

Use your pen, pencil, or keyboard freely to highlight and distill the text:

crit

6a

- **Distinguish main ideas from supporting ideas.** Look for the central idea (the thesis), for the main idea of each paragraph or section, and for the evidence supporting ideas.
- **Learn key terms.** Understand both their meanings and their applications.
- **Identify the connections among ideas.** Be sure you see why the author moves from point A to point B to point C and how those points work together to support the central idea. It often helps to outline the text or summarize it (see p. 152).
- **Distinguish between facts and opinions.** Especially when reading an argument, tease apart the facts from the author's opinions that may or may not be based on facts. (See pp. 188–89 for more on facts and opinions.)
- **Add your own comments.** In the margins or separately, note links to other readings or to class discussions, questions to explore further, possible topics for your writing, points you find especially strong or weak.

An example of critical reading

The following samples show how a student, Charlene Robinson, approached Thomas Sowell's "Student Loans." After her first reading, Robinson went through Sowell's text more slowly and added her comments and questions. Here are the first four paragraphs with her annotations:

> The first lesson of economics is scarcity: There is never enough of anything to fully satisfy all those who want it.   *fact*
>
> The first lesson of politics is to disregard the first lesson of economics. When politicians discover some group that is being vocal about not having as much as they want, the "solution" is to give them more. Where do politicians get this "more"? They <u>rob Peter to pay Paul.</u>

opinion—basic contradiction between economics and politics

⟵ *biblical reference?*

After a while, of course, they discover that Peter doesn't have enough. Bursting with compassion, politicians rush to the rescue. Needless to say, they do not admit that robbing Peter to pay Paul was a dumb idea in the first place. On the contrary, they now rob Tom, Dick, and Harry to help Peter.

ironic and dismissive language

The latest chapter in this long-running saga is that politicians have now suddenly discovered that many college students graduate heavily in debt. To politicians it follows, as the night follows the day, that the government should come to their rescue with the taxpayers' money.

politicians = fools? or irresponsible

After reading the text, Robinson wrote about it in the journal she kept on her computer. She divided the journal into two columns, one each for the text and her responses. Here is the portion pertaining to the preceding paragraphs:

crit

6a

Text	Responses
Economics teaches lessons (1), and politics (politicians) and economics are at odds	Is economics truer or more reliable than politics? More scientific?
Politicians don't accept econ. limits—always trying to satisfy "vocal" voters by giving them what they want (2)	Politicians do spend a lot of our money. Is that what they're elected to do, or do they go too far?
"Robbing Peter to pay Paul" (2)— from the Bible (the Apostles)?	
Politicians support student loan program with taxpayer funds bec. of "vocal" voters (2-4): another ex. of not accepting econ. limits	I support the loan program, too. Are politicians being irresponsible when they do? (Dismissive language underlined on copy.)

You should try to answer the questions about meaning that you raise in your annotations and your journal, and that may take another reading or some digging in other sources, such as dictionaries and encyclopedias. Recording in your journal what you think the author means will help you build an understanding of the text, and a focused attempt to summarize will help even more (see the next page). Such efforts will resolve any confusion you feel, or they will give you the confidence to say that your confusion is the fault of the author, not the reader.

Exercise 6.2 Reading

Read Sowell's essay on pages 148–49 at least twice, until you think you understand what the author is saying. Either on these pages or separately, note your questions and reactions in writing, as student writer Charlene Robinson did for the first four paragraphs. Look up any words you don't know, and try to answer your questions. You might want to discuss the essay with your classmates as well.

6b Summarizing

Video
tutorial

A good way to master the content of a text and to see its strengths and weaknesses is to **summarize** it: reduce it to its main points *using your own words*. Assignments sometimes call for brief summaries, as when you summarize the plot in a critical essay about a novel (p. 765). Summary is also an essential tool in research papers and other writing that draws on sources (pp. 633–34). In fact, summarizing is such a useful skill that some instructors give it as a separate assignment. In showing how summary can reveal the meaning of a text, this section will help you learn to summarize for any purpose.

A summary should state in as few words as possible the main ideas of a passage. When you need to summarize a few paragraphs or a brief article, your summary should not exceed one-fifth the length of the original. For longer works, such as chapters of books or whole books, your summary should be quite a bit shorter in proportion to the original. A procedure for drafting a summary appears in the following box.

crit
6b

Writing a summary

Video
tutorial

- ■ **Understand the meaning.** Look up words or concepts you don't know so that you understand the author's sentences and how they relate to one another.
- ■ **Understand the organization.** Work through the text to identify its sections—single paragraphs or groups of paragraphs focused on a single topic. To understand how parts of a work relate to one another, try drawing a tree diagram or creating an outline (pp. 43–47).
- ■ **Distill each section.** Write a one- or two-sentence summary of each section you identify. Focus on the main point of the section, omitting examples, facts, and other supporting evidence.
- ■ **State the main idea.** Write a sentence or two capturing the author's central idea.
- ■ **Support the main idea.** Write a full paragraph (or more, if needed) that begins with the central idea and supports it with the sentences that summarize sections of the work. The paragraph should concisely and accurately state the thrust of the entire work.
- ■ *Use your own words.* By writing, you re-create the meaning of the work in a way that makes sense for you. You also avoid plagiarism.
- ■ *Cite the source.* If you use a summary in writing that you do for others, always acknowledge the source.

Summarizing even a passage of text can be tricky. Here we'll look at attempts to summarize the following material from an introductory biology textbook:

Original text

As astronomers study newly discovered planets orbiting distant stars, they hope to find evidence of water on these far-off celestial bodies, for water is the substance that makes possible life as we know it here on Earth. All organisms familiar to us are made mostly of water and live in an environment dominated by water. They require water more than any other substance. Human beings, for example, can survive for quite a few weeks without food, but only a week or so without water. Molecules of water participate in many chemical reactions necessary to sustain life. Most cells are surrounded by water, and cells themselves are about 70–95% water. Three-quarters of Earth's surface is submerged in water. Although most of this water is in liquid form, water is also present on Earth as ice and vapor. Water is the only common substance to exist in the natural environment in all three physical states of matter: solid, liquid, and gas.

—Neil A. Campbell and Jane B. Reece, Biology

The first attempt to summarize this passage accurately restates ideas in the original, but it does not pare the passage to its essence:

crit

6b

Draft summary

Astronomers look for water in outer space because life depends on it. It is the most common substance on Earth and in living cells, and it can be a liquid, a solid (ice), or a gas (vapor).

The work of astronomers and the three physical states of water add color and texture to the original, but they are asides to the key concept that water sustains life because of its role in life. The following revision narrows the summary to this concept:

Revised summary

Water is the most essential support for life—the dominant substance on Earth and in living cells and a component of life-sustaining chemical processes.

When Charlene Robinson summarized Thomas Sowell's "Student Loans," she first drafted the following sentence about paragraphs 1–4:

Draft summary

As much as politicians would like to satisfy voters by giving them everything they ask for, the government cannot afford a student loan program.

Rereading the sentence and Sowell's paragraphs, Robinson saw that this draft misread the text by asserting that the government cannot afford student loans. She realized that Sowell's point is more complicated than that and rewrote her summary:

Revised summary

As their support of the government's student loan program illustrates, politicians ignore the economic reality that using resources to benefit one group (students in debt) involves taking the resources from another group (taxpayers).

Caution Using your own words when writing a summary not only helps you understand the meaning but also constitutes the first step in avoiding plagiarism, discussed on pages 3–5 and 648–54. The second step is to cite the source when you use the summary in something written for others.

Note Do not count on the AutoSummarize function on your word processor for summarizing texts that you may have copied onto your computer. The summaries are rarely accurate, and you will not gain the experience of interacting with the texts on your own.

Exercise 6.3 Summarizing

Start where Robinson's summary of Thomas Sowell's essay ends (at paragraph 5) to summarize the entire essay. Your summary, in your own words, should not exceed one paragraph. For additional exercises in summarizing, see page 641.

6c Developing a critical response

crit
6c

Once you've grasped the content of what you're reading—what the author says—then you can turn to understanding what the author does not say outright but suggests or implies or even lets slip. At this stage you are concerned with the purpose or intention of the author and with how he or she carries it out. Depending on what you are reading and why, you may examine evidence, organization, attitude, use of language, and other elements of the text.

Critical thinking and reading consist of four operations: analyzing, interpreting, synthesizing, and (often) evaluating. Although we'll look at them one by one, these operations interrelate and overlap. Indeed, the first three are often combined under the general label *analysis,* and evaluation is sometimes taken for granted as a result of the process.

In the following pages, we use two quite different examples to show how critical reading can work: *People* magazine and Sowell's "Student Loans."

Guidelines for analysis, interpretation, and synthesis

Video
tutorial

- ▨ What is the purpose of your reading?
- ▨ What questions do you have about the work, given your purpose?
- ▨ What elements does the most interesting question highlight? What elements might you ignore as a result?
- ▨ How do you interpret the meaning and significance of the elements? What are your assumptions about the work? What do you infer about the author's assumptions?
- ▨ What patterns can you see in (or synthesize from) the elements? How do the elements relate? How does this whole work relate to other works?
- ▨ What do you conclude about the work? What does this conclusion add to the work?

1 Analyzing

Analysis is the separation of something into its parts or elements, the better to understand it. To see these elements in what you are reading, begin with a question that reflects your purpose in analyzing the text: why you're curious about it or what you're trying to make out of it. This question will serve as a kind of lens that highlights some features and not others.

Here are some questions you might ask about *People* magazine, listed along with the elements that each question highlights:

Questions for analysis	Elements
Does *People* challenge or perpetuate stereotypes?	Stereotypes: explicit and implicit stereotypes or challenges in the magazine
Does the magazine offer positive role models for its readers?	Role models: text and photographs presenting positive or negative role models
Does the magazine's editorial material (articles and accompanying photographs) encourage readers to consume goods and entertainment?	Encouragement of consumption: references to goods and entertainment, focus on consumers, equation of consumption with happiness or success

crit

6c

As these examples show, a question for analysis concentrates your attention on relevant features and eliminates irrelevant features. To answer the question in the preceding list about *People*'s encouragement of consumption, you would focus on items that feature consumption and the products consumed: photographs of designer clothes and celebrities' well-appointed homes, articles on the authors of best-selling books and the stars of new movies. At the same time, you would skip over items that have little or no relevance to consumption, such as uplifting stories about families or the physically challenged.

Analyzing Thomas Sowell's "Student Loans" (pp. 148–49), you might ask these questions:

Questions for analysis	Elements
What is Sowell's attitude toward politicians?	References to politicians: content, words, tone
How does Sowell support his assertions about the loan program's costs?	Support: evidence, such as statistics and examples

A difference in the kinds of questions asked is a key distinction among academic disciplines. A sociologist neatly outlined three disciplines' approaches to poverty:

Political science does a wonderful job looking at poverty as a policy issue. Economics does an equally wonderful job looking at it from an

income-distribution perspective. But sociology asks how people in poverty live and what they aspire to.

Even within disciplines, approaches may differ. The sociologist
quoted above may focus on how people in poverty live, but another
may be more interested in the effects of poverty on cities or the
changes in the poor population over the last fifty years. (See Chapters 49–52 for more on the disciplines' analytical questions.)

2 Interpreting

Identifying the elements of something is of course only the
beginning: you also need to interpret the meaning or significance of
the elements and of the whole. Interpretation usually requires you
to infer the author's **assumptions,** opinions or beliefs about what is
or what could or should be. (*Infer* means to draw a conclusion
based on evidence.)

The word *assumption* here has a more specific meaning than it
does in everyday usage, where it may stand for expectation (*I assume
you'll pay*), speculation (*It was a mere assumption*), or error (*The report
was riddled with assumptions*). Defined more strictly as what a person
supposes to be true, assumptions are unavoidable. We all adhere to
certain values and beliefs; we all form opinions. We live our lives by
such assumptions.

Though pervasive, assumptions are not always stated outright.
Speakers and writers may judge that their audience already understands and accepts their assumptions; they may not even be aware
of their assumptions; or they may deliberately refrain from stating
their assumptions for fear that the audience will disagree. That is
why your job as a critical thinker is to interpret what the assumptions are.

Reasonable inferences

Exercise

Like an author deciding what to say in an article, the publishers
of *People* magazine make assumptions that guide their selection of
content for the magazine. One set of assumptions, perhaps the most
important, concerns what readers want to see: as a for-profit enter-
prise, the magazine naturally aims to maintain and even expand its
readership (currently about 3.4 million each week). If your analysis
of the magazine's editorial material reveals that much of it features
consumer products, you might infer the following:

> Reasonable   The publishers of *People* assume that the magazine's read-
> ers are consumers who want to see and hear about goods
> and entertainment.

Nowhere in *People* will you find a statement of this assumption, but
the evidence implies it.

Similarly, Thomas Sowell's "Student Loans" (pp. 148–49) is
based on certain assumptions, some obvious, some not so obvious.

crit
6c

If you were analyzing Sowell's attitude toward politicians, as suggested earlier, you would focus on his statements about them. Sowell says that they "disregard the first lesson of economics" (paragraph 2), which implies that they ignore important principles (knowing that Sowell is an economist himself makes this a reasonable assumption on your part). Sowell also says that politicians "rob Peter to pay Paul," are "[b]ursting with compassion," "do not admit . . . a dumb idea," are characters in a "long-running saga," and arrive at the solution of spending taxes "as the night follows the day"—that is, inevitably (paragraphs 2–4). From these statements and others, you can infer the following:

> Reasonable Sowell assumes that politicians become compassionate when a cause is loud and popular, not necessarily just, and they act irresponsibly by trying to solve the problem with other people's (taxpayers') money.

crit

6c

Unreasonable inferences

Interpreting assumptions gives you greater insight into an author's intentions. But it's crucial that inferences fit the evidence of the text, as do the previous inferences about *People* and Sowell's essay. Sometimes it's tempting to read too much into the text, as in the next examples:

> Faulty *People*'s publishers deliberately skew the magazine's editorial material to promote products on which they receive kickbacks. [The inference is far-fetched, even absurd. It would be reasonable only if there were hard evidence of kickbacks.]

> Faulty Sowell thinks that politicians should not be entrusted with running the country. [The inference misreads Sowell. Although he does not outline a solution for politicians' irresponsibility, there's no evidence that he would overhaul our democratic political system.]

Faulty inferences like these are often based on the reader's *own* assumptions about the text or its subject. When thinking and reading critically, you need to look hard at *your* ideas, too.

3 Synthesizing

If you stopped at analysis and interpretation, critical thinking and reading might leave you with a pile of elements and possible meanings but no vision of the whole. With **synthesis** you make connections among parts *or* among wholes. You use your perspective—your knowledge and beliefs—to create a new whole by drawing conclusions about relationships and implications.

Video
tutorial

A key component of academic reading and writing, synthesis receives attention in the next chapter (pp. 173–75) and then in the context of research writing (pp. 626–28). Sometimes you'll respond directly to a text, as in the following two conclusions. The first pulls together the earlier analysis of *People* magazine's editorial content and the interpretation of the publisher's assumptions about readers:

> Conclusion   *People* magazine appeals to its readers' urge to consume by displaying, discussing, and glamorizing consumer goods.

The next statement, about Thomas Sowell's essay "Student Loans," connects Sowell's assumptions about politicians to a larger idea also implied by the essay:

> Conclusion   Sowell's view that politicians are irresponsible with taxpayers' money reflects his overall opinion that the laws of economics, not politics, should drive government.

crit
6c

Often synthesis will take you outside the text to its surroundings. The following questions can help you investigate the context of a work:

- **How does the work compare with works by others?** For instance, how does *People's* juxtaposition of articles and advertisements compare with that in similar magazines, such as *Us Weekly, Entertainment Weekly,* and *Interview*? Or how have other writers responded to Sowell's views on student loans?

- **How does the work fit into the context of other works by the same author or group?** What distinguishes *People* from the many other magazines published by Time Inc., such as *Time, Sports Illustrated, Family Circle,* and *Fortune*? How do Sowell's views on student loans typify, or not, the author's other writings on political and economic issues?

- **What cultural, economic, or political forces influence the work?** Why, for instance, are *People* and other celebrity magazines increasingly popular with readers? What other examples might Sowell have given to illustrate his view that economics, not politics, should determine government spending?

- **What historical forces influence the work?** How does *People* reflect changes in the ways readers choose magazines? How has the indebtedness of college students changed over the past four decades?

To create links among the elements of a work or between a work and its context, it helps (again) to write while reading and thinking. The active reading recommended earlier is the place to start, as you note your questions and opinions about the text. You can also create connections with a combination of writing and drawing: start with your notes, expand them as needed to take account of context, and draw connections between related thoughts with lines and arrows. (On a word processor you can use the Highlight function or different colors to link related ideas, or use the

Comment function to annotate connections.) You want to open up your thinking, so experiment freely.

With synthesis, you create something different from what you started with. To the supermarket shopper reading *People* while standing in line, the magazine may be entertaining and inconsequential. To you—after a critical reading in which you analyze, interpret, and synthesize—the magazine is (at least in part) a significant vehicle of our consumer culture. The difference depends entirely on the critical reading.

4 Evaluating

Many critical reading and writing assignments end at analysis, interpretation, and synthesis: you explain your understanding of what the author says and doesn't say. Only if you are expected to evaluate the work will you state and defend the judgments you've made about its quality and its significance.

You'll inevitably form judgments while reading the work: *What a striking series of images* or *That just isn't enough evidence*. In evaluating, you collect your judgments, determine that they are generally applicable and are themselves not trivial, and turn them into assertions: *The poet creates fresh, intensely vivid images. The author does not summon the evidence to support his case.* And you support these statements with citations from the text.

Evaluation takes a certain amount of confidence. You may think that you lack the expertise to cast judgment on another's writing, especially if the text is difficult or the author well known. True, the more informed you are, the better a critical reader you are. But conscientious reading and analysis will give you the internal authority to judge a work *as it stands* and *as it seems to you,* against your own unique experiences, observations, and attitudes.

The following box gives questions that can help you evaluate many kinds of works. There's more on evaluation (including evaluation of online sources) on pages 612–25. For arguments and in academic disciplines, you'll require additional, more specific criteria. See Chapters 8 and 48–52.

crit
6c

Video
tutorial

Guidelines for evaluation

- What are your reactions to the work? What in the work are you responding to?
- How sound are the work's central idea and evidence?
- How well does the author achieve his or her purpose? How worthwhile is the purpose?
- How authoritative, trustworthy, and sincere is the author?

(continued)

Video
tutorial

Guidelines for evaluation
(continued)

- How unified and coherent is the work? Do its parts all support a central idea and clearly relate to one another?
- What do color, graphics, or (online) sound or video contribute to the work? Do such elements add meaning or merely decoration?
- What is the overall quality and significance of the work?
- Do you agree or disagree with the work? Can you support, refute, or extend it?

crit

6c

Exercise

Exercise 6.4 Thinking critically

Following are three numbered statements about the communications media. Use systematic critical thinking to understand not only what each statement says but also why its author might have said it. As in the example, do your thinking in writing: the act of writing will help you think, and your notes will help you discuss your ideas with your classmates.

Example:

Statement: Every year sees the disappearance of more locally owned hardware stores because big-box stores such as Home Depot and Walmart force them out of business.

Analysis: Why did the author make this statement? Certain words reveal the author's purpose: *disappearance of more locally owned hardware stores; because; big-box stores force them out of business.*

Interpretation: *More locally owned hardware stores* means others have disappeared. *Because* specifies cause. *Force* implies coercion, predator to prey. Author's assumptions: Big-box stores behave like predators. The predatory behavior of big-box stores causes the disappearance of locally owned stores. The more hardware stores there are, the better.

Synthesis: The author objects to the predatory behavior of big-box stores, which he or she holds responsible for eliminating locally owned stores and reducing the total number of hardware stores.

Evaluation: This biased statement against big-box stores holds them responsible for the shrinking number of hardware stores. But are the large companies solely responsible? Do they offer value in return? And why is the shrinking necessarily bad?

1. Newspapers, magazines, and news Web sites are better news sources than television because they demand reading, not just viewing.
2. Radio call-in shows are the true democratic forum, giving voice to people of all persuasions.
3. Participation in online communities threatens to undermine our ability to interact face to face.

Exercise 6.5 Reading an essay critically

Reread Thomas Sowell's "Student Loans" (pp. 148–49) in order to form your own critical response to it. Follow the guidelines for analysis, interpretation, synthesis, and evaluation in the boxes on pages 154 and 159–60. Focus on any elements suggested by your question about the text: perhaps assumptions, evidence, organization, use of language, tone, authority, vision of education or of students. Be sure to write while reading and thinking; your notes will help your analysis and enhance your creativity, and they will be essential for writing about the selection (Exercise 7.5, p. 185).

Exercise 6.6 Reading a magazine critically

Do your own critical reading of *People* or another magazine. What do you see beyond the obvious? What questions does your reading raise? Let the guidelines on pages 154 and 159–60 direct your response, and do your work in writing.

Exercise

6d Viewing visuals critically

crit

6d

Every day we are bombarded with visuals—pictures on billboards, commercials on television, graphs and charts in newspapers and textbooks, to name just a few examples. Most visuals slide by without our noticing them, or so we think. But visuals, sometimes even more than text, can influence us covertly. Their creators have purposes, some worthy, some not, and understanding those purposes requires critical reading. The method parallels that in the previous sections for reading text critically: write while reading, preview, read for comprehension, analyze, interpret, synthesize, and (often) evaluate.

1 Writing while reading a visual

Writing as you read a visual helps you view it deliberately and allows you to record your impressions precisely. If possible, print a copy of the visual or scan it into your reading journal, and write your comments in the margins or separately. The example on the next page shows how one student annotated an advertisement he was reading.

2 Previewing a visual

Your first step in exploring a visual is to form initial impressions of its origin and purpose and to note its distinctive features. This previewing process is like the one for previewing a text (p. 147):

- **What do you see?** What is most striking about the visual? What is its subject? What is the gist of any text or symbols? What is the overall effect of the visual?
- **What are the facts of publication?** Where did you first see the visual? Do you think the visual was created especially for that location or for others as well? What can you tell about when the visual was created?
- **What do you know about the person or group that created the visual?** For instance, was the creator an artist, scholar, news

Annotation of an advertisement

Advertisement for *BoostUp.org*

organization, or corporation? What seems to have been the creator's purpose?

- **What is your preliminary response?** What about the visual interests, confuses, or disturbs you? Are the form, style, and subject familiar or unfamiliar? How might your knowledge, experiences, and values influence your reception of the visual?

3 Reading a visual

Reading a visual requires the same level of concentration as reading a text. Plan to spend more than one session working with the visual to absorb its meaning and purpose and then to analyze and maybe challenge its message.

Try to answer the following questions about the visual. If some answers aren't clear at this point, skip the question until later.

- **What is the purpose?** Is the visual mainly explanatory, conveying information, or is it argumentative, trying to convince readers of something or to persuade them to act? What information or point of view does it seem to want to get across?
- **Who is the intended audience?** What does the source of the visual, including its publication facts, tell about the visual creator's expectations for readers' knowledge, interests, and attitudes? What do the features of the visual itself add to your impression?
- **What do any words or symbols add?** Whether located on the visual or outside it (such as in a caption), do words or symbols add information, focus your attention, or alter your impression?
- **What action, change, people, places, or things are shown?** Does the visual tell a story? Do its characters or other features tap into your knowledge, or are they unfamiliar?
- **What is the form?** Is the visual a photograph, advertisement, painting, graph, diagram, cartoon, or something else? How do its content and apparent purpose and audience relate to its form?

The following notes by a student, Matthew Greene, illustrate the results of asking questions like these about the advertisement opposite. Greene first saw this ad on a bus shelter and then found it online so that he could examine it more closely. He annotated a copy of the ad and filled out his ideas in his reading journal:

Details of the ad	Responses
Gray background: street, sidewalk, wall, blocked-up window	The grim landscape conveys a feeling of emptiness, hopelessness.
Teen dressed in T-shirt, jeans, and a backward baseball cap, standing off to the side with hands in pockets	The clothing seems typical for an urban high school student. Positioned at the edge of the photo, he looks to be on his own, even isolated.
Message from "Danny R." taped to the top of the photo with another message underneath	The message is an offer of help, probably directed at the boy. Danny R. looks to be a friend—is he trying to help the boy stay in school? Is the message underneath also from Danny R.? Taped messages break up the gray = hope for the boy.
Logo at lower right and words "Help Kody graduate at BoostUp.org."	The boy in the picture must be Kody. This is a direct appeal to readers to find out more. What is *BoostUp.org*? How can I help Kody graduate?

Analyzing a visual

Elements for analysis

Sample
document

Sample
document

As when analyzing a written work, you analyze a visual by identifying its elements. The visual elements you might consider appear in the box below. Keep in mind that a visual is a *composition* whose every element likely reflects a deliberate effort to communicate. Still, few visuals include all the elements, and you can narrow the list further by posing a question about the visual you are reading.

Elements of visuals

crit

6d

Video
tutorial

- **Emphasis:** Most visuals pull your eyes to certain features: a graph line moving sharply upward, a provocative figure, bright color, thick lines, and so on. The cropping of a photograph or the date range in a chart will also reflect what the visual's creator considers most important.

- **Narration:** Most visuals tell stories, whether in a sequence (a TV commercial or a graph showing changes over time) or at a single moment (a photograph, a painting, or a pie chart).

- **Point of view:** The creator of the visual considers both the viewer's physical relation to the subject—for instance, whether it is seen head-on or from above—and the viewer's assumed attitude toward the subject.

- **Arrangement:** Patterns among colors or forms, figures in the foreground and background, and elements that are juxtaposed or set apart contribute to the visual's meaning and effect.

- **Color:** Colors can direct the viewer's attention and convey the creator's attitude toward the subject. Color may also suggest a mood, an era, a cultural connection, or another frame for viewing the visual.

- **Characterization:** The figures and objects in a visual have certain qualities—sympathetic or not, desirable or not, and so on. Their characteristics reflect the roles they play in the visual's story.

- **Context:** The source of a visual or the background in a visual affects its meaning, whether it is a graph from a scholarly journal or a photo of a car on a sunny beach.

- **Tension:** Visuals often communicate a problem or seize attention with features that seem wrong, such as misspelled or misaligned words, distorted figures, or controversial relations between characters.

- **Allusions:** An **allusion** is a reference to something the audience is likely to recognize and respond to. Examples include a cultural symbol such as a dollar sign, a mythological figure such as a unicorn, or a familiar movie character such as Darth Vader from *Star Wars*.

Question for analysis

You can focus your analysis of elements by framing your main interest in the visual as a question. Matthew Greene concentrated his analysis of the *BoostUp.org* ad by asking the question *Does the ad move readers to learn more about* BoostUp.org *and how they can help teens to graduate?* The question led Greene to focus on certain elements of the ad and to ignore others:

Elements of the ad	Responses
Emphasis	The grayness and the placement of Kody at the far left put primary emphasis on the boy's isolation. Danny R.'s message receives secondary emphasis.
Narration	The taped-on message suggests a story and connection between Kody and Danny R. Danny R. might be a friend, relative, or mentor. From the direct appeal in the word bubble, it appears that Danny R. is trying to help Kody graduate by offering to help him with schoolwork.
Arrangement	The ad places Danny R. and Kody together on the left side of the page, with Danny's message a bright spot on the dull landscape. The appeal to help Kody graduate is subtle and set on its own—the last thing readers look at. It also pulls the elements together so that the ad makes sense.
Color	The lack of color in most of the photo emphasizes Kody's isolation. The whiteness of Danny R.'s message relieves the grayness, like a ray of hope.

Sample visuals for analysis

The following visuals give you a chance to analyze selective elements in a line graph, a photograph, and two Web pages. Questions in the annotations can help to open up your thinking.

Elements in a line graph

Color and emphasis: What do the title and labels say you are looking at? How does color focus your attention?

Narration: What story does the graph tell about the changing uses of media?

Context: The graph comes from a reputable research organization, the Pew Research Center for the People and the Press. What does that information contribute to your understanding of the graph?

Main news source for adults ages 18–29, 2001–10

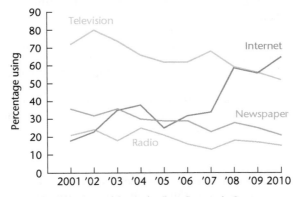

Graph adapted from the Pew Research Center for the People and the Press

Elements in a photograph

Emphasis: What is the focus of the photograph? What are your eyes drawn to?

Characterization: What does the man seem to be feeling? Consider especially his mouth and eyes.

Narration: What story or stories might the photograph tell?

Arrangement: What is interesting about the arrangement of elements?

Color: What does the black-and-white presentation contribute to the image? How might the image differ in full color?

Allusion: What symbol do you see? What meaning does it give to the photograph?

Photograph by Steve Simon

The screen shots opposite are from *AIDS Clock,* an interactive Web site sponsored by the United Nations Population Fund (*www.unfpa.org/aids_clock*). The top image is the home page, displaying a traditional world map. The bottom image appears when viewers click on "Resize the map": now each country's size reflects the number of its people who live with HIV, the virus that causes AIDS. (For example, South Africa grows while the United States shrinks.) The large blue number at the top changes every twelve seconds.

Note See also pages 204–09 for information on reading visuals that make arguments and on identifying distortions and other misrepresentations in visuals.

5 Interpreting a visual

The strategies for interpreting a visual parallel those for interpreting a written text (pp. 156–57). In this process you look more deeply at the elements, considering them in relation to the likely assumptions and intentions of the visual's creator. You aim to draw

crit
6d

Elements of Web pages

Emphasis and color: What elements on these pages draw your attention? How does color distinguish and emphasize elements?

Narration: What story do the two Web pages tell? What does each map contribute to the story? What does the blue number contribute? (Notice that the number changes from the first screen to the second.)

Arrangement: What does the arrangement of elements on the pages contribute to the story being told?

Tension: How do you respond to the distorted map in the second image? What does the distortion contribute to your view of the Web site's effectiveness?

Context: How does knowing the Web site's sponsoring organization, the United Nations Population Fund, affect your response to these images?

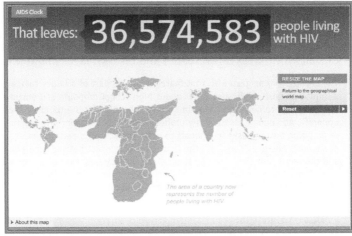

AIDS Clock Web pages, 2011

crit
6d

reasonable inferences about *why* the visual looks as it does. Here's a reasonable inference about the *BoostUp.org* advertisement on page 162:

> Reasonable   The creators of the *BoostUp.org* ad assume that readers want teens to graduate from high school.

This inference is supported by the ad's text: the word bubble connecting to the *BoostUp.org* logo specifically says, "Help Kody graduate at BoostUp.org." In contrast, the next inference is *not* reasonable because it leaps to a conclusion that is not supported by the ad:

> Faulty   The creators of the *BoostUp.org* ad want readers to help improve the quality of education in the United States.

crit
6d

The ad implies that readers believe education is important, but it does not suggest that readers should take steps to change the educational system.

6 Synthesizing ideas about a visual

As discussed on pages 157–59, with synthesis you take analysis and interpretation a step further to consider how a work's elements and underlying assumptions mesh: How do the elements and assumptions relate to one another? What is the overall message of the visual? You may also expand your synthesis to view the whole visual in a larger context: How does the work compare with works by others? How does the work fit into the context of other works by the same author or group? What cultural, economic, political, or historical forces influence the work?

Placing a visual in its context often requires research. For instance, to learn more about the assumptions underlying the *BoostUp.org* advertisement and the goals of the larger ad campaign, Matthew Greene visited the Web sites of *BoostUp.org* and the Ad Council, one of the ad's sponsors. The following entry from his reading journal synthesizes this research and his own ideas about the ad:

> The *BoostUp.org* magazine ad that features Kody is part of a larger campaign designed to raise public awareness about high school dropouts and encourage pubic support to help teens stay in school. Sponsored by the US Army and the nonprofit Ad Council, *BoostUp.org* profiles high school seniors who are at risk of dropping out and asks individuals to write the students personal messages of support. Ads like "Kody" are the first point of contact between the public and the teens, but they don't by themselves actually help the teens. For that, readers need to visit *BoostUp.org*. Thus the ad's elements work together like pieces of a puzzle, with the solution to be found only on the Web site.

7 Evaluating a visual

If your critical reading moves on to evaluation, you'll form judgments about the quality and significance of the visual. Questions to ask for evaluation appear in the box on pages 159–60. Briefly: Is the message of the visual accurate and fair, or is it distorted and biased? Can you support, refute, or extend the message? Does the visual achieve its apparent purpose, and is the purpose worthwhile? How does the visual affect you?

See Matthew Greene's paper on pages 183–85 for an evaluation of the *BoostUp.org* advertisement.

Exercise 6.7 Viewing a visual critically

Review the list of visual elements on page 164 and then take another close look at the *BoostUp.org* advertisement on page 162. Using the guidelines on the preceding pages, draw your own conclusions about the ad. Write while reading and thinking to help yourself concentrate and develop ideas. A writing suggestion based on this activity appears in Exercise 7.6, page 185.

crit

6d

Exercise 6.8 Viewing a visual critically

Select the graph on page 165, the photograph on page 166, or the Web pages on page 167 to examine in more detail. Using the guidelines on the preceding pages, read the visual(s) methodically and critically. Write down your ideas. A writing suggestion based on this activity appears in Exercise 7.7, page 185.

Exercise 6.9 Comparing visuals critically

Two visuals in this section—the advertisement and the photograph—use people as subjects to reinforce their messages. The other visuals—a line graph and Web pages—center on data and maps. Using the guidelines on the preceding pages, compare these visuals, focusing on each one's emphasis. How effective are these emphases? Write down your responses. A writing suggestion based on this activity appears in Exercise 7.8, page 185.

7

Writing in Academic Situations

The academic disciplines differ widely in their subjects and approaches, but they all share the common goal of building knowledge through questioning, research, and communication. The differences among disciplines lie mainly in the kinds of questions asked, the kinds of research done to find the answers, and the genres, or types of writing, used to communicate the answers, such as case studies, research reports, literary analyses, and reviews of others' writings.

Exercise

Both a discipline's concerns and the kind of writing create an academic writing situation, which in turn shapes your choice of subject, definition of purpose, conception of audience, use of genre, choice of structure and content, selection of documentation style, and even use of language. This chapter introduces academic writing situations in general. Chapters 49–52 detail the particular goals and expectations for writing about literature and in other humanities, the social sciences, and the natural and applied sciences.

7a   Determining purpose, audience, and genre

Like any writing, academic writing occurs in a particular situation created by your assignment and by your subject, purpose, audience, and genre. The assignment and subject will be different for each project, but some generalizations can be made about the other elements. (If you haven't already done so, read Chapter 2 of this book for discussion of writing situations and their elements.)

1   Purpose

For most academic writing, your general purpose will be mainly explanatory or mainly argumentative. That is, you will aim to explain your subject by analyzing, describing, or reporting on it so that readers understand it as you do; or you will aim to gain readers'

mycomplab

Visit *mycomplab.com* for the eText and for resources and
170   more exercises on writing in academic situations.

agreement with a debatable idea about the subject. (See pp. 18–19 for more on general and specific purposes and Chapters 8–9 for more on argument.) Although the general purpose for writing may not be stated outright in an assignment, it will probably be implied, as you can see in these two abbreviated assignments:

Explanation

Compare the depiction of war in two films viewed this semester, considering plots, characters, dialog, battle scenes, production designs, and other elements of the films.

Argument

What ideology do you see informing the movies of director Steven Spielberg? What beliefs about the world do his choices convey, whether explicitly or implicitly, intentionally or unintentionally? Support your claim with evidence from at least four of Spielberg's movies, considering plots, characters, dialog, production designs, and other elements.

7a

Your specific purpose—including your subject and how you hope readers will respond—depends on the genre, the kind of writing that you're doing. (See the next page.) For instance, in a literature review for a biology class, you want readers to understand the research area you're covering, the recent contributions made by researchers, the issues needing further research, and the sources you consulted. Not coincidentally, these topics correspond to the major sections of a literature review. In following the standard format, you both help to define your purpose and begin to meet the discipline's (and thus your instructor's) expectations.

Your specific purpose will be more complex as well. You take a course to learn about a subject and the ways experts think about it. Your writing, in return, contributes to the discipline through the knowledge you uncover and the lens of your perspective. At the same time, as a student you want to demonstrate your competence with research, evidence, format, and other requirements of the discipline.

2 Audience

Many academic writing assignments will specify or assume an educated audience or an academic audience. Such readers look for writing that is clear, balanced, well-organized, and well-reasoned. Other assignments will specify or assume an audience of experts on your subject, readers who look in addition for writing that meets the subject's requirements for claims and evidence, organization, language, format, and other qualities discussed in Chapters 48–52.

Much of your academic writing will have only one reader besides you: the instructor of the course for which you are writing. Instructors fill two main roles as readers:

- **They represent the audience you are addressing.** They may actually be members of the audience, as when you address academic readers or subject experts. Or they may imagine themselves as members of your audience—reading, for instance, as if they sat on the city council. In either case, they're interested in how effectively you write for the audience.

- **They serve as coaches,** guiding you toward achieving the goals of the course and, more broadly, toward the academic aims of building and communicating knowledge.

Like everyone else, instructors have preferences and peeves, but you'll waste time and energy trying to anticipate them. Do attend to written and spoken directions for assignments, of course. But otherwise view your instructors as representatives of the community you are writing for. Their responses will be guided by the community's aims and expectations and by a desire to teach you about them.

7a

3 Genre

Many academic writing assignments will suggest the genre in which you are to write—the kind of writing and/or the format. Sometimes the genre is prescribed, such as the literature review mentioned earlier, with its standard content and format. Often genre is implied, as in the two assignments about movies on page 171: both require analysis and comparison, but the first asks for explanation and the second asks for argument. In these cases, responses would most likely be conventional academic essays—introduction, thesis statement, supporting paragraphs, conclusion—with additional features for analyzing and comparing subjects, explaining them, or arguing about them.

Whether genre is specified or implied in your assignment, you are being asked to demonstrate your ability to write competently in that genre. If it is unfamiliar to you, take time to learn its features and conventions. This book contains examples of the genres listed below. Studying these samples along with the surrounding explanations and annotations will give you a good sense of how other writers have worked within genre conventions.

Informative essay (p. 51)
Personal response to a text (p. 73)
Informative Web site (p. 133)
Literacy narrative posted to a blog (p. 134)
PowerPoint slides for an oral presentation (p. 141)
Critique of a text (p. 181)
Critique of a visual (p. 183)
Argument essays (pp. 226 and 775)
Essay exam (p. 223)
Research papers (pp. 718 and 746)
Annotated bibliography (p. 612)
Literary analyses (pp. 746, 771, 775, and 778)
Research report (p. 826)
Laboratory report (p. 842)

In addition, common assignments in literature, other humanities, the social sciences, and the natural and applied sciences are described in pages 765, 781, 800, and 830–31, respectively. And Chapter 11 contains examples of genres used in public writing: complaint letter, application letter and résumé, memo, report, proposal, flyer, newsletter, and brochure.

7b Writing in response to texts

Academic knowledge building depends on reading, analyzing, and expanding on the work of others. Thus many academic writing assignments require you to respond to one or more texts—not only written products such as short stories and journal articles but also visual communications such as images, charts, films, and advertisements. As you form a response to a text, you integrate, or synthesize, its ideas and information with yours to come to your own conclusions. As you write your response, you support your ideas about the text by citing evidence from it.

7b

Note A common academic assignment, the research paper, expects you to consult and respond to multiple texts in order to support and extend your ideas (see Chapters 41–46). This section focuses on responding directly to a single text, but the skills involved apply to research writing as well.

1 Deciding how to respond

When an assignment asks you to respond directly to a text, you might take one of the following approaches. (Note that the word *author* refers to a photographer, painter, or other creator as well as to a writer.)

- Agree with and extend the author's ideas, exploring related ideas and providing additional examples.
- Agree with the author on some points but disagree on others.
- Disagree with the author on one or more main points.
- Explain how the author achieves a particular effect, such as evoking a historical period or balancing opposing views.
- Analyze the overall effectiveness of a text—for example, how well a writer supports a thesis with convincing evidence or whether an advertisement succeeds in its unstated purpose.

2 Forming a response

You will likely have an immediate response to at least some of the texts you analyze: you may agree or disagree strongly with what the author is saying. But for some other responses, you may need time and thought to determine what the author is saying and what you think about it.

Whatever your assignment, your first task is to examine the text or texts thoroughly so that you're sure you understand what the author says outright and also assumes or implies. You can use the process of critical reading described in the previous chapter to take notes on the text, summarize it, and develop a critical response. Then, as you write, you can use the tips in the following box to convey your response to readers.

Video
tutorial

7b

Responding to a text

- Make sure your writing has a point—a central idea, or thesis, that focuses your response. (For more on developing a thesis, see pp. 36–40.)
- Include a very brief summary if readers may be unfamiliar with your subject. But remember that your job is not just to report what the text says or what a visual shows; it is to *respond* to the work from your own critical perspective. (For more on summary, see pp. 152–54.)
- Center each paragraph on an idea of your own that supports your thesis. Generally, state the idea outright, in your own voice.
- Support the paragraph idea with evidence from the text—quotations, paraphrases, details, and examples.
- Conclude each paragraph with your interpretation of the evidence. As a general rule, avoid ending paragraphs with source evidence; instead, end with at least a sentence that explains what the evidence shows.

Video
tutorial

3 Emphasizing synthesis in your response

Following the suggestions in the preceding box will lead you to show readers the synthesis you achieved by thinking critically about the text. That is, you integrate your perspective with that of the author in order to support a conclusion of your own about the work.

A key to synthesis is deciding how to present evidence from your reading and observation in your writing. Especially when you are writing about a relatively unfamiliar subject, you may be tempted to let a text or other source do the talking for you through extensive summary or quotations. However, your voice is crucial in academic writing, where readers expect to see you managing ideas and information to make your points. A typical paragraph of text-based writing follows the pattern outlined in the preceding box: the writer's own idea, evidence from the text, and the writer's interpretation of the evidence. You can see this pattern in the following paragraph from an essay that appears later in this chapter (p. 182):

The most fundamental and most debatable assumption underlying Sowell's essay is that higher education is a kind of commodity that not everyone is entitled to. In order to diminish the importance of graduates' average debt from education loans, Sowell claims that	Writer's idea Evidence and interpretation

a car loan will probably be higher (131). This comparison between education and an automobile implies that the two are somehow equal as products and that an affordable higher education is no more a right than a new car is. Sowell also condemns the "irresponsible" students who drop out of school and "the increasingly easy availability of college to people who are not very serious about getting an education" (132). But he overlooks the value of encouraging education, including the education of those who don't finish college or who aren't scholars. For many in the United States, education has a greater value than that of a mere commodity like a car. And even from an economic perspective such as Sowell's, the cost to society of an uneducated public needs to be taken into account. By failing to give education its due, Sowell   Writer's conclusion undermines his argument at its core.

    —Charlene Robinson, "Weighing the Costs"

7c

This example meets an important goal of synthesis in academic writing: Robinson finds **balance** in her own and Sowell's claims so that her claims are reasonable and believable. Disagreeing with Sowell, Robinson might simply have dismissed his claims as "ridiculous" and moved on. Instead, she takes a more serious and impartial approach by giving Sowell's claims a fair hearing and detailing the flaws and omissions she sees. Thus she gives readers a chance to evaluate for themselves both Sowell's and her own claims.

Note Effective synthesis requires careful handling of evidence from the text (quotations, paraphrases, and summaries) so that the evidence meshes smoothly into your sentences and yet is clearly distinct from your own ideas. See pages 642–47 on integrating borrowed material.

7c   Choosing structure and content

Many academic writing assignments will at least imply how you should organize your paper and even how you should develop your ideas. As with the literature review mentioned earlier, the required genre will suggest discrete parts, each with its own requirements for content. Even a direct response to a text, whose content depends on the text and the response, still implies certain requirements: you are asked to make a claim and to support the claim with specific evidence. Sometimes you may also be expected to show that you understand what others think about the text.

For most academic assignments, the broad aims of building and exchanging knowledge determine features that are common across disciplines. Follow these general guidelines for your academic writing, supplementing them as indicated with others elsewhere in this book:

■ **Develop a main point for your writing.** Depending on the genre, the main point may be a claim or thesis, a summary of findings, or a conclusion based on primary research that you have conducted, such as an experiment, an observation, a survey, or an interview. For more on thesis statements, see pages 36–40. For more on writing assignments in other disciplines, see pages 765, 781, 800, and 830–31.

■ **Support the main point with evidence,** drawn usually from your reading, personal experience, or primary research. The kinds of evidence will depend on the discipline you're writing in and the type of paper you're doing. For more on evidence in the disciplines, see pages 765 (literature), 780–81 (other humanities), 799–800 (social sciences), and 830 (natural and applied sciences).

■ **Synthesize.** Put your sources to work for you by thinking critically about them. Integrate them into your own perspective in your own voice. For more on synthesis, see pages 173–75 in this chapter and pages 626–28 in the discussion of research writing.

■ **Acknowledge sources fully, including online sources.** *Not* acknowledging sources is plagiarism, and it undermines the knowledge-sharing foundation of academic writing. See below.

■ **Organize clearly within the framework of the type of writing you're doing.** Develop your ideas as simply and directly as your purpose and content allow. Clearly relate sentences, paragraphs, and sections so that readers always know where they are in the paper's development.

⟨**CULTURE LANGUAGE**⟩ These features are not universal. In some cultures academic writers may be indirect, may assume that readers will discover the thesis, or may be expected to consult only well-known sources and to adhere to the sources' ideas. In US colleges and universities, students are expected to look for relevant and reliable sources, well known or not, and to use sources mainly to support their own ideas.

7d Acknowledging sources

Aside from your own experience and the data you gather through primary research, any sources you use in writing must be acknowledged fully. When you cite sources responsibly, you become a partner in the academic discussion of a subject and contribute to the knowledge about it. Such active construction of knowledge is at the heart of academic work, and it depends on sharing ideas and on trusting that writers will credit others whose work they borrow. If you fail to acknowledge sources, you undermine this knowledge building and trust and you plagiarize, which can be punishable. Thus it is important to understand what plagiarism is and how to use sources responsibly and honestly. You can rely on this book as a resource, consulting the following discussions:

- Building academic integrity, pages 3–5.
- Avoiding plagiarism and documenting sources, pages 648–58.
- Citing sources in MLA style for English and some other humanities (pp. 667–713), Chicago style for history, philosophy, and some other humanities (pp. 785–96), APA style for the social sciences (pp. 804–23), and CSE style for the natural sciences (pp. 834–41).

7e

CULTURE LANGUAGE Cultures have different definitions of a writer's responsibility to sources. In some cultures, for instance, a writer need not cite sources that are well known. In the United States, in contrast, a writer is obligated to cite all sources. Recognizing differences between practices in your native culture and in the United States can help you adapt to the expectations of US academic writing.

7e Using academic language

American academic writing relies on a dialect called standard American English. The dialect is also used in business, government, the media, and other sites of social and economic power where people of diverse backgrounds must communicate with one another. It is "standard" not because it is better than other forms of English, but because it is accepted as the common language, much as the dollar bill is accepted as the common currency.

Video
tutorial

In writing, standard American English varies a great deal, from the formality of an academic research report to the more relaxed language of this handbook to informal e-mails between coworkers in a company. Even in academic writing, standard American English allows much room for the writer's own tone and voice, as these passages on the same topic show:

More formal

Responsibility for the widespread problem of obesity among Americans depends on the person or group describing the problem and proposing a solution. Some people believe the cause lies with individuals who make poor eating choices

Drawn-out phrasing, such as *widespread problem of obesity among Americans*.

for themselves and parents who feed unhealthy foods to their children. Others take strong issue with the food industry, citing food manufacturers and fast-food chains that create and advertise food that is high in sugar, fat, and sodium. Still others place responsibility on American society as a whole for preferring a sedentary lifestyle centered on screen-based activities such as watching television and using computers for video games and social interaction.

> More complicated sentence structures, such as *take strong issue with the food industry, citing food manufacturers and fast-food chains that create and advertise.* . . .

> More formal vocabulary: *responsibility, children, television.*

Less formal

Who or what is to blame for the obesity epidemic depends on who is talking and what they want to do about the problem. Some people blame eaters for making bad choices and parents for feeding their kids unhealthy foods. Others demonize food manufacturers and fast-food chains for creating and advertising sugary, fatty, and sodium-loaded food. Still others point to Americans generally for spending too much time in front of screens watching TV, playing video games, or going on *Facebook*.

> More informal phrasing, such as *obesity epidemic.*

> Less complicated sentence structures, such as *demonize food manufacturers and fast-food chains for creating and advertising.* . . .

> More informal vocabulary: *blame, kids, TV.*

As different as they are, both examples illustrate several common features of academic language:

- **Its formality varies depending on the writer's voice and audience.** For instance, the first passage might reflect the writer's preference for more formal language and also an audience of experts in the field who expect a serious, measured approach. Addressing peers instead of experts, the same writer might still sound more formal than the second writer does—perhaps retaining the formal vocabulary—but might also shorten sentences and tighten phrasing.

- **It follows the conventions of standard American English for grammar and usage.** These conventions are detailed in guides to the dialect, such as this handbook.

- **It uses a standard vocabulary,** not one that only some groups understand, such as slang, an ethnic or regional dialect, or another language. See pages 525–28 for more on specialized vocabularies.

- **It *does not use* the informalities of everday speech, texting, and instant messaging.** These informalities include incomplete sentences, slang, no capital letters, and shortened spellings (*u* for *you*, *b4* for *before*, *thru* for *through*, and so on.) (See p. 502 for more on these forms.)

- **It generally uses the third person (*he, she, it, they*).** The first-person *I* is sometimes appropriate to express personal opinions, but academic writers tend to avoid it and make conclusions speak for themselves. The first-person *we* can connect with readers and invite them to think along, but, again, many academic writers avoid it. The second-person *you* is appropriate only in addressing readers directly (as in this handbook), and even then it may seem condescending or too chummy. Definitely avoid using or implying *you* in conversational expressions such as *You know what I mean* and *Don't take this the wrong way.*

- **It is authoritative and neutral.** In the examples on the facing page, the writers express themselves confidently, not timidly (as in *Explaining the causes of obesity requires the reader's patience because . . .*). They also refrain from hostility (*The food industry's callous attitude toward health . . .*) and enthusiasm (*The food industry's clever and appealing advertisements . . .*).

At first, the diverse demands of academic writing may leave you groping for an appropriate voice. In an effort to sound fresh and confident, you may write too casually, as if speaking to friends or family:

7e

Too casual

Getting the truth about the obesity epidemic in the US requires some heavy lifting. It turns out that everyone else is to blame for the problem— big eaters, reckless corporations, and all those Americans who think it's OK to be a couch potato.

In an effort to sound "academic," you may produce wordy and awkward sentences:

Wordy and awkward

The responsibility for the problem of widespread obesity among Americans depends on the manner of defining the problem and the proposals for its solution. In some discussions, the cause of obesity is thought to be individuals who are unable or unwilling to make healthy choices in their own diets and parents who similarly make unhealthy choices for their children. [The passive voice in this example—*cause . . . is thought to be* instead of *people blame*—adds to its wordiness and indirection. See pp. 320–22 for more on verb voice.]

The cure for writing too informally or too stiffly is to read academic writing so that the language and style become familiar and to edit your own writing so that it sounds similar. (See pp. 67–69.) With experience and practice, you will develop a voice that is sufficiently formal but still authentic and natural, as in the examples opposite.

CULTURE LANGUAGE If your first language is not English or is an English dialect besides standard American, you know well the power of communicating with others who share your language. Learning to write standard American English in no way requires you to abandon your first language. Like most multilingual people, you are probably already adept at switching between languages as the situation demands—speaking one way with your relatives, say, and another way with an employer. As you practice academic writing, you'll develop the same flexibility with it.

Exercise

Exercise 7.1 Using academic language

Revise the following paragraph to make the language more academic while keeping the factual information the same.

> If you buy into the stereotype of girls chatting away on their cell phones, you should think again. One of the major wireless companies surveyed 1021 cell phone owners for a period of five years and—surprise!—reported that guys talk on cell phones more than girls do. In fact, guys were way ahead of girls, using an average of 571 minutes a month compared to 424 for girls. That's 35% more time on the phone! The survey also asked about conversations on land lines, and while girls still beat the field, the guys are catching up.

Exercise 7.2 Considering your past work: Writing in academic situations

Look back at a paper you wrote for a course in high school or college. To what extent does it share the features of academic writing discussed in this chapter? How does it differ? Write a revision plan for making the paper more academic.

Exercise

Exercise 7.3 Considering your native language or dialect

What main similarities do you notice between writing in your native language or dialect and writing for US college courses? What differences do you notice? Consider especially audience, purpose, content, structure, and the expression of ideas. Which aspects of writing for US college courses are easiest for you? Which ones are more difficult? Why?

Exercise

7f Examining sample critical responses

A critical response to a text or a visual, often called a **critique**, is a common academic assignment. The specifics depend on the discipline, but the principles illustrated here apply across disciplines.

Note Critical writing is *not* summarizing. You might summarize to clarify a text or a visual for yourself, and you may briefly summarize a work in your larger piece of writing. But in critical writing you go further to bring your own perspective to the work.

1 Writing critically about a text

Student paper

The following essay by the student Charlene Robinson responds to Thomas Sowell's essay "Student Loans" (pp. 148–49). Robinson arrived at her response, an argument, through the process of critical reading outlined in the previous chapter and then by gathering and organizing her ideas, developing a thesis about Sowell's text that synthesized his ideas and hers, and drafting and revising until she believed she had supported her thesis with sufficient evidence from her own experience and from Sowell's text.

Robinson did not assume that her readers would see the same things in Sowell's essay or share her views, so her essay offers evidence of Sowell's ideas in the form of direct quotations, summaries, and paraphrases (restatements in her own words). Robinson documents these borrowings from Sowell using the style of the Modern Language Association (MLA): the numbers in parentheses are page numbers in the book containing Sowell's essay, listed at the end as a work cited. (See Chapter 46 for more on MLA style.)

Weighing the Costs

In the essay "Student Loans," the economist Thomas Sowell challenges the US government's student-loan program for three main reasons: a scarce resource (taxpayers' money) goes to many undeserving students, a high number of recipients fail to repay their loans, and the easy availability of money has led to both lower academic standards and higher college tuitions. Sowell wants his readers to "weigh the costs of things" (133) in order to see, as he does, that the loan program should not receive so much government funding. Sowell wrote his essay in the 1990s, but the argument he makes is still heard frequently today and is worth examining. Does Sowell provide the evidence of cost and other problems to lead the reader to agree with his argument? The answer is no, because hard evidence is less common than debatable and unsupported assumptions about students, scarcity, and the value of education.

Sowell's portrait of student-loan recipients is questionable. It is based on averages, some statistical and some not, but averages are often deceptive. For example, Sowell cites college graduates' low average debt of $7,000 to $9,000 (131) without giving the full range of statistics or acknowledging that when he was writing many students' debt was much higher. (Today the average debt itself is much higher.) Similarly, Sowell dismisses "heart-rending stories" of "the low-income student with a huge debt" as "not at all typical" (132), yet he invents his own exaggerated version of the typical loan recipient: an affluent slacker ("Rockefellers" and "Vanderbilts") for whom college is a "place to hang out for a few years" sponging off the government, while his or her parents clear a profit from making use of the loan program (132). Although such students (and parents) may well exist, are they really typical? Sowell does not offer any data one way or the other—for instance, how many loan recipients come from each income group, what percentage of loan funds go to each group, how many loan recipients receive significant help from their parents, and how many receive none. Together, Sowell's statements and omissions cast doubt on the argument that students don't need or deserve the loans.

Another set of assumptions in the essay has to do with "scarcity": "There is never enough of anything to fully satisfy all those who want it,"

Margin annotations:

Introduction

Summary of Sowell's essay

Robinson's critical question

Thesis statement

First main point

Evidence for first point: paraphrases and quotations from Sowell's text

Evidence for first point: Sowell's omissions

Conclusion of first point: Robinson's interpretation

Transition to second main point

Second main point	Sowell says (131). This statement appeals to readers' common sense, but the "lesson" of scarcity does not necessarily apply to the student-loan program.
Evidence for second point: Sowell's omissions	Sowell omits many important figures needed to prove that the nation's resources are too scarce to support the program, such as the total cost of the program, its percentage of the total education budget and the total federal budget, and its cost compared to the cost of defense, Medicare, and other expensive programs. Moreover, Sowell does not mention the interest paid by loan recipients, even though the interest must offset some of the costs of running the program and covering unpaid loans. Thus
Conclusion of second point: Robinson's interpretation	his argument that there isn't enough money to run the student loan program is unconvincing.
Third main point	The most fundamental and most debatable assumption underlying Sowell's essay is that higher education is a kind of commodity that not everyone is entitled to. In order to diminish the importance of graduates' average
Evidence for third point: paraphrases and quotations from Sowell's text	debt from education loans, Sowell claims that a car loan will probably be higher (131). This comparison between education and an automobile implies that the two are somehow equal as products and that an affordable higher education is no more a right than a new car is. Sowell also condemns the "irresponsible" students who drop out of school and "the increasingly easy availability of college to people who are not very serious about getting an education"
Evidence for third point: Sowell's omissions	(132). But he overlooks the value of encouraging education, including the education of those who don't finish college or who aren't scholars. For many in the United States, education has a greater value than that of a mere commodity like a car. And even from an economic perspective such as Sowell's, the cost to soci-
Conclusion of third point: Robinson's interpretation	ety of an uneducated public needs to be taken into account. By failing to give education its due, Sowell undermines his argument at its core.
Conclusion	Sowell writes with conviction, and his concerns are valid: high
Acknowledgment of Sowell's concerns	taxes, waste, unfairness, declining educational standards, obtrusive government. However, the essay's flaws make it unlikely that Sowell could convince readers who do not already agree with him. He does
Summary of three main points	not support his portrait of the typical loan recipient, he fails to demonstrate a lack of resources for the loan program, and he neglects the special nature of education compared to other services and products. Sowell may
Return to theme of introduction: weighing costs	have the evidence to back up his assumptions, but by omitting it he himself does not truly weigh the costs of the loan program.
Work cited in MLA style (p. 676)	Work Cited Sowell, Thomas. "Student Loans." *Is Reality Optional? and Other Essays.* Stanford: Hoover, 1993. 131-33. Print.

—Charlene Robinson (student)

2 Writing critically about a visual

The following essay, by the student Matthew Greene, responds to the *BoostUp.org* advertisement on page 162. As we saw in the previous chapter, Greene examined the ad over several stages, each time discovering more in it and gradually developing his own ideas. In his paper Greene takes pains to be sure that readers will see the ad as he does: he reproduces it, captions it, and clearly describes its features. He cites his sources using MLA style (Chapter 46). (All but one of Greene's text citations lack page numbers because the sources themselves are not numbered.)

Caution A visual is a source just as a written work is, and like a written source it must be acknowledged. Greene cites the *BoostUp.org* ad in the caption. (MLA style does not require him to cite it again in his list of works cited.) If Greene published his paper online, he would also need to seek the copyright owner's permission to use the ad. See pages 651–54 for more about acknowledging sources and pages 655–56 for more about permissions for online publication.

Student paper

7f

Giving a Boost

How many commuters paused, as I did, to puzzle over a bus shelter advertisement that shows a teenage boy standing in a sea of gray street, sidewalk, and wall? (See fig. 1.) Were other readers curious about the

Introduction

Description of advertisement

Fig. 1. An advertisement for *BoostUp.org* encourages viewers to visit its Web site and support students who are at risk of dropping out of high school. From "High School Dropout Prevention"; *Ad Council*; Ad Council, 2007; Web; 10 Apr. 2008.

Caption giving the ad's main idea and source

message from "Danny R.," taped to the top of the photograph, that reads, "Hey—let me know if you want some help with school work this weekend. I'm around"? Did they follow the ad's instruction: "HELP KODY GRADUATE AT BOOSTUP.ORG"? If they did, they probably appreciated how effective the ad

Thesis statement

is. Through its photograph, taped-on message, and direct appeal, it encourages readers to find out how they can help students stay in high school.

Background information on the ad campaign

The *BoostUp.org* campaign is sponsored by the nonprofit Ad Council and the US Army. It aims to raise public awareness about high school dropouts and encourage public support to help teens stay in school ("High School"). When people visit *BoostUp.org*, they can learn about particular at-risk students and mentoring programs in their communities; and users of *YouTube* and *Facebook* can send support through those sites ("What"). First, though, people have to visit the site, and that's where "Kody" and similar ads come in. They are very effective at making people curious enough to go to the site and concerned enough to participate in the campaign.

7f

First main point

The main image in the *BoostUp.org* ad—the photograph of a teenager wearing a T-shirt, baggy jeans, and a backward baseball cap—

Evidence for first point: analysis of photograph

presents the boy as especially isolated. The cropping of the photograph pushes him to one side and makes him seem small amid hard gray surfaces. His off-center stance, hands in pockets, and glance to the side all heighten

Conclusion of first point: Greene's interpretation

the sense that he is alone, vulnerable, and in need of a friend or help. At the same time, nothing in the photograph suggests that the boy is causing trouble or planning it. He's just very much by himself.

Second main point

The second major element in the ad, Danny R.'s message in the upper left corner, counters the photograph in two ways. First, with the offer to

Evidence for second point: analysis of message

help with school work over the weekend, Danny R. shows that he is someone who knows and cares about the person he's writing to. It isn't immediately clear who this person is, but if it's the boy in the photograph then he isn't as alone as he first seems. Second, Danny R.'s message is literally taped on the photo, over another message that can't be read. This covered message

Conclusion of second point: Greene's interpretation

implies that Danny R. is not the only support the boy has. Together, the messages break up the bleak grayness that the photograph depicts as the boy's world, offering hope that the boy has friends who want to help him.

Third main point

The third important element in the ad—the word bubble in the lower right—pulls together the other two elements. The word bubble is a direct

Evidence for third point: analysis of word bubble

appeal to readers to get involved. It is less prominent than the other two elements, so it is probably the final place readers look when scanning the ad. It suggests that the boy is named Kody and that he is at risk of not graduat-

Conclusion of third point: Greene's interpretation

ing. Yet the text still does not say what *BoostUp.org* is or how readers can help Kody there. Some mystery remains to attract readers to the Web site.

The creators of this advertisement seem to assume that readers see dropping out as a negative step for high school students. Thus the ad is designed to draw readers in by showing Kody's world, providing an example of an encouraging message, and inviting visits to *BoostUp.org.* Once there, readers may be moved, as I was, to offer a "boost" of their own to Kody and his classmates.

Conclusion

Works Cited

"High School Dropout Prevention." *Ad Council.* Ad Council, 2007. Web. 18 Apr. 2008.

"What Is Boost?" *BoostUp.org.* US Army and Ad Council, 2007. Web. 15 Apr. 2008.

—Matthew Greene (student)

Works cited in MLA style

No works-cited entry for advertisement because the caption provides complete source information

Exercise 7.4 Responding to critiques

Read Charlene Robinson's and Matthew Greene's essays carefully. Do you think the authors' critiques are accurate and fair? Are they perceptive? Do the authors provide enough evidence to convince you of their points? Do they miss anything you would have mentioned? Write your responses to one of the essays in a brief critique of your own.

Exercise

Exercise 7.5 Writing critically about a text

Write an essay based on your own critical reading of Thomas Sowell's "Student Loans" (Exercise 6.1, p. 147). Your critique may be entirely different from Charlene Robinson's, or you may have developed some of the same points. If there are similarities, they should be expressed and supported in your own way, in the context of your own critical perspective.

Exercise 7.6 Writing critically about a visual

Write an essay based on your own critical reading of the *BoostUp.org* advertisement (Exercise 6.7, p. 169). Your critique may be entirely different from Matthew Greene's, or you may have developed some of the same points. If there are similarities, they should be expressed and supported in your own way, in the context of your own critical perspective.

Exercise 7.7 Writing critically about a visual

Write an essay based on your critical reading of the graph on page 165, the photograph on page 166, or the Web pages on page 167 (Exercise 6.8, p. 169).

Exercise 7.8 Writing critically about several visuals

Write an essay based on your critical reading and comparison of the visuals in the previous chapter (Exercise 6.9, p. 169).

8

Reading Arguments Critically

Argument is writing that attempts to open readers' minds to an opinion, change readers' own opinions, or move readers to action. A good argument is neither a cold exercise in logic nor an attempt to beat others into submission. It is a work of negotiation and problem solving in which both writer and reader search for the knowledge that will create common ground between them.

Of course, not all arguments are "good." Whether deliberately or not, some are unclear, incomplete, misleading, or downright false. The negotiation fails; the problem remains unsolved. This chapter will help you read written arguments critically, including visual arguments, and the next chapter will help you write effective arguments.

CULTURE LANGUAGE The ways of reading and writing arguments described in this chapter and the next may be uncomfortable to you if your native culture approaches such writing differently. In some cultures, for example, a writer is expected to begin indirectly, to avoid asserting his or her opinion outright, or to establish a compromise rather than argue a position. In American academic and business settings, readers and writers look or aim for a well-articulated opinion, evidence gathered from many sources, and a direct and concise argument for the opinion.

8a Recognizing the elements of argument

Few arguments are an easy read. Most demand the attentive critical reading discussed in Chapter 6. (If you haven't read pp. 147–60, you should do so before continuing.) As a reader of argument, your purpose will almost always be the same: you'll want to know whether you should be convinced by the argument. This purpose focuses your attention on the elements that make an argument convincing, or not.

In a scheme adapted from the work of the British philosopher Stephen Toulmin, an argument has three main elements.

mycomplab

Visit *mycomplab.com* for the eText and for resources and more exercises on reading arguments critically.

186

- Claims: positive statements that require support. In a written argument the central claim is stated outright in a **thesis statement** (see p. 36). This central claim is what the argument is about. For instance:

  In both its space and its equipment, the college's chemistry laboratory is outdated.

  Several minor claims, such as that the present equipment is inadequate, will contribute to the central assertion.

- Evidence: the facts, examples, expert opinions, and other information that support the claims. (Toulmin calls evidence *data* or *grounds*, terms that indicate both its specificity and its work as an argument's foundation.) Evidence to support the preceding claim might include the following:

  The present lab's age and size
  An inventory of equipment
  The testimony of chemistry professors

  Like the claims, the evidence is always stated outright.

- Assumptions: the writer's underlying (and often unstated) beliefs, opinions, principles, or inferences that tie the evidence to the claims. (Toulmin calls these assumptions *warrants:* they justify making the claims on the basis of the evidence provided.) For instance, the following assumption might connect the evidence of professors' testimony with the claim that a new lab is needed:

  Chemistry professors can reliably evaluate the present lab's quality.

In the following pages, we'll examine each of these elements along with several others: tone and language, reasonableness, and common errors in reasoning. Charlene Robinson's "Weighing the Costs" in the previous chapter (pp. 181–82) provides a good example of critically reading an argument for its claims, evidence, and assumptions.

arg
8a

Questions for critically reading an argument

- What **claims** does the writer make?
- What kinds and quality of **evidence** does the writer provide to support the claims?
- What **assumptions** underlie the argument, connecting evidence to claims? Are they clear and believable?
- What is the writer's **tone**? How does the writer use **language**?
- Is the writer **reasonable**?
- Is the argument **logical**? Does it contain any **fallacies**?
- Are you convinced? Why or why not?

Checklist

8b Testing claims

The claims or assertions in an argument will likely be statements of opinion, fact, belief, or prejudice. It's important to distinguish between the kinds of statements and to analyze the definitions of terms.

1 Recognizing opinions

An **opinion** is a judgment based on facts and arguable on the basis of facts. Reasonable people could and probably do disagree over opinions, and they are potentially changeable: with more facts, a writer might change opinions partly or wholly.

The thesis statement of an effective argument is an opinion, often one of the following:

■ A claim about past or present reality:

In both its space and its equipment, the college's chemistry laboratory is outdated.

Academic cheating increases with students' economic insecurity.

■ A claim of value:

The new room fees are unjustified given the condition of the dormitories.

Computer music pirates undermine the system that encourages the very creation of music.

■ A recommendation for a course of action, often a solution to a perceived problem:

The college's outdated chemistry laboratory should be replaced incrementally over the next five years.

Schools and businesses can help to resolve the region's traffic congestion by implementing car pools and rewarding participants.

The backbone of an argument consists of specific claims that support the thesis statement. These may be statements of opinion, too, or they may state facts or beliefs.

Opinions do not make arguments by themselves. As a critical reader, you must satisfy yourself that the writer has specified the evidence for the opinions and that the assumptions linking claims and evidence are clear and believable.

2 Recognizing facts

A **fact** may be a verifiable statement—that is, one that can be proved as true:

Last year tuition increased by 16%.

Or it may be an inference from verifiable facts:

Over their lifetimes, four-year-college graduates earn almost twice as much as high-school graduates.

A claim of fact does not work as the thesis of an argument. Although people often dispute facts, they are not fundamentally arguable because ultimately they can be verified. Facts have another important role in argument, providing crucial evidence for other claims (see pp. 190–91).

3 Recognizing beliefs

A **belief** is a conviction based on cultural or personal faith, morality, or values:

Abortion is legalized murder.

Capital punishment is legalized murder.

The primary goal of government should be to provide equality of opportunity for all.

arg

8b

Such statements are often called opinions because they express viewpoints, but unlike opinions they are not based on facts and other evidence. Since they cannot be disproved by facts or even contested on the basis of facts, they cannot serve as the central or supporting claims of an argument. However, beliefs can play a significant role in argument. Appeals to readers' beliefs can serve as a kind of evidence by tapping into emotions (see pp. 192 and 219–21), and beliefs often form the assumptions that link claims and evidence (see pp. 192 and 194–95).

4 Recognizing prejudices

One kind of assertion that has no place in argument is a **prejudice,** an opinion based on insufficient or unexamined evidence:

Women are bad drivers.

Fat people are jolly.

Teenagers are irresponsible.

Athletes are unintelligent.

People who use wheelchairs have cognitive disabilities.

Unlike a belief, a prejudice is testable: it can be contested and disproved on the basis of facts. Very often, however, we form prejudices or accept them from others—parents, friends, the communications media—without questioning their meaning or testing their truth. Writers who display prejudice do not deserve your confidence and agreement.

When reading arguments that appear online, you should be especially vigilant for claims of belief or prejudice that pose as considered opinions. Anyone with a computer and an Internet connection can post anything on the Internet, without passing it through an editorial screening like that undergone by books and by articles in journals and magazines. The filtering of such material is entirely up to the reader.

5 Looking for defined terms

In any argument, but especially in arguments about abstract ideas, the clear and consistent definition of terms is essential. In the following claim, the writer is not clear about what she means by the crucial term *justice:*

> Over the past few decades, justice has deteriorated so badly that it almost does not exist anymore.

The word *justice* is **abstract:** it does not refer to anything specific or concrete and in fact has varied meanings. (The five definitions in *The American Heritage Dictionary* include "the principle of moral rightness" and "the administration and procedure of law.") When the writer specifies her meaning, her assertion is much clearer:

> If by *justice* we mean treating people fairly, punishing those who commit crimes, and protecting the victims of those crimes, then justice has deteriorated badly over the past few decades.

Writers who use highly abstract words such as *justice, equality,* and *success* have a responsibility to define them. If the word is important to the argument, such a definition may take an entire paragraph. As a reader you should evaluate the writer's definitions before you accept his or her assertions. (See p. 102 for more on definition and a paragraph defining the abstract word *quality.*)

8c Weighing evidence

Exercise

In argument, evidence demonstrates the validity of the writer's claims. If the evidence is inadequate or questionable, the claims are at best doubtful.

1 Recognizing kinds of evidence

Writers draw on several kinds of evidence to support their claims.

Evidence for argument

Video
tutorial

- Facts: verifiable statements
- Statistics: facts expressed in numbers
- Examples: specific cases
- Expert opinions: the judgments of authorities
- Appeals to readers' beliefs or needs

Facts

Facts are statements whose truth can be verified or inferred (see pp. 188–89). Facts employing numbers are **statistics:**

> Of those polled, 62% stated a preference for a flat tax.

In 2010 there were 1,430,895 men and women on active duty in the US armed forces.

The average American household consists of 2.58 persons.

Numbers may be implied:

Earth is closer to the sun than Saturn is.
The cost of medical care is rising.

Or a fact may involve no numbers at all:

The city council adjourned without taking a vote.
The President vetoed the bill.

Examples

Examples are specific instances of the point being made, including historical precedents and personal experiences. The passage below uses a personal narrative as partial support for the claim in the first sentence:

> Besides broadening students' knowledge, required courses can also introduce students to possible careers that they otherwise would have known nothing about. Somewhat reluctantly, I enrolled in a psychology course to satisfy the requirement for work in social science. But what I learned in the course about human behavior has led me to consider becoming a clinical psychologist instead of an engineer.

Expert opinions

Expert opinions are the judgments formed by authorities on the basis of their own examination of the facts. In the following passage the writer cites the opinion of an expert to support the claim in the first sentence:

> Despite the fact that affirmative action places some individuals at a disadvantage, it remains necessary to right the wrongs inflicted historically on whole groups of people. Howard Glickstein, a past director of the US Commission on Civil Rights, maintains that "it simply is not possible to achieve equality and fairness" unless the previous grounds for discrimination (such as sex, race, and national origin) are now considered as grounds for admission to schools and jobs (26).

As this passage illustrates, a citation of expert opinion should always refer you to the source, here indicated by the author's name, Glickstein, and the page number in parentheses, "(26)." Such a citation is also generally accompanied by a reference to the expert's credentials. See pages 645 and 657–58.

(CULTURE LANGUAGE) In some cultures a person with high standing in government, society, or organized religion may be considered an authority on many different subjects. In American academic and business settings, authority comes from study, learning, and experience: the more knowledge a person can demonstrate about a subject, the more authority he or she has. See page 193 on relevant evidence.

arg
8c

Appeals to beliefs or needs

A writer's **appeal to beliefs or needs** asks you to accept an assertion in part because you already accept it as true without evidence or because it coincides with your needs. Each of the following examples combines such an appeal (second sentence) with a summary of factual evidence (first sentence).

> Thus the chemistry laboratory is outdated in its equipment. In addition, its shabby, antiquated appearance shames the school, making it seem a second-rate institution. [Appeals to readers' belief that their school is or should be first-rate.]

> That police foot patrollers reduce crime has already been demonstrated. Such officers might also restore our sense that our neighborhoods are orderly, stable places. [Appeals to readers' need for order and stability.]

arg

8c

(For more on beliefs, see p. 189. For more on appeals to emotion, see pp. 219–21.)

2 Judging the reliability of evidence

To be convinced by evidence, you should see it as reliable. The test of reliability for an appeal to beliefs or needs is specific to the situation: whether it is appropriate for the argument and correctly gauges how you, the reader, actually feel (see p. 220). With the other kinds of evidence, the standards are more general and apply to any argument.

Video
tutorial

Criteria for weighing evidence

- Is it **accurate**: trustworthy, exact, undistorted?
- Is it **relevant**: authoritative, pertinent, current?
- Is it **representative**: true to context?
- Is it **adequate**: plentiful, specific?

Accuracy

Accurate evidence is true:

- It is drawn from trustworthy sources.
- It is quoted exactly.
- It is presented with the original meaning undistorted.

Reading an argument in favor of gun control, you might expect the writer to cite some procontrol sources, which are undoubtedly biased. But you should also look for anticontrol sources (representing the opposite bias) and neutral sources (attempting to be unbiased). If the writer quotes an expert, the quotation should present the expert's true meaning, not just a few words that appear to support the writer's argument. (As a reader you may have difficulty judging the accuracy of quotations if you are not familiar with the expert's opinions.)

Not just opinions but also facts and examples may be misinterpreted or distorted. Suppose you were reading an argument for extending a three-year-old law allowing the police to stop vehicles randomly as a means of apprehending drunk drivers. If the author cited statistics showing that the number of drunk-driving accidents dropped in the first two years of the law but failed to note that the number rose back to the previous level in the third year, then the evidence would be distorted and thus inaccurate. You or any reader would be justified in questioning the entire argument, no matter how accurate the rest seemed.

Relevance

Relevant evidence pertains to the argument:

- It comes from sources with authority on the subject.
- It relates directly to the point the writer is making.
- It is current.

arg

8c

If you are reading an argument against a method of hazardous-waste disposal and the writer offers his church minister's opinion as evidence, you should accept the evidence only if the minister is an authority on the subject and her expertise is up to date. If she is an authority on Method A and not Method B, you should accept her authority only about Method A. If the writer relates his own experience of living near a hazardous-waste site, you should accept the story as relevant only if it pertains to his thesis. His authority in this case is that of a close observer and a citizen. (See also pp. 200–01 on the fallacy of false authority.)

Representativeness

Representative evidence is true to its context:

- It reflects the full range of the sample from which it is said to be drawn.
- It does not overrepresent any element of the sample.

In an essay arguing that dormitories should stay open during school holidays, a writer might say that "the majority of the school's students favor leaving the dormitories open." But that writer would mislead you and other readers if the claim were based only on a poll of her roommates and dormitory neighbors. A few dormitory residents could not be said to represent the entire student body, particularly the nonresident students. To be representative, the poll would have to take in many more students and the respondents would have to reflect the proportions of resident and nonresident students on campus.

Adequacy

Adequate evidence is sufficient:

- It is plentiful enough to support the writer's assertions.
- It is specific enough to support the writer's assertions.

A writer arguing against animal abuse should not hope to win you over solely with statements about her personal experiences and claims of her opinions. Her experience may indeed be relevant evidence if, say, she has worked with animals or witnessed animal abuse. And her opinions are indeed important to the argument, so that you know what she thinks. But even together her experiences and opinions are not adequate evidence: they cannot substitute entirely for facts, nonpersonal examples, and the opinions of experts to demonstrate abuse and describe the scope of the problem.

8d Discovering assumptions

Assumptions connect evidence to claims: they are the opinions or beliefs that explain why a particular piece of evidence is relevant to a particular claim. As noted in Chapter 6 on critical thinking, assumptions are not flaws in arguments but necessities: we all acquire beliefs and opinions that shape our view of the world. Here are examples of beliefs that you, or people you know, may hold:

Criminals should be punished.
Hard work is virtuous.
Teachers' salaries are too low.

Assumptions are inevitable in argument, but they aren't neutral. For one thing, an assumption can weaken an argument. Say that a writer claims that real estate development should be prevented in your town. As evidence for this claim, the writer offers facts about past developments that have replaced older buildings. But the evidence is relevant to the claim only if you accept the writer's extreme assumptions that old buildings are always worthy and new development is always bad.

In such a case, the writer's bias may not even be stated. Hence a second problem: in arguments both sound and unsound, assumptions are not always explicit. Following are a claim and evidence forming a reasonable argument. What is the unstated assumption?

Claim

The town should create a plan to manage building preservation and new development.

Evidence

Examples of how such plans work; expert opinions on how and why both preservation and development are needed.

In this instance the assumption is that neither uncontrolled development nor zero development is healthy for the town. If you can accept this assumption, you should be able to accept the writer's claim (though you might still disagree over particulars).

Here are tips for dealing with assumptions:

Guidelines for analyzing assumptions

- What are the assumptions underlying the argument? How does the writer connect claims with evidence?
- Are the assumptions believable? Do they express your values? Do they seem true in your experience?
- Are the assumptions consistent with one another? Is the argument's foundation solid, not slippery?

Video tutorial

8e Watching language, hearing tone

arg
8e

Tone is the expression of the writer's attitudes toward himself or herself, toward the subject, and toward the reader (see p. 22 for a discussion). Tone can tell you quite a bit about the writer's intentions, biases, and trustworthiness. For example:

> Some women cite personal growth as a reason for pursuing careers while raising children. Of course, they are equally concerned with the personal growth of the children they relegate to "child-care specialists" while they work.

In the second sentence this writer is being **ironic,** saying one thing while meaning another. The word *relegate* and the quotation marks with *child-care specialists* betray the writer's belief that working mothers may selfishly neglect their children for their own needs. Irony can sometimes be effective in argument, but here it marks the author as insincere in dealing with the complex issues of working parents and child care.

When reading arguments, you should be alert to the author's language. Look for words that **connote,** or suggest, certain attitudes and evoke certain responses in readers. (Notice your own responses to these word pairs with related meanings but different connotations: *daring/foolhardy, dislike/detest, glad/joyous, angry/rabid, freedom/license.*) Connotative language is no failure in argument; indeed, the strongest arguments use it skillfully to appeal to readers' hearts as well as their minds (see pp. 219–21). But be suspicious if the language runs counter to the substance of the argument.

Look also for evasive words. **Euphemisms,** such as *attack of a sexual nature* for "rape" or *peace-keeping force* for a war-making army, are supposedly inoffensive substitutes for words that may frighten or offend readers (see pp. 528–29). In argument, though, they are sometimes used to hide or twist the truth. An honest, forthright arguer will avoid them.

Finally, watch carefully for sexist, racist, and other biased language that reveals deep ignorance or, worse, entrenched prejudice on the part of the writer. Obvious examples are *broad* for woman and *fag* for homosexual. (See pp. 529–32 for more on such language.)

The **reasonableness** of an argument is the sense you get as a reader that the author is being fair and sincere. The reasonable writer does not conceal or distort facts, hide prejudices, mask belief as opinion, manipulate you with language, or resort to any of dozens of devices used unconsciously by those who don't know better and deliberately by those who do.

Reasonableness involves all the elements of argument examined so far: claims, evidence, assumptions, and language. In addition, the fair, sincere argument always avoids so-called fallacies (covered in the next section), and it acknowledges the opposition.

Judging whether a writer deals adequately with his or her opposition is a fairly simple matter for the reader of argument. By definition, an arguable issue has more than one side. Even if you have no preconceptions about a subject, you will know that another side exists. If the writer pretends otherwise or dismisses the opposition too quickly, you are justified in questioning the honesty and fairness of the argument. (For the more complicated business of *writing* an acknowledgment of opposing views, see pp. 221–22.)

Exercise 8.1 Reading arguments critically

Following are two brief arguments. Though not directly opposed, the two arguments do represent different stances on environmental issues. Read each argument critically, following the process outlined in Chapter 6 (pp. 145–60) and answering the questions in the box on page 187 (questions about claims, evidence, assumptions, and the other elements of argument). Develop your responses in writing so that you can refer to them for later exercises and class discussion.

The Environmental Crisis Is Not Our Fault

I am as responsible as most eco-citizens: I bike everywhere; I don't 1
own a car; I recycle newspapers, bottles, cans, and plastics; I have a vegetable garden in the summer; I buy organic products; and I put all vegetable waste into my backyard compost bin, probably the only one in all of Greenwich Village. But I don't at the same time believe that I am saving the planet, or in fact doing anything of much consequence about the various eco-crises around us. What's more, I don't even believe that if "all of us" as individuals started doing the same it would make any but the slightest difference.

Leave aside ozone depletion and rain forest destruction—those are 2
patently corporate crimes that no individual actions can remedy to any degree. Take, instead, energy consumption in this country. In the most recent figures, residential consumption was 7.2% of the total, commercial 5.5%, and industrial 23.3%; of the remainder, 27.8% was transportation (about one-third of it by private car) and 36.3% was electric generation (about one-third for residential use). Individual energy use, in sum, was something like 28% of total consumption. Although you and I cutting down on energy consumption would have some small effect (and should be done), it is surely the energy consumption of industry

and other large institutions such as government and agribusiness that needs to be addressed first. And it is industry and government that must be forced to explain what their consumption is for, what is produced by it, how necessary it is, and how it can be drastically reduced.

The point is that the ecological crisis is essentially beyond "our" control, as citizens or householders or consumers or even voters. It is not something that can be halted by recycling or double-pane insulation. It is the inevitable by-product of our modern industrial civilization, dominated by capitalist production and consumption and serviced and protected by various institutions of government, federal to local. It cannot possibly be altered or reversed by simple individual actions, even by the actions of the millions who take part in Earth Day—even if they all go home and fix their refrigerators and from then on walk to work. Nothing less than a drastic overhaul of this civilization and an abandonment of its ingrained gods—progress, growth, exploitation, technology, materialism, anthropocentricity, and power—will do anything substantial to halt our path to environmental destruction, and it's hard to see how life-style solutions will have an effect on that. ₃

What I find truly pernicious about such solutions is that they get people thinking they are actually making a difference and doing their part to halt the destruction of the earth: "There, I've taken all the bottles to the recycling center and used my string bag at the grocery store; I guess that'll take care of global warming." It is the kind of thing that diverts people from the hard truths and hard choices and hard actions, from the recognition that they have to take on the larger forces of society—corporate and governmental—where true power, and true destructiveness, lie. ₄

And to the argument that, well, you have to start somewhere to raise people's consciousness, I would reply that this individualistic approach does not in fact raise consciousness. It does not move people beyond their old familiar liberal perceptions of the world, it does nothing to challenge the belief in technofix or write-your-Congressperson solutions, and it does not begin to provide them with the new vocabulary and modes of thought necessary for a true change of consciousness. We need, for example, to think of recycling centers not as the answer to our waste problems, but as a confession that the system of packaging and production in this society is out of control. Recycling centers are like hospitals; they are the institutions at the end of the cycle that take care of problems that would never exist if ecological criteria had operated at the beginning of the cycle. Until we have those kinds of understandings, we will not do anything with consciousness except reinforce it with the same misguided ideas that created the crisis. ₅

—Kirkpatrick Sale

Global Warming Statists Threaten Our Liberty

Life, liberty, and the pursuit of happiness—"unalienable rights" cited by our Founding Fathers in the Declaration of Independence—are now at risk as left-wing activists seek to curtail our liberties and personal choices to save the planet from supposedly man-made global warming. ₁

No one is saying global climate change doesn't exist. We all know the hot era of the dinosaurs later gave way to the frigid Ice Age. Throughout recorded human history, with and without the presence of factories and other factors blamed for today's alleged rising temperatures, there have been many warming and cooling trends. ₂

What is unresolved is the role man actually plays in climate change. 3
It is easy to be skeptical of the man-made global warming hysterics when
the scientific data remain inconclusive and uncontrollable events, such
as volcanic eruptions, can do more harm to the atmosphere than man.

Despite all the ambiguity, our liberties are at the peril of this dubi- 4
ous theory.

Cars and trucks are at the top of the leftist hit list. Special interest 5
groups' attacks, particularly on the SUV, spurred lawmakers to dictate
the type of cars and trucks available for consumers in the new energy bill
by mandating increased vehicle gas mileage. To meet the proposed
increase in the corporate average fuel economy (CAFE) standard of
35 miles per gallon, vehicles will inevitably become smaller and lighter.
Consumers who need or prefer bigger and safer vehicles will have fewer
choices as manufacturers struggle to meet new government fuel
mandates. As a result, the freedom of consumer choice will be greatly
diminished.

Even lighting your house is now in the crosshairs. Politicians and ac- 6
tivists want to invade our homes and empty our wallets when they call
for replacing incandescent light bulbs with more costly and energy-
efficient compact fluorescent light bulbs (CFLs). To remove any element
of consumer choice in the matter, the recent passage of the energy bill
will phase out the old bulbs and force consumers to purchase only the
federally approved CFLs. While CFLs are said to last longer and reduce
power-plant emissions of carbon dioxide, they have a number of draw-
backs. Not only is the initial cost of a CFL bulb up to ten times higher,
but they emit far less light. CFLs also contain the toxic element mercury,
which means they may require special means of disposal and pose a
health risk should they break.

What you eat is also a target. Animal rights groups want people to 7
adopt a vegan diet because they consider farm animals a significant
source of "greenhouse gases." People for the Ethical Treatment of Animals (PETA) is even criticizing Al Gore—who won the Nobel Peace Prize
for his global warming activism—for ignoring this alleged connection.
The ads show an image of Gore holding a chicken drumstick with a
tagline: "Too Chicken to Go Vegetarian? Meat Is the No. 1 Cause of
Global Warming."

Despite the numerous flaws and ambiguities in trying to link human 8
behavior and global warming, activists and their allies in govenment use
emotion and alarmism to make their case. They are seeking to cut off
any reasonable debate and silence their critics by saying these people are
motivated by corporate and personal greed and don't care about pollution. That, however, is hardly the case.

Critics of the global warming agenda are motivated instead by a 9
love of freedom and civil liberties. They want a discussion based on logic
and facts that will address any problems without depriving us of liberty
and personal choice. They do not want to sacrifice our way of life based
on fears of an unproven theory.

After all, the loss of liberty is a greater cause of alarm than global 10
warming.

—Deneen Borelli, *The National Center
for Public Policy Research*

8g Recognizing fallacies

Fallacies—errors in argument—fall into two groups. Some evade the issue of the argument. Others treat the argument as if it were much simpler than it is.

Exercise

1 Recognizing evasions

The central claim of an argument defines an issue or question: Should real estate development be controlled? Should drug testing be mandatory in the workplace? An effective argument faces the central issue squarely with relevant opinions, beliefs, and evidence. An ineffective argument dodges the issue.

arg
8g

Begging the question

A writer **begs the question** by treating an opinion that is open to question as if it were already proved or disproved. In essence, the writer begs readers to accept his or her ideas from the start.

> The college library's expenses should be reduced by cutting subscriptions to useless periodicals. [Begged questions: Are some of the library's periodicals useless? Useless to whom?]

> The fact is that political campaign financing is too corrupt to be reformed. [Begged questions: How corrupt is campaign financing? Does corruption, even if extensive, put campaign financing beyond reform?]

Non sequitur

In a **non sequitur** a writer asserts or implies a connection between ideas when no logical relation exists. *Non sequitur* means "it does not follow" in Latin: the second idea does not follow from the first. Usually the problem is an unstated assumption that links the ideas but is false, as in these examples:

> She uses a wheelchair, so she must be unhappy. [Unstated assumption: People who use wheelchairs are unhappy.]

> Kathleen Newsome has my vote for mayor because she has the best-run campaign organization. [Unstated assumption: A good campaign organization means that the candidate is well qualified for the job.]

Red herring

A **red herring** is literally a kind of fish that might be drawn across a path to distract a bloodhound from a scent it's following. In argument, a red herring is an irrelevant issue intended to distract readers from the relevant issues. The writer changes the subject rather than pursue the argument.

Checklist of fallacies

Checklist

Evasions

- **Begging the question:** treating an opinion that is open to question as if it were already proved or disproved.
- **Non sequitur** ("it does not follow"): drawing a conclusion based on a false assumption.
- **Red herring:** introducing an irrelevant issue to distract readers.
- **False authority:** citing as expert opinion the views of a person who is not an expert.
- **Inappropriate appeals:**

  Appealing to readers' fear or pity.
  Snob appeal: appealing to readers' wish to be like those who are more intelligent, famous, rich, and so on.
  Bandwagon: appealing to readers' wish to be part of the group.
  Flattery: appealing to readers' intelligence, taste, and so on.
  Argument ad populum ("to the people"): appealing to readers' general values, such as patriotism or love of family.
  Argument ad hominem ("to the man"): attacking the opponent rather than the opponent's argument.

Oversimplifications

- **Hasty generalization** (jumping to a conclusion): asserting an opinion based on too little evidence.
- **Sweeping generalization:** asserting an opinion as applying to all instances when it may apply to some, or to none. **Absolute statements** and **stereotypes** are variations.
- **Reductive fallacy:** generally, oversimplifying causes and effects.
- **Post hoc fallacy:** assuming that *A* caused *B* because *A* preceded *B*.
- **Either/or fallacy (false dilemma):** reducing a complicated question to two alternatives.
- **False analogy:** exaggerating the similarities in an analogy or ignoring key differences.

A campus speech code is essential to protect students, who already have enough problems coping with rising tuition. [Tuition costs and speech codes are different subjects. What protections do students need that a speech code will provide?]

Instead of developing a campus speech code that will infringe on students' First Amendment rights, administrators should be figuring out how to prevent yet another tuition increase. [Again, tuition costs and speech codes are different subjects. How would the code infringe on rights?]

False authority

Arguments often cite as evidence the opinions of people who are experts on the subject (see p. 191). But writers use **false authority** when they cite as an expert someone whose expertise is doubtful or nonexistent.

Jason Bing, a recognized expert in corporate finance, maintains that pharmaceutical companies do not test their products thoroughly enough. [Bing's expertise in corporate finance bears no apparent relation to the testing of pharmaceuticals.]

According to Helen Liebowitz, the Food and Drug Administration has approved sixty dangerous drugs in the last two years alone. [Who is Helen Liebowitz? On what authority does she make this claim?]

Inappropriate appeals

Appeals to readers' emotions are common in effective arguments. But such appeals must be relevant and must supplement rather than substitute for facts, examples, and other evidence.

Writers sometimes ignore the question with **appeals to readers' fear or pity.**

arg
8g

By electing Susan Clark to the city council, you will prevent the city's economic collapse. [Trades on people's fears. Can Clark singlehandedly prevent economic collapse? Is collapse even likely?]

She should not have to pay taxes because she is an aged widow with no friends or relatives. [Appeals to people's pity. Should age and loneliness, rather than income, determine a person's tax obligation?]

Sometimes writers ignore the question by appealing to readers' sense of what other people believe or do. One approach is **snob appeal,** inviting readers to accept an assertion in order to be identified with others they admire.

As any literate person knows, James Joyce is the best twentieth-century novelist. [But what qualities of Joyce's writing make him a superior novelist?]

Blake Lively has an account at Big City Bank, and so should you. [A celebrity's endorsement does not guarantee the worth of a product, a service, an idea, or anything else.]

A similar tactic invites readers to accept an assertion because everybody else does. This is the **bandwagon approach.**

As everyone knows, marijuana use leads to heroin addiction. [What is the evidence?]

Yet another diversion involves **flattery** of readers, in a way inviting them to join in a conspiracy.

We all understand campus problems well enough to see the disadvantages of such a policy. [What are the disadvantages of the policy?]

The **argument ad populum** ("argument to the people") asks readers to accept a conclusion based on shared values or even prejudices and nothing else.

Any truly patriotic American will support the President's action. [But why is the action worth taking?]

One final and very common kind of inappropriate emotional appeal addresses *not* the pros and cons of the issue itself but the real or imagined negative qualities of the people who hold the opposing view. This kind of argument is called **ad hominem,** Latin for "to the man."

One of the scientists has been treated for emotional problems, so his pessimism about nuclear waste merits no attention. [Do the scientist's previous emotional problems invalidate his current views?]

arg
8g

2 Recognizing oversimplifications

To **oversimplify** is to conceal or ignore complexities in a vain attempt to create a neater, more convincing argument than reality allows.

Hasty generalization

A **hasty generalization,** also called **jumping to a conclusion,** is a claim based on too little evidence or on evidence that is unrepresentative. (See also p. 193.)

It is disturbing that several of the youths who shot up schools were users of violent video games. Obviously, these games can breed violence, and they should be banned. [A few cases do not establish the relation between the games and violent behavior. Most youths who play violent video games do not behave violently.]

From the way it handled this complaint, we can assume that the consumer protection office has little intention of protecting consumers. [One experience with the office does not demonstrate its intention or overall performance.]

Sweeping generalization

Whereas a hasty generalization comes from inadequate evidence, a **sweeping generalization** probably is not supportable at all. One kind of sweeping generalization is the **absolute statement** involving words such as *all, always, never,* and *no one* that allow no exceptions. Rarely can evidence support such terms. Moderate words such as *some, sometimes, rarely,* and *few* are more reasonable.

Another common sweeping generalization is the **stereotype,** a conventional and oversimplified characterization of a group of people.

People who live in cities are unfriendly.
Californians are fad-crazy.
Women are emotional.
Men can't express their feelings.

(See also pp. 529–32 on sexist and other biased language.)

Reductive fallacy

The **reductive fallacy** oversimplifies (or reduces) the relation between causes and their effects. The fallacy (sometimes called **oversimplification**) often involves linking two events as if one caused the other directly, whereas the causes may be more complex or the relation may not exist at all. For example:

> Poverty causes crime. [If so, then why do people who are not poor commit crimes? And why aren't all poor people criminals?]
>
> The better a school's athletic facilities are, the worse its academic programs are. [The sentence assumes a direct cause-and-effect link between athletics and scholarship.]

Post hoc fallacy

arg

8g

Related to the reductive fallacy is the assumption that because *A* preceded *B*, then *A* must have caused *B*. This fallacy is called in Latin *post hoc, ergo propter hoc*, meaning "after this, therefore because of this," or the **post hoc fallacy** for short.

> In the two months since he took office, Mayor Holcomb has allowed crime in the city to increase by 12%. [The increase in crime is probably attributable to conditions existing before Holcomb took office.]
>
> The town council erred in permitting the adult bookstore to open, for shortly afterward two women were assaulted. [It cannot be assumed without evidence that the women's assailants visited or were influenced by the bookstore.]

Either/or fallacy

In the **either/or fallacy** (also called **false dilemma**), the writer assumes that a complicated question has only two answers, one good and one bad, both bad, or both good.

> City police officers are either brutal or corrupt. [Most city police officers are neither.]
>
> Either we permit mandatory drug testing in the workplace or productivity will continue to decline. [Productivity is not necessarily dependent on drug testing.]

False analogy

An **analogy** is a comparison between two essentially unlike things for the purpose of definition or illustration. In arguing by analogy, a writer draws a likeness between things on the basis of a single shared feature and then extends the likeness to other features. For instance, the "war on drugs" equates a battle against a foe with a program to eradicate (or at least reduce) sales and use of illegal drugs. Both involve an enemy, a strategy of overpowering the enemy, a desired goal, officials in uniform, and other similarities.

Analogy can only illustrate a point, never prove it: just because things are similar in one respect, they are not *necessarily* alike in other respects. In the fallacy called **false analogy,** the writer assumes such a complete likeness. Here is the analogy of the war on drugs taken to its false extreme:

> To win the war on drugs, we must wage more of a military-style operation. Prisoners of war are locked up without the benefit of a trial by jury, and drug dealers should be, too. Soldiers shoot their enemy on sight, and officials who encounter big drug operators should be allowed to shoot them, too. Military traitors may be executed, and corrupt law enforcers could be, too.

arg
8h

Exercise

Exercise 8.2   Identifying and revising fallacies

Fallacies tend to appear together, as each of the following sentences illustrates. Identify at least one fallacy in each sentence. Then revise the sentences to make them more reasonable.

1. The American government can sell nuclear technology to nonnuclear nations, so why can't individuals, who after all have a God-given right to earn a living as they see fit?
2. A successful marriage demands a maturity that no one under twenty-five possesses.
3. Students' persistent complaints about the grading system prove that it is unfair.
4. People watch television because they are too lazy to talk or read or because they want mindless escape from their lives.
5. Racial tension is bound to occur when people with different backgrounds are forced to live side by side.

Exercise 8.3   Identifying fallacies in arguments

Analyze the two arguments on pages 196–98 for fallacies. To what extent do any fallacies weaken either argument? Explain.

Exercise 8.4   Identifying fallacies online

Exercise

At *blogsearch.google.com* or *groups.yahoo.com,* find a conversation about drug testing in the workplace, environmental pollution, violence in the media, or any other subject that interests you and that is debatable. Read through the arguments made in the conversation, noting the fallacies you see. List the fallacious statements as well as the types of fallacies they illustrate, keeping in mind that a given statement may illustrate more than a single type.

8h   Reading visual arguments

Arguments can be visual as well as verbal. Advertisements often provide the most vivid and memorable examples of visual argument, but writers in almost every field—from astronomy to music to physiology—support their claims with photographs, charts, graphs, diagrams, and other figures.

Like a written argument, a visual argument has three main elements: claims, evidence, and assumptions. To read visual arguments critically, you analyze all three elements.

1 Testing claims

Sample document

Claims are positive statements that require support (see pp. 187, 188–90). In a visual argument, claims may be made by composition as well as by content, with or without accompanying words. Here are a few examples of visual claims:

arg

8h

Visual	A magnetic sticker shaped like a ribbon and decorated with the colors and symbols of the American flag, positioned prominently on a car.
Claim	I support American troops overseas, and you should, too.
Visual	A photograph framing hundreds of chickens crammed into small cages, resembling familiar images of World War II concentration camps.
Claim	Commercial poultry-raising practices are cruel and unethical.
Visual	A chart with dramatically contrasting bars that represent the optimism, stress, and weight reported by people before and after they participated in a program of daily walking.
Claim	Daily exercise leads to a healthier and happier life.
Visual	A cartoon featuring affluent-looking young adults on an affluent-looking college campus, conversing and frowning sadly as they gaze downhill at rough-looking teens in a dilapidated schoolyard. The caption reads, "Yes, it's sad what's happening to schools today. But everyone knows that throwing money at the problem isn't the solution."
Claim	Better funding makes for better schools.

The advertisement on the next page is one in the "Army Strong" series that the United States Army runs for recruitment. As noted in the annotations, the ad makes several claims both in the photograph and in the text.

2 Weighing evidence

The kinds of evidence provided in visuals parallel those found in written arguments (see pp. 190–92):

Sample document

■ **Facts can be verified by observation or research.** In visual arguments facts may be data, as in a graph showing a five-year rise in oil prices or in the text of the US Army advertisement promising "one of over 150 career opportunities." Facts may also be based

Claims in a visual

Visual claim: Serving in the US Army requires technical knowledge and skill.

Visual claim: The US Army provides soldiers with technical knowledge and skill.

Text claim: Service in the US Army can give soldiers technical expertise that they may have thought was beyond them.

BELIEVING IN YOURSELF IS STRONG.
ACHIEVING WHAT YOU NEVER
BELIEVED POSSIBLE IS ARMY STRONG.

There's strong. And then there's Army Strong.
There is no limit to the things you can learn from one of over 150 career
opportunities available to you in the Army. You can also receive money for college.
Find out more at goarmy.com/strong.

U.S. ARMY
ARMY STRONG.

Advertisement by the United States Army

on or inferred from data, as in the statement that the army provides "money for college."

■ **Examples illustrate and reinforce a point.** Visual arguments often focus on an instance of the argument's claims. In the army ad, the soldier using and surrounded by technical equipment is an example supporting the claim that the army gives soldiers technical training.

■ **Expert opinions** are the findings of subject-matter authorities based on their research and experience. A visual argument might present a chart from an expert showing a trend in, say, unemployment among high school graduates.

■ **Appeals to beliefs or needs** reinforce readers' values or truths. Many visual arguments appeal to beliefs about how things ought to be (for instance, an antidrug ad featuring a teenager refusing peer pressure) or how things should not be (a Web site for an antihunger campaign featuring images of emaciated children).

When you read a visual as an argument, judge the evidence with the same criteria as for a written argument. Use the following questions:

- **Is the evidence accurate?** Analyze a visual for its fairness, precision, and trustworthiness. For example, a graph claiming to show changes in college living expenses between 2000 and 2010 should identify the source and purpose of the research, supply data for all the years, and clarify the definition of *living expenses* (the cost of room and board only, or transportation, recreation, and other expenses as well?).

- **Is the evidence relevant and adequate?** Ask whether the visual pertains to the claims made in the larger argument and sufficiently demonstrates its own claims. In an article on eating disorders, for instance, a relevant and adequate visual might be a graph showing average weights and heights of people who have anorexia. However, a photograph of a skinny celebrity would be merely sensationalistic unless the subject had publicly confirmed that her low weight resulted from an eating disorder.

8h

- **Does the evidence represent the context?** Check whether the visual reflects the full range of the sample it's drawn from and does not overrepresent or hide important elements of the subject. For example, the US Army ad conveys the soldier's ease and competence with technical equipment, which is presumably the result of his training. At the same time, the photo and text do not address the possible disadvantages of military service, such as separation from family, injury, or even death.

The annotation on the following graph demonstrates one way of analyzing visual evidence for this claim: *The teen birthrate has dropped steadily since 1990.* The data come from the Centers for Disease Control and Prevention (CDC), a US agency and a reputable source. But the data are incomplete, so the graph is misleading.

Incomplete and unreliable evidence in a visual

The graph shows a steady decrease in birthrate, as claimed, but 2005 is not very recent. In fact, later data showed *increases* in the birthrate—facts that undercut the claim about a steady decline since 1990.

Sample
document

arg

8h

3 Discovering assumptions

Like a written argument, a visual argument is based on **assumptions**—the creator's ideas, often unstated, about why the evidence relates to the claims (see pp. 194–95). In visual arguments many assumptions involve the creator's beliefs about the audience, as detailed below. The examples analyze the US Army ad on page 206.

- ▣ **Who readers are and where they will see the argument.** The army ad has appeared in magazines with young adult readers who might be interested in the possibility of training, education, and life change.
- ▣ **What readers already know about the subject.** Although most readers are familiar with the military, the army presumably considers readers less familiar with its opportunities for training and life change.
- ▣ **How familiar readers are with the purpose, format, and style of the argument.** With hundreds of print, TV, and online ads, the "Army Strong" campaign has become a fixture in US culture. Each new ad fits into the framework established by its predecessors.
- ▣ **Whether readers are likely to lean toward the argument's claims.** The advertiser clearly assumes that the photograph in the ad will attract the attention of young men and women who are interested in technology. At the same time, it seems to assume that readers need to be persuaded to join the army.
- ▣ **What kinds of information, ideas, and images readers will find persuasive.** The advertiser seems to assume that a strictly factual claim about the benefits of joining the army would not be persuasive enough to readers, so it combines a headline and photo that emphasize appealing qualities of competence, strength, and personal development.

4 Recognizing fallacies

Fallacies, or errors in argument, are sometimes accidental, but they are often used deliberately to manipulate readers' responses. All the fallacies of written arguments discussed on pages 199–204 may appear in visual arguments as well. Here we'll focus on examples of the two main categories.

Evasions

Evasions attempt to deflect the reader from the central claim of the argument. One evasion is **snob appeal,** inviting readers to think or be like someone they admire. Look again at the US Army ad on page 206. The soldier is clearly comfortable and competent with the equipment, and the ad appeals to the reader's wish to be someone who is equally as capable and fulfilled. If you join the US Army, the ad says subtly, you too may become strong. The ad does have some substance in its specific and verifiable claim of "over 150 career opportunities" and "money for college," but the soldier in quiet command of his equipment makes a stronger claim.

Oversimplifications

Oversimplifications imply that subjects are less complex than they are. An example is the **hasty generalization,** a claim that is based on too little evidence or that misrepresents the facts. The fallacy appears in the following graph, which is intended to support this claim: *After a steep decline over the preceding five years, the teen birthrate shot up in 2006 and 2007.* At first, the graph appears to demonstrate the claim, but a close look reveals that it—as well as the claim it supports—badly misrepresents the data.

arg
8h

Fallacy in a visual

The vertical axis lacks a zero point and covers a small span, thus misrepresenting and exaggerating both the decline and the increase in the birthrate.

The corrected graph below uses exactly the same data, but they tell a different story because they are presented without manipulation.

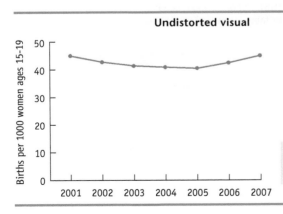

Undistorted visual

The vertical axis starts at zero and covers a large span, thus showing accurately just a gradual decline and a slight increase.

Exercise 8.5 Reading a visual argument

The following advertisement (a billboard) is from a campaign to discourage drunk driving. Examine the ad closely and jot down your answers to the following questions.

1. Who appears to be the intended audience?
2. What claim does the ad make about language and behavior?
3. What evidence supports the claim? How effective is it?
4. What assumptions underlie the argument, connecting evidence to claims?
5. How does the visual organization (repetition of the photograph, placement of the text) make the argument more or less effective?
6. Is the argument persuasive to you? Why or why not?

arg

8h

Exercise 8.6 Identifying fallacies in visual arguments

Locate a current or historical source with extreme views on a subject, such as a sensationalist tabloid newspaper or an example of wartime propaganda (from any nation or era). Photocopy or print a visual that seems especially rife with fallacies and, referring to the complete list of fallacies on page 200, find as many as possible in the visual. The following sites can help you begin your search:

Tabloids

National Enquirer (US): *nationalenquirer.com*
Daily Mail (Great Britain): *www.dailymail.co.uk*

World War II propaganda

Northwestern University (American images): *digital.library.northwestern.edu/ wwii-posters*

Calvin College (German images): *www.calvin.edu/academic/cas/gpa*

9

Writing an Argument

In composing an argument, you try to clarify an issue or solve a problem by finding the common ground between you and your readers. Using critical thinking, you develop and test your own ideas. Using a variety of techniques, you engage readers in an attempt to narrow the distance between your views and theirs.

9a Finding a subject

An argument subject must be arguable—that is, reasonable people will disagree over it and be able to support their positions with evidence. This sentence implies a number of *do*s and *don't*s:

Exercise

Tests for an argument subject

A good subject:

- Concerns a matter of opinion—a conclusion drawn from evidence.
- Can be disputed: others might take a different position.
- *Will* be disputed: it is controversial.
- Is something you care about and know about or want to research.
- Is narrow enough to argue in the space and time available.

A bad subject:

- Cannot be disputed because it concerns a fact, such as the distance to Saturn or the functions of the human liver.
- Cannot be disputed because it concerns a personal preference or belief, such as a liking for a certain vacation spot or a moral commitment to vegetarianism.
- *Will not* be disputed because few if any disagree over it—the virtues of a secure home, for instance.

Video tutorial

Additional help on subjects for writing appears earlier in this book:

- Working with a specific assignment, pages 14–15.
- Working with a general assignment, page 15.
- Narrowing a subject to a question, pages 15–17.

mycomplab

Visit *mycomplab.com* for the eText and for resources and more exercises on writing arguments.

CULTURE LANGUAGE Choosing a subject for argument may seem difficult if you're not familiar with what people in the United States find debatable. One way to find a subject is to scout online discussion groups, such as those listed at *groups.yahoo.com*, for subjects on which there is a range of opinion. Another approach is to read a newspaper every day for at least a week, looking for issues that involve or interest you. Following the development of the issues in articles, editorials, and letters to the editor will give you a sense of how controversial they are, what the positions are, and what your position might be.

arg
9b

✳
Exercise

Exercise 9.1 Finding a subject for argument

Explain why each subject below is or is not appropriate for argument. Refer to the box on the previous page if you need help.

1. Granting of athletic scholarships
2. Care of automobile tires
3. Censoring the Web sites of hate groups
4. History of the town park
5. Housing for the homeless
6. Billboards in urban residential areas or in rural areas
7. Animal testing for cosmetics research
8. Cats versus dogs as pets
9. Ten steps in recycling wastepaper
10. Benefits of being a parent

9b Conceiving a thesis statement

The **thesis** is the main idea of your paper (see pp. 36–40). In an argument the **thesis statement** makes the claim that you want your readers to accept or act on. Here are two thesis statements on the same subject:

> The new room fees are unjustified given the condition of the dormitories.

> The administration should postpone the new room fees at least until conditions in the dormitories are improved.

Your thesis statement must satisfy the same requirements as your subject (see the box on the previous page). But it must also specify the basis for your claim. In both thesis statements above, the basis for protesting the room fees is that the dorms are in poor condition.

Note that the writer of either of these arguments must clarify the definition of *condition(s)* if the argument is to be clear and reasonable. Always take pains to define abstract and general terms that are central to your argument, preferably in or just after the thesis statement. (See p. 190.)

Exercise 9.2 Conceiving a thesis statement

For each subject in Exercise 9.1 that you deemed arguable, draft a tentative thesis statement that specifies the basis for an argument. If you prefer, choose five arguable subjects of your own and draft a thesis statement for each one. One thesis statement should interest you enough to develop into a complete argument in later exercises.

9c Analyzing your purpose and your audience

Your purpose in argument is, broadly, to engage readers in order to convince them of your position or persuade them to act. But arguments have more specific purposes as well, such as the following:

To strengthen the commitment of existing supporters
To win new supporters from the undecided or uninformed
To get the opposition to reconsider
To inspire supporters to act
To deter the undecided from acting

It's no accident that each of these purposes characterizes the audience (*existing supporters, the undecided,* and so on). In argument, even more than in other kinds of writing, achieving your purpose depends on the response of your readers, so you need a sense of who they are and where they stand. The "Questions about audience" on pages 20–21 can help you identify readers' knowledge, beliefs, and other pertinent information. In addition, you need to know how readers stand on your subject—not only whether they agree or disagree generally, but also which specific assertions they will find more or less convincing.

Your purpose can help you fill in this information. If you decide to address supporters or opponents, you essentially select readers with certain inclinations and ignore other readers who may tune in. If you decide to win new supporters from those who are undecided on your topic, you'll have to imagine skeptical readers who will be convinced only by an argument that is detailed, logical, and fair. Like you when you read an argument critically, these skeptical readers seek to be reasoned with, not manipulated into a position or hammered over the head.

Exercise 9.3 Analyzing purpose and audience
Specify a purpose and a likely audience for the thesis statement you chose to develop in Exercise 9.2. What do purpose and audience suggest about the way you should develop the argument?

9d Using reason

As a reader of argument, you seek evidence for the writer's claims and clear reasoning about the relationship of evidence to claims. As a writer of argument, you seek to provide what the reader needs in a way that furthers your case.

The thesis of your argument is a conclusion you reach by reasoning about evidence. Two common processes of reasoning are

Student
paper

arg
9d

induction and deduction—methods of thinking that you use all the time even if you don't know their names. You can think of induction and deduction as two different ways of moving among claims, evidence, and assumptions—the elements of argument derived from Stephen Toulmin's work (pp. 186–87).

1 Reasoning inductively

When you're about to buy a used car, you consult friends, relatives, and consumer guides before deciding what kind of car to buy. Using **inductive reasoning,** you make specific observations about cars (your evidence) and you induce, or infer, a **generalization** (or claim) that Model X is the most reliable. Writing a paper on the effectiveness of print advertising, you might also use inductive reasoning:

> First analyze statistics on advertising in print, on the Web, and in other media (evidence).
>
> Then read comments by advertisers, publishers, and others who place and sell advertising (more evidence).
>
> Finally, form a conclusion that print remains the most cost-effective advertising medium (generalization).

This reasoning builds from the evidence to the claim, with assumptions connecting evidence to claim. By predicting something about the unknown based on what you know, you create new knowledge out of old.

Inductive reasoning

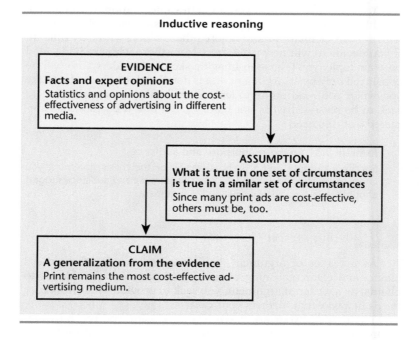

The more evidence you accumulate, the more probable it is that your generalization is true. Note, however, that absolute certainty is not possible. At some point you must *assume* that your evidence justifies your generalization, for yourself and your readers. Most errors in inductive reasoning involve oversimplifying either the evidence or the generalization. See pages 199–204 on fallacies.

2 Reasoning deductively

You use **deductive reasoning** when you proceed from your generalization that Model X is the most reliable used car to your own specific circumstances (you want to buy a used car) to the conclusion (or claim) that you should buy a Model X car. Like induction, deduction uses the elements of argument—claims, evidence, and assumptions—but with it you apply old information to new.

arg
9d

Deductive reasoning

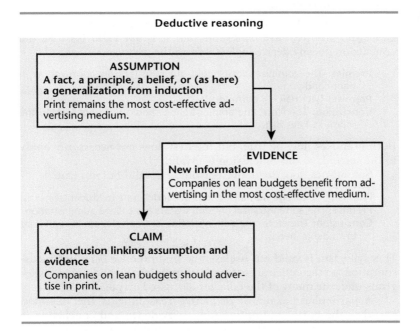

The deductive syllogism

The conventional way of displaying a deductive argument is in a **syllogism:**

Premise: All human beings are mortal. [A generalization, fact, principle, or belief that you assume to be true.]
Premise: I am a human being. [New information: a specific case of the first premise.]
Conclusion: Therefore, I am mortal.

As long as the premises of a syllogism are true, the conclusion derives logically and certainly from them. If you want the school administration to postpone new room fees for one dormitory, your deductive argument might be expressed in this syllogism:

> **Premise:** The administration should not raise fees on dorm rooms in poor condition.
> **Premise:** The rooms in Polk Hall are in poor condition.
> **Conclusion:** Therefore, the administration should not raise fees on the rooms in Polk Hall.

The force of deductive reasoning depends on the reliability of the premises and the care taken to apply them in drawing conclusions. The reasoning process is **valid** if the premises lead logically to the conclusion. It is **true** if the premises are believable.

<table><tr><td>arg
9d</td></tr></table>

Problems with syllogisms

Sometimes the reasoning in a deductive argument is true because the premises are believable, but it is *not* valid because the conclusion doesn't derive logically from the premises:

> **Premise:** The administration should not raise fees on dorm rooms in poor condition.
> **Premise:** Tyler Hall is a dormitory.
> **Conclusion:** Therefore, the administration should not raise fees on the rooms in Tyler Hall.

Both premises may be true, but the first does not *necessarily* apply to the second, so the conclusion is invalid.

Sometimes, too, deductive reasoning is valid but *not* true:

> **Premise:** All college administrations are indifferent to students' needs.
> **Premise:** The administration of Central State is a college administration.
> **Conclusion:** Therefore, the administration of Central State is indifferent to students' needs.

This syllogism is valid but useless: the first premise is an untrue assumption, so the entire argument is untrue. Invalid and untrue syllogisms underlie many of the fallacies discussed on pages 199–204.

A particular hazard of deductive reasoning is the **unstated premise:** the basic assumption linking evidence and conclusion is not stated but implied. Here the unstated premise is believable and the argument is reasonable:

> Ms. Stein has worked with drug addicts for fifteen years, so she knows a great deal about their problems. [Unstated premise: Anyone who has worked fifteen years with drug addicts knows about their problems.]

But when the unstated premise is wrong or unfounded, the argument is false. For example:

> As a senator, Jane Lightbow must receive money illegally from lobbyists. [Unstated premise: All senators receive money illegally from lobbyists.]

Tests for inductive and deductive reasoning

Induction

Video
tutorial

- Have you stated your evidence clearly?
- Is your evidence complete enough and good enough to justify your claim? What is the assumption that connects evidence and claim? Is it believable?
- Have you avoided fallacies?

Deduction

- What are the premises leading to your conclusion? Look especially for unstated premises.
- What does the first premise assume? Is the assumption believable?
- Does the first premise necessarily apply to the second premise?
- Is the second premise believable?
- Have you avoided fallacies?

arg

9d

To avoid such false conclusions, you may be tempted to make your claims sound more reasonable. But even a conclusion that sounds reasonable must be supportable. For instance, changing *must* to *might* modifies the unstated assumption about Senator Lightbow:

> As a senator, Jane Lightbow might receive money illegally from lobbyists. [Unstated premise: *Some* senators receive money illegally from lobbyists.]

But it does not necessarily follow that Senator Lightbow is one of the "some." The sentence, though logical, is not truly reasonable unless evidence demonstrates that Senator Lightbow should be linked with illegal activities.

Exercise 9.4 Reasoning inductively

Study the facts below and then evaluate each of the numbered conclusions on the next page. Which of the generalizations are reasonable given the evidence, and which are not? Why?

Exercise

In 2009–10 each American household viewed a weekly average of 58 hours and 10 minutes of television (including DVDs and videos.)

Each individual viewed an average of 19 hours and 21 minutes every week.

Those viewing the most television per week (31 hours and 27 minutes) were women over age 55.

Those viewing the least television per week (15 hours and 54 minutes) were children ages 6–12.

Households earning under $30,000 a year watched an average of 59 hours and 57 minutes a week.

Households earning more than $60,000 a year watched an average of 56 hours and 32 minutes a week.

1. Households with incomes under $30,000 tend to watch more television than average.
2. Women watch more television than men.
3. Nonaffluent people watch less television than affluent people.
4. Women over age 55 tend to watch more television than average.
5. Children watch less television than critics generally assume.

Exercise 9.5 Reasoning deductively

Convert each of the following statements into a syllogism. (You may have to state unstated assumptions.) Use the syllogism to evaluate both the validity and the truth of the statement.

Example:

DiSantis is a banker, so he does not care about the poor.

Premise: Bankers do not care about the poor.
Premise: DiSantis is a banker.
Conclusion: Therefore, DiSantis does not care about the poor.

The statement is untrue because the first premise is untrue.

1. The mayor opposed pollution controls when he was president of a manufacturing company, so he may not support new controls or vigorously enforce existing ones.
2. Information on corporate Web sites is unreliable because the sites are sponsored by for-profit entities.
3. Schroeder is a good artist because she trained at Parsons, like many other good artists.
4. Wealthy athletes who use their resources to help others deserve our particular appreciation.
5. Jimson is clearly a sexist because she has hired only one woman.

9e Using evidence

Whether your argument is reasonable or not depends heavily on the evidence you marshal to support it. The kinds of evidence and the criteria for evaluating evidence are discussed in detail on pages 190–94. Finding evidence is discussed under research writing on pages 587–610. Evaluating sources of evidence, including Web and other online sources, is discussed under research writing on pages 612–25.

The kind and quantity of evidence you use should be determined by your purpose, your subject, and the needs of your audience. Some arguments, such as an appeal for volunteer help in a soup kitchen, will rely most heavily on examples (including perhaps a narrative of your own experience) and on appeals to readers' beliefs. Other arguments, such as a proposal for mandatory side air bags in cars, will rely much more on statistics and expert opinions. Most arguments, including these, will mingle facts, examples, expert opinions, and appeals to readers' beliefs and needs.

In using evidence for argument, you'll need to be especially wary of certain traps that carelessness or zeal can lure you into. These traps are described in the following box.

Responsible use of evidence

Video tutorial

- ■ **Don't distort.** You mislead readers when you twist evidence to suit your argument—for instance, when you claim that crime in your city occurs five times more often than it did in 1955, without mentioning that the population is also seven times larger.
- ■ **Don't stack the deck.** Ignoring damning evidence is like cheating at cards. You must deal forthrightly with the opposition. (See pp. 221–22.)
- ■ **Don't exaggerate.** Watch your language. Don't attempt to manipulate readers by characterizing your own evidence as *pure* and *rock-solid* and the opposition's as *ridiculous* and *half-baked*. Make the evidence speak for itself.
- ■ **Don't oversimplify.** Avoid forcing the evidence to support more than it can. (See also pp. 202–04.)
- ■ **Don't misquote.** When you cite experts, quote them accurately and fairly.

arg

9f

Exercise 9.6 Using reason and evidence in your argument

Develop the structure and evidence for the argument you began in Exercises 9.2 and 9.3 (pp. 212 and 213). (You may want to begin drafting at this stage.) Is your argument mainly inductive or mainly deductive? Use the box on page 217 to test the reasoning of the argument. Use the boxes on page 192 and above to test your evidence.

9f Reaching your readers

To reach your readers in argument, you appeal directly to their reason and emotions, you present yourself as someone worth heeding, and you account for views opposing your own.

1 Appealing to readers

In forming convictions about arguable issues, we generally interpret the factual evidence through the filter of our values, beliefs, tastes, desires, and feelings. You may object to placing the new town dump in a particular wooded area because the facts suggest that the site is not large enough and that prevailing winds will blow odors back through the town. But you may also have fond memories of playing in the wooded area as a child, feelings that color your interpretation of the facts and strengthen your conviction that the dump should be placed elsewhere. Your conviction is partly rational, because it is based on evidence, and partly emotional, because it is also based on feelings.

Rational and emotional appeals

In most arguments you will combine **rational appeals** to readers' capacities for reasoning logically between evidence and claims with **emotional appeals** to readers' beliefs and feelings. The following passages, all arguing the same view on the same subject, illustrate how either a primarily rational or a primarily emotional appeal may be weaker than an approach that uses both:

Rational appeal

Advertising should show more people who are physically challenged. The millions of Americans with disabilities have considerable buying power, yet so far advertisers have made no attempt to tap that power. [Appeals to the logic of financial gain.]

Emotional appeal

Advertising should show more people who are physically challenged. By keeping people with disabilities out of the mainstream depicted in ads, advertisers encourage widespread prejudice against disability, prejudice that frightens and demeans those who hold it. [Appeals to a sense of fairness and open-mindedness.]

Rational and emotional appeals

Advertising should show more people who are physically challenged. The millions of Americans with disabilities have considerable buying power, yet so far advertisers have made no attempt to tap that power. Further, by keeping people with disabilities out of the mainstream depicted in ads, advertisers encourage widespread prejudice against disability, prejudice that frightens and demeans those who hold it.

arg
9f

The third passage, in combining both kinds of appeal, gives readers both rational and emotional bases for agreeing with the writer.

For an emotional appeal to be successful, it must be appropriate for the audience and the argument:

- It must not misjudge readers' actual feelings.
- It must not raise emotional issues that are irrelevant to the claims and the evidence. See pages 201–02 for a discussion of specific inappropriate appeals, such as the bandwagon approach.

One further caution: Visuals and multimedia can reinforce your claims with a strong emotional appeal, but they must be relevant to your claims, and you must explain their relevance in your text and captions.

Ethical appeal

A third kind of approach to readers, the **ethical appeal**, is the sense you give of being a competent, fair, trustworthy person. A sound argument backed by ample evidence—a rational appeal—will convince readers of your knowledge and reasonableness. (So will your acknowledging the opposition. See the facing page.) Appropriate emotional appeals will demonstrate that you share readers' beliefs and needs. An argument that is concisely written and correct in grammar, spelling, and other matters will underscore your competence. In addition, a sincere and even tone will assure readers that you are a balanced person who wants to reason with them.

A sincere and even tone need not exclude language with emotional appeal—words such as *frightens* and *demeans* at the end of the third example on the previous page. But avoid certain forms of expression that will mark you as unfair:

- Insulting words, such as *idiotic* or *fascist*.
- Biased language, such as *rednecks* or *fags*. (See pp. 529–31.)
- Sarcasm—for instance, using the phrase *What a brilliant idea* to indicate contempt for the idea and its originator.
- Exclamation points! They'll make you sound shrill!

See also page 195 on tone.

arg
9f

2 Responding to opposing views

A good test of your fairness in argument is how you handle possible objections. Assuming your thesis is indeed arguable, then others can marshal their own evidence to support a different view or views. By dealing squarely with those opposing views, you show yourself to be honest and fair. You strengthen your ethical appeal and thus your entire argument.

Before or while you draft your essay, list for yourself all the opposing views you can think of. You'll find them in your research, by talking to friends and classmates, and by critically thinking about your own ideas. You can also look for a range of views in an online discussion that deals with your subject. Two places to start are the *Yahoo!* archive of discussion groups at *groups.yahoo.com* and the *Google* blog directory at *blogsearch.google.com*.

Rebutting opposing views

A common way to handle opposing views is to state them, refute those you can, grant the validity of others, and demonstrate why, despite their validity, the opposing views are less compelling than your own. The following paragraph illustrates this approach:

> For Springfield to become a first-rate academic institution, it will need to reduce its funding of intercollegiate sports in favor of academic programs. The athletic director argues against a reduction on the grounds that the team programs *Statement of opposing view*
>
> more than pay for themselves. It is true that the surpluses from the team programs have gone into the general university fund. *Concession that opposing view is partly valid*
>
> However, this argument misses the point that the team programs *Demonstration that opposing view is irrelevant*

demand too many resources to begin with for an institution whose main priorities should be academic. Some members of the athletic department have acknowledged that intercollegiate sports could manage with budget cuts of 20 percent. — Evidence for author's claim

Committing the savings to academic programs would establish a more appropriate balance between the competing goals of athletic power and academic strength. — Author's claim

Finding common ground

A somewhat different approach to addressing opposing views, developed by the psychologist Carl Rogers, emphasizes the search for common ground. A **Rogerian argument** can be especially helpful when you expect readers to resist your claims. You start by showing that you understand readers' views and by establishing points on which you and readers agree and disagree. Creating a connection in this way can encourage readers to hear you out as you argue your own claims. Recast as a Rogerian argument, the preceding example might read as follows:

The Springfield community thus seems united in the goal of making the university a first-rate academic institution, but it differs over whether to help pay for the needed improvements by reducing funds for intercollegiate sports. Most of us who support this step do value the sports, and we appreciate the athletic director's point that the team programs more than pay for themselves, contributing surpluses to the general university fund. — Focus on points of agreement

We certainly do not propose that the university abandon the sports altogether or even dramatically cut their funding. — Rejection of more extreme solutions

However, some members of the athletic department have acknowledged that intercollegiate sports could manage with budget cuts of 20 percent. — Evidence for author's claim

Thus we seek this manageable reduction so that Springfield can continue as a sports power while also putting more resources to work for academic excellence. — Author's claim

Exercise 9.7 Identifying appeals

Exercise

Identify each passage below as primarily a rational appeal or primarily an emotional appeal. Which passages make a strong ethical appeal as well?

1. Use of the Web may contribute to the global tendency toward breadth rather than depth of knowledge. Relying on those most essential skills—pointing and clicking—our brightest minds may now never encounter, much less read, the works of Plato and Shakespeare.
2. Thus the data collected by these researchers indicate that a mandatory sentence for illegal possession of handguns may lead to a reduction in handgun purchases.

3. Most broadcasters worry that further government regulation of television programming could breed censorship—certainly, an undesirable outcome. Yet most broadcasters also accept that children's television is a fair target for regulation.

4. Anyone who cherishes life in all its diversity could not help being appalled by the mistreatment of laboratory animals. The so-called scientists who run the labs are misguided.

5. Many experts in constitutional law have warned that the rule violates the right to free speech. Yet other experts have viewed the rule, however regretfully, as necessary for the good of the community as a whole.

Exercise 9.8 Reaching your readers

Continuing your argument-in-progress from Exercise 9.6 (p. 219), analyze whether your claims are rational or emotional and whether the mix is appropriate for your audience and argument. Analyze your ethical appeal, too, considering whether it can be strengthened. Then make a list of possible opposing views. Think freely at first, not stopping to censor views that seem far-fetched or irrational. When your list is complete, decide which views must be taken seriously and why, and develop a response to each one.

arg

9g

9g Organizing your argument

All arguments include the same parts, but depending on the type of argument the organization can vary:

Student paper

■ **Introduction:** Commonly, the introduction establishes the significance of the subject or the scope of the problem, provides the background, and usually includes the thesis statement. However, if you think your readers may have difficulty accepting your thesis statement before they see at least some support for it, then it may come later in the paper. In a Rogerian argument, you might use the introduction to emphasize the common ground between you and readers and delay stating the thesis until the conclusion.

■ **Body:** The body paragraphs state and develop the claims supporting the thesis, using clearly relevant evidence. The arrangement of the claims can vary widely, as can their position relative to the response to opposing views. See the next page.

■ **Response to opposing views:** The response to opposing views details and addresses those views, finding common ground, demonstrating the arguments' greater strengths, or conceding the opponent's points. For some arguments, readers will be satisfied to see opposing views dealt with at the end. For others, each claim will invite its own objections, and those opposing views will need to be addressed claim by claim. When readers' resistance may be very strong, the Rogerian approach of discussing and conceding opposing views right away can establish a common understanding that opens readers to the argument's claims.

■ **Conclusion:** The conclusion completes the argument. Often it restates the thesis, summarizes the supporting claims, and makes a final appeal to readers. In a Rogerian argument, the conclusion often states the thesis as a solution, giving ground and inviting the audience to do the same.

For more on introductions and conclusions, see pages 110–15.

You may want to experiment with various organizations—for instance, trying out your strongest claims first or last in the body, stating claims outright or letting the evidence build to them, answering the opposition near the beginning or near the end or claim by claim. You can do this experimentation on paper, of course, but it's easier on a computer. Try rearranging your outline as described on page 37. Or try rearranging your draft (work with a copy) by cutting and pasting parts of it for different emphases.

arg
9h

Video tutorial

Organizing an argument's body and response to opposing views

A common scheme

Claim 1 and evidence
Claim 2 and evidence
Claim X and evidence
Response to opposing views

A variation

Claim 1 and evidence
Response to opposing views
Claim 2 and evidence
Response to opposing views
Claim X and evidence
Response to opposing views

The Rogerian scheme

Common ground and conces-
    sion to opposing views
Claim 1 and evidence
Claim 2 and evidence
Claim X and evidence

The problem-solution scheme

The problem: claims and evidence
The solution: claims and evidence
Response to opposing views

Exercise 9.9 Organizing your argument

Continuing from Exercise 9.8 (p. 223), develop a structure for your argument. Consider especially how you will introduce it, how you will arrange your claims, where you will place your responses to opposing views, and how you will conclude.

9h Revising your argument

When you revise your argument, do it in at least two stages—revising underlying meaning and structure, and editing more superficial elements. The checklists on pages 61 and 68–69 can be a guide. Supplement them with the checklist opposite, which encourages you to think critically about your own argument.

Checklist for revising an argument

Checklist

Thesis

- What is your thesis? Where is it stated?
- In what ways is your thesis statement an arguable claim?

Reasoning

- If your thesis derives from induction, where have you related the evidence to your generalization?
- If your thesis derives from deduction, is your syllogism both true and valid?
- Have you avoided fallacies in reasoning?

Evidence

- Where have you provided the evidence readers need?
- Where might your evidence not be accurate, relevant, representative, or adequate? (Answer this question from the point of view of a neutral or even skeptical reader.)

Appeals

- Where have you considered readers' probable beliefs and values?
- How are your rational appeals and emotional appeals appropriate for your readers?
- What is your ethical appeal? How can you improve it?

Opposing views

- What opposing views have you answered?
- How successfully have you refuted opposing views? (Again, consider the neutral or skeptical reader.)

Organization

- How clearly does your argument move from one point to the next?
- How appropriate is your organization, given the likely views of your readers?

arg
9i

Exercise 9.10 Writing and revising your argument
Draft and revise the argument you have developed in the exercises in this chapter. Use the revision checklists on page 61 and above to review your work.

9i Examining a sample argument

The following essay by the student Aimee Lee illustrates the principles discussed in this chapter. As you read the essay, notice especially the organization, the relation of claims and supporting evidence (including illustrations), the kinds of appeals Lee makes, and the ways she responds to opposing views.

Awareness, Prevention, Support:

A Proposal to Reduce Cyberbullying

Introduction: identification of the problem

My roommate and I sat in front of her computer staring at the vicious message under her picture. She quickly removed the tag that identified her, but the comments already posted on the photo proved that the damage was done. While she slept, my roommate had become the victim of a cyberbully. She had joined an increasing number of college students who are targeted in texts, e-mails, social-networking sites, and other Web sites that broadcast photographs, videos, and comments. My roommate's experi-

Thesis statement: proposal for a solution to the problem

ence alerted me that our campus needs a program aimed at awareness and prevention of cyberbullying and support for its victims.

Although schoolyard bullying typically ends with high school graduation, cyberbullying continues in college. According to data gathered by

Evidence of the problem: published research

researchers at the Massachusetts Aggression Reduction Center (MARC) of Bridgewater State College, cyberbullying behavior decreases when students enter college, but it does not cease. Examining the experiences of first-year students, the researchers found that 8% of college freshmen had been cyberbullied at college and 3% admitted to having cyberbullied another student (Englander, Mills, and McCoy 217-18). In a survey of fifty-two freshmen, I

Evidence of the problem: student's own research

found further evidence of cyberbullying on this campus. I asked two questions: (1) Have you been involved in cyberbullying as a victim, a bully, or both? (2) If you answered "no" to the first question, do you know anyone who has been involved in cyberbullying as a victim, a bully, or both? While a large majority of the students I surveyed (74%) have not been touched by cyberbullying, a significant number (26%) have been involved personally or know someone who has, as shown in fig. 1. Taken together, the evidence demonstrates that cyberbullying is significant in colleges and specifically on our campus.

Pie chart showing results of student's research

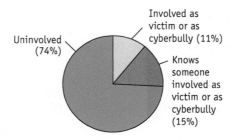

Uninvolved (74%)

Involved as victim or as cyberbully (11%)

Knows someone involved as victim or as cyberbully (15%)

Fig. 1. Involvement in cyberbullying among fifty-two first-year students.

Explanation of proposed solution: goals of the program

The proposed "Stop Cyberbullying" program aims to reduce the behavior through a month-long campaign of awareness, prevention, and support modeled on the college's "Alcohol Awareness Month" program. The program can raise awareness of cyberbullying by explaining what cyberbullying is and by informing students about the college's code of conduct, which prohibits cyberbullying behavior but which few people read. The program can work to prevent cyberbullying by appealing to students to treat those around them respectfully. And, with the participation of the counseling department, the program can provide support for victims, their friends, and others involved in the behavior.

If adopted, the program can use online and print media to get the message out to the entire college community. For instance, an extensive brochure distributed to first-year students and available through the counseling center can describe cyberbullying and how it violates the college's code of conduct, give strategies for avoiding it, and provide resources for help. During the month-long campaign, flyers posted on campus (see fig. 2) can also raise awareness of the problem, and brief postings to the college's Web site, *Facebook* page, and *Twitter* feed can reach students who take online and hybrid classes as well as those in traditional classes.

Explanation of proposed solution: specific actions

arg
9i

Have YOU been a victim of cyberbullying? Have you read something about yourself that made you feel embarrassed, intimidated, or just bad?

Are YOU a cyberbully? Have you sent a message or posted something that you knew would make someone feel embarrassed, intimidated, or just bad?

Do YOU know someone who is being cyberbullied or who is bullying somone else?

Together WE can BREAK the cycle:
• **Wait before you post!** Think about who may read it and how they might respond.
• **Be informed about our campus code of conduct** and what it says about cyberbullying.
• **Get help if you need it.** The counseling office is available to help you cope with or stop cyberbullying.

**You can help
stop cyberbullying**
www.mrcc.edu/cyberbullying

STOP

Visual evidence of program publicity

Fig. 2. Sample flyer for proposed "Stop Cyberbullying" program.

Because this college already has a code of conduct in place and because the state has recently enacted anti-bullying legislation that includes cyberbullying, some students and administrators may contend that enough is being done to deal with the problem. To the administration's credit, the code of conduct contains specific language about online behavior, but promises of punishment for proven allegations do not address several aspects of the problem.

Anticipation of objection: code of conduct does enough

First, cyberbullies are sometimes anonymous. To accuse another student of cyberbullying, the victim needs to know the identity of the bully.

Response to objection: anonymity of cyberbullies

While postings on *Facebook* are attached to real names, most college gossip sites are anonymous. On such sites, a cyberbully can post photographs, videos, and aggressive messages under the cover of anonymity.

Response to objection: invisibility of the problem

Second, even when the identities of cyberbullies are known, the bullying is often invisible to those in a position to take action against it. According to Ikuku Aoyama and Tony L. Talbert at Baylor University, cyberbullying occurs frequently in groups of people who know each other and who attack and retaliate: students are rarely "pure bullies" or "pure victims" but instead are often part of a "bully-victim group" (qtd. in Laster). Moreover, even if students want to separate from bullying groups, Englander, Mills, and McCoy found that they probably will not report cyberbullying incidents to authorities because they generally believe that administrators are unlikely to do anything (221). Thus counselors and administrators who may be interested in helping students to cope are often unaware of the problem.

arg
9i

Response to objection: conduct codes ineffective

Third, conduct codes rarely affect cyberbullying. While some cyberbullying has resulted in tragedy, many aggressive incidents do not rise to the level of punishable offenses ("Cyberbullying"). More often they consist of a humiliating photograph or a mean message—hurtful, to be sure, but not necessarily in violation of the law or the code of conduct. Indeed, the hurdles to getting recourse through official channels are fairly high.

Conclusion

Given its hidden nature and the inability of punitive measures to stop it, cyberbullying needs another approach—namely, a program that teaches students to recognize and regulate their own behavior and provides help when they find themselves in a difficult situation. This program will not heal the wound suffered by my roommate, nor will it prevent all cyberbullying. But if adopted, the program will demonstrate to the college community that the administration is aware of the problem, eager to prevent it, and willing to commit resources to support students who are affected by it.

Works cited in MLA style

Works Cited

"Cyberbullying Goes to College." *Bostonia*. Boston U, Spring 2009. Web. 18 Feb. 2011.

Englander, Elizabeth, Elizabeth Mills, and Meghan McCoy. "Cyberbullying and Information Exposure: User-Generated Content in Post-Secondary Education." *Violence and Society in the Twenty-First Century*. Spec. issue of *International Journal of Contemporary Sociology* 46.2 (2009): 213-30. Web. 21 Feb. 2011.

Laster, Jill. "Two Scholars Examine Cyberbullying among College Students." *Chronicle of Higher Education*. Chronicle of Higher Education, June 2010. Web. 18 Feb. 2011.

—Aimee Lee (student)

10

Taking Essay Exams

In writing an essay for an examination, you summarize or analyze a topic, usually in several paragraphs or more and usually within a time limit. An essay question not only tests your knowledge of a subject (as short-answer and objective questions do) but also tests your ability to think critically about what you have learned. If you have not already done so, read Chapter 6 on critical thinking and reading.

10a Preparing for an essay examination

To do well on an essay exam, you will need to understand the course content, not only the facts but also the interpretation of them and the relations between them.

- Take careful lecture notes.
- Thoughtfully, critically read the assigned texts or articles.
- Review regularly. Give the material time to sink in and stimulate your thinking.
- Create summaries. Recast others' ideas in your own words, and extract the meaning from notes and texts. (See pp. 152–54 for instructions on summarizing.)
- Prepare notes or outlines to reorganize the course material around key topics or issues. One technique is to create and answer likely essay questions. For instance, in a business course you might focus on the advantages and disadvantages of several approaches to management. In a short-story course you might locate a theme running through all the stories you have read by a certain author or from a certain period. Working through such topics can help you anticipate questions, master the material, and allocate your time during the actual exam.

10b Planning your time and your answer

When you first receive an exam, take a few minutes to get your bearings and plan an approach. The time will not be wasted.

Visit *mycomplab.com* for the eText and for resources and exercises on essay exams.

- Read the exam all the way through at least once. Don't start answering any questions until you've seen them all.
- Weigh the questions. Determine which questions seem most important, which ones are going to be most difficult for you, and approximately how much time you'll need for each question. (Your instructor may help by assigning a point value to each question as a guide to its importance or by suggesting an amount of time for you to spend on each question.)

Planning continues when you turn to an individual essay question. Resist the temptation to rush right into an answer without some planning, for a few minutes can save you time later and help you produce a stronger essay.

10b

- Read the question at least twice. You will be more likely to stick to the question and answer it fully.
- Examine the words in the question and consider their implications. Look especially for words such as *describe, define, explain, summarize, analyze, evaluate,* and *interpret,* each of which requires a different kind of response. Here, for example, is an essay question whose key term is *explain:*

Question
Given humans' natural and historical curiosity about themselves, why did a scientific discipline of anthropology not arise until the 20th century? Explain, citing specific details.

See the box on the facing page and consult earlier discussions of such terms on pages 33–35 and 98–108.

- Make a brief outline of the main ideas you want to cover. Use the back of the exam sheet or booklet for scratch paper. In the outline below, a student planned her answer to the question above.

Outline
1. Unscientific motivations behind 19th-c anthro.
   Imperialist/colonialist govts.
   Practical goals
   Nonobjective and unscientific (Herodotus, Cushing)
2. 19th-c ethnocentricity (vs. cultural relativism)
3. 19th-c anthro. = object collecting
   20th-c shift from museum to univ.
   Anthro. becomes acad. disc. and professional (Boas, Malinowski)

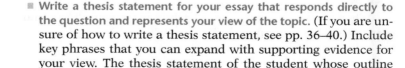

Exercise

- Write a thesis statement for your essay that responds directly to the question and represents your view of the topic. (If you are unsure of how to write a thesis statement, see pp. 36–40.) Include key phrases that you can expand with supporting evidence for your view. The thesis statement of the student whose outline

Sample instructions for essay examinations

Sample instructions	Key terms	Strategies for answers	Examples of wrong answers
Define *dyslexia* and compare and contrast it with two other learning disabilities.	Define	Specify the meaning of *dyslexia*—distinctive characteristics, ways the impairment works, etc.	Feelings of children with dyslexia. Causes of dyslexia.
	Compare and contrast	Analyze similarities and differences (severity, causes, treatments, etc.).	Similarities without differences, or vice versa.
Analyze the role of Horatio in *Hamlet*.	Analyze	Break Horatio's role into its elements (speeches, relations with other characters, etc.).	Plot summary of *Hamlet*. Description of Horatio's personality.
Explain the effects of the drug Thorazine.	Explain	Set forth the facts and theories objectively.	Argument for or against Thorazine.
	Effects	Analyze the consequences.	Reasons for prescribing Thorazine.
Discuss term limits for elected officials.	Discuss	Explain and compare the main points of view on the issue.	Analysis of one view. Argument for or against one view.
Summarize the process that resulted in the Grand Canyon.	Summarize	Distill the subject to its main points, elements, or steps.	Detailed description of the Grand Canyon.
How do you evaluate the Laffer curve as a predictor of economic growth?	Evaluate	Provide your opinion of significance or value, supported with evidence.	Explanation of the Laffer curve, without evaluation. Comparison of the Laffer curve and another predictor, without evaluation.

Video tutorial

10b

appears above concisely previews a three-part answer to the sample question:

Thesis statement

Anthropology did not emerge as a scientific discipline until the 20th century because of the practical and political motivations behind 19th-century ethnographic studies, the ethnocentric bias of Western researchers, and a conception of culture that was strictly material.

10c Starting the essay

An essay exam does not require a smooth and inviting opening. Instead, begin by stating your thesis immediately and giving an overview of the rest of your essay. Such a capsule version of your answer tells your reader (and grader) generally how much command you have and also how you plan to develop your answer. It also gets you off to a good start.

The opening statement should address the question directly and exactly, as it does in the successful essay answer beginning on the next page. In contrast, the opening of the unsuccessful essay (p. 234) restates the question but does not answer it, nor does the opening provide any sense of the writer's thesis.

10d Developing the essay

Student paper

Develop your essay as you would develop any piece of sound academic writing:

- Observe the methods, terms, or other special requirements of the discipline in which you are writing.
- Support your thesis statement with solid generalizations, each one perhaps the topic sentence of a paragraph.
- Support each generalization with specific, relevant evidence.

If you observe a few *don't*s as well, your essay will have more substance:

- Avoid filling out the essay by repeating yourself.
- Avoid other kinds of wordiness that pad and confuse, whether intentionally or not. (See pp. 545–51.)
- Avoid resorting to purely subjective feelings. Keep focused on analysis, or whatever is asked of you. (It may help to abolish the word *I* from the essay.)

The following essays illustrate a successful and an unsuccessful answer to the sample essay question on page 230 about anthropology. Both answers were written in the allotted time of forty minutes. Marginal comments highlight their effective and ineffective elements.

Successful essay answer

Anthropology did not emerge as a scientific discipline until the 20th century because of the practical and political motivations behind 19th-century ethnographic studies, the ethnocentric bias of Western researchers, and a conception of culture that was strictly material.

Before the 20th century, ethnographic studies were almost always used for practical goals. The study of human culture can be traced back at least as far as Herodotus's investigations of the Mediterranean peoples. Herodotus was like many pre-20th-century "anthropologists" in that he was employed by a government that needed information about its neighbors, just as the colonial nations in the 19th century needed information about their newly conquered subjects. The early politically motivated ethnographic studies that the colonial nations sponsored tended to be isolated projects, and they aimed less to advance general knowledge than to solve a specific problem. Frank Hamilton Cushing, who was employed by the American government to study the Zuni tribe of New Mexico, and who is considered one of the pioneers of anthropology, didn't even publish his findings. The political and practical aims of anthropologists and the nature of their research prevented their work from being a scholarly discipline in its own right.

Anthropologists of the 19th century also fell short of the standards of objectivity needed for truly scientific study. This partly had to do with anthropologists' close connection to imperialist governments. But even independent researchers were hampered by the prevailing assumption that Western cultures were inherently superior. While the modern anthropologist believes that a culture must be studied in terms of its own values, early ethnographers were ethnocentric: they judged "primitive" cultures by their own "civilized" values. "Primitive" peoples were seen as uninteresting in their own right. The reasons to study them, ultimately, were to satisfy curiosity, to exploit them, or to prove their inferiority. There was even some debate as to whether so-called savage peoples were human.

Finally, the 19th century tended to conceive of culture in narrow, material terms, often reducing it to a collection of artifacts. When not working for a government, early ethnographers usually worked for a museum. The enormous collections of exotica still found in many museums today are the legacy of this 19th-century object-oriented conception of anthropology, which ignored the myths, symbols, and rituals the objects related to. It was only when the museum tradition was broadened to include all aspects of a culture that anthropology could come into existence as a scientific discipline. When anthropologists like Franz Boas and Bronislaw Malinowski began to publish their findings for others to read and criticize and began to move from the museum to the university, the discipline gained stature and momentum.

In brief, anthropology required a whole series of ideological shifts to become modern. Once it broke free of its purely practical bent, the cultural prejudices of its practitioners, and the narrow

Introduction stating thesis	
Direct answer to question and preview of three-part response	
First main point: practical aims	
Example	
Example	
Second main point: ethnocentricity	
Third main point (with transition *Finally*): focus on objects	
Examples	
Conclusion, restating thesis supported by essay	

conception that limited it to a collection of objects, anthropology could grow into a science.

Unsuccessful essay answer

Introduction, not answering question

No thesis statement or sense of direction

Irrelevant information

The discipline of anthropology, the study of humans and their cultures, actually began in the early 20th century and was strengthened by the Darwinian revolution, but the discipline did not begin to take shape until people like Franz Boas and Alfred Kroeber began doing scientific research among nonindustrialized cultures. (Boas, who was born in Germany but emigrated to the US, is the father of the idea of historical particularism.)

Cliché added to language of question without answering question

Wheel spinning, positioning contemporary anthropology as a scientific discipline

Since the dawn of time, humans have always had a natural curiosity about themselves. Art and literature have always reflected this need to understand human emotions, thought, and behavior. Anthropology is yet another reflection of this need. Anthropologists have a different way of looking at human societies than artists or writers. Whereas the latter paint an individualistic, impressionistic portrait of the world they see, anthropologists study cultures systematically, scientifically. They are thus closer to biologists. They are *social scientists*, with the emphasis on both words.

Not *Another reason* but the first reason given

Assertion without support

Another reason why anthropology did not develop until the 20th century is that people in the past did not travel very much. The expansion of the automobile and the airplane has played a major role in the expansion of the discipline.

Next three paragraphs: discussion of pioneers showing familiarity with their work but not answering question

Cushing's important work among the Zuni Indians in New Mexico is a good example of the transition between 19th-century and 20th-century approaches to anthropology. Cushing was one of the first to develop the method of *participant observation*. Instead of merely coming in as an outsider, taking notes, and leaving, Cushing actually lived among the Zuni, dressing like them and following their customs. In this way, he was able to build a relationship of trust with his informants, learning much more than someone who would have been seen as an outsider.

Padding with repetition

Irrelevant information

Franz Boas, as mentioned earlier, was another anthropology pioneer. A German immigrant, Boas proposed the idea of *historical particularism* as a response to the prevailing theory of *cultural evolution*. Cultural evolution is the idea that cultures gradually evolve toward higher levels of efficiency and complexity. Historical particularism is the idea that every culture is unique and develops differently. Boas developed his theory to counter those who believed in cultural evolution. Working with the Kwakiutl Indians, he was also one of the first anthropologists to use a native assistant to help him gain access to the culture under study.

Vague assertion without support

Irrelevant and empty conclusion

A third pioneer in anthropology was Malinowski, who developed a theory of *functionalism*—that culture responds to biological, psychological, and other needs. Malinowski's work is extremely important and still influential today.

Anthropologists have made great contributions to society over the course of the past century. One can only hope that they will continue the great strides they have made, building on the past to contribute to a bright new future.

10e Rereading the essay

The time limit on an essay examination does not allow for the careful rethinking and revision you would give an essay or research paper. You need to write clearly and concisely the first time. But try to leave yourself a few minutes after finishing the entire exam for rereading the essay (or essays) and doing touch-ups.

- **Correct mistakes:** illegible passages, misspellings, grammatical errors, and accidental omissions.
- **Verify that your thesis is accurate**—that it is, in fact, what you ended up writing about.
- **Ensure that you have supported all your generalizations.** Cross out irrelevant ideas and details, and add any information that now seems important. (Write on another page, if necessary, keying the addition to the page on which it belongs.)

11

Public Writing

Writing outside of college, such as for business or for community work, resembles academic writing in many ways. It usually involves the same basic writing process, discussed in Part 1: assessing the writing situation, developing what you want to say, freely working out your meaning in a draft, and revising and editing so that your writing will achieve your purpose with readers. It often involves research, as discussed in Part 9. And it involves the standards of conciseness, appropriate and exact language, and correct grammar and usage discussed in Parts 3–8.

But public writing has its own conventions, too. They vary widely depending on what you're writing and why, whether it is a proposal for your job or a flyer announcing a dinner for a community group. This chapter covers several types of public writing: business letters and memos (next page); job applications (p. 242); business reports

Exercise

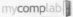
my**comp**lab

Visit *mycomplab.com* for the eText and for resources and exercises on job applications, business reports, and other kinds of public writing.

and proposals (p. 244); and flyers, newsletters, and brochures for community work (p. 247).

Note Wizards or templates can help you format documents such as letters, résumés, and brochures. Be sure the format is appropriate for your writing situation, and remember that a formatting tool can do nothing to help you express your ideas effectively.

CULTURE LANGUAGE Public writing in the United States, especially in business, favors efficiency. If you are accustomed to public writing in another culture, the US style may seem abrupt or impolite. A business letter elsewhere may be expected to begin with polite questions about the addressee or with compliments for the addressee's company, whereas US business letters are expected to come right to the point. (See the letters in this chapter for examples.)

11a Writing business letters and memos

When you write in business, you are addressing busy people who want to see quickly why you are writing and how they should respond to you. A wordy letter or a memo with grammatical errors may prevent you from getting what you want, either because the reader cannot understand your wish or because you present yourself poorly.

In all business writing, follow these general guidelines:

- State your purpose right at the start.
- Be straightforward, clear, concise, objective, and courteous.
- Observe conventions of grammar and usage, which make your writing clear and impress your audience with your care.
- Use a standard format. Your audience will expect it.

1 Using a standard format for letters

Use either unlined white paper measuring $8\frac{1}{2}$" × 11" or what is called letterhead stationery with your address at the top of the sheet. Print the letter single-spaced, with double space between elements, on only one side of a sheet.

The two most common forms for business letters—the full block and the modified block—are illustrated on the next page and on page 243, respectively. Annotations on the samples indicate spacing, margins, and other aspects of format.

The letter

Return-address heading Unless you're using letterhead stationery, the return-address heading gives your address (but not your name) and the date. If you are using letterhead, add only the date.

Inside address The inside address shows the name, title, and complete address of the person you are writing to. (See pp. 238–39 for abbreviations of state names.)

Business letter (block style)

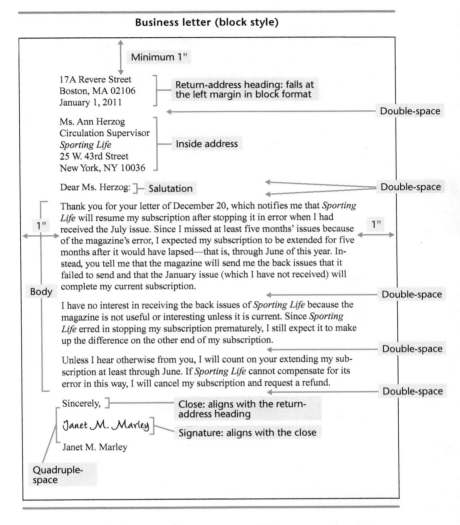

Salutation The salutation greets the addressee. Whenever possible, address your letter to a specific person. (Contact the company or department to ask whom to address.) If you can't find a person's name, then use a job title (*Dear Human Resources Manager, Dear Customer Service Manager*) or use a general salutation (*Dear Smythe Shoes*). Use *Ms.* as the title for a woman when she has no other title, when you don't know how she prefers to be addressed, or when you know that she prefers to be addressed as *Ms.* If you know a woman prefers to be addressed as *Mrs.* or *Miss*, use the appropriate title.

Body The body of the letter, containing its substance, begins at the left margin in both letter styles. Instead of indenting the first line of each paragraph, place an extra line of space between paragraphs so that they are readily visible.

Close The letter's close should reflect the level of formality in the salutation. For formal letters, *Cordially, Yours truly,* and *Sincerely* are common closes. For less formal letters, you may choose to use *Regards, Best wishes,* or the like. Only the first word of the close is capitalized, and the close is followed by a comma.

Signature The signature of a business letter falls below the close and has two parts. One is your name typed on the fourth line below the close. The other is your handwritten signature, which fills the space between the close and your typed name. The signature should consist only of your name, as you would sign checks and other documents.

Other information Below the signature at the left margin, you may want to include additional information such as *Enc. 3* (indicating that there are three enclosures with the letter) or *cc: Margaret Newton* (indicating that a copy is being sent to the person named).

The envelope

The envelope should accommodate the letter once it is folded horizontally in thirds. For addresses, use the common Postal Service abbreviations shown below and opposite.

11a

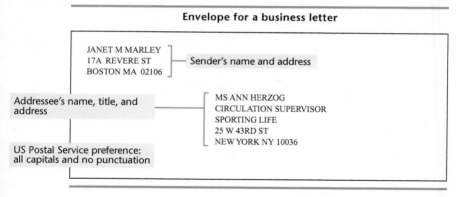

Envelope for a business letter

JANET M MARLEY
17A REVERE ST
BOSTON MA 02106 — Sender's name and address

Addressee's name, title, and address

MS ANN HERZOG
CIRCULATION SUPERVISOR
SPORTING LIFE
25 W 43RD ST
NEW YORK NY 10036

US Postal Service preference: all capitals and no punctuation

Street names

Avenue	AVE	Expressway	EXPY	Place	PL
Boulevard	BLVD	Freeway	FWY	Road	RD
Circle	CIR	Highway	HWY	Square	SQ
Corner	CNR	Lane	LN	Street	ST
Court	CT	Parkway	PKY	Turnpike	TPKE

Compass points

North	N	West	W	Southwest	SW
East	E	Northeast	NE	Northwest	NW

State names

Alabama	AL	Arizona	AZ	California	CA
Alaska	AK	Arkansas	AR	Colorado	CO
Connecticut	CT	Massachusetts	MA	Oklahoma	OK
Delaware	DE	Michigan	MI	Oregon	OR
District of		Minnesota	MN	Pennsylvania	PA
Columbia	DC	Mississippi	MS	Puerto Rico	PR
Florida	FL	Missouri	MO	Rhode Island	RI
Georgia	GA	Montana	MT	South Carolina	SC
Hawaii	HI	Nebraska	NE	South Dakota	SD
Idaho	ID	Nevada	NV	Tennessee	TN
Illinois	IL	New		Texas	TX
Indiana	IN	Hampshire	NH	Utah	UT
Iowa	IA	New Jersey	NJ	Vermont	VT
Kansas	KS	New Mexico	NM	Virginia	VA
Kentucky	KY	New York	NY	Washington	WA
Louisiana	LA	North Carolina	NC	West Virginia	WV
Maine	ME	North Dakota	ND	Wisconsin	WI
Maryland	MD	Ohio	OH	Wyoming	WY

11a

2 Writing requests and complaints

Letters and e-mails in which you request something—for instance, a pamphlet, information about a product, a T-shirt advertised in a magazine—must be specific and accurate about the item you are requesting. The letter or e-mail should describe the item completely and, if applicable, include a copy or description of the advertisement or other source that prompted your request.

Sample document

Letters and e-mails in which you complain about a product or a service (such as a wrong billing from the telephone company) should be written in a reasonable but firm tone. (See the sample letter on p. 237.) Assume that the addressee is willing to resolve the problem when he or she has the relevant information. In the first sentence, say what you are writing about. Then provide as much background as needed, including any relevant details from past correspondence (as in the sample letter). Describe exactly what you see as the problem, sticking to facts and avoiding discourse on the company's social responsibility or your low opinion of its management. Proceed concisely from one point to the next without repeating yourself, and always include your opinion of how the problem can be solved. Many companies are required by law to establish a specific procedure for complaints about products and services. If you know of such a procedure, be sure to follow it.

Sample document

3 Writing business memos

Unlike business letters, which address people in other organizations, business memos address people within the same organization. A memo can be quite long, such as a sales plan for a particular region, or it may deal briefly with a specific topic, such as an answer to a question, a progress report, or an evaluation. The content of the

Sample document

memo comes quickly to the point and disposes of it efficiently. Use the following tips to make a memo's content effective:

- **State your reason for writing in the first sentence.** You might outline a problem, make a request, refer to a request that prompted the memo, or briefly summarize new findings. Do not, however, waste words with expressions like *The purpose of this memo is. . . .*
- **Devote the first paragraph to a succinct presentation of your solution, recommendation, answer, or evaluation.** The first paragraph should be short, and by its end your reader should know precisely what to expect from the rest of the memo: the details and reasoning that support your conclusion.
- **Deliver the support in the body of the memo.** The paragraphs may be numbered or bulleted to highlight the main divisions of your message. A long memo may need headings (see p. 122).
- **Use an appropriate level of formality.** Typically, business correspondence grows more formal as the rank and number of intended readers increase. But even when addressing a few colleagues at your own level, your writing should show respect for the situation and the colleagues.
- **Write concisely.** Keep your sentences short and your language simple, using technical terms only when your readers will understand them. Say only what readers need to know.
- **Provide contact information.** Give the recipients your e-mail address, phone number, and mailing address.

Memos are usually sent as e-mails or as word-processing documents attached to e-mails. Keep the following guidelines in mind when you use e-mail for a memo, and also consult pages 5–7 on using e-mail and other electronic communication:

- **Consider whom to address.** Confine the list of recipients to those who need to read your message. Similarly, avoid sending replies to a large group—look at who will receive your message before you hit Reply All.
- **Provide context for the message.** In the subject line and opening sentences, give an overview of your subject and purpose.
- **Don't say anything you wouldn't say face to face or in a printed document.** The messages you send are going to people, not merely inboxes, so craft your messages with the recipients in mind. Furthermore, most companies save e-mail and can retrieve it if questions arise about your conduct or performance.
- **Check your work.** Avoid the shortcuts of texting and tweeting, and proofread for errors in grammar, punctuation, and spelling.

The following samples illustrate common formats for memos sent as e-mail messages and as word-processing documents.

11a

E-mail memo

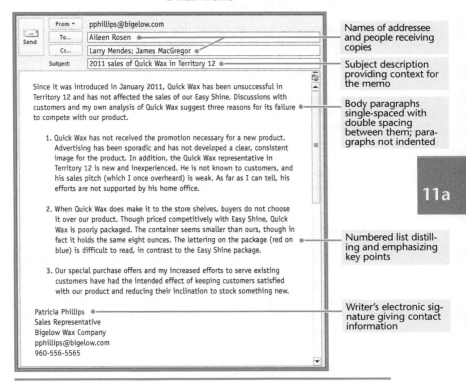

Names of addressee and people receiving copies

Subject description providing context for the memo

Body paragraphs single-spaced with double spacing between them; paragraphs not indented

11a

Numbered list distilling and emphasizing key points

Writer's electronic signature giving contact information

Word-processed or printed memo

To: Aileen Rosen
Cc: Larry Mendes; James MacGregor
From: Patricia Phillips, Territory 12
Date: February 26, 2011
Subject: 2011 sales of Quick Wax in Territory 12

Since it was introduced in January 2011, Quick Wax has been unsuccessful in Territory 12 and has not affected the sales of our Easy Shine. Discussions with customers and my own analysis of Quick Wax suggest three reasons for its failure to compete with our product.

   1. Quick Wax has not received the promotion necessary for a new product. Advertising has been sporadic and

Names of addressee and people receiving copies, writer's name, and date

Subject description giving context for the memo

Body paragraphs single-spaced with double spacing between them; paragraphs not indented

11b Writing a job application

In applying for a job or requesting a job interview, send both a résumé and a cover letter. If you need to submit your application electronically, see the tips beginning near the bottom of this page.

1 Writing the cover letter

Sample
document

The cover letter should be formatted in block style (p. 237) or modified block style (opposite). In composing the letter, use the sample opposite and the following guidelines:

11b

- Interpret your résumé for the particular job. Don't detail your entire résumé, reciting your job history. Instead, highlight and reshape only the relevant parts.
- Announce at the outset what job you seek and how you heard about it.
- Include any special reason you have for applying, such as a specific career goal.
- Summarize your qualifications for this particular job, including relevant facts about education and employment and emphasizing notable accomplishments. Mention that additional information appears in an accompanying résumé.
- Describe your availability. At the end of the letter, mention that you are free for an interview at the convenience of the addressee, or specify when you will be available (for instance, when your current job or classes leave you free).

2 Writing and formatting the résumé

Sample
document

The résumé that accompanies your letter of application should provide information in table format that allows a potential employer to evaluate your qualifications. The résumé should include your name and address, the position you seek, your education and employment history, any special skills or awards, and how to obtain your references. All the information should fit on one uncrowded page unless your education and experience are extensive. See the sample on page 244 for writing and formatting a résumé that you will submit in print.

Employers may want to add your résumé to a computerized database of applicants. The employers may scan your printed résumé to convert it to an electronic file, which they can then store in an appropriate database. Or they may ask you to provide the résumé electronically, either attaching it to or embedding it in an e-mail message. If an employer requests a scannable or electronic résumé, use the following guidelines and consult the sample on page 245.

- Keep the design simple for accurate scanning or electronic transmittal. Avoid images, unusual type, more than one column, vertical or horizontal lines, italics, and underlining.

Job-application letter (modified block style)

> Return-address heading:
> falls to the right of center ⎯
> in modified block format

3712 Swiss Avenue
Dallas, TX 75204
March 2, 2011

Raymond Chipault
Human Resources Manager
Dallas News
Communications Center
Dallas, TX 75222

Dear Mr. Chipault:

In response to your posting in the English Department of Southern Methodist University, I am applying for the summer job of part-time editorial assistant for the *Dallas News*.

I am now enrolled at Southern Methodist University as a sophomore, with a dual major in English literature and journalism. My courses so far have included news reporting, copy editing, and electronic publishing. I worked a summer as a copy aide for my hometown newspaper, and for two years I have edited and written sports stories and features for the university newspaper. My feature articles cover subjects as diverse as campus elections, parking regulations, visiting professors, and speech codes.

As the enclosed résumé and writing samples indicate, my education and knowledge of newspaper work prepare me for the opening you have.

I am available for an interview at your convenience and would be happy to show more samples of my writing. Please e-mail me at ianirv@mail.smu .edu or call me at 214-744-3816.

> Close and signature:
> align with the return- ⎯
> address heading

Sincerely,

Ian M. Irvine

Ian M. Irvine

Enc.

11b

■ **Use concise, specific words to describe your skills and experience.** The employer's computer may use keywords (often nouns) to identify the résumés of suitable job candidates, and you want to ensure that your résumé includes the appropriate keywords. Name your specific skills—for example, the computer programs you can operate—and write concretely with words like *manager* (not *person with responsibility for*) and *reporter* (not *staff member who reports*). Look for likely keywords in the employer's description of the job you seek.

Résumé (print)

Name and contact information	**Ian M. Irvine**	3712 Swiss Avenue Dallas, TX 75204 214-744-3816 ianirv@mail.smu.edu

Desired position stated simply and clearly

Position desired   Part-time editorial assistant.

Education before work experience for most college students

Education   *Southern Methodist University*, 2009 to present.
Current standing: sophomore.
Major: English literature and journalism.
Journalism courses: news reporting, copy editing, electronic publishing, communication arts, broadcast journalism.

Abilene (Texas) Senior High School, 2005-09.
Graduated with academic, college-preparatory degree.

Headings marking sections, set off with space and highlighting

Employment history   2009 to present. Reporter, *Daily Campus*, student newspaper of Southern Methodist University.
Write regular coverage of baseball, track, and soccer teams.
Write feature stories on campus policies and events. Edit sports news, campus listings, features.

Conventional use of capital letters: yes for proper nouns and after periods; no for job titles, course names, department names, and so on

Summer 2010. Copy aide, *Abilene Reporter-News*.
Assisted reporters with copy routing and research.

Summer 2009. Painter, Longhorn Painters, Abilene.
Prepared and painted exteriors and interiors of houses.

Special skills   Fluent in Spanish.
Proficient in Internet research and word processing.

Standard, consistent type font

References   Available on request:

Placement Office
Southern Methodist University
Dallas, TX 75275

11c Writing business reports and proposals

Sample document

Reports and proposals are text-heavy documents, sometimes lengthy, that convey information such as the results of research, a plan for action, or a recommendation for change. As with other business correspondence, you will prepare a report or proposal for a specific purpose, and you will be addressing interested but busy readers.

Résumé (scannable or electronic)

Ian M. Irvine
3712 Swiss Avenue
Dallas, TX 75204
214-744-3816
ianirv@mail.smu.edu

KEYWORDS: Editor, editorial assistant, publishing, electronic publishing.

OBJECTIVE
Part-time editorial assistant.

EDUCATION
Southern Methodist University, 2009 to present.
Major: English literature and journalism.
Journalism courses: news reporting, copy editing, electronic publishing,
communication arts, broadcast journalism.

Abilene (Texas) Senior High School, 2005-09.
Academic, college preparatory degree.

EMPLOYMENT HISTORY
Reporter, Daily Campus, Southern Methodist University, 2009 to present.
Writer of articles for student newspaper on sports teams, campus policies,
and local events. Editor of sports news, campus listings, and features.

Copy aide, Abilene Reporter-News, Abilene, summer 2010.
Assistant to reporters, routing copy and doing research.

Painter, Longhorn Painters, Abilene, summer 2009.
Preparation and painting of exteriors and interiors of houses.

SPECIAL SKILLS
Fluent in Spanish.
Proficient in Internet research and word processing.

REFERENCES
Available on request:
Placement Office
Southern Methodist University
Dallas, TX 75275

Accurate keywords, allowing the employer to place the résumé into an appropriate database

Simple design, avoiding unusual type, italics, multiple columns, decorative lines, and images

Standard font easily read by scanners

Every line aligning at left margin

Reports and proposals usually divide into sections. The sections vary depending on purpose, but often they include a summary, which tells the reader what the document is about; a statement of the problem or need, which justifies the report or proposal; a statement of the plan or solution, which responds to the problem or need; and a recommendation or evaluation. Consider the following guidelines and samples.

Sample
document

■ **Do your research.** To write a successful report or proposal, you must be well informed. Be alert to where you have enough information or where you don't.

■ **Focus on the purpose of each section.** Stick to the point of each section, saying only what you need to say, even if you have additional information. Each section should accomplish its purpose and contribute to the whole.

■ **Follow an appropriate format.** In many businesses, reports and proposals have specific formatting requirements. If you are unsure about the requirements, ask your supervisor.

Report

Descriptive title conveying report's contents

Standard format: summary, statement of the problem, solutions, and (not shown) recommendations

Major sections delineated by headings

Formal tone, appropriate to a business-writing situation

Single spacing with double spacing between paragraphs and around the list

Bulleted list emphasizing alternative solutions

Canada Geese at ABC Institute:
An Environmental Problem

Summary

The flock of Canada geese on and around ABC Institute's grounds has grown dramatically in recent years to become a nuisance and an environmental problem. This report reviews the problem, considers possible solutions, and proposes that ABC Institute and the US Fish and Wildlife Service cooperate to reduce the flock by humane means.

The Problem

Canada geese began living at Taylor Lake next to ABC Institute when they were relocated there in 1985 by the state game department. As a nonmigratory flock, the geese are present year-round, with the highest population each year occurring in early spring. In recent years the flock has grown dramatically. The Audubon Society's annual Christmas bird census shows a thirty-fold increase from the 37 geese counted in 1986 to the 1125 counted in 2010.

The principal environmental problem caused by the geese is pollution of grass and water by defecation. Geese droppings cover the ABC Institute's grounds as well as the park's picnicking areas. The runoff from these droppings into Taylor Lake has substantially affected the quality of the lake's water, so that local authorities have twice (2009 and 2010) issued warnings against swimming.

Possible Solutions

The goose overpopulation and resulting environmental problems have several possible solutions:

• Harass the geese with dogs and audiovisual effects (light and noise) so that the geese choose to leave. This solution is inhumane to the geese and unpleasant for human neighbors.
• Feed the geese a chemical that will weaken the shells of their eggs and thus reduce growth of the flock. This solution is inhumane to the geese and also impractical, because geese are long-lived.
• Kill adult geese. This solution is, obviously, inhumane to the geese.
• Thin the goose population by trapping and removing many geese (perhaps 600) to areas less populated by humans, such as wildlife preserves.

Though costly (see figures below), the last solution is the most humane. It would be harmless to the geese, provided that sizable netted enclosures are used for traps. [Discussion of solution and "Recommendations" section follow.]

Internal proposal

Springfield Veterans Administration Hospital

To: Jefferson Green, Director, Finance and Operations
From: Kate Goodman, Director, ReadingWorks   *KG*
Date: March 5, 2011
Subject: Budget proposal for ReadingWorks Awards Dinner

OVERVIEW

ReadingWorks requests funding for an awards dinner.

NEED

ReadingWorks, the literacy center operated by Springfield VA Hospital, has for 6 years served between 50 and 70 patients/students a year with a small paid staff and a corps of dedicated volunteers. In the past year the center's paid staff and 20 volunteers provided more than 1260 hours of literacy tutoring to 67 students, an increase of 14 students over last year. I want to recognize the efforts and accomplishments of our students and tutors by holding an awards dinner for them and their families.

PLAN

I propose the following event for Friday, May 20, 7:30 to 10:30 PM: dinner and nonalcoholic beverages for approximately 135 students, tutors, and their guests; entertainment; and certificates for approximately 20 students and tutors. I request the use of Suite 42 because it can accommodate as many as 200 people as well as caterers and a DJ. Hospital staff will need to have the room ready by 6:00 PM on May 20.

BUDGET

Dinner and beverages for about 135 attendees	$2700
Music for two hours	200
Certificates	50
TOTAL	$2950

Bids from local businesses are attached.

PERSONNEL

Five hospital employees will be needed to set up, take down, and clean Suite 42 before and after the dinner.

Side annotations:

Memo format for internal proposal (p. 239)

"Overview": statement of proposal

"Need": justification for the request

Formal tone appropriate for a proposal

"Plan": explanation of request

"Budget" and "Personnel": details on the proposal's requirements

Single spacing with double spacing between sections

11d Writing for community work

At some point in your life, you're likely to volunteer for a community organization such as a soup kitchen, a daycare center, a literacy program, or a tutoring center for immigrants learning English. Many college courses involve service learning, in which you do such volunteer work, write about the experience for your course, and write *for* the organization you're helping.

Sample document

The writing you do for a community group may include flyers (below), newsletters (opposite), and brochures (p. 250). Two guidelines in particular will help you prepare effective projects:

- Craft each document for its purpose and audience. You are trying to achieve a specific aim with your readers, and the approach and tone you use will influence their responses. If, for example, you are writing letters to local businesses to raise funds for a homeless shelter, bring to mind the people who will read your letter. How can you best persuade those readers to donate money?

Flyer

11d

FIRST ANNUAL AWARDS DINNER

ReadingWorks

Springfield VA Hospital

Large type and color focusing a distant reader's attention on important information: what's happening, when, where, and who is invited

White space drawing viewers' eyes to main message and creating flow among elements

WHEN

Friday night
May 20
7:30 to 10:30

For information
contact ReadingWorks
209-556-1212

Color highlighting key information

WHERE

Suite 42
Springfield VA Hospital

WHO

Students, tutors, and their families are invited to join us for an evening of food and music as we celebrate their efforts and accomplishments.

Less important information set in smaller type

ReadingWorks of Springfield Veterans Administration Hospital
111 South Springdale Drive
Springfield, MI 45078

▪ **Expect to work with others.** Much public writing is the work of more than one person. Even if you draft the document on your own, others will review the content, tone, and design. Such collaboration is rewarding, but it sometimes requires patience and goodwill. See pages 75–78 for advice on collaborating.

The illustrations in this section show documents prepared for ReadingWorks, a literacy program. See also pages 236–41 and 244–47 on business letters, memos, and proposals, as well as pages 139–41 on *PowerPoint* presentations.

Newsletter

ReadingWorks

Springfield Veterans Administration Hospital   **SUMMER 2011**

From the director

Can you help? With more and more learners in the ReadingWorks program, we need more and more tutors. You may know people who would be interested in participating in the program, if only they knew about it.

Those of you who have been tutoring VA patients in reading and writing know both the great need you fulfill and the great benefits you bring to the students. New tutors need no special skills—we'll provide the training—only patience and an interest in helping others.

We've scheduled an orientation meeting for Friday, September 9, at 6:30 PM. Please come and bring a friend who is willing to contribute a couple of hours a week to our work.

Thanks,
Kate Goodman

IN THIS ISSUE

FIRST ANNUAL AWARDS DINNER

A festive night for students and tutors

The first annual ReadingWorks Awards Dinner on May 20 was a great success. Springfield's own Golden Fork provided tasty food and Amber Allen supplied lively music. The students decorated Suite 42 on the theme of books and reading. In all, 127 people attended.

The highlight of the night was the awards ceremony. Nine students, recommended by their tutors, received certificates recognizing their efforts and special accomplishments in learning to read and write:

Ramon Berva
Edward Byar
David Dunbar
Tony Garnier
Chris Guigni
Akili Haynes
Josh Livingston
Alex Obeld
B. J. Resnansky

In addition, nine tutors received certificates commemorating five years of service to ReadingWorks:

Anita Crumpton
Felix Cruz-Rivera
Bette Elgen

Kayleah Bortoluzzi
Harriotte Henderson
Ben Obiso
Meggie Puente
Max Smith
Sara Villante

Congratulations to all!

PTSD: New Guidelines

Most of us are working with veterans who have been diagnosed with post-traumatic stress disorder. Because this disorder is often complicated by alcoholism, depression, anxiety, and other problems, the National Center for PTSD has issued some guidelines for helping PTSD patients in ways that reduce their stress.

• The hospital must know your tutoring schedule, and you need to sign in and out before and after each tutoring session.

• To protect patients' privacy, meet them only in designated visiting and tutoring areas, never in their rooms.

• Treat patients with dignity and respect, even when (as sometimes happens) they grow frustrated and angry. Seek help from a nurse or orderly if you need it.

Annotations in right margin:

Multicolumn format allowing room for headings, articles, and other elements on a single page

Two-column heading emphasizing the main article

Elements helping readers skim for highlights: spacing, varied font sizes, lines, and a bulleted list

Color focusing readers' attention on banner, headlines, and table of contents

Lively but uncluttered overall appearance

Box in the first column highlighting table of contents

11d

Brochure

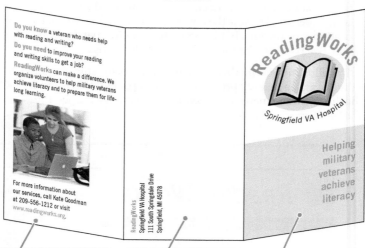

Do you know a veteran who needs help with reading and writing?

Do you need to improve your reading and writing skills to get a job?

ReadingWorks can make a difference. We organize volunteers to help military veterans achieve literacy and to prepare them for life-long learning.

For more information about our services, call Kate Goodman at 209-556-1212 or visit www.readingworks.org.

ReadingWorks
Springfield VA Hospital
111 South Springdale Drive
Springfield, MI 45078

ReadingWorks

Springfield VA Hospital

Helping military veterans achieve literacy

Panel 2: The right page when the cover is opened, the first one readers see, containing key information

Panel 6: The back, usually including the return address and space for a mailing label and postage

Panel 1: The cover, drawing readers' attention to the group's name, purpose, and affiliation

ReadingWorks
Springfield VA Hospital

OUR MISSION
- We provide workshops and formal lessons for veterans wishing to develop their reading and writing skills
- We train volunteers to tutor veterans one on one.
- We maintain outreach programs to provide access to literacy training for all veterans.
- We create literacy resources and share them with others who promote literacy for veterans.

OUR SERVICES
One-on-one tutoring
One to three hours a week with a trained volunteer tutor.

Workshops and classes
Small-group meetings centered on reading and writing, computer skills, and English as a second language.
Library
Books and other resources for students at various literacy levels.
Computer lab
Five computers with high-speed Internet access and a full range of software.

OUR TUTORS
The goodwill and generosity of our volunteer tutors allows us to reach out to those who have served our country.
If you or someone you know can join our team, contact Kate Goodman at 209-556-1212.

Hours
12:00 to 8:00, Mon., Wed.
9:00 to 5:00, Tues., Thurs., Fri.
Eligibility
Any veteran of the US military is eligible for our services.
How to reach us
Springfield VA Hospital
Room 172, first floor
111 South Springdale Drive
Springfield, MI 45078
209-556-1212
www.readingworks.org

Panel 3: The left page when the cover is opened, reinforcing the message of panel 2

Varied type, color, and photographs, adding visual interest and focusing readers' attention

Panels 4 and 5: The inside panels, containing contact information and other details

12

Understanding Sentence Grammar

Video
tutorial

Grammar describes how language works. Following the rules of standard English grammar is what allows you to communicate with others across barriers of personality, region, class, or ethnic origin. If you are a native English speaker, you follow these rules mostly unconsciously. But when you're trying to improve your communication, making the rules conscious and learning the language for them can help.

Grammar reveals a lot about a sentence, even if you don't know the meanings of all the words:

The rumfrums prattly biggled the pooba.

You don't know what this sentence means, but you can infer that some things called *rumfrums* did something to a *pooba*. They *biggled* it, whatever that means, in a *prattly* way. Two grammatical cues, especially, make this sentence like *The students easily passed the test*:

- **Word forms.** The ending *-s* means more than one *rumfrum*. The ending *-ed* means that *biggled* is an action that happened in the past. The ending *-ly* means that *prattly* probably describes *how* the rumfrums biggled.
- **Word order.** *Rumfrums biggled pooba* resembles a common sequence in English: something (*rumfrums*) performed some action (*biggled*) to or on something else (*pooba*). Since *prattly* comes right before the action, it probably describes the action.

This chapter explains how such structures work and shows how practicing with them can help you communicate more effectively.

Grammar checkers A grammar checker can both offer assistance and cause problems as you compose sentences. Look for the cautions and tips for using a checker in this and the next five parts of this book. For more information about grammar checkers, see pages 71–72.

mycomplab

Visit *mycomplab.com* for the eText and for resources and more exercises on sentence grammar.

252

12a Understanding the basic sentence

The **sentence** is the basic unit of thought. Its grammar consists of words with specific forms and functions arranged in specific ways.

1 Identifying subjects and predicates

Most sentences make statements. First the **subject** names something; then the **predicate** makes an assertion about the subject or describes an action by the subject.

Subject	Predicate
Art	thrives.

Video tutorial

The **simple subject** consists of one or more nouns or pronouns, whereas the **complete subject** also includes any modifiers. The **simple predicate** consists of one or more verbs, whereas the **complete predicate** adds any words needed to complete the meaning of the verb plus any modifiers.

Exercise

Sometimes, as in the short example *Art thrives*, the simple and complete subject and predicate are the same. More often, they are different:

gram

12a

                 Subject   Predicate

    ┌──── complete ────┐   ┌──── complete ────┐
            ┌── simple ──┐   ┌ simple
Some contemporary <u>art</u>   **<u>stirs</u> controversy.**

    ┌──── complete ────┐   ┌──────── complete ────────┐
     ┌── simple ──→   ←── simple ──→
<u>Critics</u> and the <u>media</u>   **<u>discuss</u> and <u>dispute</u> its value.**

In the second example, the simple subject and simple predicate are both **compound:** in each, two words joined by *and* serve the same function.

Note If a sentence contains a word group such as *that makes it into established museums* or *because we dispute its quality,* you may be tempted to mark the subject and verb in the word group as the subject and verb of the sentence. But these word groups are subordinate clauses, made into modifiers by the words they begin with: *that* and *because.* See pages 272–73 for more on subordinate clauses.

CULTURE LANGUAGE The subject of an English sentence may be a noun (*art*) or a pronoun that refers to the noun (*it*), but not both. (See p. 255.)

Faulty	<u>Art it</u> can stir controversy.
Revised	<u>Art</u> can stir controversy.
Revised	<u>It</u> can stir controversy.

When identifying the subject and the predicate of a sentence, be aware that some English words can serve as both nouns and verbs. For example, *visits* in the following sentences functions as a verb and as a noun:

She <u>visits</u> the museum every Saturday. [Verb.]
Her <u>visits</u> are enjoyable. [Noun.]

See also page 256.

Tests to find subjects and predicates

The tests below use the following example:

Art that makes it into museums has often survived controversy.

Identify the subject.

■ Ask *who* or *what* is acting or being described in the sentence.

Complete subject   art that makes it into museums

■ **Isolate the simple subject by deleting modifiers**—words or word groups that don't name the actor of the sentence but give information about it. In the example, the word group *that makes it into museums* does not name the actor but modifies it.

Simple subject   art

Identify the predicate.

■ **Ask what the sentence asserts about the subject:** what is its action, or what state is it in? In the example, the assertion about *art* is that it *has often survived controversy.*

Complete predicate   has often survived controversy

■ **Isolate the verb, the simple predicate, by changing the time of the subject's action.** The simple predicate is the word or words that change as a result.

Example   Art . . . has often survived controversy.
Present   Art . . . often survives controversy.
Future   Art . . . will often survive controversy.
Simple predicate   has survived

---

2 Identifying the basic words: Nouns and verbs

The following five simple sentences consist almost entirely of two quite different kinds of words:

Subject	Predicate
The earth	trembled.
The earthquake	destroyed the city.
The result	was chaos.
The government	sent the city aid.
The citizens	considered the earthquake a disaster.

The words in the subject position name things, such as *earth, earthquake,* and *government.* In contrast, the words in the predicate position express states or actions, such as *trembled, destroyed,* and *sent.*

The parts of speech

Nouns name persons, places, things, ideas, or qualities: *Roosevelt, girl, Kip River, coastline, Koran, table, strife, happiness.* (See below.)

Pronouns usually substitute for nouns and function as nouns: *I, you, he, she, it, we, they, myself, this, that, who, which, everyone.* (See p. 257.)

Verbs express actions, occurrences, or states of being: *run, bunt, inflate, become, be.* (See the next page.)

Adjectives describe or modify nouns or pronouns: *gentle, small, helpful.* (See p. 262.)

Adverbs describe or modify verbs, adjectives, other adverbs, or whole groups of words: *gently, helpfully, almost, really, someday.* (See p. 262.)

Prepositions relate nouns or pronouns to other words in a sentence: *about, at, down, for, of, with.* (See pp. 264–65.)

Conjunctions link words, phrases, and clauses. **Coordinating conjunctions** and **correlative conjunctions** link words, phrases, or clauses of equal importance: *and, but, or, nor; both . . . and, not only . . . but also, either . . . or.* (See pp. 278–79.) **Subordinating conjunctions** introduce subordinate clauses and link them to main clauses: *although, because, if, whenever.* (See p. 273.)

Interjections express feeling or command attention, either alone or in a sentence: *hey, oh, darn, wow.*

Exercise

gram
12a

The subject and predicate words work in different ways. *Citizen* can become *citizens*, but not *citizened*. *Destroyed* can become *destroys*, but not *destroyeds*. Grammar reflects such differences by identifying the **parts of speech** or **word classes** shown in the box above. Except for *the* and *a*, which simply point to and help identify the words after them, the five sentences about the earthquake consist entirely of nouns and verbs.

Nouns

Meaning

Nouns name. They may name a person (*Angelina Jolie, LeBron James, Jackson, astronaut*), a thing (*chair, book, Mt. Rainier*), a quality (*pain, mystery, simplicity*), a place (*city, Washington, ocean, Red Sea*), or an idea (*reality, peace, success*).

Video
tutorial

Form

Most nouns form the **possessive** to indicate ownership or source. Singular nouns usually add an apostrophe plus *-s* (*Auden's poems*); plural nouns usually add just an apostrophe (*citizens' rights*).

Nouns also change form to distinguish between singular (one) and plural (more than one). Most nouns add *-s* or *-es* for the plural: *earthquake, earthquakes; city, cities.* Some nouns have irregular plurals: *woman, women; child, children.*

 Some useful rules for forming noun plurals appear on pages 559–60. The irregular plurals must be memorized. Note that some English nouns are not considered countable and do not have plural forms. Examples of these **noncount nouns** are *equality, anger, oxygen,* and *equipment*. (See also pp. 344–45.)

Nouns with *the, a,* and *an*

Nouns are often preceded by *the* or *a* (*an* before a vowel sound: *an apple*). These words are usually called **articles** or **determiners** and always indicate that a noun follows.

> *CULTURE LANGUAGE* See pages 345–46 for the rules governing the use of *the, a/an,* or no article at all before a noun.

Verbs

Meaning

Verbs express an action (*bring, change, grow*), an occurrence (*become, happen*), or a state of being (*be, seem*).

Form

Most verbs can be recognized by two changes in form:

- Most verbs add *-d* or *-ed* to indicate a difference between present and past time: *They play today. They played yesterday.* Some verbs indicate past time irregularly: *eat, ate; begin, began* (see pp. 297–99).
- Most present-time verbs add *-s* or *-es* with subjects that are singular: *The bear escapes. It runs. The woman begins. She sings.* The exceptions are *be* and *have,* which change to *is* and *has.*

(See Chapter 14, pp. 294–310, for more on verb forms.)

Helping verbs

Certain forms of all verbs can combine with other words such as *do, have, can, might, will,* and *must.* These other words are called **helping verbs** or **auxiliary verbs.** In phrases such as *could run, will be running,* and *has escaped,* they help to convey time and other attributes. (See Chapter 14, pp. 296, 302–06.)

A note on form and function

In different sentences an English word may serve different functions, take correspondingly different forms, and belong to different word classes. For example:

> The government sent the city aid. [*Aid* functions as a noun.]
> Governments aid citizens. [*Aid* functions as a verb.]

Because words can function in different ways, we must always determine how a particular word works in a sentence before we can identify what part of speech it is. **The *function* of a word in a sentence always determines its part of speech in that sentence.**

Pronouns

Most **pronouns** substitute for nouns and function in sentences as nouns do. In the following sentence all three pronouns—*who, they, their*—refer to *nurses:*

> Some nurses who have families prefer the night shift because they have more time with their children.

The most common pronouns are the **personal pronouns** (*I, you, he, she, it, we, they*) and the **relative pronouns** (*who, whoever, which, that*). Most of them change form to indicate their function in the sentence—for instance, *He called me. I called him back.* (See Chapter 13 for a discussion of these form changes.)

Exercise 12.1 Identifying subjects and predicates

In the following sentences, insert a vertical line between the complete subject and the complete predicate. Underline each simple subject once and each simple predicate twice. Then use each sentence as a model to create a sentence of your own.

Exercise

gram
12a

> *Example:*
> The <u>pony</u>, the light <u>horse</u>, and the draft <u>horse</u> | <u><u>are</u></u> three types of domestic horses.
>
> *Sample imitation:* Toyota, Honda, and Nissan are three brands of Japanese cars.

1. The leaves fell.
2. October ends soon.
3. The orchard owners made apple cider.
4. They examined each apple carefully for quality.
5. Over a hundred people will buy cider at the roadside stand.

Exercise 12.2 Identifying nouns, verbs, and pronouns

In the following sentences identify all words functioning as nouns with *N*, all words functioning as verbs with *V*, and all pronouns with *P*.

Exercise

> *Example:*
>
>   P   V   N   N
> <u>They</u> <u>took</u> the <u>tour</u> through the <u>museum</u>.

1. The trees died.
2. They caught a disease.
3. The disease was a fungus.
4. It ruined a special grove.
5. Our great-grandfather planted the grove ninety years ago.

Exercise 12.3 Using nouns and verbs

Identify each of the following words as a noun, as a verb, or as both. Then create sentences of your own, using each word in each possible function.

Exercise

Example:
fly
Noun and verb.
The <u>fly</u> sat on the meat loaf. [Noun.] The planes <u>fly</u> low. [Verb.]

1.	wish	6.	label
2.	tie	7.	door
3.	swing	8.	company
4.	mail	9.	whistle
5.	spend	10.	glue

Exercise

gram
12a

3 Forming sentence patterns with nouns and verbs

English builds all sentences on the five basic patterns shown in the box on the facing page. As the diagrams indicate, the patterns differ in their predicates because the relation between the verb and the remaining words is different.

CULTURE LANGUAGE Word order in English sentences may not correspond to word order in the sentences of your native language. For instance, some other languages prefer the verb first in the sentence, whereas English strongly prefers the subject first, then the verb, then any other words. The main exceptions to the word patterns discussed here appear on pages 282–83: questions, commands, passive sentences, and sentences with postponed subjects. See also pages 381–87 on positioning modifiers in sentences.

Pattern 1: The earth trembled.

In the simplest pattern the predicate consists only of the verb. Verbs in this pattern do not require following words to complete their meaning and thus are called **intransitive** (from Latin words meaning "not passing over").

Subject	Predicate
	Intransitive verb
The earth	trembled.
The hospital	may close.

Pattern 2: The earthquake destroyed the city.

In pattern 2 the predicate consists of a verb followed by a noun that identifies who or what receives the action of the verb. This noun is a **direct object.** Verbs that require direct objects to complete their meaning are called **transitive** ("passing over"): the verb transfers the action from subject to object.

Subject	Predicate	
	Transitive verb	*Direct object*
The earthquake	destroyed	the city.
Education	opens	doors.

The five basic sentence patterns

Subject   Predicate

1. **Subject** → **Verb (intransitive)**

   The earth   trembled.

2. **Subject** → **Verb (transitive)** → **Direct object**

   The earthquake   destroyed   the city.

3. **Subject** → **Verb (linking)** → **Subject complement: noun or adjective**

   The result   was   chaos.

4. **Subject** → **Verb (transitive)** → **Indirect object** → **Direct object**

   The government   sent   the city   aid.

5. **Subject** → **Verb (transitive)** → **Direct object** → **Object complement: noun or adjective**

   The citizens   considered   the earthquake   a disaster.

gram

12a

CULTURE LANGUAGE The distinction between transitive verbs (pattern 2) and intransitive verbs (pattern 1) is important because only transitive verbs may be used in the passive voice, when the subject is acted upon: *The city was destroyed by the earthquake*. (See pp. 320–21.) Your dictionary says whether a verb is transitive or intransitive, often with an abbreviation such as *tr.* or *intr.* Some verbs (*begin, learn, read, write,* and others) can be both transitive and intransitive.

Pattern 3: The result was chaos.

In pattern 3 the predicate also consists of a verb followed by a noun, but here the noun renames or describes the subject. We could write the sentence *The result = chaos*. The verb serving as an equal sign is a **linking verb** because it links the subject and the following description. The linking verbs include *be, seem, appear, become, grow, remain, stay, prove, feel, look, smell, sound,* and *taste*. The word that describes the subject is called a **subject complement** (it complements, or completes, the subject).

Subject	Predicate	
	Linking verb	*Subject complement*
The result	was	chaos.
The man	became	an accountant.

Subject complements in this sentence pattern may also be adjectives, words such as *tall* and *hopeful* (see p. 262):

Subject	Predicate	
	Linking verb	*Subject complement*
The result	was	chaotic.
The apartments	seem	expensive.

Pattern 4: The government sent the city aid.

In pattern 4 the predicate consists of a verb followed by two nouns. The second noun, *aid,* is a direct object (see pattern 2). But the first noun, *city,* is an **indirect object,** identifying to or for whom the action of the verb is performed. The direct object and indirect object refer to different things, people, or places.

gram
12a

Subject	Predicate		
	Transitive verb	*Indirect object*	*Direct object*
The government	sent	the city	aid.
One company	offered	its employees	bonuses.

A number of verbs can take indirect objects, including those above and *allow, bring, buy, deny, find, get, leave, make, pay, read, sell, show, teach,* and *write.*

CULTURE
LANGUAGE With some verbs that express action done to or for someone, the indirect object must be turned into a phrase beginning with *to* or *for.* In addition, the phrase must come after the direct object. The verbs that require these changes include *admit, announce, demonstrate, explain, introduce, mention, prove, recommend, say,* and *suggest.*

	indirect object	direct object
Faulty	The manual explains <u>workers</u> the new <u>procedure.</u>	

	direct object	*to* phrase
Revised	The manual explains the new <u>procedure to workers.</u>	

Pattern 5: The citizens considered the earthquake a disaster.

In pattern 5, as in pattern 4, the predicate consists of a verb followed by two nouns. But in pattern 5 the first noun is a direct object and the second noun renames or describes it. Here the second noun is an **object complement** (it complements, or completes, the object):

Subject	Predicate		
	Transitive verb	*Direct object*	*Object complement*
The citizens	considered	the earthquake	a disaster.
The class	elected	Kate O'Day	president.

Like a subject complement (pattern 3), an object complement may be a noun or an adjective, as below:

Subject	Predicate		
	Transitive verb	*Direct object*	*Object complement*
The citizens	considered	the earthquake	disastrous.
Success	makes	some people	nervous.

Exercise 12.4 Identifying sentence patterns

In the following sentences, identify each verb as intransitive, transitive, or linking. Then identify each direct object (DO), indirect object (IO), subject complement (SC), and object complement (OC).

Exercise

gram
12b

> *Example:*
>
> transitive
> verb   IO   DO   DO
> Children give their parents both headaches and pleasures.

1. Many people find New York City exciting.
2. Tourists flock to New York each year.
3. Often they visit Times Square first.
4. The square's lights are astounding.
5. The flashing signs sell visitors everything from TVs to underwear.

Exercise 12.5 Creating sentences

Create sentences by using each of the following verbs in the pattern indicated. (For the meanings of the abbreviations, see the directions for Exercise 12.4.) You may want to change the form of the verb.

> *Example:*
> give (S-V-IO-DO)
> Sam gave his brother a birthday card.

1. laugh (S-V)
2. elect (S-V-DO-OC)
3. steal (S-V-DO)
4. catch (S-V-DO)
5. bring (S-V-IO-DO)
6. seem (S-V-SC)
7. call (S-V-DO-OC)
8. become (S-V-SC)
9. buy (S-V-IO-DO)
10. study (S-V)

12b Expanding the basic sentence with single words

Most of the sentences we read, write, or speak are more complex and also more informative and interesting than those examined so far. Most sentences contain one or more of the following: (1) modifying words (discussed here); (2) word groups, called phrases and clauses (p. 264); and (3) combinations of two or more words or word groups of the same kind (p. 278).

1 Using adjectives and adverbs

The simplest expansion of sentences occurs when we add modifying words to describe or limit the nouns and verbs. Modifying words add details:

> Recently, the earth trembled.
> The earthquake <u>nearly</u> destroyed the <u>old</u> city.
> The <u>federal</u> government <u>soon</u> sent the city aid.
> The grant was a <u>very generous</u> one but disappeared <u>too quickly</u>.

The underlined words represent two different parts of speech:

gram

12b

- **Adjectives** describe or modify nouns and pronouns. They specify which one, what quality, or how many.

old	city		generous	one		two	pears
adjective	noun		adjective	pronoun		adjective	noun

- **Adverbs** describe or modify verbs, adjectives, other adverbs, and whole groups of words. They specify when, where, how, and to what extent.

nearly	destroyed		too	quickly
adverb	verb		adverb	adverb

very	generous		Unfortunately,	taxes will rise.
adverb	adjective		adverb	word group

An *-ly* ending often signals an adverb, but not always: *friendly* is an adjective; *never, not,* and *always* are adverbs. The only way to tell whether a word is an adjective or an adverb is to determine what it modifies.

Adjectives and adverbs appear in three forms:

- **Positive:** The basic form, the one listed in the dictionary: *good, green, angry; badly, quickly, angrily.*
- **Comparative:** The form that indicates a greater degree of the quality named by the word: *better, greener, angrier; worse, more quickly, more angrily.*
- **Superlative:** The form that indicates the greatest degree of the quality named: *best, greenest, angriest; worst, most quickly, most angrily.*

(For further discussion of these forms, see p. 340.)

2 Using other words as modifiers

Nouns and special forms of verbs may sometimes serve as modifiers of other nouns. In combinations such as *office buildings,* *Thanksgiving prayer,* and *shock hazard,* the first noun modifies the second. In combinations such as *singing birds, corrected papers,* and *broken finger,* the first word is a verb form modifying the following noun. (These modifying verb forms are discussed in more detail on pp. 267–68.) Again, the part of speech to which we assign a word always depends on its function in a sentence.

Exercise 12.6   Identifying and using adjectives and adverbs

Identify the adjectives and adverbs in the following sentences. Then use each sentence as a model for creating a sentence of your own.

Exercise

> *Example:*
>
>   adjective   adverb   adjective
> The <u>red</u> barn sat <u>uncomfortably</u> among <u>modern</u> buildings.
>
> *Sample imitation:* The little girl complained loudly to her busy mother.

1. The blue water glistened in the hot afternoon sunlight.
2. Happily, children dipped their toes in the cool lake.
3. Excitedly, some of the children hopped into the water.
4. Cautious parents watched from their shady porches.
5. The children played contentedly until the day finally ended.

Exercise 12.7   Using verb forms as modifiers

Use each of the following verb forms to modify a noun in a sentence of your own.

Exercise

> *Example:*
>
> smoking
> Only a <u>smoking cigar</u> remained.

1. scrambled	5. painted	8. ripened
2. twitching	6. written	9. known
3. rambling	7. charging	10. driven
4. typed		

Exercise 12.8   Sentence combining: Single-word modifiers

To practice expanding the basic sentence patterns with single-word modifiers, combine each group of sentences below into one sentence. You will have to delete and rearrange words.

Exercise

> *Example:*
>
> Paris offers tourists food. Paris offers food proudly. The food is delicious.
>
> Paris <u>proudly</u> offers tourists <u>delicious</u> food.

1. The turn of the century ushered in technology and materials. The century was the twentieth. The technology was improved. The materials were new.
2. A skeleton made the construction of skyscrapers possible. The skeleton was sturdy. It was made of steel.
3. By 1913 the Woolworth Building, with its ornaments, stood 760 feet (55 stories). The building was towering. The ornaments were Gothic.
4. At 1450 feet the Willis Tower in Chicago doubles the height of the Woolworth Building. The doubling is now. The Woolworth height is puny. The puniness is relative.
5. Skyscrapers became practical in 1857 when Elisha Graves Otis built the elevator. It was the first elevator. The elevator was safe. It served passengers.

12c   Expanding the basic sentence with word groups

Most sentences we read or write contain word groups that serve as nouns and modifiers. Such word groups enable us to combine several bits of information into one sentence and to make the relations among them clear, as in the following sentence:

subject

When the experiment succeeded, the <u>researchers</u>, excited by the

verb   object

results, <u>expanded</u> the <u>study</u> to enroll more patients.

Attached to *researchers expanded the study,* the skeleton of this sentence, are three groups of words that add related information: *When the experiment succeeded, excited by the results, to enroll more patients.* These constructions are phrases and clauses:

- A *phrase* is a group of related words that lacks either a subject or a predicate or both: *excited by the results, to enroll more patients.*
- A *clause* contains both a subject and a predicate: *When the experiment succeeded* and *the researchers expanded the study* are both clauses, though only the second can stand alone as a sentence.

1   Using prepositional phrases

Podcast

Prepositions are connecting words. Unlike nouns, verbs, and modifiers, which may change form, prepositions never change form. As the box opposite shows, many prepositions signal relationships of time or space; others signal relationships such as addition, comparison or contrast, cause or effect, concession, condition, opposition, possession, and source. Notice that some prepositions consist of more than one word.

A preposition connects a noun or pronoun to another word in the sentence: *Robins nest <u>in</u> trees.* The noun or pronoun so connected

Common prepositions

Time or space (position or direction)			Other relationships (addition, comparison, etc.)	
about	by	out of	according to	in spite of
above	down	outside	as	instead of
across	during	over	as for	like
after	for	past	aside from	of
against	from	since	because of	on account of
along	in	through	concerning	regarding
along with	inside	throughout	despite	regardless of
among	inside of	till	except	unlike
around	into	to	except for	with
at	near	toward	excepting	without
before	next to	under	in addition to	
behind	off	underneath		
below	on	until		
beneath	onto	up		
beside	on top of	upon		
between	out	within		
beyond				

gram

12c

✳
Exercise

(*trees*) is the **object of the preposition.** The preposition plus its object and any modifiers is a **prepositional phrase:**

Preposition	Object
on	the surface
upon	entering the room
from	where you are standing
except for	ten employees

Prepositional phrases function as adjectives (modifying nouns) or as adverbs (modifying verbs, adjectives, or other adverbs). As modifiers, they add details that make sentences clearer and more interesting for readers.

Life on a raft was an opportunity for adventure.
adjective phrase   adjective phrase

Huck Finn rode the raft by choice.
                           adverb phrase

CULTURE LANGUAGE The meanings and idiomatic uses of English prepositions can be difficult to master; most must be memorized or looked up in a dictionary. (A list of dictionaries for English as a second language appears on p. 535.) See pages 309–10 for two-word verbs that include prepositions, such as *look after,* and see pages 540–41 for idioms with prepositions.

Punctuating prepositional phrases

Since a prepositional phrase lacks a subject and a predicate, it should not be punctuated as a complete sentence. If it is, the result is a **sentence fragment** (Chapter 17):

Fragment   Toward the sun.

The phrase must be attached to another group of words containing both a subject and a predicate:

Revised   The plane turned <u>toward the sun</u>.

A prepositional phrase that introduces a sentence is set off with punctuation, usually a comma, unless it is short (see p. 447):

<u>According to the newspaper and other sources</u>, the governor has reluctantly decided to veto the bill.
In 1865 the Civil War finally ended.

A prepositional phrase that interrupts or concludes a sentence is *not* set off with punctuation when it is essential to the meaning of the word or words it modifies (see p. 451):

The announcement <u>of a tuition increase</u> surprised no one.
Students expected new fees <u>for the coming year</u>.

When an interrupting or concluding prepositional phrase is *not* essential to meaning, but merely adds information to the sentence, then it *is* set off with punctuation, usually a comma or commas (see p. 450):

The governor, <u>according to the newspaper and other sources</u>, has reluctantly decided to veto the bill.

As all the preceding examples illustrate, a preposition and its object are not separated by a comma.

Exercise 12.9   Identifying prepositional phrases

Identify the prepositional phrases in the following passage. Indicate whether each phrase functions as an adjective or as an adverb, and underline the word that the phrase modifies.

Example:

┌── adverb ──┐   ┌── adverb ──┐┌── adjective ──┐
After an hour I finally <u>arrived</u> at the <u>home</u> of my professor.

On July 3, 1863, at Gettysburg, Pennsylvania, General Robert E. Lee gambled unsuccessfully for a Confederate victory in the American Civil War. The battle of Pickett's Charge was one of the most disastrous conflicts of the war. Confederate and Union forces faced each other on parallel ridges separated by almost a mile of open fields. After an artillery bombardment of the Union position, nearly 12,000 Confederate infantry marched toward the Union ridge. The Union guns had been silent but

gram
12c

suddenly roared against the approaching Confederates. Within an hour, perhaps half of the Confederate soldiers lay wounded or dead.

Exercise 12.10 Sentence combining: Prepositional phrases

To practice writing sentences with prepositional phrases, combine each group of sentences below into one sentence that includes one or two prepositional phrases. You will have to add, delete, and rearrange words. Some items have more than one possible answer.

Exercise

> *Example:*
> I will start working. The new job will pay the minimum wage.
> I will start working <u>at a new job</u> <u>for the minimum wage</u>.

1. The slow loris protects itself well. Its habitat is Southeast Asia. It possesses a poisonous chemical.
2. The loris frightens predators when it exudes this chemical. The chemical comes from a gland. The gland is on the loris's upper arm.
3. The loris's chemical is highly toxic. The chemical is not like a skunk's spray. Even small quantities of the chemical are toxic.
4. A tiny dose can affect a human. The dose would get in the mouth. The human would be sent into shock.
5. Predators probably can sense the toxin. They detect it at a distance. They use their nasal organs.

gram
12c

2 Using verbals and verbal phrases

Verbals are special verb forms such as *smoking* or *hidden* or *to win* that can function as nouns (*smoking is dangerous*) or as modifiers (*the hidden money, the urge to win*).

Exercise

Note A verbal *cannot* stand alone as the complete verb in the predicate of a sentence. For example, *The man smoking* and *The money hidden* are not sentences but sentence fragments (see p. 352). Any verbal must combine with a helping verb to serve as the predicate of a sentence: *The man was smoking. The money is hidden.*

Because verbals cannot serve alone as sentence predicates, they are sometimes called **nonfinite verbs** (in essence, they are "unfinished"). **Finite verbs,** in contrast, can make an assertion or express a state of being without a helping verb (they are "finished"). Either of the following two tests can distinguish finite and nonfinite verbs.

Tests for finite and nonfinite verbs (verbals)

Test 1 Does the word require a change in form when a third-person subject changes from singular to plural?

Yes Finite verb: *It sings. They sing.*

No Nonfinite verb (verbal): *bird singing, birds singing*

(continued)

Tests for finite and nonfinite verbs (verbals)
(continued)

Test 2 Does the word require a change in form to show the difference in present, past, and future?

Yes   Finite verb: *It sings. It sang. It will sing.*

No   Nonfinite verb (verbal): *The bird singing is a robin.*
                                     The bird singing was a robin.
                                     The bird singing will be a robin.

There are three kinds of verbals: participles, gerunds, and infinitives.

Participles

All verbs have two participle forms, a present and a past. The **present participle** consists of the dictionary form of the verb plus the ending *-ing*: *beginning, completing, hiding.* The **past participle** of most verbs consists of the dictionary form plus *-d* or *-ed*: *believed, completed.* Some common verbs have an irregular past participle, such as *begun* or *hidden.* (See pp. 297–99.)

Both present and past participles function as adjectives to modify nouns and pronouns:

Shopping malls sometimes frustrate shoppers.

Shoppers may feel trapped.

CULTURE / LANGUAGE The present and past participles of verbs that express feelings have different meanings. The present participle modifies the thing that causes the feeling: *It was a boring lecture.* The past participle modifies the thing that experiences the feeling: *The bored students slept.* See page 343.

Gerunds

Gerund is the name given to the *-ing* form of the verb when it serves as a noun:

subject
Strolling through stores can exhaust the hardiest shopper.

object
Many children learn to hate shopping.

Present participles and gerunds can be distinguished *only* by their function in a sentence. When the *-ing* form functions as an adjective (*a teaching degree*), it is a present participle. When the *-ing* form functions as a noun (*Teaching is difficult*), it is a gerund.

CULTURE / LANGUAGE In English, always use a gerund, not any other verb form, as the object of a preposition:

Faulty   Diners are prohibited from <u>to smoke</u>.
Revised   Diners are prohibited from <u>smoking</u>.

See also the culture-language note below.

Infinitives

The **infinitive** is the *to* form of the verb, the dictionary form preceded by the infinitive marker *to: to begin, to hide, to run.* Infinitives may function as adjectives, nouns, or adverbs:

adjective
The question to answer is why shoppers endure mall fatigue.

noun
The solution for mall fatigue is to leave.

adverb
Still, shoppers find it difficult to quit.

CULTURE•LANGUAGE Infinitives and gerunds may follow some English verbs and not others and may differ in meaning after a verb:

The cowboy stopped <u>to sing</u>. [He stopped to do the activity.]
The cowboy stopped <u>singing</u>. [He finished the activity.]

(See pp. 307–09.)

gram
12c

Verbal phrases

Participles, gerunds, and infinitives—like other verb forms—may take subjects, objects, or complements, and they may be modified by adverbs. The verbal and all the words immediately related to it make up a **verbal phrase.** With verbal phrases, we can create concise sentences packed with information.

Like participles, **participial phrases** always serve as adjectives, modifying nouns or pronouns:

Buying things, most shoppers feel themselves in control.

They make selections determined by personal taste.

Gerund phrases, like gerunds, always serve as nouns:

subject
Shopping for clothing and other items satisfies personal needs.

object of preposition
Malls are good at creating such needs.

Infinitive phrases may serve as nouns, adverbs, or adjectives:

sentence subject   subject complement
To design a mall is to create an artificial environment.
noun phrase   noun phrase

Malls are designed to make shoppers feel safe.
adverb phrase

The environment supports the impulse to shop for oneself.
adjective phrase

Note When an infinitive or infinitive phrase serves as a noun after verbs such as *hear, help, let, make, see,* and *watch,* the infinitive marker *to* is omitted: *We all heard her <u>tell</u>* [not *to tell*] *the story.*

Punctuating verbals and verbal phrases

Verbal phrases punctuated as complete sentences are sentence fragments (Chapter 17). A complete sentence must contain a subject and a finite verb (p. 267):

> Fragment <u>Treating</u> the patients kindly.
> Revised <u>She treats</u> the patients kindly.

A verbal or verbal phrase serving as a modifier is almost always set off with a comma when it introduces a sentence (see p. 447):

> To pay tuition, some students work at two jobs.

A modifying verbal or verbal phrase that interrupts or concludes a sentence is *not* set off with punctuation when it is essential to the meaning of the word or words it modifies (see p. 450):

> Jobs paying well are hard to find.

gram
12c

When an interrupting or concluding verbal modifier is *not* essential to meaning but merely adds information to the sentence, it *is* set off with punctuation, usually a comma or commas (see p. 450):

> One good job, paying twelve dollars an hour, was filled in fifteen minutes.

Exercise 12.11 Identifying verbals and verbal phrases

The following sentences contain participles, gerunds, and infinitives as well as participial, gerund, and infinitive phrases. First underline each verbal or verbal phrase. Then indicate whether it is used as an adjective, an adverb, or a noun.

> *Example:*
>
> adjective   adverb
> <u>Laughing</u>, the talk-show host prodded her guest <u>to speak</u>.

1. Written in 1850 by Nathaniel Hawthorne, *The Scarlet Letter* tells the story of Hester Prynne.
2. Shunned by the community, Hester endures her loneliness.
3. Hester is humble enough to withstand her Puritan neighbors' cutting remarks.
4. Enduring the cruel treatment, the determined young woman refuses to leave her home.
5. By living a life of patience and unselfishness, Hester eventually becomes the community's angel.

Exercise 12.12 Sentence combining: Verbals and verbal phrases

Exercise

To practice writing sentences with verbals and verbal phrases, combine each of the following pairs of sentences into one sentence. You will have to add, delete, change, and rearrange words. Each item has more than one possible answer.

> *Example:*
> My father enjoyed mean pranks. For instance, he hid the neighbor's cat.
> My father enjoyed mean pranks such as hiding the neighbor's cat.

1. Air pollution is a health problem. It affects millions of Americans.
2. The air has been polluted mainly by industries and automobiles. It contains toxic chemicals.
3. Environmentalists pressure politicians. They think politicians should pass stricter laws.
4. Many politicians waver. They are not necessarily against environmentalism.
5. The problems are too complex. They cannot be solved easily.

3 Using absolute phrases

Absolute phrases consist of a noun or pronoun and a participle, plus any modifiers:

┌——— absolute phrase ———┐
Many ethnic groups, their own place established, are making way for new arrivals.

┌——— absolute phrase———┐ ┌——— absolute phrase———┐
Their native lands left behind, an uncertain future looming, immigrants face many obstacles.

gram

12c

These phrases are called *absolute* (from a Latin word meaning "free") because they have no specific grammatical connection to a noun, verb, or any other word in the rest of the sentence. Instead, they modify the entire rest of the sentence, adding information.

Notice that absolute phrases, unlike participial phrases, always contain a subject. Compare the following sentences:

┌——participial phrase ┐
For many immigrants learning English, the language introduces American culture.

┌——————— absolute phrase—————┐
The immigrants having learned English, their opportunities widen.

We often omit the participle from an absolute phrase when it is some form of *be,* such as *being* or *having been*:

┌——— absolute phrase———┐
Two languages [being] at hand, bilingual citizens in fact have many cultural and occupational advantages.

Punctuating absolute phrases

Absolute phrases are always set off from the rest of the sentence with punctuation, usually a comma or commas (see also p. 454):

> Their future more secure, these citizens will make room for new arrivals.
> These citizens, their future more secure, will make room for new arrivals.

Exercise

Exercise 12.13   Sentence combining: Absolute phrases

To practice writing sentences with absolute phrases, combine each pair of sentences below into one sentence that contains an absolute phrase. You will have to add, delete, change, and rearrange words.

Example:
The flower's petals wilted. It looked pathetic.
<u>Its petals wilted</u>, the flower looked pathetic.

1. Geraldine Ferraro's face beamed. She enjoyed the crowd's cheers after her nomination for Vice President.
2. A vacancy had occurred. Sandra Day O'Connor was appointed the first female Supreme Court justice.
3. The vote was complete. Madeleine Albright was confirmed as the first female secretary of state.
4. Her appointment was confirmed. Condoleezza Rice became the first female national security adviser.
5. The election was over. Nancy Pelosi became the first female speaker of the House of Representatives.

gram

12c

4 Using subordinate clauses

A **clause** is any group of words that contains both a subject and a predicate. There are two kinds of clauses, and the distinction between them is important:

■ A *main* or *independent clause* makes a complete statement and can stand alone as a sentence: *The sky darkened.*

■ A *subordinate* or *dependent clause* is just like a main clause except that it begins with a subordinating word: *when the sky darkened*; *because he wants it*; *whoever calls.* The subordinating word reduces the clause to a single part of speech—an adjective, an adverb, or a noun—that supports the idea in a main clause. Because it only modifies or names something, a subordinate clause cannot stand alone as a sentence (see the discussion of punctuation on p. 275). (The word *subordinate* means "secondary" or "controlled by another." It comes from the Latin *sub*, "under," and *ordo*, "order.")

Exercise

The following examples show the differences between main and subordinate clauses:

┌──────────main clause──────────┬─main clause─┐
The school teaches parents. It is unusual.

┌──────────subordinate clause──────────┬─main clause─┐
Because the school teaches parents, it is unusual.

┌──────────main clause──────────┬──────main clause──────┐
Some parents avoid their children's schools. They are often illiterate.

┌──────────main clause──────────┐
Parents who are illiterate often avoid their children's schools.
        └subordinate clause┘

Two kinds of subordinating words introduce subordinate clauses: subordinating conjunctions and relative pronouns.

Subordinating conjunctions

Subordinating conjunctions, like prepositions, never change form in any way. In the following box they are arranged by the relationships they signal. (Some fit in more than one group.)

Common subordinating conjunctions

Cause or effect	Condition	Comparison or contrast	Space or time
as	even if	as	after
because	if	as if	as long as
in order that	if only	as though	before
since	provided	rather than	now that
so that	since	than	once
Concession	unless	whereas	since
although	when	whether	till
as if	whenever	while	until
even if	whether	**Purpose**	when
even though		in order that	whenever
though		so that	where
		that	wherever
			while

CULTURE LANGUAGE Learning the meanings of subordinating conjunctions can help you to express your ideas clearly. Note that each one conveys its meaning on its own. It does not need help from another function word, such as the coordinating conjunction *and, but, for,* or *so* (see p. 278).

Faulty Even though the parents are illiterate, but their children may read well. [*Even though* and *but* have the same meaning, so both are not needed.]

Revised Even though the parents are illiterate, their children may read well.

Relative pronouns

Unlike subordinating conjunctions, **relative pronouns** usually act as subjects or objects in their own clauses, and two of them (*who* and *whoever*) change form accordingly (see pp. 291–92).

Relative pronouns

which	what	who (whose, whom)
that	whatever	whoever (whomever)

---

gram
12c

Subordinate clauses

Subordinate clauses function as adjectives, adverbs, or nouns.

Adjective clauses

Adjective clauses modify nouns and pronouns. They usually begin with the relative pronoun *who, whom, whose, which,* or *that,* although a few adjective clauses begin with *when* or *where* (standing for *in which, on which,* or *at which*). The pronoun is the subject or object of the clause it begins. The clause ordinarily falls immediately after the noun or pronoun it modifies:

Parents who are illiterate often have bad memories of school.

Schools that involve parents are more successful with children.

One school, which is open year-round, helps parents learn to read.

The school is in a city where the illiteracy rate is high.

Adverb clauses

Like adverbs, **adverb clauses** modify verbs, adjectives, other adverbs, and whole groups of words. They usually tell how, why, when, where, under what conditions, or with what result. They always begin with subordinating conjunctions.

The school began teaching parents when adult illiteracy gained national attention.

At first the program was not as successful as its founders had hoped.

Because it was directed at people who could not read, advertising had to be inventive.

Noun clauses

Noun clauses function as subjects, objects, and complements in sentences. They begin with *that, what, whatever, who, whom, whoever, whomever, when, where, whether, why,* or *how.* Unlike adjective and adverb clauses, noun clauses *replace* a word (a noun) within a clause; therefore, they can be difficult to identify.

sentence subject
Whether the program would succeed depended on door-to-door advertising.

object of verb
Teachers explained in person how the program would work.

object of preposition
A few parents were anxious about what their children would think.

Elliptical clauses

A subordinate clause that is grammatically incomplete but clear in meaning is an **elliptical clause** (*ellipsis* means "omission"). The meaning of the clause is clear because the missing element can be supplied from the context. Most often the elements omitted are the pronouns *that, which,* and *whom* or the predicate from the second part of a comparison.

Skepticism and fear were among the feelings [that] the parents voiced.

The parents knew their children could read better than they [could read].

Punctuating subordinate clauses

Subordinate clauses punctuated as complete sentences are sentence fragments (Chapter 17). Though a subordinate clause contains a subject and a predicate and thus resembles a complete sentence, it also begins with a subordinating word that makes it into an adjective, adverb, or noun. A single part of speech cannot stand alone as a complete sentence.

gram

12c

Fragment	Because a door was ajar.
Revised	A door was ajar.
Revised	The secret leaked because a door was ajar.

A subordinate clause serving as an adverb is almost always set off with a comma when it introduces a sentence (see p. 447):

Although the project was almost completed, it lost its funding.

A modifying subordinate clause that interrupts or concludes a main clause is *not* set off with punctuation when it is essential to the meaning of the word or words it modifies (see p. 451):

The woman who directed the project lost her job.
The project lost its funding because it was not completed on time.

When an interrupting or concluding subordinate clause is *not* essential to meaning, but merely adds information to the sentence, it *is* set off with punctuation, usually a comma or commas (see pp. 450–51):

The project lost its funding, although it was almost completed.
The director, who holds a PhD, sought new funding.

Exercise 12.14 Identifying subordinate clauses

Identify the subordinate clauses in the following sentences. Then indicate whether each is used as an adjective, an adverb, or a noun. If the clause is a noun, indicate what function it performs in the sentence.

Example:

noun

The article explained <u>how one could build an underground house.</u>
[Object of *explained*.]

1. Scientists who want to catch the slightest signals from space use extremely sensitive receivers.
2. Even though they have had to fight for funding, these scientists have persisted in their research.
3. The research is called SETI, which stands for Search for Extraterrestrial Intelligence.
4. The theory is that intelligent beings in space are trying to get in touch with us.
5. Scientists do not yet know what frequency these beings would use to send signals.

Exercise 12.15   Sentence combining: Subordinate clauses

To practice writing sentences with subordinate clauses, combine each pair of main clauses into one sentence. Use either subordinating conjunctions or relative pronouns as appropriate, referring to the lists on page 273 if necessary. You will have to add, delete, and rearrange words. Each item has more than one possible answer.

Example:

She did not have her tire irons with her. She could not change her bicycle tire.

<u>Because she did not have her tire irons with her,</u> she could not change her bicycle tire.

1. Moviegoers expect something. Movie sequels should be as exciting as the original films.
2. A few sequels are good films. Most sequels are poor imitations of the originals.
3. A sequel to a blockbuster film arrives in the theater. Crowds quickly line up to see it.
4. Viewers pay to see the same villains and heroes. They remember these characters fondly.
5. Afterward, viewers often grumble about filmmakers. The filmmakers rehash tired plots and characters.

5 Using appositives

An **appositive** is usually a noun that renames another noun nearby, most often the noun just before the appositive. (The word *appositive* derives from a Latin word that means "placed near to" or "applied to.") An **appositive phrase** includes modifiers as well.

Bizen ware, a dark stoneware, has been produced in Japan since the fourteenth century.

The name Bizen comes from the location of the kilns used to fire the pottery.

All appositives can replace the words they refer to: *A dark stoneware has been produced in Japan.*

Appositives are often introduced by words and phrases such as *or, that is, such as, for example,* and *in other words*:

Bizen ware is used in the Japanese tea ceremony, that is, <u>the Zen Buddhist observance that links meditation and art.</u>

Appositives are economical alternatives to adjective clauses containing a form of *be*:

Bizen ware, <u>[which is] a dark stoneware</u>, has been produced in Japan since the fourteenth century.

Although most appositives are nouns that rename other nouns, they may also be and rename other parts of speech, such as the verb *thrown* in the sentence below:

The pottery is thrown, or <u>formed on a potter's wheel.</u>

Punctuating appositives

Appositives punctuated as complete sentences are sentence fragments (see Chapter 17). To correct such fragments, you can usually connect the appositive to the main clause containing the word referred to:

Fragment   An exceedingly tall man with narrow shoulders.

Revised   He stood next to a basketball player, <u>an exceedingly tall man with narrow shoulders.</u>

An appositive is *not* set off with punctuation when it is essential to the meaning of the word it refers to (see p. 451):

The verb *howl* comes from the Old English verb *houlen.*

When an appositive is *not* essential to the meaning of the word it refers to, it *is* set off with punctuation, usually a comma or commas (see p. 451):

<u>An aged elm,</u> the tree was struck by lightning.
The tree, <u>an aged elm,</u> was struck by lightning.
Lightning struck the tree, <u>an aged elm.</u>

A nonessential appositive is sometimes set off with a dash or dashes, especially when it contains commas (see p. 493):

Three people—<u>Will, Erica, and Alex</u>—object to the new procedure.

A concluding appositive is sometimes set off with a colon (see p. 491):

Two principles guide the judge's decisions: <u>justice and mercy.</u>

Exercise 12.16   Sentence combining: Appositives

To practice writing sentences with appositives, combine each pair of sentences into one sentence that contains an appositive. You will have to delete and rearrange words. Some items have more than one possible answer.

Example:

The largest land animal is the elephant. The elephant is also one of the most intelligent animals.

The largest land animal, the elephant, is also one of the most intelligent animals.

1. Some people perform amazing feats when they are very young. These people are geniuses from birth.
2. John Stuart Mill was a British philosopher. He had written a history of Rome by age seven.
3. Two great artists began their work at age four. They were Paul Klee and Gustav Mahler.
4. Mahler was a Bohemian composer of intensely emotional works. He was also the child of a brutal father.
5. Paul Klee was a Swiss painter. As a child he was frightened by his own drawings of devils.

gram

12d

12d   Compounding words, phrases, and clauses

A **compound construction** combines words that are closely related and equally important. It makes writing clearer and more economical because it pulls together linked information.

Headaches can be controlled by biofeedback. Heart rate can be controlled by biofeedback.

┌──────compound subject──────┐
Headaches and heart rate can be controlled by biofeedback.

Without medication, biofeedback cures headaches. It steadies heart rate. It lowers blood pressure. It relaxes muscles.

┌──────────── compound predicate ────────────┐
Without medication, biofeedback cures headaches, steadies heart rate, lowers blood pressure, and relaxes muscles.

1 Using coordinating conjunctions and correlative conjunctions

Two kinds of words create compound constructions: coordinating and correlative conjunctions. **Coordinating conjunctions** are few and do not change form. In the following box the relationship that each conjunction signals appears in parentheses.

Coordinating conjunctions

and (*addition*)   nor (*alternative*)   for (*cause*)   yet (*contrast*)
but (*contrast*)   or (*alternative*)   so (*effect*)

To remember the coordinating conjunctions, use the word *fanboys: for, and, nor, but, or, yet, so.*

The coordinating conjunctions *and, but, nor,* and *or* always connect words or word groups of the same kind—that is, two or more nouns, verbs, adjectives, adverbs, phrases, subordinate clauses, or main clauses:

Biofeedback or simple relaxation can relieve headaches.
Biofeedback is effective but costly.
Relaxation also works well, and it is inexpensive.

The conjunctions *for* and *so* connect only main clauses. *For* indicates cause; *so* indicates effect.

Biofeedback can be costly, for the training involves technical equipment and specialists.

Relaxation can be difficult to learn alone, so some people do seek help from specialists.

gram
12d

Some coordinating conjunctions pair up with other words to form **correlative conjunctions.** In the following box the relationship each conjunction signals appears in parentheses.

Common correlative conjunctions

both . . . and (*addition*)   neither . . . nor (*negation*)
not only . . . but also (*addition*)   whether . . . or (*alternative*)
not . . . but (*substitution*)   as . . . as (*comparison*)
either . . . or (*alternative*)

Both biofeedback and relaxation can relieve headaches.

The techniques require neither psychotherapy nor medication.

The headache sufferer learns not only to recognize the causes of headaches but also to control those causes.

Punctuating compounded words, phrases, and clauses

Two words, phrases, or subordinate clauses that are connected by a coordinating conjunction are *not* separated by a comma (see pp. 461–62):

> The library needs <u>renovation and rebuilding</u>.
>
> The work will begin <u>after spring term but before fall term</u>.

When two *main* clauses are joined into one sentence with a coordinating conjunction, a comma precedes the conjunction (see p. 444):

> The project will be lengthy<u>,and</u> everyone will suffer some inconvenience.

When two main clauses are joined *without* a coordinating conjunction, they must be separated with a semicolon to avoid the error called a comma splice (see p. 361):

> The work cannot be delayed<u>;</u> it's already overdue.

In a series of three or more items, commas separate the items, with *and* usually preceding the last item (see p. 455):

> The renovated library will feature <u>new study carrels, new shelving, and a larger reference section</u>.

Semicolons sometimes separate the items in a series if they are long or contain commas (see p. 470).

A comma also separates two or more adjectives when they modify a noun equally and are not joined by a coordinating conjunction (see p. 455):

> <u>Cracked, crumbling</u> walls will be repaired.

The comma does *not* separate adjectives when the one nearer the noun is more closely related to it in meaning (see p. 456):

> <u>New reading</u> lounges will replace the old ones.

gram
12d

2 Using conjunctive adverbs

One other kind of connecting word, called a **conjunctive adverb,** relates only main clauses, not words, phrases, or subordinate clauses. In the box opposite, the conjunctive adverbs are arranged by the relationships they signal.

It's important to distinguish between conjunctive adverbs and conjunctions (coordinating and subordinating) because they demand different punctuation (see the facing page). Conjunctive adverbs are *adverbs*: they describe the relation of ideas in two clauses, and, like most adverbs, they can move around in their clause:

> Relaxation techniques have improved; <u>however,</u> few people know them.
>
> Relaxation techniques have improved; few people know them, <u>however</u>.

In contrast, conjunctions bind two clauses into a single grammatical unit, and they cannot be moved.

Common conjunctive adverbs

Addition	Emphasis	Comparison or contrast	Cause or effect	Time
also	certainly	however	accordingly	finally
besides	indeed	in comparison	as a result	meanwhile
further	in fact	in contrast	consequently	next
furthermore	still	instead	hence	now
in addition	undoubtedly	likewise	similarly	then
incidentally		nevertheless	therefore	thereafter
moreover		nonetheless	thus	
		otherwise		
		rather		

> Although few people know them, relaxation techniques have improved. [The subordinating conjunction can't be moved: *Few people know them although, relaxation techniques have improved.*]

> Relaxation techniques have improved, but few people know them. [The coordinating conjunction can't be moved: *Relaxation techniques have improved, few people know them but.*]

gram
12d

Note Some connecting words have more than one use. *After, until,* and some other words may be either prepositions or subordinating conjunctions. Some prepositions, such as *behind* and *in,* can serve also as adverbs, as in *He trailed behind.* And some conjunctive adverbs, particularly *however,* may also serve simply as adverbs in sentences such as *However much the books cost, we must have them for our classes.* Again, the part of speech of a word depends on its function in a sentence.

Punctuating sentences containing conjunctive adverbs

Because the two main clauses related by a conjunctive adverb remain independent units, they must be separated by a semicolon. If they are separated by a comma, the result is a comma splice (Chapter 18):

> Comma splice Interest rates rose, therefore, real estate prices declined.
> Revised Interest rates rose; therefore, real estate prices declined.

A conjunctive adverb is almost always set off from its clause with a comma or commas (see p. 452):

> The decline was small; however, some home owners suffered unexpected losses.

> The decline was small; some home owners, however, suffered unexpected losses.

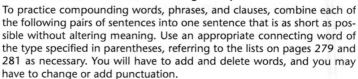

Exercise 12.17 Sentence combining: Compound constructions

To practice compounding words, phrases, and clauses, combine each of the following pairs of sentences into one sentence that is as short as possible without altering meaning. Use an appropriate connecting word of the type specified in parentheses, referring to the lists on pages 279 and 281 as necessary. You will have to add and delete words, and you may have to change or add punctuation.

Example:

The encyclopedia had some information. It was not detailed enough. (*Conjunctive adverb.*)

The encyclopedia had some information; however, it was not detailed enough.

1. All too often people assume that old age is not a productive time. Many people in their nineties have had great achievements. (*Conjunctive adverb.*)
2. In his nineties the philosopher Bertrand Russell spoke vigorously for international peace. He spoke for nuclear disarmament. (*Correlative conjunction.*)
3. Grandma Moses did not retire to an easy chair. She began painting at age seventy-six and was still going at one hundred. (*Conjunctive adverb.*)
4. The American dancer and choreographer Martha Graham choreographed works after she was eighty. The American dancer and choreographer Merce Cunningham choreographed works after he was eighty. (*Coordinating conjunction.*)
5. The architect Frank Lloyd Wright designed his first building at age twenty. He designed his last building at age ninety. (*Coordinating conjunction.*)

12e Changing the usual word order

So far, all the examples of basic sentence structure have been similar: the subject of the sentence comes first, naming the performer of the predicate's action, and the predicate comes second. This arrangement describes most English sentences, but four kinds of sentences change the order.

Questions

In most questions the predicate verb or a part of it precedes the subject:

verb   subject ┌──verb──┐
Have interest rates been rising?

verb subject verb
Did rates rise?

verb subject verb
Why did rates rise today?

subject verb
What is the answer? [Normal subject-verb order.]

Commands

In commands the subject *you* is omitted:

verb   verb
Think of the options.   Watch the news.

Passive sentences

Generally, the subject performs the action of a verb in the **active voice.** But sometimes the subject *receives* the action of a verb in the **passive voice:**

subject   verb
Active   Kyong wrote the paper.

subject —— verb ——┐
Passive   The paper was written by Kyong.

See pages 320–21 for more on forming the passive voice, and see pages 321–22 on overuse of the passive voice.

Sentences with postponed subjects

The subject follows the predicate in two sentence patterns. The normal order may be reversed for emphasis:

Henry comes here. [Normal order.]
Here comes Henry. [Reversed order.]

Or the word *there* or *it* may postpone the subject:

verb   subject
There will be eighteen people attending the meeting.

verb   ┌————— subject—————┐
It was surprising that Marinetti was nominated.

There and *it* in such sentences are called **expletives.** Expletive sentences have their uses, but they can also be wordy and unemphatic (see pp. 550–51).

CULTURE / LANGUAGE When you use an expletive construction, be careful to include *there* or *it.* Only commands and some questions can begin with verbs.

Faulty   No one predicted the nomination. Were no polls showing Marinetti ahead.

Revised   No one predicted the nomination. There were no polls showing Marinetti ahead.

Exercise 12.18   Forming questions and commands

Form a question and a command from the following noun and verb pairs.

Example:
wood, split
Did you split all this wood? Split the wood for our fire.

1. water, boil   3. table, set   5. telephone, use
2. music, stop   4. dice, roll

gram
12e

Exercise

Exercise 12.19 Rewriting passives and expletives

Rewrite each passive sentence below as active, and rewrite each expletive construction to restore normal subject-predicate order. (For additional exercises with the passive voice and with expletives, see pp. 322, 402, and 552.)

Example:

All the trees in the park were planted by the city.
<u>The city planted</u> all the trees in the park.

1. The screenplay for *Monster's Ball* was cowritten by Milo Addica and Will Rokos.
2. The film was directed by Marc Foster.
3. There was only one performance in the movie that received an Academy Award.
4. It was Halle Berry who won the award for best actress.
5. Berry was congratulated by the press for being the first African American to win the award.

12f Classifying sentences

We describe and classify sentences in two different ways: by function (statement, question, command, exclamation, and so on) or by structure. Four basic sentence structures are possible: simple, compound, complex, and compound-complex. Each structure gives different emphasis to the sentence's main idea or ideas and to any supporting information.

1 Writing simple sentences

A **simple sentence** consists of a single main clause and no subordinate clause:

┌─────────── main clause ───────────┐
Last summer was unusually hot.

┌────────────────────── main clause ──────────────────────┐
The summer made many farmers leave the area for good or reduced them to bare existence.

2 Writing compound sentences

A **compound sentence** consists of two or more main clauses and no subordinate clause. The clauses may be joined by a coordinating conjunction and a comma, by a semicolon alone, or by a conjunctive adverb and a semicolon.

┌──── main clause ────┐   ┌──── main clause ────┐
Last July was hot, but August was even hotter.

┌──────── main clause ────────┐ ┌──────── main clause ────────┐
The hot sun scorched the earth; the lack of rain killed many crops.

┌──────── main clause ────────┐   ┌─main clause─┐
This summer was also dry; however, it was cooler.

3 Writing complex sentences

A **complex sentence** contains one main clause and one or more subordinate clauses:

```
┌──main clause──┐ ┌──────────── subordinate clause ──────────────┐
Rain finally came, although many had left the area by then.
```

```
   ┌──────────────────── main clause ────────────────────┐ ┌────── subordinate clause ──────
Those who remained were able to start anew because the government
      subordinate clause
┌─────────────────────┐
came to their aid.
```

Notice that length does not determine whether a sentence is complex or simple; both kinds can be short or long.

4 Writing compound-complex sentences

A **compound-complex sentence** has the characteristics of both the compound sentence (two or more main clauses) and the complex sentence (at least one subordinate clause):

```
┌──────────── subordinate clause ────────────┐ ┌─────────── main clause ───────────┐
When government aid finally came, many people had already been re-
┌─────────────────────────┐ ┌─────────── main clause ───────────┐
duced to poverty and others had been forced to move.
```

Exercise 12.20 Identifying sentence structures

Mark the main clauses and subordinate clauses in the following sentences. Identify each sentence as simple, compound, complex, or compound-complex.

Example:

```
┌──────────────── main clause ────────────────┐ ┌────── subordinate clause ──────
The police began patrolling more often when crime in the neigh-
┌──────────────────────┐
borhood increased. [Complex sentence.]
```

1. Joseph Pulitzer endowed the Pulitzer Prizes.
2. Pulitzer, incidentally, was the publisher of the New York newspaper *The World.*
3. Although the first prizes were for journalism and letters only, Pulitzers are now awarded in music and other areas.
4. For example, Berke Breathed won for his *Bloom County* comic strip, and Roger Reynolds won for his musical composition *Whispers out of Time.*
5. Although only one prize is usually awarded in each category, in 2010 Sheri Fink's "The Deadly Choices at Memorial" won a prize for investigative journalism, and it shared the honor with "Tainted Justice" by Barbara Laker and Wendy Ruderman.

Exercise 12.21 Sentence combining: Sentence structures

Combine each of the following sets of simple sentences to produce the kind of sentence specified in parentheses. You will have to add, delete, change, and rearrange words.

Exercise

Example:
The traffic passed the house. It never stopped. (*Complex.*)
The traffic that passed the house never stopped.

1. Recycling takes time. It reduces garbage in landfills. (*Compound.*)
2. People begin to recycle. They generate much less trash. (*Complex.*)
3. White tissues and paper towels biodegrade more easily than dyed ones. People still buy dyed papers. (*Complex.*)
4. The cans are aluminum. They bring recyclers good money. (*Simple.*)
5. Environmentalists have hope. Perhaps more communities will recycle newspaper and glass. Many citizens refuse to participate. (*Compound-complex.*)

13

Case of Nouns and Pronouns

Video
tutorial

Case is the form of a noun or pronoun that shows the reader how it functions in a sentence—that is, whether it functions as a subject, as an object, or in some other way. As shown in the box on the next page, only *I, we, he, she, they,* and *who* change form for each case. Thus these pronouns are the focus of this chapter.

Exercise

The **subjective case** generally indicates that the word is a subject or a subject complement. (See pp. 253 and 259–60.)

subject
<u>She and Novick</u> discussed the proposal.

subject
The proposal ignores many <u>who</u> need help.

subject complement
The disgruntled planners were <u>she and Novick</u>.

The **objective case** generally indicates that the word is the object of a verb or preposition. (See pp. 258–61 and 264–65.)

object of verb
The proposal disappointed <u>her and Novick</u>.

mycomplab

Visit *mycomplab.com* for the eText and for resources and more exercises on noun and pronoun case.

Case forms of nouns and pronouns

	Subjective	Objective	Possessive
Nouns	boy	boy	boy's
	Jessie	Jessie	Jessie's
Personal pronouns			
Singular			
1st person	I	me	my, mine
2nd person	you	you	your, yours
3rd person	he	him	his
	she	her	her, hers
	it	it	its
Plural			
1st person	we	us	our, ours
2nd person	you	you	your, yours
3rd person	they	them	their, theirs
Relative and interrogative pronouns			
	who	whom	whose
	whoever	whomever	—
	which, that, what	which, that, what	—
Indefinite pronouns	everybody	everybody	everybody's

Video tutorial

case
13

object
of verb / object
of verb

A colleague <u>whom</u> they respected let <u>them</u> down.

object of
preposition

Their opinion of <u>him</u> suffered.

The **possessive case** generally indicates ownership or source:

<u>Her</u> counterproposal is in preparation.
<u>Theirs</u> is the more defensible position.
The problem is not <u>his</u>.

Do not use an apostrophe to form the possessive of personal pronouns: *yours* (not *your's*); *theirs* (not *their's*). (See p. 478. See also p. 475 for the possessive forms of nouns, which do use apostrophes.)

Grammar checkers A grammar checker may flag some problems with pronoun case, but it will also miss a lot. For instance, one checker spotted the error in *We asked <u>whom</u> would come* (should be *<u>who</u> would come*), but it overlooked *We dreaded <u>them</u> coming* (should be *<u>their</u> coming*).

Video tutorial

 In standard American English, *-self* pronouns do not change form to show function. Their only forms are

myself, yourself, himself, herself, itself, ourselves, yourselves, themselves.
Avoid nonstandard forms such as *hisself, ourself,* and *theirselves.*

| Faulty | Novick presented the proposal hisself. |
| Revised | Novick presented the proposal himself. |

13a Use the subjective case for compound subjects and for subject complements.

Podcast

In compound subjects use the same pronoun form you would
use if the pronoun stood alone as a subject:

subject
She and Novick will persist.

subject
The others may lend their support when she and Novick get a hearing.

If you are in doubt about the correct form, try the test in the box
below.

**case
13a**

A test for case forms in compound constructions

1. Identify a compound construction (one connected by *and, but, or, nor*).

   [He, Him] and [I, me] won the prize.
   The prize went to [he, him] and [I, me].

2. Write a separate sentence for each part of the compound.

   [He, Him] won the prize. [I, Me] won the prize.
   The prize went to [he, him]. The prize went to [I, me].

3. Choose the pronouns that sound correct.

   He won the prize. I won the prize. [Subjective.]
   The prize went to him. The prize went to me. [Objective.]

4. Put the separate sentences back together.

   He and I won the prize.
   The prize went to him and me.

After a linking verb, such as a form of *be,* a pronoun renaming
the subject (a subject complement) should be in the subjective case:

subject complement
The ones who care most are she and Novick.

subject
complement
It was they whom the mayor appointed.

If this construction sounds stilted to you, use the more natural order:
She and Novick are the ones who care most. The mayor appointed them.

13b Use the objective case for compound objects.

In compound objects use the same pronoun form you would use if the pronoun stood alone as an object:

Podcast

direct object
The mayor nominated <u>Zhu and him</u>.

indirect object
The mayor gave <u>Zhu and him</u> awards.

object of preposition
Credit goes equally to <u>them and the mayor</u>.

If you are in doubt about the correct form, try the test in the box opposite.

Exercise 13.1 Choosing between subjective and objective pronouns

From the pairs in brackets, select the appropriate subjective or objective pronoun(s) for each of the following sentences.

Exercise

Example:
"Between you and [I, me]," the seller said, "this deal is a steal."
"Between you and <u>me</u>," the seller said, "this deal is a steal."

case
13d

1. Lisa and [I, me] were competing for places on the relay team.
2. The fastest runners at our school were [she, her] and [I, me], so [we, us] expected to make the team.
3. [She, Her] and [I, me] were friends but also intense rivals.
4. The time trials went badly, excluding both [she, her] and [I, me] from the team.
5. Next season [she, her] and [I, me] are determined to earn places on the team.

13c Use the appropriate case when the plural pronoun *we* or *us* occurs with a noun.

Whether to use *we* or *us* with a noun depends on the use of the noun:

object of
preposition
Freezing weather is welcomed by <u>us</u> skaters.

subject
<u>We</u> skaters welcome freezing weather.

13d In appositives the case of a pronoun depends on the function of the word described or identified.

appositive
object of verb   identifies object
The class elected two <u>representatives</u>, DeShawn and <u>me</u>.

subject   appositive
                identifies subject
Two representatives, DeShawn and I, were elected.

If you are in doubt about case in an appositive, try the sentence without the word the appositive identifies: *The class elected De-Shawn and me. DeShawn and I were elected.*

Exercise 13.2 Choosing between subjective and objective pronouns

From the pairs in brackets, select the appropriate subjective or objective pronoun for each of the following sentences.

Example:

Convincing [we, us] veterans to vote yes will be difficult.
Convincing us veterans to vote yes will be difficult.

1. Obtaining enough protein is important to [we, us] vegetarians.
2. Instead of obtaining protein from meat, [we, us] vegetarians get our protein from other sources.
3. Jeff claims to know only two vegetarians, [he, him] and Helena, who avoid all animal products, including milk.
4. Some of [we, us] vegetarians eat fish, which is a good source of protein.
5. [We, Us] vegetarians in my family, my parents and [I, me], drink milk and eat fish.

13e The case of a pronoun after *than* or *as* in a comparison depends on the meaning.

When a pronoun follows *than* or *as* in a comparison, the case of the pronoun indicates what words may have been omitted. When the pronoun is subjective, it must serve as the subject of an omitted verb:

subject
Some critics like Glass more than he [does].

When the pronoun is objective, it must serve as the object of an omitted verb:

object
Some critics like Glass more than [they like] him.

13f Use the objective case for pronouns that are subjects or objects of infinitives.

subject of
infinitive
The school asked him to speak.

object of
infinitive
Students chose to invite him.

case
13f

13g Use *who* or *whom* depending on function.

To choose between *who* and *whom*, *whoever* and *whomever*, you need to figure out whether the word serves as a subject or as an object. Use *who* where you would use *he* or *she*—all ending in vowels. Use *whom* where you would use *him* or *her*—all ending in consonants.

Podcast

Exercise

1 At the beginning of a question, use *who* for a subject and *whom* for an object.

subject⟶
<u>Who</u> wrote the policy?

object ⟵
<u>Whom</u> does it affect?

A test for *who* versus *whom* in questions

1. **Pose the question.**

   [Who, Whom] makes that decision?
   [Who, Whom] does one ask?

2. **Answer the question, using a personal pronoun.** Choose the pronoun that sounds correct, and note its case.

   [She, Her] makes that decision. She makes that decision. [Subjective.]
   One asks [she, her]. One asks her. [Objective.]

3. **Use the same case (*who* or *whom*) in the question.**

   Who makes that decision? [Subjective.]
   Whom does one ask? [Objective.]

---

case

13g

Note In speech the subjective case *who* is commonly used whenever it is the first word of a question, regardless of whether it is a subject or an object. But formal writing requires a distinction between the forms:

Spoken <u>Who</u> should we credit?

object ⟵
Written <u>Whom</u> should we credit?

2 In a subordinate clause, use *who* or *whoever* for a subject, *whom* or *whomever* for an object.

The case of a pronoun in a subordinate clause depends on its function in the clause, regardless of whether the clause itself functions as a subject, an object, or a modifier:

subject ⟶
Credit <u>whoever</u> wrote the policy.

object ←———
Research should reveal <u>whom</u> to credit.

Note Don't let expressions such as *I think* and *she says* confuse you when they come between the subject *who* and its verb:

subject ———————→
He is the one <u>who</u> the polls say will win.

To choose between *who* and *whom* in such constructions, delete the interrupting phrase: *He is the one <u>who</u> will win.*

A test for *who* versus *whom* in subordinate clauses

1. Locate the subordinate clause.

   Few people know [<u>who, whom</u>] they should ask.
   They are unsure [<u>who, whom</u>] makes the decision.

2. Rewrite the subordinate clause as a separate sentence, substituting a personal pronoun for *who, whom*. Choose the pronoun that sounds correct, and note its case.

   They should ask [<u>she, her</u>]. They should ask her. [Objective.]
   [<u>She, Her</u>] makes the decision. She makes the decision. [Subjective.]

3. Use the same case (*who* or *whom*) in the subordinate clause.

   Few people know whom they should ask. [Objective.]
   They are unsure who makes the decision. [Subjective.]

Exercise

Exercise 13.3 Choosing between *who* and *whom*

From the pairs in brackets, select the appropriate form of the pronoun in each of the following sentences.

> *Example:*
> My mother asked me [who, whom] I was going out with.
> My mother asked me <u>whom</u> I was going out with.

1. The judges awarded first prize to Inez, [<u>who, whom</u>] they believed gave the best performance.
2. Inez beat the other contestants [<u>who, whom</u>] competed against her.
3. She is a consummate performer, singing to [<u>whoever, whomever</u>] would listen.
4. [<u>Who, Whom</u>] in the school has not heard Inez sing?
5. [<u>Who, Whom</u>] has she not performed for?

Exercise

Exercise 13.4 Sentence combining: *Who* versus *whom*

Combine each of the following pairs of sentences into one sentence that contains a clause beginning with *who* or *whom*. Be sure to use the appropriate case form. You will have to add, delete, and rearrange words. Each item may have more than one possible answer.

case
13g

Example:
David is the candidate. We think David deserves to win.
David is the candidate <u>who</u> we think deserves to win.

1. Some children have undetected hearing problems. These children may do poorly in school.
2. They may not hear important instructions and information from teachers. Teachers may speak softly.
3. Classmates may not be audible. The teacher calls on those classmates.
4. Some hearing-impaired children may work harder to overcome their disability. These children get a lot of encouragement at home.
5. Some hearing-impaired children may take refuge in fantasy friends. They can rely on these friends not to criticize or laugh.

13h   Ordinarily, use a possessive pronoun or noun immediately before a gerund.

case

13h

A **gerund** is the *-ing* form of a verb (*running, sleeping*) used as a noun (p. 268). Like nouns, gerunds are commonly preceded by possessive nouns and pronouns: *our vote* (noun), *our voting* (gerund).

The coach disapproved of their lifting weights.

The coach's disapproving was a surprise.

A noun or pronoun before an *-ing* verb form is not always possessive. Sometimes the *-ing* form will be a present participle modifying the preceding word:

Everyone had noticed him weightlifting. [Emphasis on *him*.]
               objective   participle
               pronoun

Everyone had noticed his weightlifting. [Emphasis on the activity.]
               possessive gerund
               pronoun

Note that a gerund usually is not preceded by the possessive when the possessive would create an awkward construction:

Awkward	A rumor spread about <u>everybody's</u> on the team wanting to quit.
Less awkward	A rumor spread about <u>everybody</u> on the team wanting to quit.
Better	A rumor spread <u>that everybody</u> on the team <u>wanted</u> to quit.

Exercise 13.5   Revising: Case
Revise all inappropriate case forms in the following paragraph, and explain the function of each case form.

Exercise

Written four thousand years ago, *The Epic of Gilgamesh* tells of the friendship of Gilgamesh and Enkidu. Gilgamesh was a bored king who his people thought was too harsh. Then he met Enkidu, a wild man whom had lived with the animals in the mountains. Immediately, him and Gilgamesh wrestled to see whom was more powerful. After hours of struggle, Enkidu admitted that Gilgamesh was stronger than him. Now the friends needed adventures worthy of the two strongest men on earth. Gilgamesh said, "Between you and I, mighty deeds will be accomplished, and our fame will be everlasting." Among their acts, Enkidu and him defeated a giant bull, Humbaba, and cut down the bull's cedar forests. Them bringing back cedar logs to Gilgamesh's treeless land won great praise from the people. When Enkidu died, Gilgamesh mourned his death, realizing that no one had been a better friend than him. When Gilgamesh himself died many years later, his people raised a monument praising Enkidu and he for their friendship and their mighty deeds of courage.

Note See page 349 for an exercise involving case along with other aspects of grammar.

14

Verbs

The verb is the most complicated part of speech in English, changing form to express a wide range of information.

Verb Forms

All verbs except *be* have five basic forms. The first three are the verb's **principal parts.**

- The *plain form* is the dictionary form of the verb. When the subject is a plural noun or the pronoun *I, we, you,* or *they,* the plain form indicates action that occurs in the present, occurs habitually, or is generally true.

Visit *mycomplab.com* for the eText and for resources and more exercises on verb forms.

Terms used to describe verbs

Tense

The time of the verb's action—for instance, present (*kick*), past (*kicked*), future (***will** kick*). (See p. 311.)

Mood

The attitude of the verb's speaker or writer—the difference, for example, in *I kick the ball, Kick the ball,* and *I suggested that she kick the ball.* (See p. 318.)

Voice

The distinction between the **active,** in which the subject performs the verb's action (*I kick the ball*), and the **passive,** in which the subject is acted upon (*The ball is kicked by me*). (See p. 320.)

Person

The verb form that reflects whether the subject is speaking (*I/we kick the ball*), spoken to (*You kick the ball*), or spoken about (*She kicks the ball*). (See p. 324.)

Number

The verb form that reflects whether the subject is singular (*The girl kicks the ball*) or plural (*Girls kick the ball*). (See p. 324.)

vb
14

A few artists live in town today.
They hold classes downtown.

■ The *past-tense form* indicates that the action of the verb occurred before now. It usually adds -*d* or -*ed* to the plain form, although some irregular verbs form it in other ways (see p. 297).

Many artists lived in town before this year.
They held classes downtown. [Irregular verb.]

■ The *past participle* is the same as the past-tense form, except in most irregular verbs. It combines with forms of *have* or *be* (*has climbed, was created*), or by itself it modifies nouns and pronouns (*the sliced apples*).

Artists have lived in town for decades.
They have held classes downtown. [Irregular verb.]

■ The *present participle* adds -*ing* to the verb's plain form. It combines with forms of *be* (*is buying*), modifies nouns and pronouns (*the boiling water*), or functions as a noun (*Running exhausts me*).

A few artists are living in town today.
They are holding classes downtown.

▪ **The -s form ends in -s or -es.** When the subject is a singular noun, a pronoun such as *everyone,* or the personal pronoun *he, she,* or *it,* the -s form indicates action that occurs in the present, occurs habitually, or is generally true.

The artist lives in town today.
She holds classes downtown.

The verb *be* has eight forms rather than the five forms of most other verbs:

Plain form	be
Present participle	being
Past participle	been

	I	*he, she, it*	*we, you, they*
Present tense	am	is	are
Past tense	was	was	were

CULTURE LANGUAGE If standard American English is not your native language or dialect, you may have difficulty with the -s forms of verbs (as in *He skis, and he runs*), with their past-tense forms (*They skied, and they ran*), or with their past participles (*We have skied, and we have run*). See pages 297–99 and 301–02 for more on these forms.

vb
14

Helping verbs

Helping verbs, also called **auxiliary verbs,** combine with some verb forms to indicate time and other kinds of meaning, as in *can run, was sleeping, had been eaten.* These combinations are **verb phrases.** Since the plain form, present participle, or past participle in any verb phrase always carries the principal meaning, it is sometimes called the **main verb.**

	Verb phrase	
	Helping	*Main*
Artists	can	train others to draw.
The techniques	have	changed little.

These are the most common helping verbs:

Forms of *be*: be, am, is, are, was, were, been, being
Forms of *have*: have, has, had, having
Forms of *do*: do, does, did

be able to	had better	must	used to
be supposed to	have to	ought to	will
can	may	shall	would
could	might	should	

CULTURE LANGUAGE The helping verbs of standard American English may be problematic if you are used to speaking another language or dialect. See pages 302–06 for more on helping verbs.

14a Use the correct forms of regular and irregular verbs.

Most verbs are **regular;** that is, they form their past tense and past participle by adding *-d* or *-ed* to the plain form.

Plain form	Past tense	Past participle
live	lived	lived
act	acted	acted

Since the past tense and past participle are the same, the forms of regular verbs do not often cause problems (but see pp. 301–02).

About two hundred English verbs are **irregular;** that is, they form their past tense and past participle in some irregular way.

Plain form	Past tense	Past participle
begin	began	begun
break	broke	broken
sleep	slept	slept

You can see the difference between a regular and an irregular verb in these examples:

Plain form	Today the birds twitter.
	Today the birds sing.
Past tense	Yesterday the birds twittered.
	Yesterday the birds sang.
Past participle	In the past the birds have twittered.
	In the past the birds have sung.

vb

14a

The box on the next two pages lists the forms of many irregular verbs. Check this box or a dictionary if you have any doubt about a verb's principal parts. If a dictionary lists only the plain form, the verb is regular: both the past tense and the past participle add *-d* or *-ed* to the plain form. If the verb is irregular, the dictionary will list the plain form, the past tense, and the past participle in that order (*go, went, gone*). If the dictionary gives only two forms (as in *think, thought*), then the past tense and the past participle are the same.

Grammar checkers A grammar checker may flag incorrect forms of irregular verbs, but it may also fail to do so. For example, a checker did not flag *The runner had steal second base* (*stolen* is correct). When in doubt about the forms of irregular verbs, refer to the box on the next two pages or consult a dictionary.

 Some English dialects use verb forms that differ from those of standard American English: for instance, *drug* for *dragged, growed* for *grew, come* for *came,* or *went* for *gone.* In situations requiring standard American English, use the forms in the following box or in a dictionary.

| Faulty | They have went to the movies. |
| Revised | They have gone to the movies. |

Principal parts of common irregular verbs

Plain form	Past tense	Past participle
arise	arose	arisen
be	was, were	been
become	became	become
begin	began	begun
bid	bid	bid
bite	bit	bitten, bit
blow	blew	blown
break	broke	broken
bring	brought	brought
burst	burst	burst
buy	bought	bought
catch	caught	caught
choose	chose	chosen
come	came	come
cut	cut	cut
dive	dived, dove	dived
do	did	done
draw	drew	drawn
dream	dreamed, dreamt	dreamed, dreamt
drink	drank	drunk
drive	drove	driven
eat	ate	eaten
fall	fell	fallen
find	found	found
flee	fled	fled
fly	flew	flown
forget	forgot	forgotten, forgot
freeze	froze	frozen
get	got	got, gotten
give	gave	given
go	went	gone
grow	grew	grown
hang (suspend)	hung	hung
hang (execute)	hanged	hanged
have	had	had
hear	heard	heard
hide	hid	hidden
hold	held	held
keep	kept	kept
know	knew	known
lay	laid	laid
lead	led	led
leave	left	left
lend	lent	lent
let	let	let
lie	lay	lain

vb
14a

Plain form	Past tense	Past participle
lose	lost	lost
pay	paid	paid
prove	proved	proved, proven
ride	rode	ridden
ring	rang	rung
rise	rose	risen
run	ran	run
say	said	said
see	saw	seen
set	set	set
shake	shook	shaken
shrink	shrank, shrunk	shrunk, shrunken
sing	sang, sung	sung
sink	sank, sunk	sunk
sit	sat	sat
sleep	slept	slept
slide	slid	slid
speak	spoke	spoken
spring	sprang, sprung	sprung
stand	stood	stood
steal	stole	stolen
swim	swam	swum
swing	swung	swung
take	took	taken
teach	taught	taught
tear	tore	torn
throw	threw	thrown
wear	wore	worn
write	wrote	written

vb

14a

Exercise 14.1 Using irregular verbs

For each irregular verb in brackets, give either the past tense or the past participle, as appropriate, and identify the form you used.

Exercise

Example:

Though we had [hide] the cash box, it was [steal].

Though we had <u>hidden</u> the cash box, it was <u>stolen</u>. [Two past participles.]

1. The world population has [grow] by two-thirds of a billion people in less than a decade.
2. In 2000 it [break] the 6 billion mark.
3. Experts have [draw] pictures of a crowded future.
4. They predict that the world population may have [slide] up to as much as 10 billion by the year 2050.
5. Though the food supply [rise] in the last decade, the share to each person [fall].

14b Distinguish between *sit* and *set, lie* and *lay,* and *rise* and *raise.*

The forms of *sit* and *set, lie* and *lay,* and *rise* and *raise* are easy to confuse:

Plain form	Past tense	Past participle
sit	sat	sat
set	set	set
lie	lay	lain
lay	laid	laid
rise	rose	risen
raise	raised	raised

In each of these confusing pairs, one verb is **intransitive** (it does not take an object) and one is **transitive** (it does take an object). (See pp. 258–59 for more on this distinction.)

vb
14b

Intransitive

The patients lie in their beds. [*Lie* means "recline" and takes no object.]

Visitors sit with them. [*Sit* means "be seated" or "be located" and takes no object.]

Patients' temperatures rise. [*Rise* means "increase" or "get up" and takes no object.]

Transitive

Orderlies lay the dinner trays on tables. [*Lay* means "place" and takes an object, here *trays*.]

Orderlies set the trays down. [*Set* means "place" and takes an object, here *trays*.]

Nursing aides raise the shades. [*Raise* means "lift" or "bring up" and takes an object, here *shades*.]

Exercise

Exercise 14.2 Distinguishing *sit/set, lie/lay, rise/raise*

Choose the correct verb from the pair given in brackets. Then supply the past tense or past participle, as appropriate.

Example:

After I washed all the windows, I [lie, lay] down the squeegee and then I [sit, set] the table.

After I washed all the windows, I laid down the squeegee and then I set the table.

1. Yesterday afternoon the child [lie, lay] down for a nap.
2. The child has been [rise, raise] by her grandparents.
3. Most days her grandfather has [sit, set] with her, reading her stories.
4. She has [rise, raise] at dawn most mornings.
5. Her toys were [lie, lay] out on the floor.

| 14c | Use the *-s* and *-ed* forms of the verb when they are required. | |

Exercise

Speakers of some English dialects and nonnative speakers of English sometimes omit the *-s* and *-ed* verb endings when they are required in standard American English.

Note If you tend to omit these endings in writing, practice pronouncing them when speaking or when reading correct verbs aloud, such as those in the examples here. The spoken practice can help you remember the endings in writing.

Grammar checkers A grammar checker will flag many omitted *-s* and *-ed* endings from verbs, such as in *he ask* and *was ask.* But it will miss many omissions, too.

Required *-s* ending

Use the *-s* form of a verb when *both* of these situations hold:

- The subject is a singular noun (*boy*), an indefinite pronoun (*everyone*), or *he, she,* or *it.* These subjects are **third person,** used when someone or something is being spoken about.
- The verb's action occurs in the present.

vb
14c

The letter <u>asks</u> [not <u>ask</u>] for a quick response.
Delay <u>costs</u> [not <u>cost</u>] money.

Be especially careful with the *-s* forms of *be* (*is*), *have* (*has*), and *do* (*does, doesn't*). These forms should always be used to indicate present time with third-person singular subjects.

The company <u>is</u> [not <u>be</u>] late in responding.
It <u>has</u> [not <u>have</u>] problems.
It <u>doesn't</u> [not <u>don't</u>] have the needed data.
The contract <u>does</u> [not <u>do</u>] depend on the response.

In addition, *be* has the *-s* form *was* in the past tense with *I* and with third-person singular subjects:

The company <u>was</u> [not <u>were</u>] in trouble before.

Except for the past tense *I was,* the pronouns *I* and *you* and all plural subjects do *not* take the *-s* form of verbs:

I <u>am</u> [not <u>is</u>] a student.
You <u>are</u> [not <u>is</u>] also a student.
They <u>are</u> [not <u>is</u>] students, too.

Required *-ed* or *-d* ending

The *-ed* or *-d* verb form is required in *any* of the following situations:

■ The verb's action occurred in the past:

Yesterday the company <u>asked</u> [not <u>ask</u>] for more time.

■ The verb form functions as a modifier:

The data <u>concerned</u> [not <u>concern</u>] should be retrievable.

■ The verb form combines with a form of *be* or *have*:

The company is <u>supposed</u> [not <u>suppose</u>] to be the best.
It has <u>developed</u> [not <u>develop</u>] an excellent reputation.

Watch especially for a needed *-ed* or *-d* ending when it isn't pronounced clearly in speech, as in *asked, discussed, mixed, supposed, walked,* and *used.*

Exercise

Exercise 14.3 Using *-s* and *-ed* verb endings

Supply the correct form of each verb in brackets. Be careful to include *-s* and *-ed* (or *-d*) endings where they are needed for standard English.

A teacher sometimes [ask] too much of a student. In high school I was once [punish] for being sick. I had [miss] some school, and I [realize] that I would fail a test unless I had a chance to make up the classwork. I [discuss] the problem with the teacher, but he said I was [suppose] to make up the work while I was sick. At that I [walk] out of the class. I [receive] a failing grade then, but it did not change my attitude. Today I still balk when a teacher [make] unreasonable demands or [expect] miracles.

vb
14d

14d Use helping verbs with main verbs appropriately.

Exercise

Helping verbs combine with main verbs to form verb phrases (see p. 296).

Common helping verbs

Forms of *be:* be, am, is, are, was, were, been, being
Forms of *have:* have, has, had, having
Forms of *do:* do, does, did

be able to	had better	must	used to
be supposed to	have to	ought to	will
can	may	shall	would
could	might	should	

Grammar checkers A grammar checker often spots omitted helping verbs and incorrect main verbs with helping verbs, but sometimes it does not. A checker flagged *Many been fortunate* and *She working* but overlooked other examples on the following pages.

1 Use helping verbs when they are required.

Standard American English requires helping verbs in certain situations:

- The main verb ends in *-ing*.

  Researchers <u>are</u> conducting fieldwork all over the world. [Not <u>Researchers conducting</u>. . . .]

- The main verb is *been* or *be*.

  Many <u>have</u> been fortunate in their discoveries. [Not <u>Many been</u>. . . .]
  Some <u>could</u> be real-life Indiana Joneses. [Not <u>Some be</u>. . . .]

- The main verb is a past participle, such as *talked, begun,* or *thrown*.

  Their discoveries <u>were</u> covered in newspapers and magazines. [Not <u>Their discoveries covered</u>. . . .]

  Often the researchers <u>have</u> done TV interviews. [Not <u>the researchers done</u>. . . .]

In every example above, omitting the helping verb would create an incomplete sentence, or **sentence fragment** (see Chapter 17). In a complete sentence, some part of the verb (helping or main) must be capable of changing form to show changes in time: *I run, I <u>ran</u>; you <u>are</u> running, you <u>were</u> running* (see p. 353). But a present participle (*conducting*), an irregular past participle (*been*), and the plain form *be* cannot change form in this way. They need helping verbs to work as sentence verbs.

vb
14d

2 Combine helping verbs and main verbs appropriately for your meaning.

Helping verbs and main verbs combine into verb phrases in specific ways.

Note The main verb in a verb phrase (the one carrying the main meaning) does not change to show a change in subject or time: *she has <u>studied</u>, you had <u>studied</u>*. Only the helping verb may change.

Form of *be* + present participle

The **progressive tenses** indicate action in progress (see p. 314). Create them with *be, am, is, are, was, were,* or *been* followed by the main verb's present participle:

She <u>is working</u> on a new book.

Be and *been* always require additional helping verbs to form the progressive tenses:

can	might	should		have	
could	must	will	} be working	has	} been working
may	shall	would		had	

When forming the progressive tenses, be sure to use the *-ing* form of the main verb:

Faulty Her ideas are <u>grow</u> more complex. She is <u>developed</u> a new approach to ethics.

Revised Her ideas are <u>growing</u> more complex. She is <u>developing</u> a new approach to ethics.

Form of *be* + past participle

The **passive voice** of the verb indicates that the subject *receives* the action of the verb (see p. 320). Create the passive voice with *be, am, is, are, was, were, being,* or *been* followed by the main verb's past participle:

Her latest book <u>was completed</u> in four months.

Be, being, and *been* always require additional helping verbs to form the passive voice:

| have
has
had | } been completed | am
is
are | was
were | } being completed |

will <u>be</u> completed

Be sure to use the main verb's past participle for the passive voice:

Faulty Her next book will be <u>publish</u> soon.

Revised Her next book will be <u>published</u> soon.

Note Only transitive verbs may form the passive voice:

Faulty A philosophy conference <u>will be occurred</u> in the same week. [*Occur* is not a transitive verb.]

Revised A philosophy conference <u>will occur</u> in the same week.

See pages 321–22 for advice on when to use and when to avoid the passive voice.

Forms of *have*

Four forms of *have* serve as helping verbs: *have, has, had, having.* One of these forms plus the main verb's past participle creates one of the **perfect tenses,** those expressing action completed before another specific time or action (see p. 313):

Some students <u>have complained</u> about the laboratory.
Others <u>had complained</u> before.

Will and other helping verbs sometimes accompany forms of *have* in the perfect tenses:

Several more students <u>will have complained</u> by the end of the week.

Forms of *do*

Do, does, and *did* have three uses as helping verbs, always with the plain form of the main verb:

- To pose a question: *How did the trial end?*
- To emphasize the main verb: *It did end eventually.*
- To negate the main verb, along with *not* or *never*: The judge *did not withdraw*.

Be sure to use the main verb's plain form with any form of *do*:

| Faulty | The judge did remained in court. |
| Revised | The judge did remain in court. |

Modals

The modal helping verbs include *can, may, should, would,* and several two- and three-word combinations, such as *have to* and *be able to*. (See p. 302 for a list of helping verbs.) Use the plain form of the main verb with a modal unless the modal combines with another helping verb (usually *have*):

| Faulty | The equipment can detects small vibrations. It should have detect the change. |
| Revised | The equipment can detect small vibrations. It should have detected the change. |

Modals convey various meanings. The ones following are the most common:

- Ability: *can, could, be able to*

  The equipment can detect small vibrations. [Present.]
  The equipment could detect small vibrations. [Past.]
  The equipment is able to detect small vibrations. [Present. Past: was able to. Future: will be able to.]

- Possibility: *could, may, might; could/may/might have* + past participle

  The equipment could fail. [Present.]
  The equipment may fail. [Present or future.]
  The equipment might fail. [Present or future.]
  The equipment may have failed. [Past.]

- Necessity or obligation: *must, have to, be supposed to*

  The lab must purchase a backup. [Present or future.]
  The lab has to purchase a backup. [Present or future. Past: had to.]
  The lab will have to purchase a backup. [Future.]
  The lab is supposed to purchase a backup. [Present. Past: was supposed to.]

vb
14d

■ Permission: *may, can, could*

> The lab <u>may spend</u> the money. [Present or future.]
> The lab <u>can spend</u> the money. [Present or future.]
> The lab <u>could spend</u> the money. [Present or future, more tentative.]
> With budget approval, the lab <u>could have spent</u> the money. [Past.]

■ Intention: *will, shall, would*

> The lab <u>will spend</u> the money. [Future.]
>
> <u>Shall</u> we <u>offer</u> advice? [Future. Use *shall* for questions requesting opinion or consent.]
>
> We <u>would have offered</u> advice. [Past.]

■ Request: *could, can, would*

> <u>Could</u> [or <u>Can</u> or <u>Would</u>] you please <u>obtain</u> a bid? [Present or future.]

■ Advisability: *should, had better, ought to; should have* + past participle

vb

14d

> You <u>should obtain</u> three bids. [Present or future.]
> You <u>had better obtain</u> three bids. [Present or future.]
> You <u>ought to obtain</u> three bids. [Present or future.]
> You <u>should have obtained</u> three bids. [Past.]

■ Past habit: *would, used to*

> In years past we <u>would obtain</u> five bids.
> We <u>used to obtain</u> five bids.

Exercise 14.4   Using helping verbs

Exercise

Add helping verbs in the following sentences where they are needed for standard English.

> *Example:*
> The story been told for many years.
> The story <u>has</u> been told for many years.

1. For as long as I can remember, I been writing stories.
2. While I living with my grandparents one summer, I wrote mystery stories.
3. Nearly every afternoon I sat at the computer and wrote about two brothers who solved mysteries while their mother be working.
4. By the end of the summer, I written four stories.
5. I was very happy when one of my stories published in the school newspaper.

Exercise 14.5   Revising: Helping verbs plus main verbs

Exercise

Revise the following sentences so that helping verbs and main verbs are used correctly. Mark the number preceding any sentence that is already correct.

Example:

The college testing service has test as many as five hundred students at one time.

The college testing service has <u>tested</u> as many as five hundred students at one time.

1. A report from the Bureau of the Census has confirm a widening gap between rich and poor.
2. As suspected, the percentage of people below the poverty level did increased over the last decade.
3. The richest 1% of the population is make 17% of all the income.
4. These households will keeping an average of $1.3 million each after taxes.
5. The average middle-income household will retain about $55,000.

14e   Use a gerund or an infinitive after a verb as appropriate.

Nonnative speakers of English may find it difficult to see whether a gerund or an infinitive should follow a verb. A **gerund** is the *-ing* form of a verb used as a noun (*opening*). An **infinitive** is the plain form of a verb preceded by *to* (*to open*). (See pp. 268–69 for more on these forms.)

vb
14e

✳
Exercise

Gerunds and infinitives may follow certain verbs but not others. Sometimes the use of a gerund or an infinitive with the same verb changes the meaning.

Grammar checkers   A grammar checker will spot some but not all errors in matching gerunds or infinitives with verbs. For example, a checker failed to flag *I practice <u>to swim</u>* and *I promise <u>helping out</u>.* Use the lists given here and a dictionary of English as a second language to determine whether an infinitive or a gerund is appropriate. (See p. 535 for a list of ESL dictionaries.)

Either gerund or infinitive

A gerund or an infinitive may follow these verbs with no significant difference in meaning:

begin	hate	love
can't bear	hesitate	prefer
can't stand	intend	start
continue	like	

The pump began <u>working</u>.
The pump began <u>to work</u>.

Meaning change with gerund or infinitive

With four verbs, a gerund has quite a different meaning from an infinitive:

forget	stop
remember	try

The engineer stopped <u>eating</u>. [He no longer ate.]
The engineer stopped <u>to eat</u>. [He stopped in order to eat.]

Gerund, not infinitive

Do not use an infinitive after these verbs:

admit	discuss	mind	recollect
adore	dislike	miss	resent
appreciate	enjoy	postpone	resist
avoid	escape	practice	risk
consider	finish	put off	suggest
deny	imagine	quit	tolerate
detest	keep	recall	understand

Faulty   He finished <u>to eat</u> lunch.
Revised   He finished <u>eating</u> lunch.

Infinitive, not gerund

vb
14e

Do not use a gerund after these verbs:

agree	decide	mean	refuse
appear	expect	offer	say
ask	have	plan	wait
assent	hope	pretend	want
beg	manage	promise	wish
claim			

Faulty   He decided <u>checking</u> the pump.
Revised   He decided <u>to check</u> the pump.

Noun or pronoun + infinitive

Some verbs may be followed by an infinitive alone or by a noun or pronoun and an infinitive. The presence of a noun or pronoun changes the meaning.

ask	dare	need	wish
beg	expect	promise	would like
choose	help	want	

He expected <u>to watch</u>.
He expected <u>his workers</u> <u>to watch</u>.

Some verbs *must* be followed by a noun or pronoun before an infinitive:

admonish	cause	convince	force
advise	challenge	encourage	hire
allow	command	forbid	instruct

invite	persuade	teach	urge
order	remind	tell	warn
permit	request	train	

He instructed his workers to watch.

Do not use *to* before the infinitive when it follows one of these verbs and a noun or pronoun:

feel	make ("force")
have	see
hear	watch
let	

He let his workers learn by observation.

Exercise 14.6 Revising: Verbs plus gerunds or infinitives

Revise the following sentences so that gerunds or infinitives are used correctly with verbs. Mark the number preceding any sentence that is already correct.

Example:
A politician cannot avoid to alienate some voters.
A politician cannot avoid alienating some voters.

1. A program called *Boostup.org* encourages students to finish high school.
2. People supporting this program hope that students will at least postpone to drop out of school.
3. Adults who want to help can promise mentoring a student.
4. Because of *Boostup.org*, many students who might have dropped out now plan going to college.
5. The organization persuades volunteers signing up via its Web site, *Facebook* page, and *Twitter* feed.

vb
14f

14f Use the appropriate particles with two-word verbs.

Standard American English includes some verbs that consist of two words: the verb itself and a **particle**, a preposition or adverb that affects the meaning of the verb. For example:

Look up the answer. [Research the answer.]
Look over the answer. [Examine the answer.]

The meanings of these two-word verbs are often quite different from the meanings of the individual words that make them up. (There are some three-word verbs, too, such as *put up with* and *run out of*.)

Exercise

A dictionary of English as a second language will define two-word verbs and say whether the verb may be separated in a sentence, as explained below. (See p. 535 for a list of ESL dictionaries.) A grammar checker will rarely recognize misused two-word verbs.

Note Many two-word verbs are more common in speech than in more formal academic or business writing. For formal writing, consider using *research* instead of *look up, examine* or *inspect* instead of *look over.*

Inseparable two-word verbs

Verbs and particles that may not be separated by any other words include the following:

call on	go over	run into	stay up
catch on	grow up	run out of	take care of
come across	keep on	speak up	turn out
get along	look for	speak with	turn up at
get up	look into	stand up	work for
give in	play around	stay away	
go on	run across		

Faulty   Children <u>grow</u> quickly <u>up</u>.
Revised   Children <u>grow up</u> quickly.

Separable two-word verbs

Most two-word verbs that take direct objects may be separated by the object:

Parents <u>help out</u> their children.
Parents <u>help</u> their children <u>out</u>.

If the direct object is a pronoun, the pronoun *must* separate the verb from the particle:

Faulty   Parents <u>help out</u> them.
Revised   Parents <u>help</u> them <u>out</u>.

The separable two-word verbs include the following:

bring up	give back	make up	throw out
call off	hand in	point out	try on
call up	hand out	put away	try out
drop off	help out	put back	turn down
fill out	leave out	put off	turn on
fill up	look over	take out	wrap up
give away	look up	take over	

Exercise 14.7 Revising: Verbs plus particles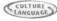

The two- and three-word verbs in the following sentences are underlined. Some are correct as given, and some are not because they should or should not be separated by other words. Revise the verbs and other

Exercise

vb
14f

words that are incorrect. Consult the lists on the preceding page or an ESL dictionary if necessary to determine whether verbs are separable.

Example:

Hollywood producers never seem to <u>come up with</u> entirely new plots, but they also never <u>run</u> new ways <u>out of</u> to present old ones.

Hollywood producers never seem to come up with [correct] entirely new plots, but they also never <u>run out of</u> new ways to present old ones.

1. American movies treat everything from <u>going out with</u> someone to <u>making up</u> an ethnic identity, but few people <u>look</u> their significance <u>into</u>.
2. While some viewers <u>stay away from</u> topical films, others <u>turn</u> at the theater <u>up</u> simply because a movie has sparked debate.
3. Some movies attracted rowdy spectators, and the theaters had to <u>throw out</u> them.
4. Filmmakers have always been eager to <u>point</u> their influence <u>out</u> to the public.
5. Everyone agrees that filmmakers will <u>keep</u> creating controversy <u>on</u>, if only because it can <u>fill up</u> theaters.

Tense

t
14

Exercise

Tense shows the time of a verb's action. The box on the next page defines and illustrates the tense forms for a regular verb in the active voice. (See pp. 297 and 320 on regular verbs and voice.)

Grammar checkers A grammar checker can provide little help with incorrect verb tenses and tense sequences because correctness usually depends on meaning. You'll have to proofread carefully yourself to catch errors in tense or tense sequence.

CULTURE LANGUAGE In standard American English, a verb conveys time and sequence through its form. In some other languages and English dialects, various markers besides verb form may indicate the time of a verb. For instance, in African American Vernacular English, *I be attending class on Tuesday* means that the speaker attends class every Tuesday. But to someone who doesn't know the dialect, the sentence could mean last Tuesday, this Tuesday, or every Tuesday. In standard American English, the intended meaning is indicated by verb tense:

I <u>attended</u> class on Tuesday. [Past tense indicates *last* Tuesday.]

I <u>will attend</u> class on Tuesday. [Future tense indicates *next* Tuesday.]

I <u>attend</u> class on Tuesday. [Present tense indicates habitual action, *every* Tuesday.]

mycomplab

Visit *mycomplab.com* for the eText and for resources and more exercises on verb tense.

Video
tutorial

Tenses of a regular verb (active voice)

Present Action that is occurring now, occurs habitually, or is generally true

Simple present Plain form or -s form	Present progressive *Am*, *is*, or *are* plus *-ing* form
I walk.	I am walking.
You/we/they walk.	You/we/they are walking.
He/she/it walks.	He/she/it is walking.

Past Action that occurred before now

Simple past Past-tense form (-*d* or *-ed*)	Past progressive *Was* or *were* plus *-ing* form
I/he/she/it walked.	I/he/she/it was walking.
You/we/they walked.	You/we/they were walking.

Future Action that will occur in the future

Simple future Plain form plus *will*	Future progressive *Will be* plus *-ing* form
I/you/he/she/it/we/they will walk.	I/you/he/she/it/we/they will be walking.

Present perfect Action that began in the past and is linked to the present

Present perfect *Have* or *has* plus past participle (-*d* or *-ed*)	Present perfect progressive *Have been* or *has been* plus *-ing* form
I/you/we/they have walked.	I/you/we/they have been walking.
He/she/it has walked.	He/she/it has been walking.

Past perfect Action that was completed before another past action

Past perfect *Had* plus past participle (-*d* or *-ed*)	Past perfect progressive *Had been* plus *-ing* form
I/you/he/she/it/we/they had walked.	I/you/he/she/it/we/they had been walking.

Future perfect Action that will be completed before another future action

Future perfect *Will have* plus past participle (-*d* or *-ed*)	Future perfect progressive *Will have been* plus *-ing* form
I/you/he/she/it/we/they will have walked.	I/you/he/she/it/we/they will have been walking.

 Use the appropriate tense to express your meaning.

Video
tutorial

Many errors in verb tense are actually errors in verb form like those discussed earlier. Still, the present tense, the perfect tenses, and the progressive tenses can cause problems.

1 Observe the special uses of the present tense.

The present tense has several distinctive uses:

Action occurring now

She understands the problem.
We define the problem differently.

Habitual or recurring action

Banks regularly undergo audits.
The audits monitor the banks' activities.

A general truth

The mills of the gods grind slowly.
The earth is round.

Discussion of literature, film, and so on (see also p. 766)

Huckleberry Finn has adventures we all envy.
In that article, the author examines several causes of crime.

Future time

Next week we draft a new budget.
Funding ends in less than a year.

t
14g

(In the last two examples, time is really indicated by *Next week* and *in less than a year.*)

2 Observe the uses of the perfect tenses.

The perfect tenses generally indicate action completed before another specific time or action. (The term *perfect* derives from the Latin *perfectus*, "completed.") The present perfect tense also indicates action begun in the past and continued into the present. The perfect tenses consist of a form of *have* plus the verb's past participle.

present perfect
The dancer has performed here only once. [The action is completed at the time of the statement.]

present perfect
Critics have written about the performance ever since. [The action began in the past and continues now.]

past perfect
The dancer had trained in Asia before his performance. [The action was completed before another past action.]

future perfect
He will have danced here again by the end of the year. [The action begins now or in the future and will be completed by a specified time in the future.]

CULTURE
LANGUAGE
With the present perfect tense, the words *since* and *for* are followed by different information. After *since*, give a specific point in time: *The United States has been a*

member of the United Nations <u>since 1945</u>. After *for,* give a span of time: *The United States has been a member of the United Nations <u>for many decades</u>*.

---

3 Observe the uses of the progressive tenses.

The progressive tenses indicate continuing (therefore progressive) action. In standard American English the progressive tenses consist of a form of *be* plus the verb's *-ing* form (present participle). (The words *be* and *been* must be combined with other helping verbs. See p. 304.)

_{present progressive}
The team <u>is improving</u>.

_{past progressive}
Last year the team <u>was losing</u>.

_{future progressive}
The owners <u>will be watching</u> for signs of improvement.

_{present perfect progressive}
Sports writers <u>have been expecting</u> an upturn.

_{past perfect progressive}
New players <u>had been performing</u> well.

_{future perfect progressive}
If the season goes badly, fans <u>will have been watching</u> their team lose for ten straight years.

Note Verbs that express unchanging conditions (especially mental states) rather than physical actions do not usually appear in the progressive tenses. These verbs include *adore, appear, believe, belong, care, doubt, hate, have, hear, imagine, know, like, love, mean, need, own, prefer, realize, remember, see, sound, taste, think, understand,* and *want*.

> Faulty   She <u>is wanting</u> to study ethics.
> Revised   She <u>wants</u> to study ethics.

14h   Use the appropriate sequence of verb tenses.

The term **sequence of tenses** refers to the relation between the verb tense in a main clause and the verb tense in a subordinate clause or phrase. The tenses should change when necessary to reflect changes in actual or relative time. (For a discussion of tense shifts—changes *not* required by meaning—see p. 377.)

1 Use the appropriate tense sequence with infinitives.

The **present infinitive** is the verb's plain form preceded by *to*. It indicates action *at the same time* as or *later* than that of the verb:

Exercise

verb: infinitive:
present perfect   present

She <u>would have liked</u> <u>to see</u> [not <u>to have seen</u>] change before now.

The verb's **perfect infinitive** consists of *to have* followed by the past participle, as in *to have talked, to have won*. It indicates action *earlier* than that of the verb:

verb: infinitive:
present   perfect

Other researchers <u>would like</u> [not <u>would have liked</u>] <u>to have seen</u> change as well.

2 Use the appropriate tense sequence with participles.

The present participle shows action occurring *at the same time* as that of the verb:

participle: verb:
present   past perfect

<u>Testing</u> a large group, the researcher <u>had posed</u> multiple-choice questions.

The past participle and the present perfect participle show action occurring *earlier* than that of the verb:

participle: verb:
past   past

<u>Prepared</u> by earlier failures, she <u>knew</u> not to ask open questions.

participle: verb:
present perfect   past

<u>Having tested</u> many people, she <u>understood</u> the process.

t seq

14h

3 Use the appropriate tense sequence with the past or past perfect tense.

When the verb in the main clause is in the past or past perfect tense, the verb in the subordinate clause must also be past or past perfect:

main clause: subordinate clause:
past   past

The researchers <u>discovered</u> that people <u>varied</u> widely in their knowledge of public events.

main clause: subordinate clause:
past   past perfect

The variation <u>occurred</u> because respondents <u>had been born</u> in different decades.

main clause: subordinate clause:
past perfect   past

None of them <u>had been born</u> when Warren G. Harding <u>was</u> President.

Exception Always use the present tense for a general truth, such as *The earth is round*:

main clause: subordinate clause:
past   present

Most <u>understood</u> that popular Presidents <u>are</u> not necessarily good Presidents.

4 Use the appropriate tense sequence in conditional sentences.

A **conditional sentence** states a factual relation between cause and effect, makes a prediction, or speculates about what might happen. Such a sentence usually contains a subordinate clause beginning with *if, when,* or *unless* along with a main clause stating the result. The three kinds of conditional sentences use distinctive verbs.

Factual relation

Statements linking factual causes and effects use matched tenses in the subordinate and main clauses:

subordinate clause: main clause:
present   present
When a voter <u>casts</u> a ballot, he or she <u>has</u> complete privacy.

subordinate clause: main clause:
past   past
When voters <u>registered</u> in some states, they <u>had</u> to pay a poll tax.

Prediction

Predictions generally use the present tense in the subordinate clause and the future tense in the main clause:

subordinate clause: main clause:
present   future
Unless citizens <u>regain</u> faith in politics, they <u>will</u> not <u>vote</u>.

Sometimes the verb in the main clause consists of *may, can, should,* or *might* plus the verb's plain form: *If citizens <u>regain</u> faith, they <u>may vote</u>.*

Speculation

The verbs in speculations depend on whether the linked events are possible or impossible. For possible events in the present, use the past tense in the subordinate clause and *would, could,* or *might* plus the verb's plain form in the main clause:

subordinate clause: main clause:
past   *would* + plain form
If voters <u>had</u> more confidence, they <u>would vote</u> more often.

Use *were* instead of *was* in the subordinate clause, even when the subject is *I, he, she, it* or a singular noun. (See p. 319 for more on this distinctive verb form.)

subordinate clause: main clause:
past   *would* + plain form
If the voter <u>were</u> more confident, he or she <u>would vote</u> more often.

For impossible events in the present—events that are contrary to fact—use the same forms as above (including the distinctive *were* when applicable):

subordinate clause: main clause:
past   *might* + plain form
If Lincoln <u>were</u> alive, he <u>might inspire</u> confidence.

t seq

14h

For impossible events in the past, use the past perfect tense in the subordinate clause and *would, could,* or *might* plus the present perfect tense in the main clause:

subordinate clause:
past perfect

main clause:
might + present perfect

If Lincoln <u>had lived</u> past the Civil War, he <u>might have helped</u> stabilize the country.

Exercise 14.8   Adjusting tense sequence: Past or past perfect tense

The tenses in each sentence below are in correct sequence. Change the tense of one verb as instructed. Then change the tense of infinitives, participles, and other verbs to restore correct sequence. Some items have more than one possible answer.

Exercise

Example:

Delgado will call when he reaches his destination. (Change *will call* to *called.*)

Delgado <u>called</u> when he <u>reached</u> [or <u>had reached</u>] his destination.

1. Diaries that Adolf Hitler is supposed to have written have surfaced in Germany. (*Change have surfaced to had surfaced.*)
2. Many people believe that the diaries are authentic because a well-known historian has declared them so. (*Change believe to believed.*)
3. However, the historian's evaluation has been questioned by other authorities, who call the diaries forgeries. (*Change has been questioned to was questioned.*)
4. They claim, among other things, that the paper is not old enough to have been used by Hitler. (*Change claim to claimed.*)
5. Eventually, the doubters will win the debate because they have the best evidence. (*Change will win to won.*)

Exercise 14.9   Revising: Tense sequence with conditional sentences

Supply the appropriate tense for each verb in brackets below.

Exercise

Example:

If Babe Ruth or Jim Thorpe [be] athletes today, they [remind] us that even sports heroes must contend with a harsh reality.

If Babe Ruth or Jim Thorpe <u>were</u> athletes today, they <u>might</u> [or <u>could</u> or <u>would</u>] remind us that even sports heroes must contend with a harsh reality.

1. When an athlete [turn] professional, he or she [commit] to a grueling regimen of mental and physical training.
2. If athletes [be] less committed, they [disappoint] teammates, fans, and themselves.
3. If professional athletes [be] very lucky, they [play] until age forty.
4. Unless an athlete [achieve] celebrity status, he or she [have] few employment choices after retirement.
5. If professional sports [be] less risky, athletes [have] longer careers and more choices after retirement.

Mood

Mood in grammar is a verb form that indicates the writer's or speaker's attitude toward what he or she is saying. The **indicative mood** states a fact or opinion or asks a question:

> The theater <u>needs</u> help. [Opinion.]
> The ceiling <u>is falling</u>. [Fact.]
> <u>Will</u> you <u>contribute</u> to the theater? [Question.]

The **imperative mood** expresses a command or gives a direction. It omits the subject of the sentence, *you*:

> <u>Help</u> the theater. [Command.]
> <u>Send</u> contributions to the theater. [Direction.]

The **subjunctive mood** expresses a suggestion, a requirement, or a desire, or it states a condition that is contrary to fact (that is, imaginary or hypothetical). The subjunctive mood uses distinctive verb forms.

- Suggestion or requirement: plain form with all subjects.

> The manager asked that he <u>donate</u> money. [Suggestion.]
> Rules require that every donation <u>be</u> mailed. [Requirement.]

- Desire or present condition contrary to fact: past tense; for *be,* the past tense *were* for all subjects, singular as well as plural.

> We wish that the theater <u>had</u> more money. [Desire.]
> It would be in better shape if it <u>were</u> better funded. [Present condition contrary to fact.]

- Past condition contrary to fact: past perfect.

> The theater could have been better funded if it <u>had been</u> better managed.

Note that with conditions contrary to fact, the verb in the main clause also expresses the imaginary or hypothetical with the helping verb *could, would,* or *might.* (See also pp. 316–17.)

For a discussion of keeping mood consistent within and among sentences, see page 377.

14i Use the subjunctive verb forms appropriately.

Exercise

Contemporary English uses distinctive subjunctive verb forms in only a few constructions and idioms. (For the sequence of tenses in many subjunctive sentences, see pp. 316–17.)

Grammar checkers A grammar checker may spot some simple errors in the subjunctive mood, but it may miss others. For example, a checker flagged *I wish I was home* (should be *were home*) but not *If I had a hammer, I will hammer in the morning* (should be *would hammer*).

1 Use the subjunctive in contrary-to-fact clauses beginning with *if* or expressing desire.

If the theater were saved, the town would benefit.
We all wish the theater were not so decrepit.
I wish I were able to donate money.

The indicative form *was* (*We all wish the theater was not so decrepit*) is common in speech and in some informal writing, but the subjunctive *were* is usual in formal English.

Not all clauses beginning with *if* express conditions contrary to fact. In the sentence *If Joe is out of town, he hasn't heard the news,* the verb *is* is correct because the clause refers to a condition presumed to exist.

vb

14i

2 Use *would, could,* or *might* only in the main clause of a conditional statement.

The helping verb *would, could,* or *might* appears in the main clause of a sentence expressing a condition contrary to fact. The helping verb does not appear in the subordinate clause beginning with *if*:

Not   Many people would have helped if they would have known.
But   Many people would have helped if they had known.

3 Use the subjunctive in *that* clauses following verbs that demand, request, or recommend.

Verbs such as *ask, demand, insist, mandate, recommend, request, require, suggest,* and *urge* indicate demand or suggestion. They often precede subordinate clauses beginning with *that* and containing the substance of the demand or suggestion. The verb in such a *that* clause should be in the subjunctive mood:

The board urged that everyone contribute.
The members insisted that they themselves be donors.
They suggested that each donate both time and money.

Note These constructions have widely used alternative forms that do not require the subjunctive, such as *The board urged everyone to contribute* and *The members insisted on donating.*

Exercise

Exercise 14.10 Revising: Subjunctive mood

Revise the following sentences with appropriate subjunctive verb forms.

> *Example:*
> I would help the old man if I was able to reach him.
> I would help the old man if I <u>were</u> able to reach him.

1. If John Hawkins would have known of the dangerous side effects of smoking tobacco, would he have introduced the dried plant to England in 1565?
2. Hawkins noted that if a Florida Indian was to travel for several days, he would have smoked tobacco to satisfy his hunger and thirst.
3. Early tobacco growers feared that their product would not gain acceptance unless it was perceived as healthful.
4. To prevent fires, in 1646 the General Court of Massachusetts passed a law requiring that colonists smoked tobacco only if they were five miles from any town.
5. To prevent decadence, in 1647 Connecticut passed a law mandating that one's smoking of tobacco was limited to once a day in one's own home.

vb

14i

Voice

Video tutorial

  The **voice** of a verb tells whether the subject of the sentence performs the action (**active voice**) or is acted upon (**passive voice**). In the passive voice, the actual actor may be named in a prepositional phrase (such as *by the city*) or may be omitted.

 A passive verb always consists of a form of *be* plus the past participle of the main verb: *Rents are controlled.* Other helping verbs must also be used with *be, being,* and *been*: *Rents will be controlled. Rents are being controlled. Rents have been controlled.* Only a transitive verb (one that takes an object) may be used in the passive voice. (See p. 258.)

Converting passive to active

Video tutorial

  To change a passive verb to active, name the verb's actor as the subject, use an active verb form, and convert the old subject into an object:

	subject	passive verb	
Passive	Tenants	are protected	by leases.
	new subject	active verb	old subject = object
Active	Leases	protect	tenants.

Visit *mycomplab.com* for the eText and for resources and more exercises on verb voice.

Active and passive voice

Active voice   The subject acts.

Subject = actor	Transitive verb in active voice	Direct object
The city	controls	rents.

Passive voice   The subject is acted upon.

Subject = object of action	Transitive verb in passive voice	(optional) by actor
Rents	are controlled	by the city.
Rents	are controlled.	

pass

14j

Converting active to passive

To change a transitive verb from active to passive voice, convert either an indirect object or a direct object into the subject of the sentence, and use the passive verb form:

	subject	transitive verb	indirect object	direct object
Active	The city	gives	tenants	leases.

	new subject	passive verb	direct object	
Passive	Tenants	are given	leases.	

	new subject	passive verb	old indirect object	old subject
	Leases	are given	to tenants	by the city.

14j   **Generally, prefer the active voice. Use the passive voice when the actor is unknown or unimportant.**

Because the passive omits or de-emphasizes the actor (the performer of the verb's action), it can deprive writing of vigor and is often vague or confusing. The active voice is usually stronger, clearer, and more forthright.

Podcast

Exercise

Weak passive	The <u>library</u> <u>is used</u> by students and teachers for studying and research, and the <u>plan</u> to expand it <u>has been praised</u> by many.
Strong active	<u>Students and teachers</u> <u>use</u> the library for studying and research, and <u>many</u> <u>have praised</u> the plan to expand it.

The passive voice is useful in two situations: when the actor is unknown and when the actor is unimportant or less important than the object of the action.

> The Internet was established in 1969 by the US Department of Defense. The network has been extended internationally to governments, foundations, corporations, educational institutions, and private individuals. [In the first sentence the writer wishes to stress the Internet rather than the Department of Defense. In the second sentence the actor is unknown or too complicated to name.]

> After the solution had been cooled to 10°C, the acid was added. [The person who cooled and added, perhaps the writer, is less important than the facts that the solution was cooled and acid was added. Passive sentences are common in scientific writing. See p. 832.]

Except in such situations, however, you should prefer the active voice in your writing.

Grammar checkers Most grammar checkers can be set to spot the passive voice. (See pp. 71–72.) But they can't determine when a passive verb may be appropriate for your writing, such as when you do not know the actor.

pass
14j

Exercise

Exercise 14.11   Converting between active and passive voices

To practice using the two voices of the verb, convert the following sentences from active to passive or from passive to active. (In converting from passive to active, you may have to add a subject for the new sentence.) Which version of each sentence seems more effective, and why? For additional exercises with the passive voice, see pages 284 and 402.

> *Example:*
> The aspiring actor was discovered in a nightclub.
> A talent scout discovered the aspiring actor in a nightclub.

1. When the Eiffel Tower was built in 1889, it was thought by the French to be ugly.
2. At that time many people still resisted industrial technology.
3. The tower's naked steel construction epitomized this technology.
4. Beautiful ornament was expected to grace fine buildings.
5. Further, the tower could not even be called a building because it had no solid walls.

Exercise

Exercise 14.12   Revising: Verb forms, tense, mood

Mark all the verbs and verbals in the following paragraph and correct their form, tense, or mood if necessary.

> For centuries the natives of Melanesia, a group of islands laying northeast of Australia, have practice an unusual religion. It began in the eighteenth century when European explorers first have visited the islands. The natives were fascinated by the rich goods or "cargo" possessed by the explorers. They saw the wealth as treasures of the gods, and cargo cults eventually had arisen among them. Over the centuries

some Melanesians turned to Christianity in the belief that the white man's religion will bring them the white man's treasures. During World War II, US soldiers, having arrived by boat and airplane to have occupied some of the islands, introduced new and even more wonderful cargo. Even today some leaders of the cargo cults insist that the airplane is worship as a vehicle of the Melanesians' future salvation.

Note See page 349 for an exercise involving verbs along with other aspects of grammar.

15

Agreement

Agreement helps readers understand the relations between elements in a sentence. Subjects and verbs agree in number and person:

More Japanese Americans live in Hawaii and California than elsewhere.
   subject   verb

Daniel Inouye was the first Japanese American in Congress.
 subject verb

Pronouns and their **antecedents**—the words they refer to—agree in person, number, and gender:

Inouye makes his home in Hawaii.
antecedent pronoun

Hawaiians value his work for them.
antecedent   pronoun

15a Make subjects and verbs agree in number.

Most subject-verb agreement problems arise when endings are omitted from subjects or verbs or when the relation between sentence parts is uncertain.

Video
tutorial

---

mycomplab

Visit *mycomplab.com* for the eText and for resources and more exercises on subject-verb and pronoun-antecedent agreement.

Person and number in subject-verb agreement

| Person | Number | |
	Singular	Plural
First	I eat.	We eat.
Second	You eat.	You eat.
Third	He/she/it eats.	They eat.
	The bird eats.	Birds eat.

Video
tutorial

Grammar checkers A grammar checker will catch many simple errors in subject-verb agreement, such as *Addie and John is late,* and some more complicated errors, such as *Is Margaret and Kyle going with us?* (should be *are* in both cases). But a checker failed to flag *The old group has gone their separate ways* (should be *have*) and offered a wrong correction for *The old group have gone their separate ways*, which is already correct.

vb agr

15a

Exercise

1 **The -s and -es endings work differently for nouns and verbs.**

An *-s* or *-es* ending does opposite things to nouns and verbs: it usually makes a noun *plural,* but it always makes a present-tense verb *singular.* Thus a singular noun as subject will not end in *-s,* but its verb will. A plural noun as subject will end in *-s,* but its verb will not. **Between them, subject and verb use only one -s ending.**

Singular	Plural
The boy plays.	The boys play.
The bird soars.	The birds soar.

The only exceptions to these rules involve the nouns that form irregular plurals, such as *child/children, woman/women.* The irregular plural still requires a plural verb: The *children play.*

CULTURE LANGUAGE If your first language or dialect is not standard American English, subject-verb agreement may be difficult, especially for these reasons:

■ Some English dialects omit the *-s* ending for singular verbs or use the *-s* ending for plural verbs.

Nonstandard	The voter resist change.
Standard	The voter resists change.
Standard	The voters resist change.

The verb *be* changes spelling for singular and plural in both present and past tenses. (See also p. 296.)

| Nonstandard | Taxes is high. They was raised just last year. |
| Standard | Taxes are high. They were raised just last year. |

Summary of subject-verb agreement

▦ Basic subject-verb agreement (opposite):

singular singular
subject verb

The kite flies.

plural plural
subject verb

The kites fly.

✳ Exercise

▦ Words between subject and verb (p. 326):

The kite with two tails flies badly. The tails of the kite compete.

▦ Subjects joined by *and* (p. 326):

The kite and the bird are almost indistinguishable.

▦ Subjects joined by *or* or *nor* (p. 327):

The kite or the bird dives. Kites or birds fill the sky.

▦ Indefinite pronoun as subject (p. 327):

No one knows. All the spectators wonder.

▦ Collective noun as subject (p. 328):

A flock appears. The flock disperse.

vb agr

15a

▦ Verb preceding subject (p. 329):

Is the kite or the bird blue? Are the kite and the bird both blue?

▦ Linking verb (p. 329):

The kite is a flier and a dipper.

▦ *Who, which, that* as subject (p. 329):

The kite that flies longest wins. Kites that fall lose.

▦ Subject with plural form and singular meaning (p. 330):

Aeronautics plays a role in kite flying.

▦ Title or word named as word (p. 330):

Kite Dynamics is one title. *Vectors* is a key word.

Have also has a distinctive *-s* form, *has*:

Nonstandard   The new tax have little chance of passing.
Standard   The new tax has little chance of passing.

▦ Some other languages change all parts of verb phrases to match their subjects. In English verb phrases, however, only the helping verbs *be, have,* and *do* change for different subjects. The modal helping verbs—*can, may, should, will,* and others—do not change:

| Nonstandard | The tax <u>mays</u> pass next year. |
| Standard | The tax <u>may</u> pass next year. |

The main verb in a verb phrase also does not change for different subjects:

| Nonstandard | The tax may <u>passes</u> next year. |
| Standard | The tax may <u>pass</u> next year. |

2 **Subject and verb should agree even when other words come between them.**

Podcast

When the subject and verb are interrupted by other words, make sure the verb agrees with the subject:

vb agr
15a

The survival of hibernating frogs in freezing temperatures <u>is</u> [not <u>are</u>] fascinating.

A chemical reaction inside the cells of the frogs <u>stops</u> [not <u>stop</u>] the formation of ice crystals.

Note Phrases beginning with *as well as, together with, along with,* and *in addition to* do not change the number of the subject:

The president, together with the deans, <u>has</u> [not <u>have</u>] agreed to improve the computer labs.

If you really mean *and* in such a sentence, use it. Then the subject is compound, and the verb should be plural: *The president and the deans have agreed to improve the computer labs.*

3 **Subjects joined by *and* usually take plural verbs.**

Video
tutorial

Two or more subjects joined by *and* usually take a plural verb, whether one or all of the subjects are singular:

Frost and Roethke <u>were</u> contemporaries.

Frost, Roethke, Stevens, and Pound <u>are</u> among the great American poets.

Exceptions When the parts of the subject form a single idea or refer to a single person or thing, they take a singular verb:

Avocado and bean sprouts <u>is</u> a California sandwich.

When a compound subject is preceded by the adjective *each* or *every,* the verb is usually singular:

Each man, woman, and child has a right to be heard.

But a compound subject *followed* by *each* takes a plural verb:

The man and the woman each have different problems.

4 When parts of a subject are joined by *or* or *nor,* the verb agrees with the nearer part.

When all parts of a subject joined by *or* or *nor* are singular, the verb is singular; when all parts are plural, the verb is plural.

Either the painter or the carpenter knows the cost.

The cabinets or the bookcases are too costly.

When one part of the subject is singular and the other plural, avoid awkwardness by placing the plural part closer to the verb so that the verb is plural:

Awkward   Neither the owners nor the contractor agrees.

Revised   Neither the contractor nor the owners agree.

When the subject consists of nouns and pronouns of different person requiring different verb forms, the verb agrees with the nearer part of the subject. Reword if this construction is awkward:

Awkward   Either Juarez or I am responsible.

Revised   Either Juarez is responsible, or I am.

5 With an indefinite pronoun such as *anybody* or *all,* use a singular or plural verb as appropriate.

An **indefinite pronoun** is one that does not refer to a specific person or thing. Most indefinite pronouns take a singular verb, but some take a plural verb and some take a singular *or* a plural verb.

vb agr
15a

((•
Podcast

Common indefinite pronouns

Singular			Singular or plural	Plural
anybody	everyone	nothing	all	both
anyone	everything	one	any	few
anything	much	somebody	more	many
each	neither	someone	most	several
either	nobody	something	none	
everybody	no one		some	

Exercise

The singular indefinite pronouns refer to a single unspecified person or thing, and they take a singular verb:

Something smells.   Neither is right.

The plural indefinite pronouns refer to more than one unspecified thing, and they take a plural verb:

Both are correct.   Several were invited.

The other indefinite pronouns take a singular or a plural verb depending on whether the word they refer to is singular or plural. The word may be stated in the sentence:

All of the money is reserved for emergencies. [*All* refers to *money.*]

All of the funds are reserved for emergencies. [*All* refers to *funds.*]

The word referred to by the pronoun may also be implied:

All are planning to attend. [*All* implies "all the people."]

All is lost. [*All* implies "everything."]

None may be singular even when referring to a plural word, especially to emphasize the meaning "not one": *None* [*Not one*] *of the animals has a home.*

CULTURE LANGUAGE   See page 347 for the distinction between *few* ("not many") and *a few* ("some").

vb agr

15a

6 Collective nouns such as *group* take singular or plural verbs depending on meaning.

Podcast

A **collective noun** has singular form but names a group of individuals or things—for example, *army, audience, committee, crowd, family, group, team.* As a subject, a collective noun may take a singular or plural verb, depending on the context. When the group acts as one unit, use a singular verb:

The team has won five of the last six meets.

But when the group's members act separately, use the plural form of the verb:

The old team have gone their separate ways.

If a combination such as *team have* seems awkward, reword the sentence: *The members of the old team have gone their separate ways.*

The collective noun *number* may be singular or plural. Preceded by *a,* it is plural; preceded by *the,* it is singular.

A number of people are in debt.

The number of people in debt is very large.

CULTURE LANGUAGE In English some noncount nouns (nouns that don't form plurals) are collective nouns because they name groups: for instance, *furniture, clothing, mail.* These noncount nouns usually take singular verbs: *Mail arrives daily.* But some of these nouns take plural verbs, including *clergy, military, people, police,* and any collective noun that comes from an adjective, such as *the poor, the rich, the young, the elderly.* If you mean one representative of the group, use a singular noun such as *police officer* or *poor person.*

7 The verb agrees with the subject even when it precedes the subject.

The verb precedes the subject mainly in questions and in constructions beginning with *there* or *here* and a form of *be*:

Is voting a right or a privilege?

Are a right and a privilege the same thing?

There are differences between them.

In constructions beginning with *there* or *here,* you may use *is* before a compound subject when the first element in the subject is singular:

Here lies both the problem and its solution.

Word order may sometimes be reversed for emphasis. The verb still agrees with its subject:

From the mountains comes an eerie, shimmering light.

8 A linking verb agrees with its subject, not the subject complement.

A linking verb such as *is* or *are* should agree with its subject, usually the first element in the sentence, not with the noun or pronoun serving as a subject complement (see pp. 259–60):

The child's sole support is her court-appointed guardians.

Her court-appointed guardians are the child's sole support.

9 *Who, which,* and *that* take verbs that agree with their antecedents.

When used as subjects, *who, which,* and *that* refer to another word in the sentence, called the **antecedent.** The verb agrees with the antecedent:

vb agr
15a

Mayor Garber ought to listen to the people who work for her.

Bardini is the only aide who has her ear.

Agreement problems often occur with *who, which,* or *that* when the sentence includes *one of the* or *the only one of the*:

Bardini is one of the aides who work unpaid. [Of the aides who work unpaid, Bardini is one.]

Bardini is the only one of the aides who knows the community. [Of the aides, only one, Bardini, knows the community.]

CULTURE LANGUAGE In phrases like those above beginning with *one of the,* be sure the noun is plural: *Bardini is one of the aides* [not *aide*] *who work unpaid.*

10 Nouns with plural form but singular meaning, such as *news,* take singular verbs.

Some nouns with plural form (that is, ending in -*s*) are usually regarded as singular in meaning. They include *athletics, economics, mathematics, measles, mumps, news, physics, politics,* and *statistics,* as well as place names such as *Athens, Wales,* and *United States.*

After so long a wait, the news has to be good.

Statistics is required of psychology majors.

A few of these words take plural verbs only when they describe individual items rather than whole bodies of activity or knowledge: *The statistics prove him wrong.*

Measurements and figures ending in -*s* may also be singular when the quantity they refer to is a unit:

Three years is a long time to wait.

Three-fourths of the library consists of reference books.

11 Titles and words named as words take singular verbs.

When your sentence subject is the name of a corporation, the title of a work (such as a book), or a word you are defining or describing, the verb should be singular even if the name, title, or word is plural:

Hakada Associates is a new firm.

Dream Days remains a favorite book.

Folks is a down-home word for *people.*

Exercise 15.1 Revising: Subject-verb agreement

Revise the verbs in the following sentences as needed to make subjects and verbs agree in number. If the sentence is already correct as given, mark the number preceding it.

Exercise

> *Example:*
> Each of the job applicants type sixty words per minute.
> Each of the job applicants <u>types</u> sixty words per minute.

1. Weinstein & Associates is a consulting firm that tries to make businesspeople laugh.
2. Results from recent research shows that humor relieves stress.
3. Reduced stress in businesses in turn reduce illness and absenteeism.
4. In special conferences held by one consultant, each of the participants practice making the others laugh.
5. One consultant to many companies suggest cultivating office humor with practical jokes such as a rubber fish in the water cooler.
6. When employees or their manager regularly post cartoons on the bulletin board, office spirit usually picks up.
7. When someone who has seemed too easily distracted is entrusted with updating the cartoons, his or her concentration often improves.
8. In the face of levity, the former sourpuss becomes one of those who hides bad temper.
9. Reduced stress can also reduce friction within an employee group, which then work more productively.
10. Every one of the consultants caution, however, that humor has no place in life-affecting corporate situations such as employee layoffs.

pn agr
15b

15b **Make pronouns and their antecedents agree in person, number, and gender.**

Video
tutorial

The **antecedent** of a pronoun is the noun or other pronoun to which the pronoun refers.

Homeowners fret over their tax bills.
antecedent   pronoun

Its constant increases make the tax bill a dreaded document.
pronoun   antecedent

Since a pronoun derives its meaning from its antecedent, the two must agree in person, number, and gender.

Exercise

Grammar checkers A grammar checker cannot help with agreement between pronoun and antecedent because it cannot recognize the intended relation between the two.

CULTURE LANGUAGE The gender of a pronoun should match its antecedent, not a noun that the pronoun may modify: *Sara Young invited her* [not *his*] *son to join the company's staff.* Also, nouns in English have only neuter gender unless they specifically refer to males or females. Thus nouns such as *book, table, sun,* and *earth* take the pronoun *it*: *I am reading a new book.* <u>*It*</u> *is inspiring.*

Person, number, and gender in pronoun-antecedent agreement

	Number	
Person	*Singular*	*Plural*
First	*I*	*we*
Second	*you*	*you*
Third	*he, she, it,* indefinite pronouns, singular nouns	*they,* plural nouns
Gender		
Masculine	*he,* nouns naming males	
Feminine	*she,* nouns naming females	
Neuter	*it,* all other nouns	

pn agr

15b

Video tutorial

1 Antecedents joined by *and* usually take plural pronouns.

Two or more antecedents joined by *and* usually take a plural pronoun, whether one or all of the antecedents are singular:

Mr. Bartos and I cannot settle our dispute.

The dean and my adviser have offered their help.

Exceptions When the compound antecedent refers to a single idea, person, or thing, then the pronoun is singular:

My friend and adviser offered her help.

When the compound antecedent follows *each* or *every,* the pronoun is singular:

Every girl and woman took her seat.

2 When parts of an antecedent are joined by *or* or *nor,* the pronoun agrees with the nearer part.

When the parts of an antecedent are connected by *or* or *nor,* the pronoun should agree with the part closer to it:

Tenants or owners must present their grievances.

Either the tenant or the owner will have her way.

When one subject is plural and the other singular, the sentence will be awkward unless you put the plural one second:

Awkward   Neither the tenants nor the owner has yet made her case.

Revised   Neither the owner nor the tenants have yet made their case.

Summary of pronoun-antecedent agreement

- Basic pronoun-antecedent agreement:

  antecedent   pronoun
  Old Faithful spews its columns of water, each of them over 115 feet high.

- Antecedents joined by *and* (opposite):

  Old Faithful and Giant are geysers known for their height.

- Antecedents joined by *or* or *nor* (opposite):

  Either Giant or Giantess ejects its column the highest.

- Indefinite words as antecedents (below):

  Each of the geysers has its own personality.

  Each person who visits has his or her favorites.

  Some return to their favorites year after year.

- Collective nouns as antecedents (p. 335):

  A crowd amuses itself watching Old Faithful.

  Afterward the crowd go their separate ways.

pn agr
15b

---

3 With an indefinite word as antecedent, such as *anyone* or *person*, use a singular or plural pronoun as appropriate.

Indefinite words do not refer to any specific person or thing. They include **indefinite pronouns** such as *anyone, everybody,* and *no one* (see p. 327 for a list). They also include **generic nouns,** or singular nouns that refer to typical members of a group, as in *The individual has rights* or *The job requires a person with computer skills.*

Most indefinite pronouns and all generic nouns are singular in meaning. When they serve as antecedents, they take singular pronouns:

Each of the animal shelters in the region has its population of homeless pets.
indefinite
pronoun

Every worker in our shelter cares for his or her favorite animal.
    generic
    noun

Four indefinite pronouns are plural in meaning: *both, few, many, several.* As antecedents, they take plural pronouns:

Many of the animals show affection for their caretakers.

Six indefinite pronouns may be singular or plural in meaning: *all, any, more, most, none, some.* As antecedents, they take singular pronouns if they refer to singular words, plural pronouns if they refer to plural words:

Most of the shelter's equipment was donated by its original owner. [*Most* refers to *equipment*.]

Most of the veterinarians donate their time. [*Most* refers to *veterinarians*.]

None may be singular even when referring to a plural word, especially to emphasize the meaning "not one": *None* [*Not one*] *of the shelters has increased its capacity.*

Most agreement problems arise with the singular indefinite words. We often use these words to mean something like "many" or "all" rather than "one" and then refer to them with plural pronouns, as in *Everyone has their own locker* or *A person can padlock their locker.* Often, too, we mean indefinite words to include both masculine and feminine genders and thus resort to *they* instead of the generic *he*—the masculine pronoun referring to both genders, as in *Everyone deserves his privacy.* (For more on the generic *he*, which many readers view as sexist, see p. 531.)

Although some experts accept *they, them,* and *their* with singular indefinite words, most do not, and many teachers and employers regard the plural as incorrect. To be safe, work for agreement between singular indefinite words and the pronouns that refer to them, using the options in the following box.

pn agr

15b

Ways to correct agreement with indefinite words

- Change the indefinite word to a plural, and use a plural pronoun to match:

Faulty	Every athlete deserves their privacy.
Revised	**Athletes** deserve their privacy.

- Rewrite the sentence to omit the pronoun:

Faulty	Everyone is entitled to their own locker.
Revised	Everyone is entitled to **a** locker.

- Use *he or she* (*him or her, his or her*) to refer to the indefinite word:

Faulty	Now everyone has their private space.
Revised	Now everyone has **his or her** private space.

However, used more than once in several sentences, *he or she* quickly becomes awkward. (Many readers do not accept the alternative *he/she.*) Using the plural or omitting the pronoun will usually correct agreement problems and create more readable sentences.

---

4 With a collective noun as antecedent, such as *group* or *team,* use a singular or plural pronoun depending on meaning.

Collective nouns such as *army, committee, family, group,* and *team* have singular form but may be referred to by singular or plural pronouns, depending on the meaning intended. When the group acts as a unit, the pronoun is singular:

The committee voted to disband itself.

When the members of the group act separately, the pronoun is plural:

The old team have gone their separate ways.

In the last example, note that the verb and pronoun are consistent in number (see also p. 376).

Inconsistent   The old team has gone their separate ways.

Consistent   The old team have gone their separate ways.

If a combination such as *team have . . . their* seems awkward, reword the sentence: *The members of the old team have gone their separate ways.*

> CULTURE LANGUAGE   In standard American English, collective nouns that are noncount nouns (they don't form plurals) usually take singular pronouns: *The mail sits in its own basket.* A few noncount nouns take plural pronouns, including *clergy, military, people, police, the rich,* and *the poor*: *The police support their unions.* (See also pp. 328–29.)

pn agr

15b

Exercise 15.2   Revising: Pronoun-antecedent agreement
Revise the following sentences so that pronouns and their antecedents agree in person and number. Some items have more than one possible answer. Try to avoid the generic *he* (see opposite). If you change the subject of a sentence, be sure to change verbs as necessary for agreement. If the sentence is already correct as given, mark the number preceding it.

Example:
Each of the Boudreaus' children brought their laundry home at Thanksgiving.

All of the Boudreaus' children brought their laundry home at Thanksgiving. *Or:* Each of the Boudreaus' children brought laundry home at Thanksgiving. *Or:* Each of the Boudreaus' children brought his or her laundry home at Thanksgiving.

1. Each girl raised in a Mexican American family in the Rio Grande Valley of Texas hopes that one day they will be given a *quinceañera* party for their fifteenth birthday.
2. Such celebrations are very expensive because it entails a religious service followed by a huge party.
3. A girl's immediate family, unless they are wealthy, cannot afford the party by themselves.

4. The parents will ask each close friend or relative if they can help with the preparations.
5. Surrounded by her family and attended by her friends and their escorts, the *quinceañera* is introduced as a young woman eligible for Mexican American society.

Exercise 15.3 Adjusting for agreement

Exercise

In the sentences below, subjects agree with verbs and pronouns agree with antecedents. Make the change specified in parentheses after each sentence, and then revise the sentence as necessary to maintain agreement. Some items have more than one possible answer.

Example:

The student attends weekly conferences with her teacher. (*Change The student to Students.*)

<u>Students</u> <u>attend</u> weekly conferences with <u>their</u> teacher.

1. The giant panda is endangered. (*Change The giant panda to Giant pandas.*)
2. A conservationist estimates that fewer than two thousand giant pandas live in central China, their natural habitat, because the bamboo forests there are shrinking. (*Change A conservationist to Conservationists.*)
3. The giant panda eats bamboo and gains most of its nutrition from its leaves and stalks. (*Change The giant panda to Giant pandas.*)
4. At the Wolong Wildlife Refuge in China, researchers breed pandas in captivity and release a cub into the wild when it is old enough to survive on its own. (*Change a cub to the cubs.*)
5. A zoo in the United States wishes to raise awareness of the giant panda's plight by breeding a pair of adults and allowing the public to view the adorable cub while it is young. (*Change A zoo to Zoos, a pair to pairs, and cub to the cubs.*)

pn agr

15b

Exercise 15.4 Revising: Agreement

Revise the sentences in the following paragraphs to correct errors in agreement between subjects and verbs or between pronouns and their antecedents. Try to avoid the generic *he.*

The writers Richard Rodriguez and Maxine Hong Kingston, despite their differences, shares one characteristic: their parents was immigrants to California. A frequent theme of their writings are the difficulties of growing up with two languages and two cultures.

A child whose first language is not English is often ridiculed because they cannot communicate "properly." Rodriguez learned Spanish at home, but at school everyone expected him to use their language, English. He remembers his childish embarrassment because of his parents' poor English. College and graduate school, which usually expands one's knowledge, widened the gap between Rodriguez and his Latino culture. His essays suggests that he lost a part of himself, a loss that continue to bother him.

Kingston spoke Chinese at home and also learned her first English at school. She sometimes write of these experiences, but more often she write to recover and preserve her Chinese culture. *The Woman Warrior,* which offer a blend of autobiography, family history, and mythic tales, describe the struggle of Kingston's female relatives. *China Men* focus on Kingston's male ancestors; each one traveled to Hawaii or California to make money for their wife back in China. Kingston's work, like Rodriguez's essays, reflect the tension and confusion that the child of immigrants often feel when they try to blend two cultures.

Note See page 349 for an exercise involving agreement along with other aspects of grammar.

16

Adjectives and Adverbs

Adjectives and adverbs are modifiers that describe, restrict, or otherwise qualify the words to which they relate.

Video tutorial

Functions of adjectives and adverbs

Adjectives modify	nouns:	serious student
	pronouns:	ordinary one
Adverbs modify	verbs:	warmly greet
	adjectives:	only three people
	adverbs:	quite seriously
	phrases:	nearly to the edge of the cliff
	clauses:	just when we arrived
	sentences:	Fortunately, she is employed.

Many of the most common adjectives are familiar one-syllable words such as *bad, strange, large,* and *wrong.* Many others are formed by adding endings such as *-al, -able, -ful, -less, -ish, -ive,* and *-y* to nouns or verbs: *optional, fashionable, beautiful, fruitless, self-ish, expressive, dreamy.*

Most adverbs are formed by adding *-ly* to adjectives: *badly, strangely, largely, beautifully.* But note that we cannot depend on *-ly*

Video tutorial

Video tutorial

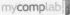
Visit *mycomplab.com* for the eText and for resources and more exercises on adjectives and adverbs.

Exercise

to identify adverbs, since some adjectives also end in *-ly* (*fatherly*, *lonely*) and since some common adverbs do not end in *-ly* (*always*, *here*, *not*, *now*, *often*, *there*). Thus the only sure way to distinguish between adjectives and adverbs is to determine what they modify.

Grammar checkers A grammar checker will spot some but not all problems with misused adjectives and adverbs. For instance, a checker flagged *Some children suffer bad* and *Chang was the most wisest person in town* and *Jenny did not feel nothing*. But it did not flag *Educating children good is everyone's focus.*

CULTURE LANGUAGE In standard American English an adjective does not change along with the noun it modifies to show plural number: *white* [not *whites*] *shoes*, *square* [not *squares*] *spaces*. Only nouns form plurals.

16a Use adjectives only to modify nouns and pronouns.

Adjectives modify only nouns and pronouns. Do not use adjectives instead of adverbs to modify verbs, adverbs, or other adjectives:

Faulty	The groups view family values different.
Revised	The groups view family values differently.

Be especially careful not to use *good* and *bad* in place of *well* and *badly*.

Faulty	Educating children good is everyone's focus.
Revised	Educating children well is everyone's focus.

Faulty	Some children suffer bad.
Revised	Some children suffer badly.

CULTURE LANGUAGE Choosing between *not* and *no* can be a challenge. Use *not* to make a verb or an adjective negative:

They do not learn. They are not happy. They have not been in class.

(See pages 386–87 for where to place *not* in relation to verbs and adjectives.) Use *no* to make a noun negative:

No child likes to fail. No good school fails children.

Place *no* before the noun or any other modifier.

16b Use an adjective after a linking verb to modify the subject. Use an adverb to modify a verb.

Video
tutorial

A **linking verb** is one that links, or connects, a subject and its complement, either a noun (*They are golfers*) or an adjective (*He is* *lucky*). (See also pp. 258–59.) Linking verbs are forms of *be,* the verbs associated with our five senses (*look, sound, smell, feel, taste*), and a few others (*appear, seem, become, grow, turn, prove, remain, stay*).

Some of these verbs may or may not be linking, depending on their meaning in the sentence. When the word after the verb modifies the subject, the verb is linking and the word should be an adjective: *He feels strong*. When the word modifies the verb, however, it should be an adverb: *He feels strongly about that.*

Two word pairs are especially troublesome in this context. One is *bad* and *badly:*

Podcast

The weather grew bad.
    linking adjective
    verb

She felt bad.
    linking adjective
    verb

Flowers grow badly in such soil.
    verb adverb

The other pair is *good* and *well*. *Good* serves only as an adjective. *Well* may serve as an adverb with a host of meanings or as an adjective meaning only "fit" or "healthy."

Decker trained well.
  verb adverb

She felt well.
  linking adjective
  verb

Her health was good.
  linking adjective
  verb

ad

16c

| **16c** | **After a direct object, use an adjective to modify the object and an adverb to modify the verb.** |

After a direct object, an adjective modifies the object, whereas an adverb modifies the verb of the sentence. (See p. 258 for more on direct objects.)

Campus politics made Mungo angry.
    adjective

Mungo repeated the words angrily.
    adverb

You can test whether a modifier should be an adjective or an adverb by trying to separate it from the direct object. If you can separate it, it should be an adverb: *Mungo angrily repeated the words.* If you cannot separate it, it is probably an adjective.

> The instructor considered the student's work thorough. [The adjective can be moved in front of *work* (*student's thorough work*), but it cannot be separated from *work*.]

> The instructor considered the student's work thoroughly. [The adverb can be separated from *work*. Compare *The instructor thoroughly considered the student's work*.]

Exercise

Exercise 16.1 Revising: Adjectives and adverbs

Revise the following sentences so that adjectives and adverbs are used appropriately. If any sentence is already correct as given, mark the number preceding it.

Example:
The announcer warned that traffic was moving very slow.
The announcer warned that traffic was moving very <u>slowly</u>.

1. People who take their health serious often believe that movie-theater popcorn is a healthy snack.
2. Nutrition information about movie popcorn may make these people feel different.
3. One large tub of movie popcorn has twelve hundred calories and sixty grams of saturated fat—both surprisingly high numbers.
4. Once people are aware of the calories and fat, they may feel badly about indulging in this classic snack.
5. People who want to eat good should think twice before ordering popcorn at the movies.

ad
16d

Podcast

Exercise

16d Use the comparative and superlative forms of adjectives and adverbs appropriately.

Adjectives and adverbs can show degrees of quality or amount with the endings *-er* and *-est* or with the words *more* and *most* or *less* and *least*. Most modifiers have three forms:

Positive The basic form listed in the dictionary	Comparative A greater or lesser degree of the quality	Superlative The greatest or least degree of the quality
Adjectives		
red	redder	reddest
awful	more/less awful	most/least awful
Adverbs		
soon	sooner	soonest
quickly	more/less quickly	most/least quickly

If sound alone does not tell you whether to use *-er/-est* or *more/most*, consult a dictionary. If the endings can be used, the dictionary will list them. Otherwise, use *more* or *most*.

1 Use the correct forms of irregular adjectives and adverbs.

Certain adjectives and adverbs are irregular: they change the spelling of their positive form to show comparative and superlative degrees.

Degrees of irregular adjectives and adverbs

Positive	Comparative	Superlative
Adjectives		
good	better	best
bad	worse	worst
little	littler, less	littlest, least
many ⎫		
some ⎬	more	most
much ⎭		
Adverbs		
well	better	best
badly	worse	worst

2 Use either *-er/-est* or *more/most*, not both.

A double comparative or double superlative combines the *-er* or *-est* ending with the word *more* or *most*. It is redundant.

Chang was the wisest [not most wisest] person in town.
He was smarter [not more smarter] than anyone else.

ad

16d

3 Use the comparative for comparing two things and the superlative for comparing three or more things.

It is the shorter of her two books. [Comparative.]
The Yearling is the most popular of the six books. [Superlative.]

In conversation the superlative form is often used to compare only two things: *When two people argue, the angriest one is usually wrong.* But the distinction between the forms should be observed in writing.

4 Use comparative or superlative forms only for modifiers that can logically be compared.

Some adjectives and adverbs cannot logically be compared— for instance, *perfect, unique, dead, impossible, infinite,* and related adverbs such as *perfectly* and *impossibly.* These absolute words can be preceded by adverbs like *nearly* and *almost* that mean "approaching," but they cannot logically be modified by *more* or *most* (as in *most perfect*). This distinction is sometimes ignored in speech, but it should always be made in writing:

Not   He was the most unique teacher we had.
But   He was a unique teacher.

Exercise 16.2   Revising: Comparatives and superlatives

Revise the sentences below so that the comparative and superlative forms of adjectives and adverbs are appropriate for formal usage. Mark the number preceding any sentence that is already correct.

Example:

Attending classes full time and working at two jobs was the most impossible thing I ever did.

Attending classes full time and working at two jobs was <u>impossible</u> [or <u>the hardest thing I ever did</u>].

1. Charlotte was the older of the three Brontë sisters, all of whom were novelists.
2. Some readers think Emily Brontë's *Wuthering Heights* is the most saddest novel they have ever read.
3. Of the other two sisters, Charlotte and Anne, Charlotte was probably the more talented.
4. Critics still argue about whether Charlotte or Emily wrote more better.
5. Certainly this family of women novelists was the most unique.

16e   Watch for double negatives.

In a **double negative** two negative words such as *no, not, none, neither, barely, hardly,* or *scarcely* cancel each other out. Some double negatives are intentional: for instance, *She was <u>not unhappy</u>* indicates with understatement that she was indeed happy. But most double negatives say the opposite of what is intended: *Jenny did <u>not feel nothing</u>* asserts that Jenny felt other than nothing, or something. For the opposite meaning, one of the negatives must be eliminated or changed to a positive: *She felt <u>nothing</u>* or *She did <u>not feel anything</u>.*

Faulty   The IRS <u>cannot hardly</u> audit all tax returns. <u>None</u> of its audits <u>never</u> touch many cheaters.

Revised   The IRS <u>cannot</u> audit all tax returns. Its audits <u>never</u> touch many cheaters.

Exercise 16.3   Revising: Double negatives

Identify and revise the double negatives in the following paragraph. Each error may have more than one correct revision.

Interest in books about the founding of the United States seems to vary with the national mood. Americans show hardly no interest in books about the founders when things are going well in the United States. However, when Americans can't barely agree on major issues, sales of books about the Revolutionary War era increase. During such periods, one cannot go to no bookstore without seeing several new volumes about John Adams, Thomas Jefferson, and other founders. When Americans feel they don't have nothing in common, their increased interest in the early leaders may reflect a desire for unity.

16f Use nouns sparingly as modifiers.

We often use one noun to modify another. For example:

child care   flood control   security guard

Such phrases can be both clear and concise, but overuse of noun modifiers can lead to flat, even senseless, writing. To avoid awkwardness or confusion, observe two principles. First, prefer possessives or adjectives as modifiers:

Exercise

Not	A student takes the state medical <u>board</u> exams to become a <u>dentist</u> technician.
But	A student takes the state medical <u>board's</u> exams to become a <u>dental</u> technician.

Second, use only short nouns as modifiers and use them only in two- or three-word sequences:

Confusing	Minimex maintains a <u>plant employee relations improvement program</u>.
Revised	Minimex maintains a program <u>for improving</u> relations <u>among plant employees</u>.

ad
16g

16g Distinguish between present and past participles as adjectives.

Both present participles and past participles may serve as adjectives: *a burning building, a burned building*. As in the examples, the two participles usually differ in the time they indicate.

But some present and past participles—those derived from verbs expressing feeling—can have altogether different meanings. The present participle modifies something that causes the feeling: *That was a frightening storm* (the storm frightens). The past participle modifies something that experiences the feeling: *They quieted the frightened horses* (the horses feel fright).

The following participles are among the ones that are likely to be confused:

Exercise

amazing/amazed
amusing/amused
annoying/annoyed
astonishing/astonished
boring/bored
confusing/confused
depressing/depressed
embarrassing/embarrassed
exciting/excited
exhausting/exhausted

fascinating/fascinated
frightening/frightened
frustrating/frustrated
interesting/interested
pleasing/pleased
satisfying/satisfied
shocking/shocked
surprising/surprised
tiring/tired
worrying/worried

Exercise

Exercise 16.4 Revising: Present and past participles

Revise the adjectives in the following sentences as needed to distinguish between present and past participles. If the sentence is already correct as given, mark the number preceding it.

Example:

The subject was embarrassed to many people.
The subject was <u>embarrassing</u> to many people.

1. Several critics found Alice Walker's *The Color Purple* to be a fascinated book.
2. One confused critic wished that Walker had deleted the scenes set in Africa.
3. Another critic argued that although the book contained many depressed episodes, the overall impact was excited.
4. Since other readers found the book annoyed, this critic pointed out its many surprised qualities.
5. In the end most critics agreed that the book was a satisfied novel.

ad
16h

Video tutorial

Exercise

16h Use *a, an, the,* and other determiners appropriately.

Determiners are special kinds of adjectives that mark nouns because they always precede nouns. Some common determiners are *a, an,* and *the* (called **articles**) and *my, their, whose, this, these, those, one, some,* and *any.* They convey information to readers—for instance, by specifying who owns what, which one of two is meant, or whether a subject is familiar or unfamiliar.

Native speakers of standard American English can rely on their intuition when using determiners, but speakers of other languages and dialects often have difficulty with them. In standard English the use of determiners depends on the context they appear in and the kind of noun they precede:

- Proper noun: Names a particular person, place, or thing and begins with a capital letter: *February, Joe Allen, Red River.* Most proper nouns are not preceded by determiners.

- Count noun: Names something that is countable in English and can form a plural: *girl/girls, apple/apples, child/children.* A singular count noun is always preceded by a determiner; a plural count noun sometimes is.

- Noncount noun: Names something not usually considered countable in English and so does not form a plural. A noncount noun is sometimes preceded by a determiner. Here is a sample of noncount nouns, sorted into groups by meaning:

Abstractions: confidence, democracy, education, equality, evidence, health, information, intelligence, knowledge, luxury, peace, pollution, research, success, supervision, truth, wealth, work

Food and drink: bread, candy, cereal, flour, meat, milk, salt, water, wine

Emotions: anger, courage, happiness, hate, joy, love, respect, satisfaction

Natural events and substances: air, blood, dirt, gasoline, gold, hair, heat, ice, oil, oxygen, rain, silver, smoke, weather, wood

Groups: clergy, clothing, equipment, furniture, garbage, jewelry, junk, legislation, machinery, mail, military, money, police, vocabulary

Fields of study: architecture, accounting, biology, business, chemistry, engineering, literature, psychology, science

A dictionary of English as a second language will say whether a noun is a count noun, a noncount noun, or both. (See p. 535 for recommended dictionaries.)

Note Many nouns can be both count and noncount nouns:

The library has a room for readers. [*Room* is a count noun meaning "walled area."]

The library has room for reading. [*Room* is a noncount noun meaning "space."]

Grammar checkers Partly because the same noun may fall into different groups, a grammar checker is an unreliable guide to missing or misused articles and other determiners. For instance, a checker flagged the omitted *a* before *Scientist* in *Scientist developed new processes;* it did not flag the omitted *a* before *new* in *A scientist developed new process;* and it mistakenly flagged the correctly omitted article *the* before *Vegetation* in *Vegetation suffers from drought.*

ad

16h

1 Use *a, an,* and *the* where they are required.

With singular count nouns

A or *an* precedes a singular count noun when the reader does not already know its identity, usually because you have not mentioned it before:

A scientist in the school's chemistry department developed a process to strengthen metals. [*Scientist* and *process* are being introduced for the first time.]

The precedes a singular count noun that has a specific identity for the reader, for one of the following reasons:

▪ You have mentioned the noun before:

A scientist in the school's chemistry department developed a process to strengthen metals. The scientist patented the process. [*Scientist* and *process* were identified in the preceding sentence.]

▪ You identify the noun immediately before or after you state it:

The most productive laboratory is the research center in the chemistry department. [*Most productive* identifies *laboratory. In the chemistry department* identifies *research center*. And *chemistry department* is a shared facility.]

▪ **The noun names something unique—the only one in existence:**

The sun rises in the east. [*Sun* and *east* are unique.]

▪ **The noun names an institution or facility that is shared by the community of readers:**

Many men and women aspire to the presidency. [*Presidency* is a shared institution.]

The cell phone has changed communication. [*Cell phone* is a shared facility.]

The is not used before a singular noun that names a general category:

Sherman said that war is hell. [*War* names a general category.]

The war in Iraq left many wounded. [*War* names a specific war.]

With plural count nouns

A or *an* never precedes a plural noun. *The* does not precede a plural noun that names a general category. *The* does precede a plural noun that names specific representatives of a category.

Men and women are different. [*Men* and *women* name general categories.]

The women formed a team. [*Women* refers to specific people.]

With noncount nouns

A or *an* never precedes a noncount noun. *The* does precede a noncount noun when it names specific representatives of a general category:

Vegetation suffers from drought. [*Vegetation* names a general category.]

The vegetation in the park withered or died. [*Vegetation* refers to specific plants.]

With proper nouns

A or *an* never precedes a proper noun. *The* generally does not precede a proper noun:

Garcia lives in Boulder.

There are exceptions, however. For instance, we generally use *the* before plural proper nouns (*the Murphys, the New England Patriots*) and the names of groups and organizations (*the Department of Justice, the Sierra Club*), ships (*the Lusitania*), oceans (*the Pacific*), mountain ranges (*the Alps*), regions (*the Middle East*), rivers (*the Mississippi*), and some countries (*the United States, the Netherlands*).

2 Use other determiners appropriately.

The uses of English determiners besides articles also depend on context and kind of noun. The following determiners may be used as indicated with singular count nouns, plural count nouns, or noncount nouns.

With any kind of noun (singular count, plural count, noncount)

> *my, our, your, his, her, its, their*
> possessive nouns (*boy's, boys'*)
> *whose, which(ever), what(ever)*
> *some, any, the other*
> *no*

> <u>Their</u> account is overdrawn. [Singular count.]
> <u>Their</u> funds are low. [Plural count.]
> <u>Their</u> money is running out. [Noncount.]

Only with singular nouns (count and noncount)

> *this, that*

> <u>This</u> account has some money. [Count.]
> <u>That</u> information may help. [Noncount.]

Only with noncount nouns and plural count nouns

> *most, enough, other, such, all, all of the, a lot of*

> <u>Most</u> money is needed elsewhere. [Noncount.]
> <u>Most</u> funds are committed. [Plural count.]

Only with singular count nouns

> *one, every, each, either, neither, another*

> <u>One</u> car must be sold. [Singular count.]

Only with plural count nouns

> *these, those*
> *both, many, few, a few, fewer, fewest, several*
> *two, three,* and so forth

> <u>Two</u> cars are unnecessary. [Plural count.]

Note *Few* means "not many" or "not enough." *A few* means "some" or "a small but sufficient quantity."

> <u>Few</u> committee members came to the meeting.
> <u>A few</u> members can keep the committee going.

Do not use *much* with a plural count noun:

> <u>Many</u> [not <u>Much</u>] members want to help.

Only with noncount nouns

> *much, more, little, a little, less, least, a large amount of*

> <u>Less</u> luxury is in order. [Noncount.]

> Note *Little* means "not many" or "not enough." *A little* means "some" or "a small but sufficient quantity."

> <u>Little</u> time remains before the conference.
> The members need <u>a little</u> help from their colleagues.

Do not use *many* with a noncount noun:

> <u>Much</u> [not <u>Many</u>] work remains.

Exercise

ad
16h

Exercise 16.5 Revising: Articles

For each blank below, indicate whether *a, an, the,* or no article should be inserted.

From _____ native American Indians who migrated from _____ Asia 20,000 years ago to _____ new arrivals who now come by _____ planes, _____ United States is _____ nation of foreigners. It is _____ country of immigrants who are all living under _____ single flag.

Back in _____ seventeenth and eighteenth centuries, at least 75% of the population came from _____ England. However, between 1820 and 1975 more than 38 million immigrants came to this country from elsewhere in _____ Europe. Many children of _____ immigrants were self-conscious and denied their heritage; many even refused to learn _____ native language of their parents and grandparents. They tried to "Americanize" themselves. The so-called Melting Pot theory of _____ social change stressed _____ importance of blending everyone together into _____ kind of stew. Each nationality would contribute its own flavor, but _____ final stew would be something called "American."

This Melting Pot theory was never completely successful. In the last half of the twentieth century, _____ ethnic revival changed _____ metaphor. Many people now see _____ American society as _____ mosaic. Americans are once again proud of their heritage, and _____ ethnic differences make _____ mosaic colorful and interesting.

Exercise 16.6 Revising: Adjectives and adverbs

Exercise

Revise the following paragraph so that it conforms to formal usage of adjectives and adverbs.

Americans often argue about which professional sport is better: basketball, football, or baseball. Basketball fans contend that their sport offers more action because the players are constant running and shooting. Because it is played indoors in relative small arenas, basketball allows fans to be more closer to the action than the other sports do. Fans point to how graceful the players fly through the air to the hoop. Football fanatics say they don't hardly stop yelling once the game begins. They cheer when their team executes a real complicated play good. They roar more louder when the defense stops the opponents in a goal-line stand.

They yell loudest when a fullback crashes in for a score. In contrast, the supporters of baseball believe that it might be the most perfect sport. It combines the one-on-one duel of pitcher and batter struggling valiant with the tight teamwork of double and triple plays. Because the game is played slow and careful, fans can analyze and discuss the manager's strategy. Besides, they don't never know when they might catch a foul ball as a souvenir. However, no matter what the sport, all fans feel happily only when their team wins.

Exercise on Chapters 13–16   Revising: Grammatical sentences

The following paragraphs contain errors in pronoun case, verb forms, subject-verb agreement, pronoun-antecedent agreement, and the forms of adjectives and adverbs. Revise the paragraphs to correct the errors.

Occasionally, musicians become "crossover artists" whom can perform good in more than one field of music. For example, Wynton and Branford Marsalis was train in jazz by their father, the great pianist Ellis Marsalis. Both of the sons has became successful classical artists. Branford's saxophone captures the richness of pieces by Ravel and Stravinsky. Wynton's albums of classical trumpet music from the Baroque period has brung him many awards. Still, if he was to choose which kind of music he likes best, Wynton would probable choose jazz. In contrast to the Marsalises, violinist Nigel Kennedy growed up studying and performing classical music. In his teens he began playing jazz and even rock music. Today he is known almost as good for his interpretations of Miles Davis and Jimi Hendrix as he is for his classical performances.

Some vocalists sing in several genres. For example, Renée Fleming, one of the great opera sopranos, have recorded popular music. Her technique on the song "In Your Eyes" is nearly perfect, yet she sounded as if she was simply trying to sing proper. Another singer, Bobby McFerrin, been successful singing both pop and classical music. He has won pop Grammy awards, but he is equal able to sing classical pieces *a capella* (without musical accompaniment). His voice's remarkable range and clarity allows him to imitate many musical instruments.

Still other musicians has founded success as crossover composers. The former Beatle Paul McCartney is best known as a pop singer and songwriter, but he has also wrote scores for symphony orchestra, opera, and ballet. Two well-known pop stars, Bono and the Edge from the band U2, had compose music for the Broadway musical *Spider-Man*. Each of these men have showed their ability to adapt to other musical styles.

All of these artists has shown great musicianship in new fields. They are willing to test and stretch their talents, and each of we music fans benefit.

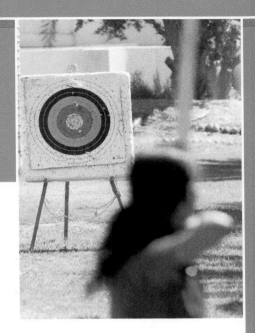

Clear Sentences

PART 4

17

Sentence Fragments

Video
tutorial

Exercise

A **sentence fragment** is part of a sentence that is set off as if it were a whole sentence by an initial capital letter and a final period or other end punctuation. Although writers occasionally use fragments deliberately and effectively (see p. 359), readers perceive most fragments as serious errors because, expecting complete sentences, they find partial sentences distracting or confusing. (Before reading further, you may find it helpful to review pp. 253–54 and 272–75 on sentences and clauses.)

Complete sentence versus sentence fragment

A *complete sentence* or *main clause*

- contains a subject and a predicate verb (*The wind blows*)
- and is not a subordinate clause (beginning with a word such as *because* or *who*).

A *sentence fragment*

- lacks a predicate verb (*The wind blowing*)
- or lacks a subject (*And blows*)
- or is a subordinate clause not attached to a complete sentence (*Because the wind blows*).

Grammar checkers A grammar checker can spot many but not all sentence fragments, and it may flag sentences that are actually correct commands, such as *Continue reading*.

17a **Test your sentences for completeness, and revise any fragments.**

Three tests will help you determine whether a word group punctuated as a sentence is actually a complete sentence. If the word group does not pass *all three* tests, it is a fragment and needs to be revised.

---

mycomplab

Visit *mycomplab.com* for the eText and for resources and more exercises on sentence fragments.

Tests for complete sentences

Perform *all three* of the following tests to be sure your sentences are complete.

1. Find the predicate verb.
2. Find the subject.
3. Make sure the clause is not subordinate.

Test 1: Find the predicate verb.

Look for a predicate verb in the group of words. Some fragments lack any verb at all:

Video tutorial

| Fragment | Uncountable numbers of sites on the World Wide Web. |
| Revised | Uncountable numbers of sites <u>make up</u> the World Wide Web. |

Other fragments may include a verb form but not a **finite verb,** one that changes form as indicated below. A verbal does not change; it cannot serve as a predicate verb without the aid of a helping verb.

	Finite verbs in complete sentences	Verbals in sentence fragments
Singular	The network <u>grows</u>.	The network <u>growing</u>.
Plural	Networks <u>grow</u>.	Networks <u>growing</u>.
Present	The network <u>grows</u>.	
Past	The network <u>grew</u>.	The network <u>growing</u>.
Future	The network <u>will grow</u>.	

CULTURE LANGUAGE Some languages allow forms of *be* to be omitted as helping or linking verbs. But English requires stating forms of *be*:

frag

17a

| Fragments | The network <u>growing</u>. It <u>much</u> larger than its developers anticipated. |
| Revised | The network <u>is</u> growing. It <u>is</u> much larger than its developers anticipated. |

Test 2: Find the subject.

If you find a finite, predicate verb, look for its subject by asking *who* or *what* performs the action or makes the assertion of the verb. The subject of the sentence will usually come before the verb. If there is no subject, the word group is probably a fragment:

| Fragment | And <u>has great popular appeal</u>. |
| Revised | And <u>the Web</u> has great popular appeal. |

In one kind of complete sentence, a command, the subject *you* is understood: [*You*] *Experiment with the Web.*

CULTURE LANGUAGE Some languages allow the omission of the sentence subject, especially when it is a pronoun. But in English, except in commands, the subject is always stated:

Fragment	Web commerce has expanded dramatically. Has hurt traditional stores.
Revised	Web commerce has expanded dramatically. It has hurt traditional stores.

Test 3: Make sure the clause is not subordinate.

A subordinate clause usually begins with a subordinating word:

Subordinating conjunctions			Relative pronouns	
after	once	until	that	who/whom
although	since	when	which	whoever/whomever
as	than	where		whose
because	that	whereas		
if	unless	while		

(See p. 273 for a longer list of subordinating conjunctions.)

Subordinate clauses serve as parts of sentences (as nouns or modifiers), not as whole sentences:

Fragment	When the government devised the Internet.
Revised	The government devised the Internet.
Revised	When the government devised the Internet, no expansive computer network existed.
Fragment	The reason that the government devised the Internet.
Revised	The reason that the government devised the Internet was to provide secure links among departments and defense contractors.

frag

17a

Note Questions beginning with *how, what, when, where, which, who, whom, whose,* and *why* are not sentence fragments: *Who was responsible? When did it happen?*

Revising sentence fragments

Video
tutorial

Almost all sentence fragments can be corrected in one of the two ways shown in the following box. The choice depends on the importance of the information in the fragment.

Revision of sentence fragments

Option 1

Rewrite the fragment as a complete sentence. This revision gives the information in the fragment the same importance as that in other complete sentences.

Fragment	A major improvement in public health occurred with the widespread use of vaccines. Which protected children against life-threatening diseases.
Revised	A major improvement in public health occurred with the widespread use of vaccines. They protected children against life-threatening diseases.

Two main clauses may be separated by a semicolon instead of a period (p. 467).

Option 2

Combine the fragment with a main clause. This revision makes the information in the fragment subordinate to the information in the main clause.

Fragment	The polio vaccine eradicated the disease from most of the globe. The first vaccine to be used widely.
Revised	The polio vaccine, the first to be used widely, eradicated the disease from most of the globe.

Punctuating corrected fragments

In the last example in the box, commas separate the inserted phrase from the rest of the sentence because the phrase is not essential to the meaning of any word in the main clause but simply adds information (see p. 449). When a phrase or subordinate clause *is* essential to the meaning of a word in the main clause, a comma or commas do *not* separate the two elements:

frag
17a

Fragment	High school students often use the Web to research colleges. That they might want to visit in person.
Revised	High school students often use the Web to research colleges that they might want to visit in person.

Sometimes a fragment may be combined with the main clause using a colon or a dash (see pp. 491 and 493–94, respectively):

Fragment	Some colleges recruit students from all over the United States. Large cities, suburbs, small towns, and rural areas.
Revised	Some colleges recruit students from all over the United States: large cities, suburbs, small towns, and rural areas.
Fragment	The colleges strive to bring together diverse groups of students. Young people with different backgrounds, experiences, and dreams for the future.
Revised	The colleges strive to bring together diverse groups of students—young people with different backgrounds, experiences, and dreams for the future.

Exercise 17.1 Identifying and revising sentence fragments

Apply the tests for completeness to each of the following word groups. If a word group is a complete sentence, mark the number preceding it. If it is a sentence fragment, revise it in two ways: by making it a complete sentence, and by combining it with a main clause written from the information given in other items.

Example:
And could not find his money. [The word group has a verb (*could . . . find*) but no subject.]
Revised into a complete sentence: And <u>he</u> could not find his money.
Combined with a new main clause: <u>He was lost</u> and could not find his money.

1. In an interesting article about vandalism against works of art.
2. The motives of the vandals varying widely.
3. Those who harm artwork are usually angry.
4. But not necessarily at the artist or the owner.
5. For instance, a man who hammered at Michelangelo's *Pietà*.
6. And knocked off the Virgin Mary's nose.
7. Because he was angry at the Roman Catholic Church.
8. Which knew nothing of his grievance.
9. Although many damaged works can be repaired.
10. Usually even the most skillful repairs are forever visible.

---

frag
17c

17b A subordinate clause is not a complete sentence.

Subordinate clauses contain both subjects and verbs, but they always begin with a subordinating conjunction (*although, if,* and so on) or a relative pronoun (*who, which, that,* and so on). (See pp. 272–75.) Subordinate clauses serve as nouns or modifiers, but they cannot stand alone as complete sentences.

To correct a subordinate clause set off as a sentence, combine it with the main clause or remove or change the subordinating word to create a main clause.

Fragment	Many pine trees bear large cones. <u>Which appear in August.</u>
Revised	Many pine trees bear large cones, which appear in August.
Revised	Many pine trees bear large cones. <u>They</u> appear in August.

17c A verbal phrase or a prepositional phrase is not a complete sentence.

A **verbal phrase** consists of an infinitive (*to choose*), a past participle (*chosen*), or a present participle or gerund (*choosing*) together with any objects and modifiers it may have (see pp. 267–70). A verbal phrase is a noun or modifier and cannot serve as the verb in a complete sentence:

Fragment	For many of the elderly, their house is their only asset. <u>Offering some security but no income.</u>
Revised	For many of the elderly, their house is their only asset, offering some security but no income.
Revised	For many of the elderly, their house is their only asset. <u>It offers</u> some security but no income.

A **prepositional phrase** is a modifier consisting of a preposition (such as *in, on, to,* or *with*) together with its object and any modifiers (see pp. 264–66). A prepositional phrase cannot stand alone as a complete sentence:

Fragment	<u>In a squeeze between a valuable asset and little income.</u> Eventually many elderly people sell their homes.
Revised	In a squeeze between a valuable asset and little income, eventually many elderly people sell their homes.
Revised	<u>Many elderly people are</u> in a squeeze between a valuable asset and little income. Eventually they may sell their homes.

CULTURE LANGUAGE Some English prepositions consist of two or three words: *as well as, along with, in addition to, on top of,* and others. Don't let prepositions of more than one word mislead you into writing sentence fragments.

| Fragment | In today's retirement communities, the elderly may have health care, housekeeping, and new friends. <u>As well as financial security.</u> |
| Revised | In today's retirement communities, the elderly may have health care, housekeeping, and new friends as well as financial security. |

frag

17d

17d Any word group lacking a subject or a verb or both is not a complete sentence.

We often follow a noun with a modifier. No matter how long the noun and its modifier are, they cannot stand alone as a sentence:

Fragments	<u>People waving flags and cheering.</u> <u>Lined the streets for the parade.</u>
Revised	People waving flags and cheering lined the streets for the parade.
Fragment	<u>Veterans who fought in Vietnam.</u> They are finally being honored.
Revised	Veterans who fought in Vietnam are finally being honored.

Appositives are nouns, or nouns and their modifiers, that rename or describe other nouns (see pp. 276–77). They cannot stand alone as sentences:

Fragment	When I was a child, my favorite adult was an old uncle. A re-<u>tired sea captain who always told me long stories of wild adventures in faraway places.</u>
Revised	When I was a child, my favorite adult was an old uncle, a retired sea captain who always told me long stories of wild adventures in faraway places.

Compound predicates are predicates made up of two or more verbs and their objects, if any (see p. 278). A verb or its object cannot stand alone as a sentence:

Fragment	Uncle Marlon drew out his tales. <u>And embellished them.</u>
Revised	Uncle Marlon drew out his tales and embellished them.

Fragment	He described characters he had met. <u>And storms at sea.</u>
Revised	He described characters he had met and storms at sea.

Note Beginning a sentence with a coordinating conjunction such as *and* or *but* can lead to a sentence fragment. Check every sentence you begin with a coordinating conjunction to be sure it is complete.

frag

17d

Exercise

Exercise 17.2 Revising: Sentence fragments

Correct any sentence fragment below either by combining it with a main clause or by making it a main clause. If an item contains no sentence fragment, mark the number preceding it.

Example:

Jujitsu is good for self-protection. Because it enables one to overcome an opponent without the use of weapons.

Jujitsu is good for self-protection because it enables one to overcome an opponent without the use of weapons.

1. Human beings who perfume themselves. They are not much different from other animals.
2. Animals as varied as insects and dogs release *pheromones*. Chemicals that signal other animals.
3. Human beings have a diminished sense of smell. And do not consciously detect most of their own species' pheromones.
4. The human substitute for pheromones may be perfumes. Especially musk and other fragrances derived from animal oils.
5. Some sources say that humans began using perfume to cover up the smell of burning flesh. During sacrifices to the gods.
6. Perfumes became religious offerings in their own right. Being expensive to make, they were highly prized.
7. The earliest historical documents from the Middle East record the use of fragrances. Not only in religious ceremonies but on the body.

8. In the nineteenth century chemists began synthesizing perfume oils. Which previously could be made only from natural sources.
9. The most popular animal oil for perfume today is musk. Although some people dislike its heavy, sweet odor.
10. Synthetic musk oil would help conserve a certain species of deer. Whose gland is the source of musk.

17e Be aware of the acceptable uses of incomplete sentences.

Podcast

A few word groups lacking the usual subject-predicate combination are not sentence fragments because they conform to the expectations of most readers. They include commands (*Move along. Shut the window.*); exclamations (*Oh no!*); questions and answers (*Where next? To Kansas.*); and descriptions in employment résumés (*Weekly volunteer in a soup kitchen.*). Another kind of incomplete sentence, occurring in special situations, is the transitional phrase (*So much for the causes, now for the results. One final point.*).

Experienced writers sometimes use sentence fragments when they want to achieve a special effect. Such fragments appear more in informal than in formal writing. Unless you are experienced and thoroughly secure in your own writing, you should avoid all fragments and concentrate on writing clear, well-formed sentences.

frag
17e

Exercise 17.3 Revising: Sentence fragments

Revise the following paragraph to eliminate sentence fragments by combining them with main clauses or rewriting them as main clauses.

Exercise

Baby red-eared slider turtles are brightly colored. With bold patterns on their yellowish undershells. Which serve as a warning to predators. The bright colors of skunks and other animals. They signal that the animals will spray nasty chemicals. In contrast, the turtle's colors warn largemouth bass. That the baby turtle will actively defend itself. When a bass gulps down a turtle. The feisty baby claws and bites. Forcing the bass to spit it out. To avoid a similar painful experience. The bass will avoid other baby red-eared slider turtles. The turtle loses its bright colors as it grows too big. For a bass's afternoon snack.

Note See page 398 for an exercise involving sentence fragments along with comma splices, fused sentences, and other sentence errors.

18

Comma Splices and Fused Sentences

Exercise

A sentence or main clause contains at least a subject and a predicate, which together express a complete thought that can stand alone (see p. 253). When two main clauses fall together, readers need a signal that one clause is ending and another is beginning. The following box shows the ways to provide this signal.

Punctuation of two or more main clauses

■ Separate main clauses with periods.

> Main clause   .   Main clause   .

Hybrid cars are popular with consumers. Automakers are releasing new models.

■ Link main clauses with a coordinating conjunction and a comma.

> Main clause   ,   for   and   or
>   so   but   nor   main clause   .
>   yet

Hybrid cars are popular with consumers, and automakers are releasing new models.

■ Link main clauses with a semicolon.

> Main clause   ;   main clause   .

Hybrid cars are popular with consumers; automakers are releasing new models.

---

mycomplab

360   Visit *mycomplab.com* for the eText and for resources and more exercises on comma splices and fused sentences.

■ Relate main clauses with a semicolon and a conjunctive adverb or transitional expression.

| Main clause | **;** | *however,*
for example,
etc. | **,** | main clause | **.** |

Hybrid cars are popular with consumers**;** as a result**,** automakers are releasing new models.

Video
tutorial

With a comma splice or a fused sentence, two main clauses run together without one of the signals listed in the box, and readers often must reread for sense. A **comma splice** joins (or splices) main clauses *only* with a comma, not with a coordinating conjunction as well:

Comma splice

The ship was huge, its mast stood eighty feet high.

A **fused sentence** (or **run-on sentence**) joins main clauses with no punctuation at all:

Podcast

Fused sentence

The ship was huge its mast stood eighty feet high.

Exception Experienced writers sometimes use a comma without a coordinating conjunction between very brief main clauses that are grammatically parallel:

cs/fs

18

He's not a person**,** he's a monster.

However, many readers view such punctuation as incorrect. Unless you are certain that your readers will not object to the comma in a sentence like this one, separate the clauses with periods or semicolons, as described in this chapter.

Grammar checkers A grammar checker can detect many comma splices, but it will miss most fused sentences. For example, a checker flagged *Money is tight, we need to spend carefully* but not *Money is tight we need to spend carefully*. A checker may also question sentences that are actually correct, such as *Money being tighter now than before, we need to spend carefully*. Verify that revision is actually needed on any flagged sentence.

CULTURE LANGUAGE An English sentence may not include more than one main clause unless the clauses are separated by a comma and a coordinating conjunction or by a semicolon or colon. If your native language does not have such a rule or has accustomed you to writing long sentences, you may need to edit your English writing especially for comma splices and fused sentences.

Revision of comma splices and fused sentences

1. Underline the main clauses in your draft.

   <u>Sailors trained on the ship</u> <u>they learned about wind and sails.</u> <u>Trainees who took the course ranged from high school students to Navy officers.</u> <u>The ship was built in 1910,</u> <u>it had sailed ever since.</u> In almost a century, <u>it had circled the globe forty times.</u> <u>It burned in 2001</u> <u>its cabins and decks were destroyed.</u>

2. Focus on sentences that contain two or more main clauses.

3. If nothing falls between the clauses or only a comma does, revise in one of the following ways. The choice depends on the relation you want to establish between the clauses, as explained below and opposite.

   Separate main clauses with a period.

   Sailors trained on the ship**.** They learned about wind and sails.

   Separate main clauses with a comma and a coordinating conjunction.

   The ship was built in 1910**,** and it had sailed ever since.

   Separate main clauses with a semicolon.

   The ship was built in 1910**;** it had sailed ever since.

   Subordinate one clause to the other, depending on which clause is more important.

   When it burned in 2001**,** its cabins and decks were destroyed.

---

cs

18a

Comma Splices

18a Separate two main clauses with a comma *only* when they are joined by a coordinating conjunction.

Video tutorial

A comma cannot separate main clauses unless they are linked by a coordinating conjunction (*and, but, or, nor, for, so, yet*). Readers expect the same main clause to continue after a comma alone. When they find themselves reading a second main clause before they realize they have finished the first, they may have to reread.

You have several options for revising comma splices.

Making separate sentences

Revising a comma splice by making separate sentences from the main clauses will always be correct. The period is not only correct

but preferable when the ideas expressed in the two main clauses are
only loosely related:

| Comma splice | Chemistry has contributed much to our understanding of foods, many foods such as wheat and beans can be produced in the laboratory. |
| Revised | Chemistry has contributed much to our understanding of foods. Many foods such as wheat and beans can be produced in the laboratory. |

CULTURE LANGUAGE Making separate sentences may be the best option
if you are used to writing very long sentences in
your native language and often write comma splices in English.

Inserting a coordinating conjunction

When the ideas in the main clauses are closely related and
equally important, you may correct a comma splice by inserting the
appropriate coordinating conjunction immediately after the comma
to join the clauses:

| Comma splice | Some laboratory-grown foods taste good, they are nutritious. |
| Revised | Some laboratory-grown foods taste good, and they are nutritious. |

Using a semicolon

If the relation between the ideas expressed in the main clauses
is very close and obvious without a conjunction, you can separate
the clauses with a semicolon.

| Comma splice | Good taste is rare in laboratory-grown vegetables, they are usually bland. |
| Revised | Good taste is rare in laboratory-grown vegetables; they are usually bland. |

CS
18a

Subordinating one clause

When the idea in one clause is more important than that in the
other, you can express the less important idea in a phrase or a subordinate clause. (See p. 273 for a list of subordinating conjunctions
and pp. 413–15 for more on subordination.) Subordination is often
more effective than forming separate sentences because it defines
the relation between ideas more precisely:

Comma splice	The vitamins are adequate, the flavor is deficient.
Revised	The vitamins are adequate. The flavor is deficient. [Both ideas receive equal weight.]
Improved	Even though the vitamins are adequate, the flavor is deficient. [Emphasis on the second idea.]

18b Separate main clauses related by *however, for example,* and so on.

Two kinds of words that are not conjunctions describe how one main clause relates to another:

- **Conjunctive adverbs,** such as *consequently, finally, hence, however, indeed, therefore,* and *thus.* (See p. 281 for a longer list.)
- **Other transitional expressions,** such as *even so, for example, in fact, of course, to the right,* and *to this end.* (See pp. 94–95 for a longer list.)

When two main clauses are related by a conjunctive adverb or a transitional expression, they must be separated by a period or by a semicolon. The adverb or expression is also generally set off by a comma or commas (see p. 452):

Comma splice	Healthcare costs are higher in the United States than in many other countries, <u>consequently</u> health insurance is also more costly.
Revised	Healthcare costs are higher in the United States than in many other countries. <u>Consequently,</u> health insurance is also more costly.
Revised	Healthcare costs are higher in the United States than in many other countries; <u>consequently,</u> health insurance is also more costly.

Conjunctive adverbs and transitional expressions are different from coordinating conjunctions (*and, but,* and so on) and subordinating conjunctions (*although, because,* and so on):

- **Unlike conjunctions, conjunctive adverbs and transitional expressions do not join two clauses into a grammatical unit.** They merely describe the way two clauses relate in meaning.
- **Unlike conjunctions, conjunctive adverbs and transitional expressions can be moved within a clause** (see also pp. 280–81). No matter where in the clause an adverb or expression falls, though, the clause must be separated from another main clause by a period or semicolon.

Comma splice

The increased time devoted to watching television is not the only cause of the decline in reading ability, <u>however,</u> it is one of the important causes.

Revised with a period

The increased time devoted to watching television is not the only cause of the decline in reading ability. <u>However,</u> it is one of the important causes.

Revised with a semicolon

The increased time devoted to watching television is not the only cause of the decline in reading ability; however, it is one of the important causes.

The increased time devoted to watching television is not the only cause of the decline in reading ability; it is, however, one of the important causes.

Exercise 18.1   Identifying and revising comma splices

Correct each comma splice below in *two* of the ways described on pages 362–63. If an item contains no comma splice, mark the number preceding it.

Exercise

> *Example:*
> Carolyn still had a headache, she could not get the child-proof cap off the aspirin bottle.
>
> Carolyn still had a headache because she could not get the child-proof cap off the aspirin bottle. [Subordination.]
>
> Carolyn still had a headache, for she could not get the child-proof cap off the aspirin bottle. [Coordinating conjunction.]

1. Money has a long history, it goes back at least as far as the earliest records.
2. Many of the earliest records concern financial transactions, indeed, early history must often be inferred from commercial activity.
3. Every known society has had a system of money, though the objects serving as money have varied widely.
4. Sometimes the objects have had real value, in modern times, however, their value has been more abstract.
5. Cattle, fermented beverages, and rare shells have served as money, each one had actual value for the society.

fs

18c

━━━━━ Fused Sentences ━━━━━

18c Combine two main clauses only with an appropriate conjunction or punctuation mark between them.

When two main clauses are joined without a word to connect them or a punctuation mark to separate them, the result is a **fused** or **run-on sentence.** Fused sentences can rarely be understood on first reading, and they are never acceptable in standard written English.

Video tutorial

> Fused   The policy is not well defined it confuses many employees.

Fused sentences may be corrected in the same ways as comma splices. See pages 362–63.

Separate sentences

The policy is not well defined. It confuses many employees.

Comma and coordinating conjunction

The policy is not well defined, and it confuses many employees.

Semicolon

The policy is not well defined; it confuses many employees.

Subordinating conjunction

Because the policy is not well defined, it confuses many employees.

Exercise 18.2   Identifying and revising fused sentences

Exercise

Revise each of the fused sentences below in *two* of the four ways shown above.

Example:

Tim was shy he usually refused invitations.
Tim was shy, so he usually refused invitations.
Tim was shy; he usually refused invitations.

1. Throughout history money and religion were closely linked there was little distinction between government and religion.
2. The head of state and the religious leader were often the same person all power rested in one ruler.
3. These powerful leaders decided what objects would serve as money their backing encouraged public faith in the money.
4. Coins were minted of precious metals the religious overtones of money were then strengthened.
5. People already believed the precious metals to be divine their use in money intensified its allure.

Exercise 18.3   Sentence combining to avoid comma splices and fused sentences

Exercise

Combine each pair of sentences below into one sentence without creating a comma splice or fused sentence. Combine sentences by (1) supplying a comma and coordinating conjunction, (2) supplying a semicolon, or (3) subordinating one clause to the other. You will have to add, delete, or change words as well as punctuation.

Example:

The sun sank lower in the sky. The colors gradually faded.

As the sun sank lower in the sky, the colors gradually faded. [The first clause is subordinated to the second.]

1. The exact origin of paper money is unknown. It has not survived as coins, shells, and other durable objects have.
2. Perhaps goldsmiths were also bankers. Thus they held the gold of their wealthy customers.
3. The goldsmiths probably gave customers receipts for their gold. These receipts were then used in trade.

4. The goldsmiths were something like modern-day bankers. Their receipts were something like modern-day money.
5. The goldsmiths became even more like modern-day bankers. They began issuing receipts for more gold than they actually held in their vaults.

Exercise 18.4 Revising: Comma splices and fused sentences

Identify and revise the comma splices and fused sentences in the following paragraph.

Exercise

All those parents who urged their children to eat broccoli were right, the vegetable really is healthful. Broccoli contains sulforaphane, moreover, this mustard oil can be found in kale and Brussels sprouts. Sulforaphane causes the body to make an enzyme that attacks carcinogens, these substances cause cancer. The enzyme speeds up the work of the kidneys then they can flush harmful chemicals out of the body. Other vegetables have similar benefits however, green, leafy vegetables like broccoli are the most efficient. Thus wise people will eat their broccoli it could save their lives.

Note See page 398 for an exercise involving comma splices and fused sentences along with other sentence errors.

19

Pronoun Reference

A **pronoun** such as *it* or *they* derives its meaning from its **antecedent,** the noun it substitutes for. Therefore, a pronoun must refer clearly and unmistakably to its antecedent in order for the meaning to be clear. A sentence such as *Jim told Mark he was not invited* is not clear because the reader does not know whether *he* refers to Jim or to Mark.

Video tutorial

One way to make pronoun reference clear is to ensure that the pronoun and antecedent agree in person, number, and gender (see pp. 331–32). The other way is to ensure that the pronoun refers unambiguously to a single, close, specific antecedent.

mycomplab

Visit *mycomplab.com* for the eText and for resources and more exercises on pronoun reference.

Principal causes of unclear pronoun reference

■ **More than one possible antecedent (below):**

| Confusing | To keep birds from eating seeds, soak <u>them</u> in blue food coloring. |
| Clear | To keep birds from eating seeds, soak the seeds in blue food coloring. |

■ **Antecedent too far away (facing page):**

| Confusing | Employees should consult with their supervisor <u>who</u> require personal time. |
| Clear | Employees <u>who</u> require personal time should consult with their supervisor. |

■ **Antecedent only implied (p. 370):**

| Confusing | Many children begin reading on their own by watching television, but <u>this</u> should probably be discounted in government policy. |
| Clear | Many children begin reading on their own by watching television, but <u>such self-instruction</u> should probably be discounted in government policy. |

See also pages 372–73.

---

ref

19a

Grammar checkers A grammar checker cannot recognize unclear pronoun reference. For instance, a checker did not spot any of the problems in Exercise 19.2 on page 373.

CULTURE LANGUAGE An English pronoun does need a clear antecedent nearby, but don't use both a pronoun and its antecedent as the subject of the same sentence or clause: *Jim* [not *Jim he*] *told Mark to go alone.* (See also p. 392.)

19a Make a pronoun refer clearly to one antecedent.

Podcast

When either of two nouns can be a pronoun's antecedent, the reference will not be clear:

| Confusing | Emily Dickinson is sometimes compared with Jane Austen, but <u>she</u> was quite different. |

Revise such a sentence in one of two ways:

■ **Replace the pronoun with the appropriate noun:**

| Clear | Emily Dickinson is sometimes compared with Jane Austen, but <u>Dickinson</u> [or <u>Austen</u>] was quite different. |

Exercise

■ **Avoid repetition by rewriting the sentence.** If you use the pronoun, make sure it has only one possible antecedent:

Clear   Despite occasional comparison, Emily Dickinson and Jane Austen were quite different.

Clear   Though sometimes compared with her, Emily Dickinson was quite different from Jane Austen.

Sentences that report what someone said, using verbs such as *said* or *told*, often require direct rather than indirect quotation:

Confusing   Juliet Noble told Ann Torre that she was next in line for the job.

Clear   Juliet Noble told Ann Torre, "I am next in line for the job."

Clear   Juliet Noble told Ann Torre, "You are next in line for the job."

Note Avoid the awkward device of using a pronoun followed by the appropriate noun in parentheses, as in the following example:

Weak   Noble and Torre had both hoped for the job, so she (Noble) was disappointed.

Improved   Noble was disappointed because she and Torre had both hoped for the job.

19b   **Place a pronoun close enough to its antecedent to ensure clarity.**

ref

19b

A clause beginning *who, which,* or *that* generally should fall immediately after the word to which it refers:

Confusing   Jody found a lamp in the attic that her aunt had used.

Clear   In the attic Jody found a lamp that her aunt had used.

Even when only one word could possibly serve as the antecedent of a pronoun, the relationship between the two may still be unclear if they are widely separated:

Confusing   Jane Austen had little formal education but was well educated at home. Far from living an isolated life in the English countryside, the Austens were a large family with a wide circle of friends who provided entertainment and cultural enrichment. They also provided material for her stories.

Clear   Jane Austen had little formal education but was well educated at home. Far from living an isolated life in the English countryside, the Austens were a large family with a wide circle of friends who provided entertainment and cultural enrichment. They also provided material for Jane Austen's stories.

Exercise

Exercise 19.1   Revising: Ambiguous and remote pronoun reference

Rewrite the following sentences to eliminate unclear pronoun reference. If you use a pronoun in your revision, be sure that it refers to only one antecedent and that it falls close enough to its antecedent to ensure clarity.

Example:

Saul found an old gun in the rotting shed that was just as his grandfather had left it.

In the rotting shed Saul found an old <u>gun that</u> was just as his grandfather had left it.

1. There is a difference between the heroes of today and the heroes of earlier times: they have flaws in their characters.
2. Baseball fans still admire Babe Ruth, Pete Rose, and Mark McGwire even though they could not be perfect.
3. Fans liked Rose for having his young son serve as batboy when he was in Cincinnati.
4. The reputation Rose earned as a gambler and tax evader may overshadow his reputation as a ballplayer, but it will survive.
5. Rose amassed an unequaled record as a hitter, using his bat to do things no one else has ever done. It stands even though Rose was banned from baseball.

ref

19c

19c Make a pronoun refer to a specific antecedent, not an implied one.

A pronoun should refer to a specific noun or other pronoun. The reader can only guess at the meaning of a pronoun when its antecedent is only implied by the context, not stated outright.

1 Use *this, that, which,* and *it* cautiously.

Exercise

The most common kind of implied reference occurs when the pronoun *this, that, which,* or *it* refers to a whole idea or situation described in the preceding clause, sentence, or even paragraph. Such reference, often called **broad reference,** is acceptable only when the pronoun refers clearly to the entire preceding clause. In the following sentence, *which* could not possibly refer to anything but the whole preceding clause:

I can be kind and civil to people, <u>which</u> is more than you can.
— George Bernard Shaw

But if a pronoun might confuse a reader, you should avoid using it or provide an appropriate noun:

Confusing The British knew little of the American countryside, and they had no experience with the colonists' guerilla tactics. This gave the colonists an advantage.

Clear The British knew little of the American countryside, and they had no experience with the colonists' guerrilla tactics. This ignorance and inexperience gave the colonists an advantage.

2 *It* and *they* should have definite antecedents.

Although common in speech, using *it* and *they* to refer to indefinite antecedents is inappropriate in writing.

Confusing In Chapter 4 of this book, it describes the early flights of the Wright brothers.

Clear Chapter 4 of this book describes the early flights of the Wright brothers.

Confusing Even in reality TV shows, they present a false picture of life.

Clear Even reality TV shows present a false picture of life.

Clear Even in reality TV shows, the producers present a false picture of life.

3 Implied nouns are not clear antecedents.

A noun may be implied in some other word or phrase, as *happiness* is implied in *happy*, *driver* is implied in *drive*, and *mother* is implied in *mother's*. But a pronoun cannot refer clearly to an implied noun, only to a specific, stated one:

Confusing In Cohen's report she made claims that led to a lawsuit.

Clear In her report Cohen made claims that led to a lawsuit.

Confusing Her reports on psychological development generally go unnoticed outside it.

Clear Her reports on psychological development generally go unnoticed outside the field.

4 Titles of papers are not clear antecedents.

The title of a paper is entirely separate from the paper itself, so a pronoun should not be used in the opening sentence of a paper to refer to the title:

ref
19c

Title	How to Row a Boat
Confusing	This is not as easy as it looks.
Revised	Rowing a boat is not as easy as it looks.

19d Use *you* only to mean "you, the reader."

You should clearly mean "you, the reader." The context must be appropriate for such a meaning:

| Inappropriate | In the fourteenth century you had to struggle simply to survive. |
| Revised | In the fourteenth century one [or a person] had to struggle simply to survive. |

Writers sometimes drift into *you* because *one, a person, the individual,* or a similar indefinite word can be difficult to sustain. Sentence after sentence, the indefinite word may sound stuffy, and it requires the sexist *he* or the awkward *he or she* for pronoun-antecedent agreement (see pp. 333–34). To avoid these difficulties, try using plural nouns and pronouns:

| Original | In the fourteenth century one had to struggle simply to survive. |
| Revised | In the fourteenth century people had to struggle simply to survive. |

19e Use the pronoun *it* only one way in a sentence.

We use *it* idiomatically in expressions such as *It is raining.* We use *it* to postpone the subject in sentences such as *It is true that more jobs are available to women today.* And we use *it* as a personal pronoun in sentences such as *Nicole wanted the book, but she couldn't find it.* All these uses are standard, but two of them in the same passage can confuse the reader:

| Confusing | It is true that the Constitution sets limits, but it is also flexible. |
| Clear | The Constitution does set limits, but it is also flexible. |

19f Use *who, which,* and *that* for appropriate antecedents.

The relative pronouns *who, which,* and *that* commonly refer to persons, animals, or things. *Who* refers most often to persons but may also refer to animals that have names:

Podcast

ref
19f

Dorothy is the girl who visits Oz.
Her dog, Toto, who accompanies her, gives her courage.

Which refers to animals and things:

The Orinoco River, which is 1600 miles long, flows through Venezuela into the Atlantic Ocean.

That refers to animals and things and occasionally to persons when they are collective or anonymous:

The rocket that failed cost millions.
Infants that walk need constant tending.

(See also p. 451 for the use of *which* and *that* in nonessential and essential clauses.)

The possessive *whose* generally refers to people but may refer to animals and things to avoid awkward and wordy *of which* constructions:

The book whose binding broke was rare. [Compare *The book of which the binding broke was rare.*]

Exercise 19.2 Revising: Indefinite and inappropriate pronoun reference

Many of the pronouns in the following sentences do not refer to specific, appropriate antecedents. Revise the sentences as necessary to make them clear.

Exercise

ref
19f

Example:
In Glacier National Park, they have moose, elk, and wolves.
Moose, elk, and wolves live in Glacier National Park.

1. "Life begins at forty" is a cliché many people live by, and this may well be true.
2. When she was forty, Pearl Buck's novel *The Good Earth* won the Pulitzer Prize.
3. Buck was a novelist which wrote primarily about China.
4. In *The Good Earth* you have to struggle, but fortitude is rewarded.
5. Buck received much critical praise and earned over $7 million, but she was very modest about it.
6. Kenneth Kaunda, past president of Zambia, was elected to it in 1964, at age forty.
7. When Catherine I became empress of Russia at age forty, they feared more than loved her.
8. At forty, Paul Revere made his famous ride to warn American revolutionary leaders that the British were going to arrest them. This gave the colonists time to prepare for battle.
9. In the British House of Commons they did not welcome forty-year-old Nancy Astor as the first female member when she entered in 1919.
10. In 610 CE, Muhammad, age forty, began to have a series of visions that became the foundation of the Muslim faith. Since then, millions of people have become one.

Exercise

Exercise 19.3   Revising: Pronoun reference

Revise the following paragraph so that each pronoun refers clearly to a single specific and appropriate antecedent.

> In Charlotte Brontë's *Jane Eyre*, she is a shy young woman that takes a job as governess. Her employer is a rude, brooding man named Rochester. He lives in a mysterious mansion on the English moors, which contributes an eerie quality to Jane's experience. Eerier still are the fires, strange noises, and other unexplained happenings in the house; but Rochester refuses to discuss this. Eventually, they fall in love. On the day they are to be married, however, she learns that he has a wife hidden in the house. She is hopelessly insane and violent and must be guarded at all times, which explains his strange behavior. Heartbroken, Jane leaves the moors, and many years pass before they are reunited.

Note See page 398 for an exercise involving unclear pronoun reference along with sentence fragments, comma splices, and other sentence errors.

20

Shifts

Podcast

Inconsistencies in grammatical elements will confuse your readers and distort your meaning. The box on the facing page shows ways to correct inconsistencies, or **shifts,** in nouns, pronouns, and verbs.

Shifts are likely to occur while you are trying to piece together meaning during drafting. But during editing you should make the grammatical elements of your sentences consistent.

Grammar checkers A grammar checker cannot recognize most shifts in sentences. Proofread your work on your own, looking carefully for inconsistencies.

mycomplab

Visit *mycomplab.com* for the eText and for resources and more exercises on shifts.

Ways to correct shifts

First draft

A |bank| |owes| more to its customers than |is held| in ————— Shift in verb voice

reserve. |It| |kept| enough assets to meet reasonable ————— Shift in verb tense

withdrawals, but panicked |customers| may demand ————— Shift in number

all their deposits. Then demands will exceed sup-

plies, and |banks| will fail. These days, a |person's| ————— Shifts in number and person

losses are not likely to be great because the govern-

ment insures |your| deposits.

Revised

A bank owes more to its customers than **it holds** in reserve. It **keeps** enough assets to meet reasonable withdrawals, but panicked customers may demand all their deposits. Then demands will exceed supplies, and **the bank** will fail. These days, the losses of **customers** are not likely to be great because the government insures **their** deposits.

20a Keep a sentence or related sentences consistent in person and number.

shift

20a

Person in grammar refers to the distinction among the person talking (first person), the person spoken to (second person), and the person, object, or concept being talked about (third person). **Number** refers to the distinction between one (singular) and more than one (plural).

Shifts in person

Most shifts in person occur because we can refer to people in general, including our readers, either in the third person (*a person, one*; *people, they*) or in the second person (*you*):

Video tutorial

People should not drive when <u>they</u> have been drinking.
<u>One</u> should not drive when <u>he or she</u> has been drinking.
<u>You</u> should not drive when <u>you</u> have been drinking.

Although any one of these possibilities is acceptable in an appropriate context, a mixture of them is inconsistent:

Shift in person	If a <u>person</u> works hard, <u>you</u> can gain satisfaction.
Revised	If <u>you</u> work hard, <u>you</u> can gain satisfaction.
Revised	If a <u>person</u> works hard, <u>he or she</u> can gain satisfaction.
Better	If <u>people</u> work hard, <u>they</u> can gain satisfaction.

Shifts in number

Inconsistency in number occurs most often between a pronoun and its antecedent (see pp. 331–32):

Shift in number	If a <u>student</u> does not understand a problem, <u>they</u> should consult the instructor.
Revised	If a <u>student</u> does not understand a problem, <u>he or she</u> should consult the instructor.
Better	If <u>students</u> do not understand a problem, <u>they</u> should consult the instructor.
Or	A <u>student who</u> does not understand a problem should consult the instructor.

Note Generic nouns and most indefinite pronouns take singular pronouns with a definite gender: *he, she,* or *it.* When we use a generic noun like *student* or *person* or an indefinite pronoun like *everyone* or *each,* we often mean to include both males and females. To indicate this meaning, use *he or she* rather than *he* (as in the first of the preceding revisions) or, better still, rewrite in the plural or rewrite to avoid the inconsistent pronoun (as in the second and third of the revisions). See pages 333–34 for more discussion and examples.

Inconsistency in number can also occur between other words (usually nouns) that relate to each other in meaning.

Inconsistent	All the <u>boys</u> have a good <u>reputation</u>.
Revised	All the <u>boys</u> have good <u>reputations</u>.

shift
20a

The consistency in the revised sentence is called **logical agreement** because the nouns are consistent (the *boys* have *reputations,* not a single *reputation*).

Exercise 20.1 Revising: Shifts in person and number

Exercise

Revise the following sentences to make them consistent in person and number.

Example:

A plumber will fix burst pipes, but they won't repair waterlogged appliances.

<u>Plumbers</u> will fix burst pipes, but they won't repair waterlogged appliances.

1. When a taxpayer is waiting to receive a tax refund from the Internal Revenue Service, you begin to notice what time the mail carrier arrives.
2. If the taxpayer does not receive a refund check within six weeks of filing a return, they may not have followed the rules of the IRS.
3. If a taxpayer does not include a Social Security number on a return, you will have to wait for a refund.

4. When taxpayers do not file their return early, they will not get a refund quickly.
5. If one makes errors on the tax form, they might even be audited,
thereby delaying a refund even longer.

20b Keep a sentence or related sentences consistent in tense and mood.

Shifts in tense

Within a sentence or from one sentence to another, certain
changes in tense may be required to indicate changes in actual or
relative time (see pp. 314–15). The following changes are necessary:

Video
tutorial

> Ramon <u>will graduate</u> from college thirty-one years after his father <u>ar-</u>
> <u>rived</u> in the United States.

In speech we often shift tenses even when they don't reflect changes
in time. But in writing, changes that are not required by meaning
distract readers. Unnecessary shifts between past and present in
passages narrating a series of events are particularly confusing:

Exercise

| Shift in tense | Immediately after Booth <u>shot</u> Lincoln, Major Rathbone <u>threw</u> himself upon the assassin. But Booth <u>pulls</u> a knife and <u>plunges</u> it into the major's arm. |
| Revised | Immediately after Booth <u>shot</u> Lincoln, Major Rathbone <u>threw</u> himself upon the assassin. But Booth <u>pulled</u> a knife and <u>plunged</u> it into the major's arm. |

Use the present tense consistently to describe what an author
has written, including the action in literature or a film:

shift

20b

| Shift in tense | The main character in the novel <u>suffers</u> psychologically because he <u>has</u> a clubfoot, but he eventually <u>triumphed</u> over his disability. |
| Revised | The main character in the novel <u>suffers</u> psychologically because he <u>has</u> a clubfoot, but he eventually <u>triumphs</u> over his disability. |

Shifts in mood

Shifts in the mood of verbs occur most frequently in directions
when the writer moves between the imperative mood (*Unplug the
appliance*) and the indicative mood (*You should unplug the appliance*). (See p. 296.) Directions are usually clearer and more concise
in the imperative, as long as its use is consistent:

| Shift in mood | <u>Cook</u> the mixture slowly, and <u>you should stir</u> it until the sugar is dissolved. |
| Revised | <u>Cook</u> the mixture slowly, and <u>stir</u> it until the sugar is dissolved. |

Exercise

Exercise 20.2 Revising: Shifts in tense and mood

Revise each of the following sentences to make it consistent in tense and mood.

Example:

Jenna rounded the base and keeps running until she slides into second.
Jenna rounded the base and <u>kept</u> running until she <u>slid</u> into second.

1. When your cholesterol count is too high, adjusting your diet and exercise level reduced it.
2. After you lowered your cholesterol rate, you decrease the chances of heart attack and stroke.
3. First eliminate saturated fats from your diet; then you should consume more whole grains and raw vegetables.
4. To avoid saturated fats, substitute turkey and chicken for beef, and you should use cholesterol-free salad dressing and cooking oil.
5. A regular program of aerobic exercise, such as walking or swimming, improves your cholesterol rate and made you feel much healthier.

20c Keep a sentence or related sentences consistent in subject and voice.

shift
20c

When a verb is in the **active voice**, the subject names the actor: *Megan passed the carrots*. When a verb is in the **passive voice**, the subject names the receiver of the action: *The carrots were passed [by Megan]*. (See pp. 320–22.)

A shift in voice may sometimes help focus the reader's attention on a single subject, as in *The candidate campaigned vigorously and was nominated on the first ballot*. However, most shifts in voice also involve shifts in subject. They are unnecessary and confusing.

Exercise

Shift in subject and voice	Internet blogs cover an enormous range of topics. Opportunities for people to discuss pet issues are provided on these sites.
Revised	Internet blogs cover an enormous range of topics and provide opportunities for people to discuss pet issues.

Exercise 20.3 Revising: Shifts in subject and voice

Make the following sentences consistent in subject and voice.

Example:

At the reunion they ate hot dogs and volleyball was played.
At the reunion they ate hot dogs and <u>played volleyball</u>.

1. If students learn how to study efficiently, much better grades will be made on tests.
2. Conscientious students begin to prepare for tests immediately after the first class is attended.

3. Before each class all reading assignments are completed, and the students outline the material and answer any study questions.
4. In class they listen carefully and good notes are taken.
5. Questions are asked by the students when they do not understand the professor.

20d Keep a quotation or a question consistently direct or indirect.

Direct quotations or questions report the exact words of a quotation or question:

"I am the greatest," bragged Muhammad Ali.
In his day few people asked, "Is he right?"

Indirect quotations or questions report that someone said or asked something, but not in the exact words:

Muhammad Ali bragged that he was the greatest.
In his day few people asked whether he was right.

Shifts between direct and indirect quotations or questions are difficult to follow.

Shift in quotation	Kapek reported that the rats avoided the maze and "as of this writing, none responds to conditioning."
Revised (indirect)	Kapek reported that the rats avoided the maze and that as of his writing none responded to conditioning.
Revised (direct)	Kapek reported, "The rats avoid the maze. As of this writing, none responds to conditioning."
Shift in question	The reader wonders whether the experiment failed or did it perhaps succeed?
Revised (indirect)	The reader wonders whether the experiment failed or whether it perhaps succeeded.
Revised (direct)	Did the experiment fail? Or did it perhaps succeed?

shift
20d

For more on quotations, see pages 458–60 (commas with signal phrases such as *she said*), 481–88 (quotation marks), and 642–47 (integrating quotations into your writing). For more on questions, see pages 441–42.

Exercise 20.4 Revising: Shifts in direct and indirect quotations and questions

Revise each of the following sentences twice, once to make it consistently direct, once to make it consistently indirect. You will have to guess at the exact wording of direct quotations and questions that are now stated indirectly.

Exercise

Example:

We all wonder what the next decade will bring and will we thrive or not?

Direct: <u>What will the next decade bring?</u> Will we thrive or not?

Indirect: We all wonder what the next decade will bring and <u>whether we will thrive or not.</u>

1. One anthropologist says that the functions of marriage have changed and "nowhere more dramatically than in industrialized cultures."
2. The question even arises of whether siblings may marry and would the union be immoral?
3. The author points out, "Sibling marriage is still illegal everywhere in the United States" and that people are still prosecuted under the law.
4. She says that incest could be considered a universal taboo and "the questions asked about the taboo vary widely."
5. Some ask is the taboo a way of protecting the family or whether it may be instinctive.

Exercise 20.5 Revising: Shifts

Exercise

Revise the following paragraph to eliminate unnecessary shifts in person, number, tense, mood, and voice.

shift
20d

Driving in snow need not be dangerous if you practice a few rules. First, one should avoid fast starts, which prevent the wheels from gaining traction and may result in the car's getting stuck. Second, drive more slowly than usual, and you should pay attention to the feel of the car: if the steering seemed unusually loose or the wheels did not seem to be grabbing the road, slow down. Third, avoid fast stops, which lead to skids. One should be alert for other cars and intersections that may necessitate that the brakes be applied suddenly. If you need to slow down, the car's momentum can be reduced by downshifting as well as by applying the brakes. When braking, press the pedal to the floor only if you have antilock brakes; otherwise, the pedal should be pumped in short bursts. If you feel the car skidding, the brakes should be released and the wheel should be turned into the direction of the skid, and then the brakes should be pressed or pumped again. If one repeated these motions, the skid would be stopped and the speed of the car would be reduced.

Note See page 398 for an exercise involving shifts along with sentence fragments, comma splices, and other sentence errors.

21

Misplaced and Dangling Modifiers

When reading a sentence in English, we depend principally on the arrangement of the words to tell us how they are related. In writing, we may create confusion if we fail to connect modifiers to the words they modify.

Video tutorial

Grammar checkers A grammar checker cannot recognize most problems with modifiers. For instance, a checker failed to flag the misplaced modifiers in *Gasoline high prices affect usually car sales* or the dangling modifier in *The vandalism was visible passing the building.*

Misplaced Modifiers

A modifier is **misplaced** if readers can't easily relate it to the word it modifies. Misplaced modifiers may be awkward, confusing, or even unintentionally funny.

21a Place modifiers where they will clearly modify the words intended.

Readers tend to link a modifying word, phrase, or clause to the nearest word it could modify: *I saw a man in a green hat.* Thus the writer must place the phrase so that it clearly modifies the intended word and not some other.

Podcast

Exercise

| Confusing | He served steak to the men on paper plates. |
| Revised | He served the men steak on paper plates. |

| Confusing | Many dogs are killed by cars and trucks roaming unleashed. |
| Revised | Many dogs roaming unleashed are killed by cars and trucks. |

Visit *mycomplab.com* for the eText and for resources and more exercises on misplaced and dangling modifiers.

Ways to revise misplaced modifiers

■ **Place modifiers clearly** (previous page and below).

Confusing	Listening to music can cause hearing loss <u>at high levels</u>.
Revised	Listening to music at high levels can cause hearing loss.

■ **Place limiting modifiers carefully** (facing page).

Confusing	The women <u>only</u> reached the summit on their last climb.
Revised	The women reached the summit only on their last climb.

■ **Make each modifier refer to only one grammatical unit** (facing page).

Confusing	Students who fail to complete assignments <u>often</u> receive poor grades.
Revised	Students who often fail to complete assignments receive poor grades.
Revised	Students who fail to complete assignments receive poor grades often.

■ **Keep grammatical units together** (pp. 384–85).

Awkward	The owner ordered the dog <u>to not bark</u>.
Revised	The owner ordered the dog not **to bark**.

■ **Place adverbs and adjectives conventionally** (pp. 386–87).

Awkward	Once endangered, bald eagles were spotted <u>seldom</u> in the eastern United States.
Revised	Once endangered, bald eagles were seldom spotted in the eastern United States.

mm
21a

Confusing	This is the only chocolate chip cookie in a bag that tastes like Mom's. [Actual advertisement.]
Revised	This is the only <u>bagged</u> [or <u>packaged</u>] chocolate chip cookie that tastes like Mom's.

Exercise

Exercise 21.1 Revising: Misplaced phrases and clauses

Revise the following sentences so that phrases and clauses clearly modify the appropriate words.

Example:
I came to enjoy flying over time.
<u>Over time</u> I came to enjoy flying.

1. Women have contributed much to knowledge and culture of great value.
2. Emma Willard founded the Troy Female Seminary, the first institution to provide a college-level education for women in 1821.

3. Sixteen years later Mary Lyon founded Mount Holyoke Female Seminary, the first true women's college with directors and a campus who would sustain the college even after Lyon's death.
4. *Una* was the first US newspaper, which was founded by Pauline Wright Davis in 1853, that was dedicated to gaining women's rights.
5. Mitchell's Comet was discovered in 1847, which was named for Maria Mitchell.

21b Place limiting modifiers carefully.

Limiting modifiers include *almost, even, exactly, hardly, just, merely, nearly, only, scarcely,* and *simply.* In speech these modifiers often occur before the verb, regardless of the words they are intended to modify. In writing, however, these modifiers should fall immediately before the word or word group they modify to avoid any ambiguity:

Unclear   She only found that fossil on her last dig.

Revised   She found only that fossil on her last dig.

Revised   She found that fossil only on her last dig.

Exercise 21.2 Using limiting modifiers

Use each of the following limiting modifiers in two versions of the same sentence.

Example:
only
He is the only one I like. He is the one only I like.

1. almost   3. hardly   5. nearly
2. even   4. simply

21c Make each modifier refer to only one grammatical element.

A modifier can modify only *one* element in a sentence—the subject, the verb, or some other element. A **squinting modifier** seems confusingly to refer to either of two words:

Squinting   Snipers who fired on the soldiers often escaped capture.

Clear   Snipers who often fired on the soldiers escaped capture.

Clear   Snipers who fired on the soldiers escaped capture often.

When an adverb modifies an entire main clause, as in the last example, it can usually be moved to the beginning of the sentence: *Often, snipers who fired on the soldiers escaped capture.*

Exercise

Exercise 21.3 Revising: Squinting modifiers

Revise each sentence twice so that the squinting modifier applies clearly first to one element and then to the other.

Example:

The work that he hoped would satisfy him completely frustrated him.
The work that he hoped would <u>completely</u> satisfy him frustrated him.
The work that he hoped would satisfy him frustrated him <u>completely</u>.

1. People who sunbathe often can damage their skin.
2. Sunbathers who apply a sunscreen frequently block some of the sun's harmful ultraviolet rays.
3. Men and women who lie out in the sun often have leathery, dry skin.
4. Doctors tell sunbathers when they are older they risk skin cancer.
5. People who stay out of the sun usually will have better skin and fewer chances of skin cancer.

21d Keep subjects, verbs, and objects together.

Exercise

English sentences tend to move from subject to verb to object. The movement is so familiar that modifiers between these elements can be awkward.

A subject and verb may be separated by an adjective that modifies the subject: *The hurricane, which hit the city with ferocious winds, damaged many homes and public buildings.* But an adverb of more than a word usually stops the flow of the sentence:

mm
21e

           subject ┌──── adverb ────┐ verb
Awkward   The city, after the hurricane, began massive rebuilding.

       ┌──── adverb ────┐ subject   verb
Revised   After the hurricane, the city began massive rebuilding.

Even a one-word adverb will be awkward between a verb and its object:

               ┌─── verb ───┐adverb   object
Awkward   The hurricane had damaged <u>badly</u> many homes in the city.

                 ┌── verb ──┐   object
Revised   The hurricane had <u>badly</u> damaged many homes in the city.
                        adverb

21e Keep parts of infinitives or verb phrases together.

An **infinitive** consists of the marker *to* plus the plain form of a verb: *to produce, to enjoy.* The two words in an infinitive are widely regarded as a grammatical unit that should not be split apart by a modifier:

                                               infinitive
Awkward   The weather service expected temperatures to <u>not</u> rise.

Revised   The weather service expected temperatures <u>not</u> to rise.

ᵧ infinitive ᵧ

A split infinitive may sometimes be natural and preferable, though it may still bother some readers:

Several US industries expect to <u>more than</u> triple their use of robots.

Here the split infinitive is more economical than the alternatives, such as *Several US industries expect to increase their use of robots by more than three times.*

A **verb phrase** consists of a helping verb plus a main verb, as in *will call, was going, had been writing* (see p. 296). A single-word adverb may be inserted after the helping verb in a verb phrase (or the first helping verb if more than one): *Scientists have <u>lately</u> been using spacecraft to study the sun.* But when longer adverbs interrupt verb phrases, the result is almost always awkward:

Awkward   People who have osteoporosis can, by increasing their daily intake of calcium and vitamin D, improve their bone density.

Revised   By increasing their daily intake of calcium and vitamin D, people who have osteoporosis can improve their bone density.

> **CULTURE LANGUAGE** In an English question, place a one-word adverb immediately after the subject:

Will spacecraft <u>ever</u> be able to leave the solar system?

mm

21e

Exercise 21.4 Revising: Separated sentence parts

Revise the following sentences to connect separated parts (subject-predicate, verb-object, verb phrase, infinitive).

Exercise

Example:
Most children have by the time they are seven lost a tooth.
<u>By the time they are seven</u>, most children have lost a tooth.

1. Myra Bradwell founded in 1868 the *Chicago Legal News.*
2. Bradwell was later denied, although she had qualified, admission to the Illinois Bar Association.
3. In an attempt to finally gain admission to the bar, she carried the case to the Supreme Court, but the justices decided against her.
4. Bradwell was determined that no other woman would, if she were qualified, be denied entrance to a profession.
5. The Illinois legislature finally passed, in response to Bradwell's persuasion, a bill ensuring that no one on the basis of gender would be restricted from a profession.

21f   Position adverbs with care.

A few adverbs may be difficult for nonnative speakers of English.

Adverbs of frequency

Adverbs of frequency include *always, never, often, rarely, seldom, sometimes,* and *usually.* They appear at the beginning of a sentence, before a one-word verb, or after the helping verb in a verb phrase:

                     verb phrase   adverb

Awkward   Robots have put <u>sometimes</u> humans out of work.

                     helping   main
                     verb   adverb   verb

Revised   Robots have <u>sometimes</u> put humans out of work.

                   adverb   verb phrase

Revised   <u>Sometimes</u> robots have put humans out of work.

Adverbs of frequency always follow the verb *be*:

                     adverb verb

Awkward   Robots <u>often</u> are helpful to workers.

                     verb adverb

Revised   Robots are <u>often</u> helpful to workers.

When *rarely, seldom,* and other negative adverbs of frequency begin a sentence, the normal subject-verb order changes. (See also p. 431.)

                     adverb verb subject

<u>Rarely</u> are robots simple machines.

Adverbs of degree

Adverbs of degree include *absolutely, almost, certainly, completely, especially, extremely, hardly,* and *only.* They fall just before the word modified (an adjective, another adverb, sometimes a verb).

                     adjective adverb

Awkward   Robots have been useful <u>especially</u> in making cars.

                     adverb   adjective

Revised   Robots have been <u>especially</u> useful in making cars.

Adverbs of manner

Adverbs of manner include *badly, sweetly, tightly,* and others that describe how something is done. They usually fall after the verb:

                     adverb   verb

Awkward   Robots <u>smoothly</u> work on assembly lines.

                     verb   adverb

Revised   Robots work <u>smoothly</u> on assembly lines.

The adverb *not*

When the adverb *not* modifies a verb, place it after the helping verb (or the first helping verb if more than one):

mm
21f

	helping verb	main verb	
Faulty	Robots do	think	not.

	helping verb		main verb
Revised	Robots do		not think.

Place *not* after a form of *be: Robots are not thinkers.*

When *not* modifies another adverb or an adjective, place it before the other modifier: *Robots are not sleek machines.*

21g Arrange adjectives appropriately.

English follows distinctive rules for arranging two or three adjectives before a noun. (A string of more than three adjectives before a noun is rare.) The order depends on the meaning of the adjectives, as indicated in the following table:

Determiner	Opinion	Size or shape	Color	Origin	Material	Noun used as adjective	Noun
many						state	**laws**
	striking		green	Thai			**birds**
a	fine			German			**camera**
this		square			wooden		**table**
all						business	**reports**
the			blue		litmus		**paper**

See pages 455–56 on punctuating adjectives before a noun.

Exercise 21.5 Revising: Placement of adverbs
and adjectives

Revise the sentences below to correct the positions of adverbs or adjectives. If a sentence is already correct as given, mark the number preceding it.

Example:

Gasoline high prices affect usually car sales.
High gasoline prices usually affect car sales.

1. Some years ago Detroit cars often were praised.
2. Luxury large cars especially were prized.
3. Then a serious oil shortage led drivers to value small foreign cars that got good mileage.
4. When gasoline ample supplies returned, consumers bought again American large cars and trucks.
5. Consumers not were loyal to the big vehicles when gasoline prices dramatically rose.

Dangling Modifiers

21h Relate dangling modifiers to their sentences.

Exercise

A **dangling modifier** does not sensibly modify anything in its sentence:

Dangling   Passing the building, the vandalism became visible.

Dangling modifiers usually introduce sentences, contain a verb form, and imply but do not name a subject. In the preceding example, the implied subject is the someone or something passing the building. Readers assume that this implied subject is the same as the subject of the sentence (*vandalism* in the example), but vandalism does not pass buildings. The modifier "dangles" because it does not connect sensibly to the rest of the sentence.

Certain kinds of modifiers are the most likely to dangle:

■ Participial phrases:

Dangling   Passing the building, the vandalism became visible.

Revised   As we passed the building, the vandalism became visible.

■ Infinitive phrases:

Dangling   To understand the causes, vandalism has been studied.

Revised   To understand the causes, researchers have studied vandalism.

dm

21h

■ Prepositional phrases in which the object of the preposition is a gerund:

Dangling   After studying the problem, vandals are now thought to share certain characteristics.

Revised   After studying the problem, researchers think that vandals share certain characteristics.

■ Elliptical clauses in which the subject and perhaps the verb are omitted:

Dangling   When destructive, researchers have learned that vandals are more likely to be in groups.

Revised   When vandals are destructive, researchers have learned, they are more likely to be in groups.

Dangling modifiers are especially likely when the verb in the main clause is in the **passive voice** instead of the **active voice,** as in *vandalism has been investigated* and *vandals are thought.* (See pp. 320–21 for more on the passive voice.)

Identifying and revising dangling modifiers

- Identify the modifier's subject. If the modifier lacks a stated subject (as *when in diapers* does), identify what the modifier describes.
- Compare the subject of the modifier and the subject of the sentence. Verify that what the modifier describes is in fact the subject of the main clause. If it is not, the modifier probably dangles.
- Revise as needed. Either (*a*) recast the dangling modifier with a stated subject of its own, or (*b*) change the subject of the main clause to be what the modifier describes.

	┌────── modifier ──────┐	subject
Dangling	When in diapers, my mother remarried.	
Revision *a*	When I was in diapers, my mother remarried.	
Revision *b*	When in diapers, I attended my mother's second wedding.	

Video tutorial

Note A modifier may be dangling even when the sentence elsewhere contains a word the modifier might seem to describe, such as *vandals* below:

Dangling   When destructive, researchers have learned that vandals are more likely to be in groups.

In addition, a dangling modifier may fall at the end of a sentence:

Dangling   The vandalism was visible passing the building.

dm
21h

Revising dangling modifiers

Revise most dangling modifiers in one of two ways, depending on what you want to emphasize in the sentence.

- Change the subject of the main clause to a word the modifier properly describes:

Dangling   To express themselves, graffiti decorate walls.

Revised   To express themselves, <u>some youths decorate</u> walls with graffiti.

- Rewrite the dangling modifier as a complete clause with its own stated subject and verb:

Revised   <u>Because some youths need</u> to express themselves, <u>they</u> decorate walls with graffiti.

Exercise 21.6   Revising: Dangling modifiers

Revise the following sentences to eliminate any dangling modifiers. Each item has more than one possible answer.

Exercise

Example:

Driving north, the vegetation became increasingly sparse.

Driving north, <u>we noticed that</u> the vegetation became increasingly sparse.

<u>As we drove north</u>, the vegetation became increasingly sparse.

1. Drawing conclusions from several formal studies, pets can improve people's emotional well-being.
2. Suffering from Alzheimer's and unable to recognize her husband, one woman's ability to identify her beloved dog was unaffected.
3. Once subject to violent outbursts, a companion dog calmed an autistic boy.
4. Facing long hospital stays, pet-therapy dogs can cheer up patients.
5. To understand why people with serious illnesses often respond well to animals, pet therapy is being studied.

Exercise 21.7 Sentence combining: Placing modifiers

Exercise

Combine each pair of sentences below into a single sentence by rewriting one as a modifier. Make sure the modifier applies clearly to the appropriate word. You will have to add, delete, and rearrange words, and you may find that more than one answer is possible in each case.

Example:

Zach demanded a hearing from the faculty. Zach wanted to appeal the decision.

<u>Wanting to appeal the decision</u>, Zach demanded a hearing from the faculty.

dm
21h

1. Evening falls in the Central American rain forests. The tungara frogs begin their croaking chorus.
2. Male tungara frogs croak loudly at night. The "songs" they sing are designed to attract female frogs.
3. But predators also hear the croaking. They gather to feast on the frogs.
4. The predators are lured by their croaking dinners. The predators include bullfrogs, snakes, bats, and opossums.
5. The frogs hope to mate. Their nightly chorus can result in death instead.

Exercise 21.8 Revising: Misplaced and dangling modifiers

Exercise

Revise the following paragraph to eliminate any misplaced or dangling modifiers.

Central American tungara frogs silence several nights a week their mating croaks. When not croaking, the chance that the frogs will be eaten by predators is reduced. The frogs seem to fully believe in "safety in numbers." They more than likely will croak along with a large group rather than by themselves. By forgoing croaking on some nights, the frogs' behavior prevents the species from "croaking."

Note See page 398 for an exercise involving misplaced and dangling modifiers along with other sentence errors.

22

Mixed and Incomplete Sentences

Mixed Sentences

A **mixed sentence** contains two or more parts that are incompatible—that is, the parts do not fit together. The misfit may be in grammar or in meaning.

Grammar checkers A grammar checker may recognize a simple mixed construction such as *reason is because*, but it will fail to flag most mixed sentences.

22a Untangle sentences that are mixed in grammar.

Sentences mixed in grammar combine two or more incompatible grammatical structures.

Exercise

1 Make sure subject and verb fit together grammatically.

A mixed sentence may occur when you start a sentence with one plan and end it with another:

```
            ┌──────── modifier (prepositional phrase) ──────────┐  verb
Mixed       By paying more attention to impressions than facts leads us
            to misjudge others.
```

```
            ┌──────── modifier (prepositional phrase) ─────────┐ subject + verb
Revised     By paying more attention to impressions than facts, we misjudge
            others.
```

```
            ┌──────── subject (gerund phrase) ───────────┐ verb
Revised     Paying more attention to impressions than facts leads us to
            misjudge others.
```

Constructions that use *Just because* clauses as subjects are common in speech but should be avoided in writing:

```
            ┌── modifier (subordinate clause) ──┐┌── verb ──┐
Mixed       Just because no one is watching doesn't mean we have license
            to break the law.
```

┌——modifier (subordinate clause)——┐ subject + verb
Revised   Even when no one is watching, we don't have license to break the law.

In some mixed sentences the grammar is so jumbled that the writer has little choice but to start over:

Mixed   My long-range goal is through law school and government work I hope to help people deal with those problems we all deal with more effectively.

Revised   My long-range goal is to go to law school and then work in government so that I can help people deal more effectively with problems we all face.

A mixed sentence is especially likely when you are working on a computer and connect parts of two sentences or rewrite half a sentence but not the other half. A mixed sentence may also occur when you don't make the subject and the predicate verb carry the principal meaning. (See pp. 400–02.) If you need help identifying the subject and predicate, see pages 253–54.

2 State parts of sentences, such as subjects, only once.

In some languages other than English, certain parts of sentences may be repeated. These include the subject in any kind of clause and an object or adverb in an adjective clause. In English, however, these parts are stated only once in a clause.

mixed
22a

Repetition of subject

You may be tempted to restate a subject as a pronoun before the verb. But the subject needs stating only once in its clause.

Faulty   The liquid it reached a temperature of 110°C.
Revised   The liquid reached a temperature of 110°C.

Faulty   Gases in the liquid they escaped.
Revised   Gases in the liquid escaped.

Repetition in an adjective clause

Adjective clauses begin with *who, whom, whose, which, that, where,* and *when* (see p. 274). The beginning word replaces another word: the subject (*He is the person who called*), an object of a verb or preposition (*He is the person whom I mentioned*), or a preposition and pronoun (*He knows the office where* [*in which*] *we work*).

Do not state the word that *who, whom,* and so on replace in an adjective clause:

Faulty   The technician whom the test depended on her was burned. [*Whom* should replace *her.*]

Revised   The technician <u>whom</u> the test depended on was burned.

Adjective clauses beginning with *where* or *when* do not need an adverb such as *there* or *then*:

Faulty   Gases escaped at a moment <u>when</u> the technician was unprepared <u>then</u>.

Revised   Gases escaped at a moment <u>when</u> the technician was unprepared.

22b   Match subjects and predicates in meaning.

In a sentence with mixed meaning, the subject is said to be or do something illogical. Such a mixture is sometimes called **faulty predication** because the predicate conflicts with the subject.

Illogical equation with *be*

When a form of *be* connects a subject and a word that describes the subject (a complement), the subject and complement must be logically related:

Mixed   A <u>compromise</u> between the city and the country would be the ideal <u>place</u> to live.

Revised   A <u>community</u> that offered the best qualities of both city and country would be the ideal <u>place</u> to live.

Is when, is where

Definitions require nouns on both sides of *be*. Definition clauses beginning with *when* or *where* are common in speech but should be avoided in writing:

Mixed   An <u>examination</u> is <u>when you are tested</u> on what you know.

Revised   An <u>examination</u> is a <u>test</u> of what you know.

Reason is because

The commonly heard construction *reason is because* is redundant since *because* means "for the reason that":

Mixed   The <u>reason</u> the temple requests donations <u>is because</u> the school needs expansion.

Revised   The <u>reason</u> the temple requests donations <u>is that</u> the school needs expansion.

Revised   The temple requests donations <u>because</u> the school needs expansion.

Other mixed meanings

Mismatched subjects and predicates are not confined to sentences with *be*:

Mixed   The use of emission controls was created to reduce air pollution.

Revised   Emission controls were created to reduce air pollution.

Exercise

Exercise 22.1   Revising: Sentences mixed in grammar or meaning

Revise the following sentences so that their parts fit together both in grammar and in meaning. Each item has more than one possible answer.

Example:

When they found out how expensive pianos are is why they were discouraged.

They were discouraged <u>because</u> they found out how expensive pianos are.

When they found out how expensive pianos are, <u>they</u> were discouraged.

1. A hurricane is when the winds in a tropical depression rotate counterclockwise at more than seventy-four miles per hour.
2. Because hurricanes can destroy so many lives and so much property is why people fear them.
3. Through high winds, storm surge, floods, and tornadoes is how a hurricane can kill thousands of people.
4. Many scientists observe that hurricanes in recent years they have become more ferocious and destructive.
5. However, in the last half-century, with improved communications systems and weather satellites have made hurricanes less deadly.

Exercise 22.2   Revising: Repeated sentence parts

Revise the following sentences to eliminate any unnecessary repetition of sentence parts.

Example:

Over 87 percent of Americans they have heard of global warming.
Over 87 percent of <u>Americans have</u> heard of global warming.

1. Global warming it is caused by the gradual erosion of the ozone layer that protects the earth from the sun.
2. Scientists who study this problem they say that the primary causes of erosion are the use of fossil fuels and the reduction of forests.
3. Many nonscientists they mistakenly believe that aerosol spray cans are the primary cause of erosion.
4. One scientist whom others respect him argues that Americans have effectively reduced their use of aerosol sprays.
5. He argues that we will slow global warming only when the public learns the real causes then.

mixed
22b

Incomplete Sentences

The most serious kind of incomplete sentence is the fragment (see Chapter 17). But sentences are also incomplete when they omit one or more words needed for clarity.

Exercise

Grammar checkers A grammar checker will not flag most kinds of incomplete sentences discussed in this section.

22c Omissions from compound constructions should be consistent with grammar and idiom.

In both speech and writing, we commonly omit words not necessary for meaning, such as those bracketed in the examples below. Notice that all the sentences contain compound constructions (see p. 278):

> By 2015 automobile-emission standards will be tougher, and by 2020 [automobile-emission standards will be] tougher still.

> Some cars run on electricity and some [run] on methane or another alternative fuel.

> Environmentalists have hopes for alternative fuels and [for] public transportation.

Such omissions are possible only when you omit words that are common to all the parts of a compound construction. When the parts differ in either grammar or idiom, all words must be included in all parts:

inc

22d

> One new car gets eighty miles per gallon of gasoline; some old cars get as little as five miles per gallon. [One verb is singular, the other plural.]

> Environmentalists were invited to submit proposals and were eager to do so. [Each *were* has a different grammatical function: the first is a helping verb; the second is a linking verb.]

> They believe in and work for fuel conservation. [Idiom requires different prepositions with *believe* and *work*.]

In the sentence *My brother and friend moved to Dallas*, the omission of *my* before *friend* indicates that *brother* and *friend* are the same person. If two different persons are meant, the modifier or article must be repeated: *My brother and my friend moved to Dallas*.

(See pp. 540–41 for a list of English idioms with prepositions and pp. 420–24 for a discussion of grammatical parallelism.)

22d All comparisons should be complete and logical.

Comparisons make statements about the relation between two or more things, as in *Dogs are more intelligent than cats*.

1 State a comparison fully enough to ensure clarity.

Unclear	Automakers worry about their industry more than environmentalists.
Clear	Automakers worry about their industry more than environmentalists do.
Clear	Automakers worry about their industry more than they worry about environmentalists.

2 The items being compared should in fact be comparable.

| Illogical | The cost of a hybrid car can be greater than a gasoline-powered car. [Illogically compares a cost and a car.] |
| Revised | The cost of a hybrid car can be greater than the cost of [or that of] a gasoline-powered car. |

3 Use *any* or *any other* appropriately in comparisons.

Comparing a person or thing with all others in the same group creates two units: (1) the individual person or thing and (2) all *other* persons or things in the group. The two units need to be distinguished:

| Illogical | Los Angeles is larger than any city in California. [The sentence seems to say that Los Angeles is larger than itself.] |
| Logical | Los Angeles is larger than any other city in California. |

Comparing a person or thing with the members of a *different* group assumes separate units to begin with. The two units do not need to be distinguished with *other*:

| Illogical | Los Angeles is larger than any other city in Canada. [Canadian cities are a group to which Los Angeles does not belong.] |
| Logical | Los Angeles is larger than any city in Canada. |

4 Comparisons should state what is being compared.

Brand X gets clothes whiter. [Whiter than what?]
Brand Y is so much better. [Better than what?]

22e Include all needed prepositions, articles, and other words.

In haste or carelessness we sometimes omit small words such as prepositions and articles that are needed for clarity:

| Incomplete | Regular payroll deductions are a type painless savings. You hardly notice missing amounts, and after period of years the contributions can add a large total. |
| Revised | Regular payroll deductions are a type of painless savings. You hardly notice the missing amounts, and after a period of years the contributions can add up to a large total. |

Be careful not to omit *that* when the omission could be confusing:

Incomplete	The personnel director expects many employees will benefit from the plan. [*Many employees* seems to be the object of *expects*.]
Revised	The personnel director expects that many employees will benefit from the plan.

Attentive proofreading is the best insurance against the kinds of omissions described in this section. *Proofread all your papers carefully.* See page 73 for tips.

 If your native language or dialect is not standard American English, you may have difficulty knowing when to use the English articles *a, an,* and *the.* For guidelines on using articles, see pages 344–46.

Exercise 22.3   Revising: Incomplete sentences

Revise the following sentences so that they are complete, logical, and clear. Some items have more than one possible answer.

Exercise

Example:
Our house is closer to the bank than the subway stop.
Our house is closer to the bank than it is to the subway stop.
Our house is closer to the bank than the subway stop is.

1. The first ice cream, eaten in China in about 2000 BC, was more lumpy than the modern era.
2. The Chinese made their ice cream of milk, spices, and overcooked rice and packed in snow to solidify.
3. In the fourteenth century ice milk and fruit ices appeared in Italy and the tables of the wealthy.
4. At her wedding in 1533 to the king of France, Catherine de Médicis offered more flavors of fruit ices than any hostess offered.
5. Modern sherbets resemble her ices; modern ice cream her soft dessert of thick, sweetened cream.

inc

22e

Exercise 22.4   Revising: Mixed and incomplete sentences

Revise the following paragraph to eliminate mixed or incomplete constructions.

Exercise

The Hancock Tower in Boston is thin mirror-glass slab that rises almost eight hundred feet. When it was being constructed was when its windows began cracking, and some fell crashing to the ground. In order to minimize risks is why the architects and owners replaced over a third the huge windows with plywood until the problem could be found and solved. With its plywood sheath, the building was homelier than any skyscraper, the butt of many jokes. Eventually, however, it was discovered that the reason the windows cracked was because joint between the double panes of glass was too rigid. The solution of thicker single-pane windows was installed, and the silly plywood building crystallized into reflective jewel.

Exercise on Chapters 17–22 Revising: Clear sentences

Clarify meaning in the following paragraphs by revising sentence fragments, comma splices, fused sentences, problems with pronoun reference,
awkward shifts, misplaced and dangling modifiers, and mixed and incomplete sentences. Most errors can be corrected in more than one way.

Many people who are physically challenged. They have accomplished much. Which proves that they are not "handicapped." Confined
to wheelchairs, successful careers were forged by Bob Sampson and
Stephen Hawking. Despite Sampson's muscular dystrophy, he earned a
law degree he also worked for United Airlines for more than thirty years.
Stephen Hawking most famous for his book *A Brief History of Time*. Unable to speak, Hawking's voice synthesizer allows him to dictate his
books and conduct public lectures. And teach mathematics classes at
Cambridge University.

Franklin D. Roosevelt, Ann Adams, and Itzhak Perlman all refused let
polio destroy their lives. Indeed, Roosevelt led the United States during
two of the worst periods of its history as President. The Great Depression
and World War II. Reassured by his strong, firm voice, Roosevelt inspired
hope and determination in the American people. Ann Adams, who was
talented in art before polio paralyzed her, knew she had to continue to
be one. Having retrained herself to draw with a pencil grasped in her
teeth. She produces sketches of children and pets. That were turned into
greeting cards. The profits from the cards sustained her. Roosevelt and
Adams were stricken with polio when they were adults; Itzhak Perlman
when a child. He was unable to play sports, instead he studied the violin,
now many think he is greater than any violinist in the world.

Like Perlman, many physically challenged individuals turn to the
arts. Perhaps the reason is because the joy of artistic achievement com-
pensates for other pleasures they cannot experience. Stevie Wonder, José
Feliciano, and Andrea Bocelli all express, through their music, their souls.
Although unable to see physically, their music reveals truly how well they
see. Hearing impairment struck Ludwig van Beethoven and Marlee Matlin it did not stop them from developing their talents. Already a successful composer, many of Beethoven's most powerful pieces were written
after he became deaf. Similarly, Matlin has had excellent acting roles in
movies, plays, and television programs, indeed she won an Oscar for
Children of a Lesser God. She encourages others to develop their ability,
and many hearing-impaired actors have been inspired by her.

22

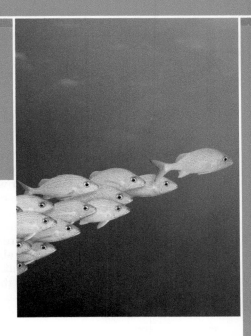

PART 5

Effective Sentences

23

Emphasizing Ideas

When you speak, your tone of voice, facial expressions, and even hand gestures work with your words and sentences to convey your meaning. When you write, your words and sentences must do that work alone. By emphasizing the main ideas in your sentences, you hold and channel readers' attention.

Grammar checkers A grammar checker may spot some problems with emphasis, such as nouns made from verbs, passive voice, wordy phrases, and long sentences that may also be flabby and unemphatic. However, no checker can help you identify the important ideas in your sentences or determine whether those ideas receive appropriate emphasis.

Video
tutorial

Ways to emphasize ideas

- Use the subjects and verbs of sentences to state key actors and actions (below).
- Use the beginnings and endings of sentences to pace and stress information (p. 402).
- Arrange series items in order of increasing importance (p. 405).
- Use an occasional balanced sentence (p. 405).
- Carefully repeat key words and phrases (p. 406).
- Set off important ideas with punctuation (p. 407).
- Write concisely (p. 408).

23a   Using subjects and verbs effectively

Exercise

The heart of every sentence is its subject, which usually names the actor, and its predicate verb, which usually specifies the subject's action: *Children* [subject] *grow* [verb]. When these elements do not identify the sentence's key actor and action, readers must find that information elsewhere and the sentence may be wordy and unemphatic.

mycomplab

Visit *mycomplab.com* for the eText and for resources and more exercises on emphasis.

In the following sentences, the subjects and verbs are underlined:

Unemphatic   The intention of the company was to expand its workforce. A proposal was also made to diversify the backgrounds and abilities of employees.

These sentences are unemphatic because their key ideas do not appear in their subjects and verbs. Revised, the sentences are not only clearer but more concise:

Revised   The company intended to expand its workforce. It also proposed to diversify the backgrounds and abilities of employees.

The constructions below usually drain meaning from a sentence's subject and verb.

Nouns made from verbs

Nouns made from verbs can obscure the key actions of sentences and add words. These nouns include *intention* (from *intend*), *proposal* (from *propose*), *decision* (from *decide*), *expectation* (from *expect*), *persistence* (from *persist*), *argument* (from *argue*), and *inclusion* (from *include*).

Unemphatic   After the company made a decision to hire more workers with disabilities, its next step was the construction of wheelchair ramps and other facilities.

Revised   After the company decided to hire more workers with disabilities, it next constructed wheelchair ramps and other facilities.

Weak verbs

Weak verbs, such as *made* and *was* in the unemphatic sentence above, tend to stall sentences just where they should be moving and often bury key actions:

Unemphatic   The company is now the leader among businesses in complying with the 1990 Americans with Disabilities Act. Its officers make speeches on the act to business groups.

Revised   The company now leads other businesses in complying with the 1990 Americans with Disabilities Act. Its officers speak on the act to business groups.

emph

23a

Passive voice

Verbs in the passive voice state actions received by, not performed by, their subjects. Thus the passive de-emphasizes the true actor of the sentence, sometimes omitting it entirely. Generally, prefer the active voice, in which the subject performs the verb's action. (See also pp. 321–22.)

| Unemphatic | The 1990 <u>law is seen</u> by most businesses as fair, but the costs of complying <u>have</u> sometimes <u>been objected to</u>. |
| Revised | Most <u>businesses see</u> the 1990 law as fair, but <u>some</u> <u>have objected to</u> the costs of complying. |

Exercise 23.1   Revising: Emphasis of subjects and verbs

Rewrite the following sentences so that their subjects and verbs identify their key actors and actions.

Example:

The issue of students making a competition over grades is a reason why their focus on learning may be lost.

<u>Students</u> who compete over grades <u>may lose</u> their focus on learning.

1. The work of many heroes was crucial in helping to emancipate the slaves.
2. The contribution of Harriet Tubman, an escaped slave herself, included the guidance of hundreds of other slaves to freedom on the Underground Railroad.
3. A return to slavery was risked by Tubman or possibly death.
4. During the Civil War she was also a carrier of information from the South to the North.
5. After the war needy former slaves were helped by Tubman's raising of money for refugees.

23b Using sentence beginnings and endings

Readers automatically seek a writer's principal meaning in the main clause of a sentence—essentially, in the subject that names the actor and the verb that usually specifies the action (see the preceding pages). Thus you can help readers understand your intended meaning by controlling the information in your subjects and the relation of the main clause to any modifiers attached to it.

Old and new information

Generally, readers expect the beginning of a sentence to contain information that they already know or that you have already introduced. They then look to the sentence ending for new information. In the unemphatic passage below, the second and third sentences both begin with new topics, while the old topics appear at the ends of the sentences. The pattern of the passage is A→B. C→B. D→A.

Unemphatic	^A<u>Education</u> often means ^B<u>controversy</u> these days, with rising
	costs and constant complaints about its inadequacies.
	But the ^C<u>value</u> of schooling should not be obscured by the

^B   ^D
controversy. The single best means of economic advance-
                                                    ^A
ment, despite its shortcomings, remains education.

In the more emphatic revision, old information begins each sentence and new information ends the sentence. The passage follows the pattern A→B. B→C. A→D.

| Revised | ^A   ^B
Education often means controversy these days, with rising costs and constant complaints about its inadequacies. But the ^B controversy should not obscure the ^C value of ^A schooling. Education remains, despite its shortcomings, ^D the single best means of economic advancement. |

Cumulative and periodic sentences

You can call attention to information by placing it first or last in a sentence, reserving the middle for incidentals:

Unemphatic	Education remains the single best means of economic advancement, despite its shortcomings. [Emphasizes shortcomings.]
Revised	Despite its shortcomings, education remains the single best means of economic advancement. [Emphasizes advancement more than shortcomings.]
Revised	Education remains, despite its shortcomings, the single best means of economic advancement. [De-emphasizes shortcomings.]

Many sentences begin with the main clause and then add modifiers to explain, amplify, or illustrate it. Such sentences are called **cumulative** (because they accumulate information as they proceed) or **loose** (because they are not tightly structured). They parallel the way we naturally think.

emph
23b

Cumulative	Education has no equal in opening minds, instilling values, and creating opportunities.
Cumulative	Most of the Great American Desert is made up of bare rock, rugged cliffs, mesas, canyons, mountains, separated from one another by broad flat basins covered with sunbaked mud and alkali, supporting a sparse and measured growth of sagebrush or creosote or saltbush, depending on location and elevation.
	—Edward Abbey

The opposite kind of sentence, called **periodic,** saves the main clause until just before the end (the period) of the sentence. Everything before the main clause points toward it.

Periodic   In opening minds, instilling values, and creating opportunities, education has no equal.

Periodic   With people from all over the world—Korean doctors, Jamaican cricket players, Vietnamese engineers, Haitian cabdrivers, Chinese athletes, Indian restaurant owners—the American mosaic is continually changing.

The periodic sentence creates suspense for readers by reserving important information for the end. But readers should already have an idea of the sentence's subject—because it was discussed or introduced in the preceding sentence—so that they know what the opening modifiers describe. A variation of the periodic sentence names the subject at the beginning, follows it with a modifier, and then completes the main clause:

Dick Hayne, who works in jeans and loafers and likes to let a question cure in the air for a while before answering it, bears all the markings of what his generation used to call a laid-back kind of guy.

—George Rush

Exercise

Exercise 23.2   Sentence combining: Beginnings and endings

Locate the main idea in each group of sentences below. Then combine each group into a single sentence that emphasizes that idea by placing it at the beginning or the end. For sentences 2–5, determine the position of the main idea by considering its relation to the previous sentences: if the main idea picks up a topic that's already been introduced, place it at the beginning; if it adds new information, place it at the end.

emph

23b

Example:

The storm blew roofs off buildings. It caused extensive damage. It knocked down trees. It severed power lines.

Main idea at beginning: The storm caused extensive damage, blowing roofs off buildings, knocking down trees, and severing power lines.

Main idea at end: Blowing roofs off buildings, knocking down trees, and severing power lines, the storm caused extensive damage.

1. Pat Taylor strode into the room. The room was packed. He greeted students called "Taylor's Kids." He nodded to their parents and teachers.
2. This was a wealthy Louisiana oilman. He had promised his "Kids" free college educations. He was determined to make higher education available to all qualified but disadvantaged students.
3. The students welcomed Taylor. Their voices joined in singing. They sang "You Are the Wind beneath My Wings." Their faces beamed with hope. Their eyes flashed with self-confidence.
4. The students had thought a college education was beyond their dreams. It seemed too costly. It seemed too demanding.

5. Taylor had to ease the costs and the demands of getting to college. He created a bold plan. The plan consisted of scholarships, tutoring, and counseling.

23c Arranging parallel elements effectively

Series

With parallelism, you use similar grammatical structures for ideas linked by *and, but,* and similar words: *Blustery winds and upturned leaves often signal thunderstorms.* (See Chapter 25.) In addition, you should arrange the parallel ideas in order of their importance:

| Unemphatic | The storm ripped the roofs off several buildings, killed ten people, and knocked down many trees in town. [Buries the most serious damage—deaths—in the middle.] |
| Emphatic | The storm knocked down many trees in town, ripped the roofs off several buildings, and killed ten people. [Arranges items in order of increasing importance.] |

You may want to use an unexpected item at the end of a series for humor or for another special effect:

Early to bed and early to rise makes a man healthy, wealthy, and dead.
—James Thurber

But be careful when creating such a series. The following series seems thoughtlessly random rather than intentionally humorous:

| Unemphatic | The painting has subdued tone, intense feeling, and a height of about three feet. |
| Emphatic | The painting, about three feet high, has subdued tone and intense feeling. |

Balanced sentences

A sentence is **balanced** when its clauses are parallel—that is, matched in grammatical structure (Chapter 25). When used carefully, balanced sentences can be especially effective in alerting readers to a strong comparison between two ideas. Read the following examples aloud to hear their rhythm.

The fickleness of the women I love is equalled only by the infernal constancy of the women who love me.   —George Bernard Shaw

In a pure balanced sentence two main clauses are exactly parallel: they match item for item.

Scratch a lover, and find a foe.   —Dorothy Parker

emph

23c

But the term *balanced* is commonly applied to sentences that are only approximately parallel or that have only some parallel parts:

> If thought corrupts language, language can also corrupt thought.
> —George Orwell

> As the traveler who has once been from home is wiser than he who has never left his own doorstep, so a knowledge of one other culture should sharpen our ability to scrutinize more steadily, to appreciate more lovingly, our own. —Margaret Mead

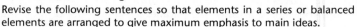

Exercise 23.3 Revising: Series and balanced elements

Exercise

Revise the following sentences so that elements in a series or balanced elements are arranged to give maximum emphasis to main ideas.

> *Example:*
>
> The campers were stranded without matches, without food or water, and without a tent.
>
> The campers were stranded without matches, without a tent, and without food or water.

1. Remembering her days as a "conductor" on the Underground Railroad made Harriet Tubman proud, but she got angry when she remembered her years as a slave.
2. Tubman wanted freedom regardless of personal danger, whereas for her husband, John, personal safety was more important than freedom.
3. Tubman proved her fearlessness in many ways: she led hundreds of other slaves to freedom, she was a spy for the North during the Civil War, and she disobeyed John's order not to run away.
4. To conduct slaves north to freedom, Tubman risked being returned to slavery, being hanged for a huge reward, and being caught by Southern patrollers.
5. After the war Tubman worked tirelessly for civil rights and women's suffrage; raising money for homes for needy former slaves was something else she did.

23d Repeating ideas

emph
23d

Repetition of words and phrases often clutters and weakens sentences, as discussed on page 549. But carefully planned repetition can be an effective means of emphasis. Such repetition often combines with parallelism. It may occur in a series of sentences (see p. 91) or in a series of words, phrases, or clauses within a sentence, as in the following examples:

> There is something uneasy in the Los Angeles air this afternoon, some unnatural stillness, some tension. —Joan Didion

> We have the tools, all the tools—we are suffocating in tools—but we cannot find the actual wood to work or even the actual hand to work it.
> —Archibald MacLeish

23e Separating ideas

When you save important information for the end of a sentence, you can emphasize it even more by setting it off from the rest of the sentence, as in the second example below:

> Mothers and housewives are the only workers who do not have regular time off, so they are the great vacationless class.
>
> Mothers and housewives are the only workers who do not have regular time off. They are the great vacationless class.
> —Anne Morrow Lindbergh

You can vary the degree of emphasis by varying the extent to which you separate one idea from the others. A semicolon provides more separation than a comma, and a period provides still more separation. Compare the following sentences:

> Most of the reading which is praised for itself is neither literary nor intellectual, but narcotic.
>
> Most of the reading which is praised for itself is neither literary nor intellectual; it is narcotic.
>
> Most of the reading which is praised for itself is neither literary nor intellectual. It is narcotic. —Donald Hall

Sometimes a dash or a pair of dashes will isolate and thus emphasize a part of a statement (see also pp. 492–93):

> His schemes were always elaborate, ingenious, and exciting—and wholly impractical.
>
> Athletics—that is, winning athletics—has become a profitable university operation.

Exercise 23.4 Emphasizing with repetition or separation

Emphasize the main idea in each of the following sentences or groups of sentences by following the instructions in parentheses: either combine sentences so that parallelism and repetition stress the main idea, or place the main idea in a separate sentence. Each item has more than one possible answer.

> *Example:*
>
> I try to listen to other people's opinions. When my mind is closed, I find that other opinions open it. And they can change my mind when it is wrong. (*Parallelism and repetition.*)
>
> I try to listen to other people's opinions, for they can open my mind when it is closed and can change my mind when it is wrong.

1. One of the few worthwhile habits is daily reading. One can read for information. One can read for entertainment. Reading can give one a broader view of the world. (*Parallelism and repetition.*)
2. Reading introduces new words. One encounters unfamiliar styles of expression through reading. (*Parallelism and repetition.*)

emph

23e

Exercise

3. Students who read a great deal will more likely write vividly, coherently, and grammatically, for they will have learned from other authors. (*Separation.*)
4. Reading gives knowledge. One gets knowledge about other cultures. One will know about history and current events. One gains information about human nature. (*Parallelism and repetition.*)
5. As a result of reading, writers have more resources and more flexibility, and thus reading creates better writers. (*Separation.*)

23f Being concise

Conciseness—brevity of expression—aids emphasis no matter what the sentence structure. Unnecessary words detract from necessary words. They clutter sentences and obscure ideas.

Weak   In my opinion the competition in the area of grades is distracting. It distracts many students from their goal, which is to obtain an education that is good. There seems to be a belief among a few students that grades are more important than what is measured by them.

Emphatic   The competition for grades distracts many students from their goal of obtaining a good education. A few students seem to believe that grades are more important than what they measure.

Techniques for tightening sentences are listed in the following box. Some of these techniques appear earlier in this chapter. All of them are covered in Chapter 39 on writing concisely.

Ways to achieve conciseness

- Make the subject and verb of each sentence identify its actor and action (pp. 400, 546):

  Avoid nouns made from verbs.
  Use strong verbs.
  Rewrite the passive voice as active.

- Cut or shorten empty words or phrases (p. 547):

  Shorten filler phrases, such as *by virtue of the fact that.*
  Cut all-purpose words, such as *area, factor.*
  Cut unneeded qualifiers, such as *in my opinion, for the most part.*

- Cut unnecessary repetition (p. 549).
- Reduce clauses to phrases and phrases to single words (p. 550).
- Avoid constructions beginning with *there is* or *it is* (p. 550).
- Combine sentences (p. 551).
- Cut or rewrite jargon (p. 551).

---

emph
23f

Video
tutorial

Exercise 23.5 Revising: Conciseness

Revise the following sentences to make them more emphatic by eliminating wordiness.

Exercise

> *Example:*
>
> The problem in this particular situation is that we owe more money than we can afford under present circumstances.
>
> The problem is that we owe more money than we can afford.

1. As far as I am concerned, customers who are dining out in restaurants in our country must be wary of suggestive selling, so to speak.
2. In suggestive selling, diners are asked by the waiter to buy additional menu selections in addition to what was ordered by them.
3. For each item on the menu, there is another food that will naturally complement it.
4. For example, customers will be presented with the question of whether they want to order french fries along with a sandwich or whether they want to order a salad along with a steak dinner.
5. Due to the fact that customers often give in to suggestive selling, they often find that their restaurant meals are more costly than they had intended to pay.

Exercise 23.6 Revising: Emphasizing ideas

Drawing on the advice in this chapter, rewrite the following paragraph to emphasize main ideas and to de-emphasize less important information.

Exercise

> These days, the choice is made by people to give "alternative" gifts for birthdays and holidays. When a donation is made to a charity or an organization in honor of the recipient, that is an alternative gift. A wrapped present is not received by the giftee. Instead, a card is sent to the giftee that explains the donation given in his or her honor. As for the alternative gift itself, a common option is money. Many other types are also possible. One organization sends livestock to rural families around the world. The use of the animals is for the families to feed themselves and to generate income by selling eggs and milk. Sewing machines are provided to city dwellers by another group. The machines allow people to start small businesses and become financially independent. Alternative gifts are ways to help others without cluttering the recipient's home, so they are the perfect choice for people who already have everything they need.

emph

23f

Note See page 434 for an exercise involving emphasis along with parallelism and other techniques for effective sentences.

24

Using Coordination and Subordination

When clearly written, your sentences show the relations between ideas and stress the more important ideas over the lesser ones. Two techniques can help you achieve such clarity:

- ▪ *Coordination* shows that two or more elements in a sentence are equally important in meaning. You signal coordination with words such as *and*, *but*, and *or*.

  equally important
  Car insurance is costly, but health insurance seems a luxury.

- ▪ *Subordination* shows that some elements in a sentence are less important than other elements for your meaning. Usually, the main idea appears in the main clause, and supporting information appears in single words, phrases, and subordinate clauses.

  less important   more important
  (subordinate clause)   (main clause)
  Because accidents and thefts occur frequently, car insurance is costly.

Grammar checkers   A grammar checker may spot some errors in punctuating coordinated and subordinated elements, and it can usually flag long sentences that may contain excessive coordination or subordination. But otherwise it can provide little help because it cannot recognize the relations among ideas in sentences.

24a   Coordinating to relate equal ideas

Exercise

By linking equally important information, you can emphasize the relations for readers. Compare the following passages:

String of simple sentences

We should not rely so heavily on oil. Coal and uranium are also overused. We have a substantial energy resource in the moving waters of our rivers. Smaller streams add to the total volume of water. The resource renews

mycomplab

Visit *mycomplab.com* for the eText and for resources and more exercises on coordination and subordination.

410

Ways to coordinate information in sentences

■ Link main clauses with a comma and a coordinating conjunction: *and, but, or, nor, for, so, yet* (p. 444).

Independence Hall in Philadelphia is faithfully restored **,** but many years ago it was in bad shape.

■ Relate main clauses with a semicolon alone or a semicolon and a conjunctive adverb: *however, indeed, thus,* etc. (pp. 467, 468).

The building was standing **;** however, it suffered from neglect.

■ Within clauses, link words and phrases with a coordinating conjunction: *and, but, or, nor* (pp. 278–79).

The people and officials of the nation were indifferent to Independence Hall or took it for granted.

■ Link main clauses, words, or phrases with a correlative conjunction: *both . . . and, not only . . . but also,* etc. (p. 279).

People not only took the building for granted but also neglected it.

itself. Oil and coal are irreplaceable. Uranium is also irreplaceable. The cost of water does not increase much over time. The costs of coal, oil, and uranium rise dramatically.

Ideas coordinated

We should not rely so heavily on oil, coal, and uranium, for we have a substantial energy resource in the moving waters of our rivers and streams. Oil, coal, and uranium are irreplaceable and thus subject to dramatic cost increases; water, however, is self-renewing and more stable in cost.

The second passage is shorter and considerably easier to understand because it links coordinate ideas with the underlined words.

coord
24a

Punctuating coordinated words, phrases, and clauses

Most coordinated words, phrases, and subordinate clauses are not punctuated with commas (see pp. 461–62). The exceptions are items in a series and coordinate adjectives:

We rely heavily on coal **,** oil **,** and uranium. [A series; see p. 455.]
Dirty **,** unhealthy air is one result. [Coordinate adjectives; see pp. 455–56.]

In a sentence consisting of two main clauses, punctuation depends on whether a coordinating conjunction, a conjunctive adverb, or no connecting word links the clauses:

Oil is irreplaceable **,** but water is self-renewing. [See pp. 444–46.]
Oil is irreplaceable **;** however, water is self-renewing. [See p. 468.]
Oil is irreplaceable **;** water is self-renewing. [See p. 467.]

1 Using coordination effectively

A string of coordinated elements—especially main clauses—creates the same effect as a string of simple sentences: it obscures the relative importance of ideas and details.

Excessive coordination	The weeks leading up to the resignation of President Richard Nixon were eventful, and the Supreme Court and the Congress closed in on him, and the Senate Judiciary Committee voted to begin impeachment proceedings, and finally the President resigned on August 9, 1974.

Such a passage needs editing to stress the important points (underlined below) and to de-emphasize the less important information:

Revised	The weeks leading up to the resignation of President Richard Nixon were eventful, as the Supreme Court and the Congress closed in on him and the Senate Judiciary Committee voted to begin impeachment proceedings. Finally, the President resigned on August 9, 1974.

2 Coordinating logically

Coordinated sentence elements should be logically equal and related, and the relation between them should be the one expressed by the connecting word. Otherwise, the result is **faulty coordination.**

Faulty	John Stuart Mill was a nineteenth-century utilitarian, and he believed that actions should be judged by their usefulness or by the happiness they cause. [The two clauses are not separate and equal: the second expands on the first by explaining what a utilitarian such as Mill believed.]
Revised	John Stuart Mill, a nineteenth-century utilitarian, believed that actions should be judged by their usefulness or by the happiness they cause.
Faulty	Mill is recognized as a utilitarian, and he did not found the utilitarian school of philosophy. [The two clauses seem to contrast, requiring *but* or *yet* between them.]
Revised	Mill is recognized as a utilitarian, but he did not found the utilitarian school of philosophy.

coord

24a

Exercise 24.1 Sentence combining: Coordination

Exercise

Combine sentences in the following passages to coordinate related ideas in the ways that seem most effective to you. You will have to supply coordinating conjunctions or conjunctive adverbs and the appropriate punctuation.

1. Many chronic misspellers do not have the time to master spelling rules. They may not have the motivation. They may rely on spelling checkers and dictionaries to catch misspellings. Most dictionaries list words under their correct spellings. One kind of dictionary is designed for chronic misspellers. It lists each word under its common

*mis*spellings. It then provides the correct spelling. It also provides the definition.

2. Henry Hudson was an English explorer. He captained ships for the Dutch East India Company. On a voyage in 1610 he passed by Greenland. He sailed into a great bay in today's northern Canada. He thought he and his sailors could winter there. The cold was terrible. Food ran out. The sailors mutinied. The sailors cast Hudson adrift in a small boat. Eight others were also in the boat. Hudson and his companions perished.

Exercise 24.2 Revising: Excessive or faulty coordination

Revise the following sentences to eliminate excessive or faulty coordination. Relate ideas effectively by adding or subordinating information or by forming more than one sentence. Each item has more than one possible answer.

Exercise

Example:

My dog barks, and I have to move out of my apartment.

Because my dog's barking disturbs my neighbors, I have to move out of my apartment.

1. Often soldiers admired their commanding officers, and they gave them nicknames, and these names frequently contained the word "old," but not all of the commanders were old.
2. General Thomas "Stonewall" Jackson was also called "Old Jack," and he was not yet forty years old.
3. Another Southern general in the Civil War was called "Old Pete," and his full name was James Longstreet.
4. The Union general Henry W. Halleck had a reputation as a good military strategist, and he was an expert on the work of a French military authority, Henri Jomini, and Halleck was called "Old Brains."
5. General William Henry Harrison won the Battle of Tippecanoe, and he received the nickname "Old Tippecanoe," and he used the name in his presidential campaign slogan "Tippecanoe and Tyler, Too," and he won the election in 1840, but he died of pneumonia a month after taking office.

sub
24b

24b Subordinating to distinguish main ideas

Exercise

With **subordination** you use words or word groups to indicate that some ideas in a sentence are less important than the idea in the main clause. In the following sentence, it is difficult to tell what is most important:

Excessive coordination	Computer prices have dropped, and production costs have dropped more slowly, and computer manufacturers have had to contend with shrinking profits.

The following revision places the point of the sentence (shrinking profits) in the main clause and reduces the rest of the information to a modifier (underlined):

Revised   Because production costs have dropped more slowly than prices, computer manufacturers have had to contend with shrinking profits.

No rules can specify what information in a sentence you should make primary and what you should subordinate; the decision will depend on your meaning. But, in general, you should consider using subordinate structures for details of time, cause, condition, concession, purpose, and identification (size, location, and the like). You can subordinate information with the structures listed in the box opposite.

In general, the shorter a subordinate structure is, the less emphasis it has. The following examples show how subordinate structures may convey various meanings with various weights. (Some appropriate subordinating words for each meaning appear in parentheses.)

Space or time (*after, before, since, until, when, while; at, in, on, until*)
The mine explosion killed six workers. The owners adopted safety measures.
After the mine explosion killed six workers, the owners adopted safety measures. [Subordinate clause.]
After six deaths in a mine explosion, the owners adopted safety measures. [Prepositional phrases.]

Cause or effect (*as, because, since, so that; because of, due to*)
Jones had been without work for six months. He was having trouble paying his bills.
Because Jones had been without work for six months, he was having trouble paying his bills. [Subordinate clause.]
Having been jobless for six months, Jones could not pay his bills. [Verbal phrase.]

Condition (*if, provided, since, unless, whenever; with, without*)
Forecasters predict a mild winter. Farmers hope for an early spring.
Whenever forecasters predict a mild winter, farmers hope for an early spring. [Subordinate clause.]
With forecasts for a mild winter, farmers hope for an early spring. [Prepositional phrase.]

Concession (*although, as if, even though, though; despite, except for, in spite of*)
The horse looked gentle. It proved hard to manage.
Although the horse looked gentle, it proved hard to manage. [Subordinate clause.]
The horse, a gentle-looking animal, proved hard to manage. [Appositive.]
The gentle-looking horse proved hard to manage. [Single word.]

Purpose (*in order that, so that, that; for, toward*)
Congress passed new immigration laws. Many Vietnamese refugees could enter the United States.

sub

24b

Ways to subordinate information in sentences

- Use a subordinate clause beginning with a subordinating conjunction: *although, because, if, whereas,* etc. (p. 273).

  Although some citizens had tried to rescue Independence Hall, they had not gained substantial public support.

- Use a subordinate clause beginning with a relative pronoun: *who, whoever, which, that* (p. 273).

  The first strong step was taken by the federal government, which made the building a national monument.

- Use a phrase (p. 264).

  Like most national monuments, Independence Hall is protected by the National Park Service. [Prepositional phrase.]

  Protecting many popular tourist sites, the service is a highly visible government agency. [Verbal phrase.]

- Use an appositive (p. 276).

  The National Park Service, a branch of the Department of Interior, also runs Yosemite and other wilderness parks.

- Use a short modifier.

  At the red brick Independence Hall, park rangers give guided tours and protect the irreplaceable building from vandalism.

Congress passed new immigration laws so that many Vietnamese refugees could enter the United States. [Subordinate clause.]

Congress passed new immigration laws, permitting many Vietnamese refugees to enter the United States. [Verbal phrase.]

Identification (*that, when, where, which, who; by, from, of*)

Old barns are common in New England. They are often painted red.

Old barns, which are often painted red, are common in New England. [Subordinate clause.]

Old barns, often painted red, are common in New England. [Verbal phrase.]

Old red barns are common in New England. [Single word.]

sub

24b

Punctuating subordinate constructions

A modifying word, phrase, or clause that introduces a sentence is usually set off from the rest of the sentence with a comma (see pp. 447–48):

Unfortunately, the bank failed.
In a little over six months, the bank became insolvent.
When the bank failed, many reporters investigated.

A modifier that interrupts or concludes a main clause is *not* set off with punctuation when it is essential to the meaning of a word or words in the clause (see p. 449):

> One article about the bank failure won a prize.
> The article that won the prize appeared in the local newspaper.
> The reporter wrote the article because the bank failure affected many residents of the town.

When an interrupting or concluding modifier is *not* essential to meaning, but simply adds information to the sentence, it *is* set off with punctuation, usually a comma or commas (see p. 449):

> The bank, over forty years old when it failed, never reopened after its doors were closed.
> The bank managers, who were cleared of any wrongdoing, all found new jobs.
> Some customers of the bank never recovered all their money, though most of them tried to do so.

Like a modifier, an appositive is set off with punctuation (usually a comma or commas) only when it is *not* essential to the meaning of the word it refers to (see p. 451):

> The bank, First City, was the oldest in town.
> Our newspaper, the *Chronicle*, was one of several reporting the story.

A dash or dashes may also be used to set off a nonessential appositive, particularly when it contains commas (see p. 493). A concluding appositive is sometimes set off with a colon (see p. 491).

1 Subordinating logically

Use subordination only for the less important information in a sentence. **Faulty subordination** reverses the dependent relation the reader expects:

sub

24b

Faulty   Ms. Angelo was in her first year of teaching, although she was a better instructor than others with many years of experience. [The sentence suggests that Angelo's inexperience is the main idea, whereas the writer meant to stress her skill *despite* her inexperience.]

Revised   Although Ms. Angelo was in her first year of teaching, she was a better instructor than others with many years of experience.

2 Using subordination effectively

Subordination can do much to organize and emphasize information. But it loses that power when you try to cram too much loosely related detail into one long sentence:

Overloaded   The boats that were moored at the dock when the hurricane, which was one of the worst in three decades, struck
were ripped from their moorings, because the owners
had not been adequately prepared, since the weather service had predicted that the storm would blow out to sea,
which storms do at this time of year.

Such sentences usually have more than one idea that deserves a
main clause, so they are best revised by sorting their details into
more than one sentence:

Revised   Struck by one of the worst hurricanes in three decades,
the boats at the dock were ripped from their moorings.
The owners were unprepared because the weather service had said that storms at this time of year blow out to
sea.

A common form of excessive subordination occurs with a string
of adjective clauses, each beginning with *which*, *who*, or *that*:

Stringy   The company opened a new plant outside Louisville, which
is in Kentucky and which is on the Ohio River, which forms
the border between Kentucky and Ohio.

To revise such sentences, recast some of the subordinate clauses as
other kinds of modifying structures:

Revised   The company opened a new plant outside Louisville, Kentucky, a city across the Ohio River from Ohio.

Exercise 24.3   Sentence combining: Subordination

Combine each of the following pairs of sentences twice, each time using
one of the subordinate structures in parentheses to make a single sentence. You will have to add, delete, change, and rearrange words.

Exercise

sub
24b

Example:

During the late eighteenth century, workers carried beverages in
brightly colored bottles. The bottles had cork stoppers. (*Clause beginning that. Phrase beginning with.*)

During the late eighteenth century, workers carried beverages in
brightly colored bottles that had cork stoppers.

During the late eighteenth century, workers carried beverages in
brightly colored bottles with cork stoppers.

1. The bombardier beetle sees an enemy. It shoots out a jet of chemicals to protect itself. (*Clause beginning when. Phrase beginning seeing.*)
2. The beetle's spray is very potent. It consists of hot and irritating
chemicals. (*Phrase beginning consisting. Phrase beginning of.*)
3. The spray's two chemicals are stored separately in the beetle's body
and mixed in the spraying gland. The chemicals resemble a nerve-
gas weapon. (*Phrase beginning stored. Clause beginning which.*)

4. The tip of the beetle's abdomen sprays the chemicals. The tip revolves like a turret on a World War II bomber. (*Phrase beginning revolving. Phrase beginning spraying.*)
5. The beetle defeats most of its enemies. It is still eaten by spiders and birds. (*Clause beginning although. Phrase beginning except.*)

Exercise

Exercise 24.4 Revising: Subordination

Rewrite the following paragraph in the way you think most effective to subordinate the less important ideas to the more important ones. Use subordinate clauses, phrases, and single words as you think appropriate.

Fewer students today are majoring in the liberal arts. I mean by "liberal arts" such subjects as history, English, and the social sciences. Students think a liberal arts degree will not help them get jobs. They are wrong. They may not get practical, job-related experience from the liberal arts, but they will get a broad education, and it will never again be available to them. Many employers look for more than a technical, professional education. They think such an education can make an employee's views too narrow. The employers want openminded employees. They want employees to think about problems from many angles. The liberal arts curriculum instills such flexibility. The flexibility is vital to the health of our society.

Exercise

Exercise 24.5 Revising: Faulty or excessive subordination

Revise the following sentences to eliminate faulty or excessive subordination. Correct faulty subordination by reversing main and subordinate structures. Correct excessive subordination by coordinating equal ideas or by making separate sentences.

sub
24b

Example:
Terrified to return home, he had driven his mother's car into a cornfield.

Having driven his mother's car into a cornfield, he was terrified to return home.

1. Genaro González is a successful writer, which means that his stories and novels have been published to critical acclaim.
2. He loves to write, although he has also earned a doctorate in psychology.
3. His first story, which reflects his consciousness of his Aztec heritage and place in the world, is titled "Un Hijo del Sol."
4. González wrote the first version of "Un Hijo del Sol" while he was a sophomore at Pan American, which is in the Rio Grande valley of southern Texas, which González calls "el Valle" in the story.
5. González's latest book, which is about a teenager and is titled *A So-Called Vacation*, is a novel about how the teen and his family live for a summer as migrant fruit pickers, which was the experience his father had when he first immigrated from Mexico.

24c Choosing clear connectors

Most connecting words signal specific and unambiguous relations; for instance, *but* clearly indicates contrast, and *because* clearly indicates cause. A few connectors, however, require careful use, either because they are ambiguous in many contexts or because they are often misused.

1 Using *as* and *while* clearly

The subordinating conjunction *as* can indicate several relations, including comparison and time:

| Comparison | The technicians work quickly, as they are required to do. |
| Time | One shift starts as the other stops. |

Avoid using *as* to indicate cause. It is unclear.

Unclear	As the experiment was occurring, the laboratory was sealed. [Time or cause intended?]
Revised	When the experiment was occurring, the laboratory was sealed. [Time.]
Revised	Because the experiment was occurring, the laboratory was sealed. [Cause.]

The subordinating conjunction *while* can indicate either time or concession. Unless the context makes the meaning of *while* unmistakably clear, choose a more exact connector:

Unclear	While technicians work in the next room, they cannot hear the noise. [Time or concession intended?]
Revised	When technicians work in the next room, they cannot hear the noise. [Time.]
Revised	Although technicians work in the next room, they cannot hear the noise. [Concession.]

2 Using *as* and *like* correctly

The use of *as* as a substitute for *whether* or *that* is considered nonstandard (it does not conform to spoken and written standard English):

| Nonstandard | They are not sure as the study succeeded. |
| Revised | They are not sure whether [or that] the study succeeded. |

Although the preposition *like* is often used as a conjunction in informal speech and in advertising (*Dirt-Away works like a soap should*), writing generally requires the conjunction *as, as if, as though,* or *that*:

| Speech | It seemed like it did succeed. |
| Writing | It seemed as if [or as though or that] it did succeed. |

sub
24c

Exercise

Exercise 24.6 Revising: Coordination and subordination

The following paragraph consists entirely of simple sentences. Use coordination and subordination to combine sentences in the ways you think most effective to emphasize main ideas.

Sir Walter Raleigh personified the Elizabethan Age. That was the period of Elizabeth I's rule of England. The period occurred in the last half of the sixteenth century. Raleigh was a courtier and poet. He was also an explorer and entrepreneur. Supposedly, he gained Queen Elizabeth's favor. He did this by throwing his cloak beneath her feet at the right moment. She was just about to step over a puddle. There is no evidence for this story. It does illustrate Raleigh's dramatic and dynamic personality. His energy drew others to him. He was one of Elizabeth's favorites. She supported him. She also dispensed favors to him. However, he lost his queen's goodwill. Without her permission he seduced one of her maids of honor. He eventually married the maid of honor. Elizabeth died. Then her successor imprisoned Raleigh in the Tower of London. Her successor was James I. The king falsely charged Raleigh with treason. Raleigh was released after thirteen years. He was arrested again two years later on the old treason charges. At the age of sixty-six he was beheaded.

Note See page 434 for an exercise involving coordination and subordination along with parallelism and other techniques for effective sentences.

25

Using Parallelism

Podcast

Parallelism gives similar grammatical form to sentence elements that have similar function and importance.

The air is dirtied by ‖ factories belching smoke
and ‖ cars spewing exhaust.

Parallel structure reinforces and highlights a close relation between compound sentence elements, whether words, phrases, or clauses.

mycomplab

Visit *mycomplab.com* for the eText and for resources and more exercises on parallelism.

The principle underlying parallelism is that form should reflect meaning: since the parts of compound constructions have the same function and importance, they should have the same grammatical form.

Exercise

Grammar checkers A grammar checker cannot recognize problems with parallelism because it cannot recognize the relations among ideas.

25a Using parallelism for coordinate elements

Use parallelism in all the situations illustrated in the box on the next page.

Video tutorial

Note Parallel elements match each other in structure, but they do not always match word for word:

The pioneers passed ‖ through the town
and ‖ into the vast, unpopulated desert.

1 Using parallelism for elements linked by coordinating conjunctions

The coordinating conjunctions *and, but, or, nor,* and *yet* always signal a need for parallelism:

The industrial base was shifting and shrinking.

Politicians rarely acknowledged the problem or proposed alternatives.

Industrial workers were understandably disturbed that they were losing their jobs and that no one seemed to care.

If sentence elements linked by coordinating conjunctions are not parallel in structure, the resulting sentence will be awkward and distracting:

Nonparallel Three reasons why steel companies kept losing money were that their plants were inefficient, high labor costs, and foreign competition was increasing.

Revised Three reasons why steel companies kept losing money were inefficient plants, high labor costs, and increasing foreign competition.

//

25a

All the words required by idiom or grammar must be stated in compound constructions (see also p. 278).

Nonparallel Given training, workers can acquire the skills and interest in other jobs. [*Skills* and *interest* require different prepositions, so both must be stated.]

Revised Given training, workers can acquire the skills for and interest in other jobs.

Patterns of parallelism

▪ Use parallel structures for elements connected by coordinating conjunctions (*and, but, or,* etc.) or correlative conjunctions (*both . . . and, neither . . . nor,* etc.):

In 1988 a Greek cyclist, backed up by | engineers,
| physiologists,
and | athletes,

broke the world's record for human flight
with neither || a boost
nor || a motor.

▪ Use parallel structures for elements being compared or contrasted:

|| Pedal power
rather than || horse power
propelled the plane.

▪ Use parallel structures for lists, outlines, or headings:

The four-hour flight was successful because
|| (1) the cyclist was very fit,
|| (2) he flew a straight course over water,
and || (3) he kept the aircraft near the water's surface.

Often, a word must be repeated to avoid confusion:

Confusing   Thoreau stood up for his principles by not paying his taxes and spending a night in jail. [Did he spend a night in jail or not?]

Revised   Thoreau stood up for his principles by not paying his taxes and by spending a night in jail.

Be sure that clauses beginning *who* or *which* are coordinated only with other *who* or *which* clauses, even when the pronoun is not repeated:

Nonparallel   Thoreau is the nineteenth-century essayist who retired to the woods and he wrote about nature.

Revised   Thoreau is the nineteenth-century essayist who retired to the woods and [who] wrote about nature.

2 Using parallelism for elements linked by correlative conjunctions

Correlative conjunctions are pairs of connectors. For example:

both . . . and   neither . . . nor   not only . . . but also
either . . . or   not . . . but   whether . . . or

//
25a

Correlative conjunctions stress equality and balance and thus emphasize the relation between elements, even long phrases and clauses. The elements should be parallel to confirm their relation:

> It is not a tax bill but a tax relief bill, providing relief not for the needy but for the greedy. —Franklin Delano Roosevelt

> At the end of the novel, Huck Finn both rejects society's values by turning down money and a home and affirms his own values by setting out for "the territory."

Most errors in parallelism with correlative conjunctions occur when the element after the second connector does not match the element after the first connector.

Nonparallel	Mark Twain refused either to ignore the moral blindness of his society or spare the reader's sensibilities. [*To* follows *either,* so it must also follow *or.*]
Revised	Mark Twain refused either to ignore the moral blindness of his society or to spare the reader's sensibilities.

Nonparallel	Huck Finn learns not only that human beings have an enormous capacity for folly but also enormous dignity. [The first element includes *that human beings have*; the second element does not.]
Revised	Huck Finn learns that human beings have not only an enormous capacity for folly but also enormous dignity.

3 Using parallelism for elements being compared or contrasted

Elements being compared or contrasted should ordinarily be cast in the same grammatical form.

> It is better to live rich than to die rich. —Samuel Johnson

Weak	The study found that most welfare recipients wanted to work rather than handouts.
Revised	The study found that most welfare recipients wanted work rather than handouts.
Revised	The study found that most welfare recipients wanted to work rather than to accept handouts.

//
25a

4 Using parallelism for lists, outlines, and headings

The elements of a list or outline that divides a larger subject are coordinate and should be parallel in structure. Parallelism is essential in the headings that divide a paper into sections (see p. 122) and in a formal topic outline (see p. 47).

Faulty	Improved
Changes in Renaissance England	Changes in Renaissance England
1. Extension of trade routes	1. Extension of trade routes
2. Merchant class became more powerful	2. Increased power of the merchant class
3. The death of feudalism	3. Death of feudalism
4. Upsurging of the arts	4. Upsurge of the arts
5. The sciences were encouraged	5. Encouragement of the sciences
6. Religious quarrels began	6. Rise of religious quarrels

Exercise

Exercise 25.1 Identifying parallel elements

Identify the parallel elements in the following sentences. How does parallelism contribute to the effectiveness of each sentence?

1. Eating an animal has not always been an automatic or an everyday affair; it has tended to be done on solemn occasions and for a special treat.   —Margaret Visser

2. They [pioneer women] rolled out dough on the wagon seats, cooked with fires made out of buffalo chips, tended the sick, and marked the graves of their children, their husbands and each other.
—Ellen Goodman

3. The mornings are the pleasantest times in the apartment, exhaustion having set in, the sated mosquitoes at rest on ceiling and walls, sleeping it off, the room a swirl of tortured bedclothes and abandoned garments, the vines in their full leafiness filtering the hard light of day, the air conditioner silent at last, like the mosquitoes.
—E. B. White

4. Aging paints every action gray, lies heavy on every movement, imprisons every thought.   —Sharon Curtin

//
25a

Exercise

Exercise 25.2 Revising: Parallelism

Revise the following sentences to make coordinate, compared, or listed elements parallel in structure. Add or delete words or rephrase as necessary.

Example:

After emptying her bag, searching the apartment, and she called the library, Emma realized she had lost the book.

After emptying her bag, searching the apartment, and calling the library, Emma realized she had lost the book.

1. The ancient Greeks celebrated four athletic contests: the Olympic Games at Olympia, the Isthmian Games were held near Corinth, at Delphi the Pythian Games, and the Nemean Games were sponsored by the people of Cleonae.

2. Each day of the games consisted of either athletic events or holding ceremonies and sacrifices to the gods.

3. In the years between the games, competitors were taught wrestling, javelin throwing, and how to box.

4. Competitors participated in running sprints, spectacular chariot and horse races, and running long distances while wearing full armor.
5. The purpose of such events was to develop physical strength, demonstrating skill and endurance, and to sharpen the skills needed for war.
6. Events were held for both men and for boys.
7. At the Olympic Games the spectators cheered their favorites to victory, attended sacrifices to the gods, and they feasted on the meat not burned in offerings.
8. The athletes competed less to achieve great wealth than for gaining honor both for themselves and their cities.
9. Of course, exceptional athletes received financial support from patrons, poems and statues by admiring artists, and they even got lavish living quarters from their sponsoring cities.
10. With the medal counts and flag ceremonies, today's Olympians sometimes seem to be proving their countries' superiority more than to demonstrate individual talent.

25b   Using parallelism to increase coherence

Video tutorial

Effective parallelism will enable you to combine in a single, well-ordered sentence related ideas that you might have expressed in separate sentences. Compare the following three sentences with the original single sentence written by H. L. Mencken:

> Slang originates in the effort of ingenious individuals to make the language more pungent and picturesque. They increase the store of terse and striking words or widen the boundaries of metaphor. Thus a vocabulary for new shades and differences in meaning is provided by slang.

> Slang originates in the effort of ingenious individuals to make the language more pungent and picturesque—to increase the store of terse and striking words, to widen the boundaries of metaphor, and to provide a vocabulary for new shades and differences in meaning.   —H. L. Mencken

Parallel structure works as well to emphasize the connections among related sentences in a paragraph:

//
25b

> *Lewis Mumford stands* high in the company of [twentieth-century] sages. A scholar of cosmic cultural reach and conspicuous public conscience, a distinguished critic of life, arts, and letters, an unequaled observer of cities and civilizations, *he is* secure in the modern pantheon of great men. *He is* also an enigma and an anachronism. A legend of epic proportions in intellectual and academic circles, *he is* surprisingly little known to the public.   —Ada Louise Huxtable

Here, Huxtable tightly binds her sentences with two layers of parallelism: the subject-verb patterns of all four sentences (italic and underlined) and the appositives of the second and fourth sentences (underlined). (See p. 92 for another illustration of parallelism among sentences.)

Exercise

Exercise 25.3 Sentence combining: Parallelism

Combine each group of sentences below into one concise sentence in which parallel elements appear in parallel structures. You will have to add, delete, change, and rearrange words. Each item has more than one possible answer.

Example:

The new process works smoothly. It is efficient, too.
The new process works smoothly <u>and efficiently</u>.

1. People can develop post-traumatic stress disorder (PTSD). They develop it after experiencing a dangerous situation. They will also have felt fear for their survival.
2. The disorder can be triggered by a wide variety of events. Combat is a typical cause. Similarly, natural disasters can result in PTSD. Some people experience PTSD after a hostage situation.
3. PTSD can occur immediately after the stressful incident. Or it may not appear until many years later.
4. Sometimes people with PTSD will act irrationally. Moreover, they often become angry.
5. Other symptoms include dreaming that one is reliving the experience. They include hallucinating that one is back in the terrifying place. In another symptom one imagines that strangers are actually one's former torturers.

Exercise 25.4 Revising: Parallelism

Exercise

Revise the following paragraph to create parallelism wherever it is required for grammar or for coherence.

The great white shark has an undeserved bad reputation. Many people consider the great white not only swift and powerful but also to be a cunning and cruel predator on humans. However, scientists claim that the great white attacks humans not by choice but as a result of chance. To a shark, our behavior in the water is similar to that of porpoises, seals, and sea lions—the shark's favorite foods. These sea mammals are both agile enough and can move fast enough to evade the shark. Thus the shark must attack with swiftness and noiselessly to surprise the prey and giving it little chance to escape. Humans become the shark's victims not because the shark has any preference or hatred of humans but because humans can neither outswim nor can they outmaneuver the shark. If the fish were truly a cruel human-eater, it would prolong the terror of its attacks, perhaps by circling or bumping into its intended victims before they were attacked.

Note See page 434 for an exercise involving parallelism along with other techniques for effective sentences.

//
25

26

Achieving Variety

In a paragraph or an essay, each sentence stands in relation to those before and after it. To make sentences work together effectively, you need to vary their length, structure, and word order to reflect the importance and complexity of ideas. Variety sometimes takes care of itself, but you can practice established techniques for achieving varied sentences:

Ways to achieve variety among sentences

- Vary the length and structure of sentences so that important ideas stand out (next page).
- Vary the beginnings of sentences with modifiers, transitional words and expressions, and occasional expletive constructions (p. 431).
- Occasionally, invert the normal order of subject, verb, and object or complement (p. 432).
- Occasionally, use a command, question, or exclamation (p. 433).

Video tutorial

A series of similar sentences will prove monotonous and ineffective, as the following passage illustrates.

> Ulysses S. Grant and Robert E. Lee met on April 9, 1865. Their meeting place was the parlor of a modest house at Appomattox Court House, Virginia. They met to work out the terms for the surrender of Lee's Army of Northern Virginia. One great chapter of American life ended with their meeting, and another began. Grant and Lee were bringing the Civil War to its virtual finish. Other armies still had to surrender, and the fugitive Confederate government would struggle desperately and vainly. It would try to find some way to go on living with its chief support gone. Grant and Lee had signed the papers, however, and it was all over in effect.

These eight sentences are all between twelve and sixteen words long (counting initials and dates), they are about equally detailed, and they all begin with the subject. We get a sense of names, dates, and events but no immediate sense of how they relate or what is most important.

Now compare the preceding passage with the actual passage written by Bruce Catton. Here the four sentences range from eleven to fifty-five words, and only one sentence begins with its subject:

When Ulysses S. Grant and Robert E. Lee met in the parlor of a modest house at Appomattox Court House, Virginia, on April 9, 1865, to work out the terms for the surrender of Lee's Army of Northern Virginia, a great chapter in American life came to a close, and a great new chapter began.

Suspenseful periodic sentence (pp. 403–04) focuses attention on meeting; details of place, time, and cause are in opening subordinate clause

These men were bringing the Civil War to its virtual finish. To be sure, other armies had yet to

Short sentence sums up

surrender, and for a few days the fugitive Confederate government would struggle desperately and vainly, trying to find some way to go on living now that its chief support was gone. But in

Cumulative sentence (p. 403) reflects lingering obstacles to peace

effect it was all over when Grant and Lee signed the papers.

Short final sentence indicates futility of further struggle

—Bruce Catton, "Grant and Lee"

The rest of this chapter suggests how you can vary your sentences for the kind of interest and clarity that Catton achieves in this passage.

Grammar checkers Some grammar checkers will flag long sentences, and you can check for appropriate variety in a series of such sentences. But generally these programs cannot help you see where variety may be needed because they cannot recognize the relative importance and complexity of your ideas.

26a Varying sentence length and structure

The sentences of a stylistically effective essay will vary most obviously in their length and the arrangement of main clauses and modifiers. The variation in length and structure makes writing both readable and clear.

var

26a

1 Varying length

In most contemporary writing, sentences vary from about ten to about forty words. When sentences are all at one extreme or the other, readers may have difficulty focusing on main ideas and seeing the relations among them:

Exercise

■ **Long sentences.** If most of your sentences contain thirty-five words or more, your main ideas may not stand out from the details that support them. Break some of the long sentences into shorter, simpler ones.

■ **Short sentences.** If most of your sentences contain fewer than ten or fifteen words, all your ideas may seem equally important and the links between them may not be clear. Try combining them with coordination (p. 410) and subordination (p. 413) to show relationships and to stress main ideas over supporting information.

2 | Rewriting strings of brief and simple sentences

A series of brief and simple sentences is both monotonous and hard to understand because it forces the reader to sort out relations among ideas. If you find that you depend on brief, simple sentences, work to increase variety by combining some of them into longer units that emphasize and link important ideas while de-emphasizing incidental information. (See Chapter 24.)

Exercise

The following examples show how a string of simple sentences can be revised into an effective piece of writing:

Monotonous | The moon is now drifting away from the earth. It moves away at the rate of about one inch a year. This movement is lengthening our days. They increase a thousandth of a second every century. Forty-seven of our present days will someday make up a month. We might eventually lose the moon altogether. Such great planetary movement rightly concerns astronomers, but it need not worry us. It will take 50 million years.

Revised | The moon is now drifting away from the earth <u>about one inch a year</u>. <u>At a thousandth of a second every century</u>, this movement is lengthening our days. Forty-seven of our present days will someday make up a month, <u>if we don't eventually lose the moon altogether</u>. Such great planetary movement rightly concerns astronomers, but it need not worry us. It will take 50 million years.

In the revision, underlining indicates subordinate structures that were simple sentences in the original. With five sentences instead of the original eight, the revision emphasizes the moon's movement, our lengthening days, and the enormous span of time involved.

var

26a

3 | Rewriting strings of compound sentences

Compound sentences are usually just simple sentences linked with conjunctions. Thus a series of them will be as weak as a series of brief, simple sentences, especially if the clauses of the compound sentences are all about the same length:

Monotonous | Physical illness may involve more than the body, for the mind may also be affected. Disorientation is common among sick people, but they are often unaware of it. They may reason abnormally, or they may behave immaturely.

Revised | Physical illness may involve the mind <u>as well as the body</u>. <u>Though often unaware of it</u>, sick people are commonly disoriented. They may reason abnormally <u>or behave immaturely</u>.

The first passage creates a seesaw effect. The revision, with some main clauses shortened or changed into modifiers (underlined), is both clearer and more emphatic. (See p. 412 for more on avoiding excessive coordination.)

Exercise

Exercise 26.1 Revising: Varied sentence structures

Rewrite the following paragraph to increase variety so that important ideas receive greater emphasis than supporting information does. You will have to change some main clauses into modifiers and then combine and reposition the modifiers and the remaining main clauses.

Charlotte Perkins Gilman was a leading intellectual in the women's movement during the first decades of the twentieth century. She wrote *Women and Economics.* This book challenged Victorian assumptions about differences between the sexes, and it explored the economic roots of women's oppression. Gilman wrote little about gaining the vote for women, but many feminists were then preoccupied with this issue, and historians have since focused their analyses on this issue. As a result, Gilman's contribution to today's women's movement has often been overlooked.

26b Varying sentence beginnings

An English sentence often begins with its subject, which generally captures old information from a preceding sentence (see pp. 402–03):

The defendant's lawyer was determined to break the prosecution's witness. She relentlessly cross-examined the stubborn witness for a week.

However, an unbroken sequence of sentences beginning with the subject quickly becomes monotonous, as shown by the unvaried passage on Grant and Lee that opened this chapter (p. 427). You can vary this subject-first pattern by adding modifiers or other elements before the subject.

Note The final arrangement of sentence elements should always depend on two concerns: the relation of a sentence to those preceding and following it and the emphasis required by your meaning.

var
26b

Adverb modifiers

Adverbs modify verbs, adjectives, other adverbs, and whole clauses. They can often fall in a variety of spots in a sentence. Consider these different emphases:

For a week, the defendant's lawyer relentlessly cross-examined the stubborn witness.

Relentlessly, the defendant's lawyer cross-examined the stubborn witness for a week.

Relentlessly, for a week, the defendant's lawyer cross-examined the stubborn witness.

Notice that the last sentence, with both modifiers at the beginning, is periodic and thus highly emphatic (see pp. 403–04).

⟨CULTURE LANGUAGE⟩ In standard American English, placing some negative adverb modifiers at the beginning of a sentence requires you to use the word order of a question, in which the verb or a part of it precedes the subject (see p. 282). These modifiers include *never, rarely, seldom,* and adverb phrases beginning *in no, not since,* and *not until.*

	adverb subject verb phrase
Faulty	Seldom a witness has held the stand for so long.

| | helping   main |
	adverb verb subject verb
Revised	Seldom has a witness held the stand for so long.

Adjective modifiers

Adjectives, modifying nouns and pronouns, may include participles and participial phrases, as in *flying geese* or *money well spent* (see pp. 268–69). These modifiers may sometimes fall at the beginning of a sentence to postpone the subject:

The witness was exhausted from his testimony, and he did not cooperate.

Exhausted from his testimony, the witness did not cooperate.

Coordinating conjunctions and transitional expressions

When the relation between two successive sentences demands, you may begin the second with a coordinating conjunction such as *and* or *but* (p. 279) or with a transitional expression such as *first, for instance, however,* or *therefore* (pp. 93–95).

The witness had expected to be dismissed after his first long day of cross-examination. But he was not.

The price of a college education has risen astronomically. For example, annual tuition at one state university climbed from $7400 to $9300 in just four years.

var

26b

Occasional expletive constructions

An expletive construction—*it* or *there* plus a form of *be*—may occasionally be useful to delay and thus emphasize the subject of the sentence:

His judgment seems questionable, not his desire.
It is his judgment that seems questionable, not his desire.

However, expletive constructions are more likely to flatten writing by adding extra words. You should use them rarely, only when you can justify doing so. (See also pp. 550–51.)

Exercise

Exercise 26.2 Revising: Varied sentence beginnings

Follow the instructions in parentheses to revise each group of sentences below: either create a single sentence that begins with an adverb or adjective modifier, or make one sentence begin with an appropriate connector.

Example:

The *Seabird* took first place. It moved quickly in the wind. (*One sentence with adjective modifier beginning <u>Moving</u>.*)

<u>Moving</u> quickly in the wind, the *Seabird* took first place.

1. Some people are champion procrastinators. They seldom complete their work on time. (*Two sentences with transitional expression.*)
2. Procrastinators may fear criticism. They may fear rejection. They will delay completing an assignment. (*One sentence with adverb modifier beginning <u>If</u>.*)
3. Procrastinators often desire to please a boss or a teacher. They fear failure so much that they cannot do the work. (*Two sentences with coordinating conjunction.*)
4. Procrastination seems a hopeless habit. It is conquerable. (*One sentence with adverb modifier beginning <u>Although</u>.*)
5. Teachers or employers can be helpful. They can encourage procrastinators. They can give procrastinators the confidence to do good work on time. (*One sentence with adjective modifier beginning <u>Helpfully encouraging</u>.*)

Exercise 26.3 Revising: Varied sentence beginnings

Exercise

Revise the following paragraph to vary sentence beginnings by using each of the following at least once: an adverb modifier, an adjective modifier, a coordinating conjunction, and a transitional expression.

Scientists in Egypt dug up 40-million-year-old fossil bones. They had evidence of primitive whales. The whale ancestors are called mesonychids. They were small, furry land mammals with four legs. These limbs were complete with kneecaps, ankles, and little toes. Gigantic modern whales have tiny hind legs inside their bodies and flippers instead of front legs. Scientists are certain that these two very different creatures share the same family tree.

var
26c

26c Inverting the normal word order

The word order of subject, verb, and object or complement is strongly fixed in English (see pp. 258–61). Thus an inverted sentence can be emphatic:

Voters once had some faith in politicians, and they were fond of incumbents. But now <u>all politicians</u>, especially incumbents, <u>voters seem to detest</u>. [The object *all politicians* precedes the verb *detests*.]

Inverting the normal order of subject, verb, and complement can be useful in two successive sentences when the second expands on the first:

Critics have not been kind to Presidents who have tried to apply the ways of private business to public affairs. Particularly explicit was the curt verdict of one critic of President Hoover: Mr. Hoover was never President of the United States; he was four years chairman of the board.

> —Adapted from Emmet John Hughes,
> "The Presidency vs. Jimmy Carter"

Inverted sentences used without need are artificial. Avoid descriptive sentences such as *Up came Ben and down went Katie's spirits.*

26d Mixing types of sentences

Most written sentences make statements. Occasionally, however, you may want to use questions, commands, or exclamations to enhance variety.

Questions may set the direction of a paragraph, as in *What does a detective do?* or *How is the percentage of unemployed workers calculated?* More often, though, the questions used in exposition or argument do not require answers but simply emphasize ideas that readers can be expected to agree with. Such **rhetorical questions** are illustrated in the following passage:

> Another word that has ceased to have meaning due to overuse is *attractive. Attractive* has become verbal chaff. Who, by some stretch of language and imagination, cannot be described as attractive? And just what is it that attractive individuals are attracting?   —Diane White

Commands occur frequently in an explanation of a process, particularly in directions, as this passage on freewriting illustrates:

> The idea is simply to write for ten minutes (later on, perhaps fifteen or twenty). Don't stop for anything. Go quickly, without rushing. Never stop to look back, to cross something out, to wonder how to spell something, to wonder what word or thought to use, or to think about what you are doing.   —Peter Elbow

Notice that the authors of these examples use questions and commands to achieve some special purpose. Variety occurs because a particular sentence type is effective for the context, not because the writer set out to achieve variety for its own sake.

Exercise 26.4 Writing varied sentences

Imagine that you are writing an essay on a transportation problem at your school. Practice varying your sentences by composing a sentence or passage to serve each purpose listed below.

Exercise

1. Write a question that could open the essay.
2. Write a command that could open the essay.
3. Write an exclamation that could open the essay.
4. For the body of the essay, write an appropriately varied paragraph of at least five sentences, including at least one short and one long sentence beginning with the subject; at least one sentence beginning

with an adverb modifier; at least one sentence beginning with a coordinating conjunction or transitional expression; and one rhetorical question or command.

Exercise

Exercise 26.5 Analyzing variety

Examine the following paragraph for sentence variety. By analyzing your own response to each sentence, try to explain why the author wrote each short or long sentence, each cumulative or periodic sentence, each sentence beginning with its subject or beginning some other way, and each question.

My earliest memory of learning to read is sitting with my grandmother on her livingroom sofa as her finger underlined the words of *Go, Dog. Go!* and I struggled to decipher them. Why did she spend so much time with me when she knew I would have every opportunity to finish high school and go to college? She listened patiently because she didn't take my education—or anyone's—for granted. The only one of her ten siblings to graduate from college, she had beaten the odds. She finished high school at the top of her class, held a full-time job while commuting to her college classes, and graduated with honors. Then she took a job at a public high school where she taught for more than thirty years. She knew that I was unaware of my opportunities, and she did not assume that I would succeed as she had. In her years of teaching, she had seen enough students struggle and drop out to know that failure often comes more easily than success. She was determined that I would be one of the successes—indeed, that I would soar. And soar I did.

Exercise

Exercise 26.6 Revising: Variety

The following paragraph consists entirely of simple sentences that begin with their subjects. As appropriate, use the techniques discussed in this chapter to vary sentences. Your goal is to make the paragraph more readable and make its important ideas stand out clearly. You will have to delete, add, change, and rearrange words.

The Italian volcano Vesuvius had been dormant for many years. It then exploded on August 24 in the year AD 79. The ash, pumice, and mud from the volcano buried two busy towns. Herculaneum is one. The more famous is Pompeii. Both towns lay undiscovered for many centuries. Herculaneum and Pompeii were discovered in 1709 and 1748, respectively. The excavation of Pompeii was the more systematic. It was the occasion for initiating modern methods of conservation and restoration. Herculaneum was simply looted of its most valuable finds. It was then left to disintegrate. Pompeii appears much as it did before the eruption. A luxurious house opens onto a lush central garden. An election poster decorates a wall. A dining table is set for breakfast.

Exercise on Chapters 23–26 Revising: Effective sentences

Revise the paragraphs below to emphasize main ideas, de-emphasize supporting information, and achieve a pleasing, clear variety in sentences. As appropriate, employ the techniques discussed in Chapters 23–26, such as using subjects and verbs effectively, subordinating and coordinating, creating parallelism, and varying sentence beginnings. Edit the finished product for punctuation.

Modern Americans owe many debts to Native Americans. Several pleasures are among the debts. Native Americans originated two fine junk foods. They discovered popcorn. Potato chips were also one of their contributions.

The introduction of popcorn to the European settlers came from Native Americans. Massasoit provided popcorn at the first Thanksgiving feast. The Aztecs offered popcorn to the Spanish explorer Hernando Cortés. The Aztecs wore popcorn necklaces. So did the natives of the West Indies. There were three ways that the Native Americans popped the corn. First, they roasted an ear over fire. The ear was skewered on a stick. They ate only some of the popcorn. They ate the corn that fell outside the flames. Second, they scraped the corn off the cob. The kernels would be thrown into the fire. Of course, the fire had to be low. Then the popped kernels that did not fall into the fire were eaten. The third method was the most sophisticated. It involved a shallow pottery vessel. It contained sand. The vessel was heated. The sand soon got hot. Corn kernels were stirred in. They popped to the surface of the sand and were eaten.

A Native American chef was responsible for devising the crunchy potato chip. His name was George Crum. In 1853 Crum was cooking at Moon Lake Lodge. The lodge was in Saratoga Springs, New York. Complaints were sent in by a customer. The man thought Crum's french-fried potatoes were too thick. Crum tried a thinner batch. These were also unsuitable. Crum became frustrated. He deliberately made the potatoes thin and crisp. They could not be cut with a knife and fork. Crum's joke backfired. The customer raved about the potato chips. The chips were named Saratoga Chips. Soon they appeared on the lodge's menu. They also appeared throughout New England. Crum later opened his own restaurant. Of course, he offered potato chips.

Now all Americans munch popcorn in movies. They crunch potato chips at parties. They gorge on both when alone and bored. They can be grateful to Native Americans for these guilty pleasures.

eff
26

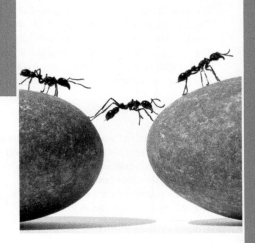

Commas, semicolons, colons, dashes, parentheses
(For explanations, consult the pages in parentheses.)

Sentences with two main clauses
The bus stopped, but no one got off. (p. 444)
The bus stopped; no one got off. (p. 467)
The bus stopped; however, no one got off. (p. 468)
The mechanic replaced the battery, the distributor cap, and the starter; but still the car would not start. (p. 470)
Her duty was clear: she had to locate the problem. (p. 489)

Introductory elements
Modifiers (p. 447)
After the argument was over, we laughed at ourselves.
Racing over the plain, the gazelle escaped the lion.
To dance in the contest, he had to tape his knee.
Suddenly, the door flew open.
With 125 passengers aboard, the plane was half full.
In 1983 he won the Nobel Prize.

Absolute phrases (p. 454)
Its wing broken, the bird hopped around on the ground.

Interrupting and concluding elements
Nonessential modifiers (p. 449)
Michael's car, which barely runs, has been impounded.
We consulted the dean, who had promised to help us.
The boy, like his sister, wants to be a pilot.
They moved across the desert, shielding their eyes from the sun.
The men do not speak to each other, although they share a car.

Nonessential appositives
Bergen's only daughter, Candice, became an actress. (p. 451)
The residents of three counties — Suffolk, Springfield, and Morrison — were urged to evacuate. (p. 493)
My father demanded one promise: that we not lie to him. (p. 491)

Essential modifiers (p. 449)
The car that hit mine was uninsured.
We consulted a teacher who had promised to help us.
The boy in the black hat is my cousin.
They were surprised to find the desert teeming with life.
The men do not speak to each other because they are feuding.

p

Essential appositives (p. 451)

Shaw's play *Saint Joan* was performed last year.

Their sons Tony, William, and Steve all chose military careers, leaving only Matthew to run the family business.

Transitional or parenthetical expressions

We suspect, however, that he will not come. (p. 452)

Jessica is respected by many people — including me. (p. 493)

George Balanchine (1904–83) was a brilliant choreographer of classical ballet. (p. 494)

Absolute phrases (p. 454)

The bird, its wing broken, hopped about on the ground.

The bird hopped about on the ground, its wing broken.

Phrases expressing contrast (p. 454)

The humidity, not just the heat, gives me headaches.

My headaches are caused by the humidity, not just the heat.

Concluding summaries and explanations

The movie opened to bad notices: the characters were judged shallow and unrealistic. (p. 490)

We had gumbo and jambalaya for dinner — a Cajun feast. (p. 493)

Items in a series

Three or more items

Chimpanzees, gorillas, orangutans, and gibbons are all apes. (p. 455)

The cities singled out for praise were Birmingham, Alabama; Lincoln, Nebraska; Austin, Texas; and Troy, New York. (p. 470)

Two or more adjectives before a noun (p. 455)

Dingy, smelly clothes decorated their room.

Dessert consisted of one tiny scoop of ice cream.

Introductory series (p. 493)

Appropriateness, accuracy, and necessity — these criteria should govern your selection of words.

Concluding series

Every word should be appropriate, accurate, and necessary. (p. 464)

Every word should meet three criteria: appropriateness, accuracy, and necessity. (p. 490)

Pay attention to your words — to their appropriateness, their accuracy, and their necessity. (p. 493)

p

27

End Punctuation

Video
tutorial

Exercise

End punctuation marks—the period, the question mark, and the exclamation point—signal the ends of sentences.

Grammar checkers A grammar checker may flag missing question marks after direct questions or incorrect combinations of marks (such as a question mark and a period at the end of a sentence), but it cannot do much else.

27a Use periods after most sentences and with some abbreviations.

1 Use a period to end a statement, mild command, or indirect question.

Statements

These are exciting and trying times.
The airline went bankrupt.

Mild commands

Please do not smoke.
Think of the possibilities.

If you are unsure whether to use an exclamation point or a period after a command, use a period. The exclamation point should be used only rarely (see p. 442).

An **indirect question** reports what someone has asked but not in the form or the exact words of the original:

Indirect questions

Students sometimes wonder whether their teachers read the papers they write.

Abused children eventually stop asking why they are being punished.

CULTURE LANGUAGE In standard American English, the reporting verb in an indirect question (for example, *asked* or *said*) usually precedes a clause that contains a subject and verb in normal order, not question order: *The reporter asked why the negotiations failed*, not *why did the negotiations fail*.

mycomplab

Visit *mycomplab.com* for the eText and for resources and more exercises on end punctuation.

2 Use periods with some abbreviations.

Use periods with abbreviations that consist of or end in small letters. Otherwise, omit periods from abbreviations.

Dr.	Mr., Mrs.	e.g.	Feb.	ft.
St.	Ms.	i.e.	p.	a.m., p.m.
PhD	BC, BCE	USA	IBM	AM, PM
BA	AD, CE	US	USMC	AIDS

Note When a sentence ends in an abbreviation with a period, don't add a second period: *My first class is at 8 a.m.*
See also pages 513–16 on uses of abbreviations in writing.

Exercise 27.1 Revising: Periods

Revise the following sentences so that periods are used correctly.

> *Example:*
> Several times I wrote to ask when my subscription ended?
> Several times I wrote to ask when my subscription ended.

1. The instructor asked when Plato wrote *The Republic*?
2. Give the date within one century
3. The exact date is not known, but it is estimated at 370 BCE
4. Dr Arn will lecture on Plato at 7:30 p.m..
5. The area of the lecture hall is only 1600 sq ft

Exercise

27b Use question marks after direct questions and sometimes to indicate doubt.

1 Use a question mark with a direct question.

What is the difference between these two people?
Will economists ever really understand the economy?

After an indirect question, use a period: *The senator asked why the bill had passed.* (See opposite.)

Questions in a series are each followed by a question mark:

The officer asked how many times the suspect had been arrested. Three times? Four times? More than that?

The use of capital letters for questions in a series is optional (see p. 505).

?
27b

Note Question marks are never combined with other question marks, exclamation points, periods, or commas:

Faulty   "What is the point?," readers ask.
Revised   "What is the point?" readers ask.

2 Use a question mark within parentheses to indicate doubt about a number or date.

The Greek philosopher Socrates was born in 470 (**?**) BC and died in 399 BC from drinking poison after having been condemned to death.

Note Don't use a question mark within parentheses to express sarcasm or irony. Express these attitudes through sentence structure and word choice. (See Chapters 23 and 38.)

Faulty   Stern's friendliness (?) bothered Crane.

Revised   Stern's <u>insincerity</u> bothered Crane.

Exercise 27.2   Revising: Question marks

Revise the following sentences so that question marks (along with other punctuation marks) are used correctly.

Exercise

Example:
"Why should I vote for you?," the woman asked the candidate.
"Why should I vote for you**?**" the woman asked the candidate.

1. In Homer's *Odyssey,* Odysseus took seven years to travel from Troy to Ithaca. Or was it eight years. Or more?
2. Odysseus must have wondered whether he would ever make it home?
3. "What man are you and whence?," asks Odysseus's wife, Penelope.
4. Why does Penelope ask, "Where is your city? Your family?"?
5. Penelope does not recognize Odysseus and asks who this stranger is?

27c Use an exclamation point after an emphatic statement, interjection, or command.

No**!** We must not lose this election**!**
Come here immediately**!**

Follow mild interjections and commands with commas or periods, as appropriate:

No**,** the response was not terrific**.**
To prolong your car's life, change its oil regularly**.**

Use exclamation points sparingly, not to express sarcasm, irony, or amazement. Rely on sentence structure and word choice to express these attitudes. (See Chapters 23 and 38.)

Faulty   After traveling 4.4 billion miles through space, *Voyager 2* was off-target by 21 miles (!).

Revised   After traveling 4.4 billion miles through space, *Voyager 2* was off-target by <u>a mere</u> 21 miles.

Relying on the exclamation point for emphasis is like crying wolf: the mark loses its power to impress the reader. Frequent exclamation points can also make writing sound overemotional:

! 27c

Overused exclamation points

Our city government is a mess! After just six months in office, the mayor has had to fire four city officials! In the same period the city councilors have done nothing but argue! And city services decline with each passing day!

Note Exclamation points are never combined with other exclamation points, question marks, periods, or commas:

Faulty   "This will not be endured!," he roared.
Revised   "This will not be endured!" he roared.

Exercise 27.3 Revising: Exclamation points

Revise the following sentences so that exclamation points (along with other punctuation marks) are used correctly. If a sentence is punctuated correctly as given, mark the number preceding it.

Exercise

> *Example:*
> "Well, now!," he said loudly.
> "Well, now!" he said loudly.

1. As the firefighters moved their equipment into place, the police shouted, "Move back!".
2. A child's cries could be heard from above: "Help me. Help."
3. When the child was rescued, the crowd called, "Hooray."
4. The rescue was the most exciting event of the day!
5. Let me tell you about it.

Exercise 27.4 Revising: End punctuation

Insert appropriate punctuation (periods, question marks, or exclamation points) where needed in the following paragraph.

Exercise

When visitors first arrive in Hawaii, they often encounter an unexpected language barrier Standard English is the language of business and government, but many of the people speak Pidgin English Instead of an excited "Aloha" the visitors may be greeted with an excited Pidgin "Howzit" or asked if they know "how fo' find one good hotel" Many Hawaiians question whether Pidgin will hold children back because it prevents communication with the *haoles,* or Caucasians, who run businesses Yet many others feel that Pidgin is a last defense of ethnic diversity on the islands To those who want to make standard English the official language of the state, these Hawaiians may respond, "Just 'cause I speak Pidgin no mean I dumb" They may ask, "Why you no listen" or, in standard English, "Why don't you listen"

Note See page 500 for a punctuation exercise combining periods with other marks of punctuation.

!
27c

28

The Comma

Video
tutorial

Commas usually function within sentences to separate elements (see the box on the next page). Omitting needed commas or inserting needless ones can confuse the reader:

| Comma needed | Though very tall Abraham Lincoln was not an overbearing man. |
| Revised | Though very tall, Abraham Lincoln was not an overbearing man. |

| Unneeded commas | The hectic pace of Beirut, broke suddenly into frightening chaos when the city became, the focus of civil war. |
| Revised | The hectic pace of Beirut broke suddenly into frightening chaos when the city became the focus of civil war. |

Grammar checkers A grammar checker will ignore many comma errors. For example, a checker failed to catch the missing commas in *The boat ran aground and we were stranded* and in *We cooked lasagna spinach and apple pie.* At the same time the checker overlooked the misused commas in *The trip was short but, the weather was perfect* and *The travelers were tempted by, the many shops, and varied restaurants.*

28a Use a comma before *and, but,* or another coordinating conjunction linking main clauses.

Exercise

The coordinating conjunctions are *and, but, or, nor, for, so,* and *yet.* When one of them links words or phrases, do not use a comma: *Dugain plays and sings Irish and English folk songs.* However, *do* use a comma when a coordinating conjunction joins main clauses. A **main clause** has a subject and a predicate (but no subordinating word at the beginning) and makes a complete statement (see p. 272).

Caffeine can keep coffee drinkers alert, and it may make them feel more energetic.

mycomplab
Visit *mycomplab.com* for the eText and for resources and more exercises on the comma.

Principal uses of the comma

■ Separate main clauses linked by a coordinating conjunction (previous and next pages):

Video tutorial

| Main clause | , | for and or
so but nor
yet | main clause | . |

The building is finished **,** but it has no tenants.

■ Set off most introductory elements (p. 447):

| Introductory element | , | main clause | . |

Unfortunately **,** the only tenant pulled out.

■ Set off nonessential elements (p. 449):

| Main clause | , | nonessential element | . |

The empty building symbolizes a weak local economy **,** which affects everyone.

| Beginning of main clause | , | nonessential element | , | end of main clause | . |

The primary cause **,** the decline of local industry **,** is not news.

■ Separate items in a series (p. 455):

| . . . | item 1 | , | item 2 | , | and
or | item 3 | . . . |

The city needs healthier businesses **,** new schools **,** and improved housing.

■ Separate coordinate adjectives (p. 455):

| . . . | first adjective | , | second adjective | | word modified | . . . |

A tall **,** sleek skyscraper is not needed.

Other uses of the comma:

Set off absolute phrases (p. 454).
Set off phrases expressing contrast (p. 454).
Separate parts of dates, addresses, long numbers (p. 457).
Separate quotations and signal phrases (p. 458).
Prevent misreading (p. 461).

See also page 461 for when *not* to use the comma.

28a

Caffeine was once thought to be safe**,** but now researchers warn of harmful effects.

Coffee drinkers may suffer sleeplessness**,** for the drug acts as a stimulant to the nervous system.

Note Do not add a comma *after* a coordinating conjunction between main clauses (see also pp. 461–62):

> Not   Caffeine increases the heart rate, and, it constricts the blood vessels.
>
> But   Caffeine increases the heart rate, and it constricts the blood vessels.

Exceptions When the main clauses in a sentence are very long or grammatically complicated, or when they contain internal punctuation, a semicolon before the coordinating conjunction will clarify the division between clauses (see p. 470):

> Caffeine may increase alertness, elevate mood, and provide energy**;** but it may also cause irritability, anxiety, stomach pains, and other ills.

When main clauses are very short and closely related in meaning, you may omit the comma between them as long as the resulting sentence is clear:

> Caffeine helps but it also hurts.

If you are in doubt about whether to use a comma in such a sentence, use it. It will always be correct.

Exercise

28a

Exercise 28.1 Punctuating linked main clauses

Insert a comma before each coordinating conjunction that links main clauses in the following sentences.

> *Example:*
>
> I would have attended the concert and the reception but I had to baby-sit for my niece.
>
> I would have attended the concert and the reception**,** but I had to baby-sit for my niece.

1. Parents once automatically gave their children the father's surname but some no longer do.
2. Instead, they bestow the mother's name for they believe that the mother's importance should be recognized.
3. The child's surname may be just the mother's or it may link the mother's and the father's with a hyphen.
4. Sometimes the first and third children will have the mother's surname and the second child will have the father's.
5. Occasionally the mother and father combine parts of their names and a new hybrid surname is born.

Exercise 28.2   Sentence combining: Linked main clauses

Combine each group of sentences below into one sentence that contains only two main clauses connected by the coordinating conjunction in parentheses. Separate the main clauses with a comma. You will have to add, delete, and rearrange words.

Exercise

> *Example:*
> The circus had come to town. The children wanted to see it. Their parents wanted to see it. (*and*)
> The circus had come to town, and the children and their parents wanted to see it.

1. Parents were once legally required to bestow the father's surname on their children. These laws have been contested in court. They have been found invalid. (*but*)
2. Parents may now give their children any surname they choose. The arguments for bestowing the mother's surname are often strong. They are often convincing. (*and*)
3. Critics sometimes question the effects of unusual surnames on children. They wonder how confusing the new surnames will be. They wonder how fleeting the surnames will be. (*or*)
4. Children with surnames different from their parents' may suffer embarrassment. They may suffer identity problems. Giving children their father's surname is still very much the norm. (*for*)
5. Hyphenated names are awkward. They are also difficult to pass on. Some observers think they will die out in the next generation. Or they may die out before. (*so*)

28b Use a comma to set off most introductory elements.

An introductory element modifies a word or words in the main clause that follows. These elements are usually set off from the rest of the sentence with a comma:

Exercise

Subordinate clause (p. 272)

Even when identical twins are raised apart, they grow up very like each other.
Because they are similar, such twins interest scientists.

Verbal or verbal phrase (p. 267)

Explaining the similarity, some researchers claim that one's genes are one's destiny.
Concerned, other researchers deny the claim.

Prepositional phrase (p. 264)

In a debate that has lasted centuries, scientists use identical twins to argue for or against genetic destiny.

28b

Transitional or parenthetical expression (pp. 94–95)

Of course, scientists can now look directly at the genes themselves.

The comma may be omitted after short introductory elements if its omission does not create confusion. (If you are in doubt, however, the comma is always correct.)

Clear	In a hundred years genetics may no longer be a mystery.
Confusing	Despite intensive research scientists still have more questions than answers.
Clear	Despite intensive research, scientists still have more questions than answers.

Commas may also be omitted after some transitional expressions when they start sentences. (See p. 452.)

Thus the debate continues.

Note Take care to distinguish -*ing* words used as modifiers from -*ing* words used as subjects, as shown in the following examples. The former almost always take a comma; the latter never do.

┌──────── modifier ────────┐   subject   verb
Studying identical twins, geneticists learn about inheritance.

┌──────── subject ────────┐   verb
Studying identical twins helps geneticists learn about inheritance.

Exercise 28.3 Punctuating introductory elements

Insert commas where needed after introductory elements in the following sentences. If a sentence is punctuated correctly as given, mark the number preceding it.

Example:

After the new library opened the old one became a student union.
After the new library opened, the old one became a student union.

1. Moving in a fluid mass is typical of flocks of birds and schools of fish.
2. Because it is sudden and apparently well coordinated the movement of flocks and schools has seemed to be directed by a leader.
3. However new studies have discovered that flocks and schools are leaderless.
4. When each bird or fish senses a predator it follows individual rules for fleeing.
5. Multiplied over hundreds of individuals these responses look as if they have been choreographed.

28b

Exercise 28.4 Sentence combining: Introductory elements

Combine each pair of sentences below into one sentence that begins with an introductory phrase or clause as specified in parentheses. Follow the introductory element with a comma. You will have to add, delete, change, and rearrange words.

Example:

The girl was humming to herself. She walked upstairs. (*Phrase beginning Humming.*)

<u>Humming to herself,</u> the girl walked upstairs.

1. Scientists have made an effort to explain the mysteries of flocks and schools. They have proposed bizarre magnetic fields and telepathy. (*Phrase beginning In.*)
2. Scientists developed computer models. They have abandoned earlier explanations. (*Clause beginning Since.*)
3. The movement of a flock or school starts with each individual. It is rapidly and perhaps automatically coordinated among individuals. (*Phrase beginning Starting.*)
4. One zoologist observes that human beings seek coherent patterns. He suggests that investigators saw purpose in the movement of flocks and schools where none existed. (*Phrase beginning Observing.*)
5. One may want to study the movement of flocks or schools. Then one must abandon a search for purpose or design. (*Phrase beginning To.*)

28c Use a comma or commas to set off nonessential elements.

Commas around part of a sentence often signal that the element is not necessary to the meaning of the sentence:

Exercise

Nonessential element

The company, <u>which is located in Oklahoma,</u> has a good reputation.

This **nonessential element** may modify or rename the word it refers to (*company* in the example), but it does not limit the word to a particular individual or group. (Because it does not restrict meaning, a nonessential element is also called a **nonrestrictive element**.) Nonessential elements are *not* essential, but punctuation *is*.

In contrast, an **essential** (or **restrictive**) element *does* limit the word it refers to:

Essential element

The company rewards employees <u>who work hard.</u>

In this example the underlined essential element cannot be omitted without leaving the meaning of *employees* too general. Because it is essential, such an element is *not* set off with commas. The element *is* essential, but punctuation is *not*.

28c

Meaning and context

The same element in the same sentence may be essential or nonessential depending on your intended meaning and the context in which the sentence appears. For example, look at the second sentence in each of the following passages:

Essential

Not all the bands were equally well received, however. The band playing old music held the audience's attention. The other groups created much less excitement. [*Playing old music* identifies a particular band.]

Nonessential

A new band called Fats made its debut on Saturday night. The band, playing old music, held the audience's attention. If this performance is typical, the group has a bright future. [*Playing old music* adds information about a band already named.]

Punctuation of interrupting nonessential elements

When a nonessential element falls in the middle of a sentence, be sure to set it off with a pair of commas, one *before* and one *after* the element. Dashes or parentheses may also set off nonessential elements (see pp. 492 and 494).

1 Use a comma or commas to set off nonessential clauses and phrases.

Clauses and phrases serving as adjectives and adverbs may be either nonessential or essential. In the following examples the underlined clauses and phrases are nonessential: they could be omitted without changing the meaning of the words they modify.

Nonessential

Elizabeth Blackwell was the first woman to graduate from an American medical school, in 1849.

A test for essential and nonessential elements

1. Identify the element.

   Hai Nguyen who emigrated from Vietnam lives in Denver.
   Those who emigrated with him live elsewhere.

2. Remove the element. Does the fundamental meaning of the sentence change?

   Hai Nguyen lives in Denver. *No.*
   Those live elsewhere. *Yes.* [Who are *Those?*]

3. If *no,* the element is *nonessential* and should be set off with punctuation.

   Hai Nguyen, who emigrated from Vietnam, lives in Denver.

   If *yes,* the element is *essential* and should *not* be set off with punctuation.

   Those who emigrated with him live elsewhere.

28c

She was a medical pioneer, helping to found the first medical college for women.

She taught at the school, which was affiliated with the New York Infirmary.

Blackwell, who published books and papers on medicine, practiced pediatrics and gynecology.

She moved to England in 1869, when she was forty-eight.

Note Most adverb clauses are essential because they describe conditions necessary to the main clause. (Adverb clauses begin with *if, because,* or another subordinating conjunction.) Set an adverb clause off with a comma or commas only when it introduces a sentence (see p. 447) or when it is truly nonessential, adding incidental information (as in the last example above) or expressing a contrast beginning *although, even though, though, whereas,* and the like.

In the following sentences, the underlined elements limit the meaning of the words they modify. Removing the elements would leave the meaning too general.

Essential

The history of aspirin began with the ancient Greeks.

Physicians who sought to relieve their patients' pains recommended chewing willow bark.

Willow bark contains a chemical that is similar to aspirin.

Aspirin is widely prescribed for pain because it is generally safe.

Note Whereas both nonessential and essential clauses may begin with *which,* only essential clauses begin with *that.* Some writers prefer *that* exclusively for essential clauses and *which* exclusively for nonessential clauses. See the Glossary of Usage, page 859, for advice on the use of *that* and *which.*

2 Use a comma or commas to set off nonessential appositives.

An **appositive** is a noun or noun substitute that renames another noun just before it. (See p. 276.) Many appositives are nonessential; thus they are set off, usually with commas.

Nonessential

Toni Morrison's fifth novel, *Beloved,* won the Pulitzer Prize in 1988.

Morrison, a native of Ohio, won the Nobel Prize in 1993.

Take care *not* to set off essential appositives; like other essential elements, they limit or define the word to which they refer.

Essential

Morrison's novel *The Bluest Eye* is about an African American girl who longs for blue eyes.

The critic Michiko Kakutani says that Morrison's work "stands radiantly on its own as an American epic."

28c

> **3** Use a comma or commas to set off transitional
> or parenthetical expressions.

Transitional expressions

Transitional expressions form links between ideas. They include conjunctive adverbs such as *however* and *moreover* as well as other words or phrases such as *for example* and *of course*. (See pp. 94–95 for a list of transitional words and phrases.) Transitional expressions are nonessential, and most of them are set off with a comma or commas:

> US workers, for example, receive fewer holidays than European workers do.

When a transitional expression links main clauses, precede it with a semicolon and follow it with a comma. (See p. 468.)

> European workers often have long paid vacations; indeed, they may receive a full month.

Exceptions The conjunctions *and, but,* and *yet* are sometimes used as transitional expressions but are never followed by commas (see p. 441). Usage varies with some other transitional expressions, depending on the expression and the writer's judgment. Many writers omit commas with expressions that we read without pauses, such as *also, hence, next, now, then,* and *thus.* The same applies to *therefore* and *instead* when they fall inside or at the ends of clauses.

> US workers therefore put in more work days. But the days themselves may be shorter.
> Then the total hours worked come out roughly the same.

Parenthetical expressions

Parenthetical expressions provide comments, explanations, digressions, or other supplementary information not essential to meaning—for example, *fortunately, unfortunately, all things considered, to be frank, in other words.* Like transitional expressions, most parenthetical expressions are set off, sometimes with commas:

> Surprisingly, the most celebrated holiday in the world is New Year's Day.

Dashes and parentheses may also set off parenthetical expressions. (See pp. 492 and 494, respectively.)

28c

> **4** Use a comma or commas to set off *yes* and *no,* tag
> questions, words of direct address, and mild interjections.

Yes and *no*

Yes, the editorial did have a point.
No, that can never be.

Tag questions
They don't stop to consider others*, *do they?
Jones should be allowed to vote*, *shouldn't he?

Direct address
Cody*, *please bring me the newspaper.
With all due respect*, *sir*, *I will not do that.

Mild interjections
Well*, *you will never know who did it.
Oh*, *they forgot all about the baby.

(You may want to use an exclamation point to set off a forceful interjection. See p. 442.)

Exercise 28.5 Punctuating essential and nonessential elements

Insert commas in the following sentences to set off nonessential elements, and delete any commas that incorrectly set off essential elements. If a sentence is correct as given, mark the number preceding it.

Exercise

> *Example:*
> Our language has adopted the word, *garage*, from the French.
> Our language has adopted the word *garage* from the French.

1. Many colleges have started campus garden programs, that aim to teach students about the benefits of sustainable farming methods and locally grown food.
2. These gardens which use organic farming techniques also provide fresh produce for the college cafeteria.
3. A garden, that is big enough to grow produce for a college cafeteria, requires a large piece of land.
4. Such a garden also needs a leader, who can choose crops that will thrive in local growing conditions.
5. Volunteers, willing to work in the garden every week, are essential as well.
6. Some campus gardeners distribute produce to people in the community who live far from a grocery store.
7. Some urban neighborhoods are called "food deserts," because they lack grocery stores that residents can reach easily on foot.
8. The colleges may distribute produce with special trucks or "veggie wagons" that drive through the urban neighborhoods.
9. The wagons deliver produce once a week although they may make two deliveries during peak harvest time.
10. A community garden planted during the academic year will fare better in the southern states where the growing season is longer than in northern states.

28c

Exercise 28.6 Sentence combining: Essential and nonessential elements

Combine each of the following pairs of sentences into one sentence that uses the element described in parentheses. Insert commas as appropriate.

Exercise

You will have to add, delete, change, and rearrange words. Some items have more than one possible answer.

> *Example:*
> Mr. Ward's oldest sister helped keep him alive. She was a nurse. (*Non-essential clause beginning who.*)
> Mr. Ward's oldest sister, who was a nurse, helped keep him alive.

1. American colonists first imported pasta from the English. The English had discovered it as tourists in Italy. (*Nonessential clause beginning who.*)
2. The English returned from their grand tours of Italy. They were called macaronis because of their fancy airs. (*Essential phrase beginning returning.*)
3. A hair style was also called *macaroni.* It had elaborate curls. (*Essential phrase beginning with.*)
4. The song "Yankee Doodle" refers to this hairdo. It reports that Yankee Doodle "stuck a feather in his cap and called it macaroni." (*Essential clause beginning when.*)
5. The song was actually intended to poke fun at unrefined American colonists. It was a creation of the English. (*Nonessential appositive beginning a creation.*)

28d Use a comma or commas to set off absolute phrases.

An **absolute phrase** modifies a whole main clause rather than any word in the clause, and it usually consists of at least a participle (such as *done* or *having torn*) and its subject (a noun or pronoun). (See p. 271.) Absolute phrases can occur at almost any point in the sentence, and they are always set off by a comma or commas:

> Household recycling having succeeded, the city now wants to extend the program to businesses.
> Many businesses, their profits already squeezed, resist recycling.

28e Use a comma or commas to set off phrases expressing contrast.

The essay needs less wit, more pith.
The substance, not the style, is important.
Substance, unlike style, cannot be faked.

Note Writers often omit commas around contrasting phrases beginning with *but*: *A full but hazy moon shone down.*

Exercise 28.7 Punctuating absolute phrases and phrases of contrast

Exercise

Insert commas in the following sentences to set off absolute phrases and phrases of contrast.

Example:
The recording contract was canceled the band having broken up.
The recording contract was canceled, the band having broken up.

1. Prices having risen rapidly the government debated a price freeze.
2. A price freeze unlike a rise in interest rates seemed a sure solution.
3. The President would have to persuade businesses to accept a price freeze his methods depending on their resistance.
4. No doubt the President his advisers having urged it would first try a patriotic appeal.
5. The President not his advisers insisted on negotiations with businesses.

28f Use commas between items in a series and between coordinate adjectives.

1 Use commas between words, phrases, or clauses forming a series.

Place commas between all elements of a **series**—that is, three or more items of equal importance:

Podcast

Anna Spingle married at the age of seventeen, had three children by twenty-one, and divorced at twenty-two.
She worked as a cook, a baby-sitter, and a crossing guard.

Some writers omit the comma before the coordinating conjunction in a series (*Breakfast consisted of coffee, eggs and kippers*). But the final comma is never wrong, and it always helps the reader see the last two items as separate:

Exercise

Confusing   Spingle's new job involves typing, filing and answering correspondence.

Clear   Spingle's new job involves typing, filing, and answering correspondence.

Exception   When items in a series are long and grammatically complicated, they may be separated by semicolons. When series items contain commas, they must be separated by semicolons. (See p. 470.)

2 Use commas between two or more adjectives that equally modify the same words.

When two or more adjectives modify the same word equally, they are said to be **coordinate.** The adjectives may be separated either by *and* or by a comma, as in the following examples.

Podcast

28f

Spingle's scratched and dented car is old, but it gets her to work.
She has dreams of a sleek, shiny car.

Punctuating two or more adjectives

1. Identify the adjectives.

   She was a <u>faithful sincere</u> friend.
   They are <u>dedicated medical</u> students.

2. Can the adjectives be reversed without changing meaning?

   She was a <u>sincere faithful</u> friend. ***Yes.***
   They are <u>medical dedicated</u> students. ***No.***

3. Can the word *and* be sensibly inserted between the adjectives?

   She was a <u>faithful and sincere</u> friend. ***Yes.***
   They are <u>dedicated and medical</u> students. ***No.***

4. If *yes* to both questions, the adjectives are coordinate and *should* be separated by a comma.

   She was a faithful**,** sincere friend.

   If *no* to both questions, the adjectives are *not* coordinate and should *not* be separated by a comma.

   They are dedicated   medical students.

Adjectives are not coordinate—and should *not* be separated by commas—when the one nearer the noun is more closely related to the noun in meaning. In each of the next examples, the second adjective and the noun form a unit that is modified by the first adjective:

   Spingle's children work at <u>various part-time</u> jobs.
   They all expect to go to a <u>nearby community</u> college.

See the box above for a test to use in punctuating adjectives.
   Note Numbers are not coordinate with other adjectives:

   Faulty   Spingle has <u>three, teenaged</u> children.
   Revised   Spingle has <u>three teenaged</u> children.

Do not use a comma between the final adjective and the noun:

   Faulty   The children hope to achieve <u>good, well-paying,</u> jobs.
   Revised   The children hope to achieve <u>good, well-paying</u> jobs.

28f

Exercise

Exercise 28.8 Punctuating series and coordinate adjectives
Insert commas in the following sentences to separate elements in series and coordinate adjectives. Mark the number preceding any sentence whose punctuation is already correct.

   Example:
   Quiet by day, the club became a noisy smoky dive at night.
   Quiet by day, the club became a noisy**,** smoky dive at night.

1. Shoes with high heels originated to protect feet from the mud garbage and animal waste in the streets.
2. The first known high heels worn strictly for fashion appeared in the sixteenth century.
3. The heels were worn by men and made of colorful silk brocades soft suedes or smooth leathers.
4. High-heeled shoes received a boost when the short powerful King Louis XIV of France began wearing them.
5. Eventually only wealthy fashionable French women wore high heels.

28g Use commas according to convention in dates, addresses, place names, and long numbers.

Use commas to separate most parts of dates, addresses, and place names: *June 20, 1950*; *24 Fifth Avenue, Suite 601*; *Cairo, Illinois*. Within a sentence, any element preceded by a comma should be followed by a comma as well, as in the examples below:

Dates

July 4, 1776, is the date the Declaration of Independence was signed.

The bombing of Pearl Harbor on Sunday, December 7, 1941, prompted American entry into World War II.

Do not use commas between the parts of a date in inverted order: *Their anniversary on 15 December 2005 was their fiftieth.* You need not use commas in dates consisting of a month or season and a year: *For the United States the war ended in August 1945.*

Addresses and place names

Columbus, Ohio, is the state capital and the location of Ohio State University.

The population of Garden City, Long Island, New York, is 30,000.

Use the address 220 Cornell Road, Woodside, California 94062, for all correspondence.

Do not use a comma between a state and a zip code.

Long numbers

Use the comma to separate the figures in long numbers into groups of three, counting from the right. With numbers of four digits, the comma is optional.

A kilometer is 3,281 feet [*or* 3281 feet].
The new assembly plant cost $7,535,000 to design and build.

> **CULTURE LANGUAGE** Usage in American English differs from that in some other languages and dialects, which use a period, not a comma, to separate the figures in long numbers.

^
28g

Exercise 28.9 Punctuating dates, addresses, place names, numbers

Insert commas as needed in the following sentences.

Example:
The house cost $27000 thirty years ago.
The house cost $27,000 thirty years ago.

1. The festival will hold a benefit dinner and performance on March 10 2012 in Asheville.
2. The organizers hope to raise more than $100000 from donations and ticket sales.
3. Performers are expected from as far away as Milan Italy and Kyoto Japan.
4. All inquiries sent to Mozart Festival PO Box 725 Asheville North Carolina 28803 will receive a quick response.
5. The deadline for ordering tickets by mail is Monday December 12 2011.

28h Use commas with quotations according to standard practice.

The words *he said, she writes,* and so on identify the source of a quotation. These **signal phrases** may come before, after, or in the middle of the quotation. A signal phrase must always be separated from the quotation by punctuation, usually a comma or commas.

Note Additional issues with quotations are discussed elsewhere in this book:

- Using quotation marks conventionally, pages 481–88.
- Selecting and transcribing quotations from sources, pages 637–39.
- Integrating source material into your text, pages 642–47.
- Acknowledging the sources of quotations to avoid plagiarism, pages 652–53 and 655–56.
- Formatting long prose quotations and poetry quotations in MLA style, pages 715–16; Chicago style, page 797; and APA style, page 826.

1 Ordinarily, use a comma with a signal phrase before or after a quotation.

In her book *You Learn by Living,* Eleanor Roosevelt says, "You must do the thing you think you cannot do."

"Knowledge is power," writes Francis Bacon.

Exceptions Do not use commas with signal phrases in the following situations:

■ Omit a comma when a signal phrase follows a quotation ending in an exclamation point or a question mark:

"Claude!" Mrs. Harrison called.
"Why must I come home?" he asked.

■ Use a colon when a complete sentence introduces a quotation:

Her statement hedged: "I will not resign unless circumstances force me to reconsider at a later time."

■ Omit commas when a quotation is integrated into your sentence structure, including a quotation introduced by *that*:

James Baldwin insists that "one must never, in one's life, accept . . . injustices as commonplace."

Baldwin thought that the violence of a riot "had been devised as a corrective" to his own violence.

2 **With an interrupted quotation, precede the signal phrase with a comma and follow it with the punctuation required by the quotation.**

Original quotation

"The shore has a dual nature, changing with the swing of the tides."

Signal phrase interrupts at comma, ends with comma

"The shore has a dual nature," observes Rachel Carson, "changing with the swing of the tides."

Original quotation

"However mean your life is, meet it and live it; do not shun it and call it hard names."

Signal phrase interrupts at semicolon, ends with semicolon

"However mean your life is, meet it and live it," Thoreau advises in *Walden*; "do not shun it and call it hard names."

Original quotation

"This is the faith with which I return to the South. With this new faith we will be able to hew out of the mountain of despair a stone of hope."

Signal phrase interrupts at end of sentence, ends with period

"This is the faith with which I return to the South," Martin Luther King, Jr., proclaimed. "With this new faith we will be able to hew out of the mountain of despair a stone of hope."

^
28h

Note Using a comma instead of a semicolon or a period after the Thoreau and King signal phrases would result in the error called a comma splice: two main clauses separated only by a comma. (See pp. 362–65.)

3 Place commas that follow quotations within quotation marks.

"Death is not the greatest loss in life**,**" claims Norman Cousins.
"The greatest loss**,**" Cousins says, "is what dies inside us while we live."

Exercise 28.10 Punctuating quotations

Insert commas or semicolons in the following sentences to correct punctuation with quotations. Mark the number preceding any sentence whose punctuation is already correct.

Example:
The shoplifter declared "I didn't steal anything."
The shoplifter declared**,** "I didn't steal anything."

1. The writer and writing teacher Peter Elbow proposes an "open-ended writing process" that "can change you, not just your words."
2. "I think of the open-ended writing process as a voyage in two stages" Elbow says.
3. "The sea voyage is a process of divergence, branching, proliferation, and confusion" Elbow continues "the coming to land is a process of convergence, pruning, centralizing, and clarifying."
4. "Keep up one session of writing long enough to get loosened up and tired" advises Elbow "long enough in fact to make a bit of a voyage."
5. "In coming to new land" Elbow says "you develop a new conception of what you are writing about."

28i Use commas to prevent misreading.

In some sentences words may run together in unintended and confusing ways unless a comma separates them:

Confusing   Soon after the business closed its doors.
Clear   Soon after**,** the business closed its doors.

Always check whether a comma added to prevent misreading might cause some other confusion or error. In the first example below, the comma prevents *pasta* and *places* from running into each other as *pasta places*, but it separates the subject (*historian*) and the verb (*places*). The revision solves both problems.

Faulty   A historian who studied pasta, places its origin in the Middle East.
Revised   A historian who studied pasta <u>says that it originated</u> in the Middle East.

Exercise

Exercise 28.11 Punctuating to prevent misreading

Insert commas in the following sentences to prevent misreading.

Example:
To Jasmine MacKenzie symbolized decadence.
To Jasmine **,** MacKenzie symbolized decadence.

1. Though happy people still have moments of self-doubt.
2. In research subjects have reported themselves to be generally happy people.
3. Among those who have life has included sufferings as well as joys.
4. Of fifty eight subjects reported bouts of serious depression.
5. For half the preceding year had included at least one personal crisis.

28j Use commas only where required.

Commas can make sentences choppy and even confusing if they are used more often than needed. The main misuses of commas are summarized in the box on the next page.

Exercise

1 Delete any comma after a subject or a verb.

Commas interrupt the movement from subject to verb to object or complement, as in the following faulty examples.

Faulty	The returning <u>soldiers, received</u> a warmer welcome than they expected. [Separation of subject and verb.]
Revised	The returning soldiers received a warmer welcome than they expected.

Faulty	They had <u>chosen, to fight</u> for their country. [Separation of verb *chosen* and object *to fight.*]
Revised	They had chosen to fight for their country.

Exception Use commas between subject, verb, and object or complement only when other words between these elements require punctuation:

Americans **,** who are preoccupied with other sports **,** have only recently developed an interest in professional soccer. [Commas set off a nonessential clause.]

2 Delete any comma that separates a pair of words, phrases, or subordinate clauses joined by a coordinating conjunction.

no ⌄
28j

When linking elements with *and, or,* or another coordinating conjunction, do not use a comma unless the elements are main clauses (see p. 444):

Faulty	Banks <u>could, and should</u> help older people manage their money. [Compound helping verb.]
Revised	Banks could and should help older people manage their money.

Principal misuses of the comma

■ **Don't use a comma after a subject or verb:**

Faulty   Anyone with breathing problems, should not exercise during smog alerts.

Revised   Anyone with breathing problems should not exercise during smog alerts.

■ **Don't separate a pair of words, phrases, or subordinate clauses joined by** *and, or,* **or** *nor:*

Faulty   Asthmatics are affected by ozone, and sulfur oxides.

Revised   Asthmatics are affected by ozone and sulfur oxides.

■ **Don't use a comma after** *and, but, although, because,* **or another conjunction:**

Faulty   Smog is dangerous and, sometimes even fatal.

Revised   Smog is dangerous and sometimes even fatal.

■ **Don't set off essential elements:**

Faulty   Even people, who are healthy, should be careful.

Revised   Even people who are healthy should be careful.

Faulty   Bruce Springsteen's song, "Born in the USA," is an anthem.

Revised   Bruce Springsteen's song "Born in the USA" is an anthem.

■ **Don't set off a series:**

Faulty   Cars, factories, and even bakeries, contribute to smog.

Revised   Cars, factories, and even bakeries contribute to smog.

■ **Don't set off an indirect quotation:**

Faulty   Experts say, that the pollutant ozone is especially damaging.

Revised   Experts say that the pollutant ozone is especially damaging.

Faulty   Older people need special assistance because they live on fixed incomes, and because they are not familiar with new accounts, and rates. [Compound subordinate clauses *because . . . because* and compound object of preposition *with.*]

Revised   Older people need special assistance because they live on fixed incomes and because they are not familiar with new accounts and rates.

Faulty   Banks, and community groups can assist the elderly, and eliminate the confusion they often feel. [Compound subject and compound predicate.]

Revised   Banks and community groups can assist the elderly and eliminate the confusion they often feel.

no ⌃
28j

3 Delete any comma after a conjunction.

The coordinating conjunctions (*and, but,* and so on) and the subordinating conjunctions (*although, because,* and so on) are not followed by commas:

Faulty   Parents of adolescents notice increased conflict at puberty, and, they complain of bickering.

Revised   Parents of adolescents notice increased conflict at puberty, and they complain of bickering.

Faulty   Although, other primates leave the family at adolescence, humans do not.

Revised   Although other primates leave the family at adolescence, humans do not.

4 Delete any commas that set off essential elements.

Commas do not set off an essential element, which limits the meaning of the word to which it refers (see p. 449):

Faulty   Hawthorne's work, *The Scarlet Letter,* was the first major American novel. [The title is essential to distinguish the novel from the rest of Hawthorne's work.]

Revised   Hawthorne's work *The Scarlet Letter* was the first major American novel.

Faulty   The symbols, that Hawthorne uses, have influenced other novelists. [The clause identifies which symbols have been influential.]

Revised   The symbols that Hawthorne uses have influenced other novelists.

Faulty   Published in 1850, *The Scarlet Letter* still resonates today, because of its theme of secret sin. [The clause is essential to explain why the novel resonates.]

Revised   Published in 1850, *The Scarlet Letter* still resonates today because of its theme of secret sin.

Quoted or italicized words are essential appositives when they limit the word they refer to (see p. 451). Do not use commas around an essential appositive:

Faulty   James Joyce's short story, "The Dead," was made into a film. [The commas imply wrongly that Joyce wrote only one story.]

Revised   James Joyce's short story "The Dead" was made into a film.

Faulty   The word, *open,* can be either a verb or an adjective.

Revised   The word *open* can be either a verb or an adjective.

no ⌃
28j

The following sentence requires commas because the quoted title is a nonessential appositive:

Her only poem about death, "Mourning Henry," was printed in the *New Yorker.*

5 Delete any comma before or after a series unless a rule requires it.

Commas separate the items *within* a series (p. 455) but do not separate the series from the rest of the sentence:

Faulty   The skills of, hunting, herding, and agriculture, sustained the Native Americans.

Revised   The skills of hunting, herding, and agriculture sustained the Native Americans.

In the sentence below, the commas around the series are appropriate because the series is a nonessential appositive (p. 451):

The four major broadcast networks, ABC, CBS, Fox, and NBC, face fierce competition from the cable and satellite networks.

However, many writers prefer to use dashes rather than commas to set off series functioning as appositives (see p. 493).

6 Delete any comma setting off an indirect quotation.

Faulty   The report concluded, that dieting could be more dangerous than overeating.

Revised   The report concluded that dieting could be more dangerous than overeating.

Exercise 28.12   Revising: Needless or misused commas

Exercise

Revise the following sentences to eliminate needless or misused commas. Mark the number preceding any sentence that is already punctuated correctly.

Example:

The portrait of the founder, that hung in the dining hall, was stolen by pranksters.

The portrait of the founder that hung in the dining hall was stolen by pranksters.

no ʌ
28j

1. Nearly 40 million US residents, speak a first language other than English.
2. After English the languages most commonly spoken in the United States are, Spanish, Chinese, and French.
3. Almost 75 percent of the people, who speak foreign languages, used the words, "good" or "very good," when judging their proficiency in English.
4. Recent immigrants, especially those speaking Spanish, Chinese, and Korean, tended to judge their English more harshly.
5. The states with the highest proportion of foreign language speakers, are New Mexico, and California.

Exercise 28.13   Revising: Commas

Insert commas in the following paragraphs wherever they are needed, and eliminate any misused or needless commas.

Exercise

Ellis Island New York reopened for business in 1990 but now the customers are tourists not immigrants. This spot which lies in New York Harbor was the first American soil seen, or touched by many of the nation's immigrants. Though other places also served as ports of entry for foreigners none has the symbolic power of, Ellis Island. Between its opening in 1892 and its closing in 1954, over 20 million people about two-thirds of all immigrants were detained there before taking up their new lives in the United States. Ellis Island processed over 2000 newcomers a day when immigration was at its peak between 1900 and 1920.

As the end of a long voyage and the introduction to the New World Ellis Island must have left something to be desired. The "huddled masses" as the Statue of Liberty calls them indeed were huddled. New arrivals were herded about kept standing in lines for hours or days yelled at and abused. Assigned numbers they submitted their bodies to the pokings and proddings of the silent nurses and doctors, who were charged with ferreting out the slightest sign of sickness, disability or insanity. That test having been passed the immigrants faced interrogation by an official through an interpreter. Those, with names deemed inconveniently long or difficult to pronounce, often found themselves permanently labeled with abbreviations, of their names, or with the names, of their hometowns. But, millions survived the examination humiliation and confusion, to take the last short boat ride to New York City. For many of them and especially for their descendants Ellis Island eventually became not a nightmare but the place where life began.

Note See page 500 for a punctuation exercise combining commas with other marks of punctuation.

29

The Semicolon

The semicolon separates equal and balanced sentence elements, usually main clauses (pp. 467–70), sometimes items in series (p. 470).

Video
tutorial

mycomplab

Visit *mycomplab.com* for the eText and for resources and more exercises on the semicolon.

Grammar checkers A grammar checker can spot a few errors in the use of semicolons. For example, a checker suggested using a semicolon after *perfect* in *The set was perfect, the director had planned every detail*, thus correcting a comma splice. But it missed the incorrect semicolon in *The set was perfect; deserted streets, dark houses, and gloomy mist* (a colon would be correct; see pp. 490–91).

Distinguishing the comma, the semicolon, and the colon

Exercise

Comma

The *comma* chiefly separates both equal and unequal sentence elements.

- It separates main clauses when they are linked by a coordinating conjunction (p. 444):

  An airline once tried to boost sales by advertising the tense alertness of its crews, but nervous fliers did not want to hear about pilots' sweaty palms.

- It separates subordinate information that is part of or attached to a main clause, such as an introductory element or a nonessential modifier (pp. 447, 449):

  Although the airline campaign failed, many advertising agencies, including some clever ones, copied its underlying message.

Semicolon

The *semicolon* chiefly separates equal and balanced sentence elements. Often the first clause creates an expectation, and the second clause fulfills the expectation.

- It separates complementary main clauses that are *not* linked by a coordinating conjunction (facing page):

  The airline campaign had highlighted only half the story; the other half was buried in the copy.

- It separates complementary main clauses that are related by a conjunctive adverb or other transitional expression (p. 468):

  The campaign should not have stressed the pilots' insecurity; instead, the campaign should have stressed the improved performance resulting from that insecurity.

Colon

The *colon* chiefly separates unequal sentence elements.

- It separates a main clause from a following explanation or summary, which may or may not be a main clause (pp. 489–91):

  Many successful advertising campaigns have used this message: the anxious seller is harder working and smarter than the competitor.

i
29

29a Use a semicolon between main clauses not joined by *and, but,* or another coordinating conjunction.

Main clauses contain a subject and a predicate and do not begin with a subordinating word (see p. 272). When you join two main clauses in a sentence, you have two primary options for separating them:

■ Insert a comma and a coordinating conjunction: *and, but, or, nor, for, so, yet.* (See p. 444.)

The drug does little to relieve symptoms**,** and it can have side effects.

■ Insert a semicolon:

The side effects are not minor**;** some leave the patient quite ill.

Note If you do not link main clauses with a coordinating conjunction and you separate them only with a comma or with no punctuation at all, you will produce a comma splice or a fused sentence. (See Chapter 18.)

Exercise 29.1   Punctuating between main clauses

Insert semicolons to separate main clauses in the following sentences.

Exercise

> *Example:*
> One man at the auction bid prudently another spent his bank account.
> One man at the auction bid prudently**;** another spent his bank account.

1. More and more musicians are playing computerized instruments more and more listeners are worrying about the future of acoustic instruments.
2. The computer is not the first new technology in music the pipe organ and saxophone were also technological breakthroughs in their day.
3. Musicians have always experimented with new technology audiences have always resisted the experiments.
4. Most computer musicians are not merely following the latest fad they are discovering new sounds and new ways to manipulate sound.
5. Few musicians have abandoned acoustic instruments most value acoustic sounds as much as electronic sounds.

Exercise 29.2   Sentence combining: Related main clauses

Combine each of the following sets of three sentences into one sentence containing only two main clauses, and insert a semicolon between the clauses. You will have to add, delete, change, and rearrange words. Most items have more than one possible answer.

Exercise

Example:

The painter Andrew Wyeth is widely admired. He is not universally admired. Some critics view his work as sentimental.

The painter Andrew Wyeth is widely but not universally admired; some critics view his work as sentimental.

1. Electronic instruments are prevalent in jazz. They are also prevalent in rock music. They are less common in classical music.
2. Jazz and rock change rapidly. They nourish experimentation. They nourish improvisation.
3. Traditional classical music does not change. Its notes and instrumentation were established by a composer. The composer was writing decades or centuries ago.
4. Contemporary classical music can not only draw on tradition. It can also respond to innovations. These are innovations such as jazz rhythms and electronic sounds.
5. Much contemporary electronic music is more than just one type of music. It is more than just jazz, rock, or classical. It is a fusion of all three.

29b Use a semicolon between main clauses related by *however, for example,* and so on.

Two kinds of words can relate main clauses: **conjunctive adverbs,** such as *consequently, hence, however, indeed,* and *thus* (see p. 281), and other **transitional expressions,** such as *even so, for example,* and *of course* (see pp. 94–95). When either type of word connects two main clauses, the clauses should be separated by a semicolon:

An American immigrant, Levi Strauss, invented blue jeans in the 1860s; eventually, his product clothed working men throughout the West.

The position of the semicolon between main clauses never changes, but the conjunctive adverb or transitional expression may move around within a clause. The adverb or expression is usually set off with a comma or commas (see p. 452):

Blue jeans have become fashionable all over the world; however, the American originators still wear more jeans than anyone else.

Blue jeans have become fashionable all over the world; the American originators, however, still wear more jeans than anyone else.

Its mobility distinguishes a conjunctive adverb or transitional expression from other connecting words, such as coordinating and subordinating conjunctions. See pages 280–81 on this distinction.

Note If you use a comma or no punctuation at all between main clauses connected by a conjunctive adverb or transitional expression, you will produce a comma splice or a fused sentence. (See Chapter 18.)

Exercise 29.3   Punctuating main clauses related by conjunctive adverbs or transitional expressions

Insert a semicolon in each of the following sentences to separate main clauses related by a conjunctive adverb or transitional expression. Also insert a comma or commas where needed to set off the adverb or expression.

Exercise

Example:

He knew that tickets for the concert would sell quickly therefore he arrived at the box office hours before it opened.

He knew that tickets for the concert would sell quickly; therefore, he arrived at the box office hours before it opened.

1. Music is a form of communication like language the basic elements however are not letters but notes.
2. Computers can process any information that can be represented numerically as a result they can process musical information.
3. A computer's ability to process music depends on what software it can run it must moreover be connected to a system that converts electrical vibration into sound.
4. Computers and their sound systems can produce many different sounds indeed the number of possible sounds is infinite.
5. The powerful music computers are very expensive therefore they are used only by professional musicians.

Exercise 29.4   Sentence combining: Main clauses related by conjunctive adverbs or transitional expressions

Combine each set of three sentences below into one sentence containing only two main clauses. Connect the clauses with the conjunctive adverb or transitional expression in parentheses, and separate them with a semicolon. Be sure the adverbs and expressions are punctuated appropriately. You will have to add, delete, change, and rearrange words. Each item has more than one possible answer.

Exercise

Example:

The Albanians censored their news. We got little news from them. And what we got was unreliable. (*therefore*)

The Albanians censored their news; therefore, the little news we got from them was unreliable.

1. Most music computers are too expensive for the average consumer. Digital keyboard instruments can be inexpensive. They are widely available. (*however*)
2. Inside the keyboard is a small computer. The computer controls a sound synthesizer. The instrument can both process and produce music. (*consequently*)
3. The person playing the keyboard presses keys or manipulates other controls. The computer and synthesizer convert these signals. The signals are converted into vibrations and sounds. (*immediately*)
4. The inexpensive keyboards can perform only a few functions. To the novice computer musician, the range is exciting. The range includes drum rhythms and simulated instruments. (*still*)

5. Would-be musicians can orchestrate whole songs. They start from just the melody lines. They need never again play "Chopsticks." (*thus*)

29c Use a semicolon to separate main clauses when they are long or contain commas, even with a coordinating conjunction.

We normally use a comma with a coordinating conjunction such as *and* or *but* between main clauses (see p. 444). But a semicolon makes a sentence easier to read when the main clauses are long and complicated or contain commas:

> By a conscious effort of the mind, we can stand aloof from actions and their consequences; and all things, good and bad, go by us like a torrent.
> —Henry David Thoreau

> I doubt if the texture of Southern life is any more grotesque than that of the rest of the nation, but it does seem evident that the Southern writer is particularly adept at recognizing the grotesque; and to recognize the grotesque, you have to have some notion of what is not grotesque and why. —Flannery O'Connor

29d Use semicolons to separate items in a series when they are long or contain commas.

We normally use commas to separate items in a series (see p. 455). But when the items are long or contain commas, semicolons help readers identify the items:

> The custody case involved Amy Dalton, the child; Ellen and Mark Dalton, the parents; and Ruth and Hal Blum, the grandparents.

> One may even reasonably advance the claim that the sort of communication that really counts, and is therefore embodied into permanent records, is primarily written; that "words fly away, but written messages endure," as the Latin saying put it two thousand years ago; and that there is no basic significance to at least fifty percent of the oral interchange that goes on among all sorts of persons, high and low.
> —Mario Pei

Exercise 29.5 Punctuating long main clauses and series items
Substitute semicolons for commas in the following sentences to separate main clauses or series items that are long or contain commas.

Example:
> After graduation he debated whether to settle in San Francisco, which was temperate but far from his parents, New York City, which was exciting but expensive, or Atlanta, which was close to home but already familiar.

Exercise

After graduation he debated whether to settle in San Francisco, which was temperate but far from his parents **;** New York City, which was exciting but expensive **;** or Atlanta, which was close to home but already familiar.

1. The Indian subcontinent is separated from the rest of the world by clear barriers: the Bay of Bengal and the Arabian Sea to the east and west, respectively, the Indian Ocean to the south, and 1600 miles of mountain ranges to the north.

2. In the north of India are the world's highest mountains, the Himalayas, and farther south are fertile farmlands, unpopulated deserts, and rain forests.

3. India is a nation of ethnic and linguistic diversity, with numerous religions, including Hinduism, Islam, and Christianity, with distinct castes and ethnic groups, and with sixteen languages, including the official Hindi and the "associate official" English.

4. Between the seventeenth and nineteenth centuries, the British colonized most of India, taking control of government, the bureaucracy, and industry, and they assumed a social position above all Indians.

5. During British rule the Indians' own unresolved differences and their frustrations with the British erupted in violent incidents such as the Sepoy Mutiny, which began on February 26, 1857, and lasted two years, the Amritsar Massacre on April 13, 1919, and violence between Hindus and Muslims during World War II that resulted in the separation of Pakistan from India.

29e Use the semicolon only where required.

Semicolons do not separate unequal sentence elements and should not be overused.

((•●

Podcast

1 Delete or replace any semicolon that separates a subordinate clause or a phrase from a main clause.

The semicolon does not separate subordinate clauses from main clauses or phrases from main clauses:

| Faulty | Pygmies are in danger of extinction; because of encroaching development. |
| Revised | Pygmies are in danger of extinction because of encroaching development. |

| Faulty | According to African authorities; only about 35,000 Pygmies exist today. |
| Revised | According to African authorities, only about 35,000 Pygmies exist today. |

;
29e

Note Many readers regard a phrase or subordinate clause set off with a semicolon as a kind of sentence fragment. (See Chapter 17.)

2 Delete or replace any semicolon that introduces a series or explanation.

Colons and dashes, not semicolons, introduce series, explanations, and so forth. (See pp. 489 and 493.)

Faulty	Teachers have heard all sorts of reasons why students do poorly; psychological problems, family illness, too much work, too little time.
Revised	Teachers have heard all sorts of reasons why students do poorly: psychological problems, family illness, too much work, too little time.
Revised	Teachers have heard all sorts of reasons why students do poorly—psychological problems, family illness, too much work, too little time.

3 Use the semicolon sparingly.

Use the semicolon only occasionally. Many semicolons in a passage, even when they are required by rule, often indicate repetitive sentence structure. To revise a passage with too many semicolons, you'll need to restructure your sentences, not just remove the semicolons. (See Chapter 26 for tips on varying sentences.)

Semicolon overused

The Make-a-Wish Foundation helps sick children; it grants the wishes of children who are terminally ill. The foundation learns of a child's wish; the information usually comes from parents, friends, or hospital staff; the wish may be for a special toy, a trip to the circus, or a visit to Disneyland. The foundation grants some wishes with its own funds; for other wishes it appeals to those who have what the child desires.

Revised

The Make-a-Wish Foundation grants the wishes of children who are terminally ill. From parents, friends, or hospital staff, the foundation learns of a child's wish for a special toy, a trip to the circus, or a visit to Disneyland. It grants some wishes with its own funds; for other wishes it appeals to those who have what the child desires.

Exercise 29.6 Revising: Misused or overused semicolons
Revise the following sentences to eliminate misused or overused semicolons, substituting other punctuation as appropriate.

> *Example:*
> The doctor gave everyone the same advice; get exercise.
> The doctor gave everyone the same advice: get exercise.

29e

Exercise

1. The main religion in India is Hinduism; a way of life as well as a theology and philosophy.
2. Unlike Christianity and Judaism; Hinduism is a polytheistic religion; with deities numbering in the hundreds.
3. Hinduism is unlike many other religions; it allows its creeds and practices to vary widely from place to place and person to person. Other

religions have churches; Hinduism does not. Other religions have principal prophets and holy books; Hinduism does not. Other religions center on specially trained priests or other leaders; Hinduism promotes the individual as his or her own priest.

4. In Hindu belief there are four types of people; reflective, emotional, active, and experimental.

5. Each type of person has a different technique for realizing the true, immortal self; which has infinite existence, infinite knowledge, and infinite joy.

Exercise 29.7   Revising: Semicolons

Insert semicolons in the following paragraph wherever they are needed. Eliminate any misused or needless semicolons, substituting other punctuation as appropriate.

Exercise

The set, sounds, and actors in the movie captured the essence of horror films. The set was ideal; dark, deserted streets, trees dipping their branches over the sidewalks, mist hugging the ground and creeping up to meet the trees, looming shadows of unlighted, turreted houses. The sounds, too, were appropriate, especially terrifying was the hard, hollow sound of footsteps echoing throughout the film. But the best feature of the movie was its actors; all of them tall, pale, and thin to the point of emaciation. With one exception, they were dressed uniformly in gray and had gray hair. The exception was an actress who dressed only in black; as if to set off her pale yellow, nearly white, long hair; the only color in the film. The glinting black eyes of another actor stole almost every scene, indeed, they were the source of all the film's mischief.

Note See page 500 for a punctuation exercise combining semicolons with other marks of punctuation.

30

The Apostrophe

Unlike other punctuation marks, which separate words, the apostrophe (') appears as *part* of a word to indicate possession or the omission of one or more letters.

Video tutorial

Uses and misuses of the apostrophe

Uses of the apostrophe

■ Use an apostrophe to form the possessives of nouns and indefinite pronouns (opposite).

Singular	Plural
Ms. Park's	the Parks'
lawyer's	lawyers'
everyone's	two weeks'

■ Use an apostrophe to form contractions (p. 478).

it's a girl	shouldn't
you're	won't

■ The apostrophe is optional for plurals of abbreviations, dates, and words or characters named as words (p. 480).

MAs or MA's	Cs or C's
1960s or 1960's	*if*s or *if*'s

Misuses of the apostrophe

■ Do not use an apostrophe plus -*s* to form the possessives of plural nouns (p. 476). Instead, first form the plural with -*s* and *then* add the apostrophe.

Not	But
the Kim's car	the Kims' car
boy's fathers	boys' fathers
babie's care	babies' care

■ Do not use an apostrophe to form plurals of nouns (p. 477).

Not	But
book's are	books are
the Freed's	the Freeds

■ Do not use an apostrophe with verbs ending in -*s* (p. 477).

Not	But
swim's	swims

■ Do not use an apostrophe to form the possessives of personal pronouns (p. 478).

Not	But
it's toes	its toes
your's	yours

30

Grammar checkers A grammar checker usually has mixed results in recognizing apostrophe errors. For instance, it may flag missing apostrophes in contractions (as in *isnt*) but may not distinguish between *its* and *it's, their* and *they're, your* and *you're, whose* and *who's*. A checker may identify some apostrophe errors in possessives but overlook others, and it may flag correct plurals. Instead of relying on your checker, try using your computer's Search or Find function to hunt for all words you have ended in *-s*. Then check each one to ensure that you have used apostrophes correctly.

30a Use the apostrophe to show possession.

Exercise

In English the **possessive case** shows ownership or possession of one person or thing by another. For nouns and indefinite pronouns, possession may be shown with an *of* phrase (*the hair of the dog, the interest of everyone*), or it may be shown with the addition of an apostrophe and, usually, an *-s* (*the dog's hair, everyone's interest*). Only certain pronouns do not use apostrophes for possession: *mine, yours, his, hers, its, ours, theirs,* and *whose* (p. 478).

Note Apostrophes are easy to misuse. Always check your drafts to ensure the following:

- Every word ending in *-s* neither omits a needed apostrophe nor adds an unneeded one.
- The apostrophe or apostrophe-plus-*s* is an *addition.* Before this addition, always spell the name of the owner or owners without dropping or adding letters: *girls* becomes *girls',* not *girl's.*

1 Add *-'s* to singular nouns and indefinite pronouns.

Bill Boughton**'s** skillful card tricks amaze children.

Some of the earth**'s** forests are regenerating.

Everyone**'s** fitness can be improved through exercise. [Indefinite pronoun.]

Add *-'s* as well to singular nouns that end in *-s*:

Henry James**'s** novels reward the patient reader.

Los Angeles**'s** weather is mostly warm.

The business**'s** customers filed suit.

√
30a

Exception We often do not pronounce the possessive *-s* of a few singular nouns ending in an *s* or *z* sound: names with more than one *s* sound (*Moses*), names that sound like plurals (*Rivers, Bridges*), and nouns followed by a word beginning in *s*. In these cases, many writers add only the apostrophe to show possession.

Podcast

Moses**'** mother concealed him in the bulrushes.

Joan Rivers' jokes offend many people.

For conscience' sake she confessed her lie.

However, usage varies widely, and the final *-s* is not wrong with words like these (*Moses's*, *Rivers's*, *conscience's*).

Podcast

2 Add -'s to plural nouns not ending in *-s*.

The bill establishes children's rights.

Publicity grabbed the media's attention.

3 Add only an apostrophe to plural nouns ending in *-s*.

Workers' incomes have not risen much over the past decade.

Many students benefit from several years' work after high school.

The Jameses' talents are extraordinary.

Note the difference in the possessives of singular and plural words ending in *-s*. The singular form usually takes the apostrophe and *-s: James's*. The plural takes only the apostrophe: *Jameses'*.

4 Add -'s only to the last word of compound words or word groups.

The council president's speech was a bore.

The brother-in-law's business failed.

Taxes are always somebody else's fault.

5 With two or more words, add -'s to one or both depending on meaning.

Individual possession

Zimbale's and Mason's comedy techniques are similar. [Each comedian has his own technique.]

Joint possession

The child recovered despite her mother and father's neglect. [The mother and father were jointly neglectful.]

Exercise 30.1 Forming possessives

Form the possessive case of each word or word group in brackets.

Example:

The [men] blood pressures were higher than the [women].

The men's blood pressures were higher than the women's.

30a

Exercise

1. In works for adults and teens, fiction writers often explore [people] relationship to nature and the environment.
2. For example, [Carl Hiaasen] inventive and humorous plots often revolve around endangered [species] habitats.
3. His [characters] personalities are often eccentric and extreme.
4. Most of [Hiaasen] books for adults and younger readers address [Florida] natural landscape and challenges to it.

5. For instance, in *Hoot*, [Hiaasen] first novel for younger readers, endangered [owls] habitat will be destroyed if a [business] plans to build a new restaurant proceed.
6. In *Flush* the main [character] father is in jail for sinking a casino boat that regularly emptied raw sewage into [Florida] water.
7. In *Scat* two [students] investigation into a [teacher] disappearance leads to an environmental mystery.
8. Two of [Margaret Atwood] recent novels are about several [individuals] survival following a devastating environmental crisis and a plague that has killed nearly all of the residents of a city.
9. The first of the two books, *Oryx and Crake*, involves characters with those names but is told from one [man] perspective, that of a character named Jimmy.
10. Readers learn [Jimmy] version of the events that have occurred.
11. Gradually readers learn about [Oryx and Crake] lives and why they are not struggling for survival along with Jimmy.
12. In the second Atwood book, *The Year of the Flood*, readers encounter a similar story, but through two [women] experiences.
13. In both books, most of the [city] residents have died from an outbreak of disease.
14. [Everyone] home is empty.
15. Some readers may be unsettled by these two [books] visions of the future.

30b Delete or replace any apostrophe in a plural noun, a singular verb, or a possessive personal pronoun.

Not all words ending in *-s* take an apostrophe. Three kinds of words are especially likely to attract unneeded apostrophes.

Plural nouns

Form most plural nouns by adding *-s* or *-es* (*boys, Smiths, families, Joneses*). Never add an apostrophe to form the plural:

Podcast

| Faulty | The unleashed dog's began traveling in a pack. |
| Revised | The unleashed dogs began traveling in a pack. |

| Faulty | The Jones' and Bass' were feuding. |
| Revised | The Joneses and Basses were feuding. |

Singular verbs

Do not add an apostrophe to present-tense verbs used with *he, she, it,* and other third-person singular subjects. These verbs always end in *-s* but *never* with an apostrophe:

| Faulty | The subway break's down less often now. |
| Revised | The subway breaks down less often now. |

| Faulty | It run's more reliably. |
| Revised | It runs more reliably. |

30b

Possessive personal pronouns

His, hers, its, ours, yours, theirs, and *whose* are possessive forms of the pronouns *he, she, it, we, you, they,* and *who.* They do not take apostrophes:

Faulty	The frog is her's, not their's. It's skin is speckled.
Revised	The frog is hers, not theirs. Its skin is speckled.

The personal pronouns are often confused with contractions, such as *it's, you're,* and *who's.* See below.

Exercise

Exercise 30.2   Distinguishing between plurals and possessives

Supply the appropriate form—possessive or plural—of each word given in brackets. Some answers require apostrophes, and some do not.

> *Example:*
> A dozen Hawaiian [shirt], each with [it] own loud design, hung in the window.
> A dozen Hawaiian shirts, each with its own loud design, hung in the window.

1. Demeter may be the oldest of the Greek [god], older than Zeus.
2. Many prehistoric [culture] had earth [goddess] like Demeter.
3. In myth she is the earth mother, which means that the responsibility for the fertility of both [animal] and [plant] is [she].
4. The [goddess] festival came at harvest time, with [it] celebration of bounty.
5. The [people] [prayer] to Demeter thanked her for grain and other [gift].

30c

30c   Use an apostrophe to indicate the omission in a standard contraction.

it is, it has	it's	let us	let's
he is	he's	does not	doesn't
she is	she's	were not	weren't
they are	they're	class of 2014	class of '14
you are	you're	of the clock	o'clock
who is, who has	who's	madam	ma'am

Contractions are common in speech and in informal writing. They may also be used to relax style in more formal kinds of writing, as they are in this handbook. But be aware that many people disapprove of contractions in any kind of formal writing.

Exercise

Note Contractions are easily confused with the possessive personal pronouns:

Contraction	Possessive pronoun
it's	its
they're	their
you're	your
who's	whose

Podcast

Faulty   Legislators know their going to have to cut the budget to eliminate it's deficit.

Revised   Legislators know they're going to have to cut the budget to eliminate its deficit.

If you tend to confuse these forms, search for both spellings throughout your drafts. Then test for correctness:

■ Use an apostrophe when you intend the word to contain the sentence verb *is, are,* or *has*: *It is* [*It's*] *a shame. It has* [*It's*] *happened. They are* [*They're*] *to blame. You are* [*You're*] *right. Who is* [*Who's*] *coming? Who has* [*Who's*] *responded?*

■ Don't use an apostrophe when you intend the word to indicate possession: *Its tail was wagging. Their car broke down. Your eyes are blue. Whose book is that?*

Exercise 30.3 Forming contractions

Form contractions from each set of words below. Use each contraction in a complete sentence.

Exercise

Example:
we are: we're
We're open to ideas.

1. she would
2. could not
3. they are
4. he is
5. do not

6. she will
7. hurricane of 1962
8. is not
9. it is
10. will not

Exercise 30.4 Revising: Contractions and personal pronouns

Revise the following sentences to correct mistakes in the use of contractions and personal pronouns. Mark the number preceding any sentence that is already correct.

30c

Example:
The agencies give they're employees they're birthdays off.
The agencies give their employees their birthdays off.

1. Many students seek help from the college writing center when their writing papers for their classes.
2. The writing center has expanded it's hours: it's now open until 10 PM every night.
3. The writing center also offers online tutoring to students whose schedules make face-to-face meetings difficult.

Exercise

4. For online tutoring, students can submit they're papers by computer when they're ready to receive help.
5. In a survey, students who use the writing center responded that it's a good source of feedback for they're writing.

30d The apostrophe is optional to mark plural abbreviations, dates, and words or characters named as words.

You'll sometimes see apostrophes used to form the plurals of abbreviations (BA's), dates (1900's), and words or characters named as words (*but*'s). However, most current style guides do not recommend the apostrophe in these cases.

BAs   PhDs
1990s   2000s

The sentence has too many *buts*.
Two *3s* end the zip code.

Note Italicize or underline a word or character named as a word (see p. 512), but not the added *-s*.

Exercise 30.5 Revising: Apostrophes

Exercise

In the following paragraph correct any mistakes in the use of the apostrophe or any confusion between contractions and possessive personal pronouns.

People who's online experiences include blogging, Web cams, and social-networking sites are often used to seeing the details of other peoples private lives. Many are also comfortable sharing they're own opinions, photographs, and videos with family, friend's, and even stranger's. However, they need to realize that employers and even the government can see they're information, too. Employers commonly put applicants names through social-networking Web sites such as *MySpace* and *Facebook*. Many large companies read their employees outbound e-mail. People can take steps to protect their personal information by adjusting the privacy settings on their social-networking pages. They can avoid posting photos of themselves that they wouldnt want an employer to see. They can avoid sending personal e-mail while their at work. Its the individuals responsibility to keep certain information private.

30d

Note See page 500 for a punctuation exercise involving apostrophes along with other marks of punctuation.

31

Quotation Marks

Quotation marks—either double (" ") or single (' ')—mainly enclose direct quotations from speech and from writing. The box on the next two pages summarizes this use and the combination of quotation marks with commas, semicolons, ellipsis marks, and other punctuation. Additional information on using quotations appears elsewhere in this book:

Video tutorial

- Using commas with signal phrases introducing quotations, pages 458–60.
- Using brackets and the ellipsis mark to indicate changes in quotations, pages 496–99.
- Quoting sources versus paraphrasing or summarizing them, pages 633–40.
- Integrating quotations into your text, pages 642–47.
- Acknowledging the sources of quotations to avoid plagiarism, pages 652–53 and 655–56.
- Formatting long prose quotations and poetry quotations in MLA style, pages 715–56; Chicago style, page 797; and APA style, page 826.

Note Always use quotation marks in pairs, one at the beginning of a quotation and one at the end.

Grammar checkers A grammar checker will help you use quotation marks in pairs by flagging a lone mark. It may also look for punctuation inside or outside quotation marks (see p. 487), but it may still fail to detect some errors.

31a   Use double quotation marks to enclose direct quotations.

Direct quotations report what someone has said or written in the exact words of the original. Enclose most direct quotations in quotation marks.

Exercise

mycomplab

Visit *mycomplab.com* for the eText and for resources and more exercises on quotation marks.

481

Handling quotations from speech or writing

Direct and indirect quotation

Direct quotation

According to Lewis Thomas, "We are, perhaps uniquely among the earth's creatures, the worrying animal. We worry away our lives."

> Note Do not use quotation marks with a direct quotation that is set off from your text. See pages 715–16 (MLA style), 797 (Chicago style), and 826 (APA style).

Quotation within quotation

Quoting a phrase by Lewis Thomas, the author adds, "We are 'the worrying animal.'"

Indirect quotation

Lewis Thomas says that human beings are unique among animals in their worrying.

Quotation marks with other punctuation marks

Commas and periods

Human beings are the "worrying animal," says Thomas.
Thomas calls human beings "the worrying animal."

Semicolons and colons

Machiavelli says that "the majority of men live content"; in contrast, Thomas calls us "the worrying animal."
Thomas believes that we are "the worrying animal": we spend our lives afraid and restless.

Question marks, exclamation points, dashes

When part of your own sentence:

Who said that human beings are "the worrying animal"?
Imagine saying that we human beings "worry away our lives"!
Thomas's phrase—"the worrying animal"—seems too narrow.

When part of the original quotation:

"Will you discuss this with me?" she asked.
"I demand that you discuss this with me!" she yelled.
"Please, won't you—" She paused.

Altering quotations

Brackets for additions

"We [human beings] worry away our lives," says Thomas.

Brackets for altered capitalization

"[T]he worrying animal" is what Thomas calls us. He says that "[w]e worry away our lives."

31a

Ellipsis marks for omissions

"We are **. . .** the worrying animal," says Thomas.

Worrying places us "uniquely among the earth's creatures**. . . .** We worry away our lives."

Punctuating signal phrases with quotations

Introductory signal phrase

He says**,** "We worry away our lives."

An answer is in these words by Lewis Thomas**:** "We are, perhaps uniquely among the earth's creatures, the worrying animal."

Thomas says that "the worrying animal" is afraid and restless.

Concluding signal phrase

We are "the worrying animal**,"** says Thomas.

"Who says**?"** she demanded.

"I do**!"** he shouted.

Interrupting signal phrase

"We are**,"** says Thomas**,** "perhaps uniquely among the earth's creatures, the worrying animal."

"I do not like the idea**,"** she said**;** "however, I agree with it."

Human beings are "the worrying animal**,"** says Thomas**.** "We worry away our lives."

"Fortunately," said the psychoanalyst Karen Horney, "analysis is not the only way to resolve inner conflicts. Life itself still remains a very effective therapist."

Notes Do not use quotation marks with a direct quotation that is set off from your text. For handling such quotations, see pp. 715–16 (MLA style), 797 (Chicago style), and 826 (APA style).

Also do not use quotation marks with an **indirect quotation**, which reports what someone said or wrote but not in the exact words:

The psychoanalyst Karen Horney remarked that analysis is but one solution to personal problems, for life is a good therapist.

(See also pp. 634–37 on paraphrasing quotations.)

" "

31b

31b Use single quotation marks to enclose a quotation within a quotation.

When you quote a writer or speaker, use double quotation marks. When the material you quote contains yet another quotation, distinguish the two by enclosing the second one in single quotation marks:

"In formulating any philosophy," Woody Allen writes, "the first consideration must always be: What can we know? Descartes hinted at the problem when he wrote, 'My mind can never know my body, although it has become quite friendly with my leg.'"

Notice that two different quotation marks appear at the end of the sentence—one single (to finish the interior quotation) and one double (to finish the main quotation).

Exercise

Exercise 31.1   Using double and single quotation marks

Insert double and single quotation marks as needed in the following sentences. Mark the number preceding any sentence that is already correct.

Example:

The purpose of this book, explains the preface, is to examine the meaning of the expression Dance is poetry.

"The purpose of this book," explains the preface, "is to examine the meaning of the expression 'Dance is poetry.'"

1. Why, the lecturer asked, do we say Bless you! or something else when people sneeze but not acknowledge coughs, hiccups, and other eruptions?
2. She said that sneezes have always been regarded differently.
3. Sneezes feel more uncontrollable than some other eruptions, she said.
4. Unlike coughs and hiccups, she explained, sneezes feel as if they come from inside the head.
5. She concluded, People thus wish to recognize a sneeze, if only with a Gosh.

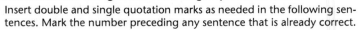

31c   Set off quotations of dialog according to standard practice.

When quoting conversations, begin a new paragraph for each speaker:

"What shall I call you? Your name?" Andrews whispered rapidly, as with a high squeak the latch of the door rose.
"Elizabeth," she said. "Elizabeth."
—Graham Greene, *The Man Within*

31c

When you quote a single speaker for more than one paragraph, put quotation marks at the beginning of each paragraph but at the end of only the last paragraph. The absence of quotation marks at the end of a paragraph tells readers that the speech is continuing.

Note Quotation marks are optional for quoting unspoken thoughts or imagined dialog:

I asked myself, "How can we solve this?"
I asked myself, How can we solve this?

31d   Put quotation marks around the titles of works that are parts of other works.

Exercise

Use quotation marks to enclose the titles of works that are published or released within larger works: see the following box. As in the second article title in the box, use single quotation marks for a quotation within a quoted title, and enclose all punctuation in the title within the quotation marks. Use italics or underlining for all other titles, such as books, plays, periodicals, and movies. (See p. 511.)

Titles to be enclosed in quotation marks

Other titles should be italicized or underlined. (See p. 511.)

Songs
"Lucy in the Sky with
   Diamonds"
"America the Beautiful"

Short poems
"Stopping by Woods on a
   Snowy Evening"
"Sunday Morning"

Articles in periodicals
"Comedy and Tragedy
   Transposed"
"Does 'Scaring' Work?"

Essays
"Politics and the English
   Language"
"Joey: A 'Mechanical Boy'"

Short stories
"The Battler"
"The Gift of the Magi"

**Page or document on a
Web site**
"Readers' Page" (on site
   Friends of Prufrock)

**Episodes of television and
radio programs**
"The Mexican Connection"
   (on *60 Minutes*)
"Cooking with Clams"
   (on *Eating In*)

Subdivisions of books
"Voyage to the Houyhnhnms"
   (Part 4 of *Gulliver's Travels*)
"The Mast Head" (Chapter 35
   of *Moby-Dick*)

Note Some academic disciplines do not require quotation marks for titles within source citations. See pages 809 (APA style) and 836–37 (CSE style).

" "

31d

Exercise

Exercise 31.2   Quoting titles
Insert quotation marks as needed for titles in the following sentences. If quotation marks should be used instead of italics, insert them.

Example:
She published an article titled Marriage in Grace Paley's An Interest in Life.

She published an article titled "Marriage in Grace Paley's 'An Interest in Life.'"

1. In Chapter 8, titled *How to Be Interesting,* the author explains the art of conversation.
2. The Beatles' song Let It Be reminds Martin of his uncle.
3. The article that appeared in *Mental Health* was titled *Children of Divorce Ask, "Why?"*
4. In the encyclopedia the discussion under Modern Art fills less than a column.
5. One prizewinning essay, *Cowgirls on Wall Street,* first appeared in *Entrepreneur* magazine.

31e Quotation marks may be used to enclose words used in a special sense.

On film sets, movable *"wild walls"* make a one-walled room seem four-walled on film.

Writers often put quotation marks around a word they are using with irony—that is, with a different or even opposite meaning than usual:

With all the *"compassion"* it could muster, the agency turned away two-thirds of those seeking help.   —Joan Simonson

Readers quickly tire of such irony, though, so use it sparingly. Prefer language that expresses your meaning exactly. (See Chapter 38.)

Note For words you are defining, use italics or underlining. (See p. 512.)

31f Use quotation marks only where they are required.

Don't use quotation marks in the titles of your papers unless they contain or are themselves direct quotations:

Not   "The Death Wish in One Poem by Robert Frost"
But   The Death Wish in One Poem by Robert Frost
Or   The Death Wish in *"Stopping by Woods on a Snowy Evening"*

Don't use quotation marks to enclose common nicknames or technical terms that are not being defined:

Not   As President, "Jimmy" Carter preferred to use his nickname.
But   As President, Jimmy Carter preferred to use his nickname.

Not   "Mitosis" in a cell is fascinating to watch.
But   Mitosis in a cell is fascinating to watch.

Don't use quotation marks in an attempt to justify or apologize for slang and trite expressions that are inappropriate to your writing. If slang is appropriate, use it without quotation marks.

Not   We should support the President in his "hour of need" rather than "wimp out" on him.

But   We should give the President the support he needs rather than turn away like cowards.

(See pp. 526 and 544 for more on slang and trite expressions.)

31g   Place other punctuation marks inside or outside quotation marks according to standard practice.

The position of another punctuation mark inside or outside a closing quotation mark depends on what the other mark is, whether it appears in the quotation, and whether a source citation immediately follows the quotation.

Podcast

1 Place commas and periods inside quotation marks.

Commas or periods fall *inside* closing quotation marks, even when (as in the third example) single and double quotation marks are combined:

Swift uses irony in his essay "A Modest Proposal."

Many first-time readers are shocked to see infants described as "delicious."

"'A Modest Proposal,'" writes one critic, "is so outrageous that it cannot be believed."

(See pp. 458–60 for the use of commas, as in the preceding example, to separate a quotation from a signal phrase such as *writes one critic*.)

Exception When a parenthetical source citation immediately follows a quotation, place any period or comma *after* the citation:

One critic calls the essay "outrageous" (Olms 26).

Partly because of "the cool calculation of its delivery" (Olms 27), Swift's satire still chills a modern reader.

See pages 673–74 for more on placing parenthetical citations.

2 Place colons and semicolons outside quotation marks.

Some years ago the slogan in elementary education was "learning by playing"; now educators are concerned with basic skills.

We all know what is meant by "inflation": more money buys less.

3 Place dashes, question marks, and exclamation points inside quotation marks only if they belong to the quotation.

When a dash, question mark, or exclamation point is part of the quotation, put it *inside* quotation marks. Don't use any other punctuation such as a period or a comma:

31g

"But must you——" Marcia hesitated, afraid of the answer.

"Go away**!**" I yelled.

Did you say, "Who is she**?**" [When both your sentence and the quotation would end in a question mark or exclamation point, use only the mark in the quotation.]

When a dash, question mark, or exclamation point applies only to the larger sentence, not to the quotation, place it *outside* quotation marks—again, with no other punctuation:

One evocative line in English poetry—"After many a summer dies the swan"—comes from Alfred, Lord Tennyson.

Who said, "Now cracks a noble heart"**?**

The woman called me "stupid"**!**

Exercise

Exercise 31.3   Revising: Quotation marks

The italic words in the following sentences are titles or direct quotations. Insert quotation marks where italics should not be used. Be sure that other marks of punctuation are correctly placed inside or outside the quotation marks.

> *Example:*
> The award-winning essay is *Science and Values.*
> The award-winning essay is **"**Science and Values.**"**

1. In the title essay of her book *The Death of the Moth and Other Essays,* Virginia Woolf describes the last moments of a *frail and diminutive body.*
2. An insect's death may seem insignificant, but the moth is, in Woolf's words, *life, a pure bead.*
3. The moth's struggle against death, *indifferent, impersonal,* is heroic.
4. Where else but in such a bit of life could one see a protest so *superb*?
5. At the end Woolf sees the moth lying *most decently and uncomplainingly composed*; in death it finds dignity.

Exercise

Exercise 31.4   Revising: Quotation marks

Insert quotation marks as needed in the following paragraphs.

In one class we talked about a passage from *I Have a Dream,* the speech delivered by Martin Luther King, Jr., on the steps of the Lincoln Memorial on August 28, 1963:

> When the architects of our republic wrote the magnificent words of the Constitution and the Declaration of Independence, they were signing a promissory note to which every American was to fall heir. This note was a promise that all men would be guaranteed the unalienable rights of life, liberty, and the pursuit of happiness.

What did Dr. King mean by this statement? the teacher asked. Perhaps we should define promissory note first. Then she explained that a person who signs such a note agrees to pay a specific sum of money on a particular date or on demand by the holder of the note.

31g

One student suggested, Maybe Dr. King meant that the writers of the Constitution and Declaration promised that all people in America should be equal.

He and over 200,000 people had gathered in Washington, DC, added another student. Maybe their purpose was to demand payment, to demand those rights for African Americans.

The whole discussion was an eye opener for those of us (including me) who had never considered that those documents make promises that we should expect our country to fulfill.

Note See page 500 for a punctuation exercise involving quotation marks along with other marks of punctuation.

32

Other Punctuation Marks

This chapter covers the colon (below), the dash (p. 492), parentheses (p. 494), brackets (p. 496), the ellipsis mark (p. 497), and the slash (p. 500).

Video tutorial

Grammar checkers A grammar checker may flag a lone parenthesis or bracket so that you can match it with another parenthesis or bracket. But most checkers cannot recognize other misuses of the marks covered here and instead simply ignore the marks.

Exercise

32a Use the colon to introduce and to separate.

The colon is mainly a mark of introduction: it signals that the words following will explain or amplify. The colon also has several conventional uses, such as in expressions of time.

Video tutorial

In its main use as an introducer, a colon is *always* preceded by a complete **main clause**—a word group that can stand alone as a

mycomplab

Visit *mycomplab.com* for the eText and for resources and more exercises on the colon, the dash, parentheses, brackets, the ellipsis mark, and the slash.

Distinguishing the colon and the semicolon

Colon

The colon is a mark of introduction that separates elements of *unequal* importance, such as statements and explanations or introductions and quotations. The first element must be a complete main clause; the second element need not be.

The business school caters to working students: it offers special evening courses in business writing, finance, and management.

The school has one goal: to train students to be responsible, competent businesspeople.

Semicolon

The semicolon separates elements of *equal* importance, almost always complete main clauses. (See p. 465.)

Few enrolling students know exactly what they want from the school; most hope generally for a managerial career.

---

sentence because it contains a subject and a predicate and does not start with a subordinating word (see p. 272 for more on main clauses). A colon may or may not be followed by a main clause. This is one way the colon differs from the semicolon (see the box above). The colon is interchangeable with the dash, though the dash is more informal and more abrupt (see p. 492).

Note Don't use a colon more than once in a sentence. The sentence should end with the element introduced by the colon.

1 Use a colon to introduce a concluding explanation, a series, an appositive, and some quotations.

Depending on your preference, a complete sentence *after* the colon may begin with a capital letter or a small letter. Just be consistent throughout an essay.

Explanation

Soul food is a varied cuisine: it includes spicy gumbos, black-eyed peas, and collard greens.

Soul food has a deceptively simple definition: the ethnic cooking of African Americans.

Sometimes a concluding explanation is preceded by *the following* or *as follows* and a colon:

A more precise definition might be the following: soul food draws on ingredients, cooking methods, and dishes that originated in Africa, were brought to the New World by slaves, and were modified or supplemented in the Caribbean and the American South.

32a

Series (p. 455)

At least three soul food dishes are familiar to most Americans: fried chicken, barbecued spareribs, and sweet potato pie.

Appositive (p. 276)

Soul food has one disadvantage: fat.

Certain expressions commonly introduce appositives, such as *namely* and *that is*. These expressions should *follow* the colon: *Soul food has one disadvantage: namely, fat.*

Quotation

The comma generally separates a signal phrase from a quotation (see p. 458). But when you introduce a quotation with a complete sentence, use a colon instead:

One soul food chef has a solution: "Soul food doesn't have to be greasy to taste good. Instead of using ham hocks to flavor beans, I use smoked turkey wings. The soulful, smoky taste remains, but without all the fat of pork."

2 Use a colon to separate titles and subtitles and the subdivisions of time.

Titles and subtitles	Time
Charles Dickens: An Introduction to His Novels	1:30 AM
Eros and Civilization: An Inquiry into Freud	12:26 PM

3 Use the colon only where required.

Use the colon only at the *end* of a main clause. Do not use it directly after a verb or preposition.

Not Two critically acclaimed movies directed by Steven Spielberg are: *Schindler's List* and *Saving Private Ryan.*

But Two critically acclaimed movies directed by Steven Spielberg are *Schindler's List* and *Saving Private Ryan.*

Not Shakespeare had the qualities of a Renaissance thinker, such as: humanism and an interest in Greek and Roman literature.

But Shakespeare had the qualities of a Renaissance thinker, such as humanism and an interest in Greek and Roman literature.

:
32a

Exercise 32.1 Revising: Colons

Insert colons as needed in the following sentences, or delete colons that are misused.

Exercise

Example:

Mix the ingredients as follows sift the flour and salt together, add the milk, and slowly beat in the egg yolk.

Mix the ingredients as follows: sift the flour and salt together, add the milk, and slowly beat in the egg yolk.

1. In remote areas of many developing countries, simple signs mark human habitation a dirt path, a few huts, smoke from a campfire.
2. In the built-up sections of industrialized countries, nature is all but obliterated by signs of human life, such as: houses, factories, skyscrapers, and highways.
3. The spectacle makes many question the words of Ecclesiastes 1.4 "One generation passeth away, and another cometh; but the earth abideth forever."
4. Yet many scientists see the future differently they hold that human beings have all the technology necessary to clean up the earth and restore the cycles of nature.
5. All that is needed is: a change in the attitudes of those who use technology.

32b   Use a dash to indicate shifts in tone or thought and to set off some sentence elements.

The dash is mainly a mark of interruption: it signals an insertion or break.

Note In your papers, form a dash with two hyphens (--) or use the character called an em dash on your word processor. Do not add extra space around or between the hyphens or around the em dash.

1   Use a dash or dashes to indicate shifts and hesitations.

Shift in tone
The novel—if one can call it that—appeared in 2010.

Unfinished thought
If the book had a plot—but a plot would be conventional.

Hesitation in dialog
"I was worried you might think I had stayed away because I was influenced by—" He stopped and lowered his eyes.
Astonished, Howe said, "Influenced by what?"
"Well, by—" Blackburn hesitated and for an answer pointed to the table.   —Lionel Trilling

2   Use a dash or dashes to emphasize nonessential elements.

Dashes may be used in place of commas or parentheses to set off and emphasize nonessential elements. (See the box on the facing page.) Dashes are especially useful when these elements are internally punctuated. Be sure to use a pair of dashes when the element interrupts a main clause.

Distinguishing dashes, commas, and parentheses

Dashes, commas, and parentheses may all set off nonessential elements.

Dashes
Dashes give the information the greatest emphasis (facing page):

Many students—including some employed by the college—disapprove of the new work rules.

Commas
Commas are less emphatic (p. 449):

Many students, including some employed by the college, disapprove of the new work rules.

Parentheses
Parentheses are the least emphatic, signaling that the information is just worth a mention (next page):

Many students (including some employed by the college) disapprove of the new work rules.

Appositive (p. 451)
The qualities Monet painted—bright sunlight, rich shadows, deep colors—abounded near the rivers and gardens he used as subjects.

Modifier
Though they are close together—separated by only a few blocks—the two neighborhoods could be in different countries.

Parenthetical expression (p. 452)
At any given time there exists an inventory of undiscovered embezzlement in—or more precisely not in—the country's businesses and banks.
—John Kenneth Galbraith

3 Use a dash to set off introductory series and concluding series and explanations.

Introductory series
Shortness of breath, skin discoloration or the sudden appearance of moles, persistent indigestion, the presence of small lumps—all these may signify cancer.

A dash sets off concluding series and explanations more informally and more abruptly than a colon does (see p. 490):

Concluding series
The patient undergoes a battery of tests—MRI, bronchoscopy, perhaps even biopsy.

32b

Concluding explanation

Many patients are disturbed by the MRI—by the need to keep still for long periods in an exceedingly small space.

4 Use the dash only where needed.

Don't use the dash when commas, semicolons, and periods are more appropriate. And don't use too many dashes. They can create a jumpy or breathy quality in writing.

Not   In all his life—eighty-seven years—my great-grandfather never allowed his picture to be taken—not even once. He claimed the "black box"—the camera—would steal his soul.

But   In all his eighty-seven years my great-grandfather did not allow his picture to be taken even once. He claimed the "black box"—the camera—would steal his soul.

Exercise 32.2 Revising: Dashes

Insert dashes as needed in the following sentences.

Exercise

Example:

What would we do if someone like Adolf Hitler that monster appeared among us?

What would we do if someone like Adolf Hitler—that monster— appeared among us?

1. The movie-theater business is undergoing dramatic changes changes that may affect what movies are made and shown.
2. The closing of independent theaters, the control of theaters by fewer and fewer owners, and the increasing ownership of theaters by movie studios and distributors these changes may reduce the availability of noncommercial films.
3. Yet at the same time the number of movie screens is increasing primarily in multiscreen complexes so that smaller films may find more outlets.
4. The number of active movie screens that is, screens showing films or booked to do so is higher now than at any time since World War II.
5. The biggest theater complexes seem to be something else as well art galleries, amusement arcades, restaurants, spectacles.

( )
32c

32c Use parentheses to enclose parenthetical expressions and labels for lists within sentences.

Parentheses *always* come in pairs: one before and one after the punctuated material.

1 Use parentheses to enclose parenthetical expressions.

Parenthetical expressions include explanations, digressions, and examples that may be helpful or interesting but are not essential to meaning. They are emphasized least when set off with a pair of parentheses instead of commas or dashes. (See the box on p. 493.)

> The population of Philadelphia (now about 1.5 million) has declined since 1950.
>
> *Ariel* (published in 1965) contains Sylvia Plath's last poems.

Note Don't put a comma before a parenthetical expression enclosed in parentheses:

> **Not** The population of Philadelphia compares with that of Phoenix, (just under 1.5 million).
>
> **But** The population of Philadelphia compares with that of Phoenix (just under 1.5 million).

If you use a comma, semicolon, or period after a parenthetical expression, place the mark *outside* the closing parenthesis:

> Philadelphia has a larger African American population (over 40%), while Phoenix has a larger Latino population (over 40%).

If you enclose a complete sentence in parentheses, capitalize the sentence and place the closing period *inside* the closing parenthesis:

> In general, coaches will tell you that scouts are just guys who can't coach. (But then, so are brain surgeons.)   —Roy Blount

2 Use parentheses to enclose labels for lists within sentences.

> Outside the Middle East, the countries with the largest oil reserves are (1) Venezuela (63 billion barrels), (2) Russia (57 billion barrels), and (3) Mexico (51 billion barrels).

When you set a list off from your text, do not enclose such labels in parentheses.

Exercise 32.3 Revising: Parentheses

Insert parentheses as needed in the following sentences.

> *Example:*
> Students can find good-quality, inexpensive furniture for example, desks, tables, chairs, sofas, even beds in thrift shops.
>
> Students can find good-quality, inexpensive furniture (for example, desks, tables, chairs, sofas, even beds) in thrift shops.

1. Many of those involved in the movie business agree that multiscreen complexes are good for two reasons: 1 they cut the costs of exhibitors, and 2 they offer more choices to audiences.
2. Those who produce and distribute films and not just the big studios argue that the multiscreen theaters give exhibitors too much power.

( )
32c

Exercise

3. The major studios are buying movie theaters to gain control over important parts of the distribution process what gets shown and for how much money.
4. For twelve years 1938–50 the federal government forced the studios to sell all their movie theaters.
5. But because they now have more competition television and DVD players, for instance, the studios are permitted to own theaters.

32d Use brackets within quotations to indicate your own comments or changes.

Brackets have specialized uses in mathematical equations, but their main use for all kinds of writing is to indicate that you have altered a quotation. If you need to explain, clarify, or correct the words of the writer you quote, place your additions in a pair of brackets:

> "That Chevron station [just outside Dallas] is one of the busiest in the nation," said a company spokesperson.

Use brackets if you need to alter the capitalization of a quotation so that it will fit into your sentence. (See also p. 505.)

> "[O]ne of the busiest in the nation" is how a company spokesperson described the station.

You may also use a bracketed word or words to substitute for parts of a quotation that would otherwise be unclear. In the following sentence, the bracketed word substitutes for *they* in the original:

> "Despite considerable achievements in other areas, [humans] still cannot control the weather and probably will never be able to do so."

See page 643 for additional examples of using brackets with quotations.

The word *sic* (Latin for "in this manner") in brackets indicates that an error in the quotation appeared in the original and was not made by you. When following MLA style, do not italicize *sic* in brackets. Most other styles—including Chicago, APA, and CSE—do italicize *sic*.

> According to the newspaper report, "The car slammed thru [sic] the railing and into oncoming traffic."

Don't use *sic* to make fun of a writer or to note errors in a passage that is clearly nonstandard or illiterate.

Note Always acknowledge the sources of quotations in order to avoid plagiarism. (See pp. 652–53 and 655–56.)

[ ]
32d

32e Use the ellipsis mark to indicate omissions from quotations and pauses in speech.

The **ellipsis mark** consists of three periods separated by space (. . .). The ellipsis mark usually indicates an omission from a quotation, although it may also show an interruption in dialog.

Exercise

Note Additional issues with quotations are discussed elsewhere in this book:

- Choosing and editing quotations, pages 637–39.
- Integrating source material into your text, pages 642–47.
- Acknowledging the sources of quotations to avoid plagiarism, pages 652–53 and 655–56. See also example 3 below.

1 The ellipsis mark substitutes for omissions from quotations.

When you omit a part of a quotation, show the omission with an ellipsis mark. All the following examples quote from the passage below about environmentalism.

Original quotation

"At the heart of the environmentalist world view is the conviction that human physical and spiritual health depends on sustaining the planet in a relatively unaltered state. Earth is our home in the full, genetic sense, where humanity and its ancestors existed for all the millions of years of their evolution. Natural ecosystems—forests, coral reefs, marine blue waters—maintain the world exactly as we would wish it to be maintained. When we debase the global environment and extinguish the variety of life, we are dismantling a support system that is too complex to understand, let alone replace, in the foreseeable future."   —Edward O. Wilson, "Is Humanity Suicidal?"

1. Omission of the middle of a sentence

"Natural ecosystems . . . maintain the world exactly as we would wish it to be maintained."

2. Omission of the end of a sentence, without source citation

"Earth is our home. . . ." [The sentence period, closed up to the last word, precedes the ellipsis mark.]

3. Omission of the end of a sentence, with source citation

"Earth is our home . . ." (Wilson 27). [The sentence period follows the source citation.]

4. Omission of parts of two or more sentences

Wilson writes, "At the heart of the environmentalist world view is the conviction that human physical and spiritual health depends on sustaining the planet . . . where humanity and its ancestors existed for all the millions of years of their evolution."

. . .
32e

5. Omission of one or more sentences

As Wilson puts it, "At the heart of the environmentalist world view is the conviction that human physical and spiritual health depends on sustaining the planet in a relatively unaltered state. . . . When we debase the global environment and extinguish the variety of life, we are dismantling a support system that is too complex to understand, let alone replace, in the foreseeable future."

6. Omission from the middle of a sentence through the end of another sentence

"Earth is our home. . . . When we debase the global environment and extinguish the variety of life, we are dismantling a support system that is too complex to understand, let alone replace, in the foreseeable future."

7. Omission of the beginning of a sentence, leaving a complete sentence

a. Bracketed capital letter

"[H]uman physical and spiritual health," Wilson writes, "depends on sustaining the planet in a relatively unaltered state." [No ellipsis mark is needed because the brackets around the *H* indicate that the letter was not capitalized originally and thus that the beginning of the sentence has been omitted.]

b. Small letter

According to Wilson, "human physical and spiritual health depends on sustaining the planet in a relatively unaltered state." [No ellipsis mark is needed because the small *h* indicates that the beginning of the sentence has been omitted.]

c. Capital letter from the original

One reviewer comments, ". . . Wilson argues eloquently for the environmentalist world view"(Hami 28). [An ellipsis mark is needed because the quoted part of the sentence begins with a capital letter and it's otherwise not clear that the beginning of the original sentence has been omitted.]

8. Use of a word or phrase

Wilson describes the earth as "our home." [No ellipsis mark needed.]

Note the following features of the examples:

32e

- ▪ **Use an ellipsis mark when it is not otherwise clear that you have left out material from the source,** as when you omit one or more sentences (examples 5 and 6) or when the words you quote form a complete sentence that is different in the original (examples 1–4 and 7c).
- ▪ **You don't need an ellipsis mark when it is obvious that you have omitted something,** such as when a bracketed capital letter or a small letter indicates omission (examples 7a and 7b) or when a phrase clearly comes from a larger sentence (example 8).

■ Place an ellipsis mark after any sentence period *except* when a parenthetical source citation follows the quotation, as in example 3. Then the sentence period falls after the citation.

If you omit one or more lines of poetry or paragraphs of prose from a quotation, use a separate line of ellipsis marks across the full width of the quotation to show the omission:

> In "Song: Love Armed" from 1676, Aphra Behn contrasts two lovers' experiences of a romance:
>
> > Love in fantastic triumph sate,
> >
> > Whilst bleeding hearts around him flowed,
> >
> > . . . .
> >
> > But my poor heart alone is harmed,
> >
> > Whilst thine the victor is, and free. (lines 1-2, 15-16)

(See pp. 715–16 for the format of displayed quotations like this one. And see p. 672 on the source-citation form illustrated here.)

2 The ellipsis mark indicates pauses or unfinished statements.

When writing dialog or when writing informally (not in academic writing), you can show hesitation or interruption with an ellipsis mark instead of a dash (p. 492).

> "I wish . . ." His voice trailed off.

Exercise 32.4 Using ellipsis marks

Use ellipsis marks and any other needed punctuation to follow the numbered instructions for quoting from the following paragraph.

Exercise

> Women in the sixteenth and seventeenth centuries were educated in the home and, in some cases, in boarding schools. Men were educated at home, in grammar schools, and at the universities. The universities were closed to female students. For women, "learning the Bible," as Elizabeth Joceline puts it, was an impetus to learning to read. To be able to read the Bible in the vernacular was a liberating experience that freed the reader from hearing only the set passages read in the church and interpreted by the church. A Protestant woman was expected to read the scriptures daily, to meditate on them, and to memorize portions of them. In addition, a woman was expected to instruct her entire household in "learning the Bible" by holding instructional and devotional times each day for all household members, including the servants.
>
> —Charlotte F. Otten, *English Women's Voices, 1540–1700*

1. Quote the fifth sentence, but omit everything from *that freed the reader* to the end.
2. Quote the fifth sentence, but omit the words *was a liberating experience that.*
3. Quote the first and sixth sentences.

. . .
32e

32f Use the slash between options and between lines of poetry.

Option

I don't know why some teachers oppose pass/fail courses.

Between options, the slash is not surrounded by extra space.

Note The options *and/or* and *he/she* should be avoided. (See the Glossary of Usage, pp. 846 and 852.)

Poetry

Many readers have sensed a reluctant turn away from death in Frost's lines "The woods are lovely, dark and deep, **/** But I have promises to keep" (13–14).

When you run lines of poetry into your text, separate them with a slash surrounded by space. (See pp. 715–16 for more on quoting poetry.)

Exercise

Exercise 32.5 Revising: Colons, dashes, parentheses, brackets, ellipsis marks, slashes

Insert colons, dashes, parentheses, brackets, ellipsis marks, or slashes as needed in the following paragraph. When different marks would be appropriate in the same place, be able to defend the choice you make.

"Let all the learned say what they can, 'Tis ready money makes the man." These two lines of poetry by the Englishman William Somerville 1645–1742 may apply to a current American economic problem. Non-American investors with "ready money" pour some of it as much as $1.3 trillion in recent years into the United States. The investments of foreigners are varied stocks and bonds, savings deposits, service companies, factories, artworks, even the campaigns of political candidates. Proponents of foreign investment argue that it revives industry, strengthens the economy, creates jobs more than 3 million, they say, and encourages free trade among nations. Opponents discuss the risks of heavy foreign investment it makes the American economy vulnerable to outsiders, sucks profits from the country, and gives foreigners an influence in governmental decision making. On both sides, it seems, "the learned say 'Tis ready money makes the man or country." The question is, whose money?

32f

Exercise on Chapters 27–32 Revising: Punctuation

The following paragraphs are unpunctuated except for end-of-sentence periods. Insert periods, commas, semicolons, apostrophes, quotation marks, colons, dashes, or parentheses where they are required. When different marks would be appropriate in the same place, be able to defend the choice you make.

Brewed coffee is the most widely consumed beverage in the world. The trade in coffee beans alone amounts to well over $6000000000 a year and the total volume of beans traded exceeds 4250000 tons a year.

Its believed that the beverage was introduced into Arabia in the fifteenth century CE probably by Ethiopians. By the middle or late sixteenth century the Arabs had introduced the beverage to the Europeans who at first resisted it because of its strong flavor and effect as a mild stimulant. The French Italians and other Europeans incorporated coffee into their diets by the seventeenth century the English however preferred tea which they were then importing from India. Since America was colonized primarily by the English Americans also preferred tea. Only after the Boston Tea Party 1773 did Americans begin drinking coffee in large quantities. Now though the US is one of the top coffee-consuming countries consumption having been spurred on by familiar advertising claims Good till the last drop Rich hearty aroma Always rich never bitter and by ubiquitous coffee bars.

Produced from the fruit of an evergreen tree coffee is grown primarily in Latin America southern Asia and Africa. Coffee trees require a hot climate high humidity rich soil with good drainage and partial shade consequently they thrive on the east or west slopes of tropical volcanic mountains where the soil is laced with potash and drains easily. The coffee beans actually seeds grow inside bright red berries. The berries are picked by hand and the beans are extracted by machine leaving a pulpy fruit residue that can be used for fertilizer. The beans are usually roasted in ovens a chemical process that releases the beans essential oil caffeol which gives coffee its distinctive aroma. Over a hundred different varieties of beans are produced in the world each with a different flavor attributable to three factors the species of plant *Coffea arabica* and *Coffea robusta* are the most common and the soil and climate where the variety was grown.

PART 7

Mechanics

33

Capitals

Video
tutorial

Exercise

Generally, capitalize a word only when a dictionary or conventional use says you must. Consult one of the style guides listed on pages 804 and 835 for special uses of capitals in the social, natural, and applied sciences.

Grammar checkers A grammar checker will flag overused capital letters and missing capitals at the beginnings of sentences. It will also spot missing capitals at the beginnings of proper nouns and adjectives—*if* the nouns and adjectives are in the checker's dictionary. For example, a checker caught *christianity* and *europe* but not *china* (for the country) or *Stephen king*.

CULTURE & LANGUAGE Conventions of capitalization vary from language to language. English, for instance, is the only language to capitalize the first-person singular pronoun (*I*), and its practice of capitalizing proper nouns but not most common nouns also distinguishes it from some other languages.

> common   proper   common
> noun   noun   pronoun   noun
> My friend Nathaniel and I both play the drums.

33a Capitalize the first word of every sentence.

Every writer should own a good dictionary.
Will inflation be curbed?
Watch out!

When quoting other writers, you must either reproduce the capital letters beginning their sentences or indicate with brackets that you have altered the source. Whenever possible, integrate the quotation into your own sentence so that its capital letters coincide with your own:

"Psychotherapists often overlook the benefits of self-deception," the author argues.

The author argues that "the benefits of self-deception" are not always recognized by psychotherapists.

mycomplab

Visit *mycomplab.com* for the eText and for resources and
504   more exercises on capital letters.

If you need to alter the capitalization in the source, indicate the change with brackets (see p. 496):

> "[T]he benefits of self-deception" are not always recognized by psychotherapists, the author argues.
>
> The author argues that "[p]sychotherapists often overlook the benefits of self-deception."

Note Capitalization of questions in a series is optional. Both examples below are correct:

> Is the population a hundred? Two hundred? More?
> Is the population a hundred? two hundred? more?

Also optional is capitalization of the first word in a complete sentence after a colon (see p. 489).

33b Capitalize most words in titles and subtitles of works.

Within your text, capitalize all the words in a title *except* the following: articles (*a, an, the*), *to* in infinitives, coordinating conjunctions (*and, but,* etc.), and prepositions (*with, between,* etc.). Capitalize even these short words when they are the first or last word in a title or when they fall after a colon or semicolon.

> *The Sound and the Fury* | *Management: A New Theory*
> "Courtship through the Ages" | "Once More to the Lake"
> *A Diamond Is Forever* | *An End to Live For*
> "Knowing Whom to Ask" | "Power: How to Get It"
> *Learning from Las Vegas* | *File under Architecture*
> "The Truth about AIDS" | *Only When I Laugh*

Always capitalize the prefix or first word in a hyphenated word within a title. Capitalize the second word only if it is a noun or an adjective or is as important as the first word.

> "Applying Stage Make-up" | *Through the Looking-Glass*
> *The Pre-Raphaelites*

Note The style guides of the academic disciplines have their own rules for capitals in titles. For instance, the preceding guidelines reflect MLA style for English and some other humanities. In contrast, APA style for the social sciences and CSE style for the sciences capitalize only the first word and proper names in book and article titles within source citations. See pages 809 (APA) and 836–37 (CSE).

33c Always capitalize the pronoun *I* and the interjection *O*. Capitalize *oh* only when it begins a sentence.

> I love to stay up at night, but, oh, I hate to get up in the morning.
> He who thinks himself wise, O heavens, is a great fool. —Voltaire

Video
tutorial

33d Capitalize proper nouns, proper adjectives, and words used as essential parts of proper nouns.

Proper nouns name specific persons, places, and things: *Shakespeare, California, World War I.* **Proper adjectives** are formed from some proper nouns: *Shakespearean, Californian.*

1 Capitalize proper nouns and proper adjectives.

Capitalize all proper nouns and proper adjectives but not the articles (*a, an, the*) that precede them.

Proper nouns and adjectives to be capitalized

Specific persons and things

Stephen King   the Leaning Tower of Pisa
Napoleon Bonaparte   Boulder Dam
Lady Gaga   the Empire State Building

Specific places and geographical regions

New York City   the Mediterranean Sea
China   Lake Victoria
Europe   the Northeast, the South
North America   the Rocky Mountains

But: northeast of the city, going south

Days of the week, months, holidays

Monday   Yom Kippur
May   Christmas
Thanksgiving   Columbus Day

Historical events, documents, periods, movements

World War II   the Middle Ages
the Vietnam War   the Age of Reason
the Boston Tea Party   the Renaissance
the Treaty of Ghent   the Great Depression
the Constitution   the Romantic Movement
the Bill of Rights   the Cultural Revolution

Government offices, departments, and institutions

House of Representatives   Polk Municipal Court
Department of Defense   Warren County Hospital
Appropriations Committee   Palo Alto City Council

Academic institutions and departments

University of Kansas   Department of Nursing
Santa Monica College   Haven High School

But: the university, college course, high school diploma

**cap
33d**

Political, social, athletic, and other organizations and associations and their members

Democratic Party, Democrats	Rotary Club, Rotarians
Sierra Club	League of Women Voters
Girl Scouts of America, Scout	Boston Celtics
B'nai B'rith	Chicago Symphony Orchestra

Races, nationalities, and their languages

Native American	Germans
African American	Swahili
Caucasian	Italian

But: blacks, whites

Religions and their followers

Christianity, Christians	Judaism, Orthodox Jews
Protestantism, Protestants	Hinduism, Hindus
Catholicism, Catholics	Islam, Muslims

Religious terms for the sacred

God	Buddha
Allah	the Bible [**but** biblical]
Christ	the Koran, the Qur'an

Note Follow your own preference in capitalizing *he, his,* or *him* when referring to God or Allah.

2 Capitalize common nouns used as essential parts of proper nouns.

Common nouns name general classes of persons, places, or things, and they usually are not capitalized. However, capitalize common nouns such as *street, avenue, park, river, ocean, lake, company, college, county,* and *memorial* when they are part of proper nouns naming specific places or institutions:

Main Street	Crum Creek
Park Avenue	Lake Superior
Garland Place	Ford Motor Company
Central Park	Madison College
Mississippi River	San Mateo County
Pacific Ocean	George Washington Memorial

3 Capitalize trade names.

Trade names identify individual brands of certain products. When a trade name loses its association with a brand and comes to refer to a product in general, it is not capitalized. Refer to a dictionary for current usage when you are in doubt about a name.

cap

33d

Scotch tape	Xerox
Chevrolet	Bunsen burner

But: nylon, thermos

33e Capitalize most titles of persons only when they precede proper names.

Professor Otto Osborne	Otto Osborne, a professor of English
Doctor Jane Covington	Jane Covington, a medical doctor
Governor Ella Moore	Ella Moore, the governor

Not   The <u>S</u>enator supported the bill.

But   The <u>s</u>enator supported the bill.

Or   <u>Senator Carmine</u> supported the bill.

Exception Many writers capitalize a title denoting very high rank even when it follows a proper name or is used alone:

Ronald Reagan, past <u>President</u> of the United States, died in 2004.

John Roberts is <u>Chief Justice</u> of the United States.

33f Avoid common misuses of capital letters.

1 Use small letters for common nouns replacing proper nouns.

Not   I am determined to take an <u>Economics</u> course before I graduate from <u>College</u>.

But   I am determined to take an <u>economics</u> course before I graduate from <u>college</u>.

Or   I am determined to take <u>Economics 101</u> before I graduate from <u>Madison College</u>.

2 Capitalize compass directions only when they refer to specific geographical areas.

The storm blew in from the <u>northeast</u> and then veered <u>south</u> along the coast. [Here *northeast* and *south* refer to general directions.]

Students from the <u>South</u> have trouble adjusting to the <u>Northeast's</u> bitter winters. [Here *South* and *Northeast* refer to specific regions.]

3 Use small letters for the names of seasons and the names of academic years and terms.

spring	autumn	senior year
summer	fall quarter	winter term

4 Capitalize the names of relationships only when they form part of or substitute for proper names.

my <u>m</u>other	the <u>f</u>ather of my friend
my <u>u</u>ncle Brad	Brad's <u>b</u>rother

I remember how <u>D</u>ad scolded us.
<u>A</u>unt Annie and <u>Uncle</u> Jake died within two months of each other.

5 Use capitals according to convention in online
   communication.

Online messages written in all-capital letters or with no capital
letters are difficult to read. Further, messages in all-capital letters
may be considered rude. Use capital letters according to rules
33a–33f in all your online communication.

Exercise 33.1 Revising: Capitals

Capitalize words as necessary in the following sentences, or substitute
small letters for unnecessary capitals. Consult a dictionary if you are in
doubt. If the capitalization in a sentence is already correct, mark the
number preceding the sentence.

Exercise

> *Example:*
> The first book on the reading list is mark twain's *a connecticut yankee
> in king arthur's court.*
>
> The first book on the reading list is Mark Twain's *A Connecticut Yan-
> kee in King Arthur's Court.*

1. San Antonio, texas, is a thriving city in the southwest.
2. The city has always offered much to tourists interested in the roots of
   spanish settlement of the new world.
3. The alamo is one of five Catholic Missions built by Priests to convert
   native americans and to maintain spain's claims in the area.
4. But the alamo is more famous for being the site of an 1836 battle
   that helped to create the republic of Texas.
5. Many of the nearby Streets, such as Crockett street, are named for
   men who gave their lives in that Battle.
6. The Hemisfair plaza and the San Antonio river link tourist and convention facilities developed during mayor Cisneros's terms.
7. Restaurants, Hotels, and shops line the River. the haunting melodies
   of "Una paloma blanca" and "malagueña" lure passing tourists into
   Casa rio and other excellent mexican restaurants.
8. The university of Texas at San Antonio has expanded, and a Medical
   Center has been developed in the Northwest part of the city.
9. Sea World, on the west side of San Antonio, entertains grandparents, fathers and mothers, and children with the antics of dolphins and seals.
10. The City has attracted high-tech industry, creating a corridor of
    economic growth between san antonio and austin and contribut-
    ing to the texas economy.

Note See page 520 for an exercise involving capitals along with
italics or underlining and other mechanics.

cap
33f

34

Italics or Underlining

Exercise

Italic type and <u>underlining</u> indicate the same thing: the word or words are being <u>distinguished</u> or emphasized. Italic type is now used almost universally in academic and business writing. Some instructors do recommend underlining, so ask your instructor for his or her preference.

Always use either italics or underlining consistently throughout a document in both text and source citations. If you are using italics, make sure that the italic characters are clearly distinct from the regular type. If you are using underlining and you underline two or more words in a row, underline the space between the words, too: <u>Criminal Statistics: Misuses of Numbers.</u>

Grammar checkers A grammar checker cannot recognize problems with italics or underlining. Use the guidelines in this chapter to edit your work.

34a Italicize or underline the titles of works that appear independently.

Within your text, italicize or underline the titles of works that are published, released, or produced separately from other works (see the box opposite). Use quotation marks for all other titles (see p. 485).

Note Italicize or underline a mark of punctuation only when it is part of the title. In newspaper titles, highlight the name of the city only when it is part of the title. And for all periodical titles, do not capitalize or highlight the article *the* when it begins the title.

> Who is the publisher of the Manchester *Guardian*?
>
> The national edition of the *New York Times* often differs substantially from the late edition.

Exceptions Legal documents, the Bible, the Koran, and their parts are generally not italicized or underlined.

> Not   They registered their *deed.*
> But   They registered their deed.

Visit *mycomplab.com* for the eText and for resources and more exercises on italics and underlining.

Titles to be italicized or underlined

Other titles should be placed in quotation marks. (See p. 485.)

Books

War and Peace
Psychology: An Introduction

Plays

Hamlet
The Phantom of the Opera

Computer software

Microsoft Internet Explorer
Google

Web sites

YouTube
Friends of Prufrock

Pamphlets

The Truth about Alcoholism
Plants of the Desert

Long musical works

Tchaikovsky's *Swan Lake*
The Beatles' *Revolver*
But: Symphony in C

Television and radio programs

All Things Considered
NBC Sports Hour

Long poems

Beowulf
Paradise Lost

Periodicals

Time
Boston Globe
Yale Law Review

Published speeches

Lincoln's *Gettysburg Address*
Pericles's *Funeral Oration*

Movies, DVDs, and videos

Schindler's List
How to Relax

Works of visual art

Michelangelo's *David*
Picasso's *Guernica*

Not   We studied the *Book of Revelation* in the *Bible*.

But   We studied the Book of Revelation in the Bible.

Many sciences do not use italics or underlining for some or all titles within source citations. (See pp. 836–37 on CSE style.)

34b Italicize or underline the names of ships, aircraft, spacecraft, and trains.

Queen Mary 2   *Orient Express*   *Apollo XI*
Challenger   *Spirit of St. Louis*   *Montrealer*

34c Italicize or underline foreign words and phrases that have not been absorbed into English.

English has adopted many foreign words and phrases—such as the French "bon voyage"—and they need not be italicized or underlined. Do italicize or underline words considered foreign, consulting a dictionary if needed.

ital

34c

The scientific name for the brown trout is *Salmo trutta.* [The Latin scientific names for plants and animals are always italicized or underlined.]

What a life he led! He was a true *bon vivant.*

The Latin *De gustibus non est disputandum* translates roughly as "There's no accounting for taste."

34d Italicize or underline words or characters named as words.

Use italics or underlining to indicate that you are citing a character or word as a word rather than using it for its meaning. Words you are defining fall under this convention:

The word *syzygy* refers to a straight line formed by three celestial bodies, as in the alignment of the earth, sun, and moon.

Some people say *th,* as in *thought,* with a faint *s* or *f* sound.

Carved into the column, twenty feet up, was a mysterious *7.*

34e Occasionally, italics or underlining may be used for emphasis.

Italics or underlining can stress an important word or phrase, especially in reporting how someone said something:

"Why on earth would *you* do that?" she cried.

But use such emphasis very rarely. Excessive underlining or italics will make your writing sound immature or hysterical:

The settlers had *no* firewood and *no* food. Many of them *starved* or *froze to death* that first winter.

34f In online communication, use alternatives for italics or underlining.

Some forms of online communication do not allow italics or underlining for the purposes described in this chapter. On Web sites, for instance, underlining often indicates a link to another site.

If you can't use italics or underlining for highlighting, type an underscore before and after the element: *Measurements coincide with those in _Joule's Handbook_.* You can also emphasize words with asterisks: *I *will not* be able to attend.*

Avoid using all-capital letters for emphasis. (See also p. 509.)

ital
34f

Exercise 34.1 Revising: Italics or underlining

In the following sentences, underline the words and phrases that need highlighting with italics or underlining and place a check mark next to words and phrases that are highlighted unnecessarily. Note that some highlighting is correct as given.

Exercise

Example:
Of Hitchcock's movies, Psycho is the scariest.
Of Hitchcock's movies, <u>Psycho</u> is the scariest.

1. Of the many Vietnam veterans who are writers, Oliver Stone is perhaps the most famous for writing and directing the films Platoon and Born on the Fourth of July.
2. Tim O'Brien has written short stories for Esquire, GQ, and Massachusetts Review.
3. Going after Cacciato is O'Brien's dreamlike novel about the horrors of combat.
4. The word Vietnam is technically two words (*Viet* and *Nam*), but most American writers spell it as *one* word.
5. American writers use words or phrases borrowed from Vietnamese, such as di di mau ("go quickly") or dinky dau ("crazy").
6. Philip Caputo's *gripping* account of his service in Vietnam appears in the book A Rumor of War.
7. Caputo's book was made into a television movie, also titled *A Rumor of War*.
8. David Rabe's plays—including The Basic Training of Pavlo Hummel, Streamers, and Sticks and Bones—depict the effects of the war *not only* on the soldiers *but also* on their families.
9. Called the *poet laureate of the Vietnam war,* Steve Mason has published two collections of poems: Johnny's Song and Warrior for Peace.
10. The Washington Post published *rave* reviews of Veteran's Day, an autobiography by Rod Kane.

Note See page 520 for an exercise involving italics or underlining along with capitals and other mechanics.

35

Abbreviations

The following guidelines on abbreviations pertain to the text of a nontechnical document. All academic disciplines use abbreviations

Video
tutorial

mycomplab

Visit *mycomplab.com* for the eText and for resources and more exercises on abbreviations.

in source citations, and much technical writing, such as in the sciences and engineering, uses many abbreviations in the document text. For the requirements of the discipline you are writing in, consult one of the style guides listed on pages 785 (humanities), 804 (social sciences), and 835 (natural and applied sciences).

Usage varies, but writers increasingly omit periods from abbreviations that consist of or end in capital letters: *US, BA, USMC, PhD.* See page 441 on punctuating abbreviations.

Grammar and spelling checkers A grammar checker may flag some abbreviations, such as *ft.* (for *foot*) and *st.* (for *street*). A spelling checker will flag abbreviations it does not recognize. But neither checker can tell you whether an abbreviation is appropriate for your writing situation or will be clear to your readers.

35a Use standard abbreviations for titles immediately before and after proper names.

Before the name	After the name
Dr. James Hsu	James Hsu, MD
Mr., Mrs., Ms., Hon., St., Rev., Msgr., Gen.	DDS, DVM, PhD, EdD, OSB, SJ, Sr., Jr.

Use abbreviations such as *Rev., Hon., Prof., Rep., Sen., Dr.,* and *St.* (for *Saint*) only if they appear before a proper name. Spell them out in the absence of a proper name:

Not	We learned to trust the Dr.
But	We learned to trust the doctor.
Or	We learned to trust Dr. Kaplan.

The abbreviations for academic degrees—*PhD, MA, BA,* and the like—may be used without a proper name: *My brother took seven years to get his PhD. I will likely take as long to earn my BA.*

35b Familiar abbreviations and acronyms are acceptable in most writing.

An **acronym** is an abbreviation that spells a pronounceable word, such as WHO, NATO, and AIDS. These and other abbreviations that use initials are acceptable in most writing as long as they are familiar to readers. Abbreviations of two or more words written in all capital letters may be written without periods (see p. 441):

Institutions	LSU, UCLA, TCU
Organizations	CIA, FBI, YMCA, AFL-CIO
Corporations	IBM, CBS, ITT
People	JFK, LBJ, FDR
Countries	US, USA

Abbreviations for nontechnical writing

- Titles before or after proper names: *Dr. Jorge Rodriguez; Jorge Rodriguez, PhD.*
- Familiar abbreviations and acronyms: *USA, AIDS.*
- *BC, BCE, AD, CE, AM, PM, no.,* and *$* with dates and numbers.
- *I.e., e.g.,* and other Latin abbreviations within parentheses and in source citations.
- *Inc., Bros., Co.,* and *&* with names of business firms.

Note If a name or term (such as *operating room*) appears often in a piece of writing, then its abbreviation (*OR*) can cut down on extra words. Spell out the full term at its first appearance, give its abbreviation in parentheses, and use the abbreviation from then on.

35c | Use *BC, BCE, AD, CE, AM, PM, no.,* and *$* only with specific dates and numbers.

44 BC	AD 1492	8:05 PM (*or* p.m.)	no. 36 (*or* No. 36)
44 BCE	1492 CE	11:26 AM (*or* a.m.)	$7.41

Not   Hospital routine is easier to follow in the AM than in the PM.

But   Hospital routine is easier to follow in the morning than in the afternoon or evening.

Note The abbreviation BC ("before Christ") always follows a date, whereas AD (*anno Domini*, Latin for "in the year of the Lord") precedes a date. Increasingly, these abbreviations are being replaced by BCE ("before the common era") and CE ("common era"), respectively. Both follow the date.

35d | Generally, reserve Latin abbreviations for source citations and comments in parentheses.

The following common Latin abbreviations are generally not italicized or underlined.

i.e.	*id est:* that is
cf.	*confer:* compare
e.g.	*exempli gratia:* for example
et al.	*et alii:* and others
etc.	*et cetera:* and so forth
NB	*nota bene:* note well

He said he would be gone a fortnight (i.e., two weeks).
Trees, too, are susceptible to disease (e.g., Dutch elm disease).
Bloom et al., editors, *Anthology of Light Verse*

ab
35d

Some writers avoid these Latin abbreviations in formal writing, even within parentheses.

35e Use *Inc., Bros., Co.,* or & (for *and*) only in official names of business firms.

Not   The Santini bros. operate a large moving firm in New York City.
But   The Santini brothers operate a large moving firm in New York City.
Or   Santini Bros. is a large moving firm in New York City.

Not   We read about the Hardy Boys & Nancy Drew.
But   We read about the Hardy Boys and Nancy Drew.

35f Spell out most units of measurement and names of places, calendar designations, people, and courses.

In most academic, general, and business writing, certain words should always be spelled out. (In source citations and technical writing, however, these words are more often abbreviated.)

Units of measurement
The dog is thirty inches [not in.] high.
The building is 150 feet [not ft.] tall.

Exception Long phrases such as *miles per hour (m.p.h.)* or *cycles per second (c.p.s.)* are usually abbreviated, with or without periods: *The speed limit on that road was once 75 m.p.h.* [or *mph*].

Geographical names
The publisher is in Massachusetts [not Mass. or MA].
He came from Auckland, New Zealand [not NZ].
She lived on Morrissey Boulevard [not Blvd.].

Exceptions The United States is often referred to as the USA or the US. In writing of the US capital, use the abbreviation DC for District of Columbia when it follows the city's name: Washington, DC.

Names of days, months, and holidays
The truce was signed on Tuesday [not Tues.], April [not Apr.] 16.
The Christmas [not Xmas] holidays were uneventful.

Names of people
Virginia [not Va.] Woolf was British.
Robert [not Robt.] Frost wrote accessible poems.

Courses of instruction
I'm majoring in political science [not poli. sci.].
Economics [not Econ.] is a difficult course.

ab
35f

Exercise 35.1 Revising: Abbreviations

Revise the following sentences as needed to correct inappropriate use of abbreviations for nontechnical writing. Mark the number preceding any sentence in which abbreviations are appropriate as written.

Exercise

Example:
One prof. lectured for five hrs.
One <u>professor</u> lectured for five <u>hours</u>.

1. In the Sept. 17, 2003, issue of *Science* magazine, Virgil L. Sharpton discusses a theory that could help explain the extinction of dinosaurs.
2. About 65 mill. yrs. ago, a comet or asteroid crashed into the earth.
3. The result was a huge crater about 10 km. (6.2 mi.) deep in the Gulf of Mex.
4. Sharpton's new measurements suggest that the crater is 50 pct. larger than scientists previously believed.
5. Indeed, 20-yr.-old drilling cores reveal that the crater is about 186 mi. wide, roughly the size of Conn.
6. The space object was traveling more than 100,000 m.p.h. and hit earth with the impact of 100 to 300 million megatons of TNT.
7. On impact, 200,000 cubic km. of rock and soil were vaporized or thrown into the air.
8. That's the equivalent of 2.34 bill. cubic ft. of matter.
9. The impact would have created 400-ft. tidal waves across the Atl. Ocean, temps. higher than 20,000 degs., and powerful earthquakes.
10. Sharpton theorizes that the dust, vapor, and smoke from this impact blocked the sun's rays for mos., cooled the earth, and thus resulted in the death of the dinosaurs.

Note See page 520 for an exercise involving abbreviations along with capitals and other mechanics.

36

Numbers

This chapter addresses the use of numbers (numerals versus words) in the text of a document. All disciplines use many more numerals in source citations.

Video
tutorial

Visit *mycomplab.com* for the eText and for resources and more exercises on numbers.

Grammar checkers A grammar checker will flag numerals beginning sentences and can be customized to ignore or to look for numerals (see pp. 71–72). But it can't tell you whether numerals or
spelled-out numbers are appropriate for your writing situation.

| 36a | Use numerals according to standard practice in the field you are writing in. |

Exercise

Always use numerals for numbers that require more than two
words to spell out:

> The leap year has 366 days.
> The population of Minot, North Dakota, is about 36,500.

In nontechnical academic writing, spell out numbers of one or two
words. A hyphenated number may be considered one word.

> Twelve nations signed the treaty.
> The ball game drew forty-two thousand people.
> Jenson lived to be ninety-nine or one hundred.

In much business writing, use numerals for all numbers over
ten (*five reasons, 11 participants*). In technical academic and business writing, such as in science and engineering, use numerals for
all numbers over ten, and use numerals for zero through nine
when they refer to exact measurements (*2 milliliters, 1 kilosecond*).
(Consult one of the style guides listed on pp. 804 and 835 for more
details.)

Notes Use a combination of numerals and words for round
numbers over a million: *26 million, 2.45 billion*. And use either all
numerals or all words when several numbers appear together in a
passage, even if convention would require a mixture:

| Inconsistent | The satellite Galatea is about twenty-six thousand miles from Neptune. It is 110 miles in diameter and orbits Neptune in just over ten hours. |
| Revised | The satellite Galatea is about 26,000 miles from Neptune. It is 110 miles in diameter and orbits Neptune in just over 10 hours. |

Avoid using two numbers in a row, which can be confusing. Rewrite
to separate the numbers:

| Confusing | Out of 530 101 children caught the virus. |
| Clear | Out of 530 children 101 caught the virus. |

CULTURE LANGUAGE In American English a comma separates the numerals in long numbers (*26,000*), and a period
functions as a decimal point (*2.06*).

num
36a

36b Use numerals according to convention for dates, addresses, and other information.

Even when a number requires one or two words to spell out, we conventionally use numerals in the following situations:

Days and years

June 18, 2000   AD 12   456 BCE   1999

Exception The day of a month may be expressed in words when it is not followed by a year (*June fifth; October first*).

Pages, chapters, volumes, acts, scenes, lines	Decimals, percentages, and fractions
Chapter 9, page 123	22.5
Hamlet, act 5, scene 3, lines 35–40	48% (*or* 48 percent) 3½

Addresses	Scores and statistics
RD 2	21 to 7
419 Stonewall Street	a mean of 26
Washington, DC 20036	a ratio of 8 to 1

Exact amounts of money	The time of day
$4.50	9:00 AM
$3.5 million (*or* $3,500,000)	2:30 PM

Exceptions Round dollar or cent amounts of only a few words may be expressed in words: *seventeen dollars; fifteen hundred dollars; sixty cents.* When the word *o'clock* is used for the time of day, also express the number in words: *two o'clock* (not *2 o'clock*).

36c Always spell out numbers that begin sentences.

For clarity, spell out any number that begins a sentence. If the number requires more than two words, reword the sentence so that the number falls later and can be expressed as a numeral:

Not   3.9 billion people live in Asia.
But   The population of Asia is 3.9 billion.

Exercise 36.1 Revising: Numbers

Revise the following sentences so that numbers are used appropriately for nontechnical writing. Mark the number preceding any sentence in which numbers are already used appropriately.

Example:
Charlie paid two hundred five dollars for used scuba gear.
Charlie paid $205 for used scuba gear.

Exercise

num

36c

1. The planet Saturn is nine hundred million miles, or nearly one billion five hundred million kilometers, from the sun.
2. A year on Saturn equals almost thirty of our years.
3. Thus, Saturn orbits the sun only two and four-tenths times during the average human life span.
4. It travels in its orbit at about twenty-one thousand six hundred miles per hour.
5. 15 to 20 times denser than Earth's core, Saturn's core measures 17,000 miles across.
6. The temperature at Saturn's cloud tops is minus one hundred seventy degrees Fahrenheit.
7. In nineteen hundred thirty-three, astronomers found on Saturn's surface a huge white spot 2 times the size of Earth and 7 times the size of Mercury.
8. Saturn's famous rings reflect almost seventy percent of the sunlight that approaches the planet.
9. The ring system is almost forty thousand miles wide, beginning 8800 miles from the planet's visible surface and ending forty-seven thousand miles from that surface.
10. Saturn also has at least sixty-two moons, ranging in size from less than one mile across to more than one-half the size of Earth's moon.

Exercise on Chapters 33–36   Revising: Mechanics

Revise the following paragraphs to correct any errors in the use of capital letters, italics or underlining, abbreviations, and numbers. (For abbreviations and numbers, follow standard practice for nontechnical writing.) Consult a dictionary as needed.

According to many sources—e.g., the Cambridge Ancient History and Gardiner's Egypt of the Pharaohs—the ancient egyptians devoted much attention to making Life more convenient and pleasurable for themselves.

Our word pharaoh for the ancient egyptian rulers comes from the egyptian word pr'o, meaning "great house." Indeed, the egyptians placed great emphasis on family residences, adding small bedrms. as early as 3500 yrs. bce. By 3000 bce, the egyptians made ice through evaporation of water at night and then used it to cool their homes. About the same time they used fans made of palm fronds or papyrus to cool themselves in the day. To light their homes, the egyptians abandoned the animal-fat lamps Humans had used for 50 thousand yrs. Instead, around 1300 bce the people of Egt. devised the 1st oil lamps.

egyptians found great pleasure in playing games. Four thousand three hundred yrs. ago or so they created one of the oldest board games known. the game involved racing ivory or stone pieces across a papyrus playing board. By three thousand bce, egyptian children played marbles with semi-precious stones, some of which have been found in gravesites at nagada, EG. Around one thousand three hundred sixty bce, small children played with clay rattles covered in silk and shaped like animals.

To play the game of love, egyptian men and women experimented with cosmetics applied to skin and eyelids. kohl, history's first eyeliner, was used by both sexes to ward off evil. 5000 yrs. ago egyptians wore wigs made of vegetable fibers or human hair. In 9 hundred bce, queen Isimkheb wore a wig so heavy that she needed assistance in walking. To adjust their make-up and wigs, egyptians adapted the simple metal mirrors devised by the sumerians in the bronze age, ornamenting them with carved handles of ivory, gold, or wood. Feeling that only those who smelled sweet could be attractive, the egyptians made deodorants from perfumed oils, e.g., cinnamon and citrus.

PART 8

Effective Words

37

Using Appropriate Language

Appropriate language suits your writing situation—your subject, purpose, and audience. Like everyone, you vary your words depending on the context in which you are speaking and writing. Look, for example, at the underlined words in these two sentences:

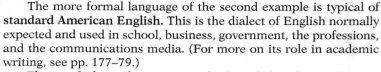

The first sentence might be addressed to friends in casual conversation. The second is more suitable for an academic audience.

Video
tutorial

The more formal language of the second example is typical of **standard American English.** This is the dialect of English normally expected and used in school, business, government, the professions, and the communications media. (For more on its role in academic writing, see pp. 177–79.)

Exercise

The vocabulary of written standard English is huge, allowing you to express an infinite range of ideas and feelings. However, it does exclude words that only some groups of people use, understand, or find inoffensive. It also excludes words and expressions that are commonly spoken but are too imprecise for writing. Whenever you doubt a word's status, consult a dictionary (see p. 534). A label such as *nonstandard, slang,* or *colloquial* tells you that the word is not generally appropriate in academic or business writing.

Grammar checkers A grammar checker can often be set to flag potentially inappropriate words, such as nonstandard dialect, slang, and gender-specific terms (*manmade, policeman*). However, the checker can flag only words listed in its dictionary of questionable words. For example, a checker flagged *businessman* as potentially sexist in *A successful businessman puts clients first,* but the checker did not flag *his* in *A successful businessperson listens to his clients.* If you use a checker to review your language, you'll still need to judge whether your words are appropriate for your writing situation. (See p. 72 for tips on customizing a grammar checker.)

mycomplab

524

Visit *mycomplab.com* for the eText and for resources and more exercises on appropriate language.

Appropriate language in academic writing

■ Use standard American English, the dialect recommended by this handbook. Slang, colloquial language, and other vocabularies are sometimes appropriate in academic writing. Nonstandard dialect, online shortcuts, and pretentious writing are rarely or never appropriate. (See below and pp. 526–29.)

Inappropriate	With a little help, <u>Web-shy folks</u> can <u>get to be hotshot surfers</u>.
Revised	With a little help, people reluctant to explore the Web can become capable users.

■ Avoid stereotypes. (See pp. 529–30.)

Stereotype	<u>Football players</u> need tutors and counselors.
Revised	Football players with poor grades need tutors and counselors.

■ Avoid sexist language. (See pp. 530–31.)

Sexist	<u>Teenage girls</u> are ideal babysitters.
Revised	Teenagers who enjoy young children are ideal babysitters.

■ Be sensitive when labeling groups. (See p. 532.)

Inappropriate	The <u>hurricane victims</u> needed immediate help.
Revised	The people affected by the hurricane needed immediate help.

37a Revising nonstandard dialect

Like many countries, the united States consists of scores of regional, social, and ethnic groups with their own distinct dialects, or versions of English. Standard American English is one of these dialects, and so are African American Vernacular English, Appalachian English, Creole, and the English of coastal Maine. All the dialects of English share many features, but each also has its own vocabulary, pronunciation, and grammar.

If you speak a dialect of English besides standard American English, be careful about using your dialect in situations where standard English is the norm, such as in academic or public writing. Dialects are not wrong in themselves, but forms imported from one dialect into another may still be perceived as unclear or incorrect. When you know standard English is expected in your writing, edit to eliminate expressions in your dialect that you know (or have been told) differ from standard English. These expressions may include *theirselves, hisn, them books,* and others labeled *nonstandard* by a dictionary. They may also include certain verb forms, as discussed

appr
37c

on pages 297–310. For help identifying and editing nonstandard language, see "⟨CULTURE LANGUAGE⟩ Guide" inside the back cover of this book.

Your participation in the community of standard English does not require you to abandon your own dialect. You may want to use it in writing you do for yourself, such as journals, notes, and drafts, which should be composed as freely as possible. You may want to quote it in an academic paper, as when analyzing or reporting conversation in dialect. And, of course, you will want to use it with others who speak it.

37b Revising the shortcuts of online communication

Rapid communication by e-mail and text or instant messaging encourages some informalities that are inappropriate for academic writing. If you use these media frequently, you may need to proofread your academic papers especially to identify and revise errors such as the following:

- **Sentence fragments.** Make sure every sentence has a subject and a predicate. Avoid fragments such as *Observing the results* and *After the meeting.* (See pp. 352–58.)

- **Missing punctuation.** Between and within sentences, use standard punctuation marks. Check especially for missing commas within sentences and missing apostrophes in possessives and contractions. (See pp. 444–60 and 473–79.)

- **Missing capital letters.** Use capital letters at the beginnings of sentences, for proper nouns and adjectives, and in titles. (See pp. 504–08.)

- **Nonstandard abbreviations and spellings.** Avoid forms such as *2* for *to* or *too*, *b4* for *before*, *bc* for *because*, *ur* for *you are* or *you're*, and + or & for *and.* (See pp. 556–65.)

37c Using slang only when appropriate

All groups of people—from musicians and computer scientists to vegetarians and golfers—create novel and colorful expressions called **slang**. The following quotation, for instance, is from an essay on the slang of "skaters" (skateboarders):

> Curtis slashed ultra-punk crunchers on his longboard, while the Rubeman flailed his usual Gumbyness on tweaked frontsides and lofty fakie ollies.
> —Miles Orkin, "Mucho Slingage by the Pool"

Among those who understand it, slang may be vivid and forceful. It often occurs in dialog, and an occasional slang expression can enliven an informal essay. Some slang, such as *dropout* (*She was a high school dropout*), has proved so useful that it has passed into the general vocabulary.

But most slang is too flippant and imprecise for effective communication, and it is generally inappropriate for college or business writing. Notice the gain in seriousness and precision achieved in the following revision:

Slang	Many students start out <u>pretty together</u> but then <u>get weird</u>.
Revised	Many students start out <u>with clear goals</u> but then <u>lose their direction</u>.

37d Using colloquial language only when appropriate

Colloquial language designates the words and expressions appropriate to everyday spoken language. Regardless of our backgrounds and how we live, we all try to *get along with* each other. We play with *kids*, *go crazy* for something, and in our worst moments try to *get back at* someone who has made us do the *dirty work*.

When you write informally, colloquial language may be appropriate to achieve the casual, relaxed effect of conversation. An occasional colloquial word dropped into otherwise more formal writing can also help you achieve a desired emphasis. But colloquial language does not provide the exactness needed in more formal college, public, and professional writing. In such writing you should generally avoid any words and expressions labeled *informal* or *colloquial* in your dictionary. Take special care to avoid **mixed diction,** a combination of standard and colloquial words:

Mixed diction	According to a Native American myth, the Great Creator <u>had a dog hanging around with him</u> when he created the earth.
Revised	According to a Native American myth, the Great Creator <u>was accompanied by a dog</u> when he created the earth.

Note See also pages 177–79 for a discussion of formal and informal language in academic writing.

37e Using regionalisms only when appropriate

Regionalisms are expressions or pronunciations peculiar to a particular area. Southerners may say they *reckon*, meaning "think" or "suppose." People in Maine invite their Boston friends to come *down* rather than *up* (north) to visit. New Yorkers stand *on* rather than *in* line for a movie.

Regional expressions are appropriate in writing addressed to local readers and may lend realism to regional description, but they should be avoided in writing intended for a general audience.

37f Revising neologisms

Neologisms are words created (or coined) so recently that they have not come into established use. An example is *advermation* (made up of *advertise* and *information*), which is a marketing message disguised as objective information. Some neologisms do become accepted as part of our general vocabulary—*motel*, coined from *motor* and *hotel*, is an example. But most neologisms pass quickly from the language. Unless such words serve a special purpose in your writing and are sure to be understood by your readers, you should avoid them.

37g Using technical words with care

All disciplines and professions rely on special words or give common words special meanings. Chemists speak of *esters* and *phosphatides*, geographers and mapmakers refer to *isobars* and *isotherms*, and literary critics write about *motifs* and *subtexts*. Such technical language allows specialists to communicate precisely and economically with other specialists who share their vocabulary. But without explanation these words are meaningless to nonspecialists. When you are writing for nonspecialists, avoid unnecessary technical terms and carefully define terms you must use.

37h Revising indirect or pretentious writing

In most writing, small, plain, and direct words are preferable to big, showy, or evasive words. Avoid euphemisms, double talk, and pretentious writing.

A **euphemism** is a presumably inoffensive word that a writer or speaker substitutes for a word deemed potentially offensive or too blunt, such as *passed away* for "died." Euphemisms appear whenever a writer or speaker wants to soften the truth, as when a governor mentions the *negative growth* (meaning "decline") in her state. Use euphemisms only when you know that blunt, truthful words would needlessly hurt or offend members of your audience.

A kind of euphemism that deliberately evades the truth is **double talk** (also called **doublespeak** or **weasel words**): language intended to confuse or to be misunderstood. Today double talk is unfortunately common in politics and advertising—the *revenue enhancement* that is really a tax, the *biodegradable* bags that last decades. Double talk has no place in honest writing.

Euphemism and sometimes double talk seem to keep company with fancy writing. Any writing that is more elaborate than its subject requires will sound **pretentious**—that is, excessively showy.

Choose your words for their exactness and economy. The big, ornate word may be tempting, but pass it up. Your readers will be grateful.

| Pretentious | Hardly a day goes by without a new revelation about the devastation of the natural world, and to a significant extent our dependence on the internal combustion engine is the culprit. Respected scientific minds coalesce around the argument that carbon dioxide emissions, such as those from automobiles imbibing gasoline, are responsible for a gradual escalation in temperatures on the earth. |
| Revised | Much of the frequent bad news about the environment can be blamed on the internal combustion engine. Respected scientists argue that carbon dioxide emissions, such as those from gas-powered cars, are warming the earth. |

37i Revising sexist and other biased language

Even when we do not mean it to, our language can reflect and perpetuate hurtful prejudices toward groups of people, especially racial, ethnic, religious, age, and sexual groups. Such biased language can be obvious—words such as *nigger, whitey, mick, kike, fag, dyke,* and *broad.* But it can also be subtle, generalizing about groups in ways that may be familiar but that are also inaccurate or unfair. For instance, people with physical disabilities are as varied a group as any other: the only thing they have in common is some form of impairment. To assume that people with disabilities share certain attitudes (shyness, helplessness, victimization, whatever) is to disregard the uniqueness of each person.

Video tutorial

Biased language reflects poorly on the user, not on the person or persons whom it mischaracterizes or insults. Unbiased language does not submit to false generalizations. It treats people as individuals and labels groups as they wish to be labeled.

1 Avoiding stereotypes of race, ethnicity, religion, age, and other characteristics

A **stereotype** is a generalization based on poor evidence, a kind of formula for understanding and judging people simply because of their membership in a group:

Men are uncommunicative.
Women are emotional.
Liberals want to raise taxes.
Conservatives are affluent.

At best, stereotypes betray an uncritical writer, one who is not thinking beyond notions received from others. Worse, they betray a writer who does not mind hurting others or even *wants* to hurt others.

In your writing, be alert for any general statements about people based on only one or a few characteristics. Be especially cautious about substituting such statements for the evidence you should be providing instead.

Stereotype	Elderly drivers should have their licenses limited to daytime driving. [Implies that all elderly people are poor night drivers.]
Revised	Drivers with impaired night vision should have their licenses limited to daytime driving.

Some stereotypes have become part of the language, but they are still potentially offensive.

Stereotype	The administrators are too blind to see the need for a new gymnasium. [Equates vision loss and lack of understanding.]
Revised	The administrators do not understand the need for a new gymnasium.

Exercise

2 Avoiding sexist language

Among the most subtle and persistent biased language is that expressing narrow ideas about men's and women's roles, position, and value in society. This **sexist language** distinguishes needlessly between men and women in such matters as occupation, ability, behavior, temperament, and maturity. Like other stereotypes, it can wound or irritate readers, and it indicates the writer's thoughtlessness or unfairness. The following box suggests ways of eliminating sexist language.

Podcast

Eliminating sexist language

■ **Avoid demeaning and patronizing language**—for instance, identifying women and men differently or trivializing either gender:

Sexist	Dr. Keith Kim and Lydia Hawkins wrote the article.
Revised	Dr. Keith Kim and Dr. Lydia Hawkins wrote the article.
Revised	Keith Kim and Lydia Hawkins wrote the article.

Sexist	Ladies are entering formerly male occupations.
Revised	Women are entering formerly male occupations.

■ **Avoid occupational or social stereotypes**, assuming that a role or profession is exclusively male or female:

Sexist	The considerate doctor commends a nurse when she provides his patients with good care.
Revised	The considerate doctor commends a nurse who provides good care for patients.

■ **Avoid referring needlessly to gender:**

Sexist   Marie Curie, <u>a woman chemist</u>, discovered radium.

Revised   Marie Curie, a chemist, discovered radium.

Sexist   The patients were tended by <u>a male nurse</u>.

Revised   The patients were tended by a nurse.

However, don't overcorrect by avoiding appropriate references to gender: *Pregnant women* [not *people*] *should avoid drinking alcohol.*

■ **Avoid using *man* or words containing *man* to refer to all human beings.** Here are a few alternatives:

businessman	businessperson
chairman	chair, chairperson
congressman	congressperson, legislator
craftsman	craftsperson, artisan
layman	layperson
mankind	humankind, humanity, human beings, people
policeman	police officer
salesman	salesperson

Sexist   <u>Man</u> has not reached the limits of social justice.

Revised   Humankind [or Humanity] has not reached the limits of social justice.

Sexist   The furniture consists of <u>manmade</u> materials.

Revised   The furniture consists of synthetic materials.

■ **Avoid the generic *he*,** the male pronoun used to refer to both genders. (See also pp. 333–34.)

Sexist   The newborn child explores <u>his</u> world.

Revised   Newborn children explore their world. [Use the plural for the pronoun and the word it refers to.]

Revised   The newborn child explores the world. [Avoid the pronoun altogether.]

Revised   The newborn child explores his or her world. [Substitute male and female pronouns.]

Use the last option sparingly—only once in a group of sentences and only to stress the singular individual.

⟨CULTURE ⟩
⟨LANGUAGE⟩ Forms of address vary widely from culture to culture. In some cultures, for instance, one shows respect by referring to all older women as if they were married, using the equivalent of the title *Mrs.* Usage in the United States is changing toward making no assumptions about marital status, rank, or other characteristics—for instance, using the title *Ms.* for a woman unless she is known to prefer *Mrs.* or *Miss.*

appr
37i

3 Using appropriate labels

We often need to label groups: *swimmers, politicians, mothers, Christians, westerners, students.* But labels can be shorthand stereotypes that slight the person labeled and ignore the preferences of the group members themselves. Showing sensitivity when applying labels reveals you to be alert to readers' needs and concerns. Although sometimes dismissed as "political correctness," such sensitivity hurts no one and helps gain your readers' trust and respect.

Video
tutorial

- Avoid labels that (intentionally or not) insult the person or group you refer to. A person with emotional problems is not a *mental patient.* A person with cancer is not a *cancer victim.* A person using a wheelchair is not *wheelchair-bound.*
- Use names for racial, ethnic, and other groups that reflect the preferences of each group's members, or at least many of them. Examples of current preferences include *African American* or *black* and *people with disabilities* (rather than *the disabled* or *the handicapped*). But labels change often. To learn how a group's members wish to be labeled, ask them directly, attend to usage in reputable periodicals, or check a recent dictionary.
- Identify a person's group only when it is relevant to the point you're making. Consider the context of the label: Is it a necessary piece of information? If not, don't use it.

A helpful reference for appropriate labels is *Guidelines for Bias-Free Writing,* by Marilyn Schwartz and the Task Force on Bias-Free Language of the Association of American University Presses.

Exercise 37.1 Revising: Appropriate words

Rewrite the following sentences as needed for standard American English. Consult a dictionary to determine whether particular words are appropriate and to find suitable substitutes.

Exercise

> *Example:*
> If negotiators blow up during contract discussions, they may mess up chances for a settlement.
>
> If negotiators <u>become angry</u> during contract discussions, they may <u>harm</u> chances for a settlement.

1. Acquired immune deficiency syndrome (AIDS) is a major deal all over the world.
2. The disease gets around primarily by sexual intercourse, exchange of bodily fluids, shared needles, and blood transfusions.
3. Those who think the disease is limited to homos, mainliners, and foreigners are quite mistaken.
4. Stats suggest that in the United States one in every five hundred college kids carries the virus.
5. A person with AIDS does not deserve to be subjected to exclusionary behavior or callousness on the part of his fellow citizens. Instead, he

has the necessity for all the compassion, medical care, and financial assistance due those who are in the extremity of illness.

6. An AIDS victim often sees a team of doctors or a single doctor with a specialized practice.
7. The doctor may help his patients by obtaining social services for them as well as by providing medical care.
8. The AIDS sufferer who loses his job may need public assistance.
9. For someone who is very ill, a full-time nurse may be necessary. She can administer medications and make the sick person as comfortable as possible.
10. Some people with AIDS have insurance, but others lack the bucks for premiums.

38

Using Exact Language

To write clearly and effectively, you will want to find the words that fit your meaning exactly and convey your attitude precisely. Don't worry too much about choosing exact words while you are drafting an essay. If the right word doesn't come to you, leave a blank. Revision (p. 58) or editing (p. 67) is the stage to consider tone, specificity, and precision.

Grammar checkers A grammar checker can provide some help with inexact language. For instance, you can set it to flag commonly confused words (such as *continuous/continual*), misused prepositions in idioms (such as *accuse for* instead of *accuse of*), and clichés. (See p. 72 on setting a checker.) But the checker can flag only words stored in its dictionary. It can't help you at all with inappropriate connotation, excessive abstraction, or other problems discussed in this chapter.

38a Using a dictionary and a thesaurus

A dictionary and a thesaurus can help you choose exact words and avoid errors in word use.

mycomplab

Visit *mycomplab.com* for the eText and for resources on exact language.

Avoiding common mistakes in word choice

■ **Make sure words have the meanings you intend.** Check a dictionary if you aren't sure of a word's meanings.

Incorrect   Increased global temperatures will effect everyone.

Revised   Increased global temperatures will affect everyone.

■ **Before you select a word suggested by a spelling checker, make sure it's the one you mean.** (See p. 71 for more on spelling checkers.)

Incorrect   The results were defiant: the experiment was a failure.

Revised   The results were definite: the experiment was a failure.

■ **Use idioms correctly.** (See pp. 540–41 for more on idioms.)

Incorrect   The planners agreed over the details of the evacuation plan.

Revised   The planners agreed **on** the details of the evacuation plan.

---

1 Using a dictionary

Video
tutorial

A dictionary defines words and provides pronunciation, grammatical functions, etymology (word history), and other information. The following sample is from *Merriam-Webster's Collegiate Dictionary*:

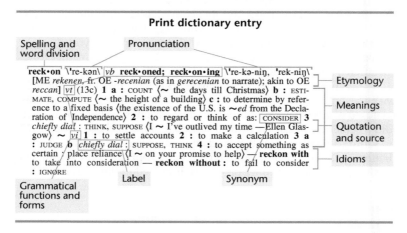

Print dictionary entry

This sample is from a print dictionary, but Merriam-Webster and others provide online dictionaries that give the same information in less abbreviated form and also allow you to hear how a word is pronounced. Here is part of the entry for *reckon* from *Merriam-Webster Online* (*merriam-webster.com*):

Partial online dictionary entry

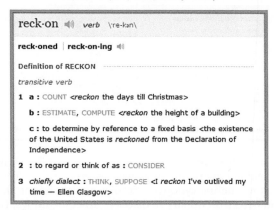

reck·on 🔊 *verb* \ˈre-kən\

reck·oned | **reck·on·ing** 🔊

Definition of RECKON ....

transitive verb

1 a : COUNT <*reckon* the days till Christmas>

  b : ESTIMATE, COMPUTE <*reckon* the height of a building>

  c : to determine by reference to a fixed basis <the existence of the United States is *reckoned* from the Declaration of Independence>

2 : to regard or think of as : CONSIDER

3 *chiefly dialect* : THINK, SUPPOSE <I *reckon* I've outlived my time — Ellen Glasgow>

Other useful online sites are *Dictionary.com* (*dictionary.com*) and *The Free Dictionary* (*thefreedictionary.com*), which provide entries from several dictionaries at once. *Dictionary.com* also offers a translater that converts text between languages, such as English to Spanish. *The Free Dictionary* offers dictionaries in more than a dozen languages besides English.

If you prefer a print dictionary, good ones, in addition to *Merriam-Webster's Collegiate*, include *American Heritage College Dictionary*, *Random House Webster's College Dictionary*, and *Webster's New World College Dictionary*. Some of these books come with CD versions as well.

⟨CULTURE + LANGUAGE⟩ If English is not your native language, you probably should have a dictionary prepared especially for students using English as a second language (ESL). Such a dictionary contains special information on prepositions, count versus noncount nouns, and many other matters. The following are reliable print ESL dictionaries, each with an online version at the URL in parentheses: *Longman Dictionary of Contemporary English* (*ldoceonline.com*), *Oxford Advanced Learner's Dictionary* (*oxfordadvancedlearnersdictionary.com*), *Merriam-Webster Advanced Learner's English Dictionary* (*learnersdictionary.com*).

2 Using a thesaurus

To find a word with the exact shade of meaning you intend, you may want to consult a thesaurus, or collection of **synonyms**—words with approximately the same meaning. A thesaurus lists most imaginable synonyms for thousand of words. For instance, here is the listing of synonyms for one meaning of *reckon* on the site *Thesaurus.com* (*thesaurus.com*):

exact
38b

Partial online thesaurus entry

Main Entry:	**reckon**
Part of Speech:	*verb*
Definition:	add up; evaluate
Synonyms:	account, appraise, approximate, calculate, call, cast, cipher, compute, conjecture, consider, count, count heads, count noses, deem, enumerate, esteem, estimate, figure, figure out, foot, gauge, guess, hold, judge, keep tabs, look upon, number, place, put, rate, regard, run down, square, sum, surmise, take account of, tally, think of, tick off, tot, tot up, total, tote, tote up, view

Because a thesaurus aims to open up possibilities, its lists of synonyms include approximate as well as precise matches. The thesaurus does not define synonyms or distinguish among them, however, so you need a dictionary to discover exact meanings. In general, don't use a word from a thesaurus—even one you like the sound of—until you are sure of its appropriateness for your meaning.

Exercise

Exercise 38.1 Using a dictionary

Consult your dictionary on five of the following words. For each word, write down (*a*) the division into syllables, (*b*) the pronunciation, (*c*) the grammatical functions and forms, (*d*) the etymology, (*e*) each meaning, and (*f*) any special uses indicated by labels. Finally, use the word in at least two sentences of your own.

1. depreciation	4. manifest	7. potlatch	10. toxic
2. secretary	5. assassin	8. plain (*adj.*)	11. steal
3. grammar	6. astrology	9. ceremony	12. obelisk

38b Using the right word for your meaning

Precisely expressing your meaning requires understanding both the denotations and the connotations of words. A word's **denotation** is the thing or idea it refers to, the meaning listed in the dictionary without reference to the emotional associations it may arouse in a reader. Using words according to their established denotations is essential if readers are to grasp your meaning. Here are a few guidelines:

- Consult a dictionary whenever you are unsure of a word's meaning.
- Distinguish between similar-sounding words that have widely different denotations:

Inexact   Older people often suffer infirmaries [places for the sick].

Exact   Older people often suffer infirmities [disabilities].

Some words, called **homonyms** (from the Greek meaning "same name"), sound exactly alike but differ in meaning: for example, *principal/principle* and *rain/reign/rein*. (See pp. 554–55 for a list of commonly confused homonyms.)

■ **Distinguish between words with related but distinct denotations:**

Inexact	Television commercials <u>continuously</u> [unceasingly] interrupt programming.
Exact	Television commercials <u>continually</u> [regularly] interrupt programming.

In addition to their emotion-free denotations, many words carry related meanings that evoke specific feelings. These **connotations** can shape readers' responses and are thus a powerful tool for writers. (At the same time they are a potential snare for readers. See p. 195.) Some connotations are personal: the word *dog*, for instance, may have negative connotations for the letter carrier who has been bitten three times. Usually, though, people agree about connotations. The following word pairs are just a few of many that have related denotations but very different connotations:

pride: sense of self-worth
vanity: excessive regard for oneself

firm: steady, unchanging, unyielding
stubborn: unreasonable, bullheaded

enthusiasm: excitement
mania: excessive interest or desire

Understanding connotation is especially important in choosing among synonyms, or words with approximately the same meanings. For instance, *cry* and *weep* both denote the shedding of tears, but *cry* more than *weep* connotes a sobbing sound accompanying the tears. *Sob* itself connotes broken, gasping crying, with tears, whereas *wail* connotes sustained sound, perhaps without tears.

Exercise 38.2 Revising: Denotation

Revise any underlined word below that is not used according to its established denotation. Circle any word used correctly. Consult a dictionary if you are uncertain of a word's precise meaning.

✳
Exercise

Example:
Sam and Dave are going to Bermuda and Hauppauge, <u>respectfully</u>, for spring vacation.
Sam and Dave are going to Bermuda and Hauppauge, <u>respectively</u>, for spring vacation.

1. Maxine Hong Kingston was <u>rewarded</u> many prizes for her first two books, *The Woman Warrior* and *China Men*.
2. Kingston <u>sites</u> her mother's tales about ancestors and ancient Chinese customs as the sources of these memoirs.
3. In her childhood Kingston was greatly <u>effected</u> by her mother's tale about a pregnant aunt who was <u>ostracized</u> by villagers.

4. The aunt gained <u>avengeance</u> by drowning herself in the village's water supply.
5. Kingston decided to make her nameless relative <u>infamous</u> by giving her <u>immortality</u> in *The Woman Warrior*.

Exercise

Exercise 38.3 Considering the connotations of words

Fill the blank in each sentence below with the most appropriate word from the list in parentheses. Consult a dictionary to be sure of your choice.

Example:

Channel 5 _____ Oshu the winner before the polls closed. (*advertised, declared, broadcast, promulgated*)

Channel 5 <u>declared</u> Oshu the winner before the polls closed.

1. AIDS is a serious health _____. (*problem, worry, difficulty, plight*)
2. Once the virus has entered the blood system, it _____ T-cells. (*murders, destroys, slaughters, executes*)
3. The _____ of T-cells is to combat infections. (*ambition, function, aim, goal*)
4. Without enough T-cells, the body is nearly _____ against infections. (*defenseless, hopeless, desperate*)
5. To prevent exposure to the disease, one should be especially _____ in sexual relationships. (*chary, circumspect, cautious, calculating*)

38c Balancing the abstract and concrete, the general and specific

To understand a subject as you understand it, your readers need ample guidance from your words. When you describe a building as *beautiful* and nothing more, you force readers to provide their own ideas of what makes a building beautiful. If readers bother (and they may not), they surely will not conjure up the image you had in mind. Use words to tell readers what you want them to know, that the beautiful building is *a sleek, silver skyscraper with blue-tinted windows*, for instance, or *a Victorian brick courthouse with tall, arched windows*.

Clear, exact writing balances abstract and general words, which outline ideas and objects, with concrete and specific words, which sharpen and solidify.

- Abstract words name ideas: *beauty, inflation, management, culture, liberal*. Concrete words name qualities and things we can know by our five senses of sight, hearing, touch, taste, and smell: *sleek, humming, rough, salty, musty*.
- General words name classes or groups of things, such as *buildings, weather,* and *birds*, and include all the varieties of the class. Specific words limit a general class, such as *buildings*, by naming a variety, such as *skyscraper, Victorian courthouse,* or *hut*.

Note that *general* and *specific* are relative terms: the same word may be more general than some words but more specific than others.

General
weather   bird
rain   parrot
downpour   cockatoo
sudden downpour   my pet cockatoo Moyshe
Specific

Abstract and general words are useful in the broad statements that set the course for your writing:

> The wild horse in America has a <u>romantic</u> history.
> We must be <u>free</u> from <u>government interference</u> in our <u>affairs</u>.
> <u>Relations</u> between the sexes today are only a <u>little</u> more <u>relaxed</u> than they were in the past.

But the sentences following these would have to develop the ideas with concrete and specific details. When your meaning calls for an abstract or general word, make sure you define it, explain it, and narrow it. Look at how concrete and specific information turns vague sentences into exact ones in the following examples:

> Vague   The size of his hands made his smallness real. [How big were his hands? How small was he?]
>
> Exact   Not until I saw his delicate, doll-like hands did I realize that he stood a full head shorter than most other men.

> Vague   The long flood caused a lot of awful destruction in the town. [How long did the flood last? What destruction did it cause? Why was the destruction awful?]
>
> Exact   The flood waters, which rose swiftly and then stayed stubbornly high for days, killed at least six townspeople and made life a misery for the hundreds who had to evacuate their ruined homes and stores.

Note You can use your computer's Find function to help you find and revise abstract and general words that you tend to overuse. Examples of such words might include *nice, interesting, things, very, good, a lot, a little,* and *some.*

Exercise 38.4   Revising: Concrete and specific words

Make the following paragraph vivid by expanding the sentences with appropriate details of your own choosing. Substitute concrete and specific words for the abstract and general ones that are underlined.

Exercise

> I remember <u>clearly</u> how <u>awful</u> I felt the first time I <u>attended</u> Mrs. Murphy's second-grade class. I had <u>recently</u> moved from a <u>small</u> town in Missouri to a <u>crowded</u> suburb of Chicago. My new school looked <u>big</u> from the outside and seemed <u>dark</u> inside as I <u>walked</u> down the <u>long</u> corridor toward the classroom. The class was <u>noisy</u> as I neared the door;

Exercise

but when I <u>entered</u>, <u>everyone</u> became <u>quiet</u> and <u>looked</u> at me. I felt uncomfortable and <u>wanted</u> a place to hide. However, in a <u>loud</u> voice Mrs. Murphy <u>directed</u> me to the front of the room to introduce myself.

Exercise 38.5   Using concrete and specific words

For each abstract or general word below, give at least two other words or phrases that illustrate increasing specificity or concreteness. Consult a dictionary as needed. Use the most specific or concrete word from each group in a sentence of your own.

Example:

awake, <u>watchful</u>, <u>vigilant</u>

<u>Vigilant</u> guards patrol the buildings.

1. fabric
2. delicious
3. car
4. narrow-minded
5. reach (*verb*)
6. green
7. walk (*verb*)
8. flower
9. serious
10. pretty
11. teacher
12. nice
13. virtue
14. angry
15. crime

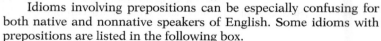

38d Using idioms

   Idioms are expressions in any language whose meanings cannot be determined simply from the words in them or whose component words cannot be predicted by any rule of grammar; often, they violate conventional grammar. Examples of English idioms include *put up with, plug away at,* and *make off with.*

Video
tutorial

   Idioms involving prepositions can be especially confusing for both native and nonnative speakers of English. Some idioms with prepositions are listed in the following box.

Exercise

Idioms with prepositions

abide <u>by</u> a rule
    <u>in</u> a place or state
accords <u>with</u>
according <u>to</u>
accuse <u>of</u> a crime
adapt <u>from</u> a source
    <u>to</u> a situation
afraid <u>of</u>
agree <u>on</u> a plan as a group
    <u>to</u> someone else's plan
    <u>with</u> a person
angry <u>with</u>
aware <u>of</u>
based <u>on</u>

capable <u>of</u>
certain <u>of</u>
charge <u>for</u> a purchase
    <u>with</u> a crime
concur <u>in</u> an opinion
    <u>with</u> a person
contend <u>for</u> a principle or prize
    <u>with</u> an obstacle
dependent <u>on</u>
differ <u>about</u> or <u>over</u> a question
    <u>from</u> in some quality
    <u>with</u> a person
disappointed <u>by</u> or <u>in</u> a person
    <u>in</u> or <u>with</u> a thing

familiar <u>with</u>	opposed <u>to</u>
identical <u>with</u> or <u>to</u>	part <u>from</u> a person
impatient <u>for</u> a raise	<u>with</u> a possession
<u>with</u> a person	prior <u>to</u>
independent <u>of</u>	proud <u>of</u>
infer <u>from</u>	related <u>to</u>
inferior <u>to</u>	rewarded <u>by</u> the judge
involved <u>in</u> a task	<u>for</u> something done
<u>with</u> a person	<u>with</u> a gift
oblivious <u>of</u> or <u>to</u> one's surroundings	similar <u>to</u>
<u>of</u> something forgotten	superior <u>to</u>
occupied <u>by</u> a person	wait <u>at</u> a place
<u>in</u> study	<u>for</u> a train, a person
<u>with</u> a thing	<u>on</u> a customer

exact
38d

CULTURE LANGUAGE If you are learning standard American English, you may find its prepositions difficult: their meanings can shift depending on context, and they have many idiomatic uses. In mastering the prepositions of standard English, you probably can't avoid memorization. But you can help yourself by memorizing related groups, such as those below for the very common *at, in, on, for,* and *since.*

Video
tutorial

At, in, or *on* in expressions of time

- Use *at* before actual clock time: *at 8:30.*
- Use *in* before a month, year, century, or period: *in April, in 2012, in the twenty-first century, in the next month.*
- Use *on* before a day or date: *on Tuesday, on August 3, on Labor Day.*

At, in, or *on* in expressions of place

- Use *at* before a specific place or address: *at the school, at 511 Iris Street.*
- Use *in* before a place with limits or before a city, state, country, or continent: *in the house, in a box, in Tulsa, in China, in Asia.*
- Use *on* to mean "supported by" or "touching the surface of": *on the table, on Iris Street, on page 150.*

For or *since* in expressions of time

- Use *for* before a period of time: *for an hour, for two years.*
- Use *since* before a specific point in time: *since 1999, since Friday.*

A dictionary of English as a second language is the best source for the meanings of prepositions; see the recommendations on page 535. In addition, some reference works focus on prepositions. See *Essential Idioms in English* or volume 1 (*Verbs with Prepositions and Particles*) of the *Oxford Dictionary of Current Idiomatic English.*

exact

38e

Exercise

Exercise 38.6 Using prepositions in idioms

Insert the preposition that correctly completes each idiom in the following sentences. Consult the box on pages 540–41 or a dictionary as needed.

> *Example:*
>
> I disagree _____ many feminists who say women should not be homemakers.
>
> I disagree with many feminists who say women should not be homemakers.

1. Children are waiting longer to become independent _____ their parents.
2. According _____ US Census data for young adults ages eighteen to twenty-four, 57% of men and 47% of women live full-time with their parents.
3. Some of these adult children are dependent _____ their parents financially.
4. In other cases, the parents charge their children _____ housing, food, and other living expenses.
5. Many adult children are financially capable _____ living independently but prefer to save money rather than contend _____ high housing costs.

38e Using figurative language

Figurative language (or a **figure of speech**) departs from the literal meanings (the denotations) of words, usually by comparing very different ideas or objects:

> Literal   As I try to write, I can think of nothing to say.
> Figurative As I try to write, my mind is a slab of black slate.

When you use figurative language imaginatively and carefully, it can capture your meaning more precisely and emotionally than literal language.

Figurative language is common in speech. Having *slept like a log*, you may get up to find it *raining cats and dogs*. But the rapid exchange of speech leaves little time for inventiveness, and most figures of daily conversation, like those above, are worn and hackneyed. Writing gives you time to reject the tired figure and to search out fresh, concrete words and phrases.

The two most common figures of speech are the simile and the metaphor. Both compare two things of different classes, often one abstract and the other concrete. A **simile** makes the comparison explicit and usually begins with *like* or *as*:

> Whenever we grow, we tend to feel it, as a young seed must feel the weight and inertia of the earth when it seeks to break out of its shell on its way to becoming a plant.   —Alice Walker

> To hold America in one's thoughts is like holding a love letter in one's hand—it has so special a meaning.   —E. B. White

Instead of stating a comparison, a **metaphor** implies it, omitting such words as *like* or *as*:

> I cannot and will not cut my conscience to fit this year's fashions.
> —Lillian Hellman

> A school is a hopper into which children are heaved while they are young and tender; therein they are pressed into certain standard shapes and covered from head to heels with official rubber stamps.
> —H. L. Mencken

Two other figures of speech are personification and hyperbole. **Personification** treats ideas and objects as if they were human:

> The economy consumes my money and gives me little in return.

> I could hear the whisper of snowflakes, nudging each other as they fell.

Hyperbole deliberately exaggerates:

> She appeared in a mile of billowing chiffon, flashing a rhinestone as big as an ostrich egg.

> He yelled so loud that his voice carried to the next county.

To be successful, figurative language must be fresh and unstrained, calling attention not to itself but to the writer's meaning. One kind of figurative language gone wrong is the **mixed metaphor**, in which the writer combines two or more incompatible figures. Since metaphors often generate visual images in the reader's mind, a mixed metaphor can be laughable:

> Mixed   Various thorny problems that we try to sweep under the rug continue to bob up all the same.

To revise a mixed metaphor, follow through consistently with just one image:

> Improved   Various thorny problems that we try to weed out continue to thrive all the same.

Exercise 38.7 Analyzing figurative language

Identify each figure of speech in the following sentences as a simile or a metaphor, and analyze how it adds to the writer's meaning.

Exercise

1. A distant airplane, a delta wing out of nightmare, made a gliding shadow on the creek's bottom that looked like a stingray crossing upstream. —Annie Dillard
2. Her roots ran deep into the earth, and from those roots she drew strength enough to hold still against all the forces of chance and disorder. —N. Scott Momaday
3. As a member of the winning team (the graduating class of 1940) I had outdistanced unpleasant sensations by miles. I was headed for the freedom of open fields. —Maya Angelou
4. All artists quiver under the lash of adverse criticism.
—Catherine Drinker Bowen

Exercise

5. Every writer, in a roomful of writers, wants to be the best, and the judge, or umpire, or referee is soon overwhelmed and shouted down like a chickadee trying to take charge of a caucus of crows.

—James Thurber

Exercise 38.8 Using figurative language

Invent appropriate figurative language of your own (simile, metaphor, hyperbole, or personification) to describe each of the following scenes or qualities, and use each figure in a sentence.

Example:

The attraction of a lake on a hot day
The small waves <u>like fingers beckoned</u> us irresistibly.

1. The sound of a kindergarten classroom
2. People waiting in line to buy tickets to a rock concert
3. The politeness of strangers meeting for the first time
4. A streetlight seen through dense fog
5. The effect of watching television for ten hours straight

38f Using fresh, not trite, expressions

Trite expressions, or **clichés,** are phrases so old and so often repeated that they have become stale. They include the following:

acid test	ladder of success
add insult to injury	moving experience
better late than never	needle in a haystack
beyond the shadow of a doubt	point with pride
brought back to reality	ripe old age
cold, hard facts	shoulder the burden
cool as a cucumber	smart as a whip
crushing blow	sneaking suspicion
easier said than done	sober as a judge
face the music	stand in awe
flat as a pancake	strong as an ox
green with envy	thin as a rail
hard as a rock	tired but happy
heavy as lead	tried and true
hit the nail on the head	untimely death
hour of need	wise as an owl

Besides these old phrases, stale writing may also depend on fashionable words that are losing their effect: for instance, *lifestyle, enhance, awesome, fantastic,* and *caring.*

Many trite expressions were once fresh and forceful, but constant use has dulled them. They, in turn, will dull your writing by suggesting that you have not thought about what you are saying and have resorted to the easiest phrase.

Clichés may slide into your drafts while you are trying to express your meaning. In editing, then, be wary of any expression you have heard or used before. Substitute fresh words of your own or restate the idea in plain language.

Trite | A healthful <u>lifestyle enhances</u> your ability to <u>go for the gold</u> and allows you to <u>enjoy life to the fullest</u>.

Revised | <u>Living healthfully helps</u> you <u>perform well</u> and enjoy life <u>thoroughly</u>.

Exercise 38.9 Revising: Trite expressions

Revise the following sentences to eliminate trite expressions.

Exercise

Example:

The basketball team had almost seized victory, but it faced the test of truth in the last quarter of the game.

The basketball team <u>seemed about to win</u>, but the <u>real test</u> came in the last quarter of the game.

1. The disastrous consequences of the war have shaken the small nation to its roots.
2. Prices for food have shot sky high, and citizens have sneaking suspicions that others are making a killing on the black market.
3. Medical supplies are so few and far between that even civilians who are as sick as dogs cannot get treatment.
4. With most men fighting or injured or killed, women have had to bite the bullet and bear the men's burden in farming and manufacturing.
5. Last but not least, the war's heavy drain on the nation's pocketbook has left the economy in a shambles.

39

Writing Concisely

Concise writing makes every word count. Conciseness is not the same as mere brevity: detail and originality should not be cut along with needless words. Rather, the length of an expression should be appropriate to the thought.

You may find yourself writing wordily when you are unsure of your subject or when your thoughts are tangled. It's fine, even

mycomplab

Visit *mycomplab.com* for the eText and for resources and more exercises on writing concisely.

Video
tutorial

Ways to achieve conciseness

Wordy (87 words)

The highly pressured nature of critical-care nursing is due to the fact that the patients have life-threatening illnesses. Critical-care nurses must have possession of steady nerves to care for patients who are critically ill and very sick. The nurses must also have possession of interpersonal skills. They must also have medical skills. It is considered by most health-care professionals that these nurses are essential if there is to be improvement of patients who are now in critical care from that status to the status of intermediate care.

Focus on subject and verb, and cut or shorten empty words and phrases.

Avoid nouns made from verbs.

Cut unneeded repetition.

Combine sentences.

Change passive voice to active voice.

Revise *there is* constructions.

Cut unneeded repetition, and reduce clauses and phrases.

Concise (37 words)

Critical-care nursing is highly pressured because the patients have life-threatening illnesses. Critical-care nurses must possess steady nerves and interpersonal and medical skills. Most health-care professionals consider these nurses essential if patients are to improve to intermediate care.

necessary, to stumble and grope while drafting. But you should straighten out your ideas and eliminate wordiness during revision and editing.

Grammar checkers Any grammar checker will identify at least some wordy structures, such as repeated words, weak verbs, passive voice, and *there is* and *it is* constructions. But a checker can't identify all potentially wordy structures, nor can it tell you whether a structure is appropriate for your ideas.

CULTURE LANGUAGE As you'll see in this chapter's examples, wordiness is not a problem of incorrect grammar. A sentence may be perfectly grammatical but still contain unneeded words that make it unclear or awkward.

39a Focusing on the subject and verb

Exercise

Using the subjects and verbs of your sentences for the key actors and actions will reduce words and emphasize important ideas. (See pp. 400–02 for more on this topic.)

Wordy	The <u>reason</u> why most of the country shifts to daylight time <u>is</u> that summer days are much longer than winter days.
Concise	Most of the <u>country</u> <u>shifts</u> to daylight time because summer days are much longer than winter days.

Focusing on subjects and verbs will also help you avoid several other causes of wordiness discussed further on pages 400–02:

Nouns made from verbs

Wordy	The <u>occurrence</u> of the winter solstice, the shortest day of the year, <u>is</u> an event occurring about December 22.
Concise	The winter <u>solstice</u>, the shortest day of the year, <u>occurs</u> about December 22.

Weak verbs

Wordy	The earth's axis <u>has</u> a tilt as the planet <u>is</u> in orbit around the sun so that the northern and southern hemispheres <u>are</u> alternately in alignment toward the sun.
Concise	The earth's axis <u>tilts</u> as the planet <u>orbits</u> the sun so that the northern and southern hemispheres alternately <u>align</u> toward the sun.

Passive voice

Wordy	During its winter the northern hemisphere <u>is tilted</u> farthest away from the sun, so the nights <u>are made</u> longer and the days <u>are made</u> shorter.
Concise	During its winter the northern hemisphere <u>tilts</u> away from the sun, which <u>makes</u> the nights longer and the days shorter.

See also pages 320–21 on changing the passive voice to the active voice, as in the example above.

39b Cutting or shortening empty words and phrases

Empty words and phrases walk in place, gaining little or nothing in meaning. When you cut or shorten them, your writing will move faster and work harder.

Many empty phrases can be cut entirely:

Exercise

all things considered	in a manner of speaking
as far as I'm concerned	in my opinion
for all intents and purposes	last but not least
for the most part	more or less

Wordy	<u>In my opinion</u>, the council's proposal to improve the city center is inadequate, <u>all things considered</u>.
Concise	The council's proposal to improve the city center is inadequate.

Other empty words can be cut along with some words around them:

angle	character	kind	situation
area	element	manner	thing
aspect	factor	nature	type
case	field		

Wordy   The <u>type</u> of large expenditures on advertising that manufacturers must make is a very important <u>aspect</u> of the cost of detergents.

Concise Manufacturers' large advertising expenditures increase the cost of detergents.

Still other empty phrases can be reduced from several words to a single word:

For	Substitute
at all times	always
at the present time	now
at this point in time	now
in today's society	now
in the nature of	like
for the purpose of	for
in order to	to
until such time as	until
for the reason that	because
due to the fact that	because
because of the fact that	because
by virtue of the fact that	because
despite the fact that	although
in the event that	if
by means of	by
in the final analysis	finally

Wordy   <u>At this point in time</u>, the software is expensive <u>due to the fact that</u> it has no competition.

Corcise The software is expensive <u>now</u> <u>because</u> it has no competition.

Exercise 39.1   Revising: Subjects and verbs; empty words and phrases

Exercise

Revise the following sentences to achieve conciseness by focusing on subjects and verbs and by cutting or reducing empty words and phrases. See also page 402 for an additional exercise in focusing on subjects and verbs.

Example:

I made college my destination because of many factors, but most of all because of the fact that I want a career in medicine.

I <u>came</u> to college <u>mainly because</u> I want a career in medicine.

1. *Gerrymandering* refers to a situation in which the lines of a voting district are redrawn so that a particular party or ethnic group has benefits.

2. The name is a reference to the fact that Elbridge Gerry, the governor of Massachusetts in 1812, redrew voting districts in Essex County.
3. On the map one new district was seen to resemble something in the nature of a salamander.
4. Upon seeing the map, a man who was for all intents and purposes a critic of Governor Gerry's administration cried out, "Gerrymander!"
5. At the present time, changes may be made in the character of a district's voting pattern by a political group by gerrymandering to achieve the exclusion of rival groups' supporters.

39c   Cutting unnecessary repetition

Planned repetition and restatement can make writing more coherent (p. 91) or emphatic (p. 406). But unnecessary repetition weakens sentences:

Video
tutorial

| Wordy | Many <u>unskilled</u> workers <u>without training in a particular job</u> are unemployed <u>and do not have any work.</u> |
| Concise | Many unskilled workers are unemployed. |

The use of one word two different ways within a sentence is confusing:

| Confusing | Preschool instructors play a <u>role</u> in the child's understanding of male and female <u>roles.</u> |
| Clear | Preschool instructors <u>contribute</u> to the child's understanding of male and female <u>roles.</u> |

The simplest kind of useless repetition is the phrase that says the same thing twice. In the following examples, the unneeded words are underlined:

biography <u>of his life</u>
circle <u>around</u>
consensus <u>of opinion</u>
continue <u>on</u>
cooperate <u>together</u>
few <u>in number</u>
final completion
frank and honest exchange
the future <u>to come</u>

habitual custom
important [basic] essentials
large <u>in size</u>
puzzling <u>in nature</u>
repeat <u>again</u>
return <u>again</u>
revert <u>back</u>
square [round] <u>in shape</u>
surrounding circumstances

CULTURE LANGUAGE Phrases like those above are redundant because the main word already implies the underlined word or words. The repetition is not emphatic but tedious. A dictionary will tell you what meanings a word implies. *Assassinate,* for instance, means "murder someone well known," so the following sentence is redundant: *Abraham Lincoln was <u>assassinated and killed</u> at a theater.*

Exercise

Exercise 39.2 Revising: Unnecessary repetition

Revise the following sentences to achieve conciseness. Concentrate on eliminating repetition and redundancy.

Example:

Because the circumstances surrounding the cancellation of classes were murky and unclear, the editor of the student newspaper assigned a staff reporter to investigate and file a report on the circumstances.

Because the circumstances leading to the cancellation of classes were unclear, the editor of the student newspaper assigned a staffer to investigate and report the story.

1. Some Vietnam veterans coming back to the United States after their tours of duty in Vietnam had problems readjusting again to life in America.
2. Afflicted with post-traumatic stress disorder, a psychological disorder that sometimes arises after a trauma, some veterans had psychological problems that caused them to have trouble holding jobs and maintaining relationships.
3. Some who used to use drugs in Vietnam could not break their drug habits after they returned back to the United States.
4. The few veterans who committed crimes and violent acts gained so much notoriety and fame that many Americans thought all veterans were crazy, insane maniacs.
5. As a result of such stereotyping of Vietnam-era veterans, veterans are included in the same antidiscrimination laws that protect other victims of discrimination.

39d Reducing clauses to phrases, phrases to single words

Modifiers—subordinate clauses, phrases, and single words—can be expanded or contracted depending on the emphasis you want to achieve. (See pp. 264–77 on phrases and clauses and 413–15 on working with modifiers.) When editing your sentences, consider whether any modifiers can be reduced without loss of emphasis or clarity:

Wordy   The weight-loss industry faces new competition from lipolysis, which is a cosmetic procedure that is relatively noninvasive.

Concise   The weight-loss industry faces new competition from lipolysis, a relatively noninvasive cosmetic procedure.

39e Revising *there is* and *it is* constructions

You can postpone the sentence subject with the words *there* and *it*: *There are three points made in the text. It was not fair that only seniors could vote.* (See p. 283.) These constructions can be useful to emphasize the subject (as when introducing it for the first time) or to indicate a change in direction. But often they just add words and weaken sentences:

w
39g

| Wordy | There is a completely noninvasive laser treatment that makes people thinner by rupturing fat cells and releasing the fat into the spaces between cells. It is the expectation of some doctors that the procedure will replace liposuction. |
| Concise | A completely noninvasive laser treatment makes people thinner by rupturing fat cells and releasing the fat into the spaces between cells. Some doctors expect that the procedure will replace liposuction. |

39f Combining sentences

Often the information in two or more sentences can be combined into one tight sentence:

Video
tutorial

| Wordy | People who receive fat-releasing laser treatments can lose inches from their waists. They can also lose inches from their hips and thighs. They do not lose weight. The released fat remains in their bodies. |
| Concise | People who receive fat-releasing laser treatments can lose inches from their waists, hips, and thighs; but they do not lose weight because the released fat remains in their bodies. |

A number of exercises in this handbook give you practice in sentence combining. For a list, see "Sentence combining" in the book's index.

39g Rewriting jargon

Jargon can refer to the special vocabulary of any discipline or profession (see p. 528). But the term has also come to describe vague, inflated language that is overcomplicated, even incomprehensible. When it comes from government or business, we call it *bureaucratese.*

| Jargon | The weekly social gatherings stimulate networking by members of management from various divisions, with the aim of developing contacts and maximizing the flow of creative information. |
| Translation | The weekly parties give managers from different divisions a chance to meet and to share ideas. |

Exercise 39.3 Revising: Conciseness
Rewrite each of the following passages into a single concise sentence, using the techniques described in this chapter.

Exercise

Example:

He was taking some exercise in the park. Then several thugs were suddenly ahead of him in his path.

He was exercising [or jogging or strolling] in the park when several thugs suddenly loomed in his path.

1. Chewing gum was originally introduced to the United States by Antonio López de Santa Anna. He was the Mexican general.
2. After he had been defeated by the Texans in 1845, the general, who was exiled, made the choice to settle in New York.
3. A piece of chicle had been stashed by the general in his baggage. Chicle is the dried milky sap of the Mexican sapodilla tree.
4. There was more of this resin brought into the country by Santa Anna's friend Thomas Adams. Adams had a plan to make rubber.
5. The plan failed. Then the occasion arose for Adams to get a much more successful idea on the basis of the use to which the resin was put by General Santa Anna. That is, Adams decided to make a gum that could be chewed.

Exercise 39.4 Revising: Conciseness

Exercise

Make the following passage as concise as possible. Be merciless.

At the end of a lengthy line of reasoning, he came to the conclusion that the situation with carcinogens [cancer-causing substances] should be regarded as similar to the situation with the automobile. Instead of giving in to an irrational fear of cancer, we should consider all aspects of the problem in a balanced and dispassionate frame of mind, making a total of the benefits received from potential carcinogens (plastics, pesticides, and other similar products) and measuring said total against the damage done by such products. This is the nature of most discussions about the automobile. Instead of responding irrationally to the visual, aural, and air pollution caused by automobiles, we have decided to live with them (while simultaneously working to improve on them) for the benefits brought to society as a whole.

40

Spelling and the Hyphen

English spelling is difficult, even for some very experienced and competent writers. You can train yourself to spell better, and this chapter will help you. But you can also improve instantly by acquiring the habits listed in the following box.

Video tutorial

Ways to improve your spelling

- ▪ **Carefully proofread all your writing.** Use the proofreading tips on page 73 to help you find spelling errors.
- ▪ **Check a dictionary *every time* you doubt a spelling.** Being suspicious of your spellings and relying on a dictionary will take care of many potential spelling errors.
- ▪ **Create a list of your spelling errors.** Keep a record of words you misspell, and check the list every time you write a paper. With experience, you'll learn to recognize and correct the words you typically misspell.
- ▪ **Use a spelling checker critically.** A spelling checker can help you find spelling errors in your papers. However, its usefulness is limited because it can't spot the common error of confusing words with similar spellings, such as *now/not, to/too, their/they're/there,* and *principal/principle.* See page 71 for more on spelling checkers.

40a Recognizing typical spelling problems

Spelling well involves recognizing situations that commonly lead to misspelling: pronunciation can mislead you in several ways; different forms of the same word may have different spellings; and some words have more than one acceptable spelling.

1 Being wary of pronunciation

In English, unlike some other languages, pronunciation of words is an unreliable guide to their spelling. The same letter or

Video tutorial

Visit *mycomplab.com* for the eText and for resources and more exercises on spelling and the hyphen.

sp

40a

combination of letters may have different sounds in different words. (Say aloud these different ways of pronouncing the letters *ough*: *tough, dough, cough, through, bough.*) In addition, some words contain letters that are not pronounced clearly or at all, such as the *ed* in *asked,* the silent *e* in *swipe,* or the unpronounced *gh* in *tight.*

Pronunciation is a particularly unreliable guide in spelling **homonyms,** words that are pronounced the same although they have different spellings and meanings: *great/grate, to/too/two.* Some commonly confused homonyms and near-homonyms, such as *accept/except,* are listed below. (See p. 562 for tips on how to use spelling lists.)

Podcast

Words commonly confused

accept (to receive)
except (other than)

advice (a recommendation)
advise (to recommend)

affect (to have an influence on)
effect (a result)

all ready (prepared)
already (by this time)

allude (to refer to indirectly)
elude (to avoid)

allusion (an indirect reference)
illusion (an erroneous belief or
   perception)

ascent (a movement up)
assent (to agree, or an agreement)

bare (unclothed)
bear (to carry, or an animal)

board (a plane of wood)
bored (uninterested)

born (brought into life)
borne (carried)

brake (to stop)
break (to smash)

buy (to purchase)
by (next to)

capital (the seat of a government)
capitol (the building where a
   legislature meets)

cite (to quote an authority)
sight (the ability to see)
site (a place)

desert (to abandon)
dessert (after-dinner course)

discreet (reserved, respectful)
discrete (individual or distinct)

elicit (to bring out)
illicit (illegal)

eminent (well known)
imminent (soon to happen)

fair (average, or lovely)
fare (a fee for transportation)

forth (forward)
fourth (after *third*)

gorilla (a large primate)
guerrilla (a kind of soldier)

hear (to perceive by ear)
here (in this place)

heard (past tense of *hear*)
herd (a group of animals)

hole (an opening)
whole (complete)

its (possessive of *it*)
it's (contraction of *it is* or *it has*)

lead (heavy metal)
led (past tense of *lead*)

lessen (to make less)
lesson (something learned)

meat (flesh)
meet (to encounter, or a
   competition)

no (the opposite of *yes*)
know (to be certain)

passed (past tense of *pass*)
past (after, or a time gone by)
patience (forbearance)
patients (persons under medical care)
peace (the absence of war)
piece (a portion of something)
persecute (to oppress, to harass)
prosecute (to pursue, to take legal action against)
plain (clear)
plane (a carpenter's tool, or an airborne vehicle)
presence (the state of being at hand)
presents (gifts)
principal (most important, or the head of a school)
principle (a basic truth or law)
rain (precipitation)
reign (to rule)
rein (a strap for controlling an animal)
raise (to build up)
raze (to tear down)
right (correct)
rite (a religious ceremony)
write (to make letters)
road (a surface for driving)
rode (past tense of *ride*)

scene (where an action occurs)
seen (past participle of *see*)
seam (a junction)
seem (to appear)
stationary (unmoving)
stationery (writing paper)
straight (unbending)
strait (a water passageway)
their (possessive of *they*)
there (opposite of *here*)
they're (contraction of *they are*)
to (toward)
too (also)
two (following *one*)
waist (the middle of the body)
waste (discarded material)
weak (not strong)
week (Sunday through Saturday)
weather (climate)
whether (*if*, or introducing a choice)
which (one of a group)
witch (a sorcerer)
who's (contraction of *who is* or *who has*)
whose (possessive of *who*)
your (possessive of *you*)
you're (contraction of *you are*)

sp

40a

((•●

Podcast

---

2 **Distinguishing between different forms of the same word**

Spelling problems may occur when forms of the same word have different spellings, as in the following examples.

Verbs and nouns

Verb	Noun	Verb	Noun
advise	advice	enter	entrance
describe	description	marry	marriage
speak	speech	omit	omission

Nouns and adjectives

Noun	Adjective	Noun	Adjective
comedy	comic	height	high
courtesy	courteous	Britain	British
generosity	generous		

Irregular verbs

begin, began, begun
break, broke, broken

know, knew, known
ring, rang, rung

Irregular nouns

child, children
goose, geese
mouse, mice

shelf, shelves
tooth, teeth
woman, women

Other differences

four, forty

thief, theft

3 Using preferred spellings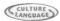

When writing for an American audience, use American spellings instead of their British equivalents. An American dictionary will show a British spelling as a variant or give it a label such as *chiefly British*.

American	British
color, humor	colour, humour
theater, center	theatre, centre
canceled, traveled	cancelled, travelled
judgment	judgement
realize	realise

40b Following spelling rules

Misspelling is often a matter of misspelling a syllable rather than the whole word. The following general rules focus on troublesome syllables, with notes for the occasional exceptions.

1 Distinguishing between *ie* and *ei*

Words like *believe* and *receive* sound alike in the second syllable, but the syllable is spelled differently. Use the familiar jingle to distinguish between *ie* and *ei*:

I before *e*, except after *c*, or when pronounced "ay" as in *neighbor* and *weigh*.

i before *e*	believe	bier	hygiene
	grief	thief	friend
ei after *c*	ceiling	conceive	perceive
	receive	deceit	conceit
ei sounded as "ay"	neighbor	weight	eight
	sleigh	freight	vein

Exceptions In some words an *ei* combination neither follows *c* nor is pronounced "ay." These words include *either, neither, foreign,* *forfeit, height, leisure, weird, seize,* and *seizure.* This sentence might help you remember some of them: *The weird foreigner neither seizes leisure nor forfeits height.*

Exercise 40.1 Distinguishing between *ie* and *ei*
Insert *ie* or *ei* in the words below. Check doubtful spellings in a dictionary.

1. br__f	5. for__gn	9. l__surely	13. h__ght
2. dec__ve	6. pr__st	10. ach__ve	14. fr__ght
3. rec__pt	7. gr__vance	11. pat__nce	15. f__nt
4. s__ze	8. f__nd	12. p__rce	16. s__ve

Exercise

2 Keeping or dropping a final *e*

Many words end with an unpronounced or silent *e*: *move, brave, late, rinse.* Drop the final *e* when adding an ending that begins with a vowel:

Video tutorial

advise + able = advisable
force + ible = forcible

surprise + ing = surprising
guide + ance = guidance

Keep the final, silent *e* when adding an ending that begins with a consonant:

battle + ment = battlement
accurate + ly = accurately

care + ful = careful
like + ness = likeness

Exceptions The silent *e* is sometimes retained before an ending beginning with a vowel. It is kept when *dye* becomes *dyeing,* to avoid confusion with *dying.* It is kept to prevent mispronunciation of words like *shoeing* (not *shoing*) and *mileage* (not *milage*). And the final *e* is often retained after a soft *c* or *g,* to keep the sound of the consonant soft rather than hard:

courageous
outrageous

changeable
manageable

noticeable
embraceable

The silent *e* is also sometimes *dropped* before an ending beginning with a consonant, when the *e* is preceded by another vowel:

argue + ment = argument
due + ly = duly
true + ly = truly

Exercise 40.2 Keeping or dropping a final *e*
Combine the following words and endings, keeping or dropping a final *e* as necessary to make correctly spelled words. Check doubtful spellings in a dictionary.

1. malice + ious	4. retire + ment	7. note + able
2. love + able	5. sue + ing	8. battle + ing
3. service + able	6. virtue + ous	9. suspense + ion

Exercise

3 Keeping or dropping a final y

Words ending in *y* often change their spelling when an ending is added to them. Change the final *y* to an *i* when it follows a consonant:

beauty, beauties	worry, worried	supply, supplies
folly, follies	merry, merrier	deputy, deputize

But keep the *y* when it follows a vowel, when the added ending is *ing*, or when the *y* ends a proper name:

day, days	cry, crying	May, Mays
obey, obeyed	study, studying	Minsky, Minskys

Exercise

Exercise 40.3 Keeping or dropping a final y

Combine the following words and endings, changing or keeping a final *y* as necessary to make correctly spelled words. Check doubtful spellings in a dictionary.

1. imply + s
2. messy + er
3. apply + ing
4. delay + ing
5. defy + ance
6. say + s
7. solidify + s
8. Murphy + s
9. supply + ed

4 Doubling consonants

Whether to double a word's final consonant depends first on the number of syllables in the word. In one-syllable words, double the final consonant when a single vowel precedes the final consonant. Otherwise, don't double the consonant.

slap, slapping	pair, paired
tip, tipping	park, parking

In words of more than one syllable, double the final consonant when a single vowel precedes the final consonant *and* the consonant ends a stressed syllable once the ending is added. Otherwise, don't double the consonant.

refer, referring	refer, reference
begin, beginning	relent, relented
occur, occurrence	despair, despairing

Exercise

Exercise 40.4 Doubling consonants

Combine the following words and endings, doubling final consonants as necessary to make correctly spelled words. Check doubtful spellings in a dictionary.

1. repair + ing
2. admit + ance
3. benefit + ed
4. shop + ed
5. conceal + ed
6. allot + ed
7. drip + ing
8. declaim + ed
9. parallel + ing

5 Attaching prefixes

Adding a prefix such as *dis*, *mis*, and *un* does not change the spelling of a word. When adding a prefix, do not drop a letter from or add a letter to the original word:

uneasy	anti-intellectual	defuse	misstate
unnecessary	disappoint	de-emphasize	misspell
antifreeze	dissatisfied	misinform	

(See also p. 566 for when to use hyphens with prefixes: *prehistory* versus *ex-student*.)

6 Forming plurals

Nouns

Most nouns form plurals by adding *s* to the singular form:

table, tables	boy, boys
carnival, carnivals	Murphy, Murphys

Boys and Murphys above add *s* to a *y* ending because the *y* follows a vowel (*boy*) or ends a proper noun (*Murphy*). When a final *y* follows a consonant in a common noun, change the *y* to *ie* before adding *s*:

baby, babies	lady, ladies

Some nouns ending in *f* or *fe* form the plural by changing the ending to *ve* before adding *s*:

leaf, leaves	wife, wives
life, lives	yourself, yourselves

Singular nouns ending in *s*, *sh*, *ch*, or *x* form the plural by adding *es*:

kiss, kisses	church, churches
wish, wishes	Jones, Joneses

(Notice that verbs ending in *s*, *sh*, *ch*, or *x* form the third-person singular in the same way. *Taxes* and *lurches* are examples.)

Nouns ending in *o* preceded by a vowel usually form the plural by adding *s*:

ratio, ratios	zoo, zoos

Nouns ending in *o* preceded by a consonant usually form the plural by adding *es*:

hero, heroes	tomato, tomatoes

Exceptions Some very common nouns form irregular plurals:

child, children	man, men
mouse, mice	woman, women

Video
tutorial

Some English nouns that were originally Italian, Greek, Latin, or French form the plural according to their original language:

analysis, analyses	datum, data
basis, bases	medium, media
beau, beaux	phenomenon, phenomena
crisis, crises	piano, pianos
criterion, criteria	thesis, theses

A few such nouns may form irregular or regular plurals: for instance, *index, indices, indexes*; *curriculum, curricula, curriculums*. The regular plural is more contemporary.

〔**CULTURE LANGUAGE**〕 Noncount nouns do not form plurals, either regularly (with an added *s*) or irregularly. Examples of noncount nouns include *equipment, courage,* and *wealth.* (See p. 345.)

Compound nouns

Form plurals of compound nouns in one of two ways. Add *s* to the last word when the component words are roughly equal in importance, whether or not they are hyphenated:

city-states	breakthroughs
painter-sculptors	bucket seats

Add *s* to a noun combined with other parts of speech:

fathers-in-law	passersby

Note, however, that most modern dictionaries give the plural of *spoonful* as *spoonfuls.*

Exercise

Exercise 40.5 Forming plurals

Make the correct plural of each of the following singular words. Check doubtful spellings in a dictionary.

1. pile	5. mile per hour	9. Bales	13. thief
2. donkey	6. box	10. cupful	14. goose
3. beach	7. switch	11. libretto	15. hiss
4. summary	8. sister-in-law	12. video	16. appendix

40c Developing spelling skills

The following techniques can help you improve your spelling. In addition, do not overrely on your computer's spelling checker (see p. 71).

1 Editing and proofreading carefully

If spelling is a problem for you, give it high priority while editing your writing (p. 67) and again while proofreading, your last chance to catch misspelled words (p. 72). Reading a draft backward, word by word, can help you spot mistakes such as switched or omitted letters in words you know. Because the procedure forces you to consider each word in isolation, it can also highlight spellings you may be less sure of. A sense of uncertainty is crucial in spotting and correcting spelling errors, even for good spellers who make relatively few errors. Listen to your own uncertainty, and let it lead you to the dictionary.

2 Using a dictionary

How can you look up a word you can't spell? Start by guessing at the spelling and looking up your guess. If that doesn't work, pronounce the word aloud to come up with other possible spellings, and look them up. Unless the word is too specialized to be included in your dictionary, trial and error will eventually pay off.

If you're using a spelling checker, it may do the guessing for you by providing alternatives for a misspelled word and highlighting a likely option. But you may still need to check a dictionary to verify your choice.

3 Pronouncing carefully

Careful pronunciation is not always a reliable guide to spelling (see p. 554), but it can keep you from misspelling words that are often mispronounced. For example:

athletics (*not* atheletics)	laboratory (*not* labratory)
disastrous (*not* disasterous)	library (*not* libary)
environment (*not* envirnment)	lightning (*not* lightening)
frustrate (*not* fustrate)	mischievous (*not* mischievious)
government (*not* goverment)	nuclear (*not* nucular)
height (*not* heighth)	recognize (*not* reconize)
history (*not* histry)	representative (*not* representive)
irrelevant (*not* irrevelant)	strictly (*not* stricly)

4 Tracking and analyzing your errors

Keep a list of the words marked "misspelled" or "spelling" or "sp" in your papers. This list will contain hints about your particular spelling problems, such as confusing *affect* and *effect* or forming plurals incorrectly. (If you need help analyzing the list, consult your writing instructor.) The list will also provide a personalized study guide, a focus for your efforts to spell better.

5 Using mnemonics

Mnemonics (pronounced with an initial *n* sound) are techniques for assisting your memory. The *er* in *letter* and *paper* can remind you that *stationery* (meaning "writing paper") has an *er* near the end; *stationary* with an *a* means "standing in place." Or the word *dome* with its long *o* sound can remind you that the building in which the legislature meets is spelled *capitol*, with an *o*. The *capital* city is spelled with *al* like *Albany*, the capital of New York. If you identify the words you have trouble spelling, you can create your own mnemonics, which may work better for you than someone else's.

6 Studying spelling lists

Exercise

Learning to spell commonly misspelled words will reduce your spelling errors. For general improvement, work with the following list of commonly misspelled words. Study only six or seven words at a time. If you are unsure of the meaning of a word, look it up in a dictionary and try using it in a sentence. Pronounce the word out loud, syllable by syllable, and write the word out. (The list of similar-sounding words on pp. 554–55 should be considered an extension of the following list.)

absence	amateur	beginning
abundance	among	belief
acceptable	amount	believe
accessible	analysis	beneficial
accidentally	analyze	benefited
accommodate	angel	boundary
accomplish	annual	breath
accumulate	answer	Britain
accuracy	apology	bureaucracy
accustomed	apparent	business
achieve	appearance	
acknowledge	appetite	calculator
acquire	appreciate	calendar
across	appropriate	caricature
actually	approximately	carrying
address	argument	cede
admission	arrest	ceiling
adolescent	ascend	cello
advice	assassinate	cemetery
advising	assimilation	certain
against	assistance	changeable
aggravate	associate	changing
aggressive	atheist	characteristic
all right	athlete	chief
all together	attendance	chocolate
allegiance	audience	choose
almost	average	chose
a lot		climbed
already	bargain	coarse
although	basically	column
altogether	because	coming

commercial
commitment
committed
committee
competent
competition
complement
compliment
conceive
concentrate
concert
condemn
conquer
conscience
conscious
consistency
consistent
continuous
controlled
controversial
convenience
convenient
coolly
course
courteous
criticism
criticize
crowd
cruelty
curiosity
curious
curriculum

deceive
deception
decide
decision
deductible
definitely
degree
dependent
descend
descendant
describe
description
desirable
despair
desperate
destroy
determine
develop
device

devise
dictionary
difference
dining
disagree
disappear
disappoint
disapprove
disastrous
discipline
discriminate
discussion
disease
disgusted
dissatisfied
distinction
divide
divine
division
doctor
drawer

easily
ecstasy
efficiency
efficient
eighth
either
eligible
embarrass
emphasize
empty
enemy
entirely
entrepreneur
environment
equipped
especially
essential
every
exaggerate
exceed
excellent
exercise
exhaust
exhilarate
existence
expense
experience
experiment
explanation
extremely

familiar
fascinate
favorite
February
fiery
finally
forcibly
foreign
foresee
forty
forward
friend
frightening
fulfill

gauge
generally
ghost
government
grammar
grief
guarantee
guard
guidance

happily
harass
height
heroes
hideous
humorous
hungry
hurriedly
hurrying
hypocrisy
hypocrite

ideally
illogical
imaginary
imagine
imitation
immediately
immigrant
incidentally
incredible
independence
independent
individually
inevitably
influential
initiate

innocuous
inoculate
insistent
integrate
intelligence
interest
interference
interpret
irrelevant
irresistible
irritable
island

jealousy
judgment

kindergarten
knowledge

laboratory
leisure
length
library
license
lieutenant
lightning
likelihood
literally
livelihood
loneliness
loose
lose
luxury
lying

magazine
maintenance
manageable
marriage
mathematics
meant
medicine
miniature
minor
minutes
mirror
mischievous
missile
misspelled
morale
morals
mortgage

mournful
muscle
mysterious

naturally
necessary
neighbor
neither
nickel
niece
ninety
ninth
noticeable
nuclear
nuisance
numerous

obstacle
occasion
occasionally
occur
occurrence
official
omission
omit
omitted
opinion
opponent
opportunity
opposite
ordinary
originally

paid
panicky
paralleled
parliament
particularly
peaceable
peculiar
pedal
perceive
perception
performance
permanent
permissible
persistence
personnel
perspiration
persuade
persuasion
physical

physiology
physique
pitiful
planning
playwright
pleasant
poison
politician
pollute
possession
possibly
practically
practice
prairie
precede
preference
preferred
prejudice
preparation
prevalent
primitive
privilege
probably
procedure
proceed
process
professor
prominent
pronunciation
psychology
purpose
pursue
pursuit

quandary
quantity
quarter
questionnaire
quiet
quizzes

realistically
realize
really
rebel
rebelled
recede
receipt
receive
recognize
recommend
reference

referred	sincerely	together
relief	sophomore	tomatoes
relieve	source	tomorrow
religious	speak	tragedy
remembrance	specimen	transferred
reminisce	speech	truly
renown	sponsor	twelfth
repetition	strategy	tyranny
representative	strength	
resemblance	strenuous	unanimous
resistance	stretch	unconscious
restaurant	strict	undoubtedly
rhyme	strictly	unnecessary
rhythm	studying	until
ridiculous	succeed	usable
roommate	successful	usually
	sufficient	
sacrifice	summary	vacuum
sacrilegious	superintendent	vegetable
safety	supersede	vengeance
satellite	suppress	vicious
scarcity	surely	villain
schedule	surprise	visible
science	suspicious	
secretary		weather
seize	teammate	Wednesday
separate	technical	weird
sergeant	technique	wherever
several	temperature	whether
sheriff	tendency	wholly
shining	than	woman
shoulder	then	women
siege	thorough	writing
significance	though	
similar	throughout	yacht

40d Using the hyphen to form or divide words

The hyphen (-) is a mark of punctuation used either to form words or to divide them at the ends of lines.

Podcast

1 Forming compound adjectives

Exercise

When two or more words serve together as a single modifier before a noun, a hyphen or hyphens form the modifying words clearly into a unit:

She is a well-known actor.
The conclusions are based on out-of-date statistics.
Some Spanish-speaking students work as translators.

When the same compound adjectives follow the noun, hyphens are unnecessary and are usually left out.

> The actor is well known.
> The statistics were out of date.
> Many students are Spanish speaking.

Hyphens are also unnecessary in compound modifiers containing an -*ly* adverb, even when the modifiers fall before the noun: *clearly defined terms; swiftly moving train.*

When part of a compound adjective appears only once in two or more parallel compound adjectives, hyphens indicate which words the reader should mentally join with the missing part:

> School-aged children should have eight- or nine-o'clock bedtimes.

2 Writing fractions and compound numbers

Hyphens join the numerator and denominator of fractions and the parts of the whole numbers twenty-one to ninety-nine:

three-fourths	twenty-four
one-half	eighty-seven

3 Forming coined compounds

Writers sometimes create (coin) temporary compounds and join the words with hyphens:

> Muhammad Ali gave his opponent a come-and-get-me look.

4 Attaching some prefixes and suffixes

Do not use hyphens with prefixes except as follows:

- With the prefixes *self-*, *all-*, and *ex-*: *self-control, all-inclusive, ex-student.*
- With a prefix before a capitalized word: *un-American.*
- With a capital letter before a word: *T-shirt.*
- To prevent misreading: *de-emphasize, anti-intellectual.*

The only suffix that regularly requires a hyphen is -*elect*, as in *president-elect.*

5 Eliminating confusion

Hyphens can prevent possible confusion:

Confusing	Doonesbury is a comic strip character. [Is Doonesbury a comic (funny) character who strips or a character in a comic strip?]
Clear	Doonesbury is a comic-strip character.

Hyphens can also clarify words with added prefixes. For example, *recreation* (*creation* with the prefix *re-*) could mean either "a new creation" or "diverting, pleasurable activity." The use of a hyphen, *re-creation*, limits the word to the first meaning. Without a hyphen the word suggests the second meaning.

6 Dividing words at the ends of lines

You can avoid occasional short lines in your documents by dividing some words between the end of one line and the beginning of the next. On a word processor, you can set the program to divide words automatically at appropriate breaks (in the Tools menu, select Language and then Hyphenation). To divide words manually, follow these guidelines:

- **Divide words only between syllables**—for instance, *win-dows*, not *wi-ndows*. Check a dictionary for correct syllable breaks.
- **Never divide a one-syllable word.**
- **Leave at least two letters on the first line and three on the second line.** If a word cannot be divided to follow this rule (for instance, *a-bus-er*), don't divide it.
- **Do not use a hyphen in breaking an electronic address** because readers may perceive any added hyphens as part of the address. The documentation styles differ in where they allow breaks in URLs. For example, MLA style allows a break only after a slash, while APA style allows a break before most punctuation marks.

Exercise 40.6 Using hyphens in compound words

Insert hyphens as needed in the following compounds. Mark all compounds that are correct as given. Consult a dictionary as needed.

Exercise

1. reimburse
2. deescalate
3. forty odd soldiers
4. little known bar
5. seven eighths
6. seventy eight
7. happy go lucky
8. preexisting
9. senator elect
10. postwar
11. two and six person cars
12. ex songwriter
13. V shaped
14. reeducate

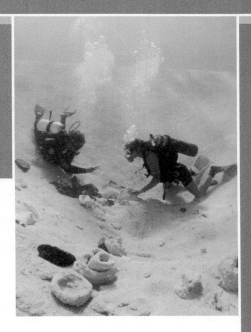

PART 9

Research Writing

41

Planning a
Research Project

If you've ever watched a TV or movie detective pursue a culprit, you know that research can be exciting. When an investigator has a goal in sight, the seemingly mundane work of digging through files, interviewing witnesses, and piecing together clues becomes a concentrated and enthusiastic search.

This same excitement can be yours when you conduct research in college. Honest and inquisitive research writing does demand close attention to details, but the work will be rewarding as you see the details steadily contributing to your own ideas and to the ideas of others. Through your research, synthesis, and writing, you will gain significant, in-depth understanding of a subject that you may not have known much about when you started, and you will add to the body of knowledge about the subject. You will become an expert in your own right.

Like most of the writing you do in college, research writing is a process that involves stages. Generally, you will pass through and return to the following stages during the course of working on a research project:

- Choosing a subject and posing a question about it
- Finding information about the subject to answer the question
- Evaluating source information and synthesizing the ideas of others with your own
- Integrating source information into your writing
- Documenting the ideas of others in source citations
- Drafting, revising, and editing the project

These topics and others are covered throughout Chapters 41–45.

The kind of paper or project you produce will be influenced by whether you are expected to report, to interpret, or to analyze sources.

- **Report:** Survey, organize, and objectively present the available evidence about a topic.

mycomplab

Visit *mycomplab.com* for the eText and for resources and more exercises on planning a research project.

570

- Interpret: Examine a range of views on a topic and argue your own conclusion about it.
- Analyze: Argue for the solution to a problem or the answer to a question based on critical thinking about texts such as scholarly or literary works. (In this context, *analysis* stands for the entire process of critical reading and writing. See pp. 144–60.)

No matter what kind of paper you write, always focus on developing your own ideas, using sources as support. Avoid the temptation to seek a "silver bullet"—that is, to locate two or three perfect sources that already say everything you want to say about your subject. Instead of merely repeating others' ideas, read and synthesize many sources so that you enter into a dialog with them and develop your own ideas.

41a

Throughout Chapters 41–45, we will follow the development of research papers by two students, Justin Malik and Vanessa Haley. Malik's work, emphasizing interpretation, receives somewhat more attention; Haley's work, emphasizing analysis, enters the discussion whenever her process differed significantly from Malik's. Both students' final papers appear in Chapter 47.

41a Starting out

With its diverse and overlapping activities, research writing demands more planning than other kinds of writing. A thoughtful plan and systematic procedures will help you anticipate your needs, schedule your time, and complete the work successfully.

1 Preparing a schedule

As soon as you receive an assignment for a research project, you can begin developing a strategy for completing it. The first step should be making a schedule that apportions the available time to the necessary work. A possible schedule appears on the next page. In it the research-writing process corresponds to the general writing process discussed in Chapters 1–3: planning or developing (steps 1–9), drafting (step 10), and revising and editing (step 11), plus the additional important stage of documenting the sources you use (steps 12–13).

2 Keeping a research journal

To keep track of your activities and ideas during research, maintain a research journal throughout the process. (See pp. 28–30 and 146–47 on journal keeping.) Make your journal portable so that you can carry it with you conveniently. Many researchers use paper notebooks, notebook computers, or mobile devices. Some schools offer students blog space for recording research and other learning activities.

Checklist

41b

Scheduling steps in research writing

(See the pages in parentheses for discussion of the steps.)

Complete
by:

_____ 1. Setting a schedule and beginning a research journal (previous page)
_____ 2. Finding a researchable subject and question (below)
_____ 3. Developing a research strategy (p. 576)
_____ 4. Finding sources, both print and electronic (p. 583), and making a working bibliography (p. 579)

_____ 5. Evaluating and synthesizing sources (pp. 612, 626)
_____ 6. Mining and interacting with sources (p. 629), often using summary, paraphrase, and direct quotation (p. 633)
_____ 7. Taking steps to avoid plagiarism (p. 648)
_____ 8. Developing a thesis statement (p. 658)

_____ 9. Creating a structure (p. 660)
_____ 10. Drafting the paper (p. 663), integrating summaries, paraphrases, and direct quotations into your ideas (p. 642)

_____ 11. Revising and editing the paper (p. 664)
_____ 12. Citing sources in your text (p. 657)
_____ 13. Preparing the list of works cited (p. 657)
_____ 14. Preparing and proofreading the final manuscript (p. 666)

_____ Final paper due

Each segment marked off by a horizontal line will occupy *roughly* one-fourth of the total time. The most unpredictable segments are the first two, so get started early enough to accommodate the unexpected.

In the research journal's dated entries, you can write about the sources you consult, the leads you want to pursue, and any difficulties you encounter. Most important, you can record your thoughts about sources, leads, dead ends, new directions, relationships, and anything else that strikes you. The very act of writing in your journal can expand and clarify your thinking.

Note The research journal is the place to track and develop your own ideas. To avoid mixing up your thoughts and those of others, keep separate notes on what your sources actually say, using one of the methods discussed on pages 630–33.

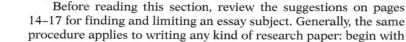

41b Finding a researchable subject and question

Video
tutorial

Before reading this section, review the suggestions on pages 14–17 for finding and limiting an essay subject. Generally, the same procedure applies to writing any kind of research paper: begin with an assigned subject or one that you want to explore and learn more about (perhaps one you've already written about without benefit of research); then narrow the subject to manageable size by asking questions about it. However, selecting and limiting a subject for a research paper can present special opportunities and problems.

1 Choosing an appropriate subject

A subject for a research paper has four primary requirements, each with corresponding pitfalls:

41b

1. Ample sources of information are available on the subject. Other researchers should have had a chance to produce evidence on the subject, weigh the evidence, and publish their conclusions. And the sources should be accessible.

   Avoid very recent subjects, such as a new medical discovery or a breaking story in today's newspaper.

2. The subject encourages research in the kinds and number of sources required by the assignment.

   Avoid (*a*) subjects that depend entirely on personal opinion and experience, such as the virtues of your hobby; and (*b*) subjects that require research in only one source, such as a straight factual biography or a how-to like "Making Lenses for Eyeglasses." (An exception to *b* is a paper in which you analyze a single work such as a novel or painting.)

3. The subject will lead you to an objective assessment of sources and to defensible conclusions. Even when you write a persuasive research paper, arguing your own point of view, the success of the argument will depend on your presenting multiple views responsibly and fairly.

   Avoid controversial subjects that rest entirely on belief or prejudice, even subjects you are passionate about, such as when human life begins or why women (or men) are superior. These subjects may certainly be disputed; however, your own views could slant your research or conclusions, and your readers are unlikely to be swayed from their own beliefs.

Checklist for a good research subject

1. Published sources are ample: the subject is not so recent that other researchers will still be discovering it.
2. Sources are diverse: the subject is neither wholly personal nor wholly factual.
3. Sources can be assessed objectively: the subject is not solely a matter of belief or prejudice.
4. Sources can be examined thoroughly in the assigned time and length: the subject is not too broad.

Checklist

4. **The subject suits the length of paper assigned and the time given for research and writing.**

Avoid broad subjects that have too many sources to survey adequately, such as a major event in history or the collected works of a poet.

41b

Exercise

2 Posing a research question

Asking a question or questions about your subject opens avenues of inquiry. In asking questions, you can consider what you already know about the subject, explore what you don't know, and begin to develop your own perspective.

The students Justin Malik and Vanessa Haley both wrote on environmental topics, but they arrived at their research questions by slightly different paths. For a composition course, Malik's instructor assigned an interpretation with a persuasive purpose but left the selection of the subject to the student. Malik had recently read newspaper articles on a subject that intrigued him: how big businesses are trying to improve their environmental records. Taking the broad subject of business and the environment as his starting point, he used clustering (see pp. 32–33) to pursue some ideas. While generating the cluster opposite, Malik found himself giving the most thought to green products—consumer goods that are promoted as friendly to the environment. Malik posed questions until he hit on a question that seemed interesting and significant: *Can buying green products make a real difference for the environment?*

In developing a topic and question for an analysis paper assigned in a composition course, Vanessa Haley followed a somewhat different procedure. Instead of starting with a general subject, as Malik did, Haley began by looking for an unresolved question, an interesting problem, or a disagreement among the experts in some field of study. She had recently been reading an anthology of writings on the environment, and she had been disturbed by how many naturalists and environmentalists view human beings not as part of "nature" but as something separate from it, usually as its destroyer. In her journal, Haley wrote this entry:

> Many writers see nature as a place for humans to retreat to, or a wonderful thing that humans are ruining. Humans aren't considered natural themselves—human civilization isn't considered natural. Human civ. is "anti-natural." Isn't such a separation unrealistic and damaging? We *are* natural. We're here to stay, and we're not going back to the Stone Age, so we'd better focus on the connections between "us" and "it" (nature) rather than just the differences. Dillard seems to do this—seems to connect human and natural worlds. People are neither better nor worse than nature but just bound up in it. "Nature is as careless as it is bountiful, and . . . with that extravagance goes a crushing waste that will one day include our own cheap lives" ("Fecundity").

Clustering for a research question

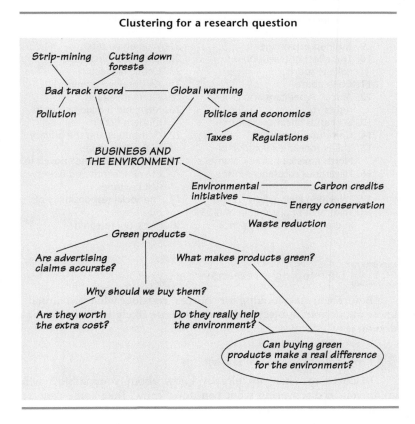

At the end of her journal entry, Haley refers to and quotes the writer Annie Dillard, one of the authors represented in the anthology. Haley decided to explore Dillard's views further by reading and analyzing more of her work. Haley's opening question for investigation, then, was *How does Annie Dillard see the place of humanity in nature?*

Exercise 41.1 Finding a topic and question

Choose three of the following subjects (or three subjects of your own), and narrow each one to at least one subject and question suitable for beginning work on a research paper. (This exercise can be the first step in a research-writing project that continues through Chapters 41–45.)

1. National security and civil rights
2. Distribution of books by conventional versus electronic means
3. Bilingual education
4. Dance in America
5. The history of women's suffrage
6. Genetically modified foods

7. Immigrants in the United States
8. Space exploration
9. Business espionage
10. The effect of television on college sports
11. Child abuse
12. African Americans and civil rights
13. Successes in cancer research
14. Computer piracy
15. The European exploration of North America before Columbus
16. Hazardous substances in the workplace
17. Television evangelism
18. Treatment or prevention of AIDS in the United States or Africa
19. Water pollution
20. Science fiction
21. Women writers
22. Campaign financing
23. Comic film actors
24. An unsolved crime
25. Alternative fuels
26. Male and female heroes in modern fiction
27. Computers and the privacy of the individual
28. Gothic or romance novels in the nineteenth and twenty-first centuries
29. The social responsibility of business
30. Stem-cell research

41c   Developing a research strategy

Before you start looking for sources, consider what you already know about your subject and where you are likely to find information on it.

1   Tapping into your own knowledge

Discovering what you already know about your subject will guide you in discovering what you don't know. Take some time at the start to write down everything you know about the subject: facts you have learned, opinions you have heard or read elsewhere, and of course your own opinions. Use one of the discovery techniques discussed in Chapter 2 to explore and develop your ideas: keeping a journal, observing your surroundings, freewriting, list making, drawing, asking the journalist's questions, using the patterns of development, or thinking critically.

When you've explored your thoughts, make a list of questions for which you don't have answers, whether factual (*How much do Americans spend on green products?*) or more open-ended (*Are they worth the higher prices?*). These questions will give you clues about the sources you need to look for first.

2   Setting goals for sources

For many research projects, you'll want to consult a mix of sources, as described on the following pages. You may start by seeking the outlines of your topic—the range and depth of opinions about it—in reference works and articles in popular periodicals or through a Web search. Then, as you refine your views and your research question, you'll move on to more specialized sources, such as scholarly books and periodicals and your own interviews or surveys. (See pp. 587–610 for more on each kind of source.)

The mix of sources you choose depends heavily on your subject. For example, Justin Malik's paper on green consumerism required the use of recent sources because environmentally friendly products are fairly new to the marketplace. Your mix of sources may also be specified by your instructor or limited by the requirements of your assignment.

41c

Library and Internet sources

The print and electronic sources available at your library or through its Web site—mainly reference works, books, and periodicals—have two big advantages over most of what you'll find on the open Web: library sources are cataloged and indexed for easy retrieval; and they are generally reliable, having been screened first by their publishers and then by the library's staff. In contrast, the Internet's retrieval systems are more difficult to use effectively, and Internet sources tend to be less reliable because most do not pass through any screening before being posted. (There are many exceptions, such as online scholarly journals and reference works. But these sources are generally available through your library's Web site as well.)

Most instructors expect research writers to consult sources found in and through the library, including print sources. But most will accept Internet sources, too, if you have used them judiciously. Even with its disadvantages, the Internet can be a valuable resource for primary sources, current information, and a diversity of views. For guidelines on evaluating both library and Internet sources, see pages 612–25.

Primary and secondary sources

Use **primary sources** when they are available or are required by your assignment. These sources are firsthand accounts, such as historical documents (letters, speeches, and so on), eyewitness reports (including articles by journalists who are on location), works of literature, reports on experiments or surveys conducted by the writer, and sources you originate (interviews, experiments, observations, or correspondence).

Many assignments will allow you to use **secondary sources,** which report and analyze information drawn from other sources, often primary ones. Examples include a reporter's summary of a controversial issue, a historian's account of a battle, a critic's reading of a poem, and a psychologist's evaluation of several studies. Secondary sources may contain helpful summaries and interpretations that direct, support, and extend your own thinking. However, most research-writing assignments expect your own ideas to go beyond those in such sources.

Scholarly and popular sources

The scholarship of acknowledged experts is essential for depth, authority, and specificity. Most instructors expect students to emphasize scholarly sources in their research. But the general-interest views and information of popular sources can help you apply more scholarly approaches to daily life.

41c

- **Check the title.** Is it technical, or does it use a general vocabulary?
- **Check the publisher.** Is it a scholarly journal (such as *Cultural Geographies*) or a publisher of scholarly books (such as Harvard University Press), or is it a popular magazine (such as *Consumer Reports* or *Newsweek*) or a publisher of popular books (such as Little, Brown)? For more on the distinction between scholarly and popular sources, see pages 594 and 614.
- **Check the length of periodical articles.** Scholarly articles are generally much longer than magazine and newspaper articles.
- **Check the author.** Have you seen the name elsewhere, which might suggest that the author is an expert?
- **Check the URL.** A Web site's URL, or electronic address, includes an abbreviation that can tell you something about the origin of the source: scholarly sources usually end in *edu, org,* or *gov,* while popular sources usually end in *com.* See pages 618–19 for more on types of Web sources.

Older and newer sources

- **Check the publication date.** For most subjects a combination of older, established sources (such as books) and current sources (such as newspaper articles, interviews, and Web sites) will provide both background and up-to-date information. Only historical subjects or very current subjects (such as social-networking Web sites) require an emphasis on one extreme or another.

Impartial and biased sources

Seek a range of viewpoints. Sources that attempt to be impartial can offer trustworthy facts and an overview of your subject. Sources with clear biases can offer a diversity of opinion. Of course, to discover bias, you may have to read the source carefully (see p. 613); but you can infer quite a bit just from a bibliographical listing.

- **Check the title.** It may reveal something about point of view. (Consider these contrasting titles uncovered by Justin Malik: "Go for the Green" versus "Where the Green Is: Examining the Paradox of Environmentally Conscious Consumption.")
- **Check the author.** You may have heard of the author before as a respected researcher (thus more likely to be objective) or as a leading proponent of a certain view (less likely to be objective).

Note Internet sources must be approached with particular care. See pages 615–25.

Sources with helpful features

Depending on your topic and how far along your research is, you may want to look for sources with features such as illustrations (which can clarify important concepts), bibliographies (which can direct you to other sources), and indexes (which can help you develop keywords for electronic searches; see pp. 586–87).

> **Exercise 41.2 Developing a research strategy**
>
> Following the suggestions on page 576, write what you already know about the topic you selected in Exercise 41.1 (pp. 575–76), and then frame some questions for which you'll need to find answers. Also in writing, consider the kinds of sources you'll probably need to consult, using the categories given on the preceding pages.

41d Making a working, annotated bibliography

When you begin searching for sources, it may be tempting to pursue each possibility as you come across it. But that approach would prove inefficient and probably ineffective. Instead, you'll want to find out the *full range* of sources available—from scholarly and popular articles to books and Web sites—and then decide on a good number to consult. For a paper of 1800 to 2500 words, try for ten to thirty promising titles as a start.

To keep track of where sources are, compile a **working bibliography** as you uncover possibilities. Record the information for a source as soon as you think you may want to use it, following the guidelines in this section. Then you'll be able to find the source when you're ready to consult it, and you'll have the information needed to cite the source in your paper.

As you look for and assess sources, your instructor may ask you to prepare an **annotated bibliography** as part of the research process or as a separate assignment. In an annotated bibliography, you summarize sources and evaluate their usefulness for your research.

1 Tracking source information

You have several options for making a working bibliography:

- **Copy source information by hand on note cards** (usually 3" × 5"), one source to a card. With this system, you can record source information no matter where you are, as long as you have a pen or pencil, and you can easily add, delete, and rearrange sources. Some instructors require that a working bibliography be submitted on note cards.

■ **Create the working bibliography on your computer or mobile device,** either typing the information yourself or downloading it from online indexes, catalogs, and other sources. You'll be able to sort sources by subject or by author and to copy bibliographic data into your paper when you prepare final source citations.

■ **Combine the two systems:** print and cut up computer-generated source listings, and then paste or tape each source on a note card.

41d

Whatever system you use, be sure to record all the information you will need. A downloaded listing, for instance, may look complete but lack the name of the database and other crucial information.

The two records below come from Justin Malik's working bibliography. The first, for a book, Malik handwrote in his research notebook. The second, for a magazine article, Malik downloaded from an online database, printed out, and then annotated with information he knew he would need.

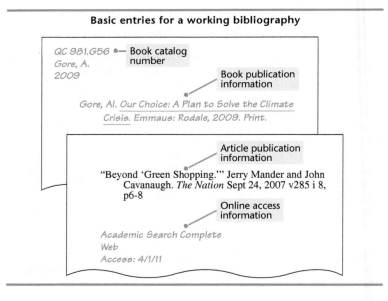

Basic entries for a working bibliography

QC 981.G56 ●— Book catalog
Gore, A.   number
2009
                    Book publication
                    information

Gore, Al. *Our Choice: A Plan to Solve the Climate
Crisis.* Emmaus: Rodale, 2009. Print.

                    Article publication
                    information

"Beyond 'Green Shopping.'" Jerry Mander and John
Cavanaugh. *The Nation* Sept 24, 2007 v285 i 8,
p6-8

                    Online access
                    information

Academic Search Complete
Web
Access: 4/1/11

2 Recording source information

When you turn in your paper, you will be expected to attach a list of the sources you have used. So that readers can check or follow up on your sources, your list must include all the information needed to find the sources, in a format readers can understand. The following box shows the information you should record for each type of source so that you will not have to retrace your steps later. See later pages for illustrations of how to locate this information for printed journal

Information for a working bibliography

For books
Library call number
Name(s) of author(s), editor(s),
    translator(s), or others listed
Title and subtitle
Publication data:
  Place of publication
  Publisher's name
  Date of publication
Other important data, such as
    edition or volume number
Medium (print, Web, etc.)

For periodical articles
Name(s) of author(s)
Title and subtitle of article
Title of periodical
Publication data:
  Volume number and issue
    number (if any) in which
    article appears
  Date of issue
  Page numbers on which
    article appears
Medium (print, Web, etc.)

For electronic sources
Name(s) of author(s)
Title and subtitle of source
Title of Web site, periodical,
    or other larger work
Publication data, such as data
    listed above for a book or

article; the publisher or sponsor
    of a Web site; and the date of
    release, revision, or online
    posting
Any publication data for the source
    in another medium (print, film,
    etc.)
Format of online source (Web site
    or page, podcast, e-mail, etc.)
Date you consulted the source
Title of any database used to
    reach the source
Complete URL (see the note
    below)
Digital Object Identifier, if any (see
    the note below)
Medium (Web, CD-ROM, etc.)

For other sources
Name(s) of author(s), creator(s),
    or others listed, such as a gov-
    ernment department, record-
    ing artist, or photographer
Title of work
Format, such as unpublished letter,
    live performance, or photograph
Publication or production data:
  Publication title
  Publisher's or producer's name
Date of publication, release, or
    production
Identifying numbers (if any)
Medium (print, typescript, etc.)

41d

Note Documentation styles vary in requiring URLs and DOIs (Digital
Object Identifiers) for citations of electronic sources. (See p. 809 for more
on DOIs.) For instance, MLA style generally does not require URLs or DOIs,
APA style generally requires DOIs if available or just home-page URLs, and
some other styles always require complete URLs. Even if you don't need the
complete URL or DOI in your final citation of a source, record it anyway so
that you'll be able to track the source down if you want to consult it again.
For a source you reach through a library database, record just a DOI if one
is available because most database URLs can't be used to locate sources.

articles (682) and books (688) and for Web sites (696), Web journal
articles (705), and sources in online databases (708).

Note Recording source information meticulously will help you
avoid accidental plagiarism because you will be less likely to omit

the information in your paper. Whenever possible, record source information in the correct format for the documentation style you will be using. That will help you avoid omitting or mixing up dates, numbers, and other data when it's time to write your citations. This book describes four documentation styles: MLA (p. 667), Chicago (p. 785), APA (p. 804), and CSE (p. 834). (Malik's first source record on p. 580 follows MLA style.) For other styles, consult one of the guides listed on pages 804 and 835. See also pages 657–58 for tips on using bibliography software to format source information.

41d

Student
paper

3 Annotating your bibliography

Annotating a working bibliography converts a simple list into a tool for assessing sources. When you discover a possible source, record not only its publication information but also the following:

- What you know about the source's content. Periodical databases and book catalogs generally include abstracts or summaries of sources that can help you with this part of the annotation.
- How you think the source may be helpful in your research. Does it offer expert opinion, statistics, an important example, or a range of views? Does it place your subject in a historical, social, or economic context?

Taking time to prepare thorough annotations can help you discover gaps that may remain in your sources and will later help you decide which sources to pursue in depth. Justin Malik annotated a bibliography entry on his computer with a summary and a note on the source features he thought would be most useful to him:

Entry for an annotated working bibliography

Publication information for source	Gore, Al. *Our Choice: A Plan to Solve the Climate Crisis*. Emmaus: Rodale, 2009. Print.
Summary of source	A sequel to Gore's *An Inconvenient Truth* that emphasizes solutions to global warming. Expands on the argument that global warming is a serious threat, with recent examples of natural disasters. Proposes ways that governments, businesses, and individuals can reduce or reverse the risks of global
Ideas on use of source	warming. Includes helpful summaries of scientific studies, short essays on various subjects, and dozens of images, tables, charts, and graphs.

As you become more familiar with your sources, you can use your initial annotated bibliography to record your evaluation of them and more detailed thoughts on how they fit into your research. See page 612 on this later stage.

Exercise 41.3 Compiling an annotated working bibliography

Prepare an annotated working bibliography of at least ten sources for a research paper on one of the following people or on someone of your own choosing. Begin by limiting the subject to a manageable size, posing a question about a particular characteristic or achievement of the person. Then consult reference works, periodical indexes, the library's book catalog, and the Web. (See pp. 587–605 for more on these resources.) For each source, record complete publication information as well as a summary and a note on the source's potential use.

1. Steven Jobs (a founder of Apple Computer), or another business entrepreneur
2. Sonia Sotomayor, or another Supreme Court justice
3. Emily Dickinson, or another writer
4. Serena Williams, or another sports figure
5. Isamu Noguchi, or another artist

42

Finding Sources

Once you have discovered a research subject and question, have developed a research strategy, and know how to make an annotated working bibliography, you're ready to find sources. This chapter discusses electronic searches and the kinds of sources, both print and electronic, that are available to you.

Video
tutorial

Note If you require sources that are not available from your own library, you may be able to obtain them from another library by mail, fax, or computer. Ask your librarian for help, and plan ahead: interlibrary loans can take a week or longer.

42a Starting with your library's Web site

As you conduct academic research, your library's Web site will be your gateway to ideas and information. Always start with your library's site, not with a public search engine such as *Google*. (*Google Scholar*, a tool that searches for scholarly articles, is discussed on pp. 594–95.) The library's site will lead you to vast resources, including

---

A tip for researchers

Take advantage of these valuable resources offered by your library:

- An **orientation**, which introduces the library's resources and explains how to reach and use the Web site and the print holdings.
- **Reference librarians**, whose job it is to help you and others navigate the library's resources. All libraries offer face-to-face consultations, and many offer e-mail and chat services. Even very experienced researchers often consult reference librarians.

Video
tutorial

books, periodical articles, and reference works that aren't available on the open Web. More important, unlike many sources you can find using a public search engine, every source you find on the library's site will have passed through filters to ensure its value. A scholarly journal article, for instance, undergoes at least three successive reviews: first, subject-matter experts deem it worth publishing in the journal; next, a database vendor deems the journal worth including in the database; and finally, your school's librarians deem the database worth subscribing to.

Google and other search engines may seem more user-friendly than the library's Web site and may seem to return plenty of sources for you to work with. Many of the sources may indeed be reliable and relevant to your research, but many more will not be. In the end, a library Web search will be more efficient and more effective than a direct Web search. (For help with evaluating sources from any resource, see pp. 612–25.)

Note Start with your library's Web site, but don't stop there. Many books, periodicals, and other excellent sources are available only on library shelves, not online, and most instructors expect research papers to be built to some extent on these resources. When you spot promising print sources while browsing a library's online databases, make records of them and then look them up at the library. You can also browse the bookshelves to discover sources.

42b Searching electronically

The way you reach your library's resources will vary depending on the way the Web site is set up. Many libraries offer separate searches of their catalogs of physical holdings (such as print books and periodicals) and of individual databases for articles. Other libraries provide a centralized search page that allows a simultaneous search of all the library's resources, including print books and e-books, print and electronic articles, and so on.

In either situation, an electronic search requires planning. A too-casual search can miss helpful sources while returning hundreds, even thousands, of irrelevant sources. Become familiar with the kinds of electronic sources available to you and with the different search strategies for each (below). And take time early in your research to develop **keywords** that name your subject for databases and Web search engines (pp. 586–87).

1 Anticipating the kinds of library sources

Your library's Web site will lead you to many kinds of electronic resources suitable for academic research.

42b

- The catalog of holdings, searchable from the library's Web site, is a database that lists all the resources that the library owns or subscribes to. Depending on the library, the catalog may include print and electronic books, journals, magazines, newspapers, reference works, and more. It may also include the holdings of other school libraries nearby or in your state.

- Online databases include indexes, bibliographies, and other reference works. They are your main route to articles in periodicals, providing publication information, summaries, and often full text. Your library subscribes to the databases and makes them available through its Web site, either on its main search page or on a separate database page. (You may also discover databases directly on the Web, but, again, the library is the more productive starting place.)

- Research guides, available through some libraries, provide points of access to the library's resources on particular subjects, such as twentieth-century English literature or social psychology.

- Databases on CD-ROM include the same information as online databases, but they must be read at a library computer terminal. Increasingly, libraries have moved away from CD-ROMs in favor of online databases.

2 Using databases and search engines

To develop keywords it helps to understand how library databases, library search engines, and public search engines work:

✳
Exercise

- A database matches your keywords to its index of authors, titles, and subject headings. The subject headings reflect the database's directory of terms and are assigned by people who have read the sources. You can find these subject headings by using your own keywords until you locate a promising source. The information for the source will list the headings under which the database indexes the source and others like it. (See p. 597 for an illustration.) You can then use those headings for further searches.

- A library's centralized search engine seeks your keywords among all the library's physical holdings and online offerings. After your initial keyword search, the engine will provide options to limit or expand your search within the library's available resources. The search engine will not return content from the open Web.

■ **A Web search engine seeks your keywords in the titles and texts of sites on the public Web.** The results will depend on how well your keywords describe your subject and anticipate the words used in sources. If you describe your subject too broadly or describe it specifically but don't match the vocabulary in relevant sources, your search will turn up few relevant sources and probably many that aren't relevant.

42b

3 Refining keywords

Exercise

Every database and search engine provides a system that you can use to refine your keywords for a productive search. The basic operations appear in the following box, but resources do differ. For instance, some assume that *AND* should link two or more keywords, while others provide options specifying "Must contain all the words" and other equivalents for the operations in the box. To learn a search engine's system, consult its Advanced Search page.

Ways to refine keywords

Video
tutorial

Most databases and many search engines work with **Boolean operators,** terms or symbols that allow you to expand or limit your keywords and thus your search.

■ **Use *AND* or + to narrow the search** by including only sources that use all the given words. The keywords *green AND products* request only the sources in the shaded area:

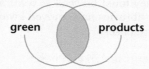

■ **Use *NOT* or – ("minus") to narrow the search** by excluding irrelevant words. *Green AND products NOT guide* excludes sources that use the word *guide*:

■ **Use *OR* to broaden the search** by giving alternative keywords. *Green AND products OR goods* allows for sources that use a synonym for *products*:

- Use parentheses or quotation marks to form search phrases. For instance, *(green products)* requests the exact phrase, not the separate words. Only sources using *green products* would turn up.
- Use wild cards to permit different versions of the same word. In *consum**, for instance, the wild card * indicates that sources may include *consume, consumer, consumerism,* and *consumption* as well as *consumptive, consumedly,* and *consummate.* The example suggests that you have to consider all the variations allowed by a wild card and whether it opens up your search too much. If you seek only two or three from many variations, you may be better off using *OR: consumption OR consumerism.* (Note that some systems use ?, :, or + for a wild card instead of *.)
- Be sure to spell your keywords correctly. Some search tools will look for close matches or approximations, but correct spelling gives you the best chance of finding relevant sources.

42c

Note You will probably have to use trial and error in developing your keywords. Because different databases have different directories and many search tools have no directory at all, you should count on occasionally running dry (turning up few or no sources) or hitting uncontrollable gushers (turning up hundreds or thousands of mostly irrelevant sources). But the process is not busywork —far from it. Besides leading you eventually to worthwhile sources, it can also teach you a great deal about your subject: how you can or should narrow it, how it is and is not described by others, what others consider interesting or debatable about it, and what the major arguments are.

42c Finding reference works

Reference works, often available online, include encyclopedias, dictionaries, digests, bibliographies, indexes, atlases, and handbooks. Your research *must* go beyond reference works; indeed, many instructors discourage students from relying on such sources for ideas and information in final papers. But reference works can help you get started:

- They can help you decide whether your subject interests you and meets the requirements for a research paper (pp. 573–74).

Video
tutorial

42c

Guide to research sources

- They can direct you to more detailed sources on your subject.
- They can help you refine keywords for electronic searches, giving you the terminology of the field you're researching.
- They can identify the main debates in a field and the proponents of each side.

Justin Malik's use of reference works illustrates how helpful such sources can be as a starting point, even for a current topic such as green products. Malik first consulted *Dictionary of Environment and Development* (to get some background on environmental issues) and *Encyclopedia of Advertising* (to explore the recent history of promotional campaigns for green products).

The following lists give the types of reference works. Ask a reference librarian if you're unsure of where to start. The librarian can also advise you which sources are available through the library's Web site, in print at the library, or directly via the Web.

42c

General encyclopedias

General encyclopedias give brief overviews and bibliographies. Covering all fields, they are convenient but very limited.

Encyclopedia Americana
Encyclopaedia Britannica
Random House Encyclopedia

Note The Web-based encyclopedia *Wikipedia* (found at *wikipedia .org*) is one of the largest reference sites on the Internet. Like any encyclopedia, *Wikipedia* can provide background information for research on a topic. But unlike other encyclopedias, *Wikipedia* is a **wiki,** a kind of Web site that can be contributed to or edited by anyone, not just reliable experts. Ask your instructor whether *Wikipedia* is an acceptable source before you use it. If you do use it, you must carefully evaluate any information you find, using the guidelines on pages 615–22.

Specialized encyclopedias, dictionaries, bibliographies

A specialized encyclopedia, dictionary, or bibliography generally covers a single field or subject. These works will give you more detailed and more technical information than a general reference work will, and many of them (especially bibliographies) will direct you to particular books and articles on your subject. For information on specialized reference works in various disciplines, consult lists elsewhere in this book:

- Literature (p. 766)
- Other humanities, including history, the arts, philosophy, and religion (p. 782)
- Social sciences, such as business and economics, criminal justice, education, and psychology (p. 802)
- Natural and applied sciences, such as biology, engineering, mathematics, and physics (p. 832)

Several databases allow you to search for reference entries across many specialized sources:

Essay and General Literature Index. Lists tens of thousands of articles and essays that appear in books (rather than periodicals) and that might not be listed elsewhere.

Oxford Reference Online. A compilation of general and specialized dictionaries, encyclopedias, and other sources.

Reference Universe. Searches the indexes and article titles in subject encyclopedias and other reference sources in a variety of disciplines.

42c Unabridged dictionaries and special dictionaries on language

Unabridged dictionaries are more comprehensive than college or abridged dictionaries. Special dictionaries give authoritative information on aspects of language. (See Chapter 38 for more on the kinds of dictionaries and how to use them.)

Unabridged dictionaries

A Dictionary of American English on Historical Principles
The Oxford English Dictionary
Webster's Third New International Dictionary of the English Language

Special dictionaries

R. W. Burchfield, ed., *The New Fowler's Modern English Usage*
Frederic G. Cassidy et al., eds., *Dictionary of American Regional English*
Robert L. Chapman, ed., *Roget's International Thesaurus*
Bryan A. Garner, *A Dictionary of Modern American Usage*
J. E. Lighter, ed., *Historical Dictionary of American Slang*
Charles T. Onions et al., eds., *The Oxford Dictionary of English Etymology*

Biographical reference works

If you want to learn about someone's life, achievements, credentials, or position, or if you want to learn the significance of a name you've come across, consult one of the following reference works:

American Men and Women of Science
American National Biography
Biography and Genealogy Master Index (citations of biographical entries in more than 3000 reference works)
Contemporary Authors
Current Biography
Dictionary of American Biography
Dictionary of American Negro Biography
Dictionary of Literary Biography
Dictionary of National Biography (British)
Dictionary of Scientific Biography
Marquis Who's Who (nearly twenty publications organized by geography, profession, and other categories)
Notable American Women
Webster's New Biographical Dictionary
World Authors

Atlases and gazetteers

Atlases are collections of maps; gazetteers are geographical dictionaries.

Britannica World Atlas
National Atlas of the United States of America
National Geographic Atlas of the World
Times Atlas of the World
Times Atlas of World History
Webster's New Geographical Dictionary

42d

Almanacs and yearbooks

Both almanacs and yearbooks are annual compilations of facts. Yearbooks record information about the previous year in a country, field, or other subject. Almanacs give facts about a variety of fields.

Americana Annual
Britannica Book of the Year
Facts on File Yearbook
Time Almanac
US Bureau of the Census, *Statistical Abstract of the United States*
World Almanac and Book of Facts

42d Finding books

Books can provide background information, subject surveys, popular views of culture, statements of scholarly theory, research results—in short, a broad range of secondary and primary sources (see p. 577).

1 Using the library catalog

Your library's catalog is searchable at computers in the library and via the library's Web site. With *WorldCat*, available through most libraries, you can also search for specific books in the catalogs of tens of thousands of libraries worldwide. You may be able to borrow books from another library in your area. Ask a librarian for assistance with remote searches and loans. And allow time for a book to be sent after your request.

All book catalogs contain similar information, though it may be organized differently from one library to the next. By far the most widely used format derives from the Library of Congress cataloging system and includes author, title, publisher, date of publication, description (number of pages, size, and other data), subject headings the book is listed under, and the library's call number (which directs you to the book's location in the stacks). See page 593 for a complete book record showing all this information.

2 Using a search strategy

Unless you seek a specific author or title, you'll want to find books with a subject or keyword search of the library's catalog. In a subject search, you start with headings found in *Library of Congress Subject Headings (LCSH)*, the massive directory under which the Library of Congress catalogs books. In a keyword search, you start with your own description of your subject as a way of locating appropriate *LCSH* headings.

The keyword approach is illustrated here by part of Justin Malik's catalog search. In his initial keyword search (screen 1), Malik used *environmentalism and products*. The search produced a number of promising books (screen 2), including the second one, *Building the Green Economy*. The complete record for this book (screen 3) showed that it was indexed under three *LCSH* subject headings: *Sustainable development—Citizen participation*; *Environmentalism—Economic aspects*; and *Green products*. Malik then used these headings to search the catalog further.

Note In addition to searching the book catalog, you can also browse the library shelves. The first part of the call number for a promising title (*HC79.E5 D3252* in the full record opposite) will

---

1. Initial keyword search of a book catalog

Library Search | Article Search

New Search   Advanced Search   What am I searching?

Search for environmentalism and products •— Keywords

GO

---

2. Book catalog search results

1 Green gone wrong : how our economy is undermining the environmental revolution (View details)
Heather Rogers 1970- New York : Scribner 2010
Book   ☐ Add to e-Shelf
Checked out (HC79.E5 R6312 2010) (Get It)
Locations

2 Building the green economy : success stories from the grassroots (View details)
Kevin Danaher 1950- Shannon Biggs; Jason Mark Sausalito, CA : PoliPointPress : Distributed by Ingram Publisher Services c2007
Book   ☐ Add to e-Shelf
Available (HC79.E5 D3252 2007) (Get It)
Locations

3 Simple steps to a greener home (View details)
Danny Seo; Gaiam Media. Louisville, CO : Gaiam Americas c2007
Audio/Visual ☐ Add to e-Shelf
Available (TH4860 .S56 2007) (Get It)
Locations

3. Book catalog full record

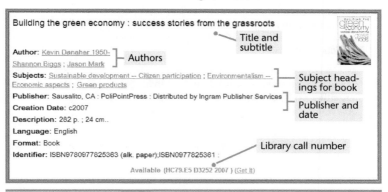

Building the green economy : success stories from the grassroots

Title and subtitle

Author: Kevin Danaher 1950-
Shannon Biggs ; Jason Mark
— Authors

Subjects: Sustainable development -- Citizen participation ; Environmentalism -- Economic aspects ; Green products
— Subject headings for book

Publisher: Sausalito, CA : PoliPointPress : Distributed by Ingram Publisher Services
Creation Date: c2007
— Publisher and date
Description: 282 p. ; 24 cm..
Language: English
Format: Book
Identifier: ISBN9780977825363 (alk. paper);ISBN0977825361 :
— Library call number

Available (HC79.E5 D3252 2007) (Get It)

42e

lead you to other books on the same subject that a catalog search might miss.

3 | Using references to books

The following can help you identify books that have information about your topic:

- *WorldCat* allows you to conduct subject, author, title, and keyword searches of library catalogs around the world. You might, for example, want to know if the author of an encyclopedia article has published any relevant books since the date of the encyclopedia. You could search for the author's name on *WorldCat* to find out.

- **Review indexes** list published reviews of books and can help you evaluate whether a book is relevant to your subject:

  Book Review Digest Plus. Summarizes and indexes reviews of books.
  Book Review Index

  For specialized review indexes, see pages 803 (social sciences) and 833 (natural and applied sciences).

42e | Finding periodicals

Periodicals include newspapers, academic journals, and magazines, either print or online. Newspapers are useful for detailed accounts of past and current events. Journals and magazines can be harder to distinguish, but their differences are important. Most college instructors expect students' research to rely more on journals than on magazines.

42e

Journals	Magazines
Examples	
American Anthropologist, Journal of Black Studies, Journal of Chemical Education	*The New Yorker, Time, Rolling Stone, People*
Availability	
Mainly college and university libraries, either on library shelves or in online databases	Public libraries, newsstands, bookstores, the open Web, and online databases
Purpose	
Advance knowledge in a particular field	Express opinion, inform, or entertain
Authors	
Specialists in the field	May or may not be specialists in their subjects
Readers	
Often specialists in the field	Members of the general public or a subgroup with a particular interest
Source citations	
Source citations always included	Source citations rarely included
Length of articles	
Usually long, ten pages or more	Usually short, fewer than ten pages
Frequency of publication	
Quarterly or less often	Weekly, biweekly, or monthly
Pagination of issues	
May be paged separately (like a magazine) or may be paged sequentially throughout an annual volume, so that issue number 3 (the third issue of the year) could open on page 327.	Paged separately, each beginning on page 1

1 Using periodical databases

Video
tutorial

Periodical databases index the articles in journals, magazines, and newspapers. Often these databases include abstracts, or summaries, of the articles, and they may offer the full texts of the articles as well. Your library subscribes to many periodical databases and to services that offer multiple databases. (See p. 598 for a list.) Most databases and services will be searchable through the library's Web site.

Note The search engine *Google* is developing *Google Scholar*, a search engine at *scholar.google.com* that seeks out scholarly articles. It is particularly useful for subjects that range across disciplines, for which discipline-specific databases can be too limited. *Google Scholar* can connect to your library's holdings if you tell it to do so under Scholar Preferences. Keep in mind, however, that *Google Scholar*'s searches are not as yet exhaustive, and they may list articles that you cannot obtain in full text. Your library is the best source for articles that are available to you, so begin there.

Selection of databases

To decide which databases to consult, you'll need to consider what you're looking for:

42e

- Does your research subject span more than one discipline? Then start with a broad database such as *Academic Search Complete, JSTOR, Lexis Nexis Academic Universe,* or *CQ Researcher*. A broad database covers many subjects and disciplines but does not index the full range of periodicals in each subject.
- Does your research subject focus on a single discipline? Then start with a discipline-specific database such as *Historical Abstracts, MLA International Bibliography, Biological Abstracts*, or *Education Search Complete*. A specific database covers few subjects but includes most of the available periodicals in each subject. If you don't know the name of an appropriate database, the library's Web site probably lists possibilities by discipline.
- Which databases most likely include the kinds of resources you need? The Web sites of most libraries allow you to narrow a database search to a particular discipline. Some libraries also provide research guides, which list potentially helpful databases for your search terms. You can then discover each database's focus by checking the description of the database (sometimes labeled "Help" or "Guide") or the list of indexed resources (sometimes labeled "Publications" or "Index"). The description will also tell you the time period the database covers, so you'll know whether you also need to consult older print indexes at the library.

Database searches

When you first search a database, use your own keywords to locate sources. The general procedure is discussed on pages 586–87. Your goal is to find at least one source that seems just right for your subject, so that you can then see what subject headings the database itself uses for such sources. Using one or more of those headings will focus and speed your search.

Justin Malik first searched *EBSCOhost Academic Search Complete*, a broad database covering more than 4500 periodicals. His keywords *green* and *products* returned more than 7000 articles, and none on the first page dealt with his subject. He then tried *green* and *products* and *environment,* getting fewer returns but still nothing usable on the first page. He stopped there to brainstorm other terms that might work better, some of them synonyms and some narrower:

green	products	environment
responsible	shopping	environmentalism
conscious	consumption	pollution
eco-friendly	advertising	waste
sustainable	economics	
	business	

42e

The three screen shots here show Malik's use of one combination of these terms, *green* and *products* and *shopping*. The first two returns (screen 2) included one source related to Malik's subject. The full record for the source (screen 3) provided an abstract of the source along with the database's headings for the article. Malik had seen one of these headings, *Consumer behavior*, in his background research, but he had thought the term might be too specialized to produce good results. Now he tried it on *Academic Search Complete* and found dozens of additional source possibilities. To broaden his search, he also tried some of the subject headings for these other sources, such as *Environmental economics and sustainable development—citizen participation*. When he thought he had found a good range of possible sources, including government publications as well as scholarly and popular articles, he moved on to other databases.

Many databases allow you to limit your search to so-called peer-reviewed or refereed journals—that is, scholarly journals whose articles have been reviewed before publication by experts in the field and then revised by the author. (Malik's initial search on *Academic Search Complete* included this limitation, as shown in screen 1 below.) Limiting your search to peer-reviewed journals can help you navigate huge databases that might otherwise return scores of unusable articles from other kinds of periodicals.

---

1. Initial keyword search of a periodical database

2. Partial keyword search results

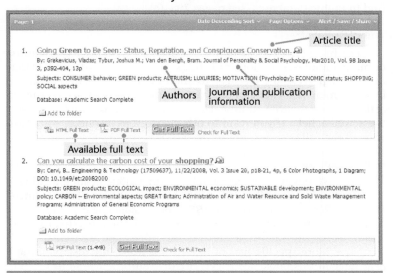

3. Full article record with abstract

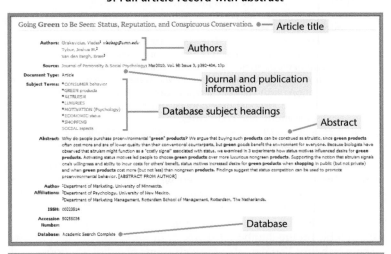

Note As you follow leads in online research, it's easy to lose track of what database you're using. You'll need this information to cite any article you obtain online, so make sure you have it. If you print search records or save them as a file, the database information will appear on the record along with other bibliographic information (see screen 3 on the previous page). For help with citing articles you find in online databases, see pages 708–09.

The use of abstracts

The full article record on the previous page shows a key feature of many databases' periodical listings: an abstract that summarizes the article. Describing research methods, conclusions, and other information, an abstract can tell you whether you want to pursue an article and thus save you time. However, the abstract cannot replace the actual article. If you want to use the work as a source, you must consult the full text.

Helpful databases

The list below includes databases to which academic libraries commonly subscribe. Some of these databases—for instance, *ProQuest Research Library* and *EBSCOhost Academic Search*—cover much the same material, so your library may not subscribe to all of them.

Note More specific lists of indexes for academic disciplines appear later in this book: see pages 767 (literature), 783–84 (other humanities), 803–04 (social sciences), and 833 (natural and applied sciences).

> *EBSCOhost Academic Search.* A periodical index covering magazines and journals in the social sciences, sciences, arts, and humanities. Many articles are available full-text.
> *InfoTrac Expanded Academic.* The Gale Group's general periodical index covering the social sciences, sciences, arts, and humanities as well as national news periodicals. It includes full-text articles.
> *LexisNexis Academic.* An index of news and business, legal, and reference information, with full-text articles. *LexisNexis* includes international, national, and regional newspapers, newsmagazines, legal and business publications, and court cases.
> *ProQuest Research Library.* A periodical index covering the sciences, social sciences, arts, and humanities, including many full-text articles.

While using databases like these, you may want to consult a **citation index** to see what has been written *about* an article or a book, as when one scholar comments on the work of another. The three main citation indexes are *Arts and Humanities Citation Index,* *Social Science Citation Index,* and *Science Citation Index.* All three are available on the database *ISI Web of Science,* which many libraries subscribe to. You can also view citations of scholarly books and articles on *Google Scholar.*

2 Locating the articles in periodicals

Many article listings you find will include or link directly to the full text of the article, which you'll be able to read online and print or e-mail to yourself. If the full text is not available online, you'll need to consult the periodical itself. Usually the article listing will also say whether the periodical is available in your library. If you don't see this information, then consult the library's list of periodicals (often called *serials*) either in the main catalog or in a separate catalog.

Your library probably holds recent issues of print periodicals in the periodicals room. Back issues are usually stored elsewhere, in one of three forms:

■ In bound volumes

■ On *microfilm,* a filmstrip showing pages side by side

■ On *microfiche,* a sheet of film with pages arranged in rows and columns.

42f

Consulting periodicals stored on microfilm or microfiche requires using a special machine, or "reader," with which you locate the page and project it on a screen. (Some readers are also attached to scanners or photocopiers.) Any member of the library's staff will show you how to operate the reader.

If the periodical you seek is not available in your library, you may be able to obtain the article by interlibrary loan. The article will probably arrive online, and there may be a fee for the service. Even electronic loans can sometimes take a week or more, so place your order early.

Note Many periodicals are available both online and in print, and most documentation styles require you to specify which version you consulted. For scholarly journals, the two versions are likely to be identical in content though not in format: for instance, the online version may not include the print version's page breaks and numbers. (However, a full-text version in PDF format reproduces the actual pages of the print journal. To open PDF files, you may need to download a program called *Acrobat Reader.*) For newspapers and magazines, the two versions often differ more: for instance, the online version may be shorter or longer than the print version, may contain fewer illustrations, or may include links to other resources.

42f Finding sources on the Web

As an academic researcher, you enter the Web in two ways: through your library's Web site, and through public search engines such as *Bing* and *Google.* The library entrance, covered in the preceding sections, is your main path to the books and periodicals that, for most subjects, should make up most of your sources. The public entrance, discussed here, can lead to a wealth of information and ideas, but it also has disadvantages that limit its usefulness for academic research:

■ **The Web is a wide-open network.** Anyone with the right tools can place information on the Internet, and even a carefully conceived search can turn up sources with widely varying reliability: journal articles, government documents, scholarly data, term papers written by high school students, sales pitches masked as objective reports, wild theories. You must be especially diligent about evaluating Internet sources (see pp. 615–25).

42f

■ **The Web changes constantly.** No search engine can keep up with the Web's daily additions and deletions, and a source you find today may be different or gone tomorrow. You should not put off consulting an online source that you think you may want to use. If it seems appropriate for your needs, take notes from it or (if the source allows) download it to your own computer. Be sure to record complete source information at the same time, and note the date you found the source. (See p. 581 for a complete list of what to record.)

■ **The Web is not all-inclusive.** Most books and many periodicals are available only via the library, not directly via the Web.

Clearly, the Web warrants cautious use. It should not be the only resource you work with.

1 Using a search engine

To find sources on the Web, you use a **search engine** that catalogs Web sites in a series of directories and conducts keyword searches. Generally, use a directory when you haven't yet refined your topic or you want a general overview. Use keywords when you have refined your topic and you seek specific information.

Current search engines

Dozens of search engines are available. The following box lists the currently most popular engines. (To reach any of them, enter its URL in the Address or Location field of your Web browser.)

Video
tutorial

Web search engines

The features of search engines change often, and new ones appear constantly. For the latest on search engines, see the links collected by *Easy Searcher* at *www.easysearcher.com*.

Directories that review sites
Infomine (*infomine.ucr.edu*)
ipl2 (*ipl.org*)
Internet Scout Project (*scout.wisc.edu/archives*)

Search engines

AlltheWeb (alltheweb.com)
AltaVista (altavista.com)
Ask.com (ask.com)
Bing (bing.com)
Dogpile (dogpile.com)
Google (google.com)
MetaCrawler (metacrawler.com)
Yahoo! (yahoo.com)

Note For a good range of sources, try out more than a single search engine, perhaps as many as four or five. No search engine can catalog the entire Web—indeed, even the most powerful engine may not include half the sites available at any given time, and most engines include only a fifth or less. In addition, most search engines accept paid placements, giving higher billing to sites that pay a fee. These so-called sponsored links are usually marked as such, but they can compromise a search engine's method for arranging sites in response to your keywords.

Customized searches

The home page of a search engine includes a field for you to type your keywords into. Generally, it will also include an Advanced Search link that you can use to customize your search. For instance, you may be able to select a range of dates, a language, or a number of results to see. Advanced Search will also explain how to use operators such as *AND* and *NOT* to limit or expand your search.

Search records

No matter which search engines you use, your Web browser includes functions that allow you to keep track of Web sources and your search:

- Use *Favorites* or *Bookmarks* to save site addresses as links. Click one of these terms near the top of the browser screen to add a site you want to return to. A favorite or bookmark remains on file until you delete it.
- Use *History* to locate sites you have visited before. The browser records sites for a certain period, such as a day, a week, or a month. (You can set the period in the browser's Tools menu.) If you forgot to bookmark a site, click History or Go to recover the site from the search history.

Note If you do Web research on a public computer, such as in a lab at school, your favorites and history probably will not be saved from one day to the next. To track sources that you may want to return to, copy the site URLs and e-mail them to yourself or save them in a file.

2 Following a sample Web search

For his initial search of the Web, Justin Malik started on *Google* with the keywords *green products*. But the search returned more than 53 *million* items, with the first page consisting entirely of sites selling products, including sponsored sites and other advertisers (see screen 1 below). Malik realized he had to alter his strategy to get more useful results. Following the same procedure he had used with a periodical database, he experimented with combinations of synonyms and narrower terms. The keywords *"green consumerism" products* did refine the search but still produced 130,000 results.

From *Google*'s Advanced Search help, Malik learned that he could specify what he wanted to see in the URLs of sources. Adding *site:.gov* limited the results to government sites, whose URLs end in *.gov*. With *"green consumerism" products site:.gov*, Malik received 197 results (see screen 2). Although the number was still large, the government origin combined with *Google*'s criteria for ranking sources gave Malik confidence that he would easily find sources to serve his needs. He continued to limit the search by replacing

1. First *Google* search results

2. *Google* results with refined keywords

site:.gov with *site:.org* (nonprofit organizations), *site:.edu* (educational institutions), and *site:.com* (commercial organizations).

Knowing that no search engine catalogs every Web site, Malik also tried his successful keywords on two other engines, *AlltheWeb* and *Dogpile*. The *AlltheWeb* search turned up an additional promising site among the first thirty. The *Dogpile* search, which worked through multiple search engines, returned about sixty more items, including many irrelevant ones but also one more possible source.

Malik's Web search illustrates the trial-and-error approach required to refine keywords so that they locate worthwhile sources. Almost any Web search will require similar persistence and patience.

42g Finding sources using social media

Online sources that you reach through interactive media can put you directly in touch with experts and others whose ideas and information may inform your research. These social media include e-mail, blogs, social-networking sites, and discussion groups. Like Web sites, they are unfiltered, so you must always evaluate them carefully. (See pp. 622–25.)

Note If your paper includes social-media correspondence that is not already public—for instance, an e-mail or a discussion-group posting—ask the author for permission to use it. Doing so advises the author that his or her ideas are about to be distributed more widely and lets the author verify that you have not misrepresented the ideas. (See also pp. 608–09 on interviews.)

1 Using e-mail

As a research tool, e-mail allows you to communicate with others who are interested in your topic. You might, for instance, carry on an e-mail conversation with a teacher at your school or interview an expert in another state to follow up on a scholarly article he or she published. (See pp. 5–7 on writing e-mail.)

2 Using blogs and social-networking sites

Blogs (Web logs) are Web sites on which an author or authors post time-stamped comments, generally centering on a common theme, in a format that allows readers to respond to the writer or to one another. You can find directories of blogs at *blogcatalog.com*. (See also pp. 133–34 for a discussion and an example of presenting writing on a blog.)

Somewhat similar to blogs, pages on social-networking sites such as *Facebook* are increasingly being used by organizations, businesses, individuals, and even scholars to communicate with others.

Like all other social media discussed in this section, blogs and pages on social-networking sites must be evaluated carefully as potential sources. Some are reliable sources of opinion and evolving scholarship, and many refer to worthy books, articles, Web sites, and other resources. But just as many are little more than outlets for their authors' gripes or self-marketing. See pages 622–25 for tips on telling the good from the bad.

3 Using discussion lists

A **discussion list** (sometimes called a **listserv** or just a **list**) uses e-mail to connect individuals who are interested in a common subject, often with a scholarly or technical focus. By sending a question to an appropriate list, you may be able to reach scores of people who know something about your topic. For an index of discussion lists, see *tile.net*.

Begin research on a discussion list by consulting the list's archive to ensure that the discussion is relevant to your topic and to see whether your question has already been answered. When you write to the list, follow the guidelines for writing e-mail on pages 5–7. And always evaluate messages you receive, following the guidelines on pages 622–25. Although many contributors are reliable experts, almost anyone with an Internet connection can post a message.

4 Using Web forums and newsgroups

Web forums and newsgroups are more open and less scholarly than discussion lists, so their messages require even more diligent evaluation. **Web forums** allow participants to join a conversation simply by selecting a link on a Web page. For a directory of forums, see *delphiforums.com*. **Newsgroups** are organized under subject headings such as *soc* for social issues and *biz* for business. For a directory of newsgroups, see *groups.google.com*.

42h Finding government publications

Government publications provide a vast array of data compilations, reports, policy statements, public records, and other historical and contemporary information. For US government publications, by far the most numerous, consult the Government Printing Office's *GPO Access* at *www.gpoaccess.gov*. Also helpful is *Google US Government Search* (*google.com/unclesam*) because it returns *.gov* (government) and *.mil* (military) documents and its ranking system emphasizes the most useful documents. Many federal, state, and local government agencies post important publications—legislation, reports, press releases—on their own Web sites. You can find lists of sites for various federal agencies by using the keywords *United States federal government* with any search engine. Use the name of a state, city, or town with *government* for state and local information. With the keywords *US Environmental Protection Agency*, Justin Malik found the following graph of the volume of municipal solid waste (MSW) produced in the United States:

Graph from a government publication

Figure 1. MSW Generation Rates, 1960 to 2009

Government Web sites can be sources for data, policy, consumer advice, and other information.

Besides what's available online, your library will have a large collection of printed government publications only if it is a depository library (that is, designated to receive such documents). If yours is a depository library, ask a librarian to help you locate the documents you seek.

42i Finding visuals, audio, and video

Visuals, audio, and video can be used as both primary and secondary sources in a research project. A painting, an advertisement, or a video of a speech might be the subject of your writing and thus a primary source. A college lecture or a podcast of a radio interview with an expert on your subject might serve as a secondary source. Because many of these sources are unfiltered—they can be posted by anyone—you must always evaluate them as carefully as you would any source you find on the open Web. (See pp. 622–25.)

Caution You must also cite every visual, audio, and video source fully in your paper, just as you cite text sources, with author, title, and publication information. In addition, some sources will require that you seek permission from the copyright holder, either the source itself or a third party such as a photographer or the creator of a video. Permission is especially likely to be required if you are submitting your project on the public Web. (See pp. 655–56 for more about online publication.) To avoid having to seek permission, you can search for visuals, audio, and video that are not protected by copyright. On *Google*, for instance, go to Advanced Search and select "Labeled for reuse." Consult a librarian at your school if you have questions.

1 Finding visuals

Pages 123–30 discuss the use of visuals as evidence in your writing. To find visuals, you have a number of options:

- **Scout for visuals while reading print or online sources.** Your sources may include charts, photographs, and other visuals that can support your ideas. When you find a visual you may want to use, photocopy or download it so you'll have it available later.
- **Create your own visuals,** such as photographs or charts. See pages 123–27 for suggestions on creating visuals.
- **Use an image search engine.** *Google, Yahoo!, AlltheWeb,* and some other search engines can be set to search for visuals, and they allow you to restrict your search to visuals that don't require reuse permission. Although search engines can find scores of visuals, the results may be inaccurate or incomplete because the sources surveyed often do not include descriptions of the visuals. (The engines search file names and any text accompanying the visuals.)
- **Use a public image database.** The following sites generally conduct accurate searches because their images are filed with information such as a description of the visual, the artist's name, and the visual's date:

Duke University, *Ad*Access (library.duke.edu/digitalcollections/adaccess).* Print advertisements spanning 1911–55.

Library of Congress, *American Memory* (*memory.loc.gov/ammem*). Maps, photographs, prints, and advertisements documenting the American experience.

Library of Congress, *Prints and Photographs Online Catalog* (*loc.gov/pictures*). Visuals from the library's collection, including those available through American Memory.

New York Public Library Digital Gallery (*digitalgallery.nypl.org/nypldigital*). Maps, drawings, photographs, and paintings from the library's collection.

Political Cartoons (*politicalcartoons.com*). Cartoons on contemporary issues and events.

42i

■ **Use a public image directory.** The following sites collect links to image sources:

Art Project (*googleartproject.com*). Selections of fine art from major museums in the United States and Europe.

Art Source (*ilpi.com/artsource/general.html*). Sources on art and architecture.

MuseumLink's Museum of Museums (*museumlink.com*). Links to museums all over the world.

Cultural Politics: Resources for Critical Analysis (*culturalpolitics.net*). Sources on advertising, fashion, magazines, toys, and other artifacts of popular culture.

Yale University Arts Library, *Image Resources* (*www.library.yale.edu/arts*). Sources on the visual and performing arts.

■ **Use a subscription database.** Your library may subscribe to the following resources:

ARTstor. Museum collections and a database of images typically used in art history courses.

Associated Press, *AccuNet/AP Multimedia Archives*. Historical and contemporary news images.

Grove Art Online. Art images and links to museum sites.

Many visuals you find will be available at no charge for copying or downloading, but some sources do charge a fee for use. Before paying for a visual, check with a librarian to see if it is available elsewhere for free.

2 Finding audio and video

Audio and video, widely available on the Web and on disc, can provide you and your readers with the experience of "being there." For example, if you are researching the media response to Martin Luther King's famous *I Have a Dream* speech and you are publishing your paper electronically, you might insert links to the speech and to TV and radio coverage of it.

■ **Audio files** such as podcasts, Webcasts, and CDs record radio programs, interviews, speeches, lectures, and music. They are available on the Web and through your library. Online sources of audio include the Library of Congress's *American Memory* (see the previous page) and podcasts at *www.podcastdirectory.com*.

■ **Video files** capture performances, public presentations and speeches, news events, and other activities. They are available on the Web and on DVD or Blu-ray disc from your library. Online sources of video include the Library of Congress's *American Memory* (see the previous page); *YouTube*, which includes commercials, historical footage, current events, and much more (*youtube.com*); and search engines such as *Google* (*video .google.com*).

42j   Generating your own sources

Some academic writing assignments will require you to consult primary sources and to conduct primary research for information of your own. In many papers this primary research will be the sole basis for your writing, as when you analyze a poem or report on an experiment you conducted. In other papers you will be expected to use primary research to support, extend, or refute the ideas of others. Three common forms of primary research are personal interviews, surveys, and observation.

1   Conducting personal interviews

A personal interview with an expert on the topic you are researching can provide the kind of information you won't find in books, articles, or Web documents. Because of the give-and-take of an interview, you can ask questions precisely geared to your topic and follow up on points of confusion and unexpected leads. In addition, quotations and paraphrases from an interview can give your paper immediacy and authority.

You can conduct an interview in person, over the telephone, or online. A personal interview is preferable if you can arrange it because you can see the person's expressions and gestures as well as hear his or her tone. But telephone and online interviews allow you to consult someone who resists a personal interview or who lives far away from you, while still retaining most advantages of interaction.

A few precautions will help you get the maximum information from an interview with the minimum disruption to the person you are interviewing:

■ **Choose your interviewee carefully.** If you do not already know whom to consult for an interview, ask a teacher in the field or do some telephone or library research. Likely sources, depending on your topic, are those who have written about your topic or something closely related, officials in government, businesspeople, even a relative, if he or she is an expert on your topic because of experience, scholarship, or both.

- **Call or write for an appointment.** Tell the person exactly why you are calling, what you want to discuss, and how long you expect the interview to take. Be true to your word on all points.
- **Prepare a list of open-ended questions to ask**—perhaps ten or twelve for a one-hour interview. Do some research on these questions ahead of the interview to discover background on the issues and your subject's published views on the issues.
- **Pay attention to your subject's answers** so that you can ask appropriate follow-up questions. Take care in interpreting answers, especially if you are online and thus can't depend on facial expressions, gestures, and tone of voice to convey the subject's attitudes. Ask for clarification when you need it.
- **Keep thorough notes.** Take notes during an in-person or telephone interview, or record the interview if you have the equipment and your subject agrees. For online interviews, save the discussion in a file of its own.
- **Verify quotations.** Before you quote your subject in your paper, check with him or her to ensure that the quotations are accurate.
- **Send a thank-you note immediately after the interview.** Promise your subject a copy of your finished paper, and send the paper promptly.

42j

2 Conducting surveys

Asking questions of a defined group of people can provide information about respondents' attitudes, behavior, backgrounds, and expectations. Use the following tips to plan and conduct a survey:

- **Decide what you want to find out.** The questions you ask should be dictated by your purpose. Formulating a **hypothesis** about your subject—a generalization that can be tested—will help you refine your purpose.
- **Define your population.** Think about the kinds of people your hypothesis is about—for instance, college men or preschool children. Plan to sample this population so that your findings will be representative.
- **Write your questions.** Surveys may contain closed questions that direct the respondent's answers (checklists and multiple-choice, true/false, or yes/no questions) or open-ended questions that allow brief, descriptive answers. Avoid loaded questions that reveal your own biases or make assumptions about subjects' answers, such as "Do you want the United States to support democracy in China?" or "How much more money does your father make than your mother?"
- **Test your questions.** Use a few respondents with whom you can

discuss the answers. Eliminate or recast questions that respondents find unclear, discomforting, or unanswerable.

- **Tally the results.** Count the actual numbers of answers, including any nonanswers.
- **Seek patterns in the raw data.** Such patterns may confirm or contradict your hypothesis. Revise the hypothesis or conduct additional research if necessary.

42j

3 Observing

Observation can be an effective way to gather fresh information on your subject. You may observe in a controlled setting—for instance, watching children at play in a child-development lab. Or you may observe in a more open setting—for instance, watching the interactions among students at a cafeteria on your campus. Use these guidelines for planning and gathering information through observation:

- **Be sure that what you want to learn *can* be observed.** You can observe people's choices and interactions, but you would need an interview or a survey to discover people's attitudes or opinions.
- **Allow ample time.** Observation requires several sessions of several hours in order to be reliable.
- **Record your impressions.** Throughout the observation sessions, take careful notes on paper, a computer, or a mobile device. Always record the date, time, and location for each session.
- **Be aware of your own bias.** Such awareness will help you avoid the common pitfall of seeing only what you expect or want to see.

Exercise 42.1   Using the library

Exercise

To become familiar with the research sources available through your library, visit both the library and its Web site for answers to the following questions. Ask a librarian for help whenever necessary.

1. Which resources does the library include on its Web site? Which resources require a visit to the library?
2. Where are reference books stored in the library? How are they cataloged and arranged? Which ones are available through the Web site? Where and in what format(s) are (*a*) *Contemporary Authors,* (*b*) *Encyclopaedia Britannica,* and (*c*) *MLA International Bibliography of Books and Articles on the Modern Languages and Literatures*?
3. Where is the catalog of the library's periodicals? Where and in what format(s) does the library have current and back issues of the following periodicals: (*a*) the *New York Times,* (*b*) *Harper's* magazine, and (*c*) *Journal of Social Psychology*?
4. What tools does the library's Web site offer for finding periodical databases that are appropriate for a particular research subject?
5. Research the focus and indexed publications of two periodical databases, such as *Academic Search Complete, JSTOR, LexisNexis, PAIS,* or *ProQuest Research Library.* What disciplines does each database seem most suited for?

6. Does the catalog cover all of the library's book holdings? If not, which books are not included, and where are they cataloged?
7. What are the library call numbers of the following books: (*a*) *The Power Broker*, by Robert Caro; (*b*) *Heart of Darkness*, by Joseph Conrad; and (*c*) *The Hero with a Thousand Faces*, by Joseph Campbell?

Exercise 42.2 Finding library sources

Locate at least six promising articles and books for the subject you began working on in the previous chapter (Exercise 41.1, p. 575, and Exercise 41.2, p. 579). Consider the sources "promising" if they seem directly to address your central research question. Following the guidelines on pages 579–82, make an annotated working bibliography of the sources. Be sure to include all the information you will need to acknowledge the sources in your final paper.

Exercise 42.3 Finding Web sources

Use at least two Web search engines to locate six or seven promising sources for your research project. Begin by developing a list of keywords that can be used to query one of the search engines (see pp. 586–87). Then try your keywords on the other search engine as well. How do the results differ? What keyword strategies worked best for finding relevant information? Add promising sources to your annotated working bibliography.

43

Working with Sources

The previous chapters helped you lay the groundwork for a research project. This chapter takes you into the most personal, most intensive, and most rewarding part of research writing: using the sources you've found to extend and support your own ideas, to make your subject your own. As before, the work of Justin Malik (on green consumerism) and Vanessa Haley (on the work of Annie Dillard) will illustrate the activity and thought that go into research writing.

〈CULTURE LANGUAGE〉 Making a subject your own requires thinking critically about sources and developing independent ideas. These goals may at first be uncomfortable if your native culture emphasizes understanding and respecting established authority more than questioning and enlarging it. This chapter offers guidance in

mycomplab

Visit *mycomplab.com* for the eText and for resources and more exercises on working with sources.

working with sources so that you can become an expert in your own right and convincingly convey your expertise to others.

Video
tutorial

43a

43a   Evaluating sources

When you evaluate sources, you look at them critically and judge them with a variety of criteria. Evaluation is one of the most challenging aspects of research because it requires you to determine whether a source is worthwhile in itself and for your research project.

1   Gaining an overview

Once you have a satisfactory working bibliography, you want to get a sense of your sources' usefulness and value.

■ **Look first at sources that seem most likely to define your subject.** Justin Malik started with a scholarly review of the literature on green consumption. Vanessa Haley turned first to a book by Annie Dillard, Haley's subject. (For a paper like Haley's that analyzes a writer's work, always begin with that work.)

■ **Scan sources to gauge the kind and extent of their ideas and information.** Don't get bogged down collecting information at this point. Instead, ensure that your sources are appropriately detailed and cover the full range of your subject—that together they promise to help you answer your research question.

■ **Update your annotated bibliography with assessments of sources.** As you take the measure of sources, add your evaluations to

---

Annotated bibliography entry with assessment

Publication information for source

> Gore, Al. *Our Choice: A Plan to Solve the Climate Crisis*. Emmaus: Rodale, 2009. Print.

Summary of source (from working bibliography)

> A sequel to Gore's *An Inconvenient Truth* that emphasizes solutions to global warming. Expands on the argument that global warming is a serious threat, with recent examples of natural disasters. Proposes ways that governments, businesses, and individuals can reduce or reverse the risks of global warming. Includes helpful summaries of scientific studies, short essays on various subjects, and dozens of images, tables, charts, and graphs.

Assessment of source

> Compelling overview of possible solutions, with lots of data that seem thorough and convincing. But the book is aimed at a general audience and doesn't have formal source citations. Can use it for broad concepts, but for data I'll have to track down Gore's scholarly sources.

your working bibliography. The writing will help you differentiate sources and start you on building connections among them. In each annotation, summarize the purpose, main argument, and any apparent bias of the source. Also note any questions you have about it. The example on the facing page comes from Justin Malik's evolving bibliography and adds to the entry on page 582.

Student paper

2 Judging relevance and reliability

43a

Not all the sources you find will prove worthwhile: some may be irrelevant to your project, and others may be unreliable. Gauging the relevance and reliability of sources is the essential task of evaluating them. If you haven't already done so, read this book's Chapters 6 and 8 on critical reading. They provide a foundation for answering the questions in the following box.

Video tutorial

Exercise

Questions for evaluating sources

For online sources, supplement these questions with those on pages 615 and 623.

Checklist

Relevance

▪ **Does the source devote some attention to your subject?** Does it focus on your subject or cover it marginally? How does it compare to other sources you've found?

▪ **Is the source appropriately specialized for your needs?** Check the source's treatment of a topic you know something about, to ensure that it is neither too superficial nor too technical.

▪ **Is the source up to date enough for your subject?** When was it published? If your subject is current, your sources should be, too.

Reliability

▪ **Where does the source come from?** Did you find it through your library or directly through the Internet? (If the latter, see the note on the next page.) Is it popular or scholarly?

▪ **Is the author an expert in the field?** Check the author's credentials in a biography (if the source includes one), in a biographical reference (see p. 590), or by a keyword search of the Web.

▪ **What is the bias of the source?** How do the author's ideas relate to those in other sources? What areas does the author emphasize, ignore, or dismiss?

▪ **Is the source fair, reasonable, and well written?** Does it provide sound reasoning and a fair picture of opposing views? Is the tone calm and objective? Is the source logically organized and error-free?

▪ **Are the author's claims well supported?** Does the author provide accurate, relevant, representative, and adequate evidence to back up his or her claims? Does the author cite sources, and if so are they reliable?

43a

Note In evaluating sources, you need to consider how they came to you. The sources you find through the library, both in print and on the Web, have been previewed for you by their publishers and by the library's staff. They still require your critical reading, but you can have some confidence in the information they contain. With online sources you reach directly, however, you cannot assume similar previewing, so your critical reading must be especially rigorous. Special tips for evaluating Web sites and other online sources begin on the next page.

3 Evaluating library sources

To evaluate sources you find through your library—either in print or on the library's Web site—look at dates, titles, summaries, introductions, headings, author biographies, and any source citations. The following criteria expand on the most important tips in the box on the previous page. On pages 616–17 you can see how Justin Malik applied these criteria to two print sources, a magazine article and a journal article, that he consulted during his research into green consumerism.

Identify the origin of the source.

Check whether a library source is popular or scholarly. Scholarly sources, such as refereed journals and university press books, are generally deeper and more reliable. But some popular sources, such as first-hand newspaper accounts and books for a general audience, are often appropriate for research projects.

Check the author's expertise.

The authors of scholarly publications tend to be experts whose authority can be verified. Check the source to see whether it contains a biographical note about the author, check a biographical reference (see p. 590), or check the author's name in a keyword search of the Web. Look for other publications by the author and for his or her job and any affiliation, such as teacher at a university, researcher with a nonprofit organization, author of general-interest books, or writer for popular magazines.

Identify the author's bias.

Every author has a point of view that influences the selection and interpretation of evidence. You may be able to learn about an author's bias from biographies, review indexes (p. 593), and citation indexes (p. 598). But also look at the source itself. How do the author's ideas relate to those in other sources? What areas does the author emphasize, ignore, or dismiss? When you're aware of sources' biases, you can acknowledge them in your writing and try to balance them.

Determine whether the source is fair, reasonable, and well written.

Even a strongly biased work should present solid reasoning and give balanced coverage to opposing views—all in an objective tone. View with suspicion any source that is not organized logically and written in clear, error-free sentences.

Analyze support for the author's claims.

Evidence should be accurate, relevant to the argument, representative of its context, and adequate for the point being made (see pp. 192–94). The author's sources should themselves be reliable.

4 Evaluating Web sites

To a great extent, the same critical reading that helps you evaluate library sources will help you evaluate Web sites that you reach directly. Just as you would not use a popular magazine such as *People* for academic research, you would not use a celebrity's Web site, a fan site, or a gossip site as a source. But Web sites that might seem worthy pose extra challenges for evaluation because they have not undergone prior screening by editors and librarians. On your own, you must distinguish scholarship from corporate promotion, valid data from invented statistics, and well-founded opinion from clever propaganda.

Video tutorial

To make such distinctions, use the strategy that is summarized in the following box and explained on pages 618–19 and 622. On pages 620–21 you can see how Justin Malik applied the strategy to two Web sites he found during his research into green consumerism.

Questions for evaluating Web sites

Supplement these questions with those on page 613.

Checklist

- ▪ **What type of site are you viewing?** What does the type lead you to expect about the site's purpose and content?
- ▪ **Who is the author or sponsor?** How credible is the person or group responsible for the site?
- ▪ **What is the purpose and bias of the site?** What does the site's author or sponsor intend to achieve? What bias do you detect?
- ▪ **What does context tell you?** What do you already know about the site's subject that can inform your evaluation? What kinds of support or other information do the site's links provide?
- ▪ **What does presentation tell you?** Is the site's design well thought out and effective? Is the writing clear and error-free?
- ▪ **How worthwhile is the content?** Are the site's claims well supported by evidence? Is the evidence from reliable sources? When was the site last updated?

(continued on p. 618)

Evaluating library sources

Video tutorial

43a

Opposite are sample pages from two library sources that Justin Malik considered for his paper on green consumerism. Malik evaluated the sources using the questions in the box on page 613 and the guidelines on pages 614–15.

Makower	Jackson
Origin	
Interview with Joel Makower published in *Vegetarian Times*, a popular magazine.	Article by Tim Jackson published in *Journal of Industrial Ecology*, a scholarly journal sponsored by two reputable universities: MIT and Yale.
Author	
Gives Makower's credentials at the beginning of the interview: the author of a book on green products and of a monthly newsletter on green businesses. Quotes another source that calls Makower the "guru of green business practice."	Includes a biography at the end of the article that describes Jackson as a professor at the University of Surrey (UK) and lists his professional activities related to the environment.
Bias	
Describes and promotes green products. Concludes with an endorsement of a for-profit Web site that tracks and sells green products.	Presents multiple views of green consumerism. Argues that a solution to environmental problems will involve green products and less consumption but in different ways than currently proposed.
Reasonableness and writing	
Presents Makower's data and perspective on distinguishing good from bad green products, using conversational writing in an informal presentation.	Presents and cites opposing views objectively, using formal academic writing.
Source citations	
Lacks source citations for claims and data.	Includes more than three pages of source citations, many of scholarly and government sources and all cited within the article.
Assessment	
Probably unreliable: Despite Makower's reputation, the article comes from a nonscholarly source, takes a one-sided approach to consumption, and depends on statistics credited only to Makower.	**Probably reliable:** The article comes from a scholarly journal, the author is an expert in the field, he discusses many views and concedes some, and his source citations confirm evidence from reliable sources.

43a

First and last pages of
an interview with Joel
Makower, published
in *Vegetarian Times*

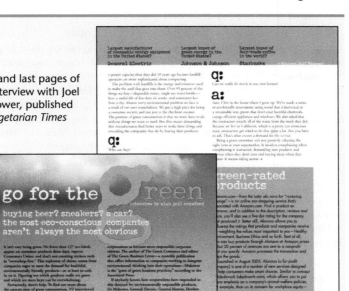

First and last pages of an
article by Tim Jackson,
published in the *Journal of
Industrial Ecology*

(continued from p. 615)

Note To evaluate a Web document, you'll often need to travel to the site's home page to discover the author or sponsor, date of publication, and other relevant information. The page you're reading may include a link to the home page. If it doesn't, you can find it by editing the URL in the Address or Location field of your browser. Working backward, delete the end of the URL up to the last slash and hit Enter. Repeat this step until you reach the home page. There you may also find a menu option, often labeled "About," that will lead you to a description of the site's author or sponsor.

43a

Determine the type of site.

Video tutorial

When you search the Web, you're likely to encounter various types of sites. Although they overlap—a primarily informational site may include scholarship as well—the types can usually be identified by their content and purposes. Here are the main types of Web sites you will find using a search engine:

- **Scholarly sites:** These sites have a knowledge-building interest, and they are likely to be reliable. They include research reports with supporting data and extensive documentation of scholarly sources. For such sites originating in the United States, the URLs generally end in *edu* (originating from a college or university), *org* (a nonprofit organization), or *gov* (a government department or agency). Sites originating in other countries will end differently, usually with a country code such as *uk* (United Kingdom), *de* (Germany), or *kr* (South Korea).

- **Informational sites:** Individuals, nonprofit organizations, corporations, schools, and government bodies all produce sites intended to centralize information on subjects as diverse as astronomy, hip-hop music, and zoo design. The sites' URLs may end in *edu, org, gov,* or *com* (originating from a commercial organization). Such sites generally do not have the knowledge-building focus of scholarly sites and may omit supporting data and documentation, but they can provide useful information and sometimes include links to scholarly and other sources.

- **Advocacy sites:** Many sites present the views of individuals or organizations that promote certain policies or actions, such as the National Rifle Association or People for the Ethical Treatment of Animals. Their URLs usually end in *org*, but they may end in *edu* or *com*. Most advocacy sites have a strong bias. Some sites include serious, well-documented research to support their positions, but others select or distort evidence.

- **Commercial sites:** Corporations and other businesses—such as automakers, electronics manufacturers, and booksellers—maintain Web sites to explain themselves, promote themselves, or sell goods and services. URLs of commercial sites usually end in *com*; however, some end in *biz*, and those of businesses based outside the United States often end in the country code. Although business sites intend to further the sponsors' profit-making purposes, they can include reliable data.

- Personal sites: The sites maintained by individuals range from diaries of a family's travels to opinions on political issues to reports on evolving scholarship. The sites' URLs usually end in *com* or *edu*. Personal sites are only as reliable as their authors, but some do provide eyewitness accounts, links to worthy sources, and other usable information. Personal sites are often blogs or pages on social-networking sites, discussed on pages 622–25.

43a

Note Informational sites called **wikis** allow anyone to contribute and edit information. Older entries on reputable wikis, such as *Wikipedia*, tend to be reliable because they have been reviewed and edited by experts, but recent entries may contain errors and even misinformation. Ask your instructor whether wikis are acceptable sources. If so, evaluate them carefully against other, more reliable sources using the guidelines in the box on page 615 and below.

Identify the author and sponsor.

A reputable site lists its authors, names the group responsible for the site, and provides information or a link for contacting the author and the sponsor. If none of this information is provided, you should not use the source. If you have only the author's or the sponsor's name, you may be able to discover more in a biographical dictionary, through a keyword search, or in your other sources. Make sure the author and the sponsor have expertise on the subject they're presenting: if an author is a doctor, for instance, what is he or she a doctor of?

Gauge purpose and bias.

A Web site's purpose determines what ideas and information it offers. Inferring that purpose tells you how to interpret what you see on the site. If a site is intended to sell a product or advocate a particular position, it may emphasize favorable ideas and information while ignoring or even distorting unfavorable information or opposing views. In contrast, if a site is intended to build knowledge—for instance, a scholarly project or journal—it will likely acknowledge diverse views and evidence.

Determining the purpose and bias of a site often requires looking beyond the first page and beneath the surface of words and images. To start, read critically what the site says about itself, usually on a page labeled "About." Be suspicious of any site that doesn't provide information about itself and its goals.

(continued on p. 622)

Evaluating Web Sites

Video
tutorial

43a

Opposite are screen shots from two Web sites that Justin Malik consulted for his paper on green consumerism. Malik evaluated the sources using the questions in the boxes on pages 613 and 615.

Allianz Knowledge Partnersite	*Nature: Climate Change*
Author and sponsor	
Site sponsor is the Allianz Group, a global insurance company partnering with well-known organizations to provide information on a variety of issues. Author of article is identified as an editor, not a scientist.	Listed author is a scientist, an expert on climate science. (Biography appears at the end of the article.) Site sponsor is the Nature Publishing Group, which also publishes the reputable science journal *Nature*.
Purpose and bias	
Educational page on a corporate-sponsored Web site with the self-stated purpose of gathering information about global issues and making it available to an international audience.	Informational site with the self-stated purpose of "publishing the most significant and cutting-edge research on the impacts of global climate change." Article expresses bias toward reducing pollution to stop climate change.
Context	
One of many sites publishing current information on climate issues.	One of many sites publishing current research on climate issues.
Presentation	
Clean, professionally designed site with mostly error-free writing.	Clean, professionally designed site with error-free writing.
Content	
Article gives basic information about climate change and provides links to other pages that expand on its claims. Probably because of the intended general (nonscientist) audience, the pages do not include citations of scholarly research.	Article is current (date below the author's name) and clearly explains an effect of climate change with references and links to scholarly sources. Other links connect to hundreds of articles elsewhere on the site about climate-related topics.
Assessment	
Probably unreliable: Despite the wealth of information in the article and its links, the material lacks the scholarly source citations necessary for its use as evidence in an academic paper.	**Probably reliable:** The article has an explicit bias toward stopping climate change, but the site sponsor has a scholarly reputation, the author is a climate expert, and the references cite scholarly and government sources.

Article published on the Web site *Allianz Knowledge Partnersite*

Article published on the Web site *Nature: Climate Change*

(continued from p. 619)

Consider context.

Your evaluation of a Web site should be informed by considerations outside the site itself. Chief among these considerations is your own knowledge. What do you already know about the site's subject and the prevailing views of it? Where does this site seem to fit into that picture? What can you learn from this site that you don't already know?

In addition, you can follow some of the site's links to see how they support, or don't support, the site's credibility. For instance, links to scholarly sources lend authority to a site—but *only* if the scholarly sources actually relate to and back up the site's claims.

Look at presentation.

Considering both the look of a site and the way it's written can illuminate its intentions and reliability. Do the site's elements all support its purpose, or is the site cluttered with irrelevant material and graphics? Is the text clearly written and focused on the purpose? Is it relatively error-free, or does it contain typos and grammatical errors? Does the site seem carefully constructed and well maintained, or is it sloppy? How intrusive are any pop-up advertisements?

Analyze content.

With information about a site's author, purpose, and context, you're in a position to evaluate its content. Are the ideas and information current, or are they dated? (Check the publication date.) Are they slanted and, if so, in what direction? Are the views and data authoritative, or do you need to balance them—or even reject them? Are claims made on the site supported by evidence drawn from reliable sources? These questions require close reading of both the text and its sources.

5 | Evaluating other online sources

Social media and multimedia require the same critical scrutiny as Web sites do. Social media—including e-mail, blogs, discussion groups, *Facebook* pages, and wikis—can be sources of reliable data and opinions, but they can also contain wrong or misleading data and skewed opinions. Multimedia—visuals, audio, and video—can provide valuable support for your ideas, but they can also mislead or distort. For example, a *YouTube* search using "I have a dream" brings up videos of Martin Luther King, Jr., delivering his famous speech as well as videos of people speaking hatefully about King and the speech.

Use the following strategy for evaluating such online sources. See pages 624–25 for Justin Malik's use of this strategy with a blog he found while researching green consumerism.

43a

Questions for evaluating social media and multimedia

Supplement these questions with those on page 613.

Checklist

- Who is the author or creator? How credible is he or she?
- What is the author's or creator's purpose? What can you tell about why the author or creator is publishing the work?
- What does the context reveal? What do responses to the work, such as responses to a blog posting or the other messages in a discussion thread, indicate about the source's balance and reliability?
- How worthwhile is the content? Are the claims made by the author or creator supported by evidence? Is the evidence from reliable sources?
- How does the source compare with other sources? Do the claims made by the author or creator seem accurate and fair, given what you've seen in sources you know to be reliable?

43a

Identify the author or creator.

Checking out the author or creator of a potential source can help you judge its reliability. You may be able to learn about the background of an author or creator with a keyword search of the Web or in a biographical dictionary. If you can't identify the author or creator at all, you can't use the source.

You can also get a sense of the interests and biases of an author or creator by tracking down his or her other work. For instance, you might check whether a blog author cites or links to other publications, look for other postings by the same author in a discussion-group archive, or use a Web search to gain an overview of a photographer's work.

Analyze the author's or creator's purpose.

What can you tell about *why* the author or creator is publishing the work? Look for claims, the use (or not) of evidence, and the treatment of opposing views. All these factors convey the person's stand on the subject and general fairness, and they will help you position the source among your other sources.

Consider the context.

Social media and multimedia are often difficult to evaluate in isolation. Looking beyond a particular contribution to the responses of others can give you a sense of context by indicating how the author or creator is regarded. On a blog or a *Facebook* page, for example, look at the comments others have posted. If you discover negative or angry responses, try to understand why: sometimes online anonymity encourages hateful responses to even quite reasonable postings.

Evaluating a blog

Opposite is a screen shot from a blog that Justin Malik consulted for his paper on green consumerism. Malik evaluated the blog using the questions in the boxes on pages 613 and 623.

Author and sponsor

Author is a climate scientist. (A link provides her credentials.) Blog sponsor is the Environmental Defense Fund, a nonprofit organization operating for more than forty years.

Purpose and bias

Advocacy site and blog with self-stated purpose of drawing on "science, economics, and law to create . . . solutions to society's most urgent environmental problems." Urges site visitors to join the organization and donate money to support its work. Posting assumes readers are somewhat familiar with the science of climate change.

Context

One of many blogs advocating and enlisting readers in action against climate change.

Presentation

Clean, professionally designed site with error-free writing.

Content

Posting is current (date under the title) and clearly explains recent findings with links to government and scholarly sources.

Assessment

Probably reliable: The site sponsor has a bias toward environmental causes, but it has a strong reputation, the author of the blog posting is an expert, and the posting cites reliable sources.

Analyze content.

A reliable source will offer evidence for claims and sources for evidence. If you don't see such support, then you probably shouldn't use the source. However, when the source is important to you and biographical information or context indicates that the author or creator is serious and reliable, you might ask him or her to direct you to supporting information.

The tone of writing can also be a clue to its purpose and reliability. In most social media, the writing tends to be more informal and may be more heated than in other kinds of sources; but look askance at writing that's contemptuous, dismissive, or shrill.

Compare with other sources.

Always consider social-media and multimedia sources in comparison to other sources so that you can distinguish singular, untested views from more mainstream views that have been subject to verification. Don't assume that a blog author's information and opinions are reliable just because you see them on other blogs. The technology allows content to be picked up instantly by other blogs, so widespread distribution indicates only popular interest, not reliability.

Posting on the blog *Climate 411*, sponsored by the
Environmental Defense Fund

Be wary of blogs that reproduce periodical articles, reports, or
other publications. Try to locate the original version of the publication to be sure it has been reproduced fully and accurately, not
quoted selectively or distorted. If you can't locate the original version, don't use the publication as a source.

Exercise 43.1 Evaluating a source

Imagine that you are researching a paper on the advertising techniques
that are designed to persuade consumers to buy products. You have
listed the following book in your working bibliography:

> Vance Packard, *The Hidden Persuaders,* revised edition, 1981.

On your own or with your classmates (as your instructor wishes), obtain
this book from a library and evaluate it as a source for your paper. Use
the guidelines on page 613.

Exercise

Exercise 43.2 Evaluating Web sites

Find and evaluate two Web sites: a commercial site, such as Microsoft's
or Apple's, and a site for a nonprofit organization, such as the American
Medical Association or Greenpeace. What do you know or can you infer
about each site's sponsor or author? What seems to be the site's purpose

Exercise

or purposes? What do the site's links contribute? How effective is the site's design? How reliable do you judge the site's information to be? How do the two sites differ in these respects?

Exercise

Exercise 43.3   Evaluating a blog

Visit *wordpress.com* or *blogcatalog.com* to find a blog on a controversial subject such as stem-cell research or animal research. Who is responsible for the blog? What can you tell about its purpose? How reliable do you judge its ideas and information to be?

43b

Exercise

Exercise 43.4   Evaluating an online discussion

Using *groups.google.com,* locate a newsgroup on a subject that interests you. (If you already participate in an online discussion group, you can use it instead.) Pick one series of at least ten related messages on a single topic. Write a brief summary of each message (see pp. 152–54 on summarizing). Then analyze and synthesize the messages to develop a one- or two-paragraph evaluation of the discussion. Which messages seem reliable? Which don't? Why?

43b   Synthesizing sources

Video
tutorial

When you begin to see the differences and similarities among sources, you move into the most significant part of research writing: forging relationships for your own purpose. This **synthesis,** an essential step in critical reading (pp. 152–54), continues through the drafting and revision of a research paper. As you read, take notes, and infer connections—say, between one writer's ideas and another's or between two works by the same author—you shape your own perspective on your subject and create new knowledge.

All kinds of connections may occur to you as you work with sources. Justin Malik, researching the environmental impacts of green consumption, found data in one study to support another source's assertions about the personal benefits of buying less. He also uncovered a central disagreement among sources over whether changing individual consumer behavior would make a significant difference on a global scale. Vanessa Haley, writing about Annie Dillard, sought and found similarities in Dillard's ideas about the place of humanity in nature, ideas expressed in varying contexts throughout Dillard's best-known book. Haley also discovered that her view of Dillard was partly supported by some of the critics she consulted but not supported by others. She knew she would have to take account of these divergent views in her paper.

Your synthesis of sources will grow more detailed and sophisticated as you proceed through the process of working with sources described in the balance of this chapter: mining and interacting with sources (pp. 629–33), deciding whether to summarize, paraphrase, or quote directly from sources (pp. 633–40), and integrating sources into your sentences (pp. 642–47). Unless, like Vanessa Haley, you are analyzing primary sources such as the works of a writer, read your sources quickly and selectively at first to obtain an overview of your subject and a sense of how the sources approach it. Instead of taking detailed notes about what sources say, record your own ideas about the sources in your research journal (p. 571) or your annotated bibliography (p. 612).

Respond to sources.

43b

One way to find your own perspective on a topic is to write down what your sources make you think. Do you agree or disagree with the author? Do you find his or her views narrow, or do they open up new approaches for you? Is there anything in the source that you need to research further before you can understand it? Does the source prompt questions that you should keep in mind while reading other sources?

Connect sources.

When you notice a link between sources, write about it. Do two sources differ in their theories or their interpretations of facts? Does one source illuminate another—perhaps commenting or clarifying or supplying additional data? Do two or more sources report studies that support a theory you've read about or an idea of your own?

Heed your insights.

Apart from ideas prompted by your sources, you are sure to come up with independent thoughts: a conviction, a point of confusion that suddenly becomes clear, a question you haven't seen anyone else ask. These insights may occur at unexpected times, so it's good practice to keep a notebook or computer handy to record them.

Draw your own conclusions.

As your research proceeds, the responses, connections, and insights you form through synthesis will lead you to answer your starting research question with a statement of your thesis (see p. 658). They will also lead you to the main ideas supporting your thesis— conclusions you have drawn from your synthesis of sources, forming the main divisions of your paper. Be sure to write them down as they occur to you.

Use sources to support your conclusions.

Effective synthesis requires careful handling of evidence from sources so that it meshes smoothly into your sentences and yet is clearly distinct from your own ideas. When drafting your paper, make sure that each paragraph focuses on an idea of your own, with the support for the idea coming from your sources. Generally, open each paragraph with your own idea, provide evidence from a source or sources with appropriate citations, and close with an interpretation of the evidence. (Avoid ending a paragraph with a source citation; instead, end with your own idea.) In this way, your paper will synthesize others' work into something wholly your own. For more on structuring paragraphs in academic writing, see pages 174–75.

43b

Exercise

Exercise 43.5 Synthesizing sources

The following three passages address the same issue, the legalization of drugs. What similarities do you see in the authors' ideas? What differences? Write a paragraph of your own in which you use these authors' views as a point of departure for your own view about drug legalization.

Perhaps the most unfortunate victims of drug prohibition laws have been the residents of America's ghettos. These laws have proved largely futile in deterring ghetto-dwellers from becoming drug abusers, but they do account for much of what ghetto residents identify as the drug problem. Aggressive, gun-toting drug dealers often upset law-abiding residents far more than do addicts nodding out in doorways. Meanwhile other residents perceive the drug dealers as heroes and successful role models. They're symbols of success to children who see no other options. At the same time the increasingly harsh criminal penalties imposed on adult drug dealers have led drug traffickers to recruit juveniles. Where once children started dealing drugs only after they had been using them for a few years, today the sequence is often reversed. Many children start using drugs only after working for older drug dealers for a while. Legalization of drugs, like legalization of alcohol in the early 1930s, would drive the drug-dealing business off the streets and out of apartment buildings and into government-regulated, tax-paying stores. It also would force many of the gun-toting dealers out of the business and convert others into legitimate businessmen.

—Ethan A. Nadelmann, "Shooting Up"

Statistics argue against legalization. The University of Michigan conducts an annual survey of twelfth graders, asking the students about their drug consumption. In 1980, 56.4% of those polled said they had used marijuana in the past twelve months, whereas in 2010 only 34.8% had done so. Cocaine use was even more reduced in the same period (22.6% to 2.9%). At the same time, twelve-month use of legally available drugs—alcohol and nicotine-containing cigarettes—remained fairly steady around 72% and 50%, respectively. The numbers of illegal drug users haven't declined nearly enough: those teenaged marijuana and cocaine users are still vulnerable to addiction and even death, and they threaten to infect their impressionable peers. But clearly the prohibition of illegal drugs has helped, while the legal status of alcohol and cigarettes has not made them less popular.

—Sylvia Runkle, "The Case against Legalization"

I have to laugh at the debate over what to do about the drug problem. Everyone is running around offering solutions—from making drug use a more serious criminal offense to legalizing it. But there isn't a real solution. I know that. I used and abused drugs, and people, and society, for two decades. Nothing worked to get me to stop all that behavior except just plain being sick and tired. Nothing. Not threats, not ten-plus years in prison, not anything that was said to me. I used until I got through. Period. And that's when you'll win the war. When all the dope fiends are done. Not a minute before.

—Michael W. Posey, "I Did Drugs Until
They Wore Me Out. Then I Stopped."

43c

Exercise 43.6 Evaluating and synthesizing sources

Look up the sources in the working bibliography you made in Exercises 42.2 and 42.3 (p. 611). Evaluate the sources for their relevance and reliability. If the sources seem unreliable or don't seem to give you what you need, expand your working bibliography and evaluate the new sources. In your research journal or annotated bibliography, write down your responses to sources, the connections you perceive among sources, and other original ideas that occur to you.

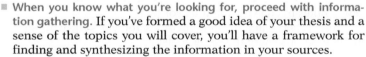

43c Mining and interacting with sources

When you have decided which sources to pursue, you may be ready to gather and synthesize information, or you may want to step back and get your bearings. Your choice will depend mainly on how familiar you are with the main issues of your subject and whether you have formed a central idea about it.

Exercise

- When you know what you're looking for, proceed with information gathering. If you've formed a good idea of your thesis and a sense of the topics you will cover, you'll have a framework for finding and synthesizing the information in your sources.
- When you're uncertain of your direction, stop to draft a thesis statement and create an outline. These steps (discussed on pp. 659–62) can help when you're attracted to several different theses or when you don't see how the various areas of your subject relate.

The following sections discuss a way of reading sources and methods of gathering and organizing information from sources.

1 Skimming and then reading

The most efficient method of reading secondary sources during research is **skimming**, reading quickly to look for pertinent information. (Primary sources usually need to be read more carefully, especially when they are the focus of your paper.) Follow these guidelines for skimming:

- **Read with a specific question in mind,** not randomly in hopes of hitting something worthwhile.
- **Consult reference aids**—tables of contents, menus, indexes, or headings—to find what you want.
- **Concentrate on headings and main ideas,** skipping material unrelated to the specific question you are researching.

When you find something relevant, read slowly and carefully to achieve a clear understanding of what the author is saying and to interpret and evaluate the material in the context of your own and others' opinions.

43c

Video
tutorial

2 Gathering and organizing information

Before you begin mining your sources, decide on categories into which your subject can be divided. (If you have previously outlined your preliminary ideas, use outline headings for these categories.) Justin Malik, for instance, divided his general subject of green consumption into these categories:

Environmental crisis
Business opportunities
Advertising messages
Benefits of green products
Environmental consequences of consumption
Activist perspectives (economic, social, and political issues)
Alternative solutions

Headings for your categories will go at the top of each of your source notes to cue you about its content.

Researchers vary in their methods for working with sources, but all methods share the same goals:

- **Keep accurate records of what sources say.** Accuracy helps prevent misrepresentation and plagiarism.
- **Keep accurate records of how to find sources.** These records are essential for retracing steps and for citing sources in the final paper. (See pp. 579–82 on recording information in a working bibliography.)
- **Synthesize sources.** Information gathering is not a mechanical process but a critical one, leading to an understanding of sources, the relationships among them and your own ideas, and their support for your ideas.

You can accomplish these goals by taking handwritten notes, typing notes into a computer or mobile device, annotating photocopies or printouts of sources, or annotating downloaded documents. On any given project, you may use all the methods. Each has advantages and disadvantages.

Note Whichever method you use, take two steps with every note, photocopy, printout, or downloaded document:

- Key the material to your outline so that you know where it goes.
- Record the source's complete publication information, or use the author's name as a shorthand reference to a list where you keep complete publication information. With a printout or a download, always record the source's URL and any DOI (Digital Object Identifier), even if you won't need them in your final source citations, so that you can return to the source if needed. Use Copy and Paste to record URLs and DOIs accurately.

43c

Handwritten notes

Writing notes by hand, either in a research notebook or on 4" × 6" cards, will prove useful when you come across a source with no computer or photocopier handy or when you need to record something brief. Handwritten notes can be risky, though. It's easy to introduce errors as you work from source to paper. And it's possible to copy source language and then later mistake and use it as your own, thus plagiarizing the source. Always take care to make accurate notes and to place big quotation marks around any passage you quote. Some researchers reduce the risk of plagiarism by summarizing or paraphrasing sources on notes instead of quoting them, as described on pages 633–37. Other researchers delay this step until drafting because it increases the risk of error.

Electronic notes

Taking notes on a computer or mobile device can streamline the path of source to note to your paper because you can import the notes into your draft as you write. If you label your files carefully, you can sort notes much as you would on note cards. (The examples on pp. 634–39 illustrate one way of labeling electronic notes.)

Computer notes have the same disadvantages as handwritten notes: the risk of introducing errors and the risk of plagiarizing. As with handwritten notes, be a stickler for accuracy and use quotation marks for quotations.

Photocopies and printouts

Photocopying from print sources or printing out online sources each has distinct advantages for researchers:

- Both methods are convenient, particularly when sources must remain in the library (for instance, bound periodicals and reference works) or when you find sources online (for instance, full-text articles or trustworthy Web pages).
- Both methods may be safer than handwritten or computer notes. Many researchers and teachers believe that photocopying or

printing out sources reduces the risks of error and plagiarism. Each method requires manipulating source material only once, not twice, to use it in your paper. And each method shows you exactly what's quoted as you work source material into your draft.

But photocopies and printouts have disadvantages, too:

- **They can discourage synthesis** by substituting busywork for thinking. You must read, question, and draw meaning from photocopies and printouts as critically as you would any other sources. Highlight or annotate the relevant passages with underlining, circles, and marginal notes about their significance for your subject. (See the example below.)

- **Source records can get lost.** You must take special care to note the publication information for sources directly on a printout or photocopy. If you don't have this information for your final paper, you can't use the source.

- **Photocopies and printouts can encourage unselective quotation.** When drafting from a complete source rather than notes on the source, you may be tempted to import whole blocks rather than the bits that advance and support your ideas. See page 638 for guidelines on judicious use of quotations.

Source printout with annotations

Environmental consequences of consumption

EPA, *Municipal Solid Waste . . .* www.epa.gov/epaoswer/non-hw/
muncpl/pubs/msw10.pdf

The breakdown, by weight, of waste generated in 2009 by product category is shown in Figure 6. Containers and packaging made up the largest portion of waste generated, 30 percent or 72 million tons. The second largest portion came from nondurable goods, which amounted to 22 percent or 53 million tons. Durable goods make up the third largest segment, accounting for 19 percent or 47 million tons. — *Packaging causes almost 1/3 of all waste . . .*

The generation and recovery of materials in the product categories, by weight and recovery as a percent of generation, are shown in Table 2. The table shows that the recovery of containers and packaging was the highest of the four product categories, with about 48 percent of the generated materials recycled. Steel, paper products, and aluminum were the most recycled materials by percentage in this category. — *. . . and less than half of it is recycled.*

Downloads

Researching online, you can usually download full-text articles, Web pages, discussion-group messages, and other materials onto your computer. If you also take notes on your computer, you can use it to organize much or all of your research and then, while drafting, import source information from one file into another.

These advantages of downloading are offset by clear disadvantages:

- **Copying and pasting downloaded source material into your paper creates a high risk of plagiarism.** You must keep clear boundaries between your own ideas and words and those of others by putting quotation marks around anything you paste in a draft or perhaps by using distinctive type fonts or colors. And make sure to record publication information as part of every downloaded document.

- **Downloading can discourage synthesis.** Even more than with photocopies and printouts, you could import a quotation into your paper without understanding it or showing how it supports your own idea. You must make an effort to analyze and interact with downloaded material. Many researchers print out downloaded sources and mark up paper copies. Alternatively, you can use your word processor's Comment and Highlight functions to annotate the electronic file or simply type your own comments into the source. (But use a different color or font!)

43d

43d Using summary, paraphrase, and quotation

Deciding whether to summarize, paraphrase, or quote directly from sources is an important step in synthesizing the sources' ideas and your own. You engage in synthesis when you use your own words to summarize an author's argument or paraphrase a significant example or when you select a significant passage to quote. Choosing summary, paraphrase, or quotation should depend on why you are using a source.

Video tutorial

Caution **Summaries, paraphrases, and quotations all require source citations. A summary or paraphrase without a source citation or a quotation without quotation marks and a source citation is plagiarism.** (See pp. 648–54 for more on plagiarism.)

1 Summarizing

When you **summarize,** you condense an extended idea or argument into a sentence or more in your own words. A full discussion of summary appears on pages 152–54, and you should read that section if you have not already done so.

Video tutorial

Summary is most useful when you want to record the gist of an author's idea without the background or supporting evidence. Justin Malik summarized the following quotation from one of his sources—the introduction by Thomas Princen, Michael Maniates, and Ken Conca to their anthology *Confronting Consumption,* page 4:

> Such intuition is even making its way, albeit slowly, into scholarly circles, where recognition is mounting that ever-increasing pressures on

ecosystems, life-supporting environmental services, and critical natural cycles are driven not only by the sheer number of resource users and the inefficiencies of their resource use, but also by the patterns of resource use themselves. In global environmental policymaking arenas, it is becoming more and more difficult to ignore the fact that overdeveloped countries must restrain their consumption if they expect underdeveloped countries to embrace a more sustainable trajectory. And while global population growth still remains a huge issue in many regions around the world—both rich and poor—per-capita growth in consumption is, for many resources, expanding eight to twelve times faster than population growth.

43d

In the following one-sentence summary, Malik picks out the kernel of the authors' passage and expresses it in his own words:

Summary of source

Environmental consequences of consumption

Princen, Maniates, and Conca 4

Overconsumption may be a more significant cause of environmental problems than increasing population is.

Notice how Malik records the authors' names and the page number in his note to avoid accidentally plagiarizing the authors' idea in his paper.

The examples below show the preceding summary in the context of a draft, the first lacking proper citation and the second with proper citation (in MLA style).

Summary with no citation (plagiarized)

Always seeking newer and better things, we consume without regard for the resources we use or the waste we leave behind. In fact, overconsumption may be a more significant cause of environmental problems than increasing population is.

Summary with proper citation (not plagiarized)

Always seeking newer and better things, we consume without regard for the resources we use or the waste we leave behind. In fact, according to Thomas Princen, Michael Maniates, and Ken Conca, overconsumption may be a more significant cause of environmental problems than increasing population is (4).

See pages 648–54 for more on plagiarism.

2 Paraphrasing

Video tutorial

When you **paraphrase,** you follow much more closely the author's original presentation, but you restate it using your own words and sentence structures. Paraphrase when you want to present or examine an author's line of reasoning but you don't feel the original words merit direct quotation. Generally, a paraphrase is briefer than the original quotation and omits examples and other details.

The note below shows how Malik might have paraphrased the passage by Princen, Maniates, and Conca given on pages 633–34. Notice the record of the authors' names and the page number, which would help Malik avoid confusing the paraphrase with his own ideas and then inadvertently plagiarizing the source in his paper.

43d

Complete paraphrase of source

Environmental consequences of consumption

Princen, Maniates, and Conca 4

Scholars are coming to believe that consumption is partly to blame for changes in ecosystems, reduction of essential natural resources, and changes in natural cycles. Policy makers increasingly see that developing nations will not adopt practices that reduce pollution and waste unless wealthy nations consume less. Rising population around the world does cause significant stress on the environment, but consumption is increasing even more rapidly than population.

This paraphrase uses simpler sentences and more common terms than the original passage, in effect translating it as shown below and on the next page. Only words that lack satisfactory synonyms—such as *ecosystems, natural, cycles,* and *population*—remain the same.

Source authors' words	Malik's paraphrase
Such intuition is even making its way, albeit slowly, into scholarly circles, where recognition is mounting that	Scholars are coming to believe that
ever-increasing pressures on ecosystems, life-supporting environmental services, and critical natural cycles are driven not only by the sheer number of resource users and the inefficiencies of their resource use, but also by the patterns of resource use themselves.	consumption is partly to blame for changes in ecosystems, reduction of essential natural resources, and changes in natural cycles.
In global environmental policy-making arenas, it is becoming more and more difficult to ignore the fact that	Policy makers increasingly see that

43d

Source authors' words	Malik's paraphrase
overdeveloped countries must restrain their consumption if they expect underdeveloped countries to embrace a more sustainable trajectory.	developing nations will not adopt practices that reduce pollution and waste unless wealthy nations consume less.
And while global population growth still remains a huge issue in many regions around the world—both rich and poor—	Rising population around the world does cause significant stress on the environment,
per-capita growth in consumption is, for many resources, expanding eight to twelve times faster than population growth.	but consumption is increasing even more rapidly than population.

Follow these guidelines when paraphrasing:

- ▣ Read the material several times to be sure you understand it.
- ▣ Restate the main ideas in your own words and sentence structures. You do not have to follow the organization of the original or restate all of it. Select and restate only what you need. If complete sentences seem too detailed or cumbersome, use phrases. Justin Malik might have written the following briefer paraphrase of the quotation by Princen, Maniates, and Conca.

Abbreviated paraphrase of source

Environmental consequences of consumption

Princen, Maniates, and Conca 4

Consumption is increasing more rapidly than population + contributing to major ecological crises. Wealthy nations have to start consuming less.

- ▣ Be careful not to distort meaning. Don't change the source's emphasis or omit connecting words, qualifiers, and other material whose absence will confuse you later or cause you to misrepresent the source. (See also p. 640.)
- ▣ Be careful not to plagiarize the source. Use your own words and sentence structures, and always provide a citation in your notes.

The following examples show the preceding abbreviated paraphrase in the context of a draft, the first lacking proper citation and the second with proper citation (in MLA style).

Paraphrase with no citation (plagiarized)

Always seeking newer and better things, we consume without regard for the resources we use or the waste we leave behind. In fact, overconsumption is increasing more rapidly than population and contributing to major ecological crises. Wealthy nations have to start consuming less.

Paraphrase with proper citation (not plagiarized)

Always seeking newer and better things, we consume without regard for the resources we use or the waste we leave behind. In fact, according to Thomas Princen, Michael Maniates, and Ken Conca, overconsumption is increasing more rapidly than population and contributing to major ecological crises. Wealthy nations have to start consuming less (4).

See pages 648–54 for more on plagiarism.

43d

CULTURE LANGUAGE If English is not your native language and you have difficulty paraphrasing the ideas in sources, try this: Before attempting a paraphrase, read the original passage several times. Then, instead of "translating" line by line, try to state the gist of the passage without looking at it. Check your effort against the original to be sure you have captured the source author's meaning and emphasis without using his or her words and sentence structures. If you need a synonym for a word, look it up in a dictionary.

3 Quoting

When you **quote** a source, you reproduce the author's exact words. Choose quotations carefully, making sure that they work for, not replace, your ideas.

Video tutorial

Deciding when to quote

Your notes from sources may include many quotations, especially if you rely on photocopies, printouts, or downloads. Whether to use a quotation in your draft, instead of a summary or paraphrase, depends on whether the source is primary or secondary and on how important the exact words are.

- Quote extensively only when you are analyzing primary sources, such as literary works and historical documents. The quotations will often be both the target of your analysis and the chief support for your ideas. You may need to quote many brief passages, integrated into your sentences, and then comment on the quotations to clarify your analysis and win readers' agreement with it. For examples, see Vanessa Haley's analysis of Annie Dillard's writing (pp. 746–51) and the three literary analyses in Chapter 49 (pp. 771–73, 774–77, and 777–80).
- Quote selectively when you are drawing on secondary sources— reports or analyses of other sources, such as a critic's view of a poem or a historian's synthesis of several eyewitness reports. Favor summaries and paraphrases over quotations, and put every quotation to each test in the box on the next page. Most papers of ten or so pages should not need more than two or three quotations that are longer than a few lines each.

Video
tutorial

43d

Tests for direct quotations from secondary sources

The author's original satisfies one of these requirements:

- The language is unusually vivid, bold, or inventive.
- The quotation cannot be paraphrased without distortion or loss of meaning.
- The words themselves are at issue in your interpretation.
- The quotation represents and emphasizes a body of opinion or the view of an important expert.
- The quotation emphatically reinforces your own idea.
- The quotation is an illustration, such as a graph, diagram, or table.

The quotation is as short as possible:

- It includes only material relevant to your point.
- It is edited to eliminate examples and other unneeded material. (For editing quotations, see the bulleted list below.)

Transcribing and using quotations

When you quote a source, either in your notes or in your draft, take precautions to avoid plagiarism or misrepresentation:

- **Copy the material carefully.** Take down the author's exact wording, spelling, capitalization, and punctuation.
- **Proofread every direct quotation at least twice.**
- **Use quotation marks around the quotation** so that later you won't confuse it with a paraphrase or summary. Be sure to transfer the quotation marks into your draft as well, unless the quotation is long. See later pages for handling long quotations in MLA style (615–16), Chicago style (797–98), and APA style (826).
- **Use brackets** to add words for clarity or to change the capitalization of letters (see pp. 496, 505).
- **Use ellipsis marks** to omit irrelevant words or sentences (see p. 497).
- **Cite the source of the quotation in your draft.** See pages 657–58 on documenting sources.

For a summary of conventions regarding quotations, see the chart on pages 482–83.

The note at the top of the facing page shows how Justin Malik might have quoted part of the passage on pages 633–34 by Princen, Maniates, and Conca, using brackets and an ellipsis mark to make the quotation more concise. Notice the record of the authors' names and the page number as well as the quotation marks around the authors' exact words—all of which would help Malik avoid plagiarizing the source in his paper.

The examples after the sample note show the quotation as part of a draft. The first lacks appropriate punctuation and proper citation; the second is corrected (in MLA style).

Quotation of source

Environmental consequences of consumption

Princen, Maniates, and Conca 4

"[E]ver-increasing pressures on ecosystems, life-supporting environmental services, and critical natural cycles are driven not only by the sheer number of resource users . . . but also by the patterns of resource use themselves."

43d

Quotation lacking quotation marks, an ellipsis mark, and a citation (plagiarized)

Increasing consumption may be as much of a threat to the environment as increasing population. In fact, ever-increasing pressures on ecosystems, life-supporting environmental services, and critical natural cycles are driven not only by the sheer number of resource users but also by the patterns of resource use themselves.

Quotation with quotation marks, an ellipsis mark, and proper citation (not plagiarized)

Increasing consumption may be as much of a threat to the environment as increasing population. According to Thomas Princen, Michael Maniates, and Ken Conca, "ever-increasing pressures on ecosystems, life-supporting environmental services, and critical natural cycles are driven not only by the sheer number of resource users . . . but also by the patterns of resource use themselves" (4).

See pages 648–54 for more on plagiarism.

4 Combining quotation, summary, and paraphrase

Using quotation in combination with summary or paraphrase can help you shape the material to suit your purposes (although you must be careful not to distort the author's meaning). The note below shows how Justin Malik might have used a combination of quotation and paraphrase to record the statement by Princen, Maniates, and Conca. Notice the record of the authors' names and the page

Combined paraphrase and quotation of source

Environmental consequences of consumption

Princen, Maniates, and Conca 4

Scholars are coming to believe that consumption as much as rising population is to blame for "ever-increasing pressures on ecosystems, life-supporting environmental services, and critical natural cycles."

number as well as the quotation marks around the authors' exact words—all of which would help Malik avoid plagiarizing the source in his paper.

The examples below show the combined paraphrase and quotation in the context of a draft. The first example cites the source but passes off the quoted language as part of the paraphrase. The second example includes the needed quotation marks.

43d

Combined paraphrase and quotation without quotation marks (plagiarized)

Always seeking newer and better things, we consume without regard for the resources we use or the waste we leave behind. According to Thomas Princen, Michael Maniates, and Ken Conca, scholars are coming to believe that consumption as much as rising population is to blame for ever-increasing pressures on ecosystems, life-supporting environmental services, and critical natural cycles (4).

Combined paraphrase and quotation with quotation marks (not plagiarized)

Always seeking newer and better things, we consume without regard for the resources we use or the waste we leave behind. According to Thomas Princen, Michael Maniates, and Ken Conca, scholars are coming to believe that overconsumption as much as rising population is to blame for "ever-increasing pressures on ecosystems, life-supporting environmental services, and critical natural cycles" (4).

See pages 648–54 for more on plagiarism.

5 Using sources accurately and fairly

When borrowing from sources, you must represent the author's meaning exactly, without distorting it. In the inaccurate summary below, the writer has stated a meaning exactly opposite that of the original. The original quotation, from the artist Henri Matisse, appears in Jack D. Flam, *Matisse on Art*, page 148.

Original	For the artist creation begins with vision. To see is itself a creative operation, requiring an effort. Everything that we see in our daily life is more or less distorted by acquired habits, and this is perhaps more evident in an age like ours when cinema posters and magazines present us every day with a flood of ready-made images which are to the eye what prejudices are to the mind.
Inaccurate summary	Matisse said that the artist can learn how to see creatively by looking at posters and magazines (qtd. in Flam 148).

The revision below combines summary and quotation to represent the author's meaning exactly:

Accurate summary	Matisse said that the artist must overcome visual "habits" and "prejudices," particularly those developed in response to images of popular culture (qtd. in Flam 148).

Exercise 43.7 Summarizing and paraphrasing

Prepare two source notes, one summarizing the entire following paragraph and the other paraphrasing the first four sentences (ending with the word *autonomy*). Use the note format illustrated in the preceding section, omitting only the subject heading.

Exercise

43d

Federal organization [of the United States] has made it possible for the different states to deal with the same problems in many different ways. One consequence of federalism, then, has been that people are treated differently, by law, from state to state. The great strength of this system is that differences from state to state in cultural preferences, moral standards, and levels of wealth can be accommodated. In contrast to a unitary system in which the central government makes all important decisions (as in France), federalism is a powerful arrangement for maximizing regional freedom and autonomy. The great weakness of our federal system, however, is that people in some states receive less than the best or the most advanced or the least expensive services and policies that government can offer. The federal dilemma does not invite easy solutions, for the costs and benefits of the arrangement have tended to balance out.

—Peter K. Eisinger et al., *American Politics,* page 44

Exercise 43.8 Combining summary, paraphrase, and direct quotation

Prepare a source note that combines paraphrase or summary and direct quotation to state the main idea of the following passage. Use the note format illustrated in the preceding section, omitting only the subject heading.

Exercise

Most speakers unconsciously duel even during seemingly casual conversations, as can often be observed at social gatherings where they show less concern for exchanging information with other guests than for asserting their own dominance. Their verbal dueling often employs very subtle weapons like mumbling, a hostile act which defeats the listener's desire to understand what the speaker claims he is trying to say (but is really not saying because he is mumbling!). Or the verbal dueler may keep talking after someone has passed out of hearing range—which is often an aggressive challenge to the listener to return and acknowledge the dominance of the speaker.

—Peter K. Farb, *Word Play,* page 107

Exercise 43.9 Gathering information from sources

Continuing from Exercise 43.6 (p. 629), as the next step in preparing a research paper, gather and organize the information from your sources. Mark every note, photocopy, printout, and download with the source's publication information and a heading related to the topics of your paper. Annotate relevant passages of photocopies, printouts, and downloads with your own ideas. For handwritten or computer notes, use direct quotation, summary, or paraphrase as seems appropriate, being careful to avoid inaccuracy and plagiarism. (If you need help recognizing plagiarism, see Chapter 44.)

43e Integrating sources into your text

Integrating source material into your sentences is key to synthesizing others' ideas with your own. Evidence drawn from sources should *back up* your conclusions, not *be* your conclusions: you don't want to let your evidence overwhelm your own voice and point of view. To emphasize your ideas, you do more than just present borrowed material; you introduce and interpret it as well.

Note Integrating borrowed material into your sentences involves several conventions discussed elsewhere in this book:

- Using commas to punctuate signal phrases, pages 458–60.
- Placing other punctuation marks with quotation marks, pages 487–88.
- Using brackets for changes in quotations, page 496 and opposite.
- Using ellipsis marks for omissions from quotations, pages 497–99.
- Punctuating and placing parenthetical citations, pages 673–75.
- Setting off long quotations from your text without quotation marks, pages 615–16 (MLA style), 797–98 (Chicago style), and 826 (APA style).

Note The examples in this and the next section use the MLA style of source documentation and also the present-tense verbs (such as *disagrees*) that are typical of much writing in the humanities. For specific variations in documentation and verb tense within the academic disciplines, see pages 645–47.

1 Introducing borrowed material

Always introduce a summary, a paraphrase, or a quotation by identifying it and by providing a smooth transition between your words and ideas and those of your source.

Links between borrowed material and your own sentences

Readers will be distracted from your point if borrowed material does not fit into your sentence. In the passage below, the writer has identified the quotation source (*one editor . . . Lyman*) but has not meshed the structures of her own and her source's sentences:

> Awkward   One editor disagrees with this view and "a good reporter does not fail to separate opinions from facts" (Lyman 52).

In the following revision the writer adds words to integrate the quotation into her sentence:

> Revised   One editor disagrees with this view, maintaining that "a good reporter does not fail to separate opinions from facts" (Lyman 52).

Alterations of quotations

To mesh your own and your source's words, you may some-times need to make a substitution or addition to the quotation, sig-naling your change with brackets:

Words added

"The tabloids [of England] are a journalistic case study in bad reporting," claims Lyman (52).

Verb form changed

A bad reporter, Lyman implies, is one who "[fails] to separate opinions from facts" (52). [The bracketed verb replaces *fail* in the original.]

Capitalization changed

"[T]o separate opinions from facts" is a goal of good reporting (Lyman 52). [In the original, *to* is not capitalized.]

Noun supplied for pronoun

The reliability of a news organization "depends on [reporters'] trustwor-thiness," says Lyman (52). [The bracketed noun replaces *their* in the original.]

43e

2 Interpreting borrowed material

You need to work borrowed material into your sentences so that readers see without effort how any quotation, paraphrase, or sum-mary contributes to your point. If you merely dump source material into your paper without explaining how you intend it to be under-stood, readers will have to struggle to understand your sentences and the relationships you are trying to establish. For example, the follow-ing passage forces us to figure out for ourselves that the writer's sen-tence and the quotation state opposite points of view.

> Dumped   Many news editors and reporters maintain that it is impossi-ble to keep personal opinions from influencing the selection and presentation of facts. "True, news reporters, like every-one else, form impressions of what they see and hear. How-ever, a good reporter does not fail to separate opinions from facts" (Lyman 52).

In the revision the underlined additions tell us how to interpret the quotation:

> Revised   Many news editors and reporters maintain that it is impossi-ble to keep personal opinions from influencing the selection and presentation of facts. Yet not all authorities agree with this view. One editor grants that "news reporters, like every-one else, form impressions of what they see and hear." But, he insists, "a good reporter does not fail to separate opinions from facts" (Lyman 52).

Signal phrases

In the revised passage on the previous page, the words *One editor grants* and *he insists* are **signal phrases**: they tell readers who the source is and what to expect in the quotations that follow. Signal phrases usually contain (1) the source author's name (or a substitute for it, such as *One editor* and *he*) and (2) a verb that indicates the source author's attitude or approach to what he or she says. In the preceding example, *grants* implies concession and *insists* implies argument. The following box gives a list of verbs that are often used in signal phrases.

43e

Verbs for signal phrases

Use verbs that convey information about source authors' attitudes or approaches. In the sentence *Smith* _____ *that the flood might have been disastrous,* filling the blank with *observes, finds,* or *insists* would create different meanings.

Note Disciplines vary in the tenses of verbs used within signal phrases. The verbs listed below are in the present tense, which is typical of writing about literature and in other humanities. In the social and natural sciences, the past tense (*asked*) or present perfect tense (*has asked*) is more common. See page 646.

Author is neutral	Author infers or suggests	Author argues	Author is uneasy or disparaging
comments	analyzes	claims	belittles
describes	asks	contends	bemoans
explains	assesses	defends	complains
illustrates	concludes	disagrees	condemns
notes	finds	holds	deplores
observes	predicts	insists	deprecates
points out	proposes	maintains	derides
records	reveals		laments
relates	shows	**Author agrees**	warns
reports	speculates	admits	
says	suggests	agrees	
sees	supposes	concedes	
thinks		concurs	
writes		grants	

Vary your signal phrases to suit your interpretation of borrowed material and also to keep readers' interest. A signal phrase may precede, interrupt, or follow the borrowed material:

Signal phrase precedes

Lyman insists that "a good reporter does not fail to separate opinions from facts" (52).

Signal phrase interrupts

"However," Lyman insists, "a good reporter does not fail to separate opinions from facts" (52).

Signal phrase follows

"[A] good reporter does not fail to separate opinions from facts," Lyman insists (52).

Background information

You can add information to a signal phrase to inform readers why you are using a source. In most cases, provide the author's name in the text, especially if the author is an expert or if readers will recognize the name:

Author named

Harold Lyman grants that "news reporters, like everyone else, form impressions of what they see and hear." But, Lyman insists, "a good reporter does not fail to separate opinions from facts" (52).

If the source title contributes information about the author or the context of the quotation, you can provide it in the text:

Title given

Harold Lyman, in his book *The Conscience of the Journalist*, grants that "news reporters, like everyone else, form impressions of what they see and hear." But, Lyman insists, "a good reporter does not fail to separate opinions from facts" (52).

Finally, if the quoted author's background and experience reinforce or clarify the quotation, you can provide those credentials in the text:

Credentials given

Harold Lyman, a newspaper editor for more than forty years, grants that "news reporters, like everyone else, form impressions of what they see and hear." But, Lyman insists, "a good reporter does not fail to separate opinions from facts" (52).

You need not always name the author, source, or credentials in your text. In fact, such introductions may get in the way when you are simply establishing facts or weaving together facts and opinions from varied sources. In the following passage, the information is more important than the source, so the name of the source is confined to a parenthetical acknowledgment:

To end the abuses of the British, many colonists were urging three actions: forming a united front, seceding from Britain, and taking control of their own international relations (Wills 325–36).

3 Following discipline styles for integrating sources

The preceding guidelines for introducing and interpreting borrowed material apply generally across academic disciplines, but there are differences in verb tense and documentation style.

English and some other humanities

Writers in English, foreign languages, and related disciplines use MLA style for documenting sources (see Chapter 46) and generally

43e

use the present tense of verbs in signal phrases. In discussing sources other than works of literature, the present perfect tense is also sometimes appropriate:

> Lyman insists . . . [present].
> Lyman has insisted . . . [present perfect].

In discussing works of literature, use only the present tense to describe both the work of the author and the action in the work:

43e

> Kate Chopin builds irony into every turn of "The Story of an Hour." For example, Mrs. Mallard, the central character, finds joy in the death of her husband, whom she loves, because she anticipates "the long procession of years that would belong to her absolutely" (23).

Avoid shifting tenses in writing about literature. You can, for instance, shorten quotations to avoid their past-tense verbs:

> Shift   Her freedom elevates her, so that "she carried herself unwittingly like a goddess of victory" (24).
>
> No shift Her freedom elevates her, so that she walks "unwittingly like a goddess of victory" (24).

History and other humanities

Writers in history, art history, philosophy, and related disciplines generally use the present tense or present perfect tense of verbs in signal phrases:

> Lincoln persisted, as Haworth has noted, in "feeling that events controlled him."[3]
>
> What Miller calls Lincoln's "severe self-doubt"[6] undermined the President's effectiveness on at least two occasions.

The raised numbers after the quotations are part of the Chicago documentation style, used in history and other disciplines and discussed on pages 785–96.

Social and natural sciences

Writers in the sciences generally use a verb's present tense just for reporting the results of a study (*The data suggest* . . .). Otherwise, they use a verb's past tense or present perfect tense in a signal phrase, as when introducing an explanation, interpretation, or other commentary. (Thus when you are writing for the sciences, generally convert the list of signal-phrase verbs on p. 644 from the present to the past or present perfect tense.)

> Lin (1999) has suggested that preschooling may significantly affect children's academic performance through high school (pp. 22–23).
>
> In an exhaustive survey of the literature published between 1990 and 2000, Walker (2001) found "no proof, merely a weak correlation, linking place of residence and rate of illness" (p. 121).

These passages conform to APA documentation style, discussed on pages 804–23. APA style, or one quite similar to it, is also used in sociology, education, nursing, biology, and many other sciences.

Exercise 43.10   Introducing and interpreting borrowed material

Drawing on the ideas in the following paragraph and using examples from your own observations and experiences, write a paragraph about anxiety. Integrate at least one direct quotation and one paraphrase from the following paragraph into your own sentences. In your paragraph identify the author by name and give his credentials: he is a professor of psychiatry and a practicing psychoanalyst.

Exercise

There are so many ways in which man is different from all the lower forms of animals, and almost all of them make us uniquely susceptible to feelings of anxiousness. Our imagination and reasoning powers facilitate anxiety; the anxious feeling is precipitated not by an absolute impending threat—such as the worry about an examination, a speech, travel—but rather by the symbolic and often unconscious representations. We do not have to be experiencing a potential danger. We can experience something related to it. We can recall, through our incredible memories, the original symbolic sense of vulnerability in childhood and suffer the feeling attached to that. We can even forget the original memory and still be stuck with the emotion—which is then compounded by its seemingly irrational quality at this time. It is not just the fear of death which pains us, but the anticipation of it; or the anniversary of a specific death; or a street, a hospital, a time of day, a color, a flower, a symbol associated with death.

—Willard Gaylin, "Feeling Anxious," page 23

44

Avoiding Plagiarism and Documenting Sources

The knowledge building that is the focus of academic writing rests on the integrity of everyone who participates, including students, in using and crediting sources. The work of a writer or creator is his or her intellectual property. You and others may borrow the work's ideas and even its words or an image, but you *must* acknowledge that what you borrowed came from someone else.

When you acknowledge sources in your writing, you are doing more than giving credit to the writer or creator of the work you consulted. You are also showing what your own writing is based on, which in turn adds to your integrity as a researcher and writer. Acknowledging sources creates the trust among scholars, students, writers, and readers that knowledge building requires.

Video tutorial

Exercise

Plagiarism (from a Latin word for "kidnapper") is the presentation of someone else's work as your own. Whether deliberate or accidental, plagiarism is a serious offense. It breaks trust, and it undermines or even destroys your credibility as a researcher and writer. In most colleges, a code of academic honesty calls for severe consequences for plagiarism: a reduced or failing grade, suspension from school, or expulsion. The way to avoid plagiarism is to acknowledge your sources: keep track of the ones you consult for each paper you write, and document them within the paper and in a list of works cited.

This chapter distinguishes between deliberate and accidental plagiarism (next page), shows how to distinguish what doesn't require acknowledgment from what does (pp. 651–54), discusses copyright issues if your project will be published or posted on the Web (pp. 655–56), and provides an overview of source documentation (pp. 657–58).

CULTURE & LANGUAGE The concepts of originality, intellectual property, and plagiarism are not universal. In some other cultures, for instance, students may be encouraged to copy the words of scholars without acknowledgment, in order to demonstrate their

Visit *mycomplab.com* for the eText and for resources and more exercises on avoiding plagiarism and documenting

sources.

Checklist for avoiding plagiarism

Know your source.

Are you using

- your own experience,
- common knowledge, or
- someone else's material?

You must acknowledge someone else's material.

Checklist

44a

Quote carefully.

- Check that every quotation exactly matches its source.
- Insert quotation marks around every quotation that you run into your text. (A quotation set off from the text does not need quotation marks. See pp. 715–16.)
- Indicate any omission from a quotation with an ellipsis mark and any addition with brackets.
- Acknowledge the source of every quotation.

Paraphrase and summarize carefully.

- Use your own words and sentence structures for every paraphrase and summary. If you have used the author's words, add quotation marks around them.
- Acknowledge the source of the idea(s) in every paraphrase or summary.

Cite sources responsibly.

- Acknowledge every use of someone else's material in each place you use it.
- Include all your sources in your list of works cited. See Chapters 46 and 50–52 for citing sources in MLA, Chicago, APA, and CSE documentation styles.

mastery of or respect for the scholars' work. In the United States, however, using an author's work without a source citation is a serious offense, whether it is accidental or intentional. When in doubt about the guidelines in this chapter, ask your instructor for advice.

44a Distinguishing deliberate from accidental plagiarism

Instructors usually distinguish between deliberate plagiarism, which is cheating, and accidental plagiarism, which often stems from a writer's inexperience with managing sources.

1 Deliberate plagiarism

Deliberate plagiarism is intentional: the writer chooses to cheat by turning in someone else's work as his or her own. Students who

Video
tutorial

44a

Plagiarism and the Internet

The Internet has made it easier to plagiarize than ever before: with just a few clicks, you can copy and paste passages or whole documents into your own files. If you do so without quoting and acknowledging your source, you plagiarize.

The Internet has also made plagiarism easier to detect. Instructors can use search engines to find specific phrases or sentences anywhere on the Web, including among scholarly publications, all kinds of Web sites, and term-paper collections. They can search term-paper sites as easily as students can, looking for similarities with papers they've received. They can also use detection software—such as *Turnitin*, *PlagiServe*, and *Glatt Plagiarism Services*—which compares students' work with other work anywhere on the Internet, seeking matches as short as a few words.

Some instructors suggest that their students use plagiarism-detection programs to verify that their own work does not include accidental plagiarism, at least not from the Internet.

deliberately plagiarize deprive themselves of an education in honest research. When their cheating is detected, the students often face stiff penalties, including expulsion.

Following are examples of deliberate plagiarism:

Copying a phrase, a sentence, or a longer passage from a source and passing it off as your own by omitting quotation marks and a source citation.

Summarizing or paraphrasing someone else's ideas without acknowledging the source in a citation.

Handing in as your own work a paper you have copied off the Web, had a friend write, or accepted from another student.

Handing in as your own work a paper you have purchased from a paper-writing service. **Paying for research or a paper does not make it your work.**

2 Accidental plagiarism

Accidental plagiarism is unintentional: grappling with complicated information and ideas in sources, the writer neglects to put quotation marks around a source's exact words or neglects to include a source citation for a quotation, paraphrase, or summary. Most instructors and schools do not permit accidental plagiarism, but they treat it less harshly than deliberate plagiarism—at least the first time it occurs.

Here are examples of accidental plagiarism:

Reading sources without taking notes on them, and then not remembering the difference between what you recently learned and what you already knew.

Copying and pasting material from a source into your document without placing quotation marks around the other writer's work.

Forgetting to add a source citation for a paraphrase. Even though a paraphrase casts another person's idea in your own words, you still need to cite the source of the idea.

Omitting a source citation for another's idea because you are unaware of the need to acknowledge the idea.

44b Knowing what you need not acknowledge

Two kinds of information do not have to be acknowledged in source citations: your own independent material and common knowledge.

1 Using your independent material

Your own independent material includes your thoughts, observations from experience, compilations of facts, or experimental results, expressed in your words or format. For example, you might offer a conclusion about crowd behavior based on watching crowds at concerts or draw a diagram from information you gathered yourself. Though you generally should describe the basis for your conclusions so that readers can evaluate your thinking, you need not cite sources for them.

Note that someone else's ideas and facts are not yours, even when you express them entirely in your own words and sentence structures. The ideas and facts require acknowledgment.

2 Using common knowledge

Common knowledge consists of the standard information of a field of study as well as folk literature and commonsense observations.

- **Standard information** includes the major facts of history, such as the dates during which Charlemagne ruled as emperor of Rome (800–14). It does *not* include interpretations of facts, such as a historian's opinion that Charlemagne was sometimes needlessly cruel in extending his power.
- **Folk literature,** such as the fairy tale "Snow White," is popularly known and cannot be traced to a particular writer. Literature traceable to a writer is *not* folk literature, even if it is very familiar.
- **Commonsense observations** are things most people know, such as that inflation is most troublesome for people with low and fixed incomes. A particular economist's idea about the effects of inflation on Chinese immigrants is *not* a commonsense observation.

As long as you express it in your own words and sentence structures, you may use common knowledge as your own.

The first time you come across an idea or a piece of information that you may want to use, record the publication information for the source. If in wider reading you repeatedly encounter the same idea or information without cited sources, then you may assume it's common knowledge. Don't take unnecessary risks, however: a source citation for common knowledge is not wrong.

44c Knowing what you *must* acknowledge

Video tutorial

You must always acknowledge other people's independent material—that is, any facts, ideas, or opinions that are not common knowledge or your own. The source may be a formal publication or release, such as a book, an article, a movie, an interview, an artwork, a comic strip, a map, a Web page, or a blog posting. The source may also be informal, such as a tweet, a posting on a *Facebook* page, an opinion you heard on the radio, or a comment by your instructor or a classmate that substantially shaped your argument. You must acknowledge summaries or paraphrases of ideas or facts as well as quotations of the language and format in which ideas or facts appear: wording, sentence structures, arrangement, and special graphics (such as a diagram).

You need to acknowledge another's material no matter how you use it, how much of it you use, or how often you use it. Whether you are quoting a single important word, paraphrasing a single sentence, or summarizing three paragraphs, and whether you are using the source only once or a dozen times, you must acknowledge the original author every time. See pages 657–58 for how to acknowledge sources and pages 673–74 for where to place source citations in relation to cited material.

1 Using copied language: Quotation marks and a source citation

Copied words and sentence structure

The following example baldly plagiarizes the original quotation from Jessica Mitford's *Kind and Usual Punishment*, page 9. Without quotation marks or a source citation, the example matches Mitford's wording (underlined) and closely parallels her sentence structure:

Original (quotation)	"The character and mentality of the keepers may be of more importance in understanding prisons than the character and mentality of the kept."
Plagiarism	But the character of prison officials (the keepers) is of more importance in understanding prisons than the character of prisoners (the kept).

To avoid plagiarism, the writer can paraphrase and cite the source (see below) or use Mitford's actual words *in quotation marks and with a source citation* (here, in MLA style):

Revision (quotation)	According to one critic of the penal system, *"*The character and mentality of the keepers may be of more importance in understanding prisons than the character and mentality of the kept*"* (Mitford 9).

44c

Changed sentence structure but copied words

Even with a source citation and with a different sentence structure, the next example is still plagiarism because it uses some of Mitford's words (underlined) without quotation marks:

Plagiarism	According to one critic of the penal system, the psychology of the kept may say less about prisons than the psychology of the keepers (Mitford 9).
Revision (quotation)	According to one critic of the penal system, the psychology of *"*the kept*"* may say less about prisons than the psychology of *"*the keepers*"* (Mitford 9).

2 Using a paraphrase or summary: Your own words and sentence structure and a source citation

Changed sentence structure but copied words

The following example changes the sentence structure of the original Mitford quotation opposite, but it still uses Mitford's words (underlined) without quotation marks or a source citation:

Plagiarism	In understanding prisons, we might focus less on the character and mentality of the kept than on those of the keepers.

To avoid plagiarism, the writer can use quotation marks and cite the source or *use his or her own words* and still *cite the source* (because the idea is Mitford's, not the writer's):

Revision (paraphrase)	Mitford holds that we may be able to learn less about prisons from the psychology of prisoners than from the psychology of prison officials (9).
Revision (paraphrase)	We may understand prisons better if we focus on the personalities and attitudes of the prison workers rather than those of the inmates (Mitford 9).

Changed words but copied sentence structure

In the next example, the writer cites Mitford and does not use her words but still plagiarizes her sentence structure. The revision changes the sentence structure as well as the words.

Plagiarism	One critic of the penal system maintains that <u>the psychology of prison officials may be more informative about prisons than the psychology of prisoners</u> (Mitford 9).
Revision (paraphrase)	One critic of the penal system maintains that we may be able to learn less from the psychology of prisoners than from the psychology of prison officials (Mitford 9).

44c

3 Using online sources

Online sources are so accessible and so easy to copy into your own documents that it may seem they are freely available, exempting you from the obligation to acknowledge them. They are not. Acknowledging online sources is somewhat trickier than acknowledging print sources, but it is no less essential: when you use material from an online source in a print or online document, you must acknowledge someone else's independent material in whatever form you find it.

Citing online sources is easier when you keep track of them as you work:

- **Record complete publication information each time you consult an online source.** Online sources may change from one day to the next or even disappear entirely. See page 581 for the information to record, such as the publication date. Without the proper information, you may not use the source.
- **Immediately put quotation marks around any text that you copy and paste into your document.** If you don't add quotation marks right away, you risk forgetting which words belong to the source and which are yours. If you don't know whose words you are using, recheck the source or do not use them.
- **Acknowledge linked sites.** If you use not only a Web site but also one or more of its linked sites, you must acknowledge the linked sites as well. The fact that one person has used a second person's work does not release you from the responsibility to cite the second work.

Exercise 44.1 Recognizing plagiarism

Exercise

The following numbered items show various attempts to quote or paraphrase a passage by George E. Vaillant. Carefully compare each attempt with the original passage. Which attempts are plagiarized, inaccurate, or both, and which are acceptable? Why?

I would agree with the sociologists that psychiatric labeling is dangerous. Society can inflict terrible wounds by discrimination, and by confusing health with disease and disease with badness.
—George E. Vaillant, *Adaptation to Life,* p. 361

1. According to George Vaillant, society often inflicts wounds by using psychiatric labeling, confusing health, disease, and badness (361).

2. According to George Vaillant, "psychiatric labeling [such as 'homosexual' or 'schizophrenic'] is dangerous. Society can inflict terrible wounds by . . . confusing health with disease and disease with badness" (361).

3. According to George Vaillant, when psychiatric labeling discriminates between health and disease or between disease and badness, it can inflict wounds on those labeled (361).

4. Psychiatric labels can badly hurt those labeled, says George Vaillant, because they fail to distinguish among health, illness, and immorality (361).

5. Labels such as "homosexual" and "schizophrenic" can be hurtful when they fail to distinguish among health, illness, and immorality.

6. "I would agree with the sociologists that society can inflict terrible wounds by discrimination, and by confusing health with disease and disease with badness" (Vaillant 361).

44d

Exercise 44.2 Revising plagiarized sentences

The following numbered items plagiarize sentences in a paragraph by Stephen Pinker. Analyze the problem in each item, and then rewrite it to quote or paraphrase correctly and add the proper source citation. (Consult pp. 667–69 if you need help with the citations.). Each item has more than one correct answer.

Exercise

> Friendship, like other kinds of altruism, is vulnerable to cheaters, and we have a special name for them: fair-weather friends. These sham friends reap the benefits of associating with a valuable person and mimic signs of warmth in an effort to become valued themselves. But when a little rain falls, they are nowhere in sight. People have an emotional response that seems designed to weed out fair-weather friends. When we are neediest, an extended hand is deeply affecting. We are moved, never forget the generosity, and feel compelled to tell the friend we will never forget it.
> —Steven Pinker, *How the Mind Works,* p. 509

1. Like other kinds of altruism, friendship is vulnerable to cheaters, people whom we call fair-weather friends.

2. According to Steven Pinker, sham friends draw advantages from being with someone they value, and they "mimic signs of warmth in an effort to become valued themselves."

3. Steven Pinker writes that people seem to have an emotional response designed to weed out fair-weather friends.

4. Pinker points out that when people are at their lowest, a sign of friendship is truly touching.

5. Pinker describes people who have received acts of friendship as moved. They do not forget the generosity, and they are compelled to say that they will never forget it.

44d Obtaining permission when publishing your work

When you use material from print or online sources in a project that will be published, you must not only acknowledge your sources but also take the additional precaution of observing copyright restrictions.

Publication means that your work will circulate outside the limited circle of a class or other group. It may appear in print media, such as magazines and newspapers, or it may appear on the Web, which is a publication medium as well. (The exception is a password-protected Web site, such as a course site, which many copyright holders regard as private.) Whether you are publishing in print or online, borrowing certain kinds or amounts of material requires you to obtain the permission of the copyright holders. You can find information about copyright holders and permissions on the copyright page of a print publication (following the title page) and on a page labeled something like "Terms of Use" on a Web site. If you don't see an explicit release for student use or publication on private Web sites, assume that you must seek permission.

The legal convention of **fair use** allows an author to use a small portion of copyrighted material without obtaining the copyright holder's permission, as long as the author acknowledges the source. The standards of fair use differ for print and online sources and are not fixed in either case. The guidelines below are conservative:

- **Text from print sources:** Quote without permission fewer than fifty words from an article or fewer than three hundred words from a book. You'll need permission to use any longer quotation from an article or book or any quotation at all from a play, poem, or song.

- **Text from online sources:** Quote without permission text that represents just a small portion of the whole—say, up to forty words out of three hundred. As with print texts, seek permission for any use of a play, poem, or song that you find online.

- **Visuals, audio, and video:** Seek permission to use any copyrighted media from either print or online sources: photographs, charts, maps, cartoons, diagrams, paintings, audio files, video files, and so on.

- **Links:** You may need to seek permission to link your site to another one—for instance, if you rely on the linked site to provide substantial evidence for your claims or if you incorporate a linked site's multimedia element (an image or a sound or video clip) into your site.

Note Although most online sources are copyrighted, much valuable material is not: either the creator does not claim copyright, or the copyright has lapsed so that the work is in the public domain. The first category includes most government documents as well as material labeled for reuse. (You can find such multimedia sources by setting your search engine to screen for them. See p. 606.) Public-domain sources include most works by authors who have been dead at least fifty years. You do not need permission to reprint from an uncopyrighted source, but *you still must cite the source.*

44e Documenting sources

Every time you borrow the words, facts, or ideas of others, you must **document** the source—that is, supply a reference (or document) telling readers that you borrowed the material and where you borrowed it from.

Editors and teachers in most academic disciplines require special documentation formats (or styles) in their scholarly journals and in students' papers. All the styles use a citation in the text that serves two purposes: it signals that material is borrowed, and it refers readers to detailed information about the source so that they can locate both the source and the place in the source where the borrowed material appears. The detailed source information appears either in footnotes or at the end of the paper.

Aside from these essential similarities, the disciplines' documentation styles differ markedly in citation form, arrangement of source information, and other particulars. Each discipline's style reflects the needs of its practitioners for certain kinds of information presented in certain ways. For instance, the currency of a source is important in the social and natural sciences, where studies build on and correct each other; thus in-text citations in these disciplines usually include a source's year of publication. In the humanities, however, currency is less important, so in-text citations do not include date of publication.

The disciplines' documentation formats are described in style guides listed elsewhere in this book for the humanities (p. 785), the social sciences (p. 804), and the natural and applied sciences (p. 835). This book also discusses and illustrates four common documentation styles:

- **MLA style,** used in English, foreign languages, and some other humanities (pp. 667–713).
- **Chicago style,** used in history, art history, philosophy, religion, and some other humanities (pp. 785–96).
- **APA style,** used in psychology and some other social sciences (pp. 804–23).
- **CSE style,** used in the biological and some other sciences (pp. 834–41).

Video tutorial

Video tutorial

Ask your instructor which style you should use. If no style is required, use the guide that's most appropriate for the discipline in which you're writing. Do follow one system for citing sources—and one system only—so that you provide all the necessary information in a consistent format.

Note Bibliography software—*Zotero, Refworks, Endnote, Knightcite,* and others—can help you format your source citations in the style of your choice. Always ask your instructors if you may use such software for your papers. The programs prompt you for needed information (author's name, book title, and so on) and then arrange, capitalize, italicize, and punctuate the information as required by the style. But no program can anticipate all the varieties of source information, nor can it substitute for your own care and attention in giving your sources complete acknowledgment using the required form.

45

Writing the Paper

Video
tutorial

Video
tutorial

Writing a research paper begins when you seek a topic and continues as you evaluate and gather information from your sources. During research, you might even pause to draft paragraphs or sections that pull your sources together to support your ideas. At some point, though, you'll need to turn your attention to the whole paper—ensuring that it has a clear thesis (below), creating a structure (p. 660), writing the complete draft (p. 663), revising and editing the paper (p. 664), and preparing the final draft (p. 666). To illustrate these stages, we continue to draw on Justin Malik's and Vanessa Haley's work.

Note This chapter complements and extends the detailed discussion of the writing situation and the writing process in Chapters 1–3, which also include tips for writing on a computer. If you haven't already done so, read Chapters 1–3 before this one.

45a Developing a thesis statement

Perhaps earlier in the research-writing process but certainly once you have gathered information from your sources, you will want to express your central idea and perspective in a thesis statement of one or two sentences. (See pp. 36–40 if you need guidance on developing a thesis statement.) Drafting a thesis statement will help you see the overall picture and organize your notes.

---

mycomplab

Visit *mycomplab.com* for eText and for resources and more exercises on writing and revising a research paper.

Justin Malik's and Vanessa Haley's work on their research papers illustrates how a thesis statement evolves to become complete and specific. Before finishing his reading on green consumerism, Malik wrote the following draft of a thesis statement:

Tentative thesis statement

Consumers need to think very carefully before buying products that claim to be green because many of them actually do more harm than good.

45a

This statement captured Malik's preliminary idea that green products may not be as beneficial to the environment as advertised. But after further reading, Malik rethought this idea. Many of his sources quoted the environmentalists' slogan "Reduce, reuse, recycle," and he began to ask whether green products meet these basic goals. That question opened up new questions: How does consumption in general affect the environment, and can green products significantly reduce this effect? With more research, Malik revised his thesis statement:

Revised thesis statement

Although green consumerism can help the environment, consumerism itself is the root of some of the most pressing ecological problems we face. To make a real difference, we must consume less.

(Malik's thesis statement consists of two sentences, the first setting up the second. Many instructors allow statements of two or more sentences as long as they build a single idea and the final sentence presents the key assertion of the paper. However, other instructors require thesis statements of a single sentence. Ask your instructor for his or her preference.)

For Vanessa Haley, framing a thesis statement for her paper on Annie Dillard required drawing together (synthesizing) Dillard's ideas about humanity and nature into a single statement of Haley's own. The first draft merely conveyed Haley's interest in Dillard:

Tentative thesis statement

Unlike many other nature writers, Dillard does not reinforce the separation between humanity and nature.

The revision stated Haley's synthesis of Dillard's ideas:

Revised thesis statement

In her encounters with nature, Dillard probes a spiritual as well as a physical identity between human beings and nature that could help to heal the rift between them.

Exercise 45.1 Developing a thesis statement

Draft and revise a thesis statement for your developing research paper. Make sure the revised version specifically asserts your main idea.

45b Creating a structure

Before starting to draft your research paper, organize your ideas and information so that you know the main divisions of your paper, the order you'll cover them in, and the important supporting ideas for each division. The goal is to create a structure that presents your ideas in a sensible and persuasive sequence and that supports ideas at each level with enough explanation and evidence. Consult the discussion of organization on pages 41–51 if you need help distinguishing general and specific information, arranging groups of information, or using a computer effectively for developing a structure.

1 Arranging ideas and support

Creating a structure for a research paper involves almost constant synthesis, the forging of relationships among ideas (see p. 626). As you arrange and rearrange source information and your own thoughts, you find connections among ideas and determine which are most important, which are merely supportive, and which are not relevant at all.

To build a structure, follow these guidelines:

- **Arrange your source information in categories** according to the subject headings you attached to each note, photocopy, or printout. Each category should correspond to a main section of your paper: a key idea of your own that supports the thesis along with the evidence for that idea.
- **Review your research journal and annotated bibliography.** Hunt for connections between sources, opinions of sources, and other thoughts that can help you organize your paper.
- **Look objectively at your categories.** If some are skimpy, with little information, consider whether you should drop the categories or conduct more research to fill them out. If most of your information falls into one or two categories, consider whether the categories are too broad and should be divided. (Does any of this rethinking affect your thesis statement? If so, revise it accordingly.)
- **Within each category, distinguish between the main idea and the supporting ideas and evidence.** Only the support should come from your sources. The main idea should be your own.

2 Using an outline

Exercise

An outline can help you shape your research and also discover potential problems, such as inadequate support and overlapping or irrelevant ideas.

Informal outline

For some research projects, you may find an **informal outline** sufficient: you list main points and supporting information in the order you expect to discuss them. Because of its informality, such an outline can help you try out different arrangements of material, even fairly early in the research process.

While examining his sources, Justin Malik experimented with an informal outline to see how his developing ideas might fit together:

Environmental crisis
    Global warming
    Resource use
    Biodiversity
    Pollution
    Waste

Consumerism
    Rising standards of living causing more waste
    Ecological effects—American vs. global
    Inequality
    Personal issues: expenses, working hours, stress, unhappiness
    Voluntary simplicity movement

Green products
    Appeal to consumers
    Advantages for businesses
    Environmental benefits
    Problems caused by manufacturing, shipping, and discarding products,
        even green products

This informal outline helped Malik decide not to continue researching consumerism (the second section) because he had more than enough to work with and the topic seemed likely to overwhelm his central question of whether buying green products can solve the environmental crisis (the last and first sections).

Formal outline

Unlike an informal outline, a **formal outline** arranges ideas tightly and in considerable detail, with close attention to hierarchy and phrasing. The example below shows the formal outline's format and schematic content:

  I. First main idea
    A. First subordinate idea
      1. First evidence for subordinate idea
        a. First detail of evidence
        b. Second detail of evidence
      2. Second evidence for subordinate idea
    B. Second subordinate idea
  II. Second main idea

In this model, levels of headings correspond to levels of importance or detail in the paper:

45b

- Main ideas (Roman numerals) are the major divisions of the paper. Each division covers a part of your thesis statement and will probably take a number of paragraphs to develop.
- Subordinate ideas (capital letters) are the building blocks. These ideas are your own and will probably take a paragraph or two to develop. They may serve as the topic sentences of paragraphs.
- Evidence (Arabic numerals) and its details (small letters) support each idea. The evidence from one or more sources will occupy much of each body paragraph. (A fourth sublevel, if needed, is labeled with Arabic numerals enclosed in parentheses.)

Each level of the outline is indented farther than the level it supports. (Your word processor may be able to help you with labels and indentions.)

A formal outline can help you decide not only what your main ideas are and how you will arrange them but also how you will support them. Some of this information may not emerge until you are drafting, however, so remain open to revising the outline as you proceed. And consider using a formal outline as a revision tool as well, creating a map of your completed first draft to check and improve the structure (see p. 60).

To be an effective organizer for your thoughts or an effective revision tool, a formal outline should be detailed and should adhere to several principles of logical arrangement, clarity, balance, and completeness. (See pp. 45–47 for examples and more details.)

- The outline should indicate which ideas are primary and which are subordinate. A long, undivided list of parallel items probably needs to be subdivided.
- Parallel headings should represent ideas of equal importance and generality. They should not overlap one another.
- Single sublevels should be avoided. They illogically divide something into only one part.

A formal outline is usually written either in phrases (a **topic outline**) or in sentences (a **sentence outline**). A complete topic outline is illustrated on page 45. A complete sentence outline accompanies Justin Malik's research paper on pages 720–21. Either is suitable for a research paper, though a sentence outline, because it requires complete statements, conveys more information.

Exercise 45.2 Creating a structure
Continuing from Exercise 45.1 (p. 659), arrange your notes into a structure. As specified by your instructor, make an informal outline or a formal sentence or topic outline to guide the drafting of your paper.

45c Drafting the paper

Beginning a draft of what will be a relatively long and complicated paper can be difficult, so it may help to remember that you do not have to proceed methodically from beginning to end.

Exercise

45c

Video
tutorial

Tips for drafting a research paper

- Reread the assignment to review your instructor's criteria. Make sure you have all the materials you'll need to meet the criteria.
- Write a quick two- or three-paragraph summary of what the paper will be about. This writing will get your juices flowing and give you a sense of direction. (Pretend you're writing to a friend if that will help loosen you up.) A version of the material you generate in this way may later prove useful for your paper's introduction or conclusion.
- Start with the section of the paper you feel most confident about. At first, skip any parts that scare you or give you undue trouble, even the introduction.
- Work in chunks, one unit or principal idea at a time. Fit the sections together only after you begin to see the draft take shape. (See below.)
- Center each section on an idea of your own. Use source material to back up the idea.
- Take great care in working with source material. Integrate sources into your own ideas (p. 642), and do not plagiarize (p. 648).
- Insert source citations as you quote, paraphrase, or summarize. Use authors' names and page numbers. (See the next page.)

---

1 Working section by section

In writing a first draft, remember that a primary reason for doing a research paper is to learn how to interpret and evaluate the evidence in sources, draw your own conclusions from the evidence, and weave the two together in a way that establishes your expertise in your subject and shows your perspective on it. (See pp. 173–75 for more discussion and an example of writing in response to texts.)

Integrating evidence with your own ideas will be easier if you view each principal idea of your paper (each Roman numeral of your outline) as a unit. Usually each principal idea requires a block of paragraphs to develop. Compose each unit as if it will stand alone (though of course you will pull the units together before your draft is complete).

- Begin each unit by stating the idea, which should be a conclusion you have drawn from reading and responding to your sources.
- Follow the statement with specific support from your sources: facts and examples; summaries, paraphrases, or quotations of secondary sources with your analysis; quotations of passages from primary sources with your analysis.

- Present fairly any disagreements among experts. Give the evidence that leads you to side with one expert or another.
- Try to remain open to new interpretations or new arrangements of ideas that occur to you.

Note Proceeding in this way will help you avoid a common trap of research writing: allowing your sources to control you, rather than vice versa. Make sure each unit of your paper centers on an idea of your own, not someone else's, and that your paragraphs are pointed toward demonstrating that idea, not merely presenting sources.

2 Tracking source citations

As you draft your paper, insert the source of each summary, paraphrase, and quotation in parentheses in the text—for instance, "(Matthews 43)," referring to page 43 in a work by Matthews. If you are conscientious about inserting these notes and carrying them through successive drafts, you will be less likely to plagiarize accidentally and you will have little difficulty documenting your sources in the final paper.

> **Exercise 45.3 Drafting your paper**
> Draft the research paper you have been developing in Chapters 41–44. Before beginning the draft, study your research journal and your source information. While drafting, follow your thesis statement and outline as closely as you need to, but stay open to new ideas, associations, and arrangements.

45d Revising and editing the paper

When you have written a first draft, take a break for at least a day so that you can gain some objectivity about your work and can read the draft critically when you begin to revise.

1 Revising

Always revise your draft first, satisfying yourself with the content and shape of the whole before trying to edit sentences and words. Begin with the advice and checklist on pages 58–64, and supplement them with the following checklist.

Checklist for revising a research paper

Checklist

Assignment
How does the draft satisfy all of the criteria stated in your instructor's assignment?

Thesis statement

How well does your thesis statement describe your subject and your perspective as they emerged during drafting?

Structure

(Outlining your draft as suggested on p. 662 can help you see structure at a glance.)

How consistently does borrowed material illuminate and support—not lead and dominate—your own ideas? How well is the importance of ideas reflected in the emphasis they receive? Will the arrangement of ideas be clear to readers?

45d

Evidence

Where might readers need more evidence in order to accept your ideas? Where might the evidence seem weak or irrelevant?

Reasonableness and clarity

How reasonable will readers find your arguments? (See pp. 213–17.) Where do you need to define terms or concepts that readers may not know or may dispute?

2 Editing

When you complete your revision—and only then—you are ready to edit. If you do not compose on a computer, copy or retype the new draft if possible so that you have a clean copy to work on. If you do compose on a computer, you can edit directly on screen or print a clean copy. (Some writers find it easier to spot errors on paper than on screen.)

For editing, consult the advice and checklist on pages 67–69. Try to read the paper from the point of view of someone who has not spent hours planning and researching but instead has come fresh to the paper. Look for lapses in sense, awkward passages, wordiness, poor transitions between ideas and evidence, unnecessary repetition, wrong or misspelled words, errors in grammar, punctuation, or mechanics—in short, anything that is likely to interfere with a reader's understanding of your meaning.

3 Completing source citations

Before you prepare your final draft (next section), you must insert final source citations into your text and prepare the list of sources for the end of the paper. See pages 657–58 on documenting sources in various disciplines' styles.

Exercise 45.4 Revising and editing your paper

Using the revision and editing checklists on pages 61 and 68–69 and the checklist and pointers here, revise and edit your research paper. Work to improve not only the presentation of ideas but also, if necessary, the ideas themselves. Make sure you have provided an in-text citation for every summary, paraphrase, and direct quotation of a source and that your list of sources is complete.

45e Preparing and proofreading the final draft

Student paper

Prepare the final draft of your paper when you have edited the text, added the source citations, and written the list of works cited. Most instructors expect research papers to be neatly typed with clear titling, double spacing, standard margins, and minimal handwritten corrections. Your instructor may have additional requirements, suggested by the discipline in which you are writing. This book explains four such document formats:

- **MLA format,** used in English, foreign languages, and some other humanities, pages 676–77 and 714–16. See also Chapter 47 for the sample research papers of Justin Malik and Vanessa Haley.
- **Chicago format,** used in history, art history, religion, philosophy, and some other humanities, pages 785–88 and 797–98.
- **APA format,** used in psychology and other social sciences, pages 808–09 and 823–26.
- **CSE format,** used in the natural and applied sciences, pages 836–37 and 841.

In any discipline, you can use a computer to present your ideas effectively and attractively with readable type fonts, headings, illustrations, and other elements. See Chapter 5 for ideas.

Before you submit your paper, proofread it carefully for typographical errors, misspellings, and other errors. (See p. 73 for proofreading tips.) Unless the errors are very numerous (more than several on a page), you can correct them by whiting out or crossing out (neatly) and inserting the correction (neatly) in ink. Don't let the pressure of a deadline prevent you from proofreading, for even minor errors can impair clarity or annoy readers and thus negate some of the hard work you have put into your project.

Exercise 45.5 Preparing and proofreading your final draft
Prepare the final draft of your research paper, following your instructor's requirements for document format. If your instructor does not specify a format, follow the MLA guidelines on pages 714–16. Proofread and correct the paper before submitting it.

46

Using MLA Documentation and Format

English, foreign languages, and some other humanities use the documentation style of the Modern Language Association, described in the *MLA Handbook for Writers of Research Papers* (7th ed., 2009).

MLA documentation style employs brief parenthetical citations within the text that direct readers to a list of works cited at the end of the text. A parenthetical citation might look like this:

Video tutorial

> Only one article mentions this discrepancy (Wolfe 62).

The name Wolfe directs readers to the article by Wolfe in the list of works cited, and the page number 62 specifies the page in the article on which the cited material appears.

This chapter presents the essentials of MLA style: what to include in a parenthetical citation (below), where to place citations (p. 673), when to use footnotes or endnotes in addition to parenthetical citations (p. 675), how to create the list of works cited (p. 676), and how to format the entire paper (p. 714).

Exercise

46a Using MLA in-text citations

1 Writing parenthetical text citations

In-text citations of sources must include just enough information for the reader to locate both of the following:

- The *source* in your list of works cited.
- The *place* in the source where the borrowed material appears.

For any kind of source, you can usually meet both these requirements by providing the author's last name and (if the source uses them) the page numbers where the material appears. The reader

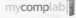
mycomplab

Visit *mycomplab.com* for the eText and for resources and more exercises on MLA documentation and format.

can find the source in your list of works cited and find the borrowed material in the source itself.

Note For most sources, you will provide the author's or authors' last names and a page reference. Do not include the title unless you are citing more than one work by exactly the same author(s) or the source has no listed author (models 5 and 6, pp. 669–70). The examples below cite a book to which neither of these exceptions applies:

Incorrect One textbook discusses the "ethical dilemmas in public relations practice" (Wilcox, Ault, and Agee, *Public Relations* 125).

Incorrect One textbook discusses the "ethical dilemmas in public relations practice" (*Public Relations* 125).

Correct One textbook discusses the "ethical dilemmas in public relations practice" (Wilcox, Ault, and Agee 125).

1. Author not named in your text

When you have not already named the author in your sentence, provide the author's last name and the page number(s), with no punctuation between them, in parentheses.

One researcher concludes that "women impose a distinctive construction on moral problems, seeing moral dilemmas in terms of conflicting responsibilities" (Gilligan 105-06).

See model 6 for the form to use when the source does not have an author. And see models 10 and 11 for the forms to use when the source does not provide page numbers.

MLA parenthetical citations

1. Author not named in your text 668
2. Author named in your text 669
3. A work with two or three authors 669
4. A work with more than three authors 669
5. A work by an author of two or more cited works 669
6. An anonymous work 670
7. A work with a corporate author 670
8. A nonprint source 670
9. A multivolume work 671
10. A one-page work, an entire work, or a work with no page or other reference numbers 671
11. A work with numbered paragraphs or sections instead of pages 672
12. A source referred to by another source (indirect source) 672
13. A literary work 672
14. The Bible 673
15. Two or more works in the same citation 673

MLA
46a

2. Author named in your text

When you have already given the author's name with the material you're citing, do not repeat it in the parenthetical citation. Give just the page number(s).

> Carol Gilligan concludes that "women impose a distinctive construction on moral problems, seeing moral dilemmas in terms of conflicting responsibilities" (105-06).

See model 6 for the form to use when the source does not list an author. And see models 10 and 11 for the forms to use when the source does not provide page numbers.

3. A work with two or three authors

If the source has two or three authors, give all their last names in the text or in the citation. Separate two authors' names with and:

> As Frieden and Sagalyn observe, "The poor and the minorities were the leading victims of highway and renewal programs" (29).

> According to one study, "The poor and the minorities were the leading victims of highway and renewal programs" (Frieden and Sagalyn 29).

With three authors, add commas and also and before the final name:

> The textbook by Wilcox, Ault, and Agee discusses the "ethical dilemmas in public relations practice" (125).

> One textbook discusses the "ethical dilemmas in public relations practice" (Wilcox, Ault, and Agee 125).

4. A work with more than three authors

If the source has more than three authors, you may list all their last names or give only the first author's name followed by et al. (the abbreviation for the Latin *et alii*, "and others"). The choice depends on what you do in your list of works cited (see p. 679).

> Increased competition means that employees of public relations firms may find their loyalty stretched in more than one direction (Wilcox et al. 417).

> Increased competition means that employees of public relations firms may find their loyalty stretched in more than one direction (Wilcox, Cameron, Reber, and Shin 417).

5. A work by an author of two or more cited works

If your list of works cited includes two or more works by the same author, then your citation must tell the reader which of the author's works you are referring to. Give the title either in the text or in a parenthetical citation. In a parenthetical citation, give the full title only if it is brief; otherwise, shorten the title to the first one, two, or three main words (excluding *A*, *An*, or *The*).

> At about age seven, children begin to use appropriate gestures with their stories (Gardner, *Arts* 144-45).

The full title of Gardner's book is *The Arts and Human Development* (see the works-cited entry on p. 680). This shortened title is italicized because the source is a book.

6. An anonymous work

MLA
46a

For a work with no named author or editor (whether an individual or an organization), use a full or shortened version of the title, as explained above. In your list of works cited, you alphabetize an anonymous work by the first main word of the title (see p. 680), so the first word of a shortened title should be the same. The following citations refer to an unsigned source titled "The Right to Die." The title appears in quotation marks because the source is a periodical article.

> One article notes that a death-row inmate may demand his own execution to achieve a fleeting notoriety ("Right" 16).

> "The Right to Die" notes that a death-row inmate may demand execution to achieve a fleeting notoriety (16).

If two or more anonymous works have the same title, distinguish them with additional information in the text citation, such as the publication date.

7. A work with a corporate author

Some works list as author a government body, association, committee, company, or other group. Cite such a work by the organization's name. If the name is long, work it into the text to avoid an intrusive parenthetical citation.

> A 2011 report by the Nevada Department of Education provides evidence of an increase in graduation rates (12).

8. A nonprint source

Cite a nonprint source such as a Web page or a DVD just as you would any other source. If your works-cited entry lists the source under the name of an author or other contributor, use that name in the text citation. The following example cites an authored source that has page numbers.

> Business forecasts for the fourth quarter tended to be optimistic (White 4).

If your works-cited entry lists the work under its title, cite the work by title in your text, as explained in model 6. The next example cites an entire work (a film on DVD) and gives the title in the text, so it omits a parenthetical citation (see model 10).

Many decades after its release, *Citizen Kane* is still remarkable for its rich black-and-white photography.

9. A multivolume work

If you consulted only one volume of a multivolume work, your list of works cited will say so (see model 30 on p. 690), and you can treat the volume as you would any book.

If you consulted more than one volume of a multivolume work, give the appropriate volume before the page number (here volume 5):

After issuing the Emancipation Proclamation, Lincoln said, "What I did, I did after very full deliberations, and under a very heavy and solemn sense of responsibility" (5: 438).

The number 5 indicates the volume from which the quotation was taken; the number 438 indicates the page number in that volume. When the author's name appears in such a citation, place it before the volume number with no punctuation: (Lincoln 5: 438).

If you are referring generally to an entire volume of a multivolume work and are not citing specific page numbers, add the abbreviation vol. before the volume number, as in (vol. 5) or (Lincoln, vol. 5) (note the comma after the author's name). Then readers will not misinterpret the volume number as a page number.

10. A one-page work, an entire work, or a work with no page or other reference numbers

When you cite a work that's only a page long or an entire work rather than a part of it, you may omit any page or other reference number. If the work you cite has an author, try to give the author's name in your text. You will not need a parenthetical citation then, but the source must still appear in your list of works cited.

Boyd deals with the need to acknowledge and come to terms with our fear of nuclear technology.

Use the same format when you cite a specific passage from a work with no page, paragraph, or other reference numbers, such as a Web source.

If the author's name does not appear in your text, put it in a parenthetical citation.

Almost 20 percent of commercial banks have been audited for the practice (Friis).

11. A work with numbered paragraphs or sections instead of pages

Some electronic sources number each paragraph or section instead of each page. In citing passages in these sources, give the paragraph or section number(s) and distinguish them from page numbers: after the author's name, put a comma, a space, and par. (one paragraph), pars. (more than one paragraph), sec., or secs.

Twins reared apart report similar feelings (Palfrey, pars. 6-7).

12. A source referred to by another source (indirect source)

When you want to use a quotation that is already in quotation marks—indicating that the author you are reading is quoting someone else—try to find the original source and quote directly from it. If you can't find the original source, then your citation must indicate that your quotation of it is indirect. In the following citation, qtd. in ("quoted in") says that Davino was quoted by Boyd.

George Davino maintains that "even small children have vivid ideas about nuclear energy" (qtd. in Boyd 22).

The list of works cited then includes only Boyd (the work consulted), not Davino.

13. A literary work

Novels, plays, and poems are often available in many editions, so your instructor may ask you to provide information that will help readers find the passage you cite no matter what edition they consult.

- **Novels:** The page number comes first, followed by a semicolon and then information on the appropriate part or chapter of the work.

  Toward the end of James's novel, Maggie suddenly feels "the thick breath of the definite—which was the intimate, the immediate, the familiar, as she hadn't had them for so long" (535; pt. 6, ch. 41).

- **Poems that are not divided into parts:** You may omit the page number and supply the line number(s) for the quotation. To prevent confusion with page numbers, precede the numbers with line or lines in the first citation; then use just the numbers.

  In Shakespeare's Sonnet 73 the speaker identifies with the trees of late autumn, "Bare ruined choirs, where late the sweet birds sang" (line 4). "In me," Shakespeare writes, "thou seest the glowing of such fire / That on the ashes of his youth doth lie . . ." (9-10).

(See pp. 775–77 for a sample paper on a poem.)

■ **Verse plays and poems that are divided into parts:** Omit a page number and cite the appropriate part—act (and scene, if any), canto, book, and so on—plus the line number(s). Use Arabic numerals for parts, including acts and scenes (3.4), unless your instructor specifies Roman numerals (III.iv).

> Later in Shakespeare's *King Lear* the disguised Edgar says, "The prince of darkness is a gentleman" (3.4.147).

(See pp. 778–80 for a sample paper on a verse play.)

■ **Prose plays:** Provide the page number followed by the act and scene, if any. See the reference to *Death of a Salesman* on page 675.

14. The Bible

When you cite passages of the Bible in parentheses, abbreviate the title of any book longer than four letters—for instance, Gen. (Genesis), 1 Sam. (1 Samuel), Ps. (Psalms), Prov. (Proverbs), Matt. (Matthew), Rom. (Romans). Then give the chapter and verse(s) in Arabic numerals.

> According to the Bible, at Babel God "did . . . confound the language of all the earth" (Gen. 11.9).

15. Two or more works in the same citation

When you refer to more than one work in a single parenthetical citation, separate the references with a semicolon.

> Two recent articles point out that a computer badly used can be less efficient than no computer at all (Gough and Hall 201; Richards 162).

Since long citations in the text can distract the reader, you may choose to cite several or more works in an endnote or footnote rather than in the text. See page 675.

2 Positioning and punctuating parenthetical citations

The following guidelines will help you place and punctuate text citations to distinguish between your own and your sources' ideas and to make your own text readable. See also pages 642–47 on editing quotations and using signal phrases to integrate source material into your sentences.

Where to place citations

Position text citations to accomplish two goals:

■ Make it clear exactly where your borrowing begins and ends.
■ Keep the citation as unobtrusive as possible.

You can accomplish both goals by placing the parenthetical citation at the end of the sentence element containing the borrowed material. This sentence element may be a phrase or a clause, and it may begin, interrupt, or conclude the sentence. Usually, as in the following examples, the element ends with a punctuation mark.

> The inflation rate might climb as high as 30 percent (Kim 164), an increase that could threaten the small nation's stability.

> The inflation rate, which might climb as high as 30 percent (Kim 164), could threaten the small nation's stability.

> The small nation's stability could be threatened by its inflation rate, which, one source predicts, might climb as high as 30 percent (Kim 164).

MLA
46a

In the last example the addition of one source predicts clarifies that Kim is responsible only for the inflation-rate prediction, not for the statement about stability.

When your paraphrase or summary of a source runs longer than a sentence, clarify the boundaries by using the author's name in the first sentence and placing the parenthetical citation at the end of the last sentence.

> Juliette Kim studied the effects of acutely high inflation in several South American and African countries since World War II. She discovered that a major change in government accompanied or followed the inflationary period in 56 percent of cases (22-23).

When you cite two or more sources in the same paragraph, position authors' names and parenthetical citations so that readers can see who said what. In the following example, the beginnings and ends of sentences clearly mark the different sources.

> Schools use computers extensively for drill-and-practice exercises, in which students repeat specific skills such as spelling words, using the multiplication facts, or, at a higher level, doing chemistry problems. But many education experts criticize such exercises for boring students and failing to engage their critical thinking and creativity. Jane M. Healy, a noted educational psychologist and teacher, takes issue with "interactive" software for children as well as drill-and-practice software, arguing that "some of the most popular 'educational' software . . . may be damaging to independent thinking, attention, and motivation" (20). Another education expert, Harold Wenglinsky of the Educational Testing Service, found in a well-regarded study that fourth and eighth graders who used computers frequently, including for drill and practice, actually did worse on tests than their peers who used computers less often (*Does It Compute?* 21). In a later article, Wenglinsky concludes that "the quantity of use matters far less than the quality of use." In schools, he says, high-quality computer work, involving critical thinking, is still rare ("In Search" 17).

How to punctuate citations

Generally place a parenthetical citation *before* any punctuation required by your sentence. If the borrowed material is a quotation, place the citation *between* the closing quotation mark and the punctuation:

> Spelling argues that during the 1970s American automobile manufacturers met consumer needs "as well as could be expected" (26), but not everyone agrees with him.

The exception is a quotation ending in a question mark or exclamation point. Then use the appropriate punctuation inside the closing quotation mark, and follow the quotation with the text citation and a period.

MLA
46a

> "Of what use is genius," Emerson asks, "if the organ . . . cannot find a focal distance within the actual horizon of human life?" ("Experience" 60). Mad genius is no genius.

When a citation appears at the end of a quotation set off from the text, place it one space *after* the punctuation ending the quotation. Do not use additional punctuation with the citation or quotation marks around the quotation.

> In Arthur Miller's *Death of a Salesman*, the most poignant defense of Willie Loman comes from his wife, Linda:
>
> > He's not the finest character that ever lived. But he's a human being, and a terrible thing is happening to him. So attention must be paid. He's not to be allowed to fall into his grave like an old dog. Attention, attention must finally be paid to such a person. (56; act 1)

(This citation of a play includes the act number as well as the page number. See p. 673.)

See the two sample research papers starting on pages 718 and 746 for further examples of placing parenthetical references in relation to summaries, paraphrases, and quotations.

3 Using footnotes or endnotes in special circumstances

Occasionally you may want to use footnotes or endnotes in place of parenthetical citations. If you need to refer to several sources at once, listing them in a long parenthetical citation could be intrusive. In that case, signal the citation with a numeral raised above the appropriate line of text and write a note beginning with the same numeral to cite the sources:

Text   At least five studies have confirmed these results.[1]

Note   1. Abbott and Winger 266-68; Casner 27; Hoyenga 78-79; Marino 36; Tripp, Tripp, and Walk 179-83.

You may also use a footnote or endnote to comment on a source or to provide information that does not fit easily in the text:

Text   So far, no one has confirmed these results.[2]

Note   2. Manter tried repeatedly to replicate the experiment, but he
            was never able to produce the high temperatures (616).

Indent a note one-half inch, type the numeral on the text line, and follow the numeral with a period and a space. If the note appears as a footnote, place it at the bottom of the page on which the citation appears, set it off from the text with quadruple spacing, and double-space the note itself. If the note appears as an endnote, place it in numerical order with the other endnotes on a page between the text and the list of works cited. Double-space all the endnotes. (See pp. 740–41 for examples of endnotes and the format for typing a page of endnotes.)

MLA
46b

Exercise

46b Preparing the MLA list of works cited

In MLA documentation style, your in-text parenthetical citations (discussed in 46a) refer the reader to complete information on your sources in a list you title Works Cited and place at the end of your paper. The list should include all the sources you quoted, paraphrased, or summarized in your paper. (If your instructor asks you to include sources you examined but did not cite, title the list Works Consulted.)

Follow this format for the list of works cited:

■ Arrange your sources in alphabetical order by the last name of the author. If an author is not given in the source, alphabetize the source by the first main word of the title (excluding *A*, *An*, or *The*).

MLA works-cited page

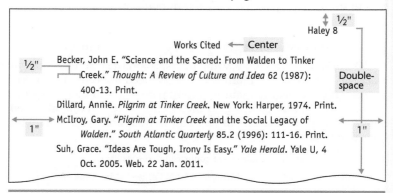

$\updownarrow$ ½"
Haley 8

Works Cited ◄— Center

½"   Becker, John E. "Science and the Sacred: From Walden to Tinker   Double-
        Creek." *Thought: A Review of Culture and Idea* 62 (1987):   space
        400-13. Print.

Dillard, Annie. *Pilgrim at Tinker Creek*. New York: Harper, 1974. Print.

◄——► McIlroy, Gary. "*Pilgrim at Tinker Creek* and the Social Legacy of   ◄——►
1"   *Walden*." *South Atlantic Quarterly* 85.2 (1996): 111-16. Print.   1"

Suh, Grace. "Ideas Are Tough, Irony Is Easy." *Yale Herald*. Yale U, 4
        Oct. 2005. Web. 22 Jan. 2011.

▪ Type the entire list double-spaced, both within and between entries.

▪ Indent the second and subsequent lines of each entry one-half inch from the left. Your word processor can format this so-called hanging indent automatically.

For complete lists of works cited, see the papers by Justin Malik (pp. 742 and 744) and Vanessa Haley (p. 751).

The box on the next two pages directs you to the MLA formats for works-cited entries. Use your best judgment in adapting the models to your particular sources. If you can't find a model that exactly matches a source you used, locate and follow the closest possible match. You will certainly need to combine formats—for instance, drawing on model 2 ("Two or three authors") and model 21 ("A book with an editor") for a book with three editors.

Note MLA style requires the publication medium for every source, such as print, Web, DVD, or television. For example, if you consulted an article in a print magazine, list the medium as Print. If you consulted a book on the Web, list the medium as Web. The models here all conform to this standard.

MLA
46b

1 Listing authors

The following models show how to handle authors' names in citing any kind of source.

1. One author

Ehrenreich, Barbara. *Dancing in the Streets: A History of Collective Joy*. New
York: Metropolitan-Holt, 2006. Print.

Give the author's full name—last name first, a comma, first name, and any middle name or initial. Omit any title, such as *Dr.* or *PhD.* End the name with a period. If your source lists an editor as author, see model 21, page 686.

2. Two or three authors

Lifton, Robert Jay, and Greg Mitchell. *Who Owns Death: Capital Punishment,
the American Conscience, and the End of Executions*. New York: Morrow,
2000. Print.

Simpson, Dick, James Nowlan, and Elizabeth O'Shaughnessy. *The Struggle for
Power and Influence in Cities and States*. New York: Longman, 2011. Print.

Give the authors' names in the order provided on the title page. Reverse the first and last names of the first author *only*, not of any other authors. Separate two authors' names with a comma and and; separate three authors' names with commas and with and before the third name. If your source lists two or three editors as authors, see model 21, page 686.

MLA works-cited models

3. More than three authors

Wilcox, Dennis L., Glen T. Cameron, Bryan H. Reber, and Jae-Hwa Shin. *Think Public Relations*. Boston: Allyn, 2010. Print.

Wilcox, Dennis L., et al. *Think Public Relations*. Boston: Allyn, 2010. Print.

You may, but need not, give all authors' names if the work has more than three authors. If you choose not to give all names, provide the name of the first author only, and follow the name with a comma and the abbreviation et al. (for the Latin *et alii*, meaning "and others"). If your source lists more than three editors as authors, see model 21, page 686.

4. The same author(s) for two or more works

Gardner, Howard. *The Arts and Human Development.* New York: Wiley, 1973.
    Print.

---. *Five Minds for the Future.* Boston: Harvard Business School P, 2007.
    Print.

Give the author's name only in the first entry. For the second and any subsequent works by the same author, substitute three hyphens for the author's name, followed by a period. Note that the three hyphens may substitute only for *exactly* the same name or names. If the second Gardner source were by Gardner and somebody else, both names would have to be given in full.

Place an entry or entries using three hyphens immediately after the entry that names the author. Within the set of entries by the same author, arrange the sources alphabetically by the first main word of the title, as in the Gardner examples (*Arts*, then *Five*).

If you cite two or more sources that list as author(s) exactly the same editor(s), follow the hyphens with a comma and ed. or eds. as appropriate. (See model 21, p. 686.)

5. A corporate author

Vault Technologies. *Turnkey Parking Solutions.* Salt Lake City: Mills, 2011.
    Print.

Corporate authors include associations, committees, institutions, government bodies, companies, and other groups. List the name of the group as author when a source gives only that name and not an individual's name.

6. Author not named (anonymous)

The Dorling Kindersley World Atlas. London: Dorling, 2010. Print.

List a work that names no author—neither an individual nor a group—by its full title. If the work is a book, italicize the title. If the work is a periodical article or other short work, enclose the title in quotation marks:

"Leaping the Wall." *Economist* 26 Mar. 2011: 51. Print.

Alphabetize the work by the title's first main word, excluding *A, An,* or *The* (*Dorling* in the first example and Leaping in the second).

2 Listing periodical print sources

Print periodicals include scholarly journals, newspapers, and magazines that are published at regular intervals (quarterly, monthly, weekly, or daily). The following list, adapted from the *MLA Handbook,* itemizes the possible elements in print periodicals, in order of their appearance in a works-cited entry.

- ▪ Author. Give the author's last name, first name, and any middle name or initial. To cite more than one author, two articles by the same author, a corporate author, or an article with no named author, see models 1–6.
- ▪ Title of the article, in quotation marks. Give the title and any subtitle. End the title with a period inside the final quotation mark.
- ▪ Title of the periodical, in italics. Omit any *A, An,* or *The* from the beginning of the title. Do not end with a period.
- ▪ Publication information. The treatment of volume and issue numbers and publication dates varies depending on the kind of periodical you are citing, as shown in models 7–18. (For the distinction between journals and magazines, see p. 594.) If you include the month of publication, abbreviate it unless it is May, June, or July.
- ▪ Page numbers of the article, without "pp."
- ▪ Medium of publication: Print, followed by a period.

MLA
46b

Articles in scholarly journals

7. An article in a journal with volume and issue numbers (print)

Bee, Robert. "The Importance of Preserving Paper-Based Artifacts in a Digital
    Age." *Library Quarterly* 78.2 (2008): 174-94. Print.

The next two pages show the basic format for an article in a periodical (a journal) and the location of the required information in the journal.

8. An article in a journal with only issue numbers (print)

Rae, Ian. "The Case for Digital Poetics." *Canadian Literature* 204 (2010):
    134-37. Print.

If a scholarly journal numbers only issues, not volumes, give the issue number alone after the journal title.

9. An abstract of a journal article or a dissertation (print)

Lever, Janet. "Sex Differences in the Games Children Play." *Social Problems*
    23.2 (1996): 478-87. *Psychological Abstracts* 63.5 (1996): item 1431.
    Print.

For an abstract of a journal article, first provide the publication information for the article, following model 7. Then give the information for the abstract. If the abstract publisher lists abstracts by item rather than page number, add item before the number. Add Abstract after the original publication information if the title of the abstracts

Format for a print journal article

Journal cover

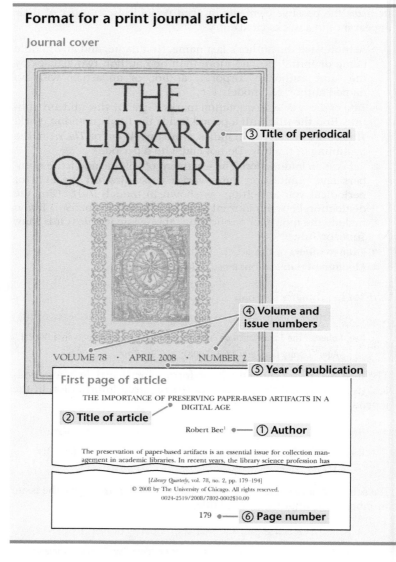

THE
LIBRARY ●—— ③ **Title of periodical**
QVARTERLY

④ **Volume and
issue numbers**

VOLUME 78 · APRIL 2008 · NUMBER 2

⑤ **Year of publication**

First page of article

THE IMPORTANCE OF PRESERVING PAPER-BASED ARTIFACTS IN A
DIGITAL AGE

② **Title of article**

Robert Bee[1] ●—— ① **Author**

The preservation of paper-based artifacts is an essential issue for collection management in academic libraries. In recent years, the library science profession has

[*Library Quarterly*, vol. 78, no. 2, pp. 179–194]
© 2008 by The University of Chicago. All rights reserved.
0024-2519/2008/7802-0002$10.00

179 ●—— ⑥ **Page number**

journal does not indicate that your source is an abstract. See model
65, page 706.

For an abstract appearing in *Dissertation Abstracts* (*DA*) or *Dissertation Abstracts International* (*DAI*), give the author's name and
the title, Diss. (for "Dissertation"), the institution granting the author's
degree, the date of the dissertation, and the publication information.

① ②
Bee, Robert. "The Importance of Preserving Paper-Based
③ ④ ⑤
Artifacts in a Digital Age." *Library Quarterly* 78.2 (2008):
⑥ ⑦
179-94. Print.

① **Author.** Give the full name—last name first, a comma, first name, and any middle name or initial. Omit *Dr., PhD,* or any other title. End the name with a period.

② **Title of article,** in quotation marks. Give the full title and any subtitle, separating them with a colon. End the title with a period inside the final quotation mark.

③ **Title of periodical,** in italics. Omit any *A, An,* or *The* from the beginning of the title. Do not end with a period.

④ **Volume and issue numbers,** in Arabic numerals, separated by a period. Do not add a period after the issue number.

⑤ **Year of publication,** in parentheses and followed by a colon.

⑥ **Inclusive page numbers of article,** without "pp." Provide only as many digits in the last number as needed for clarity, usually two.

⑦ **Medium.** Give the medium of the article, Print, followed by a period.

Steciw, Steven K. "Alterations to the Pessac Project of Le Corbusier." Diss.
U of Cambridge, England, 1986. *DAI* 46.10 (1986): 565C. Print.

See also model 40 on page 693 (entire dissertation), model 63 on page 704 (abstract on the Web), and model 65 on page 706 (abstract in an online database).

Note Most instructors expect you to consult and cite full articles, not abstracts. See page 598.

Articles in newspapers

10. An article in a national newspaper (print)

Harmanci, Reyhan. "Literary Journals Thrive, on Paper and Otherwise." *New York Times* 8 Apr. 2011, natl. ed.: A23+. Print.

MLA
46b

Give the author, the title of the article, and then the title of the newspaper as it appears on the first page (but without any *A*, *An*, or *The*). Follow the newspaper title with the day, the month, and the year of publication. (Abbreviate all months except May, June, and July.) If the newspaper lists an edition at the top of the first page, include it after the date (see natl. ed. above). If the newspaper is divided into sections that are lettered, provide the section designation before the page number when the newspaper does the same: A23+ above. (The plus sign indicates that the article continues on a later page.) If the newspaper is divided into numbered or titled sections, provide the section designation before the colon—for instance, sec. 1: 3 or Business Day sec.: 4+. End with the medium, Print.

11. An article in a local newspaper (print)

Perera, Dilshanie. "Health Department Elaborates on Latest Sharing of Services." *Town Topics* [Princeton] 16 Mar. 2011: 1+. Print.

If the city of publication does not appear in the title of a local newspaper, follow the title with the city name, not italicized, in brackets.

Articles in magazines

12. An article in a weekly or biweekly magazine (print)

Danticat, Edwidge. "A Year and a Day." *New Yorker* 17 Jan. 2011: 19-20. Print.

Give the author, title of the article, and title of the magazine. Follow the magazine title with the day, the month, and the year of publication. (Abbreviate all months except May, June, and July.) Don't place the date in parentheses, and don't provide a volume or issue number. Give the page numbers of the article and the medium, Print.

13. An article in a monthly or bimonthly magazine (print)

Hall, Stephen S. "Diseases in a Dish." *Scientific American* Mar. 2011: 40-45. Print.

Follow the magazine title with the month and the year of publication. (Abbreviate all months except May, June, and July.) Don't place the date in parentheses, and don't provide a volume or issue number. Give the page numbers of the article and the medium, Print.

Reviews, editorials, letters to the editor, interviews

14. A review (print)

Glasswell, Kathryn, and George Kamberelis. "Drawing and Redrawing the Map
of Writing Studies." Rev. of *Handbook of Writing Research*, by Charles A.
MacArthur, Steve Graham, and Jill Fitzgerald. *Reading Research Quarterly*
42.2 (2007): 304-23. Print.

Rev. is an abbreviation for "Review." The names of the authors of the
work being reviewed follow the title of the work, a comma, and by. If
the review has no title of its own, then Rev. of and the title of the
reviewed work immediately follow the name of the reviewer.

15. An editorial or a letter to the editor (print)

MLA
46b

An editorial:

"The Dollars and Cents of Bats and Farming." Editorial. *New York Times* 4 Apr.
2011, natl. ed.: A18. Print.

For an editorial with no named author, begin with the title and add
the word Editorial after the title, as in the example. For an editorial
with a named author, start with his or her name and then proceed
as in the example.

A letter to the editor:

Stasi, Dom. "Climate and Heresy." Letter. *Scientific American* Mar. 2011: 8.
Print.

Add the word Letter after the title, if there is one, or after the author's
name.

16. An interview (print)

Aloni, Shulamit. Interview. *Palestine-Israel Journal of Politics, Economics, and
Culture* 14.4 (2007): 63-68. Print.

Begin with the name of the person interviewed. If the interview
does not have a title (as in the example), add Interview after the name.
(Replace this description with the title if there is one.) You may also
add the name of the interviewer if you know it—for example,
Interview by Benson Wright. See model 75 (p. 711) to cite a broadcast interview or an interview you conduct yourself.

Articles in series or in special issues

17. An article in a series (print)

Kleinfeld, N. R. "Living at an Epicenter of Diabetes, Defiance, and Despair."
New York Times 10 Jan. 2006, natl. ed.: A1+. Print. Pt. 2 of a series,
Bad Blood, begun 9 Jan. 2006.

Cite an article in a series following the appropriate model on the preceding pages for a scholarly journal, newspaper, or magazine. If you

wish, end the entry with a description to indicate that the article is part of a series.

18. An article in a special issue (print)

Rubini, Monica, and Michela Menegatti. "Linguistic Bias in Personnel Selection." *Celebrating Two Decades of Linguistic Bias Research*. Ed. Robbie M. Sutton and Karen M. Douglas. Spec. issue of *Journal of Language and Social Psychology* 27.2 (2008): 168-81. Print.

Cite an article in a special issue of a periodical by starting with the author and title of the article. Follow with the title of the special issue, Ed., and the names of the issue's editor(s). Add Spec. issue of before the periodical title. Conclude with publication information, using the appropriate model on page 681 or 684 for a journal or magazine.

3 Listing nonperiodical print sources

Nonperiodical print sources are works that are not published at regular intervals, such as books, government publications, and pamphlets. To cite more than one author, two or more articles by the same author, a corporate author, or a source with no named author, see models 1–6.

Books

19. Basic format for a book (print)

Lahiri, Jhumpa. *Unaccustomed Earth*. New York: Knopf, 2008. Print.

Pages 688–89 show the basic format for a book and the location of the required information in the book. When other information is required, it usually falls either between the author's name and the title or between the title and the publication information, as in the following models.

20. A second or subsequent edition (print)

Bolinger, Dwight L. *Aspects of Language*. 3rd ed. New York: Harcourt, 1981. Print.

For any edition after the first, place the edition number after the title. (If an editor's name follows the title, place the edition number after the name. See model 25.) Use the appropriate designation for editions that are named or dated rather than numbered—for instance, Rev. ed. for "Revised edition."

21. A book with an editor (print)

Holland, Merlin, and Rupert Hart-Davis, eds. *The Complete Letters of Oscar Wilde*. New York: Holt, 2000. Print.

Handle editors' names like authors' names (models 1–4), but add a comma and the abbreviation ed. (one editor) or eds. (two or more editors) after the last editor's name.

22. A book with an author and an editor (print)

Mumford, Lewis. *The City in History*. Ed. Donald L. Miller. New York: Pantheon,

1986. Print.

When citing the work of the author, give his or her name first, and give the editor's name after the title, preceded by Ed. (singular only, meaning "Edited by"). When citing the work of the editor, use model 21 for a book with an editor, adding By and the author's name after the title:

Miller, Donald L., ed. *The City in History*. By Lewis Mumford. New York:

Pantheon, 1986. Print.

23. A book with a translator (print)

Alighieri, Dante. *The Inferno*. Trans. John Ciardi. New York: NAL, 1971. Print.

When citing the work of the author, as in the preceding example, give his or her name first, and give the translator's name after the title, preceded by Trans. ("Translated by").

When citing the work of the translator, give his or her name first, followed by a comma and trans. Follow the title with By and the author's name:

Ciardi, John, trans. *The Inferno*. By Dante Alighieri. New York: NAL, 1971. Print.

When a book you cite by author has a translator *and* an editor, give the translator's and editor's names in the order used on the book's title page.

24. An anthology (print)

Kennedy, X. J., and Dana Gioia, eds. *Literature: An Introduction to Fiction,*

Poetry, Drama, and Writing. 11th ed. New York: Longman, 2010. Print.

Cite an entire anthology only when citing the work of the editor or editors or when your instructor permits cross-referencing like that shown in model 26. Give the name of the editor or editors (followed by ed. or eds.) and then the title of the anthology.

25. A selection from an anthology (print)

Mason, Bobbie Ann. "Shiloh." *Literature: An Introduction to Fiction, Poetry,*

Drama, and Writing. Ed. X. J. Kennedy and Dana Gioia. 11th ed. New

York: Longman, 2010. 569-78. Print.

This listing adds the following to the anthology entry in model 24: author of selection, title of selection (in quotation marks), and inclusive

Format for a print book

Title page

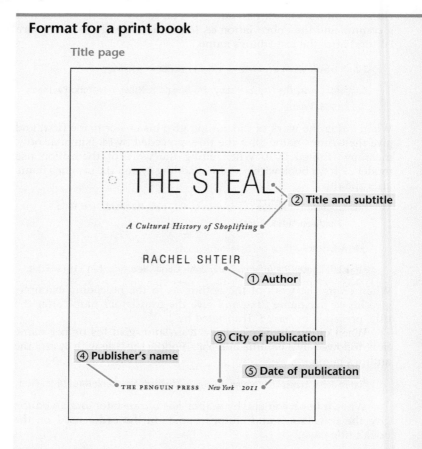

THE STEAL

② **Title and subtitle**

A Cultural History of Shoplifting

RACHEL SHTEIR

① **Author**

③ **City of publication**

④ **Publisher's name**

⑤ **Date of publication**

THE PENGUIN PRESS *New York* *2011*

MLA
46b

page numbers for the selection (without the abbreviation "pp."). If you wish, you may also supply the original date of publication for the work you are citing, after its title. See model 32 on page 691.

If the work you cite comes from a collection of works by one author that has no editor, use the following form:

> Auden, W. H. "Family Ghosts." *The Collected Poetry of W. H. Auden*. New York: Random, 1945. 132-33. Print.

26. Two or more selections from the same anthology (print)

Bradstreet, Anne. "The Author to Her Book." Kennedy and Gioia 647.

Kennedy, X. J., and Dana Gioia, eds. *Literature: An Introduction to Fiction, Poetry, Drama, and Writing*. 11th ed. New York: Longman, 2010. Print.

①   ②
Shteir, Rachel. *The Steal: A Cultural History of Shoplifting.*
     ③   ④   ⑤   ⑥
New York: Penguin, 2011. Print.

① **Author.** Give the full name—last name first, a comma, first name, and any middle name or initial. Omit *Dr., PhD,* or any other title. End the name with a period.

② **Title,** in italics. Give the full title and any subtitle, separating them with a colon. End the title with a period.

③ **City of publication.** Precede the publisher's name with its city, followed by a colon. Use only the first city if the title page lists more than one.

④ **Publisher's name.** Shorten most publishers' names ("UP" for University Press, "Little" for Little, Brown). Give both imprint and publisher's names when they appear on the title page: e.g., "Vintage-Random" for Vintage Books and Random House.

⑤ **Date of publication.** If the date doesn't appear on the title page, look for it on the next page. End the date with a period.

⑥ **Medium.** Give the medium of the book, Print, followed by a period.

MLA
46b

Merwin, W. S. "For the Anniversary of My Death." Kennedy and Gioia 834-35.

Stevens, Wallace. "Thirteen Ways of Looking at a Blackbird." Kennedy and Gioia 838-39.

When you are citing more than one selection from the same anthology, your instructor may allow you to avoid repetition by giving the anthology information in full (the Kennedy and Gioia entry) and then simply cross-referencing it in entries for the works you used. Thus the Bradstreet, Merwin, and Stevens examples replace full publication information with Kennedy and Gioia and the appropriate pages in that book. Note that each entry appears in its proper alphabetical place among other works cited. Because the specific entries cross-reference the Kennedy and Gioia anthology, they do not require the medium.

27. A scholarly article reprinted in a collection (print)

> Molloy, Francis C. "The Suburban Vision in John O'Hara's Short Stories."
> *Critique: Studies in Modern Fiction* 25.2 (1984): 101-13. Rpt. in *Short
> Story Criticism: Excerpts from Criticism of the Works of Short Fiction Writ-
> ers.* Ed. David Segal. Vol. 15. Detroit: Gale, 1989. 287-92. Print.

If the work you cite is a scholarly article that was previously printed elsewhere—for instance, in a sholarly journal—provide the complete information for the earlier publication of the piece. Follow this information with Rpt. in ("Reprinted in") and the information for the source in which you found the piece.

28. An article in a reference work (print)

> "Reckon." *Merriam-Webster's Collegiate Dictionary.* 11th ed. 2008. Print.
> Wenner, Manfred W. "Arabia." *The New Encyclopaedia Britannica: Macropaedia.*
> 15th ed. 2007. Print.

List an article in a reference work by its title (first example) unless the article is signed (second example). For works with entries arranged alphabetically, you need not include volume or page numbers. For works that are widely used and often revised, like those above, you may omit the editors' names and all publication information except any edition number, the publication year, and the medium.

For works that are specialized, give full publication information. Such works may have narrow subjects and audiences and may appear in only one edition.

> "Fortune." *Encyclopedia of Indo-European Culture.* Ed. J. P. Mallory and Douglas
> Q. Adams. London: Fitzroy, 1997. Print.

See also models 48 (p. 699) and 68 (p. 707), respectively, to cite reference works appearing on the Web or on a CD-ROM or DVD-ROM.

29. An illustrated book or graphic narrative (print)

> Wilson, G. Willow. *Cairo.* Illus. M. K. Perker. New York: Vertigo-DC Comics,
> 2005. Print.

When citing the work of the writer of a graphic narrative or illustrated book, follow the example above: author's name, title, Illus. ("Illustrated by"), and the illustrator's name. When citing the work of an illustrator, list his or her name first, followed by a comma and illus. ("illustrator"). After the title and By, list the author's name.

> Williams, Garth, illus. *Charlotte's Web.* By E. B. White. 1952. New York: Harper,
> 1999. Print.

30. A multivolume work (print)

Lincoln, Abraham. *The Collected Works of Abraham Lincoln*. Ed. Roy P. Basler.
Vol. 5. New Brunswick: Rutgers UP, 1953. Print. 8 vols.

If you use only one volume of a multivolume work, give that volume number before the publication information (Vol. 5 in the preceding example). You may add the total number of volumes at the end of the entry (8 vols. in the example).

If you use two or more volumes of a multivolume work, give the work's total number of volumes before the publication information (8 vols. in the following example). Your text citation will indicate which volume you are citing (see p. 671).

Lincoln, Abraham. *The Collected Works of Abraham Lincoln*. Ed. Roy P. Basler.
8 vols. New Brunswick: Rutgers UP, 1953. Print.

If you cite a multivolume work published over a period of years, give the inclusive years as the publication date: for instance, Cambridge: Harvard UP, 1978-90.

31. A series (print)

Bergman, Ingmar. *The Seventh Seal*. New York: Simon, 1995. Print. Mod. Film
Scripts Ser. 12.

Place the name of the series (not quoted or italicized) at the end of the entry, followed by the series number (if any) and a period. Abbreviate common words such as *modern* and *series*.

32. A republished book (print)

James, Henry. *The Bostonians*. 1886. New York: Penguin, 2001. Print.

Republished books include books reissued under new titles and paperbound editions of books originally released in hard covers. Place the original publication date after the title, and then provide the full publication information for the source you are using. If the book originally had a different title, add this title and its publication date after Rpt. of ("Reprint of") at the end of the entry—for example, Rpt. of *Thomas Hardy: A Life*. 1941.

33. The Bible (print)

The Bible. Print. King James Vers.
The Holy Bible. Trans. Ronald Youngblood et al. Grand Rapids: Zondervan,
1984. Print. New Intl. Vers.

When citing a standard version of the Bible (first example), do not italicize the title or the name of the version. You need not provide publication information. For an edition of the Bible (second example), italicize the title, provide editors' and/or translators' names, give full publication information, and add the version name at the end.

MLA
46b

34. A book with a title in its title (print)

Eco, Umberto. *Postscript to* The Name of the Rose. Trans. William Weaver.
    New York: Harcourt, 1983. Print.

When a book's title contains another book title (here *The Name of the Rose*), do not italicize the second title. When a book's title contains a quotation or the title of a work normally placed in quotation marks, keep the quotation marks and italicize both titles: *Critical Response to Henry James's "The Beast in the Jungle."*

35. Published proceedings of a conference (print)

Stimpson, Bill, ed. *2007 AWEA Annual Conference and Exhibition*. Proc. of
    Amer. Wind Energy Assn. Conf., 3-6 June 2007, New York. Red Hook:
    Curran, 2008. Print.

To cite the published proceedings of a conference, use a book model—here, an edited book (model 21). Between the title and the publication data, add information about the conference, such as its name, date, and location. You may omit any of this information that already appears in the source title. Treat a particular presentation at the conference like a selection from an anthology (model 25).

36. An introduction, preface, foreword, or afterword (print)

Donaldson, Norman. Introduction. *The Claverings*. By Anthony Trollope. New
    York: Dover, 1977. vii-xv. Print.

An introduction, foreword, or afterword is often written by someone other than the book's author. When citing such a piece, give its name without quotation marks or italics, as with Introduction above. (If the piece has a title of its own, provide it, in quotation marks, between the name of the author and the name of the book.) Follow the title of the book with By and the book author's name. Give the inclusive page numbers of the part you cite. (In the example above, the small Roman numerals refer to the front matter of the book, before page 1.)

When the author of a preface or introduction is the same as the author of the book, give only the last name after the title:

Gould, Stephen Jay. Prologue. *The Flamingo's Smile: Reflections in Natural
    History*. By Gould. New York: Norton, 1985. 13-20. Print.

37. A book lacking publication information or pagination (print)

Carle, Eric. *The Very Busy Spider*. New York: Philomel, 1984. N. pag. Print.

Some books are not paginated or do not list a publisher or a place of publication. To cite such a book, provide as much information as you can and indicate the missing information with an abbreviation: N.p. if no city of publication, n.p. if no publisher, n.d. if no publication date, and N. pag. if no page numbers.

Other nonperiodical print sources

38. A government publication (print)

United Nations. Dept. of Economic and Social Affairs. *World Youth Report 2010: Youth and Climate Change.* New York: United Nations, 2011. Print.

United States. Cong. House. Committee on Agriculture, Nutrition, and Forestry. *Food and Energy Act of 2008.* 110th Cong., 2nd sess. Washington: GPO, 2008. Print.

Wisconsin. Dept. of Public Instruction. *Bullying Prevention Program.* Madison: Wisconsin Dept. of Public Instruction, 2010. Print.

If a government publication does not list a person as author or editor, give the appropriate agency as author, as in the above examples. Provide information in the order illustrated, separating elements with periods: the name of the government, the name of the agency (which may be abbreviated), and the title and publication information. For a congressional publication (second example), give the house and committee involved before the title, and give the number and session of Congress after the title. In this example, GPO stands for the US Government Printing Office.

If a government publication lists a person as author or editor, treat the source as an authored or edited book:

Kim, Jiyul. *Cultural Dimensions of Strategy and Policy.* Carlisle: US Army War Coll., Strategic Studies Inst., 2009. Print.

See model 47 (p. 698) to cite a government publication you find on the Web.

39. A pamphlet or brochure (print)

Understanding Childhood Obesity. Tampa: Obesity Action Coalition, 2011. Print.

Most pamphlets and brochures can be treated as books. In this example, the pamphlet has no listed author, so the title comes first. If your source has an author, give his or her name first, followed by the title and publication information.

40. A dissertation (print)

McFaddin, Marie Oliver. *Adaptive Reuse: An Architectural Solution for Poverty and Homelessness.* Diss. U of Maryland, 2007. Ann Arbor: UMI, 2007. Print.

Treat a published dissertation like a book, but after the title insert Diss. ("Dissertation"), the institution granting the degree, and the year.

For an unpublished dissertation, use quotation marks rather than italics for the title and omit publication information.

> Wilson, Stuart M. "John Stuart Mill as a Literary Critic." Diss. U of Michigan, 1990. Print.

41. A letter (print)

> Buttolph, Mrs. Laura E. Letter to Rev. and Mrs. C. C. Jones. 20 June 1857. *The Children of Pride: A True Story of Georgia and the Civil War*. Ed. Robert Manson Myers. New Haven: Yale UP, 1972. 334-35. Print.

List a published letter under the writer's name. Specify that the source is a letter and to whom it was addressed, and give the date on which it was written. Treat the remaining information as with a selection from an anthology (model 25, p. 687). (See also model 15, p. 685, for the format of a letter to the editor of a periodical.)

For an unpublished letter in the collection of a library or archive, specify the writer, recipient, and date, as for a published letter. Then provide the medium, either MS ("manuscript") or TS ("typescript"). End with the name and location of the archive.

> James, Jonathan E. Letter to his sister. 16 Apr. 1970. MS. Jonathan E. James Papers. South Dakota State Archive, Pierre.

For a letter you received, give the name of the writer, specify yourself as the recipient, provide the date, and add the medium, MS or TS.

> Silva, Elizabeth. Letter to the author. 6 Apr. 2011. MS.

To cite an e-mail message or a discussion-group posting, see models 70–71 (pp. 707–08).

4 Listing nonperiodical Web sources

Video tutorial

This section shows how to cite nonperiodical sources that you find on the Web. These sources may be published only once or occasionally, or they may be updated frequently but not regularly. (Most online magazines and newspapers fall into the latter category. See p. 698.) Some nonperiodical Web sources are available only on the Web (next page); others are available in other media as well (pp. 701–03). See models 62–67 (pp. 704–06) to cite a scholarly journal that you find on the Web and any periodical that you find in an online database.

The MLA does not require a URL (electronic address) in Web source citations unless a source is hard to find without it or could be confused with another source. See model 61 (p. 703) for the form to use when citing a URL.

Note The *MLA Handbook* does not label its examples of nonperiodical Web sources as particular types. For ease of reference, the following models identify and illustrate the kinds of Web sources you are likely to encounter. If you don't see just what you need, consult the index of models on pages 678–79 for a similar source type whose format you can adapt. If your source does not include all of the information needed for a complete citation, find and list what you can.

Nonperiodical sources available only on the Web

Many nonperiodical Web sources are available only online. The following list, adapted from the *MLA Handbook*, itemizes the possible elements in a nonperiodical Web publication, in order of their appearance in a works-cited entry:

- **Name of the author or other person responsible for the source,** such as an editor, translator, or performer. See models 1–6 (pp. 677 and 679–80) for the handling of authors' names. For other kinds of contributors, see models 21–23 (editors and translators) and models 74, 76–77, and 83 (performers, directors, and so on).
- **Title of the cited work.** Use quotation marks for titles of articles, blog entries, and other sources that are parts of larger works. Use italics for books, plays, and other sources that are published independently.
- **Title of the Web site,** in italics.
- **Version or edition cited,** if any, following model 20 (p. 686)—for example, *Index of History Periodicals.* 2nd ed.
- **Publisher or sponsor of the site,** followed by a comma. If you cannot find a publisher or sponsor, use N.p. ("No publisher") instead. (See the Corbett example on p. 698.)
- **Date of electronic publication, latest revision, or posting.** If the date includes the month, abbreviate it unless it is May, June, or July. If no date is available, use n.d. ("no date") instead. (See the Corbett example on p. 698.)
- **Medium of publication:** Web.
- **Date of your access:** day, month, year. Abbreviate all months except May, June, and July.

For some Web sources, you may want to include information that is not on this list, such as the names of both the writer and the performers in a *YouTube* video.

42. A short work with a title (Web)

Murray, Amanda. "The Birth of Hip-Hop: Innovation against the Odds." *The Lemelson Center for the Study of Invention and Innovation.* Smithsonian Inst., Natl. Museum of Amer. Hist., Oct. 2010. Web. 11 Apr. 2011.

See the next two pages for an analysis of this entry and the location of the required information on the Web site. If the short work you are citing lacks an author, follow model 6 (p. 680) for an anonymous source, starting with the title as in the following example.

Format for a short work on the Web

Top of page

Bottom of page

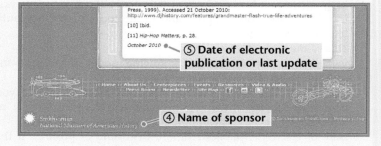

"Clean Energy." *Union of Concerned Scientists: Citizens and Scientists for Environmental Solutions.* Union of Concerned Scientists, 2010. Web. 11 Mar. 2011.

To cite a short Web source that also appears in another medium
(such as print), see models 56–60 (pp. 701–02). To cite an article
from a Web journal or from an online database, see models 62–67
(pp. 704–06).

43. A short work without a title (Web)

Cyberbullying Research Center. Home page. Cyberbullying Research Center,
2010. Web. 15 May 2011.

Murray, Amanda. "The Birth of Hip-Hop: Innovation against the
      Odots." *The Lemelson Center for the Study of Invention and*
      Innovation. Smithsonian Inst., Natl. Museum of Amer.
      Hist., Oct. 2010. Web. 11 Apr. 2011.

① **Author.** Give the full name—last name first, a comma, first name, and any middle name or initial. Omit *Dr., PhD,* or any other title. End the name with a period. If you don't see the author's name at the top of the page, look at the bottom. If no author is listed, begin with the title of the short work.

② **Title of the short work,** in quotation marks. End the title with a period inside the final quotation mark.

③ **Site title,** italicized and ending with a period.

④ **Name of the sponsor,** ending with a comma.

⑤ **Date of electronic publication or last update.** For dates that include day and month, give the day first, then month, then year. Abbreviate all months except May, June, and July. End the date with a period.

⑥ **Medium.** Give the medium of the article, Web, followed by a period.

⑦ **Date of your access.** Give the day first, then month, then year. Abbreviate all months except May, June, and July. End the date with a period.

If you are citing an untitled short work from a Web site, such as the home page of a site or a posting to a blog, insert Home page, Online posting, or another descriptive label in place of the title. Do not use quotation marks or italics for this label.

44. An entire site (Web)

Crane, Gregory, ed. *The Perseus Digital Library.* Dept. of Classics,
      Tufts U, 14 Mar. 2011. Web. 21 July 2011.

When citing an entire Web site—for instance, a scholarly project or a foundation site—include the name of the editor, author, or compiler (if available); the title of the site; the sponsor; the date of publication or most recent update; the medium (Web); and your date of access.

If your source lacks a named author or editor, begin with the site title:

> *Union of Concerned Scientists: Citizens and Scientists for Environmental Solutions.*
> Union of Concerned Scientists, 2011. Web. 11 Mar. 2011.

If your source lacks a sponsor, use the abbreviation N.p. ("No publisher"). If it lacks a publication date, use the abbreviation n.d. The source below lacks both a sponsor and a publication date:

> Corbett, John. *STARN: Scots Teaching and Resource Network.* N.p., n.d. Web. 26
> Nov. 2010.

45. An article in a newspaper (Web)

> Broad, William J. "Black Market Trinkets from Space." *New York Times.* New
> York Times, 4 Apr. 2011. Web. 8 May. 2011.

Even when an online newspaper relates to a printed version, it is treated as a nonperiodical source because the online content can change often and unpredicatably. List the author, article title, and newspaper title as in model 10 or 11 (p. 684). Then give the publisher's name and the date. End with the medium of publication (Web) and the date of your access. Use this format to adapt the models for print periodicals if you need to cite a Web newspaper review, editorial, letter to the editor, interview, or article in a series (models 14–17, p. 685).

See model 66 to cite a newspaper article in an online database.

46. An article in a magazine (Web)

> Yabroff, Jennie. "Autism Finds Its Voice." *Newsweek.* Newsweek, 16 Jan. 2011.
> Web. 15 Mar 2011.

Even when an online magazine relates to a printed version, it is treated as a nonperiodical source because the online content can change often and unpredictably. List the author, article title, and magazine title as in model 12 or 13 (p. 684). Then give the publisher's name and the date. End with the medium (Web) and the date of your access. Use this format to adapt the models for print periodicals if you need to cite a Web magazine review, editorial, letter to the editor, interview, or article in a series or special issue (models 14–18, pp. 685–86).

See model 67 to cite a magazine article in an online database.

47. A government publication (Web)

> United States. Dept. of Education. "Why Teach." *Teach.* US Dept. of
> Education, n.d. Web. 1 Mar. 2011.

See model 38 for examples of government publications in print. Provide the same information for online publications, substituting Web for print publication information and adding your date of access. The preceding example includes the names of the government and department; the title of the source, in quotation marks; the title of the Web site, in italics; the name of the sponsor; n.d. (because there is no publication date); the medium (Web); and the date of access.

48. An article in a reference work (Web)

"Yi Dynasty." *Encyclopaedia Britannica Online*. Encyclopaedia Britannica, 2011.

Web. 7 Apr. 2011.

This source does not list an author, so the entry begins with the title of the article and then proceeds as for other Web sources. If a reference article has an author, place the name before the article title, as in model 42.

For reference works that you find in print or on CD-ROM or DVD-ROM, see models 28 (p. 690) and 68 (p. 707), respectively.

49. A visual (Web)

To cite a visual that is available only on the Web, give the name of the artist or creator, the title of the work, the date of the work (if any), a word describing the type of visual (if not otherwise clear from the title of the visual or the site), the title of the Web site, the sponsor, the date of the site, the medium (Web), and your date of access. The following examples show a range of possibilities.

A work of art:

Simpson, Rick. *Overload*. *Museum of Computer Art*. Museum of Computer Art,

2008. Web. 1 Apr. 2011.

A photograph:

Touboul, Jean. *Desert 1*. 2002. Photograph. *Artmuse.net*. Jean Touboul, 2007.

Web. 14 Nov. 2010.

An advertisement:

FreeCreditReport.com. Advertisement. *Facebook*. Facebook, 2011. Web. 6 May

2011.

A map, chart, graph, or diagram:

"Greenhouse Effect." Diagram. *Earthguide*. Scripps Inst. of Oceanography,

2008. Web. 17 July 2011.

See also model 60 (p. 702) to cite a visual that appears both on a computer and in another medium; model 73 (p. 710) to cite a visual in a digital file; and models 78–82 (pp. 712–13) to cite a visual that isn't on the Web.

50. A television or radio program (Web)

Norris, Michele, host. *All Things Considered*. Natl. Public Radio, 6 Apr. 2011.
 Web. 21 Apr. 2011.

The Web sites of television and radio networks and programs often include both content that was broadcast as part of a show and content that is unique to the site. Cite either kind of source by its title or by the name of the person whose work you are citing. Identify the role of anyone but an author (host in the example). Give the site title, the sponsor, the date, the medium (Web), and the date of your access. You may also cite other contributors (and their roles) after the title, as in model 52.

See also model 74 (p. 710) to cite a television or radio program that isn't on the Web.

MLA
46b

51. A video recording (Web)

CBS News, prod. "1968 King Assassination Report." *YouTube*. YouTube, 3 Apr.
 2008. Web. 22 Feb. 2011.

Cite a video on the Web either by its title or by the name of the person whose work you are citing—in this example, the organization that produced the video. Identify the role of anyone but an author (prod. in the example). Give the video title, the site title, the sponsor, the date, the medium (Web), and the date of your access. You may also cite other contributors (and their roles) after the title, as in model 52.

See also model 53 to cite a podcast of a video recording; model 59 (p. 702) to cite a video recording or film that appears both on the Web and in another medium (such as DVD); and model 77 (p. 711) to cite a film, DVD, or video recording that isn't on the Web.

52. A sound recording (Web)

Beglarian, Eve. *Five Things*. Perf. Beglarian et al. *Earbud Music: Eve Beglarian*.
 N.p., 23 Oct. 2001. Web. 8 Mar. 2011.

Cite a musical sound recording by its title or by the name of the person whose work you are citing—in this example, the composer. (If the composer's name comes after the title, precede it with By. See the next example.) The preceding example also gives the work title, the performers of the work, the site title, the sponsor (here unknown, so replaced with N.p.), the date, the medium (Web), and the date of access.

The same format may be used for a spoken-word recording that you find on the Web:

Wasserstein, Wendy, narr. "Afternoon of a Faun." By Wasserstein. *The Borzoi
 Reader Online*. Knopf, 2001. Web. 14 Feb. 2011.

See also the next model to cite a sound podcast; model 58 to cite a sound recording that appears both on the Web and in another medium (such as CD); and model 76 (p. 711) to cite a sound recording that isn't on the Web.

53. A podcast (Web)

Glass, Ira. "Very Tough Love." *This American Life.* Chicago Public Media, 25 Mar. 2011. Web. 14 Apr. 2011.

This podcast from a radio program lists the author of a story on the show, the title of the story (in quotation marks), and the program (italicized) as well as the site title, sponsor, date, medium (Web), and access date. If a podcast does not list an author or other creator, begin with the title.

MLA

46b

54. A blog entry (Web)

Marshall, Joshua Micah. "Explosion at Nuclear Plant." *Talking Points Memo.* TPM Media, 12 Mar. 2011. Web. 21 May 2011.

To cite an entry from a blog, give the author, the title of the entry, the title of the blog or site, the name of the sponsor (or N.p. if no sponsor is named), the publication date, the medium (Web), and the date of your access. See model 43 (p. 696) to cite a blog entry without a title.

55. A wiki (Web)

"Podcast." *Wikipedia.* Wikimedia, n.d. Web. 20 Nov. 2010.

To cite an entry from a wiki, follow the above example: entry title, site title, sponsor, publication date (here n.d. because the wiki entry is undated), medium (Web), and date of access. Begin with the site title if you are citing the entire wiki.

Nonperiodical Web sources also available in print

Some sources you find on the Web may be books, poems, short stories, and other works that have been scanned from print versions. To cite such a source, generally provide the information for original print publication as well as that for Web publication. Begin your entry as if you were citing the print work, consulting models 19–41 for an appropriate format. Then, instead of giving "Print" as the medium, provide the title of the Web site you used, any version or edition number, the medium you used (Web), and the date of your access.

56. A short work with print publication information (Web)

Wheatley, Phillis. "On Virtue." *Poems on Various Subjects, Religious and Moral.* London, 1773. N. pag. *American Verse Project.* Web. 21 July 2011.

The print information for this poem follows model 25 (p. 687) for a selection from an anthology, but it omits the publisher's name because the anthology was published before 1900. The print information ends with N. pag. because the original source has no page numbers.

57. A book with print publication information (Web)

James, Henry. *The Ambassadors*. 1903. New York: Scribner's, 1909. *Oxford Text Archive*. Web. 5 May 2011.

The print information for this novel follows model 32 (p. 691) for a republished book, so it includes both the original date of publication (1903) and the publication information for the scanned book.

Nonperiodical Web sources also available in other media

Some visuals, films, and sound recordings that you find on the Web may have been published before in other media and then scanned or digitized for the Web. To cite such a source, generally provide the information for original publication as well as that for Web publication. Begin your entry as if you were citing the original, consulting models 74–84 (pp. 710–13) for an appropriate format. Then, instead of giving the original medium of publication, provide the title of the Web site you used, the medium you used (Web), and your date of access.

58. A sound recording with other publication information (Web)

"Rioting in Pittsburgh." CBS Radio, 1968. *Vincent Voice Library*. Web. 7 Dec. 2011.

For Web sound recordings with original publication information, base citations on model 76 (p. 711), adding the information for Web publication.

59. A film or video recording with other publication information (Web)

Coca-Cola. Advertisement. Dir. Haskell Wexler. 1971. *American Memory*. Lib. of Cong. Web. 8 Apr. 2011.

For Web films or videos with original publication information, base citations on model 77 (p. 711), adding the information for Web publication.

60. A visual with other publication information (Web)

Pollock, Jackson. *Lavender Mist: Number 1*. 1950. Natl. Gallery of Art, Washington. *WebMuseum*. Web. 7 Apr. 2011.

Keefe, Mike. "World Education Rankings." Cartoon. *Denver Post* 5 Apr. 2011. *PoliticalCartoons.com*. Web. 9 May 2011.

For Web visuals with original publication information, base citations on models 78–82 (pp. 712–13), adding the information for Web publication.

Citation of a URL

61. A source requiring citation of the URL (Web)

Joss, Rich. "Dispatches from the Ice: The Second Season Begins." *Antarctic Expeditions*. Smithsonian Natl. Zoo and Friends of the Natl. Zoo, 26 Oct. 2007. Web. 26 Sept. 2011. <http://nationalzoo.si.edu/ ConservationAndScience/AquaticEcosystems/Antarctica/Expedition/ FieldNew/2-FieldNews.cfm>.

The MLA does not require URLs in works-cited entries. However, you should include URLs when your instructor requires them. You should also give a URL when readers may not be able to locate a source without one. For example, using a search engine to find "Dispatches from the Ice" (the title in the example) yields more than ten hits, one of which links to the correct site but the wrong document.

If you need to include a URL, ensure accuracy by using Copy and Paste to duplicate it in a file or an e-mail to yourself. In your list of works cited, give the URL after your date of access and a period. Put angle brackets on both ends of the URL, and end with a period. Break URLs *only* after slashes—do not hyphenate.

5 Listing journals on the Web and periodicals in online databases

This section covers two kinds of periodicals: scholarly journals that you reach directly on the Web (next page) and journals, newspapers, and magazines that you reach through online databases (p. 706). Newspapers and magazines that you reach directly on the Web are typically not periodicals (because their content changes often and unpredictably), so they are covered in models 45 and 46 (p. 698).

Citations for Web journals and for periodicals in online databases resemble those for print periodicals, with some changes for the different medium. The following list, adapted from the *MLA Handbook*, itemizes the possible elements in the online periodicals, in order of their appearance in a works-cited entry.

- **Author.** Give the author's last name, first name, and any middle name or initial. To cite more than one author, two articles by the same author, a corporate author, or an article with no named author, see models 1–6.
- **Title of the article,** in quotation marks. Give the title and any subtitle. End the title with a period inside the final quotation mark.

■ **Title of the periodical,** in italics. Omit any *A, An,* or *The* from the beginning of the title. Do not end with a period.

■ **Publication information.** The treatment of volume and issue numbers and publication dates varies depending on the kind of periodical you are citing, as shown in the following models and explained with the corresponding print models on pages 681–84. If you include the month of publication, abbreviate it unless it is May, June, or July. For the distinction between journals and magazines, see page 594.

■ **Page numbers of the article,** without "pp." If the article in unpaged, give n. pag. instead.

■ **Name of the database,** in italics, if you found the source through an online database.

■ **Medium of publication:** Web, followed by a period.

■ **Date of your access:** day, month, year. Abbreviate all months except May, June, and July.

MLA
46b

Web journals consulted directly

The journals you find directly on the Web may be published only online or may be published in print versions as well. The citation format is the same in either case: begin with an appropriate print model (pp. 681–83), but replace "Print" with Web and add your access date. Because many Web journals are unpaged, you may have to substitute n. pag. for page numbers, as in the entry illustrated opposite.

62. An article in a scholarly journal (Web)

Polletta, Francesca. "Just Talk: Public Deliberation after 9/11." *Journal of*
    Public Deliberation 4.1 (2008): n. pag. Web. 7 Apr. 2011.

See the facing page for an analysis of this entry and the location of the required information in the Web journal. Use the same format to adapt the models for print periodicals if you need to cite a Web journal review, editorial, letter to the editor, interview, article in a series, or special issue (models 14–18, pp. 685–86).

For a journal article reached in an online database, see model 64.

63. An abstract of a journal article (Web)

Polletta, Francesca. "Just Talk: Public Deliberation after 9/11." *Journal of*
    Public Deliberation 4.1 (2008): n. pag. Abstract. Web. 7 Apr. 2011.

Treat a Web abstract like a Web journal article, but add Abstract between the publication information and the medium. (You may omit this label if the journal title clearly indicates that the cited work is an abstract.) See model 65 to cite an abstract in an online database.

Format for a journal article on the Web

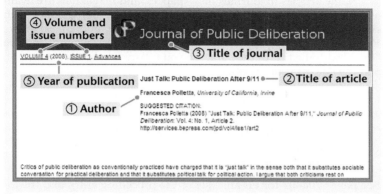

④ **Volume and issue numbers** | ③ **Title of journal** | Journal of Public Deliberation
VOLUME 4 (2008), ISSUE 1, Advances
⑤ **Year of publication** | Just Talk: Public Deliberation After 9/11 ●— ② **Title of article**
Francesca Polletta, *University of California, Irvine*
① **Author** | SUGGESTED CITATION:
Francesca Polletta (2008) "Just Talk: Public Deliberation After 9/11," *Journal of Public Deliberation:* Vol. 4: No. 1, Article 2.
http://services.bepress.com/jpd/vol4/iss1/art2

Critics of public deliberation as conventionally practiced have charged that it is "just talk" in the sense both that it substitutes sociable conversation for practical deliberation and that it substitutes political talk for political action. I argue that both criticisms rest on

　　　　① 　　　　　　　　　　　　②
Polletta, Francesca. "Just Talk: Public Deliberation after 9/11."
　　　　　　　　③ 　　　　　④ 　⑤ 　　⑥ 　　⑦
　　Journal of Public Deliberation 4.1 (2008): n. pag. Web.
　　　　⑧
　　7 Apr. 2011.

① **Author.** Give the full name—last name first, a comma, first name, and any middle name or initial. Omit *Dr., PhD,* or any other title. End the name with a period.

② **Title of article,** in quotation marks. Give the full title and any sub-title, separating them with a colon. End the title with a period inside the final quotation mark.

③ **Title of journal,** in italics. Omit any *A, An,* or *The* from the beginning of the title. Do not end with a period.

④ **Volume and issue numbers,** in Arabic numerals, separated by a period. Do not add a period after the issue number.

⑤ **Year of publication,** in parentheses and followed by a colon.

⑥ **Inclusive page numbers of the article**—or n. pag., as here, if the article is unpaged. With page numbers, do not use the abbreviation "pp.," and provide only as many digits in the last number as needed for clarity, usually two (for example, 626-42.)

⑦ **Medium.** Give the medium of the article, Web, followed by a period.

⑧ **Date of your access.** Give the day first, then month, then year. Abbreviate all months except May, June, and July. End the date with a period.

Web periodicals consulted in online databases

Many articles in journals, newspapers, and magazines are available in online databases that you reach through your library's Web site, such as *Academic Search Complete, ProQuest,* and *Project Muse.* Follow models 7–18 (pp. 681–86) for print periodicals, but replace "Print" with the title of the database you consulted, the medium (Web), and the date of your access.

64. An article in a scholarly journal (online database)

Penuel, Suzanne. "Missing Fathers: *Twelfth Night* and the Reformation of
   Mourning." *Studies in Philology* 107.1 (2010): 74-96. *Academic Search
   Complete.* Web. 10 Apr. 2011.

See pages 708–09 for an analysis of the preceding entry and the location of the required information in the database.

65. An abstract of a journal article (online database)

Penuel, Suzanne. "Missing Fathers: *Twelfth Night* and the Reformation of
   Mourning." *Studies in Philology* 107.1 (2010): 74-96. Abstract. *Academic
   Search Complete.* Web. 10 Apr. 2011.

Treat an abstract in an online database like a journal article in a database, but add Abstract between the publication information and the database title. (You may omit this label if the journal title clearly indicates that the cited work is an abstract.)

66. An article in a newspaper (online database)

Ball, Jeffrey. "Wind Power Hits a Trough." *Wall Street Journal* 5 Apr. 2011,
   eastern ed.: B1+. *LexisNexis Academic.* Web. 10 Sept. 2011.

Follow model 10 or 11 (p. 684) for citing author, title of article, title of newspaper, publication date, edition (if any), and page numbers. Add the title of the database, the medium (Web), and the date of your access.

67. An article in a magazine (online database)

Katz, Jamie. "The Painting in the Cellar." *Smithsonian* Apr. 2011: 60-65.
   Proquest Research Library. Web. 3 Aug. 2011.

Follow model 12 or 13 (p. 684) for citing author, title of article, title of magazine, publication date, and page numbers. Add the title of the database, the medium (Web), and the date of your access.

MLA
46b

6 Listing other electronic sources

Publications on CD-ROM or DVD-ROM

68. A nonperiodical CD-ROM or DVD-ROM

Nunberg, Geoffrey. "Usage in the Dictionary." *The American Heritage Dictionary of the English Language*. 4th ed. Boston: Houghton, 2000. CD-ROM.

Single-issue CD-ROMs may be encyclopedias, dictionaries, books, and other resources that are published just once, like print books. Follow models 19–37 for print books (pp. 686–93), but replace "Print" with CD-ROM or DVD-ROM. If the disc has a vendor that differs from the publisher of the work, add the vendor's place of publication, name, and publication date after the medium—for instance, Oklahoma City: Soquest, 2010.

See also models 28 (p. 690) and 48 (p. 699) to cite reference works in print and on the Web.

69. A periodical CD-ROM or DVD-ROM

Kolata, Gina. "Gauging Body Mass Index in a Changing Body." *New York Times* 28 June 2005, natl. ed.: D1+. CD-ROM. *New York Times Ondisc*. UMI-ProQuest. Sept. 2005.

Databases on CD-ROM or DVD-ROM are issued periodically—for instance, every six months or every year. The journals, newspapers, and other publications included in such a database are generally available in print as well, so your works-cited entry should give the information for both formats. Start with information for the print version, following models 7–18 (pp. 681–86). (The article here appeared in the *New York Times*.) Then replace "Print" with the medium (CD-ROM or DVD-ROM), the database title, the vendor's name (UMI-ProQuest in the example), and the database publication date.

E-mail and discussion-group postings

70. An e-mail message

Bailey, Natasha. "Re: Cairo." Message to the author. 27 Mar. 2011. E-mail.

For e-mail, give the writer's name; the title, if any, from the e-mail's subject heading, in quotation marks; Message to the author (or the name of a recipient besides you); the date of the message; and the medium, E-mail. You do not need to include the date of your access to the e-mail.

Format for a journal article in an online database

② **Title of article**

Missing Fathers: Twelfth Night and the Reformation of Mourning.

① **Author** ⑤ **Year of publication** ④ **Volume and issue numbers**

Authors: Penuel, Suzanne[1]

Source: Studies in Philology; Winter2010, Vol. 107 Issue 1, p74-96, 23p

Document Type: Literary Criticism ③ **Title of journal** ⑥ **Inclusive page numbers**

Subject Terms: *CRITICISM
*FATHERS & daughters
*INTERGENERATIONAL relations

Reviews & Products: TWELFTH Night (Theatrical production)

People: SHAKESPEARE, William, 1564-1616 — Criticism & interpretation

Abstract: A literary criticism is presented of the play "Twelfth Night," by William Shakespeare, in which the absence of fathers and what that may mean is discussed. It notes that no older generation exists in the play to hover over the young and tamp down their sexuality, yet this does not result in celebration. Instead, a feeling of loss prevails. Various passages in the verse are analyzed to shed light on mourning rituals, doubling and gender changes in some of the characters.

Author Affiliations: [1]University of South Carolina Lancaster

ISSN: 00393738

Accession Number: 46990801

Database: Academic Search Complete ⑦ **Name of database**

MLA 46b

71. A posting to a discussion group

Williams, Frederick. "Circles as Primitive." *The Math Forum @ Drexel.* Drexel U, 28 Feb. 2008. E-mail.

Cite a posting to a discussion group like a blog entry (model 54,

Penuel, Suzanne. "Missing Fathers: *Twelfth Night* and the

Reformation of Mourning." *Studies in Philology* 107.1

(2010): 74-96. *Academic Search Complete.* Web.

10 Apr. 2011.

① **Author.** Give the full name—last name first, a comma, first name, and any middle name or initial. Omit *Dr., PhD*, or any other title. End the name with a period.

② **Title of the article,** in quotation marks. End the title with a period inside the final quotation mark. (Note that the play title *Twelfth Night* is italicized within the quoted article title.)

③ **Title of journal,** in italics. Omit any *A, An,* or *The* from the beginning of the title. Do not end with a period.

④ **Volume and issue numbers,** in Arabic numerals, separated by a period. Do not add a period after the issue number.

⑤ **Year of publication,** in parentheses and followed by a colon.

⑥ **Inclusive page numbers** of article, without "pp." Provide only as many digits in the last number as needed for clarity, usually two. Use n. pag. if the article is unpaged.

⑦ **Name of the database,** in italics, ending with a period.

⑧ **Medium.** Give the medium of the article, Web, followed by a period.

⑨ **Date of your access.** Give the day first, then month, then year. Abbreviate all months except May, June, and July. End the date with a period.

p. 701). This example for a discussion-list posting includes the author's name, the title of the posting, the title of the discussion list, the name of the sponsor, the date of the posting, and the medium (E-mail). If the posting is untitled, give Online posting instead. You need not add the date of your access.

Digital files

You may want to cite a digital file that is not on the Web or on a disc, such as a PDF document, a JPEG image, or an MP3 sound recording that you downloaded onto your computer. Use the appropriate model for your kind of source (for instance, model 79 for a personal photograph), but replace the medium with the file format you're using. If you don't know the file format, use Digital file for the medium.

72. A text file (digital)

Berg, John K. "Estimates of Persons Driving While Intoxicated." *Law Enforce-ment Today* 22 Apr. 2011. PDF file.

Fernandez, Carlos. "Travels in Mexico." 2011. *Microsoft Word* file.

73. A media file (digital)

Springsteen, Bruce. "This Life." *Working on a Dream*. Columbia, 2009. MP3 file.

Girls playing basketball. Personal photograph by Granger Goetz. 2011. JPEG file.

7 Listing other print and nonprint sources

The source types covered in this section are not on a computer or, generally, in printed sources. Most of them have parallel citation formats elsewhere in this chapter when you reach them through electronic and print media. See model 16 (p. 685) to cite an interview in print. See models 49–52 (pp. 699–701) to cite visuals, television and radio programs, video recordings, and sound recordings that are available only on the Web. See models 58–60 (p. 702) to cite such sources when they are available on the Web and in other media. And see model 73 to cite such sources in digital files.

74. A television or radio program

"The Time Warp." By Zoanne Clark. Dir. Rob Corn. *Grey's Anatomy*. ABC. KGO, San Francisco, 18 Feb. 2010. Television.

Start with the title unless you are citing the work of a person or persons. The example here cites an episode title (in quotation marks) and the names of the episode's writer and director. By and Dir. identify their roles. Then the entry gives the program title (in italics), the name of the network, the call letters and city of the local station, the date, and the medium (Television). If you list individuals who worked on the entire program rather than an episode, put their names after the program title.

75. A personal or broadcast interview

Wang, Charlotte. Personal interview. 12 Mar. 2011.

Filkins, Dexter. Interview by Terry Gross. *Fresh Air*. Natl. Public Radio. WGBH,
Boston, 6 Apr. 2011. Radio.

Begin with the name of the person interviewed. For an interview you
conducted, specify Personal interview or the medium (such as Telephone
interview or E-mail interview), and then give the date. For an interview
you heard or saw, provide the title if any or Interview if there is no
title. Add the name of the interviewer if he or she is identified. Then
follow an appropriate model for the kind of source (here, a radio
program), and end with the medium (here, Radio).

76. A sound recording

MLA
46b

Rubenstein, Artur, perf. Piano Concerto no. 2 in B-flat. By Johannes Brahms.
Cond. Eugene Ormandy. Philadelphia Orch. RCA, 1972. LP.

Springsteen, Bruce. "This Life." *Working on a Dream*. Columbia, 2009. CD.

Begin with the name of the individual whose work you are citing.
Unless this person is the composer, identify his or her role, as with
perf. ("performer") in the first example. If you're citing a work identified by form, number, and key (first example), do not use quotation marks or italics for the title. If you're citing a song or song
lyrics (second example), give the title in quotation marks; then provide the title of the recording in italics. Following the title, identify
the composer or author if you haven't already, after By, and name
and identify other participants you want to mention. Then provide
the manufacturer of the recording, the date of release, and the
medium: LP in the first example, CD in the second.

77. A film, DVD, or video recording

The Joneses. Screenplay by Chris Tyrrell and Stacey Cruwys. Dir. Chris Tyrrell.
Bjort, 2010. Film.

Start with the title of the work unless you are citing the work of a person (see the next example). Generally, identify and name the director.
You may list other participants (writer, lead performers, and so on) as
you judge appropriate. For a film, end with the distributor, date, and
medium (Film).

For a DVD or videocassette, include the original release date (if
any), the distributor's name and release date, and the medium (DVD or
Videocassette).

Balanchine, George, chor. *Serenade*. Perf. San Francisco Ballet. Dir. Hilary
Bean. 1991. PBS Video, 2006. DVD.

78. A painting, photograph, or other work of visual art

Arnold, Leslie. *Seated Woman*. N.d. Oil on canvas. DeYoung Museum, San Francisco.

Sugimoto, Hiroshi. *Pacific Ocean, Mount Tamalpais*. 1994. Photograph.
Private collection.

To cite an actual work of art, name the artist and give the title (in italics) and the date of creation (or N.d. if the date is unknown). Then provide the medium of the work (such as Oil on canvas or Photograph) and the name and location of the owner, if known. (Use Private collection if not.)

For a work you see only in a reproduction, provide the complete publication information for the source you used. Omit the medium of the work itself, and replace it with the medium of the reproduction (Print in the following example). Omit such information only if you examined the actual work.

Hockney, David. *Place Furstenberg, Paris*. 1985. Coll. Art Gallery, New Paltz.
David Hockney: A Retrospective. Ed. Maurice Tuchman and Stephanie
Barron. Los Angeles: Los Angeles County Museum of Art, 1988. 247. Print.

79. A personal photograph

American white pelicans on Lake Winnebago. Personal photograph by the
author. 3 Apr. 2011.

For a personal photograph by you or by someone else, give the subject (without quotation marks or italics), the photographer, and the date. (The current edition of the *MLA Handbook* does not cover personal photographs, so this format comes from the previous edition.)

80. A map, chart, graph, or diagram

"The Sonoran Desert." Map. *Sonoran Desert: An American Deserts Handbook*. By
Rose Houk. Tucson: Western Natl. Parks Assn., 2000. 12. Print.

Unless the creator of an illustration is given on the source, list the illustration by its title. Put the title in quotation marks if it comes from another publication or in italics if it is published independently. Then add a description (Map, Chart, and so on), the publication information, and the medium (here, Print).

81. A cartoon or comic strip

Trudeau, Garry. "Doonesbury." Comic strip. *San Francisco Chronicle* 1 Sept.
2011: E6. Print.

Cite a cartoon or comic strip with the artist's name, the title (in quotation marks), the description Cartoon or Comic strip, the publication information, and the medium (here, Print).

82. An advertisement

Fusion Hybrid by Ford. Advertisement. *New Yorker* 11 Apr. 2011: 91. Print.

Cite an advertisement with the name of the product or company advertised, the description Advertisement, the publication information, and the medium (Print, Television, Radio, and so on).

83. A performance

Levine, James, cond. Boston Symphony Orch. Symphony Hall, Boston. 2 May

2010. Performance.

The New Century. By Paul Rudnick. Dir. Nicholas Martin. Mitzi E. Newhouse

Theater, New York. 6 May 2009. Performance.

For a live performance, generally base your citation on film citations (model 77). Place the title first (second example) unless you are citing the work of an individual (first example). After the title, provide relevant information about participants as well as the theater, city, and performance date. Conclude with the medium (Performance).

84. A lecture, speech, address, or reading

Fontaine, Claire. "Economics." Museum of Contemporary Art. North Miami.

5 June 2010. Address.

Give the speaker's name, the title if any (in quotation marks), the title of the meeting if any, the name of the sponsoring organization, the location of the presentation, and the date. End with a description of the type of presentation (Lecture, Speech, Address, Reading).

Although the MLA does not provide a specific style for citing classroom lectures in your courses, you can adapt the preceding format for this purpose.

Cavanaugh, Carol. Class lecture on teaching mentors. Lesley U. 4 Apr. 2011.

Lecture.

Exercise 46.1 Writing works-cited entries

Prepare works-cited entries from the following information. Follow the MLA models given in this chapter unless your instructor specifies a different style. Arrange the finished entries in alphabetical order, not numbered.

Exercise

1. An article titled "Who's Responsible for the Digital Divide?" in the March 2011 issue of the journal *Information Society,* volume 27, issue 2. The article appeared on pages 92–104. The authors are Dmitry Epstein, Erik C. Nisbet, and Tarleton Gillespie. You found the article on April 19, 2011, using the online database *Academic Search Complete.*
2. A Web article with no listed author on the Web site *Digital Divide Institute.* The sponsor of the site is DigitalDivide.org. The title of the

article is "Banking the Unbanked" and the site is dated 2010. You consulted the site on April 20, 2011.

3. A print book titled *Technology and Social Inclusion: Rethinking the Digital Divide* by Mark Warschauer. The book was published in 2003 by MIT Press in Cambridge, Massachusetts.

4. An article in the newspaper the *New York Times*, published in the national edition on December 13, 2010, on page B3. The author is Teddy Wayne. The title is "Digital Divide Is a Matter of Income." You accessed the source through the database *LexisNexis Academic* on April 19, 2011.

5. A government report you consulted online on April 20, 2011. The author is the National Telecommunications and Information Administration, an agency within the United States Department of Commerce. The title of the report is "A Nation Online: Entering the Broadband Age." It was published on the NTIA Web site in September 2004.

6. An e-mail interview you conducted with Naomi Lee on April 23, 2011.

7. A blog posting to the Web site *Code for America* by Lauren Dyson. The title is "How Will Gov 2.0 Address the Digital Divide?" The posting is dated February 15, 2011. The sponsor of the site is Code for America. You consulted the source on April 21, 2011.

46c Using MLA document format

Video
tutorial

The *MLA Handbook* provides guidelines for a fairly simple document format, with just a few elements. For guidelines on type fonts, headings, lists, illustrations, and other features that MLA style does not specify, see pages 120–30.

The samples below show the formats for the first page and a later page of a paper. For the format of the list of works cited, see pages 676–77.

Margins Use one-inch margins on all sides of every page.

Spacing and indentions Double-space throughout. Indent the first lines of paragraphs one-half inch. (See opposite for treatment of poetry and long prose quotations.)

Paging Begin numbering on the first page, and number consecutively through the end (including the list of works cited). Use Arabic numerals (1, 2, 3) positioned in the upper right, about one-half inch from the top. Place your last name before the page number in case the pages later become separated.

Identification and title MLA style does not require a title page for a paper. If your instructor asks you to supply a title page, see pages 718–19. Otherwise, follow the sample on the facing page, providing your name, the date, and other information requested by

First page of MLA paper

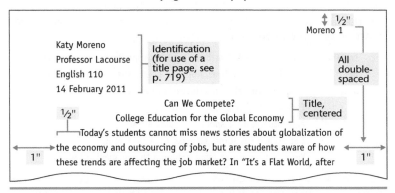

‡ ½"
Moreno 1

Katy Moreno
Professor Lacourse
English 110
14 February 2011

Identification
(for use of a
title page, see
p. 719)

All
double-
spaced

½"

Can We Compete?
College Education for the Global Economy

Title,
centered

Today's students cannot miss news stories about globalization of
the economy and outsourcing of jobs, but are students aware of how
these trends are affecting the job market? In "It's a Flat World, after

1"

1"

Later page of MLA paper

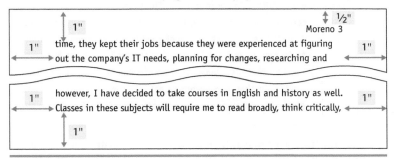

1"

‡ ½"
Moreno 3

1"

time, they kept their jobs because they were experienced at figuring
out the company's IT needs, planning for changes, researching and

1"

1"

however, I have decided to take courses in English and history as well.
Classes in these subjects will require me to read broadly, think critically,

1"

1"

your instructor. Place this identification an inch from the top of the
page, aligned with the left margin and double-spaced.

Double-space again, and center the title. Do not highlight the
title with italics, underlining, boldface, larger type, or quotation
marks. Capitalize the words in the title according to the guidelines
on page 505. Double-space the lines of the title and between the title and the text.

Poetry and long prose quotations Treat a single line of poetry
like any other quotation, running it into your text and enclosing it
in quotation marks. You may run in two or three lines of poetry as
well, separating the lines with a slash surrounded by space.

An example of Robert Frost's incisiveness is in two lines from "Death of the
Hired Man": **"**Home is the place where, when you have to go there **/** They
have to take you in**"** (119-20).

Always set off from your text a poetry quotation of more than three lines. Use double spacing above and below the quotation and for the quotation itself. Indent the quotation one inch from the left margin. *Do not add quotation marks.*

> In "The Author to Her Book," written in 1678, Anne Bradstreet characterizes her book as a child. In these lines from the poem, she captures a parent's and a writer's frustration with the imperfections of her offspring:
>
> > I washed thy face, but more defects I saw,
> > and rubbing off a spot, still made a flaw.
> > I stretched thy joints to make thee even feet,
> > Yet still thou run'st more hobbling that is meet. (13-16)

MLA
46c

Also set off a prose quotation of more than four typed lines. (See p. 637 on when to use such long quotations.) Double-space and indent as with the preceding poetry example. *Do not add quotation marks.*

> In the influential *Talley's Corner* from 1967, Elliot Liebow observes that "unskilled" construction work requires more skill than is generally assumed:
>
> > A healthy, sturdy, active man of good intelligence requires from two to four weeks to break in on a construction job. . . . It frequently happens that his foreman or the craftsman he services is not willing to wait that long for him to get into condition or to learn at a glance the difference in size between a rough 2 x 8 and a finished 2 x 10. (62)

Do not use a paragraph indention for a quotation of a single complete paragraph or a part of a paragraph. Use paragraph indentions of one-quarter inch only for a quotation of two or more complete paragraphs.

47

Two Research Papers in MLA Style

The following pages show the research papers of Justin Malik and Vanessa Haley, whose work we followed in Chapters 41–45. (Malik's paper begins on the next page, Haley's on p. 746.) Both students followed the style of the *MLA Handbook* for documenting sources and formatting their papers. Accompanying both students' papers are comments on format, source citations, and other matters.

Student paper

Exercise

mycomplab

Visit *mycomplab.com* for the eText and for resources and exercises on MLA documentation and format.

717

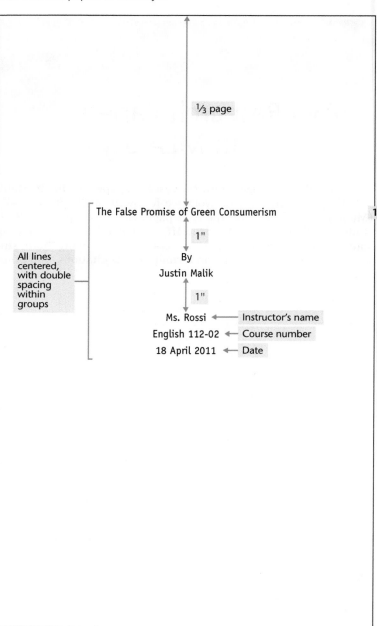

⅓ page

The False Promise of Green Consumerism

1"

By
Justin Malik

1"

Ms. Rossi ◄——— Instructor's name
English 112-02 ◄— Course number
18 April 2011 ◄— Date

All lines
centered,
with double
spacing
within
groups

1

1 **Title page format.** A title page is not required by MLA style but may be required by your instructor. If so, or if you are required to submit an outline with your paper, prepare a title page as shown opposite.

    If your instructor does not require a title page for your paper, follow MLA style: place your name, the identifying information, and the date on the first page of the paper. See Vanessa Haley's paper, page 746, for this format.

Next two pages

2 **Outline format.** If your instructor asks you to include your final outline, place it between the title page and the text and number the pages with small Roman numerals (i, ii). Follow the formatting annotations on the next two pages.

3 **Outline content.** Malik includes his final thesis statement as part of his outline so that his instructor can see how the parts relate to the whole. Notice that each main division (numbered with Roman numerals) relates to the thesis statement and that all the subdivisions relate to their main division.

    Malik casts his final outline in full sentences. Some instructors request topic outlines, in which ideas appear in phrases instead of in sentences and do not end with periods. (See p. 45 for this format.)

MLA
47

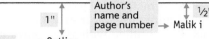

Author's name and page number → Malik i

1"   ½"

Center ⟶ Outline

2 3

Thesis statement: Although green consumerism can help the environment, consumerism itself is the root of some of the most pressing ecological problems we face. To make a real difference, we must consume less.

Double-space

I. Green products claiming to help the environment both appeal to and confuse consumers.

   A. The market for ecologically sound products is enormous.

   B. Determining whether or not a product is as green as advertised can be a challenge.

II. Green products don't solve the high rate of consumption that truly threatens the environment.

   A. Overconsumption is a significant cause of three of the most serious environmental problems.

      1. It depletes natural resources.

      2. It contributes to pollution, particularly from the greenhouse gases responsible for global warming.

      3. It produces a huge amount of solid waste.

   B. The availability of greener products has not reduced the environmental effects of consumption.

III. Since buying green products does not reduce consumption, other solutions must be found for environmental problems.

   A. Experts have proposed many far-reaching solutions, but they require concerted government action and could take decades to implement.

   B. For shorter-term solutions, individuals can change their own behavior as consumers.

      1. Precycling may be the greenest behavior that individuals can adopt.

MLA
47

Malik ii

    a. Precycling means avoiding purchase of products that use raw materials and excessive packaging.

    b. More important, precycling means avoiding purchases of new products whenever possible.

2. For unavoidable purchases, individuals can buy green products and influence businesses to embrace ecological goals.

Author's name and page number → Malik 1   ↕ ½"

1"

Title, centered → The False Promise of Green Consumerism   4‑5

They line the aisles of just about any store. They seem to dominate television and print advertising. From organic jeans to household cleaners to hybrid cars, products advertised as environmentally friendly are readily available and are so popular they're trendy. It's easy to see why Americans are buying these things in record numbers. The new wave of "green" consumer goods makes an almost irresistible promise: we can save the planet by shopping.

Double-space

Saving the planet does seem to be urgent. Thanks partly to former vice president Al Gore, who sounded the alarm in 2006 with *An Inconvenient Truth* and again in 2009 with *Our Choice,* the threat of global warming has become a regular feature in the news media and a recurring theme in popular culture.[1] Unfortunately, as Gore himself points out, climate change is just one of many environmental problems competing for our attention: the rainforests are vanishing, our air and our water are dangerously polluted, alarming numbers of species are facing extinction, and landfills are overflowing (*Our Choice* 32). All the bad news can be overwhelming, and most people feel powerless to halt the damage. Thus it is reassuring that we may be able to help by making small changes in what we buy—but that is not entirely true. Although green consumerism can help the environment, consumerism itself is the root of some of the most pressing ecological problems we face. To make a real difference, we must consume less.

1"

The market for items perceived as ecologically sound is enormous. Experts estimate that spending on green products already approaches $500 billion a year in the United States (Bhanoo). Shoppers respond well to new options, whether the purchase is as minor as a bottle of chemical-free dish soap or as major as a front-loading washing machine. Not surprisingly,

6

7

8

9‑10

11

1"

4 a Title. Malik's title clearly indicates the topic of his paper and previews his main idea. **b Paper format.** Because he provides a title page as requested by his instructor, Malik does not repeat his full name on the first page of the text. For MLA style, which omits a title page, the following would appear in the upper left of this first page:

Justin Malik

Ms. Rossi

English 112-02

18 April 2011

(See Vanessa Haley's paper, p. 746, for an example of a research paper without a title page.) Follow the formatting annotations on the facing page for margins and spacing.

MLA

47

5 Introduction. Malik offers examples of the subject of his paper—green consumer products—and suggests a reason for their popularity. He delays presenting his thesis in order to establish some background about the severity of the environmental problems that the products address. In the last sentence of this paragraph and throughout the paper, Malik builds common ground with readers by using *we* to include himself with them as sources of the problems and the solutions.

6 a Omission of a parenthetical citation. Malik does not provide a parenthetical citation for Gore's books because he names the author and titles in the text and refers to the complete works.
   b Using an endnote for supplementary information. Here Malik inserts a reference to a note at the end of the paper that gives examples of global warming as a recurring theme in popular culture. Malik signals the note with the raised numeral 1.

7 Citation of a work by an author of two or more works. To clarify which of Gore's two books he is citing, Malik gives the title in the parenthetical citation.

8 Thesis statement. Malik's introduction has led up to this statement, which asserts the claim that he will support in the paper. See page 659 for a note on thesis statements like Malik's that are expressed in two (or more) sentences.

9 Relation to outline. This paragraph begins part I of Malik's outline (see p. 720).

10 Selecting supporting evidence. Malik paraphrases and quotes two sources in this paragraph to support his point about the size of the market for green consumer products. The use of signal phrases and the placement of parenthetical citations clarify the sources of the information.

11 Citation of an article without page numbers. The Bhanoo article, which Malik found online, gave no page or other reference numbers, so the citation includes only the author's name.

businesses are responding by offering as many new eco-products as they can. Jack Neff reports in *Advertising Age* that the recent growth of green products is a "revolution" in marketing. He cites a market research report by Datamonitor: between 2007 and 2009, the number of new packaged goods labeled as green increased by 600%, and sales of organic food and beverages outpaced other options despite the higher costs (1). These new products are offered for sale at supermarkets and at stores like Walmart, Target, Home Depot, Starbucks, and Pottery Barn. It seems clear that green consumerism has grown into a mainstream interest.

    Determining whether or not a product is as green as advertised can be a challenge. Claims vary: a product might be labeled as organic, biodegradable, energy efficient, recycled, carbon neutral, renewable, or just about anything that sounds environmentally positive. However, none of these terms carries a universally accepted meaning, and no enforceable labeling regulations exist (Dahl A248). Some of the new product options offer clear environmental benefits: for instance, LED lightbulbs last fifty times longer than regular bulbs and draw about 15% of the electricity ("Lightbulbs" 26, 27), and paper made from recycled fibers saves many trees. But other "green" products just as clearly do little or nothing to help the environment: a disposable razor made with less plastic is still a disposable razor, destined for a landfill after only a few uses.

    Distinguishing truly green products from those that are not so green merely scratches the surface of a much larger issue. The products aren't the problem; it's our high rate of consumption that poses the real threat to the environment. We seek what's newer and better—whether cars, clothes, phones, computers, televisions, shoes, or gadgets—and they all require resources to

12 a Mixing quotation and paraphrase. In addition to quoting Neff, Malik paraphrases statistical information from the article that he had quoted in his original note. **b Use of an indirect source.** Neff cited Datamonitor, and Malik uses the same information. Datamonitor is thus an indirect source. Such sources are appropriate only when the cited material is not available to consult. In this case, Malik could not find a copy of the original Datamonitor report, so the indirect source is appropriate.

13 Common knowledge. Malik already knew that major stores stock green products; in fact, he had purchased many of the products he names as examples throughout the paper. Thus he treats the information as common knowledge and does not cite a source. (See p. 651 for more on common knowledge.)

14 a Anonymous source. Malik cites a magazine article for which no author is named, so he uses the title for the citation. **b Citation of a paraphrase.** Because he does give the article title in his text, Malik correctly gives the title in the citation. **c Placement of a parenthetical citation.** Malik used "Lightbulbs" only for the information on lightbulbs, so he places the parenthetical citation directly after the borrowed example.

15 Common knowledge and personal experience. Many sources mentioned the trees saved by recycled paper, so Malik treats the example as common knowledge and omits a source citation. Malik also omits a citation for the razor example, which came from his personal experience.

16 a Relation to outline. This paragraph begins part II of Malik's outline. See page 720. **b Transitional sentences.** The first two sentences of the paragraph shift the emphasis from green products (the previous section of the paper) to the environmental effects of consumption. **c Drawing conclusions.** Malik begins his discussion of the problem of consumption with his own conclusions about what he learned.

MLA

47

Malik 3

make, ship, and use them. Political scientists Thomas Princen, Michael Maniates, and Ken Conca maintain that overconsumption is a leading force behind several ecological crises, warning that

> ever-increasing pressures on ecosystems, life-supporting environmental services, and critical natural cycles are driven not only by the sheer number of resource users . . . but also by the patterns of resource use themselves. (4)

Those patterns of resource use are disturbing. In just the last half century, gross world product (the global output of consumer goods) grew at five times the rate of population growth—a difference explained by a huge rise in consumption per person. (See fig. 1.) Such growth might be good for the economy, but it is

Fig. 1. Global population, consumption, and environmental impacts, 1960-2010. Data from United Nations Development Programme; *Human Development Report: Changing Today's Consumption Patterns—For Tomorrow's Human Development* (New York: Oxford UP, 1998; print; 4); and from Earth Policy Inst.; "Data Center"; *Earth Policy Institute*; EPI, 12 Jan. 2011; Web; 16 Mar. 2011.

17 a Format of a long quotation. This quotation exceeds four typed lines, so Malik sets it off from his text without quotation marks, with double spacing throughout, and with an extra indention of ten spaces or one inch. **b Omission of an ellipsis mark.** Malik omits the first part of the quoted sentence, but he doesn't use an ellipsis mark because the small *e* in "ever" makes the omission clear. **c Use of an ellipsis mark.** Malik uses an ellipsis mark (three spaced periods) to show that he has omitted words from the quotation. **d Citation with a displayed quotation.** The parenthetical citation after the quotation falls *outside* the sentence period.

18 Synthesis of sources. Here and in the next several paragraphs, Malik integrates information from sources with his own conclusions about the significance of the data and ideas. Signal phrases and source citations clearly distinguish Malik's ideas from sources' information.

19 Use of a figure. Malik created a bar chart to show the relative increases in consumption and population and to illustrate the effects of both on the environment. He refers to the figure and elaborates on its meaning in the text.

20 a Figure caption. Malik captions the figure so that readers know how to interpret it. **b Citation of sources for data.** Following MLA style, the caption includes complete information on the two sources for the data. If this were the only use of the sources, Malik would not have to repeat the information in his list of works cited. However, he cites both sources in his text as well, so his works-cited list includes entries for them.

MLA

47

bad for the environment. As fig. 1 shows, it is accompanied by the depletion of natural resources, increases in the carbon emissions that cause global warming, and increases in the amount of solid waste disposal.

The first negative effect of overconsumption, the depletion of resources, occurs because the manufacture and distribution of any consumer product depends on the use of water, land, and raw materials such as wood, metal, and oil. Paul Hawken, a respected environmentalist, explains that just in the United States "[i]ndustry moves, mines, extracts, shovels, burns, wastes, pumps, and disposes of *4 million pounds of material* in order to provide one average . . . family's needs for a year" (qtd. in DeGraaf, Wann, and Naylor 85; emphasis added). The United Nations Development Programme's 1998 *Human Development Report* (still the most comprehensive study of the environmental impacts of consumerism) warns that many regions in the world don't have enough water, productive soil, or forests to meet the basic needs of their populations (4). More recent data from the Earth Policy Institute show that as manufacturing and per-person consumption continue to rise, the resources needed for survival continue to decline. Thus heavy consumption poses a threat not only to the environment but also to the well-being of the human race.

In addition to using up scarce natural resources, manufacturing and distributing products harms the earth by spewing pollution into the water, soil, and air. The most worrisome aspect of that pollution may be its link to global warming. As Al Gore explains, the energy needed to power manufacturing and distribution comes primarily from burning fossil fuels, a process that releases carbon dioxide and other greenhouse gases into the air. Those gases build up and trap heat in the earth's atmosphere. The result, most scientists now believe, is increasing global

21 a Integrating source material. Here and elsewhere, Malik establishes his source's credentials in a signal phrase and effectively integrates paraphrases and quotations into his own sentences. **b Editing a quotation with brackets.** By using brackets around the small *i*, Malik indicates that he changed the capitalization of the original source so that it would fit into his own sentence.

22 a Citation of an indirect source. With the use of qtd. in, Malik indicates correctly that he found the quotation by Hawken (an indirect source) in the book by DeGraaf, Wann, and Naylor (a direct source). **b Indirect sources.** Indirect sources are appropriate only when the quoted material is not available to consult. Malik's source, DeGraaf, Wann, and Naylor, gave full bibliographic information for Hawken's book, and Malik should have gone directly to it. **c Adding emphasis to a quotation.** Malik italicizes important words in the quotation. He acknowledges this change in the parenthetical citation with emphasis added, separated from the page number by a semicolon. **d Punctuation with a parenthetical citation.** The period that ends a sentence containing a quotation comes after the citation.

23 a Citation of a work with a corporate author. The source Malik cites here does not name individual authors, so he lists the sponsoring organization as author. Naming the organization in the text avoids an awkwardly long parenthetical citation. **b Citation when the author is named in your text.** Because Malik names the United Nations Development Programme in his text, he does not repeat the name in the parenthetical citation that follows his paraphrase.

24 Omission of a parenthetical citation. The Earth Policy Institute data come from an Internet source that lacks page or other identifying numbers. Since Malik names the author in his text, he doesn't include a parenthetical citation.

25 a Clarifying the boundaries of source material. The bulk of this paragraph summarizes information from Al Gore's book *An Inconvenient Truth,* surrounded by Malik's interpretation of its implications for his thesis. Malik makes the extent of the summary clear by giving Gore's name at the beginning and a parenthetical citation at the end. **b Citing a summary.** Malik condenses information from several sections of Gore's book into one brief sentence. He uses a series of page numbers (next page) to indicate the exact locations of the information in his source.

Malik 5

temperatures that will raise sea levels, expand deserts, and
cause more frequent floods and hurricanes (*Inconvenient* 26-27,
81, 118-19, 184). As the preceding bar chart shows, carbon
emissions, like production of consumer goods in general, are rising at rates out of proportion with population growth. The more
we consume, the more we contribute to global warming.

As harmful as they are, gradual global warming and the
depletion of resources half a world away can be difficult to comprehend or appreciate. A more immediate environmental effect
of our buying habits can be seen in the volumes of trash those
habits create. The US Environmental Protection Agency found
that in a single year (2009), US residents, corporations, and institutions produced 243 million tons of municipal solid waste,
amounting to "4.34 pounds per person per day" (1). Nearly a
third of that trash came just from the wrappers, cans, bottles,
and boxes used for shipping consumer goods. (See fig. 2.) Yet

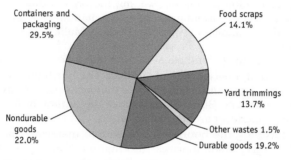

Fig. 2. Sources of municipal solid waste in the United States,
2009. Chart from United States, Environmental Protection
Agency, Solid Waste and Emergency Response; *Municipal Solid
Waste Generation, Recycling, and Disposal in the United States:
Facts and Figures for 2009*; US Environmental Protection
Agency, Dec. 2010; Web; 4 Apr. 2011.

26

27

28

29

26 **Synthesis of sources.** Rather than leave it to his readers to interpret the information provided in his chart and the paragraphs surrounding it, Malik offers his own interpretation of what the information means in the context of his thesis.

27 **Revision of a draft.** In his first draft Malik sometimes strung his source information together without interpreting it. In revising he added comments of his own (in blue) to introduce the information in the context of his ideas:

As harmful as they are, gradual global warming and the depletion of resources half a world away can be difficult to comprehend or appreciate. A more immediate environmental effect of our buying habits can be seen in the volumes of trash those habits create. The US Environmental Protection Agency found that in a single year (2009), US residents, corporations, and institutions produced 243 million tons of municipal solid waste, amounting to "4.34 pounds per person per day" (1). Nearly a third of that trash came just from the wrappers, cans, bottles, and boxes used for shipping consumer goods. (See fig. 2.) Yet the mountains of trash left over from consumption are only a part of the problem. In industrial countries overall, 90 percent of waste comes not from what gets thrown out, but from the manufacturing processes of converting natural resources into consumer products (DeGraaf, Wann, and Naylor 198). Nearly everything we buy creates waste in production, comes in packaging that gets discarded immediately, and ultimately ends up in landfills that are already overflowing.

28 **Use of a figure.** Malik uses a pie chart to show that containers and packaging account for the largest portion of solid waste produced in the United States. He refers to the figure in the preceding text.

29 **a** **Figure caption.** Malik captions the figure so that readers know how to interpret it. **b** **Citation of a source for a figure.** Following MLA style, Malik provides a source note indicating where he obtained the figure. The note includes complete information for the source. If this were the only use of the source, Malik would not have to repeat the information in his list of works cited. However, he cites the source in his text as well, so his works-cited list includes an entry for it.

the mountains of trash left over from consumption are only a part of the problem. In industrial countries overall, 90 percent of waste comes not from what gets thrown out, but from the manufacturing processes of converting natural resources into consumer products (DeGraaf, Wann, and Naylor 198). Nearly everything we buy creates waste in production, comes in packaging that gets discarded immediately, and ultimately ends up in landfills that are already overflowing.

Unfortunately, the growing popularity of green products has not reduced the environmental effects of consumption. A study conducted by economists Jeff Rubin and Benjamin Tal found that while eco-friendly and energy-efficient products have become more available, "consumption is growing by ever-increasing amounts." The authors give the example of automobiles: in the last generation, cars have become much more energy efficient, but the average American now drives 2500 more miles a year, for a net gain in energy use (4-5). At the same time, per-person waste production in the United States has risen by nearly 20% (United States 2). Greener products may reduce our cost of consumption and even reduce our guilt about consumption, but they do not reduce consumption and its effects.

If buying green won't solve the problems caused by overconsumption, what will? Politicians, environmentalists, and economists have proposed an array of far-reaching ideas, including creating a financial market for carbon credits and offsets, aggressively taxing consumption and pollution, offering financial incentives for environmentally positive behaviors, and even abandoning market capitalism altogether (de Blas).[2] However, all of these are "top-down" solutions that require concerted government action. Gaining support for any one of them, putting it into practice, and getting

30 **a** **Citation when the author is not named in your text.** Because Malik does not give the three authors' names in his text, he provides the names in the parenthetical citation along with a page number. **b** **Citation of a work with three authors.** Malik gives all three authors' last names, separating them with commas and with and before the final name.

31 **a** **Mixing quotation and paraphrase.** Malik quotes and paraphrases from Rubin and Tal's article to give readers a good sense of the issue they raise. **b** **Editing a quotation.** Malik had a long quotation by Rubin and Tal, but he selected from it only the words that supported the point he was making. The entire quotation appears in this note:

Consumer behavior

Rubin and Tal 4

"The problem is that energy efficiency is not the final objective—reducing total energy consumption must be the final objective both to the challenges of conventional oil depletion and to greenhouse gas emissions. Despite the huge gains in energy efficiency, that is simply not happening. Instead, energy consumption is growing by ever-increasing amounts. While energy use per unit of US GDP has fallen by almost 50% since 1975, total energy usage in the US economy has risen by more than 40%."

c **Punctuation with a quotation.** The period falls inside the closing quotation mark because the quotation is not immediately followed by a parenthetical citation.

32 **Drawing conclusions.** Malik ends his discussion of the environmental effects of consumption with his own conclusion about green products as a solution.

33 **a** **Relation to outline.** With this paragraph, Malik begins part III of his outline (see p. 720). **b** **Transitional question.** Malik begins the new section with a question that bridges the previous discussion and the next one.

34 **a** **Summary of sources.** Malik opted to summarize the more far-reaching solutions to overconsumption because he wanted to focus on individuals' actions. **b** **Using an endnote for citation of several sources.** Malik avoids a lengthy and obtrusive parenthetical citation by referring readers to endnote 2, which lists several sources that reinforce de Blas (see p. 740).

35 **Citation of an article without page numbers.** The de Blas article, which Malik found on the Web, has no page or other reference numbers, so the citation includes only the author's name.

MLA
47

results could take decades. In the meantime, the environment would continue to deteriorate. Clearly, short-term solutions are also essential.

The most promising short-term solution is for individuals to change their own behavior as consumers. The greenest behavior that individuals can adopt may be precycling, the term widely used for avoiding purchases of products that involve the use of raw materials. Precycling includes choosing eco-friendly products made of recycled or nontoxic materials (such as aluminum-free deodorants and fleece made from soda bottles) and avoiding items wrapped in excessive packaging (such as kitchen tools strapped to cardboard and printer cartridges sealed in plastic clamshells). More important, though, precycling means not buying new things in the first place. Renting and borrowing, when possible, saves money and resources; so does keeping possessions in good repair and not replacing them until absolutely necessary. Good-quality used items, from clothing to furniture to electronics, can be obtained for free, or very cheaply, through online communities like *Craigslist* and *Freecycle*, from thrift stores and yard sales, or by trading with friends and relatives. When consumers choose used goods over new, they can help to reduce demand for manufactured products that waste energy and resources, and they can help to keep unwanted items out of the waste stream.

Avoiding unnecessary purchases brings personal benefits as well. Brenda Lin explained in an e-mail interview that frugal living not only saves money but also provides pleasure:

> You'd be amazed at what people throw out or give away: perfectly good computers, oriental rugs, barely used sports equipment, designer clothes, you name it. . . . It's a game for me to find what

36

37

36 **a** **Common knowledge.** In his reading Malik saw many references to the concept of precycling, so he treats the information in this paragraph as common knowledge and does not cite a source for it. (See p. 651 for more on common knowledge.) **b** **Defining terms.** Because readers might not be familiar with precycling, Malik defines the concept and expands on the definition with four examples. **c** **Omission of parenthetical citations.** The precycling examples and suggestions in this paragraph are Malik's own and so do not require source citations.

37 **a** **Primary source: personal interview.** Malik tested his ideas by conducting an e-mail interview with the producer of a public-access television program about voluntary simplicity. He uses both a paraphrase and a quotation from the interview, with the subject's permission. **b** **Introducing borrowed material.** Malik paraphrases and quotes Lin as an expert, so he should have established her credentials. **c** **Editing a quotation with an ellipsis mark.** Malik uses an ellipsis mark (three spaced periods) and a period to show that he has omitted a full sentence from the quotation. **d** **Omission of a parenthetical citation.** Malik does not provide a parenthetical citation at the end of the quotation on the next page because the source (an interview) has no page or other reference numbers and the necessary information (Lin's name) appears in the text before the quotation. See page 726 for a long quotation with a parenthetical citation.

MLA

47

Malik 8

I need in other people's trash or at Goodwill.
You should see the shock on people's faces when
I tell them where I got my stuff. I get almost as
much enjoyment from that as from saving
money and helping the environment at the same
time.

Lin's experience relates to a study of the personal and social
consequences of consumerism by the sociologist Juliet B.
Schor. Schor found that the more people buy, the less happy
they tend to feel because of the stress of working longer hours
to afford their purchases (11-12). Researching the opposite effect, Schor conducted interviews with hundreds of Americans
who had drastically reduced their spending so that they would
be less dependent on paid work. For these people, she discovered, a deliberately lower standard of living improved quality
of life by leaving more time to spend with family and pursue
personal interests (136-42). Reducing consumption, it turns
out, does not have to translate into sacrifice.

For unavoidable purchases like food and light bulbs,
buying green can make a difference by influencing corporate
decisions. Some ecologists and economists believe that as
more shoppers choose earth-friendly products over their traditional counterparts—or boycott products that are clearly
harmful to the environment—more manufacturers and retailers
will look for ways to limit the environmental effects of their
industrial practices and the goods they sell (de Blas; Gore,
Inconvenient 314). Indeed, as environmental business consultant Joel Makower and his coauthors point out, Walmart,
Coca-Cola, Proctor and Gamble, Dell, and other major companies have already taken up sustainability initiatives in response to market pressure. In the process, the companies have
discovered that environmentally minded practices tend to

38

39

40

38 **Clarifying the boundaries of source material.** By mentioning Schor's name before he summarizes her findings and citing page numbers for each summary, Malik indicates which ideas are Schor's and which are his own.

39 **Parenthetical citation of more than one work.** Malik found the idea that consumer pressure can affect business behavior in two sources, so he cites both in parentheses, separating the citations with a semicolon. The first source lacked page or other reference numbers, so its citation does not include a number.

40 **Defining terms.** *Sustainability initiatives* might be unfamiliar to readers, so Malik should have defined the term or avoided it. The term refers to actions taken to reduce resource use and pollution in order to preserve the environment.

MLA
47

Malik 9

raise profits and strengthen customer loyalty (5-6). By giving
industry solid, bottom-line reasons to embrace ecological
goals, consumer demand for earth-friendly products can mag-
nify the effects of individual action.

Careful shopping can help the environment, but green
doesn't necessarily mean "Go." All consumption depletes
resources, increases the likelihood of global warming, and
creates waste, so even eco-friendly products must be used in
moderation. As individuals, we can each play a small role in
helping the environment—and help ourselves at the same
time—by not buying anything we don't really need, even if it
seems environmentally sound. Reducing our personal impact
on the earth is a small price to pay for preserving a livable
planet for future generations.

41 **Citation when the author is named in the text.** Because Malik names Makower and coauthors in his text (previous page of the paper), he gives just the page number in the parenthetical citation.

42 **Drawing a conclusion.** Rather than leave it to readers to figure out the significance of the preceding paragraph, Malik offers his own conclusion.

43 **Conclusion.** In his final paragraph Malik summarizes the main points of his paper to remind readers of both the environmental problems caused by consumption and the benefits of consuming less.

½"
Malik 10

1 space

1"

Notes ← Center

44
45

½"

Double-space

1. Just a few examples of global warming as a theme in recent popular culture include the action movies *The Day the Earth Stood Still* (2008) and *2012* (2009), the television programs *Boomtown* (2011) and *Green Home* (2011), special "green" issues of magazines ranging from *Newsweek* (2010) to *Elle* (2011), a carbon-emissions module for the computer game *SimCity* (2009), and the smartphone apps *CrazyWeather* (2010) and *LazyGreen* (2011).

2. See de Blas for in-depth explanations of these proposals. Additional governmental and institutional solutions are described in DeGraaf, Wann, and Naylor; in Gore's *Our Choice*; in Princen, Maniates, and Conca; and in United Nations Development Programme.

44 **Format of notes.** The heading Notes is centered one inch from the top of the page. (The heading would be singular—Note—if Malik had only one note.) Follow the annotations on the facing page for formatting.

45 **Endnotes for additional relevant information.** Malik uses endnotes for information and sources that are somewhat relevant to his thesis but not essential and that don't fit easily into the text. Note 1 provides several examples to support his comment that global warming has become a recurring theme in popular culture. Note 2 directs readers to a source for more information and cites several additional sources that would be obtrusive in a parenthetical citation. (See pp. 675–76 for more on supplementary notes.)

MLA

47

MLA
47

½″
Malik 11

1″

Works Cited ← Center

Bhanoo, Sindya N. "Products That Are Earth-and-Profit
    ½″ ⌐ Friendly." *New York Times*. New York Times, 11 June
        2010. Web. 23 Mar. 2011.

Dahl, Richard. "Green Washing: Do You Know What You're Buy-
        ing?" *Environmental Health Perspectives* 18.6 (2010):
        A246-52. *Academic Search Complete*. Web. 23 Mar. 2011.

de Blas, Alexandra. "Making the Shift: From Consumerism to
        Sustainability." *Ecos* 153 (2010): n. pag. Web. 25 Mar.
        2011.

DeGraaf, John, David Wann, and Thomas H. Naylor. *Affluenza:
        The All-Consuming Epidemic*. 2nd ed. San Francisco:
        Berrett-Koehler, 2005. Print.

Earth Policy Inst. "Data Center." *Earth Policy Institute*. EPI, 12
        Jan. 2011. Web. 16 Mar. 2011.

Gore, Al. *An Inconvenient Truth: The Planetary Emergency of
        Global Warming and What We Can Do about It*. Emmaus:
        Rodale, 2006. Print.

---. *Our Choice: A Plan to Solve the Climate Crisis*. Emmaus:
        Rodale, 2009. Print.

"Lightbulbs." *Consumer Reports* Oct. 2010: 26-28. Print.

Lin, Brenda. Message to the author. 21 Mar. 2011. E-mail.

Makower, Joel, et al. *State of Green Business 2011*.
        GreenBiz.com. GreenBiz Group, 2011. Web. 25 Mar.
        2011.

Neff, Jack. "Green-Marketing Revolution Defies Economic
        Turndown." *Advertising Age* 20 Apr. 2009: 1+. *Academic
        Search Complete*. Web. 25 Mar. 2011.

Princen, Thomas, Michael Maniates, and Ken Conca. Introduc-
        tion. *Confronting Consumption*. Ed. Princen, Maniates,
        and Conca. Cambridge: MIT P, 2002. 1-20. Print.

Double-
space

46
47

48

49

50

51

52

53

54
55
56

57

58

46 Format of a list of works cited. The heading Works Cited is centered at the top of the page. The entries are alphabetized by the last name of the first author or (for sources without authors) by the first main word of the title.

47 Article in a newspaper online. Here and in all other entries for Web sources, Malik provides the medium of publication, Web, and his date of access.

48 a Article in a scholarly journal consulted in an online database. b Scholarly journal that numbers volumes and issues. The issue and volume numbers for this source are 18.6.

49 a Article in a scholarly journal on the Web. b Scholarly journal that uses only issue numbers. The issue number for this source is 153. **c Article with no page numbers.** The abbreviation n. pag. indicates that the journal Malik consulted is unpaginated.

50 a Source with three authors. Malik reverses the first name and gives the other two in normal order separated by and. **b Second edition of a book.** The notation 2nd ed. follows the title. **c Print book.** Here and in all other entries for print sources, Malik provides the medium of publication, Print.

51 a Source with a corporate author. Malik lists and alphabetizes the source by its corporate author. **b Short, titled work on a Web site.** Malik lists the title of the page, the title of the Web site, the sponsor, the publication date, the medium, and his date of access. He abbreviates the sponsor's name because it is the same as the author's.

52 Print book with one author.

53 Additional source by the same author. Since the author of the previous entry is also Al Gore, in this entry Malik replaces the name with three hyphens followed by a period.

54 a Source with no listed author. Malik lists and alphabetizes the source by its title. **b Article in a print monthly magazine.**

55 Personal interview by e-mail.

56 Source with more than three authors. Malik opts to list this source with just the first author's name followed by et al. ("and others"). (See p. 680.)

57 Article in a magazine consulted in an online database.

58 a Selection from an anthology. b Introduction to a book. This source is the untitled introduction to an anthology, so Malik inserts Introduction in place of a title. Since the book is also edited by the three authors, he gives only their last names after Ed.

Malik 12

Rubin, Jeff, and Benjamin Tal. "Does Energy Efficiency Save   59
Energy?" *StrategEcon*. CIBC World Markets, 27 Nov. 2007.
Web. 23 Apr. 2011.

Schor, Juliet B. *The Overspent American: Upscaling, Downshift-*   60
ing, and the New Consumer. New York: Basic, 1998.
Print.

United Nations Development Programme. *Human Development*   61
*Report: Changing Today's Consumption Patterns—For
Tomorrow's Human Development*. New York: Oxford UP,
1998. Print.

United States. Environmental Protection Agency. Solid Waste   62
and Emergency Response. *Municipal Solid Waste Generation, Recycling, and Disposal in the United States: Facts
and Figures for 2009*. US Environmental Protection
Agency, Dec. 2010. Web. 4 Apr. 2011.

MLA
47

59 **a** **Source with two authors.** Malik reverses the first author's name and, after and, gives the second author's name in normal order. **b** **Short, titled work on a Web site.**

60 **Book with one author.**

61 **Print book with a corporate author.** The source does not list an individual as author, so Malik names the organization as author.

62 **US government source on the Web.** The source does not name an individual as author, so Malik lists as author the organization responsible for the source: first the government, then the agency, then the group within the agency.

MLA
47

Haley 1

Vanessa Haley

Professor Moisan

English 101

6 February 2011

Format of heading and title when no title page is required (see also pp. 714–15)

MLA

47

Introduction of environmental theme

Focus on issue to be resolved

Introduction of Dillard to resolve issue

Thesis statement

Acknowledgment of opposing critical view

Annie Dillard's Healing Vision

It is almost a commonplace these days that human arrogance is destroying the environment. Environmentalists, naturalists, and now the man or woman on the street seem to agree: the long-held belief that human beings are separate from nature, destined to rise above its laws and conquer it, has been ruinous.

Unfortunately, the defenders of nature tend to respond to this ruinous belief with harmful myths of their own: nature is pure and harmonious; humanity is corrupt and dangerous. Much writing about nature lacks a recognition that human beings and their civilization are as much a part of nature as trees and whales are, neither better nor worse. Yet without such a recognition, how can humans overcome the damaging sense of separation between themselves and the earth? How can humans develop realistic solutions to environmental problems that will work for humanity *and* the rest of nature?

One nature writer who seems to recognize the naturalness of humanity is Annie Dillard. In her best-known work, the Pulitzer Prize-winning *Pilgrim at Tinker Creek*, she is a solitary person encountering the natural world, and some critics fault her for turning her back on society. But in those encounters with nature, Dillard probes a spiritual as well as a physical identity between human beings and nature that could help to heal the rift between them.

Dillard is not renowned for her sense of involvement with human society. Like Henry David Thoreau, with whom she is often compared, she retreats from rather than confronts human society. The critic Gary McIlroy points out that although

Thoreau discusses society a great deal in *Walden*, he makes no attempt "to find a middle ground between it and his experiment in the woods" (113). Dillard has been similarly criticized. For instance, the writer Eudora Welty comments that

> Annie Dillard is the only person in her book, substantially the only one in her world; I recall no outside human speech coming to break the long soliloquy of the author. Speaking of the universe very often, she is yet self-surrounded and, beyond that, book-surrounded. Her own book might have taken in more of human life without losing a bit of the wonder she was after. (37)

It is true, as Welty says, that in *Pilgrim* Dillard seems detached from human society. However, she actually was always close to it at Tinker Creek. In a later book, *Teaching a Stone to Talk*, she says of the neighborhood, "This is, mind you, suburbia. It is a five-minute walk in three directions to rows of houses. . . . There's a 55 mph highway at one end of the pond, and a nesting pair of wood ducks at the other" (qtd. in Suh).

Rather than hiding from humanity, Dillard seems to be trying to understand it through nature. In *Pilgrim* she reports buying a goldfish, which she names Ellery Channing. She recalls once seeing through a microscope "red blood cells whip, one by one, through the capillaries" of yet another goldfish (124). Now watching Ellery Channing, she sees the blood in his body as a bond between fish and human being: "Those red blood cells are coursing in Ellery's tail now, too, in just that way, and through his mouth and eyes as well, and through mine" (125). Gary McIlroy observes that this blood, "a symbol of the sanctity of life, is a common bond between Dillard and the fish, between animal and human life in general, and between Dillard and other people" (115).

First response to opposing view

Second response to opposing view

Secondary source's analysis of Dillard

Combination of quotation and Haley's own analysis (next four paragraphs) interprets and synthesizes Dillard's ideas

For Dillard, the terror and unpredictability of death unify all life. The most sinister image in *Pilgrim*—one that haunts Dillard—is that of the frog and the water bug. Dillard reports walking along an embankment scaring frogs into the water when one frog refused to budge. As Dillard leaned over to investigate, the frog "slowly crumpled and began to sag.

Mixture of summary and quotation provides context and keeps quotations trim

The spirit vanished from his eyes as if snuffed. His skin emptied and dropped; his very skull seemed to collapse and settle like a kicked tent" (6). The frog was the victim of a water bug that injects poisons to "dissolve the victim's muscles and bones and organs" (6). Such events lead Dillard to wonder about a creator who would make all life "power and beauty,

Discussion of physical identity of all creatures: death and birth

grace tangled in a rapture with violence" (8). Human beings no less than frogs and water bugs are implicated in this tangle.

Dillard is equally as disturbed by birth as by death. In a chapter of *Pilgrim* called "Fecundity," she focuses on the undeniable reproductive urge of entire species. Her attitude is far from sentimental:

Comment on quotation advises reader what to look for

> I don't know what it is about fecundity that so appalls. I suppose it is the teeming evidence that birth and growth, which we value, are ubiquitous and blind, that life itself is so astonishingly cheap, that nature is as careless as it is bountiful, and that with extravagance goes a crushing waste that will one day include our own cheap lives. (160)

Quotations, including some long ones set off from the text, convey Dillard's voice as well as her ideas

The cheapness and brutality of life are problems Dillard wrestles with, wondering which is "amiss": the world, a "monster," or human beings, with their "excessive emotions" (177-78). No matter how hard she tries to leave human society, Dillard has no choice but to "bring human values to the creek" (179). The violent, seemingly pointless birth and death of all life are, spiritually,

Discussion of spiritual identity of all creatures

Haley 4

two branches of the same creek, the creek that
waters the world. . . . We could have planned
things more mercifully, perhaps, but our plan
would never get off the drawing board until we
agreed to the very compromising terms that are
the only ones that being offers. (180)

For Dillard, accepting the monstrousness as well as the beauty
of "being" is the price all living things pay for freedom.

> Haley's interpretation of Dillard's ideas

In "The Waters of Separation," the final chapter of
Pilgrim, Dillard writes about a winged maple key, or seed. At
this point in the book, the critic Sandra Humble Johnson
notes, Dillard "has been humbled and emptied; she can no
longer apply effort to her search for meaning in a parasitic
world" (4). It is the winter solstice—the shortest day of the
year. And then Dillard spies the maple key descending to earth
and germination. "It rose, just before it would have touched a
thistle, and hovered pirouetting in one spot, then twirled on
and finally came to rest" (267). The key moved, says Dillard,
"like a creature muscled and vigorous, or a creature spread
thin to that other wind, the wind of the spirit . . . , a generous, unending breath" (268). Dillard vows to see the maple
key in all of the earth and in herself. "If I am a maple key
falling, at least I can twirl" (268).

> Resolution of Dillard's concerns

According to the critic John Becker, "Annie Dillard does
not walk out on ordinary life in order to bear witness against
it"; instead, she uses the distance from other people "to make
meaning out of the grotesque disjointedness of man and nature" (408). Gary McIlroy says, nonetheless, that Dillard "does
not succeed in encompassing within her vision any but the
most fragmentary consequences for society at large" (116).
Possibly both are correct. In *Pilgrim at Tinker Creek*, Annie
Dillard suggests a vision of identity among all living things

> Conclusion: ties together divergent critical views, environmental theme, and Dillard's work

that could inform modern humanity's efforts to thrive in harmony with its environment, but she does not make the leap to practicalities. Life, she says, "is a faint tracing on the surface of a mystery. . . . We must somehow take a wider view, look at the whole landscape, really see it, and describe what's going on here" (9). The description, and acting on it, may take generations. As we proceed, however, we may be guided by Dillard's efforts to mend the disjointedness, to see that human beings and maple keys alike twirl equally.

Works Cited

Becker, John E. "Science and the Sacred: From Walden to
Tinker Creek." *Thought: A Review of Culture and Ideas* 62
(1987): 400-13. Print.

Dillard, Annie. *Pilgrim at Tinker Creek*. New York: Harper, 1974.
Print.

Johnson, Sandra Humble. *The Space Between: Literary
Epiphany in the Work of Annie Dillard*. Kent: Kent State
UP, 1992. Print.

McIlroy, Gary. "*Pilgrim at Tinker Creek* and the Social Legacy
of *Walden*." *South Atlantic Quarterly* 85.2 (1996):
111-16. Print.

Suh, Grace. "Ideas Are Tough, Irony Is Easy." *Yale Herald*. Yale
U, 4 Oct. 2005. Web. 22 Jan. 2011.

Welty, Eudora. Rev. of *Pilgrim at Tinker Creek*, by Annie Dillard.
New York Times Book Review 24 Mar. 1974: 36-37.
ProQuest Historical Newspapers. Web. 22 Jan. 2011.

MLA
47

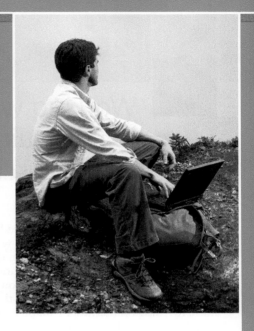

PART **10**

Writing in the Academic Disciplines

48

Working with the Goals and Requirements of the Disciplines

Chapter 7 outlines the general concerns of subject, purpose, and audience that figure in most academic writing situations. The disciplines have more in common as well: methods of gathering evidence, genre assignments for writing, scholarly tools, language conventions, and styles for source citations and document formats. This chapter introduces these common goals and requirements. The following chapters then distinguish the disciplines along the same lines, focusing on literature (Chapter 49), other humanities (50), the social sciences (51), and the natural and applied sciences (52).

Exercise

48a Using methods and evidence

The **methodology** of a discipline is the way its practitioners study their subjects—that is, how they proceed when investigating the answers to questions. Methodology relates to how practitioners analyze evidence and ideas. For instance, a literary critic and a social historian would probably approach Shakespeare's *Hamlet* quite differently: the literary critic might study the play for a theme among its poetic images; the historian might examine the play's relation to Shakespeare's context—England at the turn of the seventeenth century.

Whatever their approach, academic writers do not compose entirely out of their personal experience. Rather, they combine the evidence of their experience with that appropriate to the discipline, drawing well-supported conclusions about their subjects. The evidence of the discipline comes from research like that described in Chapters 41–43—from primary or secondary sources.

- **Primary sources** are firsthand or original accounts, such as historical documents, works of art, and reports on experiments that the writer has conducted. When you use primary sources,

mycomplab

Visit *mycomplab.com* for the eText and for resources and exercises on writing in the academic disciplines.

754

Guidelines for academic writers

- Become familiar with the methodology and the kinds of evidence appropriate for the discipline in which you are writing.
- Analyze the special demands of each assignment. The genre of the assignment, the questions you set out to answer, and the assertions you wish to support will govern how you choose your sources and evidence.
- Become familiar with the specialized tools and language of the discipline.
- Use the discipline's style for source citations and document format.

Video tutorial

you conduct original research and generate your own evidence. You might use your analysis of a painting as evidence for an interpretation of the painting. Or you might use data from your own survey of students to support your conclusions about students' attitudes.

- **Secondary sources** are books and articles written *about* primary sources. Much academic writing requires that you use such sources to spark, extend, or support your own ideas, as when you review the published opinions on your subject before contributing conclusions from your original research.

48c

48b Understanding writing assignments

For most academic writing, your primary purpose will be either to explain something to your readers or to persuade them to accept your conclusions. To achieve your purpose, you will adapt your writing process to the writing situation, particularly to your readers' likely expectations for evidence and how you use it.

Many assignments will specify or suggest the genre in which you are to write. Some genres, such as the social science report on pages 826–29 and the science report on pages 842–44, are fairly standard in their content and format. Other assignments contain key words that imply the expectations of the genre—words such as *compare, define, analyze,* and *illustrate* that express customary ways of thinking about and organizing a vast range of subjects. (See pp. 99–108 for more on the so-called patterns of development.) To be aware of the expectations for the genre in which you are writing, study the wording of each assignment carefully.

48c Using tools and language

When you write in an academic discipline, you use the scholarly tools of that discipline, particularly the research findings published as articles in scholarly journals. In addition, you may use the aids

Exercise

developed by practitioners of the discipline for efficiently and effectively approaching research, conducting it, and recording the findings. Many of these aids, such as a system for recording evidence from sources, are discussed in Chapters 41–43 and can be adapted to any discipline. Other aids are discussed in the following chapters.

Pay close attention to the texts assigned in a course and any materials given out in class, for these items may introduce you to valuable references and other research aids, and they will use the specialized language of the discipline. This specialized language allows practitioners to write to each other both efficiently and precisely. It also furthers certain concerns of the discipline, such as accuracy and objectivity. Scientists, for example, try to interpret their data objectively, so they avoid *undoubtedly, obviously,* and other words that slant conclusions. Some of the language conventions like this one are discussed in the following chapters. As you gain experience in a particular discipline, keep alert for such conventions and train yourself to follow them.

48d Following styles for source citations and document format

Most disciplines publish journals that require authors to use a certain style for source citations and a certain format for documents. In turn, most instructors in a discipline require the same of students writing papers for their courses.

When you cite your sources, you tell readers which ideas and information you borrowed and where they can find your sources. Thus source citations indicate how much knowledge you have and how broad and deep your research was. They also help you avoid **plagiarism,** the serious offense of presenting the words, ideas, and data of others as if they were your own. (See Chapter 44 on avoiding plagiarism.)

Document format specifies such features as margins and the placement of the title. But it also extends to special elements of the manuscript, such as tables or an abstract, that may be required by the discipline.

Chapters 50–52 direct you to the style guides published by different disciplines and outline the requirements of the ones used most often. If your instructor does not require a particular style, use that of the Modern Language Association, which is described and illustrated at length in Chapter 46.

49

Reading and Writing about Literature

By Sylvan Barnet

Why read literature? Let's approach this question indirectly by asking why people *write* literature. A thousand years ago a Japanese writer, Lady Murasaki, offered an answer. Here is one of her characters talking about what motivates a writer:

Exercise

> Again and again something in one's own life or in the life around one will seem so important that one cannot bear to let it pass into oblivion. There must never come a time, the writer feels, when people do not know about this.

When we read certain works—Murasaki's *The Tale of Genji* is one of them—we share this feeling; we are caught up in the writer's world, whether it is the Denmark of Shakespeare's *Hamlet* or the America of Toni Morrison's *Beloved*. We read literature because it gives us an experience that seems important, usually an experience that is both new and familiar. A common way of putting this is to say that reading broadens us and helps us understand our own experience.

49a Using the methods and evidence of literary analysis

When we read nonliterary writings, it may be enough to get the gist of the argument; in fact, we may have to work through many words to find the heart of the matter—say, three claims on behalf of capital punishment. But when we read a story, a poem, or a play, we must pay extremely close attention to what might be called the feel of the words. For instance, the word *woods* in Robert Frost's "Stopping by Woods on a Snowy Evening" has a rural, folksy quality that *forest* doesn't have, and many such small distinctions contribute to the poem's effect.

Literary authors are concerned with presenting human experience concretely, with *showing* rather than *telling*. Consider the following proverb and an unmemorable paraphrase of it.

Visit *mycomplab.com* for the eText and for resources and exercises on reading and writing about literature.

757

A rolling stone gathers no moss.

If a rock is always moving around, vegetation won't have a chance to grow on it.

The familiar original offers a small but complete world: hard (stone) and soft (moss), inorganic and organic, at rest and in motion. The original is also shapely: each noun (*stone, moss*) has one syllable, and each word of motion (*rolling, gathers*) has two syllables, with the accent on the first of the two. Such relationships unify the proverb into a pleasing whole that stays in our minds.

1 Reading a work of literature

Reading literature critically involves interacting with a text. The techniques complement those for critically reading any text, so if you haven't read Chapter 6 on such reading, you should do so. Responding critically is a matter not of making negative judgments but of analyzing the parts, interpreting their meanings, seeing how the parts relate, and evaluating significance or quality.

CULTURE LANGUAGE All readers benefit from hearing literature—particularly poetry—read out loud, but the experience can be especially helpful if standard American English is not your first language or dialect. Listening reveals the pronunciation, tone, and rhythm of the words and can illuminate structure and themes. The Academy of American Poets, at *poets.org*, offers hundreds of poems read by their authors and by others.

Previewing and responding

You can preview a literary text somewhat as you can preview any other text. You may gauge the length of the text to determine whether you can read it in one sitting, and you may read a biographical note to learn about the author. In a literary text, however, you won't find aids such as section headings or summaries that can make previewing other texts especially informative. You have to dive into the words themselves.

Do write while reading. If you own the book you are reading, don't hesitate to underline or highlight passages that especially interest you for one reason or another. Don't hesitate to annotate the margins, indicating your pleasures, displeasures, and uncertainties with remarks such as *Nice detail* or *Do we need this long description?* or *Not believable.* If you don't own the book, make these notes on separate sheets or on your computer.

An effective way to interact with a text is to keep a **reading journal.** A journal is not a diary in which you record your doings; instead, it is a place to develop and store your reflections on what you read, such as an answer to a question you may have posed in the margin of the text. You could make an entry in the form of a letter to the author or from one character to another. In many literature courses, students collaborate to develop their understanding of a literary work. In such a case, you may want to use your journal to reflect on what other students have said—for instance, why your opinion differs so much from someone else's.

You can keep a reading journal in a notebook or on your computer. Some readers prefer a two-column format like that illustrated on page 151, with summaries, paraphrases, and quotations from the text on the left and with their own responses to these passages on the right. Or you may prefer a less structured format like that illustrated on page 761.

Reading a sample story

Here is a very short story by Kate Chopin (1851–1904). (The last name is pronounced in the French way, something like "show pan.") Following the story are a student's annotations and journal entry on the story.

Kate Chopin

The Story of an Hour

Knowing that Mrs. Mallard was afflicted with a heart trouble, great care was taken to break to her as gently as possible the news of her husband's death.

It was her sister Josephine who told her, in broken sentences, veiled hints that revealed in half concealing. Her husband's friend Richards was there, too, near her. It was he who had been in the newspaper office when intelligence of the railroad disaster was received, with Brently Mallard's name leading the list of "killed." He had only taken the time to assure himself of its truth by a second telegram, and had hastened to forestall any less careful, less tender friend in bearing the sad message.

She did not hear the story as many women have heard the same, with a paralyzed inability to accept its significance. She wept at once with sudden, wild abandonment, in her sister's arms. When the storm of grief had spent itself she went away to her room alone. She would have no one follow her.

There stood, facing the open window, a comfortable, roomy armchair. Into this she sank, pressed down by a physical exhaustion that haunted her body and seemed to reach into her soul.

She could see in the open square before her house the tops of trees that were all aquiver with the new spring life. The delicious breath of rain was in the air. In the street below a peddler was crying his wares. The notes of a distant song which some one was singing reached her faintly, and countless sparrows were twittering in the eaves.

There were patches of blue sky showing here and there through the clouds that had met and piled one above the other in the west facing her window.

She sat with her head thrown back upon the cushion of the chair quite motionless, except when a sob came up into her throat and shook her, as a child who has cried itself to sleep continues to sob in its dreams.

She was young, with a fair, calm face, whose lines bespoke repression and even a certain strength. But now there was a dull stare in her

49a

eyes, whose gaze was fixed away off yonder on one of those patches of blue sky. It was not a glance of reflection, but rather indicated a suspension of intelligent thought.

There was something coming to her and she was waiting for it, fearfully. What was it? She did not know; it was too subtle and elusive to name. But she felt it creeping out of the sky, reaching toward her through the sounds, the scents, the color that filled the air.

Now her bosom rose and fell tumultuously. She was beginning to recognize this thing that was approaching to possess her, and she was striving to beat it back with her will—as powerless as her two white slender hands would have been.

When she abandoned herself a little whispered word escaped her slightly parted lips. She said it over and over under her breath: "Free, free, free!" The vacant stare and the look of terror that had followed it went from her eyes. They stayed keen and bright. Her pulses beat fast, and the coursing blood warmed and relaxed every inch of her body.

She did not stop to ask if it were not a monstrous joy that held her. A clear and exalted perception enabled her to dismiss the suggestion as trivial.

She knew that she would weep again when she saw the kind, tender hands folded in death; the face that had never looked save with love upon her, fixed and gray and dead. But she saw beyond that bitter moment a long procession of years to come that would belong to her absolutely. And she opened and spread her arms out to them in welcome.

49a

There would be no one to live for her during those coming years; she would live for herself. There would be no powerful will bending her in the blind persistence with which men and women believe they have a right to impose a private will upon a fellow creature. A kind intention or a cruel intention made the act seem no less a crime as she looked upon it in that brief moment of illumination.

And yet she had loved him—sometimes. Often she had not. What did it matter! What could love, the unsolved mystery, count for in face of this possession of self-assertion which she suddenly recognized as the strongest impulse of her being.

"Free! Body and soul free!" she kept whispering.

Josephine was kneeling before the closed door with her lips to the keyhole, imploring for admission. "Louise, open the door! I beg; open the door—you will make yourself ill. What are you doing, Louise? For heaven's sake open the door."

"Go away. I am not making myself ill." No; she was drinking in the very elixir of life through that open window.

Her fancy was running riot along those days ahead of her. Spring days, and summer days, and all sorts of days that would be her own. She breathed a quick prayer that life might be long. It was only yesterday she had thought with a shudder that life might be long.

She arose at length and opened the door to her sister's importunities. There was a feverish triumph in her eyes, and she carried herself unwittingly like a goddess of Victory. She clasped her sister's waist and together they descended the stairs. Richards stood waiting for them at the bottom.

Some one was opening the front door with a latchkey. It was Brently Mallard who entered, a little travel-stained, composedly carrying his gripsack and umbrella. He had been far from the scene of accident, and did not even know there had been one. He stood amazed at Josephine's piercing cry; at Richards' quick motion to screen him from the view of his wife.

But Richards was too late.

When the doctors came they said she had died of heart disease—of joy that kills.

Following a student's work

In this chapter we'll follow the analysis and writing of a student, Janet Vong, to see one approach to Chopin's story. Vong first annotated the story while reading it. The opening five paragraphs, with her notes, appear below:

Knowing that Mrs. Mallard was afflicted with a heart trouble, great care was taken to break to her as gently as possible the news of her husband's death. *"heart disease" at end of story*

It was her sister Josephine who told her, in broken sentences, veiled hints that revealed in half concealing. Her husband's friend Richards was there, too, near her. It was he who had been in the newspaper office when intelligence of the railroad disaster was received, with Brently Mallard's name leading the list of "killed." He had only taken the time to assure himself of its truth by a second telegram, and had hastened to forestall any less careful, less tender friend in bearing the sad message. *Too hasty, it turns out*

49a

Would men have heard differently? Is au. sexist? She did not hear the story as many women have heard the same, with a paralyzed inability to accept its significance. She wept at once with sudden, wild abandonment, in her sister's arms. When the storm of grief had spent itself she went away to her room alone. She would have no one follow her. *←old-fashioned style*

There stood, facing the open window, a comfortable, roomy armchair. Into this she sank, pressed down by a physical exhaustion that haunted her body and seemed to reach into her soul.

She could see in the open square before her house the tops of trees that were all aquiver with the new spring life. The delicious breath of rain was in the air. In the street below a peddler was crying his wares. The notes of a distant song which some one was singing reached her faintly, and countless sparrows were twittering in the eaves. *Notices spring: odd in a story of death*

Writing in her journal, Vong posed questions about the story—critical points, curiosities about characters, possible implications:

Title nothing special. What might be a better title?
Could a woman who loved her husband be so heartless? *Is* she heartless? *Did* she love him?
What are (were) Louise's feelings about her husband?
Did she want too much? *What* did she want?
Could this story happen today? Feminist interpretation?
Sister (Josephine)—a busybody?

Tricky ending—but maybe it could be true.
"And yet she had loved him—sometimes. Often she had not." Why does one
    love someone "sometimes"?
Irony: plot has reversal. Are characters ironic too?

Vong's journal entry illustrates brainstorming—the discovery technique of listing ideas (or questions) however they occur, without editing (see pp. 31–32). Another productive journal technique is focused freewriting—concentrating on a single issue (such as one of Vong's questions) and writing nonstop for a set amount of time, again without editing (p. 31).

2   Analyzing a work of literature

Like any discipline, the study of literature involves particular frameworks of analysis—particular ways of seeing literary works that help determine what elements are identified and how they are interpreted. Literary frameworks include historical or cultural criticism, which considers the effect of the author's context on a work; feminist or gender criticism, which focuses on the representation of gender in a work; and reader-response criticism, which stresses the effect of a work on its readers.

This chapter emphasizes so-called formalist criticism, which focuses on a literary work primarily as something to be understood in itself. This critical framework engages the reader immediately in the work of literature, without requiring extensive historical or cultural background, and it introduces the conventional elements of literature that all critical approaches discuss, even though they view the elements differently. The box on the next two pages lists these elements—plot, characters, setting, and so on—and offers questions about each one that can help you think constructively and imaginatively about what you read.

One significant attribute of a literary work is its meaning or themes, or what we can interpret to be its themes. Readers may well disagree over the persuasiveness of someone's argument, but they will rarely disagree over its meaning. With literature, however, disagreements over themes occur all the time because (as we have seen) literature *shows* rather than *tells*: it gives us concrete images of imagined human experiences, but it usually does not say how we ought to understand the images.

Further, readers bring to their reading not only different critical views, as noted earlier, but also different personal experiences. A woman who has recently lost her husband may interpret "The Story of an Hour" differently from most other readers. Or a story that bores a reader at age fifteen may deeply move him at twenty-five. The words on the page remain the same, but their meaning changes.

In writing about literature, we can offer only our *interpretation* of meaning rather than *the* meaning. Still, most people agree that

49a

Questions for a literary analysis

See later boxes for specific questions on fiction (p. 773), poetry (p. 774), and drama (p. 777).

Checklist

Plot

The relationships and patterns of events. Even a poem has a plot, such as a change in mood from bitterness to resignation.

What actions happen?
What conflicts occur?
How do the events connect to each other and to the whole?

Characters

The people the author creates, including the narrator of a story or the speaker of a poem.

Who are the principal people in the work?
How do they interact?
What do their actions, words, and thoughts reveal about their personalities and the personalities of others?
Do the characters stay the same, or do they change? Why?

Point of view

The perspective or attitude of the speaker in a poem or the voice who tells a story. The point of view may be **first person** (a participant, using *I*) or **third person** (an outsider, using *he, she, it, they*). A first-person narrator may be a major or a minor character in the narrative and may be **reliable** or **unreliable** (unable to report events wholly or accurately). A third-person narrator may be **omniscient** (knows what goes on in all characters' minds), **limited** (knows what goes on in the mind of only one or two characters), or **objective** (knows only what is external to the characters).

Who is the narrator (or the speaker of a poem)?
How does the narrator's point of view affect the narrative?

Tone

The narrator's or speaker's attitude, perceived through the words (for instance, joyful, bitter, or confident).

What tone (or tones) do you hear? If there is a change, how do you account for it?
Is there an ironic contrast between the narrator's tone (for instance, confidence) and what you take to be the author's attitude (for instance, pity for human overconfidence)?

Imagery

Word pictures or details involving the senses: sight, sound, touch, smell, taste.

What images does the writer use? What senses do they draw on?
What patterns are evident in the images (for instance, religious or commercial images)?
What is the significance of the imagery?

(continued)

49a

Questions for a literary analysis
(continued)

Symbolism

Concrete things standing for larger and more abstract ideas. For instance, the American flag may symbolize freedom, a tweeting bird may symbolize happiness, a dead flower may symbolize mortality.

What symbols does the author use? What do they seem to signify?

How does the symbolism relate to the other elements of the work, such as character or theme?

Setting

The place where the action happens.

What does the locale contribute to the work?

Are scene shifts significant?

Form

The shape or structure of the work.

What *is* the form? (For example, a story might divide sharply in the middle, moving from happiness to sorrow.)

What parts of the work does the form emphasize, and why?

Themes

The main ideas—conceptions of human experience suggested by the work as a whole. A theme is neither a plot (what happens) nor a subject (such as mourning or marriage). Rather it is what the author says with that plot about that subject.

Can you state each theme in a sentence? Avoid mentioning specific characters or actions; instead, write an observation applicable to humanity in general. For instance, you might state the following about Kate Chopin's "The Story of an Hour": *Happiness depends partly on freedom.*

Do certain words, passages of dialog or description, or situations seem to represent a theme most clearly?

How do the work's elements combine to develop each theme?

Appeal

The degree to which the work pleases you.

What do you especially like or dislike about the work?

Do you think your responses are unique, or would they be common to most readers? Why?

there are limits to interpretation: it must be supported by evidence from the work that a reasonable reader will find at least plausible if not totally convincing. For instance, the student who says that in "The Story of an Hour" Mrs. Mallard does not die but merely falls into a deathlike trance goes beyond the permissible limits because the story offers no evidence for such an interpretation.

3   Using evidence in writing about literature

The evidence for a literary analysis always comes from at least one primary source (the work or works being discussed) and may come from secondary sources (critical and historical works). (See pp. 754–55 for more on primary and secondary sources.) For example, if you were writing about Chopin's "The Story of an Hour," the primary material would be the story itself, and the secondary material (if you used it) might be critical studies of Chopin.

The bulk of your evidence in writing about literature will usually be quotations from the work, although you will occasionally summarize or paraphrase as well (see pp. 633–37). When using quotations, keep in mind the criteria in the box on page 769.

Your instructor will probably tell you if you are expected to consult secondary sources for an assignment. They can help you understand a writer's work, but your primary concern should always be the work itself, not what critics A, B, and C say about it. In general, then, quote or summarize secondary material sparingly. And always cite your sources.

49b

49b   Understanding writing assignments in literature

A literature instructor may ask you to write papers in one or more of the following genres. The first two are the most common.

Student paper

- A literary analysis paper: Give your ideas about a work of literature—your interpretation of its meaning, context, or representations based on specific words, characters, and events.
- A literary research paper: Combine analysis of a literary work with research about the work and perhaps about the life of its author or the context in which the author wrote the work. A literary research paper draws on both primary and secondary sources. For example, you might respond to what scholars have written about the symbolism in a play by Tennessee Williams, or you might research medieval England as a way to understand the context of Chaucer's *Canterbury Tales*.
- A personal response or reaction paper: Give your thoughts and feelings about a work of literature. For example, you might compare a novel's description of a city with your experience of the same city.
- A book review: Give a summary of a book and a judgment about the book's value. In a review of a novel, for example, you might discuss whether the plot is interesting, the characters are believable,

and the writing style is enjoyable. You might also compare the work to other works by the author.

▪ **A theater review:** Give your reactions to and opinions about a theatrical performance. You might summarize the plot of the play, describe the characters, identify the prominent themes, evaluate the other elements (writing, performances, direction, stage setting), and recommend whether others should see the performance.

49b Using the tools and language of literary analysis

1 Writing tools

The fundamental tool for writing about literature is reading critically. Asking analytical questions such as those on pages 763–64 can help you focus your ideas. In addition, keeping a reading journal can help you develop your thoughts. Keep careful, well-organized notes on any research materials. Finally, discuss the work with others who have read it. They may offer reactions and insights that will help you shape your own ideas.

2 Language considerations

49b

Video
tutorial

Use the present tense of verbs to describe both the action in a literary work (*Brently Mallard suddenly appears*) and the writing of an author (*Chopin briefly describes the view* or *In his essay he comments that . . .*). Use the past tense to describe events that actually occurred in the past (*Chopin was born in 1851*).

Some instructors discourage students from using the first-person *I* (as in *I felt sorry for the character*) in writing about literature. At least use *I* sparingly to avoid sounding egotistical. Rephrase sentences to avoid using *I* unnecessarily—for instance, *The character evokes the reader's sympathy.*

3 Research sources

In addition to the following resources on literature, you may also want to consult some on other humanities (pp. 782–85).

Specialized encyclopedias, dictionaries, and bibliographies

Cambridge Bibliography of English Literature
Cambridge Encyclopedia of Language
Cambridge Guide to Literature in English
Dictionary of Literary Biography
Handbook to Literature
Literary Criticism Index
McGraw-Hill Encyclopedia of World Drama

MLA International Bibliography
New Princeton Encyclopedia of Poetry and Poetics
Oxford Companion to American Literature
Oxford Companion to the Theatre
Oxford Dictionary of National Biography
Schomburg Center Guide to Black Literature from the Eighteenth Century to the Present

Library databases and indexes

Abstracts of Folklore Studies
Access World News
Dissertation Abstracts International (doctoral dissertations)
Early English Books Online
Eighteenth Century Collections Online
Gale Literary Resource Center
Hathi Trust
Humanities Index
LexisNexis Academic
Literary Criticism Index
Literary Index
Literature Online
MLA International Bibliography
ProQuest Historical Newspapers
World Shakespeare Bibliography

49d

Book reviews

Book Review Digest
Book Review Index

Sources on the open Web

Alex Catalog of Electronic Texts (infomotions.com/alex)
EServer (eserver.org)
ipl2 (ipl.org)
Literary Resources on the Net (ethnicity.rutgers.edu/~jlynch/Lit)
Mr. Shakespeare and the Internet (shakespeare.palomar.edu)
NINES: Nineteenth-Century Scholarship Online (www.nines.org)
Online Books Page (onlinebooks.library.upenn.edu)
Voice of the Shuttle (vos.ucsb.edu)

 Citing sources and formatting documents in writing about literature

Unless your instructor specifies otherwise, use the documentation style of the Modern Language Association (MLA), detailed in Chapter 46. In this style, parenthetical citations in the text of the paper refer to a list of works cited at the end. Sample papers illustrating this style appear in Chapter 47 as well as in this chapter.

Use MLA format for headings, margins, and other elements, as detailed on pages 714–16.

49e Drafting and revising a literary analysis

The process for writing a literary analysis is similar to that for any other kind of essay: once you've done the reading and thought about it, you need to focus your ideas, gather evidence, draft your paper, and revise it.

1 Conceiving a thesis

After reading, rereading, and making notes, you will probably be able to formulate a tentative thesis statement—an assertion of your main point, your argument. (For more on thesis statements, see pp. 36–40.) Clear the air by glancing over your notes and by jotting down a few especially promising ideas—brief statements of what you think your key points may be and their main support. One approach is to seek patterns in the work, such as recurring words, phrases, images, events, symbols, or other elements. (Go back to the work, if necessary, to expand the patterns your notes reveal.) Such patterns can help you see themes both in the work itself and in your ideas about it.

Considering Kate Chopin's "The Story of an Hour," Janet Vong at first explored the idea that Mrs. Mallard, the main character, was unrealistic and thus unconvincing. (See Vong's journal entry on pp. 761–62.) But the more Vong examined the story and her notes, the more she was impressed by a pattern of ironies, or reversals, that helped to make Mrs. Mallard believable. In her journal Vong explored the idea that the many small reversals paved the way for Mrs. Mallard's own reversal from grief to joy:

> title? "Ironies in an Hour" (?) "An Hour of Irony" (?) "Kate Chopin's Irony" (?)
> thesis: irony at end is prepared for
> chief irony: Mrs. M. dies just as she is beginning to enjoy life
> smaller ironies:
> 1. "sad message" brings her joy
> 2. Richards is "too late" at end
> 3. Richards is too early at start
> 4. "joy that kills"
> 5. death brings joy and life

From these notes Vong developed her thesis statement:

> The irony of the ending is believable partly because it is consistent with earlier ironies in the story.

This thesis statement asserts a specific idea that can be developed and convincingly argued with evidence from Chopin's story. A good thesis statement will neither assert a fact (*Mrs. Mallard dies soon after hearing that her husband has died*) nor overgeneralize (*The story is an insult to women*).

2 | Gathering evidence

In writing about literature, you use mainly evidence gathered from the work itself: quotations and sometimes paraphrases and summaries that support your ideas about the work. You can see examples of quoting and paraphrasing in Janet Vong's final draft on pages 771–72. The box below offers guidelines for using quotations in literary analysis.

Guidelines for using quotations in literary analysis

- Use quotations to support your assertions, not to pad the paper. Quote at length only when necessary to your argument.
- Specify how each quotation relates to your idea. Introduce the quotation—for example, *At the outset Chopin conveys the sort of person Richards is:* ". . ." Sometimes, comment after the quotation. (See pages 642–46 for more on integrating quotations into your writing.)
- Reproduce spelling, punctuation, capitalization, and all other features exactly as they appear in the source. See page 496 for the use of brackets when you need to add something to a quotation, and see page 497 for the use of an ellipsis mark when you need to omit something from a quotation.
- Document your sources. See pages 657–58.

Video
tutorial

49e

You may wonder how much you should summarize the plot of the work. A brief plot summary can be helpful to readers who are unfamiliar with the work. Sometimes plot elements place your ideas in the context of the work or remind readers where your quotations come from. Plot elements may even be used as evidence, as Vong uses the ironic ending of the Chopin story. But plot summary is not literary analysis, and summary alone is not sufficient evidence to support a thesis. Keep any plot summaries brief and to the point.

For a literary research paper, evidence will come from the work itself and from secondary sources such as scholarly works and critical appraisals. The thesis and principal ideas of the paper must still be your own, but you may supplement your reading of the work with the views of respected scholars or critics. Sometimes you may choose to build your own argument in part by disputing others' views. However you draw on secondary sources, remember that they must be clearly identified and documented, even when you use your own words.

Note You can find student essays on the Web that may lead you to other sources or may suggest ideas you hadn't considered. If you want to use another student's paper as a secondary source, you must evaluate it with special care because it will not have passed through a reviewing process, as an article in a scholarly journal does. (See pp. 615–25 on evaluating online sources.) You must also, of course, clearly identify and document the source: borrowing *any* other writer's ideas or words without credit is plagiarism. (See pp. 648–54.)

(See pp. 615–25 on evaluating online sources.)

3 Writing a draft

Drafting your essay is your opportunity to develop your thesis or to discover it if you haven't already. The draft below was actually Janet Vong's second: she deleted some digressions from her first draft and added more evidence for her points. The numbers in parentheses refer to the pages from which she drew the quotations. (See pp. 667–73 on this form of documentation.) Ask your instructor whether you should always give such citations, especially for a short poem or story like Chopin's.

Ironies in an Hour

After we know how the story turns out, if we reread it we find irony at the very start, as is true of many other stories. Mrs. Mallard's friends assume, mistakenly, that Mrs. Mallard is deeply in love with her husband, Brently Mallard. They take great care to tell her gently of his death. The friends mean well, and in fact they *do* well. They bring her an hour of life, an hour of freedom. They think their news is sad. Mrs. Mallard at first expresses grief when she hears the news, but soon she finds joy in it. So Richards's "sad message" (67), though sad in Richards's eyes, is in fact a happy message.

Among the ironic details is the statement that when Mallard enters the house, Richards tries to conceal him from Mrs. Mallard, but Richards is "too late" (68). This is ironic because earlier Richards has "hastened" (67) to bring his sad message; if he had been too late at the start, Brently Mallard would have arrived at home first, and Mrs. Mallard's life would not end an hour later but would simply go on as before. Yet another irony at the end of the story is the diagnosis of the doctors. The doctors say she died of "heart disease—of joy that kills" (68). In one sense the doctors are right: Mrs. Mallard has experienced a great joy. But of course the doctors totally misunderstand the joy that kills her.

The central irony resides not in the well-intentioned but ironic actions of Richards, or in the unconsciously ironic words of the doctors, but in her own life. She "sometimes" (68) loved her husband, but in a way she has been dead. Now, his apparent death brings her new life. This new life comes to her at the season of the year when "the tops of trees . . . were all aquiver with the new spring life" (67). But, ironically, her new life will last only an hour. She looks forward to "summer days" (68), but she will not see even the end of this spring day. Her years of marriage were ironic. They brought her a sort of living death instead of joy. Her new life is ironic, too. It grows out of her moment of grief for her supposedly dead husband, and her vision of a new life is cut short.

4 Revising and editing

As in other writing, use at least two drafts to revise and edit, so that you can attend separately to the big structural issues and the smaller surface problems. See pages 61 and 68–69 for general revision and editing checklists. The additional checklist below can help you with a literary analysis.

Checklist for revising a literary analysis

✓
Checklist

- **Title:** Does the title of your essay give the title and author of the work you discuss and also an idea of your approach to the work?
- **Introduction:** Does the introductory paragraph name the author and the title so that readers know exactly what work you are discussing? (Avoid opening sentences such as "In this story. . . .") Does the introduction state and develop your thesis a bit so that readers know where they will be going?
- **Organization:** How effective is the organization? The essay should not dwindle or become anticlimactic; rather, it should build up.
- **Quotations:** What evidence does each quotation provide? Do quotations let readers hear the author's voice?
- **Analysis vs. summary:** Is the essay chiefly devoted to analysis, not to summary? Summarize the plot only briefly and only to further your own ideas. A summary is not an essay.
- **Verb tenses:** Have you used the present tense of verbs to describe both the author's work and the action in the work (for example, *Chopin shows* and *Mrs. Mallard dies*)?
- **Evaluation:** How well will readers understand your evaluation of the work and what it is based on? Your evaluation may be implied (as in Janet Vong's essay on "The Story of an Hour"), or it may be explicit. In either case, give the reasons for judging the work to be effective or not, worth reading or not. It is not enough to express your likes or dislikes; readers need the support of specific evidence from the work.
- **Are all your sources documented in MLA style?**

49e

Janet Vong's final draft follows, with annotations that highlight some of its features.

An essay on fiction (no secondary sources)

Janet Vong

Mr. Romano

English 102

20 February 2011

Ironies of Life in Kate Chopin's

"The Story of an Hour"

Kate Chopin's "The Story of an Hour"—which takes only a few minutes to read—has an ironic ending: Mrs. Mallard dies just when she is

Author's name and identification in MLA format (p. 715)

Paper title incorporating author and title of analyzed work

Introduction naming author/title

beginning to live. On first reading, the ending seems almost too ironic for

belief. On rereading the story, however, one sees that the ending is believable partly because it is consistent with other ironies in the story.

Irony appears at the very start of the story. Because Mrs. Mallard's friends and her sister assume, mistakenly, that she is deeply in love with her husband, Brently Mallard, they take great care to tell her gently of his death. They mean well, and in fact they *do* well, bringing her an hour of life, an hour of joyous freedom, but it is ironic that they think their news is sad. True, Mrs. Mallard at first expresses grief when she hears the news, but soon (unknown to the others) she finds joy. So Richards's "sad message" (67), though sad in Richards's eyes, is in fact a happy message.

Among the small but significant ironic details is the statement near the end of the story that when Mallard enters the house, Richards tries to

conceal him from Mrs. Mallard, but Richards is "too late" (68). Almost at the start of the story, in the second paragraph, Richards has "hastened" (67) to bring his sad news. But if Richards had arrived too late at the start, Brently Mallard would have arrived at home first, and Mrs. Mallard's life would not end an hour later but would simply go on as before. Yet another irony at the end of the story is the diagnosis of the doctors. They say she died of "heart disease—of joy that kills" (68). In one sense they are right: Mrs. Mallard has for the last hour experienced a great joy. But of course the doctors totally misunderstand the joy that kills her. It is not joy at seeing her husband alive, but her realization that the great joy she experienced during the last hour is over.

All of these ironic details add richness to the story, but the central irony resides not in the well-intentioned but ironic actions of Richards, or in the unconsciously ironic words of the doctors, but in Mrs. Mallard's own life. She "sometimes" (68) loved her husband, but in a way she has been dead, a body subjected to her husband's will. Now, his apparent death brings her new life. Appropriately, this new life comes to her at the season of the year when "the tops of trees . . . were all aquiver with the new spring life" (67). But, ironically, her new life will last only an hour. She is "Free, free, free" (68)—but only until her husband walks through the doorway. She looks forward to "summer days" (68), but she will not see even the end of this spring day. If her years of marriage were ironic, bringing her a sort of living death instead of joy, her new life is ironic, too, not only because it grows out of her moment of grief for her supposedly dead husband, but also because her vision of "a long procession of years" (68) is cut short within an hour on a spring day.

[New page.]

New page for work cited in MLA style (p. 676)

Work Cited

Chopin, Kate. "The Story of an Hour." *An Introduction to Literature: Fiction, Poetry, and Drama.* Ed. Sylvan Barnet, William Burto, and William E. Cain. 16th ed. New York: Longman, 2011. 67-68. Print.

49f Writing about fiction, poetry, and drama

A work of literature falls into a literary genre—fiction, poetry, or drama—depending on how it is structured. The different genres of literature require different approaches in writing.

1 Writing about fiction

The "Questions for a literary analysis" on pages 763–64 will help you think about any work of literature, including a story or novel, and find a topic to write on. The following questions provide additional prompts for thinking about fiction. For an example of writing about fiction, see Janet Vong's essay analyzing Kate Chopin's "The Story of an Hour."

Student paper

49f

Questions for analyzing fiction

Checklist

- What happens in the story? For yourself, summarize the plot (the gist of the happenings). Think about what your summary *leaves out.*
- Is the story told in chronological order, or are there flashbacks or flashforwards? On rereading, what foreshadowing (hints of what is to come) do you detect?
- What conflicts does the work include?
- How does the writer develop characters? Are the characters revealed by explicit comment or through action? With which character(s) do you sympathize? Are the characters plausible? What motivates them? What do minor characters contribute to the work?
- Who tells the story? Is the narrator a character, or does the narrator stand entirely outside the characters' world? What does the narrator's point of view contribute to the story's theme? (On narrative points of view, see p. 763.)
- What is the setting? What do the time and place of the action contribute to the work?
- Are certain characters, settings, or actions symbolic? Do they stand for something in addition to themselves?
- What are the themes? That is, what does the work add up to? Do the themes reinforce your values, or do they challenge them?
- Is the title informative? Did its meaning change for you after you read the work?

2 Writing about poetry

Two types of essays on poetry are especially common. One is an analysis of some aspect of the poem in relation to the whole—for instance, the changes in the speaker's tone or the functions of meter and rhyme. The second is an explication, a line-by-line (sometimes almost word-by-word) reading that seeks to make explicit everything that is implicit in the poem. Thus an explication of the first line of Robert Frost's "Stopping by Woods on a Snowy Evening" (the line goes "Whose woods these are I think I know") might call attention to the tentativeness of the line ("I think I know") and to the fact that the words are not in the normal order ("I think I know whose woods these are"). These features might support the explanation that the poet is introducing—very quietly—a note of the *un*usual, in preparation for the experience that follows. Although one might conceivably explicate a long poem, the method is so detailed that in practice writers usually confine it to short poems or to short passages from long poems.

The "Questions for a literary analysis" on pages 763–64 will help you think about any work of literature, including a poem, and find a topic to write on. The following questions provide additional ways to think about poetry.

49f

Checklist

Questions for analyzing poetry

- What parts of the poem interest or puzzle you? What words seem especially striking or unusual?
- How can you describe the poem's *speaker* (sometimes called the *persona* or the *voice*)? The speaker may be very different from the author.
- What tone or emotion do you detect—for instance, anger, affection, sarcasm? Does the tone change during the poem?
- What is the structure of the poem? Are there stanzas (groups of lines separated by space)? If so, how is the thought related to the stanzas?
- What are the themes of the poem? What is it about? Are the themes stated or implied?
- What images do you find? Look for evocations of sight, sound, taste, touch, or smell. Is there a surprising pattern of images—say, images of business in a poem about love? What does the poem suggest symbolically as well as literally? (Trust your responses. If you don't sense a symbolic overtone, move on. Don't hunt for symbols.)

An essay on poetry with secondary sources

The sample paper opposite analyzes a short poem by Agha Shahid Ali. The paper argues for a particular interpretation of the poem, not only analyzing the poem itself but also drawing on secondary sources—that is, critical works *about* the poem. In the opening paragraph, for instance, the writer uses a brief quotation from a secondary source to establish how her interpretation differs from those of other readers. This quotation and the three later uses of secondary sources are support for the writer's points, not padding.

Note In the paper, the parenthetical citations for Ali's poem give line numbers of the poem, whereas the citations for the secondary sources give page numbers of the sources. See pages 672 and 667–68, respectively, for these two forms of citation.

Agha Shahid Ali

Postcard from Kashmir

Kashmir shrinks into my mailbox,
my home a neat four by six inches.
I always loved neatness. Now I hold
the half-inch Himalayas in my hand.

This is home. And this the closest   5
I'll ever be to home. When I return,
the colors won't be so brilliant,
the Jhelum's waters so clean,
so ultramarine. My love
so overexposed.   10

And my memory will be a little
out of focus, in it
a giant negative, black
and white, still undeveloped.

49f

Jessie Glenn
Professor Narracci
English 101
14 March 2011

Past and Future in

Agha Shahid Ali's "Postcard from Kashmir"

Most literary critics interpret Agha Shahid Ali's "Postcard from Kashmir" as a longing for a lost home, a poetic expression of the heartbreak of exile. For instance, Maimuna Dali Islam describes the speaker's futile effort "to capture his homeland" (262). However, such a reading of the poem seems too narrow. "Postcard from Kashmir" does evoke the experience of being displaced from a beloved home, but the speaker does not seem to feel an intense loss. Instead, he seems to reflect on his position of having more than one home.

Ali's brief poem consists of three stanzas and divides into two parts. In the first half, the speaker examines a postcard he has received from his former home of Kashmir (lines 1-6). In the second half, the speaker looks forward, imagining how Kashmir will look the next time he sees it and assuming that the place will be different from the idealized view of the postcard and his memory (6-14). The geography is significant. Kashmir has been in the news for many years as the focus of territorial conflict, often violent, among the bordering nations of India, Pakistan, and China. Many residents of the region have been killed, and many have left the region. One of the exiles was Ali: he moved to the United States in 1976 and lived here until his death in 2001, but he also regularly visited his family in Kashmir (Benvenuto 261, 263).

In the context of Kashmir, the literary theorist Jahan Ramazani concludes that the poem "dramatizes the . . . condition" of losing one's homeland to political turmoil (12). Yet several lines in the poem suggest that the speaker is not mourning a loss but musing about having a sense of home both in Kashmir and in the United States. This sense is evident in the opening stanza: "Kashmir shrinks into my mailbox, / my home a neat four by six inches" (1-2), with "my mailbox" conveying his current residence as home and "my home" referring to Kashmir. The dual sense of home is even more evident in the lines "This is home. And this is the closest / I'll ever be to home" (5-6). Although Maimuna Dali Islam assumes that "This" in these lines refers to the Kashmir pictured on the postcard (262), it could also or instead refer to the home attached to the mailbox.

The speaker also seems to perceive that his dual sense of home will continue into the future. The critics do not mention that the second half of the poem is written in the future tense. Beginning with "When I return" (6), the speaker makes it clear that he expects to find himself in Kashmir again, and he imagines how things will be, not how they were. Islam takes the image on the postcard as proof that "there is a place that can be captured in a snapshot" (263), but the speaker compares photography to memory, characterizing both as flawed and deceptive with terms such as "overexposed" (10) and "out of focus" (12). He acknowledges that the place won't be like the photograph: "the colors won't be so brilliant, / the Jhelum's waters so clean, / so ultramarine" (7-9). Kashmir still exists, but not as any photograph or memory has recorded it. And the speaker's relationship to his original home, his "love" (9), is changing with the place itself.

In "Postcard from Kashmir" the speaker reflects on home and displacement as he gazes into a representation of his past and considers the future. If the poem mourns a loss, as the critics suggest, it is a loss that has not happened yet, at least not completely. More convincingly, the poem captures a moment when the two homes and the past, present, and future all meet.

[New page.]

Works Cited

Ali, Agha Shahid. "Postcard from Kashmir." *The Half-Inch Himalayas*. Middletown: Wesleyan UP, 1987. 1. Print.

Benvenuto, Christine. "Agha Shahid Ali." *Massachusetts Review* 43.1 (2002): 261-73. Web. 7 Mar. 2011.

Islam, Maimuna Dali. "A Way in the World of an Asian American Existence: Agha Shahid Ali's Transimmigrant Spacing of North America and India and Kashmir."

Transnational Asian American Literature: Sites and Transits. Ed. Shirley Lim et al. Philadelphia: Temple UP, 2006. 257-73. Print.

Ramazani, Jahan. *The Hybrid Muse: Postcolonial Poetry in English.* Chicago: U of Chicago P, 2001. Print.

3 Writing about drama

Student paper

Because plays—even some one-act plays—are relatively long, analytic essays on drama usually focus on only one aspect of the play, such as the structure of the play, the function of a single scene, or a character's responsibility for his or her fate. The essay's introduction indicates what the topic is and why it is of some importance, and the introduction may also state the thesis. The conclusion often extends the analysis, showing how a study of the apparently small topic helps to illuminate the play as a whole.

The "Questions for a literary analysis" on pages 763–64 will help you think about any work of literature, including a play, and find a topic to write on. The questions in the following box provide additional prompts for thinking about drama.

Questions for analyzing drama

49f

Checklist

- How does the plot (the sequence of happenings) unfold? Does it seem plausible? If not, is the implausibility a fault? If there is more than one plot, are the plots parallel, or are they related by way of contrast?
- Are certain happenings recurrent? If so, how are they significant?
- What kinds of conflict are in the play—for instance, between two groups, two characters, or two aspects of a single character? How are the conflicts resolved? Is the resolution satisfying to you?
- How does the author develop the characters? How trustworthy are the characters when they describe themselves or others? Do some characters serve as **foils**, or contrasts, for other characters, thus helping to define the other characters? Do the characters change as the play proceeds? Are the characters' motivations convincing?
- What do the author's stage directions add to your understanding and appreciation of the play? If there are few stage directions, what do the speeches imply about the characters' manner, tone, and gestures?
- What do you make of the setting, or location? Does it help to reveal characters or themes?
- Do certain costumes or properties strike you as symbolic? See page 764 on symbolism.

An essay on drama (no secondary sources)

The following essay on William Shakespeare's *Macbeth* focuses on the title character, examining the extent to which he is and is not a tragic hero. Although the writer bases the essay on his personal response to the play, he does not simply state a preference, as if saying he likes vanilla more than chocolate; instead, he argues a case and offers evidence from the play to support his claims.

The writer delays stating his thesis fully until the final paragraph: Macbeth is a hero even though he is a villain. But this thesis is nonetheless evident throughout the essay, from the title through the opening three paragraphs (which establish a context and the case the writer will oppose) through each of the five body paragraphs (which offer five kinds of evidence for the thesis).

Note The parenthetical citations in this essay include act, scene, and line numbers—MLA style for citations of verse plays (see p. 673).

Michael Spinter
Professor Nelson
English 211, sec. 4
8 October 2010

Shakespeare's Macbeth as Hero

When people imagine a tragic hero, they probably think of a fundamentally sympathetic person who is entangled in terrifying circumstances and who ultimately dies, leaving the world a diminished place. For instance, in Shakespeare's *Hamlet* the title character must avenge his father's murder, and in doing so he performs certain actions that verge on the wrongful, such as behaving cruelly to his beloved Ophelia and his mother and killing Rosencrantz and Guildenstern. But in the end Hamlet seems fundamentally a decent man and Denmark seems the poorer for his death.

The title character of Shakespeare's *Macbeth* is different. He kills King Duncan and Duncan's grooms, kills Banquo, attempts to kill Banquo's son, and finally kills Lady Macduff and her children and her servants. True, the only people whom he kills with his own hands are Duncan and the grooms—the other victims are destroyed by hired murderers—but clearly Macbeth is responsible for all of the deaths. He could seem to be a sneaking butcher rather than a tragic hero for whom a reader can feel sympathy.

Certainly most of the other characters in the play feel no sympathy for Macbeth. Macduff calls him a "hell-kite," or a hellish bird of prey (4.3.217), a "tyrant" (5.7.14), a "hell-hound" (5.8.3), and a "coward" (5.8.23). To Malcolm he is a "tyrant" (4.3.12), "devilish Macbeth" (4.3.117), and a "butcher" (5.8.69). Readers and spectators can hardly deny the truth of these characterizations. And yet Macbeth does not seem merely villainous. It would be going too far to say that Macbeth is always sympathetic, but he is deeply interesting and not to be dismissed as an out-and-out monster. What accounts for his hold on readers' and spectators' feelings? At least five factors play their parts.

Macbeth is appealing because he is an impressive military figure. In the first extended description of Macbeth, the Captain speaks of "brave Macbeth—well he deserves that name" (1.2.16). The Captain tells how Macbeth valiantly fought on behalf of his king, and King Duncan exclaims, "O valiant cousin! Worthy gentleman!" (1.2.2). True, Macbeth sometimes cringes, such as when he denies responsibility for Banquo's death: "Thou canst not say I did it" (3.4.51). But throughout most of the play, he is a bold and courageous soldier.

Of course, Macbeth's ability as a soldier is not enough by itself to explain his appeal. He is at the same time a victim—a victim of his wife's ambition and a victim of the witches. Yes, he ought to see through his wife's schemes, and he ought to resist the witches, just as Banquo resists them, but surely Macbeth is partly tricked into crime. He is responsible, but others can imagine themselves falling as he does, and his status as a victim arouses sympathy.

Also contributing to a sense of Macbeth's humanity is the conscience he retains despite his terrible deeds. For instance, after he murders Duncan he cannot sleep at night. When he tells Lady Macbeth that he has heard a voice saying "Macbeth does murder sleep" (2.2.35), she ridicules him, but the voice is prophetic: he is doomed to sleepless nights. Macbeth's torment over his deed shows that he knows he has done wrong and that he still has some decent human feelings.

Macbeth eventually loses all of his allies, even his wife, and he then claims sympathy as a lonely, guilt-haunted figure. On this point, scene 2 of act 3 is especially significant. When Lady Macbeth asks Macbeth why he keeps to himself (line 8), he confides something of the mental stress that he is undergoing. But when she asks, "What's to be done?" (44), he cannot bring himself to tell her that he is plotting the deaths of Banquo and Fleance. Instead of further involving his wife, the only person with whom he might still have a human connection, Macbeth says, "Be innocent of the knowledge, dearest chuck . . ." (45). The word *chuck*, an affectionate form of *chick*, shows warmth and intimacy that are touching, but his refusal or his inability to confide in his wife and former partner in crime shows how fully isolated he is from all human contact. Readers and spectators cannot help feeling some sympathy for him.

Finally, Macbeth is appealing, rather than disgusting, because he speaks so eloquently. The greatness of his language compels rapt attention. Some speeches are very familiar, such as "My way of life / Is fall'n into the sear, the yellow leaf . . ." (5.3.23-24) and "Tomorrow and tomorrow and tomorrow / Creeps in this petty pace from day to day . . ." (5.5.19-20). But almost every speech Macbeth utters is equally memorable, from his first, "So foul and fair a day I have not seen" (1.3.38), to his last:

> Before my body
> I throw my warlike shield. Lay on, Macduff:
> And damned be him that first cries, "Hold, enough!" (5.8.32-34)

If readers and spectators judge Macbeth only by what he does, of course they will see a foul murderer. But if they give due weight to his bravery, his role as a

49f

victim, his tormented conscience, his isolation, and especially his moving language, then they will not simply judge Macbeth. Rather, they will see that this villain is not merely awful but awesome.

[New page.]

Work Cited

Shakespeare, William. *The Tragedy of Macbeth*. Ed. Sylvan Barnet. Rev. ed. New York: NAL, 1987. Print.

50

Writing in Other Humanities

Exercise

The humanities include literature, the visual arts, music, film, dance, history, philosophy, and religion. The preceding chapter discusses the particular requirements of reading and writing about literature. This chapter concentrates on history. Although the arts, religion, and other humanities have their own concerns, they share many important goals and methods with literature and history.

50a Using the methods and evidence of the humanities

Writers in the humanities record and speculate about the growth, ideas, and emotions of human beings. Based on the evidence of written words, artworks, and other human traces and creations, humanities writers explain, interpret, analyze, and reconstruct the human experience.

The discipline of history focuses particularly on reconstructing the past. In Greek the word for history means "to inquire": historians inquire into the past to understand its events. Then they report, explain, analyze, and evaluate the events in their context, asking such questions as what happened before or after the events or how the events were related to then existing political and social structures.

mycomplab

Visit *mycomplab.com* for the eText and for resources on writing in history, the visual arts, and other humanities.

Historians' reconstructions of the past—their conclusions about what happened and why—are always supported with reference to the written record. The evidence of history is mainly primary sources, such as eyewitness accounts and contemporary documents, letters, commercial records, and the like. For history papers, you might also be asked to support your conclusions with those in secondary sources.

In reading historical sources, you need to weigh and evaluate their evidence. If, for example, you find conflicting accounts of the same event, you need to consider the possible biases of the authors. In general, the more a historian's conclusions are supported by public records such as deeds, marriage licenses, and newspaper accounts, the more reliable the conclusions are likely to be.

50b Understanding writing assignments in the humanities

Writing assignments in the humanities often require traditional academic essays that follow the conventional pattern of introduction, thesis statement, supporting paragraphs, and conclusion. An assignment may further refine the genre with one or more of the following words:

- Explain: for instance, show how a painter developed a particular technique or clarify a general's role in a historical battle.
- Argue: assert and defend an opinion—for instance, about the meaning of a poem or the causes of a historical event.
- Analyze: examine the elements of a philosophical argument or break down the causes of a historical event.
- Interpret: infer the meaning of a film from its images or the significance of a historical event from contemporary accounts of it.
- Synthesize: find a pattern in a composer's works or in a historical period.
- Evaluate: judge the quality of an architect's design or a historian's conclusions.

See Chapters 6 and 9 for discussion of these words.

50c

Student
paper

50c Using the tools and language of the humanities

The tools and language of the humanities vary according to the discipline. Major reference works in each field, such as those listed on the next four pages, can clarify specific tools you need and language you should use.

1 Writing tools

A useful tool for the arts is to ask a series of questions to analyze and evaluate a work. (A list of such questions for reading literature appears on pp. 763–64.) In any humanities discipline, a journal—a log of questions, reactions, and insights—can help you discover and record your thoughts. (See pp. 146–47 and 571–72.)

In history the tools are those of any thorough and efficient researcher, as discussed in Chapters 41–43: a system for finding and tracking sources; a methodical examination of sources, including evaluating and synthesizing them; a system for gathering source information; and a separate system, such as a research journal, for tracking one's own evolving thoughts.

2 Language considerations

Historians strive for precision and logic. They do not guess about what happened or speculate about "what if." They avoid trying to influence readers' opinions with words having strongly negative or positive connotations, such as *stupid* or *brilliant*. Instead, historians show the evidence and draw conclusions from that. Generally, they avoid using *I* because it tends to draw attention away from the evidence and toward the writer.

50c

Writing about history demands some attention to the tenses of verbs. To refer to events that occurred in the past, historians generally use the past tense, the present perfect tense, or the past perfect tense. They reserve the present tense only for statements about the present or statements of general truths. For example:

Franklin Delano Roosevelt <u>died</u> in 1945. [Simple past.]

He <u>had contracted</u> polio at age thirty-nine. [Past perfect.]

Many historians <u>have praised</u> Roosevelt as President. [Present perfect.]

Some of his economic reforms <u>persist</u> today, such as Social Security and unemployment compensation. [Present.]

See pages 311–17 for more on verb tenses.

3 Research sources

The following lists give resources in the humanities. (Resources for literature appear on pp. 766–67.)

Specialized encyclopedias, dictionaries, and bibliographies

The arts

Architecture: From Prehistory to Post-modernity
Baker Biographical Dictionary of Music
Dictionary of Art
Encyclopedia of World Art
Film Literature Index

Film Review Index
Garland Encyclopedia of World Music
Guide to the Literature of Art History 2
Guinness Encyclopedia of Popular Music
International Encyclopedia of Dance
International Television and Video Almanac
MLA International Bibliography
New Grove Dictionary of Music and Musicians
New Grove Dictionary of Opera
Oxford Art Online
Oxford Companion to Twentieth-Century Art

History

Afro-American Reference
American Decades
American Indian Studies: A Bibliographic Guide
Dictionary of American History
Dictionary of the Middle Ages
Encyclopedia of American History
Encyclopedia of Latin American History and Culture
Encyclopedia of Russian History
Encyclopedia of World History
Harvard Guide to American History
History: Illustrated Search Strategy and Sources
Middle East Abstracts and Index
New Cambridge Modern History
Oxford Classical Dictionary

50c

Philosophy and religion

Anchor Bible Dictionary
Catholic Encyclopedia
Dictionary of the History of Ideas
Encyclopedia Judaica
Encyclopedia of Asian Philosophy
Encyclopedia of Ethics
Encyclopedia of Philosophy
Encyclopedia of Religion
Oxford Dictionary of Islam
Oxford Dictionary of the Christian Church

Library databases and indexes

America: History and Life
Art Full Text
Art Index
Arts and Humanities Citation Index
ARTStor
ATLA Religion Database
Avery Index to Architectural Periodicals
Dissertation Abstracts International (doctoral dissertations)
Film Literature Index
Historical Abstracts
Humanities Index

IIMP (*International Index of Music Periodicals*)
Index Islamicus
Index of Jewish Periodicals
JSTOR
MLA International Bibliography
Music Index
Nineteenth-Century Masterfile
Philosopher's Index
PhilPapers: Online Research in Philosophy
RILM: Abstracts of Music Literature

Book reviews

Book Review Digest
Book Review Index

Sources on the open Web

General

EDSITEment (*edsitement.neh.gov*)
Infomine (*infomine.ucr.edu*)
ipl2 (*ipl.org/div/subject*)
Library of Congress: Performing Arts Reading Room (*www.doc.gov/rr/ perform/new.internet.resources.html*)
Voice of the Shuttle Humanities (*vos.ucsb.edu*)

Art

Art History Resources on the Web (*witcombe.sbc.edu/ARTHLinks .html*)
Artnet (*artnet.com*)
ArtSource (*www.ilpi.com/artsource/welcome.html*)
World Wide Arts Resources (*wwar.com/browse.html*)

Dance

Artslynx International Dance Resources (*www.artslynx.org/dance*)
Society of Dance History Scholars (*www.sdhs.org*)

Film

CinemaSpot (*cinemaspot.com*)
Film Studies on the Internet (*guides.library.ualberta.ca/filmstudies*)
Internet Movie Database (*imdb.com*)

History

American Memory (*memory.loc.gov*)
Best of History Web Sites (*besthistorysites.net*)
National Women's History Project (*nwhp.org*)

Music

MusicMoz (*musicmoz.org*)
Music Research Institute (*performingarts.uncg.edu/ music-research-institute*)
Music Theory Online (*mtosmt.org*)
Society for American Music (*american-music.org/resources/ ResourcesOnWeb.php*)

50c

Philosophy

Philosophy Documentation Center (pdcnet.org)
PhilPapers (philpapers.org)
Stanford Encyclopedia of Philosophy (plato.stanford.edu)
Voice of the Shuttle: Philosophy (vos.ucsb.edu)

Religion

Academic Info: Religion Gateway (academicinfo.net/religion.html)
Pluralism Project (pluralism.org/directory/index.php)
Religious Studies Web Guide (people.ucalgary.ca/~lipton)
Religious Worlds (www.religiousworlds.com/index.html)

Theater

McCoy's Brief Guide to Internet Resources in Theater and Performance Studies
    (www2.stetson.edu/csata/thr_guid.html)
TheatreHistory.com (theatrehistory.com)

50d Citing sources in Chicago style

Writers in the humanities generally rely on one of the following
guides for source-citation style:

The Chicago Manual of Style, 16th ed., 2010
A Manual for Writers of Research Papers, Theses, and Dissertations, by Kate
    L. Turabian, 7th ed., rev. Wayne C. Booth, Gregory G. Colomb, and
    Joseph M. Williams, 2007
MLA Handbook for Writers of Research Papers, 7th ed., 2009

The recommendations of the *MLA Handbook* are discussed
and illustrated in Chapter 46. Unless your instructor specifies otherwise, use these recommendations for papers in English and foreign languages. In history, art history, and many other disciplines,
however, writers rely on *The Chicago Manual of Style* or the student reference adapted from it, *A Manual for Writers.*

Both books detail two documentation styles. One, used mainly
by scientists and social scientists, closely resembles the style of the
American Psychological Association, covered in Chapter 51. The
other style, used more in the humanities, calls for footnotes or endnotes and an optional bibliography. This style is described below.

1 Using Chicago notes and a bibliography

In the Chicago note style, a raised numeral in the text refers
the reader to source information in an endnote or a footnote. In
these notes, the first citation of each source contains all the information readers need to find the source. Thus your instructor may
consider a bibliography optional because it provides much the
same information. Ask your instructor whether you should use

Chic
50d

footnotes or endnotes and whether you should include a bibliography.

For both footnotes and endnotes, use single spacing for each note and double spacing between notes, as shown in the samples below. (This is the spacing recommended by *A Manual for Writers*, the student guide. For manuscripts that will be published, *The Chicago Manual* recommends double spacing throughout.) Separate footnotes from the text with a short line. Place endnotes directly after the text, beginning on a new page. For a bibliography at the end of the paper, use the format on the facing page. Arrange the sources alphabetically by the authors' last names.

Chicago footnotes

Chicago endnotes

Chicago bibliography

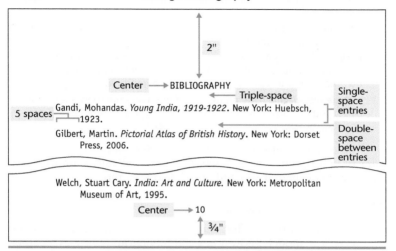

The examples below illustrate the essentials of a note and a bibliography entry.

Note

      6. Martin Gilbert, *Pictorial Atlas of British History* (New York: Dorset Press, 2006), 96.

Bibliography entry

Gilbert, Martin. *Pictorial Atlas of British History*. New York: Dorset Press, 2006.

Treat some features of notes and bibliography entries the same:

- Unless your instructor requests otherwise, single-space each note or entry, and double-space between them.
- Italicize the titles of books and periodicals.
- Enclose in quotation marks the titles of parts of books or articles in periodicals.
- Do not abbreviate publishers' names, but omit "Inc.," "Co.," and similar abbreviations.
- Do not use "p." or "pp." before page numbers.

Treat other features of notes and bibliography entries differently:

Note	Bibliography entry
Start with a number that corresponds to the note number in the text.	Do not begin with a number.
Indent the first line five spaces.	Indent the second and subsequent lines five spaces.

Note	Bibliography entry
Give the author's name in normal order.	Begin with the author's last name.
Use commas between elements such as author's name and title.	Use periods between elements.
Enclose a book's publication information in parentheses, with no preceding punctuation.	Precede a book's publication information with a period, and don't use parentheses.
Include the specific page number(s) you borrowed from, omitting "p." or "pp."	Omit page numbers except for parts of books or articles in periodicals.

You can instruct your computer to position footnotes at the bottoms of appropriate pages. It will also automatically number notes and renumber them if you add or delete one or more.

2 Following Chicago models

The Chicago models for common sources are indexed on the next page. The models show notes and bibliography entries together for easy reference. Be sure to use the numbered note form for notes and the unnumbered bibliography form for bibliography entries.

Listing authors

1. One, two, or three authors

1. Carol Gilligan, *In a Different Voice: Psychological Theory and Women's Development* (Cambridge: Harvard University Press, 1982), 27.

Gilligan, Carol. *In a Different Voice: Psychological Theory and Women's Development*. Cambridge: Harvard University Press, 1982.

1. Dennis L. Wilcox, Phillip H. Ault, and Warren K. Agee, *Public Relations: Strategies and Tactics*, 6th ed. (New York: Irwin, 2005), 182.

Wilcox, Dennis L., Phillip H. Ault, and Warren K. Agee. *Public Relations: Strategies and Tactics*. 6th ed. New York: Irwin, 2005.

2. More than three authors

2. Geraldo Lopez et al., *China and the West* (Boston: Little, Brown, 2004), 461.

Lopez, Geraldo, Judith P. Salt, Anne Ming, and Henry Reisen. *China and the West*. Boston: Little, Brown, 2004.

The Latin abbreviation et al. in the note means "and others."

3. Author not named (anonymous)

3. *The Dorling Kindersley World Atlas* (London: Dorling Kindersley, 2010), 150-51.

The Dorling Kindersley World Atlas. London: Dorling Kindersley, 2010.

Chicago note and bibliography models

Chic
50d

Listing print periodicals: Journals, newspapers, magazines

4. An article in a journal (print)

4. Janet Lever, "Sex Differences in the Games Children Play," *Social Problems* 23 (Spring 1996): 482.

Lever, Janet. "Sex Differences in the Games Children Play." *Social Problems* 23 (Spring 1996): 478-87.

For journals that are paginated continuously throughout an annual volume, include just the volume number or, for greater clarity, add the issue number, if any, or the month or season of publication. The month or season precedes the year of publication in parentheses, as above. The issue number follows the volume number:

4. Robert Bee, "The Importance of Preserving Paper-Based Artifacts in a Digital Age," *Library Quarterly* 78, no. 2 (2008): 176.

Bee, Robert. "The Importance of Preserving Paper-Based Artifacts in a Digital Age." *Library Quarterly* 78, no. 2 (2008): 174-94.

Note that the issue number and/or the month or season is required for any journal that pages issues separately or that numbers only issues, not volumes.

5. An article in a newspaper (print)

5. Reyhan Harmanci, "Literary Journals Thrive, on Paper and Otherwise," *New York Times*, April 8, 2011, national edition, A23.

Harmanci, Reyhan. "Literary Journals Thrive, on Paper and Otherwise." *New York Times*, April 8, 2011, national edition, A23.

Chicago style does not require page numbers for newspaper articles, whether in notes or in bibliography entries. Thus A23 could be omitted from the above examples.

6. An article in a magazine (print)

6. Edwidge Danticat, "A Year and a Day," *New Yorker*, January 17, 2011, 19.

Danticat, Edwidge. "A Year and a Day." *New Yorker*, January 17, 2011, 19-20.

Chicago bibliography style does not require inclusive page numbers for magazine articles, so 19-20 could be omitted from the preceding example.

7. A review (print)

7. John Gregory Dunne, "The Secret of Danny Santiago," review of *Famous All over Town,* by Danny Santiago, *New York Review of Books,* August 16, 1994, 25.

Dunne, John Gregory. "The Secret of Danny Santiago." Review of *Famous All over Town,* by Danny Santiago. *New York Review of Books,* August 16, 1994, 17-27.

Listing print books

8. Basic format for a book (print)

8. Barbara Ehrenreich, *Dancing in the Streets: A History of Collective Joy* (New York: Henry Holt, 2006), 97-117.

Ehrenreich, Barbara. *Dancing in the Streets: A History of Collective Joy.* New York: Henry Holt, 2006.

9. A book with an editor (print)

9. Hendrick Ruitenbeek, ed., *Freud as We Knew Him* (Detroit: Wayne State University Press, 1973), 64.

Ruitenbeek, Hendrick, ed. *Freud as We Knew Him*. Detroit: Wayne State University Press, 1973.

10. A book with an author and an editor (print)

10. Lewis Mumford, *The City in History,* ed. Donald L. Miller (New York: Pantheon, 1986), 216-17.

Mumford, Lewis. *The City in History*. Edited by Donald L. Miller. New York: Pantheon, 1986.

11. A translation (print)

11. Dante Alighieri, *The Inferno,* trans. John Ciardi (New York: New American Library, 1971), 51.

Alighieri, Dante. *The Inferno*. Translated by John Ciardi. New York: New American Library, 1971.

12. A later edition (print)

12. Dwight L. Bolinger, *Aspects of Language,* 3rd ed. (New York: Harcourt Brace Jovanovich, 1981), 20.

Bolinger, Dwight L. *Aspects of Language*. 3rd ed. New York: Harcourt Brace Jovanovich, 1981.

13. A work in more than one volume (print)

Citation of one volume without a title:

13. Abraham Lincoln, *The Collected Works of Abraham Lincoln,* ed. Roy P. Basler (New Brunswick: Rutgers University Press, 1953), 5:426-28.

Lincoln, Abraham. *The Collected Works of Abraham Lincoln*. Edited by Roy P. Basler. Vol. 5. New Brunswick: Rutgers University Press, 1953.

Citation of one volume with a title:

13. Linda B. Welkin, *The Age of Balanchine,* vol. 3 of *The History of Ballet* (New York: Columbia University Press, 1999), 56.

Welkin, Linda B. *The Age of Balanchine*. Vol. 3 of *The History of Ballet*. New York: Columbia University Press, 1999.

14. A selection from an anthology (print)

14. Rosetta Brooks, "Streetwise," in *The New Urban Landscape,* ed. Richard Martin (New York: Rizzoli, 2005), 38-39.

Brooks, Rosetta. "Streetwise." In *The New Urban Landscape,* edited by Richard Martin, 37-60. New York: Rizzoli, 2005.

15. A work in a series (print)

15. Ingmar Bergman, *The Seventh Seal,* Modern Film Scripts 12 (New York: Simon and Schuster, 1995), 27.

Bergman, Ingmar. *The Seventh Seal*. Modern Film Scripts 12. New York: Simon and Schuster, 1995.

16. An article in a reference work (print)

16. *Merriam-Webster's Collegiate Dictionary,* 11th ed., s.v. "reckon."

Merriam-Webster's Collegiate Dictionary. 11th ed. S.v. "reckon."

As in the example, use the abbreviation s.v. (Latin *sub verbo,* "under the word") for reference works that are alphabetically arranged.

Well-known works like the one listed in the example do not need publication information except for edition number. Chicago style generally recommends notes only, not bibliography entries, for reference works; a bibliography model is given here in case your instructor requires such entries.

Listing Web and other electronic sources

The Chicago Manual's models for documenting electronic sources mostly begin as those for print sources do. Then you add electronic publication information that will help readers locate the source. If one is available, give the Digital Object Identifier (DOI) for the source—a unique identifier that many publishers assign to periodical articles and other documents. (See model 17.) If no DOI is available, give the URL, as shown in models 18 and 19. If you retrieve an article from an online database, see model 20.

For Web pages and other electronic sources that are likely to change, *The Chicago Manual* suggests including the date of the most recent update in a statement beginning last modified (see model 22). If no date is available, give the date of your access (see model 23).

Note   Chicago style allows many ways to break DOIs and URLs at the ends of lines: after a colon or double slash and before a single slash, period, comma, hyphen, and most other marks. *Do not* break after a hyphen or add any hyphens.

Chic
50d

17. An article in a journal (Web)

17. Joseph J. Campos et al., "Reconceptualizing Emotion Regulation," *Emotion Review* 3, no. 1 (2011): 32, doi:10.1177/1754073910380975.

Campos, Joseph J., Eric A. Walle, Audun Dahl, and Alexandra Main. "Reconceptualizing Emotion Regulation." *Emotion Review* 3, no. 1 (2011): 26-35. doi:10.1177/1754073910380975.

Give a DOI if one is available (as here) or a URL if not (next two models).

18. An article in a magazine (Web)

18. Jan Swafford, "The Elusive Maestro," *Slate*, April 12, 2011, http://.www.slate.com/id/2291008.

Swafford, Jan. "The Elusive Maestro." *Slate*, April 12, 2011. http://www.slate.com/id/2291008.

19. An article in a newspaper (Web)

19. Elisabetta Povoledo, "The Little-Known Racing Legend underneath the Logo," *New York Times*, April 8, 2011, http://www.nytimes.com/2011/04/09/business/global/09iht-dallara09.html?hpw.

Povoledo, Elisabetta. "The Little-Known Racing Legend underneath the Logo." *New York Times*, April 8, 2011. http://www.nytimes.com/2011/04/09/business/global/09iht-dallara09.html?hpw.

20. An article in an online database (Web)

20. Jonathan Dickens, "Social Policy Approaches to Intercountry Adoption," *International Social Work* 52 (September 2009): 600, doi:10.1177 /0020872809337678.

Dickens, Jonathan. "Social Policy Approaches to Intercountry Adoption." *International Social Work* 52 (September 2009): 595-607. doi:10.1177 /0020872809337678.

If a database article has neither a DOI nor a URL that takes readers directly to the source, end with the name of the database:

20. Suzanne Penuel, "Missing Fathers: *Twelfth Night* and the Reformation of Mourning," *Studies in Philology* 107, no. 1 (2010): 82, Academic Search Complete.

Penuel, Suzanne. "Missing Fathers: *Twelfth Night* and the Reformation of Mourning." *Studies in Philology* 107, no. 1 (2010): 74-96. Academic Search Complete.

21. A book (Web)

21. Jane Austen, *Emma*, ed. R. W. Chapman (1816; Oxford: Clarendon, 1926; Oxford Text Archive, 2004), chap. 1, http://ota.ahds.ac.uk/Austen /Emma.1519.

Austen, Jane. *Emma*. Edited by R. W. Chapman. 1816. Oxford: Clarendon, 1926. Oxford Text Archive, 2004. http://ota.ahds.ac.uk/Austen/Emma.1519.

Provide print publication information, if any.

22. An article in a reference work (Web)

22. *Wikipedia*, s.v. "Wuhan," last modified March 31, 2011, http://en .wikipedia.org/wiki/Wuhan.

Wikipedia. S.v. "Wuhan." Last modified March 31, 2011. http://en.wikipedia .org/wiki/Wuhan.

Use the abbreviation s.v. (Latin *sub verbo*, "under the word") for reference works that are alphabetically arranged.

23. A Web page

23. "Toyota Safety," Toyota Motor Sales, accessed July 23, 2011, http://www.toyota.com/safety.

Toyota Motor Sales. "Toyota Safety." Accessed July 23, 2011. http://www .toyota.com/safety.

24. A message posted to a blog or discussion group (Web)

24. Sharyn Stein, "CFLs: Get the Whole Story," *Climate 411* (blog), January 31, 2011, http://blogs.edf.org/climate411/2011/01.

Stein, Sharyn. "CFLs: Get the Whole Story." *Climate 411* (blog). January 31, 2011. http://blogs.edf.org/climate411/2011/01.

24. Michael Tourville, "European Currency Reform," e-mail to International Finance discussion list, January 6, 2011, http://www.weg.isu.edu/finance-dl/archive/46732.

Tourville, Michael. "European Currency Reform." E-mail to International Finance discussion list. January 6, 2011. http://www.weg.isu.edu/finance-dl/archive/46732.

25. An audio or visual source (Web)

A work of art:

25. Jackson Pollock, *Shimmering Substance,* 1946, Museum of Modern Art, New York, http://moma.org/collection/conservation/pollock/shimmering_substance.html.

Pollock, Jackson. *Shimmering Substance.* 1946. Museum of Modern Art, New York. http://moma.org/collection/conservation/pollock/shimmering_substance.html.

See also model 33 to cite a work of art that you view in person.

A sound recording:

25. Ronald W. Reagan, "State of the Union Address," January 26, 1982, Vincent Voice Library, Digital and Multimedia Center, Michigan State University, http://www.lib.msu.edu/vincent/presidents/reagan.html.

Reagan, Ronald W. "State of the Union Address." January 26, 1982. Vincent Voice Library. Digital and Multimedia Center, Michigan State University. http://www.lib.msu.edu/vincent/presidents/reagan.html.

Chic
50d

A film or film clip:

25. Leslie J. Stewart, *96 Ranch Rodeo and Barbecue* (1951), 16mm, from Library of Congress, *Buckaroos in Paradise: Ranching Culture in Northern Nevada, 1945-1982,* MPEG, http://memory.loc.gov/cgi-bin/query.

Stewart, Leslie J. *96 Ranch Rodeo and Barbecue.* 1951. 16 mm. From Library of Congress, *Buckaroos in Paradise: Ranching Culture in Northern Nevada, 1945-1982.* MPEG. http://memory.loc.gov/cgi-bin/query.

26. A podcast (Web)

26. Ira Glass, "Very Tough Love," *This American Life,* podcast audio, March 25, 2011, http://www.thisamericanlife.org/radio-archives/episode/430/very-tough-love.

Glass, Ira. "Very Tough Love." *This American Life.* Podcast audio. March 25, 2011. http://www.thisamericanlife.org/radio-archives/episode/430/very-tough-love.

27. E-mail

25. Naomi Lee, "Re: Cairo," e-mail message to author, May 16, 2011.

Lee, Naomi. "Re: Cairo." E-mail message to author. May 16, 2011.

Chicago style generally recommends notes only, not bibliography entries, for personal communication. A bibliography model is given here in case your instructor requires such entries.

28. A work on CD-ROM or DVD-ROM

28. *The American Heritage Dictionary of the English Language,* 4th ed. (Boston: Houghton Mifflin, 2006), CD-ROM.

The American Heritage Dictionary of the English Language. 4th ed. Boston: Houghton Mifflin, 2006. CD-ROM.

Listing other sources

29. A government publication (print)

29. House Comm. on Agriculture, Nutrition, and Forestry, *Food and Energy Act of 2008,* 110th Cong., 2nd Sess., H.R. Doc. No. 884, at 21-22 (2008).

House Comm. on Agriculture, Nutrition, and Forestry. *Food and Energy Act of 2008.* 110th Cong. 2nd Sess., H.R. Doc. No. 884 (2008).

29. Hawaii Department of Education, *Kauai District Schools, Profile 2010-11* (Honolulu, 2011), 38.

Hawaii Department of Education. *Kauai District Schools, Profile 2010-11.* Honolulu, 2011.

30. A published letter (print)

30. Mrs. Laura E. Buttolph to Rev. and Mrs. C. C. Jones, June 20, 1857, in *The Children of Pride: A True Story of Georgia and the Civil War,* ed. Robert Manson Myers (New Haven, CT: Yale University Press, 1972), 334.

Buttolph, Laura E. Mrs. Laura E. Buttolph to Rev. and Mrs. C. C. Jones, June 20, 1857. In *The Children of Pride: A True Story of Georgia and the Civil War,* edited by Robert Manson Myers. New Haven, CT: Yale University Press, 1972.

31. A published or broadcast interview

31. Dexter Filkins, interview by Terry Gross, *Fresh Air,* NPR, April 6, 2011.

Filkins, Dexter. Interview by Terry Gross. *Fresh Air.* NPR. April 6, 2011.

32. A personal letter or interview

32. Ann E. Packer, letter to author, June 15, 2011.

Packer, Ann E. Letter to author. June 15, 2011.

32. Janelle White, interview by author, December 19, 2010.

White, Janelle. Interview by author. December 19, 2010.

33. A work of art

33. John Singer Sargent, *In Switzerland,* 1908, Metropolitan Museum of Art, New York.

Sargent, John Singer. *In Switzerland.* 1908. Metropolitan Museum of Art, New York.

34. A film, DVD, or video recording

34. George Balanchine, *Serenade,* San Francisco Ballet, performed February 2, 2000 (New York: PBS Video, 2006), DVD.

> Balanchine, George. *Serenade*. San Francisco Ballet. Performed February 2, 2000. New York: PBS Video, 2006, DVD.

35. A sound recording

> 35. Philip Glass, *String Quartet no. 5*, with Kronos Quartet, recorded 1991, Nonesuch 79356-2, 1995, compact disc.

> Glass, Philip. *String Quartet no. 5*, Kronos Quartet, Recorded 1991. Nonesuch 79356-2, 1995, compact disc.

Using shortened notes

To streamline documentation, Chicago style recommends shortened notes for sources that are fully cited elsewhere, either in a bibliography or in previous notes. Ask your instructor whether your paper should include a bibliography and, if so, whether you may use shortened notes for first references to sources as well as for subsequent references.

A shortened note contains the author's last name, the work's title (minus any initial *A*, *An*, or *The*), and the page number. Reduce long titles to four or fewer key words.

Complete note

> 4. Janet Lever, "Sex Differences in the Games Children Play," *Social Problems* 23 (Spring 1996): 482.

Complete bibliography entry

> Lever, Janet. "Sex Differences in the Games Children Play." *Social Problems* 23 (Spring 1996): 478-87.

Shortened note

> 12. Lever, "Sex Differences," 483.

You may use the Latin abbreviation ibid. (meaning "in the same place") to refer to the same source cited in the preceding note. Give a page number if it differs from that in the preceding note.

> 12. Lever, "Sex Differences," 483.
>
> 13. Gilligan, *In a Different Voice,* 92.
>
> 14. Ibid., 93.
>
> 15. Lever, "Sex Differences," 483.

Chicago style allows for in-text parenthetical citations when you cite one or more works repeatedly. In the following example, the raised number 2 refers to the source information in a note; the number in parentheses is a page number in the same source.

> British rule, observes Stuart Cary Welch, "seemed as permanent as Mount Everest."[2] Most Indians submitted, willingly or not, to British influence in every facet of life (42).

50e Formatting documents in Chicago style

Video tutorial

The following guidelines for document format come mainly from Turabian's *Manual for Writers*, which offers more specific advice than *The Chicago Manual* on the format of students' papers. See pages 786–87 for the format of footnotes, endnotes, and a bibliography. And see pages 120–23 for advice on type fonts, lists, illustrations, and other elements of document design.

Margins and spacing Use minimum one-inch margins on all pages of the body. (The first page of endnotes or the bibliography begins two inches from the top; see pp. 786–87.) Double-space your own text and between notes and bibliography entries; single-space displayed quotations (see below and the next page) and each note and bibliography entry.

First page of Chicago paper

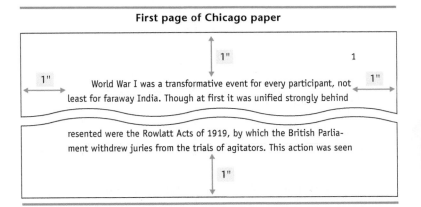

Paging Number pages consecutively from the first text page through the end (endnotes or bibliography). Use Arabic numerals (1, 2, 3) in the upper right corner of all pages except the first page of endnotes and first page of bibliography. On those pages, the number falls at the foot of the page (see pp. 786–87).

Title page On an unnumbered title page provide the title of the paper, your name, the course title, your instructor's name, and the date. (See the sample on the next page.) Use all capital letters only for the paper's title, and center everything horizontally. Single-space between adjacent lines.

Poetry and long prose quotations Display certain quotations separately from your text: three or more lines of poetry and two or more sentences of prose. Indent a displayed quotation four spaces from the left, single-space the quotation, and double-space both above it and below it. *Do not add quotation marks.*

Chic
50e

Chicago title page

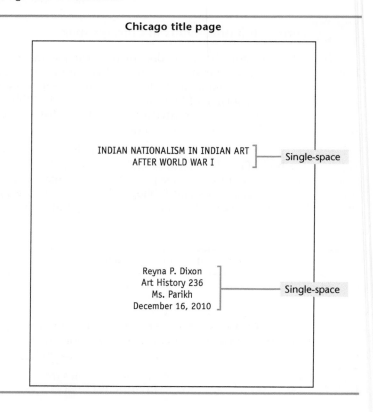

INDIAN NATIONALISM IN INDIAN ART
AFTER WORLD WAR I
— Single-space

Reyna P. Dixon
Art History 236
Ms. Parikh
December 16, 2010
— Single-space

The following example shows the format of a displayed quotation:

Gandhi articulated the principles of his movement in 1922:

> I discovered that pursuit of truth did not permit violence being inflicted on one's opponent, but that he must be weaned from error by patience and sympathy. For what appears to be truth to one may appear to be error to the other. And patience means self-suffering.[9]

51

Writing in the Social Sciences

The social sciences—including anthropology, economics, education, management, political science, psychology, and sociology—focus on the study of human behavior. As the name implies, the social sciences examine the way human beings relate to themselves, to their environment, and to one another.

Exercise

51a Using the methods and evidence of the social sciences

Researchers in the social sciences systematically pose a question, formulate a **hypothesis** (a generalization that can be tested), collect data, analyze those data, and draw conclusions to support, refine, or disprove their hypothesis. This is the scientific method developed in the natural sciences (see p. 830).

Social scientists gather data in several ways:

- They interview subjects about their attitudes and behavior, recording responses in writing or electronically. (See pp. 608–09 for guidelines on conducting an interview.)
- They conduct broader surveys using questionnaires, asking people about their attitudes and behavior. (See pp. 609–10 for guidelines on conducting a survey.)
- They make firsthand observations of human behavior, recording the observations in writing or electronically. (See p. 610 for guidelines on conducting an observation.)
- They conduct controlled experiments, structuring an environment in which to encourage and measure a specific behavior.

In their writing, social scientists explain their own research or analyze and evaluate others' research.

Social science research methods generate two kinds of data:

- *Quantitative data* are numerical, such as statistical evidence based on surveys, polls, tests, and experiments. When public-opinion

Visit *mycomplab.com* for the eText and for resources and exercises on writing in the social sciences.

pollsters announce that 47% of US citizens polled approve of the President's leadership, they are offering quantitative data gained from a survey. Social science writers present quantitative data in graphs, charts, and other illustrations that accompany their text.

- *Qualitative data* are not numerical but more subjective: they are based on interviews, firsthand observations, and inferences, taking into account the subjective nature of human experience. Examples include an anthropologist's description of the initiation rites in a culture she is studying or a psychologist's interpretation of interviews he conducted with a group of adolescents.

51b Understanding writing assignments in the social sciences

Student paper

51c

Depending on what social science courses you take, you may be asked to write in a variety of genres:

- A summary or review of research reports on the available research literature on a subject, such as infants' perception of color.
- A case analysis explains the components of a phenomenon, such as a factory closing.
- A problem-solving analysis explains the components of a problem, such as unreported child abuse, and suggests ways to solve it.
- A research paper interprets and sometimes analyzes and evaluates the writings of other social scientists about a subject, such as the effect of national appeals in advertising. An example appears in Chapter 47, pages 718–45.
- A research report explains the author's own original research or the author's attempt to replicate someone else's research. A research report begins on page 826.

Many social science disciplines have special requirements for the content and organization of each kind of assignment. The requirements appear in the style guides of the disciplines, listed on page 804. For instance, the American Psychological Association specifies the outline for research reports that is illustrated on pages 826–29. Because of the differences among disciplines and even among different kinds of papers in the same discipline, you should always ask your instructor what he or she requires for an assignment.

51c Using the tools and language of the social sciences

The following guidelines for tools and language apply to most social sciences. However, the particular discipline you are writing in, or an instructor in a particular course, may have additional requirements. Many of the research sources listed on the next several pages illustrate the disciplines' conventions.

1 Writing tools

Many social scientists rely on a **research journal** or **log**, in which they record their ideas throughout the research-writing process. Even if a research journal is not required in your courses, you may want to use one. As you begin formulating a hypothesis, you can record preliminary questions. Then when you are in the field conducting research, you can use the journal to react to the evidence you are collecting, to record changes in your perceptions and ideas, and to assess your progress. (See pp. 146–47 and 571–72 for more on journals.)

To avoid confusing your reflections on the evidence with the evidence itself, keep records of actual data—notes from interviews, observations, surveys, and experiments—separately from the journal.

2 Language considerations

Each social science discipline has specialized terminology for concepts basic to the discipline. In sociology, for example, the words *mechanism, identity,* and *deviance* have specific meanings different from those of everyday usage. And *identity* means something different in sociology, where it applies to groups of people, than in psychology, where it applies to the individual. Social scientists also use precise terms to describe or interpret research. For instance, they say *The subject expressed a feeling of* rather than *The subject felt* because human feelings are not knowable for certain; or they say *These studies indicate* rather than *These studies prove* because conclusions are only tentative.

Just as social scientists strive for objectivity in their research, they also strive to demonstrate their objectivity through language in their writing. They avoid expressions such as *I think* in order to focus attention on what the evidence shows, not the researcher's opinions. For the same reason, they also generally use the passive voice of verbs to describe their methods and results, as in *The subjects' responses were recorded.* (However, many social scientists prefer *I* to *the researcher* when they refer to their own actions, as in *I recorded the subjects' responses.* Ask your instructor for his or her preferences.) Social scientists also avoid direct or indirect expression of their personal biases or emotions, either in discussions of other researchers' work or in descriptions of research subjects. Thus one social scientist does not call another's work *sloppy* or *immaculate* and does not refer to his or her own subjects as *drunks* or *innocent victims.* Instead, the writer uses neutral language and ties conclusions strictly to the data.

51c

51c

3 Research sources

The following lists give resources in social sciences.

Specialized encyclopedias, dictionaries, and bibliographies

General
International Bibliography of the Social Sciences
International Encyclopedia of the Social and Behavioral Sciences
Dictionary of the Social Sciences

Business and economics
Advertising Age Encyclopedia of Advertising
Blackwell Encyclopedia of Management
Dictionary of Business and Management
Encyclopedia of Banking and Finance
Encyclopedia of Business Information Sources
McGraw-Hill Encyclopedia of Economics
The MIT Dictionary of Modern Economics
The New Palgrave Dictionary of Economics and the Law

Education
Encyclopedia of American Education
Encyclopedia of Education
Encyclopedia of Educational Research
The Philosophy of Education: An Encyclopedia

Political science and law
Black's Law Dictionary
Encyclopedia of Government and Politics
Information Sources of Political Science
Oxford Companion to American Law
West's Encyclopedia of American Law

Psychology, sociology, and anthropology
APA Dictionary of Psychology
Blackwell Dictionary of Sociology
Countries and Their Culture
Encyclopedia of Anthropology
Encyclopedia of Crime and Justice
Encyclopedia of North American Indians
Encyclopedia of Psychology
Encyclopedia of Sociology
Handbook of Psychology
Macmillan Dictionary of Anthropology
Race and Ethnic Relations
Sage Handbook of Sociology

Library databases and indexes

ABI/INFORM (business)
Abstracts in Anthropology
Anthropology Plus
AnthroSource
Business Periodicals Index
Business Source Premier

Communication and Mass Media Complete
Contemporary Women's Issues
Counseling and Therapy in Video
Criminal Justice Periodicals
Digital National Security Archive
Dissertation Abstracts International (doctoral dissertations)
EconLit
Education Index
Educational Resources Information Center (ERIC)
GenderWatch
Hispanic American Periodicals Index
Human Resources Abstracts
Index to Legal Periodicals
International Political Science Abstracts
Left Index
LexisNexis Academic Universe (legal publications and news sources)
National Bureau of Economic Research
PAIS International (government publications and political science journals)
PsycINFO
Social Sciences Index
Sociological Abstracts
Urban Affairs Abstracts
Wilson Business Abstracts
Worldwide Political Science Abstracts

51c

Book reviews

Index to Book Reviews in the Social Sciences

Sources on the open Web

General

Infomine (*infomine.ucr.edu*)
ipl2 (*ipl.org*)
WWW Virtual Library (*vlib.org*)

Anthropology

American Anthropological Association (*aaanet.org*)
American Folklife Center (*loc.gov/folklife*)
Anthropology Review Database (*wings.buffalo.edu/ARD*)
National Anthropological Archives (*www.nmnh.si.edu/naa*)

Business and economics

Biz/ed (*www.bized.co.uk/learn/index.html*)
globalEDGE (*globaledge.msu.edu*)
Resources for Economists on the Internet (*rfe.org*)

Education

Educator's Reference Desk (*eduref.org*)
The Gateway to 21st Century Skills (*thegateway.org*)
Annenberg Learner (*learner.org*)
US Department of Education (*ed.gov*)

Ethnic and gender studies

Gender Inn (*www.uni-koeln.de/phil-fak/englisch/datenbank/e_index.htm*)

*Internet Resources for Ethnic Studies (www2.lib.udel.edu/subj/ethst/
    internet.htm)*
*National Women's History Project Resource Center (www.nwhp.org/
    resourcecenter/index.php)*
Voice of the Shuttle: Gender Studies (vos.ucsb.edu)
Women and Gender Studies Web Sites (libr.org/wss/wsslinks)

Political science and law
Legal Information Institute (www.law.cornell.edu)
US Supreme Court Media (www.oyez.org)
Political Science Resources (politicsresources.net)
Thomas Legislative Information on the Internet (thomas.loc.gov)
Ultimate Political Science Links (upslinks.net)

Psychology
Encyclopedia of Psychology (www.psychology.org)
National Institute of Mental Health (www.nimh.nih.gov)
PsychCentral (psychcentral.com)
Psych Web (psywww.com)

Sociology
SocioSite (sociosite.net)
SocioWeb (socioweb.com)

51d Citing sources in APA style

Video tutorial

Some of the social sciences publish style guides that advise practitioners how to organize, document, and type papers in those fields. The following is a partial list:

American Anthropological Association, *AAA Style Guide,* 2009 (*www.aaanet
    .org/publications/guidelines.cfm*)
American Political Science Association, *Style Manual for Political Science,*
    2006 (*www.ipsonet.org/data/files/APSAStyleManual2006.pdf*)
American Psychological Association, *Publication Manual of the American
    Psychological Association,* 6th ed., 2010
American Sociological Association, *ASA Style Guide,* 4th ed., 2010
Linguistic Society of America, "LSA Style Sheet," published every Decem-
    ber in *LSA Bulletin*
A Uniform System of Citation (law), 19th ed., 2010

APA
51d

By far the most widely used style is that of the American Psycholog-ical Association (APA), so we detail it here. Always ask your instruc-tor in any class whether to use APA or another style.

Note The APA provides answers to frequently asked questions at *www.apastyle.org/learn/faqs/index.aspx.*

1 Using APA parenthetical text citations

In APA documentation style, parenthetical citations within the text refer the reader to a list of sources at the end of the text. A parenthetical citation contains the author's last name, the date of

APA parenthetical text citations

1. Author not named in your text *805*
2. Author named in your text *805*
3. A work with two authors *806*
4. A work with three to five authors *806*
5. A work with six or more authors *806*
6. A work with a group author *806*
7. A work with no author or an anonymous work *807*
8. One of two or more works by the same author(s) *807*
9. Two or more works by different authors *807*
10. An indirect source *807*
11. An electronic source *807*

publication, and sometimes the page number from which material is borrowed.

Note When you cite the same source more than once in a paragraph, APA style does not require you to repeat the date beyond the first citation as long as it's clear what source you refer to. Do give the date in every citation if your source list includes more than one work by the same author(s).

1. Author not named in your text

One critic of Milgram's experiments questions whether the researchers behaved morally toward their subjects (Baumrind, 1988).

When you do not name the author in your text, place in parentheses the author's last name, the date of the source, and sometimes the page number as explained below. Separate the elements with commas. Position the reference so that it is clear what material is being documented *and* so that the reference fits as smoothly as possible into your sentence structure. (See pp. 673–74 for guidelines.)

Unless none is available, the APA requires a page or other identifying number for a direct quotation and recommends an identifying number for a paraphrase:

In the view of one critic of Milgram's experiments (Baumrind, 1988), the subjects "should have been fully informed of the possible effects on them" (p. 34).

Use an appropriate abbreviation before the number—for instance, p. for *page* and para. for *paragraph*. The identifying number may fall by itself in parentheses, as in the preceding example, or it may fall with the author and date: (Baumrind, 1988, p. 34). See also model 11, page 807.

2. Author named in your text

Baumrind (1988) insisted that the subjects in Milgram's study "should have been fully informed of the possible effects on them" (p. 34).

When you use the author's name in the text, do not repeat it in the reference. Place the source date in parentheses after the author's

APA
51d

name. Place any page or paragraph reference either after the borrowed material (as in the example) or with the date: (1988, p. 34).

3. A work with two authors

Bunning and Ellis (2010) revealed significant communication differences between teachers and students.

One study (Bunning & Ellis, 2010) revealed significant communication differences between teachers and students.

When given in the text, two authors' names are connected by and. In a parenthetical citation, they are connected by an ampersand, &.

4. A work with three to five authors

Pepinsky, Dunn, Rentl, and Corson (1999) demonstrated the biases evident in gestures.

In the first citation of a work with three to five authors, name all the authors.

In the second and subsequent references to a work with three to five authors, generally give only the first author's name, followed by et al. (Latin abbreviation for "and others"):

In the work of Pepinsky et al. (1999), the loaded gestures included head shakes and eye contact.

However, two or more sources published in the same year could shorten to the same form—for instance, two references shortening to Pepinsky et al., 1999. In that case, cite the last names of as many authors as you need to distinguish the sources, and then give et al.: for instance, (Pepinsky, Dunn, et al., 1999) and (Pepinsky, Bradley, et al., 1999).

5. A work with six or more authors

One study (McCormack et al., 2010) explored children's day-to-day experience of living with a speech impairment.

For six or more authors, even in the first citation of the work, give only the first author's name, followed by et al. If two or more sources published in the same year shorten to the same form, give additional names as explained with model 4.

6. A work with a group author

The students' later work improved significantly (Lenschow Research, 2009).

For a work that lists an institution, agency, corporation, or other group as author, treat the name of the group as if it were one person's name. If the name is long and has a familiar abbreviation, you may use the abbreviation in the second and subsequent citations. For example, you might abbreviate American Psychological Association as APA.

7. A work with no author or an anonymous work

One article ("Leaping the Wall," 2011) examines Internet freedom and censorship in China.

For a work with no named author, use the first two or three words of the title in place of an author's name, excluding an initial *The, A,* or *An.* Italicize book and journal titles, place quotation marks around article titles, and capitalize the significant words in all titles cited in the text. (In the reference list, however, do not use quotation marks for article titles, and capitalize only the first word in all but periodical titles. See p. 809.)

For a work that lists "Anonymous" as the author, use that word in the citation: (Anonymous, 2011).

8. One of two or more works by the same author(s)

At about age seven, most children begin to use appropriate gestures to reinforce their stories (Gardner, 1973a).

When you cite one of two or more works by the same author(s), the date will tell readers which source you mean—as long as your reference list includes only one source published by the author(s) in that year. If your reference list includes two or more works published by the same author(s) *in the same year,* the works should be lettered in the reference list (see p. 811). Then your text citation should include the appropriate letter with the date: 1973a above.

9. Two or more works by different authors

Two studies (Marconi & Hamblen, 1999; Torrence, 2007) found that monthly safety meetings can dramatically reduce workplace injuries.

List the sources in alphabetical order by their authors' names. Insert a semicolon between sources.

10. An indirect source

Supporting data appeared in a study by Wong (as cited in Gallivan, 2011).

The phrase as cited in indicates that the reference to Wong's study was found in Gallivan. Only Gallivan then appears in the list of references.

11. An electronic source

Ferguson and Hawkins (2006) did not anticipate the "evident hostility" of participants (para. 6).

Electronic sources can be cited like printed sources, usually with the author's last name and the publication date. When quoting or paraphrasing electronic sources that number paragraphs instead of pages, provide the paragraph number preceded by para. If the

APA
51d

source does not number pages or paragraphs but does include headings, list the heading under which the quotation appears and then (counting paragraphs yourself) the number of the paragraph in which the quotation appears—for example, (Endter & Decker, 2010, Method section, para. 3). When the source does not number pages or paragraphs or provide frequent headings, omit any reference number.

2 | Using an APA reference list

In APA style, the in-text parenthetical citations refer readers to the list of sources at the end of the text. Title this list References and include in it the full publication information for every source you cited in your paper. Place the list at the end of the paper, and number its page(s) in sequence with the preceding pages.

The following sample shows the format of the first page of the APA reference list:

APA reference list

DATING VIOLENCE ON CAMPUS ← Header and page number (see p. 823) → 8

↕ ½"

References ← Center

½" or 5–7 spaces Cates, R. L., Rutter, C. H., Karl, J., Linton, M., & Smith, K. (2000). Premarital abuse: A social psychological perspective. *Journal of Family Issues, 13*(1), 79-90.

1" → Cortes, L. (2009). Beyond date rape: Violence during courtship. *Electronic Journal of Intimate Violence, 5*(2). Retrieved from http://www.ejiv.org

Glaser, R., & Rutter, C. H. (Eds.). (1999). Familial violence [Special issue]. *Family Relations, 38*(4).

Double-space

1"

APA 51d

Arrangement Arrange sources alphabetically by the author's last name. If there is no author, alphabetize by the first main word of the title.

Spacing Double-space everything in the references, as shown in the sample, unless your instructor requests single spacing. (If you do single-space the entries themselves, always double-space *between* them.)

Indention As illustrated in the sample, begin each entry at the left margin, and indent the second and subsequent lines five to seven spaces or one-half inch. Your word processor can create this so-called hanging indent automatically.

Punctuation Separate the parts of the reference (author, date, title, and publication information) with a period and one space. Do not use a final period in references that conclude with a DOI or URL (see pp. 815–16).

Authors For works with up to seven authors, list all authors with last name first, separating names and parts of names with commas. Use initials for first and middle names even when names are listed fully on the source itself. Use an ampersand (&) before the last author's name. See model 3, page 811, for the treatment of eight or more authors.

Publication date Place the publication date in parentheses after the author's or authors' names, followed by a period. Generally, this date is the year only, though for some sources (such as magazine and newspaper articles) it includes the month and sometimes the day as well.

Titles In titles of books and articles, capitalize only the first word of the title, the first word of the subtitle, and proper nouns; all other words begin with small letters. In titles of journals, capitalize all significant words (see p. 505 for guidelines). Italicize the titles of books and journals. Do not italicize or use quotation marks around the titles of articles.

City and state of publication For sources that are not periodicals (such as books or government publications), give the city of publication, a comma, the two-letter postal abbreviation of the state, and a colon. Omit the state if the publisher is a university whose name includes the state name, such as University of Arizona.

Publisher's name Also for nonperiodical sources, give the publisher's name after the place of publication and a colon. Shorten names of many publishers (such as Morrow for William Morrow), and omit *Co.*, *Inc.*, and *Publishers*. However, give full names for associations, corporations, and university presses (such as Harvard University Press), and do not omit *Books* or *Press* from a publisher's name.

Page numbers Use the abbreviation p. or pp. before page numbers in books and in newspapers. Do *not* use the abbreviation for journals and magazines. For inclusive page numbers, include all figures: 667-668.

Digital Object Identifier (DOI) Many publishers assign a DOI to journal articles and other documents. A DOI functions as a unique identifier and link to the text. When a DOI is available, include it in your source citation. (For example, see model 7, p. 812.) Do not add a period at the end of a DOI.

See the next page for an index to APA reference-list models. If you don't see a model for the kind of source you used, try to find one that comes close, and provide ample information so that readers can trace the source. Often you will have to combine models to cite a source accurately.

APA

51d

APA reference-list models

Listing authors

1. One author

Rodriguez, R. (1982). *A hunger of memory: The education of Richard Rodriguez.*
    Boston, MA: Godine.

The initial R. appears instead of the author's first name, even though the author's full first name appears on the source. In this book title, only the first words of the title and subtitle and the proper name are capitalized.

2. Two to seven authors

Nesselroade, J. R., & Baltes, P. B. (1999). *Longitudinal research in behavioral studies.* New York, NY: Academic Press.

With two to seven authors, separate authors' names with commas and use an ampersand (&) before the last author's name.

3. Eight or more authors

Wimple, P. B., Van Eijk, M., Potts, C. A., Hayes, J., Obergau, W. R., Smith, H., . . . Zimmer, S. (2001). *Case studies in moral decision making among adolescents.* San Francisco, CA: Jossey-Bass.

For a work by eight or more authors, list the first six authors' names, insert an ellipsis mark (three spaced periods), and then give the last author's name.

4. A group author

Lenschow Research. (2009). *Trends in secondary curriculum.* Baltimore, MD: Arrow Books.

For a work with a group author—such as a research group, a committee, a government agency, or a corporation—begin the entry with the group name. In the reference list, alphabetize the work as if the first main word (excluding any *The, A,* or *An*) were an author's last name.

5. Author not named (anonymous)

Merriam-Webster's collegiate dictionary (11th ed.). (2008). Springfield, MA: Merriam-Webster.

The Conversation. (2011, April 11). *Time, 177*(14), 4.

When no author is named, list the work under its title and alphabetize it by the first main word (excluding any *The, A, An*).

For a work whose author is actually given as "Anonymous," use that word in place of the author's name and alphabetize it as if it were a name:

Anonymous. (2006). *Teaching research, researching teaching.* New York, NY: Alpine Press.

6. Two or more works by the same author(s) published in the same year

Gardner, H. (1973a). *The arts and human development.* New York, NY: Wiley.

Gardner, H. (1973b). *The quest for mind: Piaget, Lévi-Strauss, and the structuralist movement.* New York, NY: Knopf.

When citing two or more works by exactly the same author(s), published in the same year, arrange them alphabetically by the first main word of the title and distinguish the sources by adding a letter to the date. Both the date and the letter are used in citing the source in your text (see p. 807).

When citing two or more works by exactly the same author(s) but *not* published in the same year, arrange the sources in order of their publication dates, earliest first.

Listing print periodicals: Journals, newspapers, magazines

7. An article in a journal (print)

Campos, J. J., Walle, E. A., Dahl, A., & Main, A. (2011). Reconceptualizing emotion regulation. *Emotion Review, 3,* 26-35. doi:10.1177 /1754073910380975

Pages 814–15 show the basic format for a print journal article and the location of the required information in the journal.

Note Some journals number the pages of issues consecutively throughout a year, so that each issue after the first begins numbering where the previous issue left off—say, at page 132 or 416. For this kind of journal, give the volume number after the title, as above. The page numbers are enough to guide readers to the issue you used. Other journals and most magazines start each issue with page 1. For these journals and magazines, place the issue number in parentheses and not italicized immediately after the volume number. See model 10.

8. An abstract of a journal article (print)

Emery, R. E. (2006). Marital turmoil: Interpersonal conflict and the children of discord and divorce. *Psychological Bulletin, 92,* 310-330. Abstract obtained from *Psychological Abstracts,* 2007, *69,* Item 1320.

When you cite the abstract of an article rather than the article itself, give full publication information for the article, followed by Abstract obtained from and the information for the collection of abstracts, including title, date, volume and issue numbers, and either page number or other reference number (Item 1320 in the example).

9. An article in a newspaper (print)

Wade, N. (2011, April 15). Ancient clicks hint language is Africa-born. *The New York Times,* pp. A1, A3.

Give month *and* day along with year of publication. Use *The* in the newspaper name if the paper itself does. Precede the page number(s) with p. or pp.

10. An article in a magazine (print)

Walsh, B. (2011, April 11). The gas dilemma. *Time, 177*(14), 40-48.

Give the full date of the issue: year, followed by a comma, month, and day (if any). Give all page numbers even when the article appears

APA 51d

on discontinuous pages, without "pp." If a magazine has volume and issue numbers, provide both because magazine issues are paginated separately. (See the note in model 7.)

11. A review (print)

Dinnage, R. (1987, November 29). Against the master and his men [Review of the book *A mind of her own: The life of Karen Horney*, by S. Quinn]. *The New York Times Book Review*, 10-11.

If the review is not titled, use the bracketed information as the title, keeping the brackets.

Listing print books

12. Basic format for a book (print)

Ehrenreich, B. (2007). *Dancing in the streets: A history of collective joy*. New York, NY: Holt.

Give the author's or authors' names, following models 1–4. Then give the complete title, including any subtitle. Italicize the title, and capitalize only the first words of the title and subtitle. End the entry with the city and state of publication and the publisher's name. (See p. 785 for how to treat these elements.)

13. A book with an editor (print)

Dohrenwend, B. S., & Dohrenwend, B. P. (Eds.). (1999). *Stressful life events: Their nature and effects*. New York, NY: Wiley.

List the editors' names as if they were authors, but follow the last name with (Eds.).—or (Ed.). with only one editor. Note the periods inside and outside the final parenthesis.

14. A book with a translator (print)

Trajan, P. D. (1927). *Psychology of animals* (H. Simone, Trans.). Washington, DC: Halperin.

The name of the translator appears in parentheses after the title, followed by a comma, Trans., a closing parenthesis, and a final period.

15. A later edition (print)

Bolinger, D. L. (1981). *Aspects of language* (3rd ed.). New York, NY: Harcourt Brace Jovanovich.

The edition number in parentheses follows the title and is followed by a period.

16. A work in more than one volume (print)

Lincoln, A. (1953). *The collected works of Abraham Lincoln* (R. P. Basler, Ed.). (Vol. 5). New Brunswick, NJ: Rutgers University Press.

Format for a print journal article

Journal cover

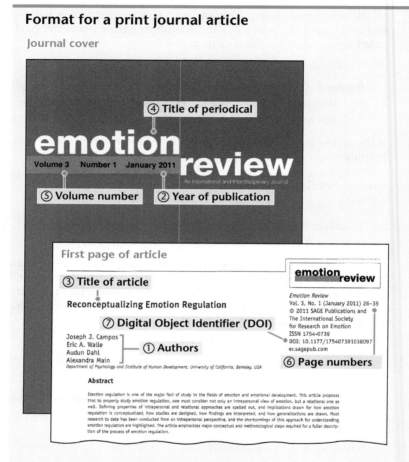

④ **Title of periodical**

emotion
Volume 3 Number 1 January 2011 **review**
An International and Interdisciplinary Journal

⑤ **Volume number**   ② **Year of publication**

First page of article

③ **Title of article**

Reconceptualizing Emotion Regulation

⑦ **Digital Object Identifier (DOI)**

Joseph J. Campos
Eric A. Walle
Audun Dahl   ① **Authors**
Alexandra Main
Department of Psychology and Institute of Human Development, University of California, Berkeley, USA

emotion review

Emotion Review
Vol. 3, No. 1 (January 2011) 26–35
© 2011 SAGE Publications and
The International Society
for Research on Emotion
ISSN 1754-0739
DOI: 10.1177/17540739103809 7
er.sagepub.com

⑥ **Page numbers**

Abstract

Emotion regulation is one of the major foci of study in the fields of emotion and emotional development. This article proposes that to properly study emotion regulation, one must consider not only an intrapersonal view of emotion, but a relational one as well. Defining properties of intrapersonal and relational approaches are spelled out, and implications drawn for how emotion regulation is conceptualized, how studies are designed, how findings are interpreted, and how generalizations are drawn. Most research to date has been conducted from an intrapersonal perspective, and the shortcomings of this approach for understanding emotion regulation are highlighted. The article emphasizes major conceptual and methodological steps required for a fuller description of the process of emotion regulation.

APA
51d

Lincoln, A. (1953). *The collected works of Abraham Lincoln* (R. P. Basler, Ed.). (Vols. 1-8). New Brunswick, NJ: Rutgers University Press.

The entry on the previous page cites a single volume (5) in the eight-volume set. The entry above cites all eight volumes. Use Vol. or Vols. in parentheses and follow the closing parenthesis with a period. In the absence of an editor's name, this description would follow the title directly: *The collected works of Abraham Lincoln* (Vol. 5).

17. An article or a chapter in an edited book (print)

Paykel, E. S. (1999). Life stress and psychiatric disorder: Applications of the clinical approach. In B. S. Dohrenwend & B. P. Dohrenwend (Eds.), *Stressful life events: Their nature and effects* (pp. 239-264). New York, NY: Wiley.

①
Campos, J. J., Walle, E. A., Dahl, A., & Main, A. (2011).
③   ④   ⑤
Reconceptualizing emotion regulation. *Emotion Review, 3,*
⑥   ⑦
26-35. doi:10.1177/1754073910380975

① **Authors.** Give each author's last name, first initial, and any middle initial. Separate names from initials with commas, and use &
before the last author's name. Omit *Dr., PhD,* or any other title.
See models 1–4 (pp. 810–11) for how to cite single and multiple
authors.

② **Year of publication,** in parentheses and followed by a period.

③ **Title of article.** Give the full article title and any subtitle, separating them with a colon. Capitalize only the first words of the title
and subtitle, and do not place the title in quotation marks.

④ **Title of periodical,** in italics. Capitalize all significant words and
end with a comma.

⑤ **Volume number,** italicized and followed by a comma. Include
just the volume number when all the issues in each annual volume are paginated in one sequence. Include the issue number
only when the issues are paginated separately.

⑥ **Inclusive page numbers of article,** without "pp." Do not omit
any numerals.

⑦ **Digital Object Identifier (DOI).** If the print article lists a DOI,
give it at the end with no period. (See p. 809 for more on
DOIs.)

APA
51d

Give the publication date of the collection (1999 here) as the publication date of the article or chapter. After the article or chapter title
and a period, say In and then provide the editors' names (in normal
order), (Eds.) and a comma, the title of the collection, and the page
numbers of the article in parentheses.

Listing Web and other electronic sources

In APA style, most electronic references begin as those for print
references do: author, date, title. Then you add information on how
to retrieve the source.

■ Give a source's **Digital Object Identifier (DOI),** not the URL, when
a DOI is available. You may find the DOI on the source or by

clicking on "Article" or "Cross-Ref." See models 18, 23, and 25 for examples of DOIs.

- ▪ **Give the URL when a DOI is not available.** Provide the URL in a statement beginning Retrieved from. For most sources, use the home page URL of the Web site where your source can be found. (See models 19 and 22.) Use the complete URL only if the source is hard to find from the home page. (See model 32.)
- ▪ **Do not add a period after a DOI or a URL.**
- ▪ **Break a DOI or URL from one line to the next only before punctuation,** such as a period or a slash. (But break after the two slashes in http://.) Do not hyphenate a URL or a DOI.
- ▪ **Generally, do not provide the date of your access.** Give the date only if the source is likely to change or if it lacks a publication date or version number. See model 29 for use of an access date.

If you don't see a model for your particular source, consult the index of models on page 810 for a similar source type whose format you can adapt. If your source does not include all of the information needed for a complete citation, find and list what you can.

18. A journal article with a Digital Object Identifier (DOI) (Web)

Cunningham, J. A., & Selby, P. (2007). Relighting cigarettes: How common is it? *Nicotine and Tobacco Research, 9*, 621-623. doi:10.1080 /14622200701239688

Pages 818–19 show the basic format for a periodical article that you access either directly online or through an online database, as well as the location of the required information on the source.

19. A journal article without a DOI (Web)

Polletta, F. (2008). Just talk: Public deliberation after 9/11. *Journal of Public Deliberation, 4*(1). Retrieved from http://services.bepress.com/jpd

When a journal article does not have a DOI, give the URL of the journal's home page in a statement beginning Retrieved from. Do not add a period at the end of the URL.

20. A periodical article in an online database (Web)

Rosen, I. M., Maurer, D. M., & Darnall, C. R. (2008). Reducing tobacco use in adolescents. *American Family Physician, 77*, 483-490. Retrieved from http://www.aafp.org/online/en/home/publications/journals/afp.html

Generally, do not give the name of the database in which you found your source, because readers may not be able to find the source the same way you did. Instead, use a search engine to find the home page of the periodical and give the home page URL, as above.

If you don't find the home page of the periodical, then give the database name in your retrieval statement, as in the next example:

Smith, E. M. (1926, March). Equal rights—internationally! *Life and Labor Bulletin, 4,* 1-2. Retrieved from Women and Social Movements in the United States, 1600-2000, database.

21. An abstract of a journal article (Web)

Polletta, F. (2008). Just talk: Public deliberation after 9/11. *Journal of Public Deliberation, 4*(1). Abstract retrieved from http://services.bepress.com/jpd

22. An article in a newspaper (Web)

Broad, W. J. (2011, April 4). Black market trinkets from space. *The New York Times.* Retrieved from http://www.nytimes.com

Give the URL of the newspaper's home page in the retrieval statement. If you found the article in an online database, see model 20.

23. An article in a magazine (Web)

Hamzelou, J. (2011, April 17). How antidepressants boost growth of new brain cells. *New Scientist, 203*(24), 15. doi:10.1038/mp.2011.26

If the magazine article includes a DOI, give it as here. Otherwise, give the URL of the magazine's home page in a retrieval statement like the one for a newspaper article in model 22. If you found the article in an online database, see model 20.

24. Periodical content that appears only online (Web)

Osnos, E. (2011, April 11). Journey to the west [Supplemental material]. *The New Yorker.* Retrieved from http://www.newyorker.com

If you cite material from a periodical's Web site that is not included in the print version of the publication, add [Supplemental material] after the title and give the URL of the publication's home page.

25. A review (Web)

Bond, M. (2008, December 18). Does genius breed success? [Review of the book *Outliers: The story of success,* by M. Gladwell]. *Nature, 456,* 785. doi:10.1038/456874a

Cite an online review like a print review (model 11, p. 813), concluding with retrieval information (here, a DOI).

26. A report or other material from the Web site of an organization or government (Web)

Greene, D. L., & Plotkin, S. E. (2011, January). *Reducing greenhouse gas emissions from U.S. transportation.* Retrieved from the Pew Center on Global Climate Change website: http://www.pewclimate.org

Treat the title of an independent Web document like the title of a

Format for a journal article on the Web

Top of page

Bottom of page

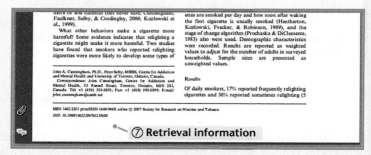

APA
51d

book. Provide the name of the publishing organization as part of the retrieval statement when the publisher is not listed as the author, as in the example on the previous page.

If the document you cite is difficult to locate from the organization's home page, give the complete URL in the retrieval statement:

> Union of Concerned Scientists. (2010). *Clean vehicles.* Retrieved from
>
> http://www.ucsusa.org/clean_vehicles

If the document you cite is undated, use the abbreviation n.d. in place of the publication date and give the date of your access in the retrieval statement:

> U.S. Department of Education. (n.d.). *Teach.* Retrieved April 23, 2011, from
>
> http://www.teach.gov

①   ②   ③

Cunningham, J. A., & Selby, P. (2007). Relighting cigarettes: How

④   ⑤   ⑥

common is it? *Nicotine and Tobacco Research, 9*, 621-623.

⑦

doi:10.1080/14622200701239688

① **Authors.** Give each author's last name, first initial, and any middle initial. Separate names from initials with commas, and use & before the last author's name. Omit *Dr., PhD,* or any other title. See models 1–4 (pp. 810–11) to cite single and multiple authors.

② **Year of publication,** in parentheses and followed by a period.

③ **Title of article.** Give the full article title and any subtitle, separating them with a colon. Capitalize only the first words of the title and subtitle, and do not place the title in quotation marks.

④ **Title of periodical,** in italics. Capitalize all significant words and end with a comma.

⑤ **Volume number,** italicized and followed by a comma. See page 812 for when to include the issue number.

⑥ **Inclusive page numbers of article,** without "pp." Do not omit any numerals.

⑦ **Retrieval information,** either a DOI (shown here) or a URL (model 19). See model 20 for how to cite an article without a DOI that you retrieve from a database.

27. A book (Web)

Reuter, P. (Ed.). (2010). *Understanding the demand for illegal drugs.* Retrieved from http://books.nap.edu/catalog.php?record_id=12976

For a book available only online, replace the publisher's city, state, and name with a DOI if one is available (see model 18) or with a retrieval statement, as above. See models 14–17 (pp. 813–14) to cite variations in book entries: a translator, a later edition, a book in more than one volume, and an article or a chapter in a book.

For an electronic version of a print book, add the format in brackets:

Freud, S. (1920). *Dream psychology: Psychoanalysis for beginners* (M. D. Eder, Trans.). [iPad version]. Retrieved from http://www.apple.com/itunes

28. An article in a reference work (Web)

Wood, R. (1998). Community organization. In W. A. Swatos, Jr. (Ed.), *Encyclopedia of religion and society.* Retrieved from http://hirr.hartsem.edu/ency/commorg.htm

If the entry you cite has no named author, begin with the title of the entry and then the date. Use a DOI instead of a URL if the source has one.

29. An article in a wiki (Web)

Clinical neuropsychology. (2010, November 12). Retrieved April 15, 2011, from Wikipedia: http://en.wikipedia.org/wiki/Clinical_neuropsychology

Give your date of retrieval for sources that are likely to change, such as this wiki.

30. A dissertation (Web)

A dissertation in a commercial database:

McFaddin, M. O. (2007). *Adaptive reuse: An architectural solution for poverty and homelessness* (Doctoral dissertation). Available from ProQuest Dissertations and Theses database. (ATT 1378764)

If a dissertation is from a commercial database, give the name of the database in the retrieval statement, followed by the accession or order number in parentheses.

A dissertation in an institutional database:

Chang, J. K. (2003). *Therapeutic intervention in treatment of injuries to the hand and wrist* (Doctoral dissertation). Retrieved from http://medsci.archive.liasu.edu/61724

If a dissertation is from an institution's database, give the URL in the retrieval statement.

See also model 38 (p. 822) for examples of print dissertations.

31. A podcast (Web)

Glass, I. (Producer). (2011, March 25). Very tough love [Audio podcast]. *This American life.* Retrieved from http://thisamericanlife.org

32. A film or video recording (Web)

CBS News (Producer). (1968, April 4). *1968 King assassination report* [Video file]. Retrieved from http://www.youtube.com/watch?v=cmOBbxgxKvo

If the film or video you cite is difficult to locate from the home page of the Web site, give the complete URL in the retrieval statement, as in the example.

APA
51d

33. A visual (Web)

United Nations Population Fund (Cartographer). (2005). *Percent of population living on less than $1/day* [Demographic map]. Retrieved from http://www.unfpa.org

34. A message posted to a blog or discussion group (Web)

Sharma, A. (2011, April 15). How effective is lifestyle management of obesity? [Web log post]. Retrieved from http://www.drsharma.ca

Include postings to blogs and discussion groups in your list of references only if they are retrievable by others. (The source above is retrievable by a search of the home page URL.) Follow the message title with [Web log post], [Electronic mailing list message], or [Online forum comment]. Include the name of the blog or discussion group in the retrieval statement if it isn't part of the URL.

35. A personal communication (text citation)

At least one member of the research team has expressed reservations about the design of the study (L. Kogod, personal communication, February 6, 2011).

Personal e-mail and other online postings that are not retrievable by others should be cited only in the text, not in the list of references.

Listing other sources

36. A report (print)

Gerald, K. (2003). *Medico-moral problems in obstetric care* (Report No. NP-71). St. Louis, MO: Catholic Hospital Association.

Treat a printed report like a book, but provide any report number in parentheses after the title, with no punctuation between them.

For a report from the Educational Resources Information Center (ERIC), provide the ERIC document number in parentheses at the end of the entry:

Jolson, M. K. (2001). *Music education for preschoolers* (Report No. TC-622). New York, NY: Teachers College, Columbia University. (ERIC Document Reproduction Service No. ED264488)

37. A government publication (print)

Hawaii. Department of Education. (2011). *Kauai district schools, profile 2010-11*. Honolulu, HI: Author.

Stiller, A. (2010). *Historic preservation and tax incentives*. Washington, DC: U.S. Department of the Interior.

If no person is named as the author, list the publication under the name of the sponsoring agency. When the agency is both the author and the publisher, use Author in place of the publisher's name, as in the first example.

For legal materials such as court decisions, laws, and testimony at hearings, the APA recommends formats that correspond to conventional legal citations. The following example of a congressional hearing includes the full title, the number of the Congress, the page number where the hearing transcript starts in the official publication, and the date of the hearing.

> *Medicare payment for outpatient physical and occupational therapy services: Hearing before the Committee on Ways and Means, House of Representatives,* 110th Cong. 3 (2007).

38. A dissertation (print)

A dissertation abstracted in DAI:

> Steciw, S. K. (1986). Alterations to the Pessac project of Le Corbusier. *Dissertation Abstracts International, 46*(6), 565C.

An unpublished dissertation:

> Hernandez, A. J. (2005). *Persistent poverty: Transient work and workers in today's labor market* (Unpublished doctoral dissertation). University of Illinois, Urbana-Champaign.

39. An interview (print)

> Schenker, H. (2007). No peace without third-party intervention [Interview with Shulamit Aloni]. *Palestine-Israel Journal of Politics, Economics, and Culture, 14*(4), 63-68.

List a published interview under the interviewer's name, and provide the title, if any, without italics or quotation marks. If there is no title, or if the title does not indicate the interview format or the interviewee (as in the example), add a bracketed explanation. End with the publication information for the kind of source the interview appears in (here, a journal).

An interview you conduct yourself should not be included in the list of references. Instead, use an in-text parenthetical citation, as shown in model 35 (p. 821) for a personal communication.

40. A motion picture

> American Psychological Association (Producer). (2001). *Ethnocultural psychotherapy* [DVD]. Available from http://www.apa.org/videos
>
> Tyrrell, C. (Director). (2010). *The Joneses* [Motion picture]. United States: Bjort Productions.

Depending on whose work you are citing, begin with the name or names of the creator, director, producer, or primary contributor, followed by the function in parentheses. (The second example would begin with the producer's name if you were citing the motion picture as a whole, not specifically the work of the director.) Add the medium in brackets after the title: [Motion picture] (for film), [DVD], or [Videocassette]. For a work in wide circulation (second example), give the country of origin and the studio that released the picture. For a work that is not widely circulated (first example), give the distributor's address or URL.

41. A musical recording

Springsteen, B. (2002). Empty sky. On *The rising* [CD]. New York, NY: Columbia.

Begin with the name of the writer or composer. (If you cite another artist's recording of the work, provide this information after the title of the work—for example, [Recorded by E. Davila].) Give the medium in brackets ([CD], [LP], and so on). Finish with the city, state, and name of the recording label.

42. A television series or episode

Rhimes, S. (Executive producer). (2011). *Grey's anatomy* [Television series]. New York, NY: ABC.

Cahn, D. (Writer), & Allen, D. (Director). (2011). Not responsible [Television series episode]. In S. Rhimes (Executive producer), *Grey's anatomy*. New York, NY: ABC.

For a television series, begin with the producer's name and identify his or her function in parentheses. Add [Television series] after the series title, and give the city and name of the network. For an episode, begin with the writer and then the director, identifying the function of each in parentheses, and add [Television series episode] after the episode title. Then provide the series information, beginning with In and the producer's name and function, giving the series title, and ending with the city and name of the network.

51e Formatting documents in APA style

Use the following guidelines and samples to prepare documents in APA format. Check with your instructor for any modifications to this format.

Video tutorial

Note See pages 808–09 for the APA format of a reference list. And see pages 120–30 for guidelines on type fonts, lists, tables and figures, and other elements of document design.

Margins Use one-inch margins on the top, bottom, and both sides.

Spacing and indentions Double-space everywhere. (The only exception is tables and figures, where related data, labels, and other elements may be single-spaced.) Indent paragraphs and displayed quotations one-half inch or five to seven spaces.

Paging Begin numbering on the title page, and number consecutively through the end (including the reference list). Provide a header about one-half inch from the top of every page, as shown in the samples on these pages. The header consists of the page number on the far right and your full or shortened title on the far left. Type the title in all-capital letters. On the title page only, precede the title with the label Running head and a colon. Omit this label on all other pages.

Title page Include the full title, your name, the course title, the instructor's name, and the date. (See below.) Type the title on the top half of the page, followed by the identifying information, all centered horizontally and double-spaced.

APA title page

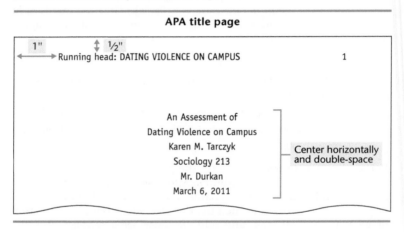

Abstract Summarize (in a maximum of 120 words) your subject, research method, findings, and conclusions. (See below.) Put the abstract on a page by itself.

APA abstract

APA
51e

Body Begin with a restatement of the paper's title and then an introduction (not labeled). (See the next page.) The introduction presents the problem you researched, your method, the relevant background (such as related studies), and the purpose of your research.

First page of APA body

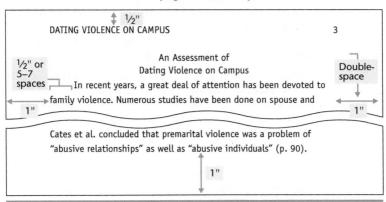

After the introduction, a section labeled **Method** provides a detailed discussion of how you conducted your research, including a description of the research subjects, any materials or tools you used (such as questionnaires), and the procedure you followed. In the illustration below, the label **Method** is a first-level heading and the label **Sample** is a second-level heading.

Later page of APA body

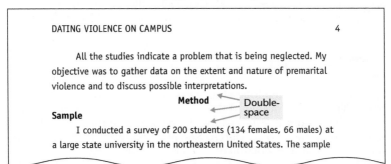

APA
51e

Format headings (including a third level, if needed) as follows:

First-Level Heading

Second-Level Heading

    Third-level heading. Run this heading into the text paragraph with a standard paragraph indention.

The **Results** section (labeled with a first-level heading) summarizes the data you collected, explains how you analyzed them, and presents them in detail, often in tables, graphs, or charts.

The **Discussion** section (labeled with a first-level heading) interprets the data and presents your conclusions. (When the discussion is brief, you may combine it with the previous section under the heading **Results and Discussion**.)

The References section, beginning a new page, includes all your sources. See pages 808–09 for an explanation and sample.

Long quotations Run into your text all quotations of forty words or less, and enclose them in quotation marks. For quotations of more than forty words, set them off from your text by indenting all lines one-half inch or five spaces, double-spacing throughout.

> Echoing the opinions of other Europeans at the time, Freud (1961) had a poor view of Americans:
>
>> The Americans are really too bad. . . . Competition is much more pungent with them, not succeeding means civil death to every one, and they have no private resources apart from their profession, no hobby, games, love or other interests of a cultured person. And success means money. (p. 86)

Do not use quotation marks around a quotation displayed in this way.

Illustrations Present data in tables, graphs, or charts, as appropriate. (See the sample on p. 828 for a clear table format to follow.) Begin each illustration on a separate page. Number each kind of illustration consecutively and separately from the other (Table 1, Table 2, etc., and Figure 1, Figure 2, etc.). Refer to all illustrations in your text—for instance, (see Figure 3). Generally, place illustrations immediately after the text references to them. (See pp. 123–30 for more on illustrations.)

51f Examining a sample social science paper

Below and on the following pages are excerpts from a sociology paper. The student followed the organization described on the preceding pages both in establishing the background for her study and in explaining her own research. She also followed the APA style of source citation and document format, although page borders and running heads are omitted here and only the required page breaks are indicated.

Excerpts from a research report

[Title page.]

An Assessment of
Dating Violence on Campus
Karen M. Tarczyk
Sociology 213
Mr. Durkan
March 6, 2011

[New page.]

Abstract

Little research has examined the patterns of abuse and violence occurring within couples during courtship. With a questionnaire administered to a sample of college students, the extent and nature of such abuse and violence were investigated. The results, some interpretations, and implications for further research are discussed.

[New page.]

An Assessment of Dating
Violence on Campus

In recent years, a great deal of attention has been devoted to family violence. Numerous studies have been done on spouse and child abuse. However, violent behavior occurs in dating relationships as well, yet the problem of dating violence has been relatively ignored by sociological research. It should be examined further because the premarital relationship is one context in which individuals learn and adopt behaviors that surface later in marriage.

The sociologist James Makepeace (1989) contended that courtship violence is a "potential mediating link" between violence in one's family of orientation and violence in one's later family of procreation (p. 103). Studying dating behaviors at Bemidji State University in Minnesota, Makepeace reported that one-fifth of the respondents had had at least one encounter with dating violence. He then extended these percentages to students nationwide, suggesting the existence of a major hidden social problem.

More recent research supports Makepeace's. Cates, Rutter, Karl, Linton, and Smith (2000) found that 22.3% of respondents at Oregon State University had been either the victim or the perpetrator of premarital violence. Another study (Cortes, 2005) found that so-called date rape, while much more publicized and discussed, was reported by many fewer woman respondents (2%) than was other violence during courtship (21%).

[The introduction continues.]

All these studies indicate a problem that is being neglected. My objective was to gather data on the extent and nature of premarital violence and to discuss possible interpretations.

Method

Sample

I conducted a survey of 200 students (134 females, 66 males) at a large state university in the northeastern United States. The sample consisted of students enrolled in an introductory sociology course.

[The explanation of method continues.]

The Questionnaire

A questionnaire exploring the personal dynamics of relationships was distributed during regularly scheduled class. Questions were answered anonymously in a 30-minute time period. The survey consisted of three sections.

[The explanation of method continues.]

Section 3 required participants to provide information about their current dating relationships. Levels of stress and frustration, communication between partners, and patterns of decision making were examined. These variables were expected to influence the amount of violence in a relationship. The next part of the survey was adopted from Murray Strauss's Conflict Tactics Scales (1992). These scales contain 19 items designed to measure conflict and the means of conflict resolution, including reasoning, verbal aggression, and actual violence.

Results

The questionnaire revealed significant levels of verbal aggression and threatened and actual violence among dating couples. A high number of students, 50% (62 of 123 subjects), reported that they had been the victim of verbal abuse. In addition, almost 14% of respondents (17 of 123) admitted being threatened with some type of violence, and more than 14% (18 of 123) reported being pushed, grabbed, or shoved. (See Table 1.)

[The explanation of results continues.]

[Table on a page by itself.]

Table 1

Incidence of Courtship Violence

Type of violence	Number of students reporting	Percentage of sample
Insulted or swore	62	50.4
Threatened to hit or throw something	17	13.8
Threw something	8	6.5
Pushed, grabbed, or shoved	18	14.6
Slapped	8	6.5
Kicked, bit, or hit with fist	7	5.7
Hit or tried to hit with something	2	1.6
Threatened with a knife or gun	1	0.8
Used a knife or gun	1	0.8

Discussion

Violence within premarital relationships has been relatively ignored. The results of the present study indicate that abuse and force do occur in dating relationships. Although the percentages are small, so was the sample. Extending them to the entire campus population would mean significant numbers. For example, if the nearly 6% incidence of being kicked, bitten, or hit with a fist is typical, then 300 students of a 5,000-member student body might have experienced this type of violence. [The discussion continues.]

If the courtship period is characterized by abuse and violence, what accounts for it? The other sections of the survey examined some variables that appear to influence the relationship. Level of stress and frustration, both within the relationship and in the respondent's life, was one such variable. The communication level between partners, both the frequency of discussion and the frequency of agreement, was another. [The discussion continues.]

The method of analyzing the data in this study, utilizing frequency distributions, provided a clear overview. However, more tests of significance and correlation and a closer look at the social and individual variables affecting the relationship are warranted. The courtship period may set the stage for patterns of married life. It merits more attention.

[New page.]

References

Cates, R. L., Rutter, C. H., Karl, J., Linton, M., & Smith, K. (2000). Premarital abuse: A social psychological perspective. *Journal of Family Issues, 13,* 79-90.

Cortes, L. (2005). Beyond date rape: Violence during courtship. *Electronic Journal of Intimate Violence, 5*(2). Retrieved from http://www.ejiv.org

Glaser, R., & Rutter, C. H. (Eds.). (1999). Familial violence [Special issue]. *Family Relations, 38*(4).

Makepeace, J. M. (1989). Courtship violence among college students. *Family Relations, 28*(6), 97-103.

Strauss, M. L. (1992). *Conflict Tactics Scales.* New York, NY: Sociological Tests.

52

Writing in the Natural and Applied Sciences

The natural and applied sciences include biology, chemistry, physics, mathematics, engineering, computer science, and their branches. Their purpose is to understand natural and technological phenomena. (A *phenomenon* is a fact or event that can be known by

Exercise

mycomplab

Visit *mycomplab.com* for the eText and for resources on writing in the natural and applied sciences.

the senses.) Scientists conduct experiments and write to explain the step-by-step processes in their methods of inquiry and discovery.

52a   Using the methods and evidence of the sciences

Scientists investigate phenomena by the **scientific method,** a process of continual testing and refinement.

The scientific method

Video
tutorial

- Observe carefully. Accurately note all details of the phenomenon being researched.
- Ask questions about the observations.
- Formulate a *hypothesis,* or preliminary generalization, that explains the observed facts.
- Test the hypothesis with additional observation or controlled experiments.
- If the hypothesis proves accurate, formulate a *theory,* or unified model, that explains *why.*
- If the hypothesis is disproved, revise it or start anew.

52b

Scientific evidence is almost always quantitative—that is, it consists of numerical data obtained from the measurement of phenomena. These data are called **empirical** (from a Greek word for "experience"); they result from observation and experience, generally in a controlled laboratory setting but also (as sometimes in astronomy or biology) in the natural world. Often the empirical evidence for scientific writing comes from library research into other people's reports of their investigations. Surveys of known data or existing literature are common in scientific writing.

52b   Understanding writing assignments in the sciences

Student
paper

No matter what your assignment, you will be expected to document and explain your evidence carefully so that anyone reading can check your sources and replicate your research. It is important for your reader to know the context of your research—both the previous experimentation and research on your particular subject (acknowledged in the survey of the literature) and the physical conditions and other variables surrounding your own work.

Assignments in the natural and applied sciences include the following genres:

- A summary distills a research article to its essence in brief, concise form. (Summary is discussed in detail on pp. 152–54.)
- A laboratory report explains the procedure and results of an experiment conducted by the writer. (See p. 842 for an example.)

- A critique summarizes and critically evaluates a scientific report.
- A research report explains the experimental research of other scientists and the writer's own methods, findings, and conclusions.
- A research proposal reviews the relevant literature and explains a plan for further research.

A laboratory report has four or five major sections:

1. "Abstract": a summary of the report.
2. "Introduction" or "Objective": a review of why the study was undertaken, a summary of the background of the study, and a statement of the problem being studied.
3. "Method" or "Procedure": a detailed explanation of how the study was conducted, including any statistical analysis.
4. "Results": an explanation of the major findings (including unexpected results) and a summary of the data presented in graphs and tables.
5. "Discussion": an interpretation of the results and an explanation of how they relate to the goals of the experiment. This section also describes new hypotheses that might be tested as a result of the experiment. If the section is brief, it may be combined with the previous section in a single section labeled "Conclusions."

52c

In addition, laboratory or research reports may include a list of references (if other sources were consulted). They almost always include tables and figures (graphs and charts) containing the data from the research (see p. 843).

52c Using the tools and language of the sciences

Tools and language concerns vary from discipline to discipline in the sciences. Consult your instructor for specifics about the field in which you are writing. You can also discover much about a discipline's tools and language from the research sources listed on the next three pages.

1 Writing tools

In the sciences a **lab notebook** or **scientific journal** is almost indispensable for accurately recording the empirical data from observations and experiments. Use such a notebook or journal for these purposes:

- Record observations from reading, from class, or from the lab.
- Ask questions and refine hypotheses.
- Record procedures.
- Record results.
- Keep an ongoing record of ideas and findings and how they change as data accumulate.

■ **Sequence and organize your material** as you compile your findings and write your report.

Make sure that your records of data are clearly separate from your reflections on the data so that you don't mistakenly confuse the two in drawing your conclusions.

2 Language considerations

Science writers prefer to use objective language that removes the writer as a character in the situation and events being explained, except as the impersonal agent of change, the experimenter. Although usage is evolving, scientists still rarely use *I* in their reports and evaluations, and they often resort to the passive voice of verbs, as in *The mixture was then subjected to centrifugal force.* This conscious objectivity focuses attention (including the writer's) on the empirical data and what they show. It discourages the writer from, say, ascribing motives and will to animals and plants. For instance, instead of asserting that the sea tortoise *developed* its hard shell *to protect* its body, a scientist would write only what could be observed: that the hard shell *covers and thus protects* the tortoise's body.

Science writers typically change verb tenses to distinguish between established information and their own research. For established information, such as that found in journals and other reliable sources, use the present tense: *Baroreceptors monitor blood pressure.* For your own and others' research, use the past tense: *The bacteria died within three hours. Marti reported some success.*

Each discipline in the natural and applied sciences has a specialized vocabulary that permits precise, accurate, and efficient communication. Some of these terms, such as *pressure* in physics, have different meanings in the common language and must be handled carefully in science writing. Others, such as *enthalpy* in chemistry, have no meanings in the common language and must simply be learned and used correctly.

3 Research sources

The following lists give resources in the sciences.

Specialized encyclopedias, dictionaries, and bibliographies

American Medical Association Encyclopedia of Medicine
Concise Encyclopedia of Computer Science
Concise Oxford Dictionary of Mathematics
CRC Handbook of Chemistry and Physics
Dorland's Illustrated Medical Dictionary
Encyclopedia of Astronomy and Astrophysics
Encyclopedia of Bioethics
Encyclopedia of Chemistry
Encyclopedia of Electronics
Encyclopedia of Environmental Science

52c

Encyclopedia of Geology
Encyclopedia of Physics
Grzimek's Animal Life Encyclopedia
Introduction to Reference Sources in Health Sciences
McGraw-Hill Encyclopedia of Science and Technology
Science and Technology in World History
Space Almanac
Van Nostrand's Scientific Encyclopedia
Wiley Encyclopedia of Electrical and Electronics Engineering
World Resources (environment)

Library databases and indexes

ACM Digital Library
Aerospace and High Technology Database
Applied Science and Technology Index
Astrophysics Data System
Biological Abstracts
Biological and Agricultural Index
Biosis Previews
Chemical Abstracts
CINAHL: Cumulative Index to Nursing and Allied Health Literature
Compendex Engineering Index
Computer Abstracts
Dissertation Abstracts International
Ecology Abstracts
Engineering Index
GeoRef
Inspec
MathSciNet: Mathematical Reviews
Medline
Pollution Abstracts
Reaxys
Science Citation Index
Scopus
Spires High Energy Physics Database
Toxline
Water Resources Abstracts
Zoological Record Plus

52c

Book reviews

Technical Book Review Index

Sources on the open Web

General

Google Directory: Science (directory.google.com/Top/Science)
Infomine (infomine.ucr.edu)
ipl2 (ipl.org/div/subject)
National Academies: Science, Engineering, and Medicine
  (www.nationalacademies.org)
Public Library of Science (www.plos.org)
WWW Virtual Library (vlib.org)

Biology
Biology Online (biology-online.org)
National Biological Information Infrastructure (www.nbii.gov)
RCSB Protein Data Bank (pdb.org)

Chemistry
American Chemical Society (chemistry.org/portal/a/c/s/1/home.html)
ChemSpy (www.chemspy.com)
ChemWeb (www.chemweb.com)

Computer science
*Computer Science: A Guide to Web Resources (libguides.library.albany
.edu/csci)*
IEEE Computer Society (computer.org)

Engineering
National Academy of Engineering (nae.edu)
TechXtra: Engineering, Mathematics, and Computing (www.techxtra.ac.uk)

Environmental science
Center for International Earth Science Information Network (ciesin.org)
EnviroLink (envirolink.org)
Environment Directory (webdirectory.com)

Geology
American Geological Institute (www.agiweb.org)
Digital Library for Earth System Education (dlese.org)
Geosource (www.library.uu.nl/geosource)
US Geological Survey Library (library.usgs.gov)

Health sciences
American Medical Association (ama-assn.org)
Centers for Disease Control and Prevention (www.cdc.gov)
Hardin MD (hardinmd.lib.uiowa.edu)
PubMed (www.ncbi.nlm.nih.gov)
World Health Organization (who.int/en)

Mathematics
Internet Mathematics Library (mathforum.org/library)
Mathematical Atlas (math-atlas.org)

Physics and astronomy
American Institute of Physics (aip.org)
Astronomy Links (astronomylinks.com)
physicsworld.com (physicsworld.com)
Science@NASA (science.nasa.gov)

CSE 52d

52d Citing sources in CSE style

Within the natural and applied sciences, practitioners use one of two styles of documentation, varying slightly from discipline to discipline. Following are some of the style guides most often consulted:

American Chemical Society, *ACS Style Guide: A Manual for Authors and Editors*, 3rd ed., 2006

American Institute of Physics, *Style Manual for Guidance in the Preparation of Papers*, 4th ed., 1997 (*www.aip.org/pubservs/style/4thed/AIP_Style_4thed.pdf*)

American Medical Association Manual of Style, 10th ed., 2007

Council of Science Editors, *Scientific Style and Format: The CSE Manual for Authors, Editors, and Publishers*, 7th ed., 2006

The most thorough and widely used of these guides is the last one, *Scientific Style and Format*, which details both styles of scientific documentation: one using author and date and one using numbers. Both types of text citation refer to a list of references at the end of the paper (see the next page). Ask your instructor which style you should use.

1 Using CSE name-year text citations

In the CSE name-year style, parenthetical text citations provide the last name of the author being cited and the source's year of publication. At the end of the paper, a list of references, arranged alphabetically by authors' last names, provides complete information on each source.

The CSE name-year style closely resembles the APA name-year style detailed on pages 804–23. You can follow the APA examples for in-text citations, making several notable changes for CSE:

- Do not use a comma to separate the author's name and the date: (Baumrind 1968, p. 34).
- Separate two authors' names with and (not "&"): (Pepinsky and DeStefano 1997).
- For sources with three or more authors, use et al. (Latin abbreviation for "and others") after the first author's name: (Rutter et al. 1996).

2 Using CSE numbered text citations

In the CSE number style, raised numbers in the text refer to a numbered list of references at the end of the paper.

Two standard references [1,2] use this term.

These forms of immunity have been extensively researched [3].

Hepburn and Tatin [2] do not discuss this project.

Assignment of numbers The number for each source is based on the order in which you cite the source in the text: the first cited source is 1, the second is 2, and so on.

Reuse of numbers When you cite a source you have already cited and numbered, use the original number again (see the last example above, which reuses the number 2 from the first example).

CSE

52d

This reuse is the key difference between the CSE numbered citations and numbered references to footnotes or endnotes. In the CSE style, each source has only one number, determined by the order in which the source is cited. With notes, in contrast, the numbering proceeds in sequence, so that each source has as many numbers as it has citations in the text.

Citation of two or more sources When you cite two or more sources at once, arrange their numbers in sequence and separate them with a comma and no space, as in the first example on the previous page.

3 Using a CSE reference list

For both the name-year and the number styles of in-text citation, provide a list, titled References, of all sources you have cited. Center this heading about an inch from the top of the page, and double-space beneath it.

The following examples show the differences and similarities between the name-year and number styles:

Name-year style

Hepburn PX, Tatin JM. 2005. Human physiology. New York (NY): Columbia University Press.

Number style

2. Hepburn PX, Tatin JM. Human physiology. New York (NY): Columbia University Press; 2005.

Spacing In both styles, single-space each entry and double-space between entries.

Arrangement In the name-year style, arrange entries alphabetically by authors' last names. In the number style, arrange entries in numerical order—that is, in order of their citation in the text.

Format In the name-year style, type all lines of entries at the left margin—do not indent. In the number style, begin the first line of each entry at the left margin and indent subsequent lines.

Authors In both styles, list each author's name with the last name first, followed by initials for first and middle names. Do not use a comma between an author's last name and initials, and do not use periods or spaces with the initials. Do use a comma to separate authors' names.

Placement of dates In the name-year style, the date follows the author's or authors' names. In the number style, the date follows the publication information (for a book) or the periodical title (for a journal, magazine, or newspaper).

Journal titles In both styles, do not italicize or underline journal titles. For titles of two or more words, abbreviate words of six or more

CSE
52d

letters (without periods) and omit most prepositions, articles, and conjunctions. Capitalize each word. For example, *Journal of Chemical and Biochemical Studies* becomes J Chem Biochem Stud, and *Hospital Practice* becomes Hosp Pract.

Book and article titles In both styles, do not italicize, underline, or use quotation marks around a book or an article title. Capitalize only the first word and any proper nouns.

Publication information for journal articles The name-year and number styles differ in the placement of the publication date (see opposite). However, after the journal title both styles give the journal's volume number, any issue number in parentheses, a colon, and the inclusive page numbers of the article, run together without space: 28:329-30 or 62(2):26-40. See model 6 on the next page.

The following box indexes the CSE models. The models include examples of both a name-year reference and a number reference for each type of source.

CSE reference-list models

CSE

52d

Listing authors

1. One author

Gould SJ. 1987. Time's arrow, time's cycle. Cambridge (MA): Harvard University Press.

1. Gould SJ. Time's arrow, time's cycle. Cambridge (MA): Harvard University Press; 1987.

2. Two to ten authors

Hepburn PX, Tatin JM, Tatin JP. 2008. Human physiology. New York (NY): Columbia University Press.

2. Hepburn PX, Tatin JM, Tatin JP. Human physiology. New York (NY): Columbia University Press; 2008.

3. More than ten authors

Evans RW, Bowditch L, Dana KL, Drumond A, Wildovitch WP, Young SL, Mills P, Mills RR, Livak SR, Lisi OL, et al. 2004. Organ transplants: ethical issues. Ann Arbor (MI): University of Michigan Press.

3. Evans RW, Bowditch L, Dana KL, Drummond A, Wildovitch WP, Young SL, Mills P, Mills RR, Livak SR, Lisi OL, et al. Organ transplants: ethical issues. Ann Arbor (MI): University of Michigan Press; 2004.

4. Author not named

Health care for children with diabetes. 2011. New York (NY): US Health Care.

4. Health care for children with diabetes. New York (NY): US Health Care; 2011.

5. Two or more cited works by the same author(s) published in the same year

Gardner H. 1973a. The arts and human development. New York (NY): Wiley.

Gardner H. 1973b. The quest for mind: Piaget, Lévi-Strauss, and the structuralist movement. New York (NY): Knopf.

(The number style does not require such forms.)

Listing print periodicals: Journals, newspapers, magazines

6. An article in a journal (print)

Campos JJ, Walle EA, Dahl A, Main A. 2011. Reconceptualizing emotion regulation. Emotion Rev. 3(1):26-35. doi:10.1177/1754073910380975

6. Campos JJ, Walle EA, Dahl A, Main A. Reconceptualizing emotion regulation. Emotion Rev. 2011;3(1):26-35. doi:10.1177/1754073910380975

If a journal article has a Digital Object Identifier (DOI), include the number at the end of the entry, as here. (See p. 809 for more on DOIs.)

7. An article in a newspaper (print)

Wade N. 2011 Apr 15. Ancient clicks hint language is Africa-born. New York Times (National Ed.). Sect. A:1 (col. 3).

7. Wade N. Ancient clicks hint language is Africa-born. New York Times (National Ed.). 2011 Apr 15;Sect. A:1 (col. 3).

8. An article in a magazine (print)

Hall S. 2011 Mar. Diseases in a dish. Scientific American. 40-45.

8. Hall S. Diseases in a dish. Scientific American. 2011 Mar:40-45.

Listing print books

9. Basic format for a book (print)

Wilson EO. 2004. On human nature. Cambridge (MA): Harvard University Press.

9. Wilson EO. On human nature. Cambridge (MA): Harvard University Press; 2004.

10. A book with an editor (print)

Jonson P, editor. 2008. Anatomy yearbook 2008. Los Angeles (CA): Anatco.

10. Jonson P, editor. Anatomy yearbook 2008. Los Angeles (CA): Anatco; 2008.

11. A selection from a book (print)

Krigel R, Laubenstein L, Muggia F. 2005. Kaposi's sarcoma. In: Ebbeson P, Biggar RS, Melbye M, editors. AIDS: a basic guide for clinicians. 2nd ed. Philadelphia (PA): Saunders. p. 100-26.

11. Kriegel R, Laubenstein L, Muggia F. Kaposi's sarcoma. In: Ebbeson P, Biggar RS, Melbye M, editors. AIDS: a basic guide for clinicians. 2nd ed. Philadelphia (PA): Saunders; 2005. p. 100-26.

Listing Web and other electronic sources

CSE references to electronic sources require additions to the basic print formats:

- Give the medium you used to find the source, in brackets: [Internet], [DVD], and so on.
- Give the date you accessed the source preceded by cited, in brackets: [cited 2009 Dec 7].
- Give the URL of an Internet source. Use an availability statement that starts with Available from: and ends with the URL. If you must break a URL from one line to the next, do so only before punctuation such as a period or a slash and do not hyphenate. Do not add a period at the end of a URL.
- Give the DOI (Digital Object Identifier) of the source if one is available. Add it at the end of the entry after a space, as in model 12. (See p. 809 for more on DOIs.)

12. An article in a journal (Web)

Grady GF. 2010. The here and now of hepatitis B immunization. Today's Med [Internet]. [cited 2010 Dec 7]; 6(2):39-41. Available from: http://www.fmrt.org/todaysmedicine/Grady050293.pdf6 doi:10.1076/262543668

12. Grady GF. The here and now of hepatitis B immunization. Today's Med [Internet]. 2010 [cited 2010 Dec 7]; 6(2):39-41. Available from: http://www.fmrt.org/todaysmedicine/Grady050293.pdf6 doi:10.1076/262543668

Give the date of your access, preceded by "cited," in brackets: [cited 2010 Dec 7] in the examples. If the article has no reference numbers (pages, paragraphs, and so on), give your calculation of its length in brackets—for instance, [about 15 p.] or [20 paragraphs].

CSE
52d

13. An article in a database (Web)

McAskill MR, Anderson TJ, Jones RD. 2005. Saccadic adaptation in neurological disorders. Prog Brain Res. 140:417-431. PubMed [Internet]. Bethesda (MD): National Library of Medicine; [cited 2011 Mar 6]. Available from: http://www.ncbi .nlm.nih.gov/PubMed

13. McAskill MR, Anderson TJ, Jones RD. Saccadic adaptation in neurological disorders. Prog Brain Res. 2005;140:417-431. PubMed [Internet]. Bethesda (MD): National Library of Medicine; [cited 2011 Mar 6]. Available from: http://www.ncbi.nlm.nih.gov/PubMed

Provide information on the database: title, [Internet], place of publication, and publisher. (If the database author is different from the publisher, give the author's name before the title.) If you see a date of publication or a copyright date for the database, give it after the publisher's name.

14. A book (Web)

Ruch BJ, Ruch DB. 2009. Homeopathy and medicine: resolving the conflict [Internet]. New York (NY): Albert Einstein College of Medicine [cited 2011 Jan 28]. Available from: http://www.einstein.edu/medicine/books/ruch.html

14. Ruch BJ, Ruch DB. Homeopathy and medicine: resolving the conflict [Internet]. New York (NY): Albert Einstein College of Medicine; 2009 [cited 2011 Jan 28]. Available from: http://www.einstein.edu/medicine/books/ruch.html

15. A Web site

American Medical Association [Internet]. 2011. Chicago (IL): American Medical Association; [cited 2011 Nov 26]. Available from: http://ama-assn.org

15. American Medical Association [Internet]. Chicago (IL): American Medical Association; 2011 [cited 2011 Nov 26]. Available from: http://ama-assn.org

16. A message posted to a discussion list

Stalinsky Q. 2011 Aug 16. More studies about hormone-replacement therapy. Woman Physicians Congress [discussion list on the Internet]. Chicago (IL): American Medical Association; [cited 2011 Aug 17]. Available from: ama-wpc@ama-assn.org

16. Stalinsky Q. More studies about hormone-replacement therapy. Woman Physicians Congress [discussion list on the Internet]. Chicago (IL): American Medical Association; 2011 Aug 16 [cited 2011 Aug 17]. Available from: ama-wpc@ama-assn.org

CSE

52d

17. A personal online communication (text citation)

One member of the research team has expressed reservation about the study design (personal communication from L. Kogod, 2011 Feb 6; unreferenced).

A personal letter or e-mail message should be cited in your text, not in your reference list. The format is the same for both the name-year and the number styles.

18. A document on CD-ROM or DVD-ROM

Reich WT, editor. 2011. Encyclopedia of bioethics [DVD-ROM]. New York (NY): Co-Health.

18. Reich WT editor. Encyclopedia of bioethics [DVD-ROM]. New York (NY): Co-Health; 2011.

Listing other sources

19. A report written and published by the same organization

Warnock M. 2006. Report of the Committee on Fertilization and Embryology. Waco (TX): Baylor University Department of Embryology. Report No.: BU/DE.4261.

19. Warnock M. Report of the Committee on Fertilization and Embryology. Waco (TX): Baylor University Department of Embryology; 2006. Report No.: BU/DE.4261.

20. A report written and published by different organizations

Hackney, JD (Rancho Los Amigos Hospital, Downey, CA). 2007. Effect of atmospheric pollutants on human physiologic function. Washington (DC): Environmental Protection Agency (US). Report No.: R-801396.

20. Hackney, JD (Rancho Los Amigos Hospital, Downey, CA). Effect of atmospheric pollutants on human physiologic function. Washington (DC): Environmental Protection Agency (US); 2007. Report No.: R-801396.

21. An audio or visual recording

Cell mitosis [DVD–ROM]. 2011. White Plains (NY): Teaching Media.

21. Cell mitosis [DVD-ROM]. White Plains (NY): Teaching Media; 2011.

52e   Formatting documents in CSE style

Scientific Style and Format is not specific about margins, spacing for headings, and other elements of document format. Unless your instructor specifies otherwise, you can use the format of the APA (pp. 823–26). The CSE exception to this style is the list of references, which is described on pages 836–37.

Video tutorial

The most troublesome aspects of manuscript preparation in the sciences are equations or formulas, tables, and figures. When typing equations or formulas, be careful to reproduce alignments, indentions, underlining, and characters accurately. If your word processor lacks special characters, leave space for them and write them in by hand.

CSE
52e

Because you will be expected to share your data with your readers, most of your writing for the sciences is likely to require illustrations to present the data in concise, readable form. Tables usually summarize raw data (see opposite for an example), whereas figures (mainly charts, graphs, and diagrams) recast the data to show noteworthy comparisons or changes. Follow the guidelines on pages 123–26 for preparing tables and figures.

52f Examining a sample science paper

The following biology paper illustrates the CSE number style for documenting sources. On page 844, passages from the paper and a reformatted list of references show the name-year style. Except for the citations and the references, the paper is formatted in APA style because CSE does not specify a format.

A laboratory report: CSE number style

[Title page.]

Exercise and Blood Pressure

Liz Garson

Biology 161

Ms. Traversa

December 13, 2010

[New page.]

Abstract

The transient elevation of blood pressure following exercise was demonstrated by pressure measurements of twenty human subjects before and after exercise.

[New page.]

Exercise and Blood Pressure
Introduction

The purpose of this experiment was to verify the changes in blood pressure that accompany exercise, as commonly reported [1,2]. A certain blood pressure is necessary for the blood to supply nutrients to the body tissues. Baroreceptors near the heart monitor pressure by determining the degree to which blood stretches the wall of the blood vessel.

[The introduction continues.]

During exercise, the metabolic needs of the muscles override the influence of the baroreceptors and result in an increase in blood pressure. This increase in blood pressure is observed uniformly (irrespective of sex or race), although men demonstrate a higher absolute systolic pressure than do women [3]. During strenuous exercise, blood pressure can rise to 40 percent above baseline [1].

Method

The subjects for this experiment were twenty volunteers from laboratory classes, ten men and ten women. All pressure measurements were performed using a standard sphygmomanometer, which was tested for accuracy. To ensure consistency, the same sphygmomanometer was used to take all readings. In addition, all measurements were taken by the same person to avoid discrepancies in method or interpretation.

The first pressure reading was taken prior to exercise as the subject sat in a chair. This pressure was considered the baseline for each subject. All subsequent readings were interpreted relative to this baseline.

In the experiment, the subjects ran up and down stairs for fifteen minutes. Immediately after exercising, the subjects returned to the laboratory to have their pressure measured. Thirty minutes later, the pressure was measured for the final time.

Results

Table 1 contains the blood pressure measurements for the male and female subjects. With the exception of subjects 3 and 14, all subjects demonstrated the expected post-exercise increase in blood pressure, with a decline to baseline or near baseline thirty minutes after exercise. The data for subjects 3 and 14 were invalid because the subjects did not perform the experiment as directed.

[Table on a page by itself.]

Table 1. Blood pressure measurements for all subjects (mmHg)

Subject	Baseline[a]	Post-exercise	30-minute reading
Male			
1	110/75	135/80	115/75
2	125/80	140/90	135/85
3	125/70	125/70	125/70
4	130/85	170/100	140/90
5	120/80	125/95	120/80
6	115/70	135/80	125/75
7	125/70	150/80	130/70
8	130/80	145/85	130/80
9	140/75	180/85	155/80
10	110/85	135/95	115/80
Female			
11	110/60	140/85	115/60
12	130/75	180/85	130/75
13	125/80	140/90	130/80
14	90/60	90/60	90/60
15	115/65	145/70	125/65
16	100/50	130/65	110/50
17	120/80	140/80	130/80
18	110/70	135/80	120/75
19	120/80	140/90	130/80
20	110/80	145/90	120/80

[a]Normal blood pressure at rest: males, 110-130/60-90; females, 110-120/50-80.

Discussion

As expected, most of the subjects demonstrated an increase in blood pressure immediately after exercise and a decline to near baseline levels thirty minutes after

CSE
52f

exercise. The usual pressure increase was 20-40 mmHg for the systolic pressure and 5-10 mmHg for the diastolic pressure.

In the two cases in which blood pressure did not elevate with exercise (subjects 3 and 14), the subjects simply left the laboratory and returned fifteen minutes later without having exercised. The experimental design was flawed in not assigning someone to observe the subjects as they exercised.

[New page.]

References

1. Guyton AC. Textbook of medical physiology. Philadelphia (PA): Saunders; 2010.

2. Rowell LB. Blood pressure regulation during exercise. Ann Med. 2004;28:329-33.

3. Gleim GW, Stachenfeld NS. Gender differences in the systolic blood pressure response to exercise. Am Heart J. 2001;121:524-30.

A laboratory report: CSE name-year style

These excerpts from the preceding paper show documentation in CSE name-year style:

The purpose of this experiment was to verify the changes in blood pressure that accompany exercise, as commonly reported (Guyton 2010; Rowell 2004).

This increase in blood pressure is observed uniformly (irrespective of sex or race), although men demonstrate a higher absolute systolic pressure than do women (Gleim and Stachenfeld 2001). During strenuous exercise, blood pressure can rise to 40 percent above baseline (Guyton 2010).

References

Gleim GW, Stachenfeld NS. 2001. Gender differences in the systolic blood pressure response to exercise. Am Heart J. 121:524-30.

Guyton AC. 2010. Textbook of medical physiology. Philadelphia (PA): Saunders.

Rowell LB. 2004. Blood pressure regulation during exercise. Ann Med. 28:329-33.

Glossary of Usage

This glossary provides notes on words or phrases that often cause problems for writers. The recommendations for standard American English are based on current dictionaries and usage guides such as the ones listed on pp. 534–35. Items labeled **nonstandard** should be avoided in academic and business settings. Those labeled **colloquial** and **slang** occur in speech and in some informal writing but are best avoided in formal college and business writing. (Words and phrases labeled *colloquial* include those labeled by many dictionaries with the equivalent term *informal*.) See Chapters 37 and 38 for further discussion of word choice and for exercises in usage. See p. 534 for a description of dictionary labels. Also see pp. 554–55 for a list of commonly confused words that are pronounced the same or similarly.

The glossary is necessarily brief. Keep a dictionary handy for all your writing, and make a habit of referring to it whenever you doubt the appropriateness of a word or phrase.

a, an Use *a* before words beginning with consonant sounds, including those spelled with an initial pronounced *h* and those spelled with vowels that are sounded as consonants: *a historian, a one-o'clock class, a university.* Use *an* before words that begin with vowel sounds, including those spelled with an initial silent *h: an organism, an L, an honor.*

The article before an abbreviation depends on how the abbreviation is read: *She was once an AEC undersecretary* (*AEC* is read as three separate letters); *Many Americans opposed a SALT treaty* (*SALT* is read as one word, *salt*).

For the use of *a/an* versus *the*, see pp. 344–46.

accept, except *Accept* is a verb meaning "receive." *Except* is usually a preposition or conjunction meaning "but for" or "other than"; when it is used as a verb, it means "leave out." *I can accept all your suggestions except the last one. I'm sorry you excepted my last suggestion from your list.*

adverse, averse *Adverse* and *averse* both mean "opposed" or "hostile." But *averse* describes the subject's opposition to something, whereas *adverse* describes something opposed to the subject: *The President was averse to adverse criticism.*

advice, advise *Advice* is a noun, and *advise* is a verb: *Take my advice; do as I advise you.*

affect, effect Usually *affect* is a verb, meaning "to influence," and *effect* is a noun, meaning "result": *The drug did not affect his driving; in fact, it seemed to have no effect at all.* But *effect* occasionally is used as a verb meaning "to bring about": *Her efforts effected a change.* And *affect* is used in psychology as a noun meaning "feeling or emotion": *One can infer much about affect from behavior.*

aggravate *Aggravate* should not be used in its colloquial meaning of "irritate" or "exasperate" (for example, *We were aggravated by her constant* *arguing*). *Aggravate* means "make worse": *The President was irritated by the Senate's indecision because he feared any delay might aggravate the unrest in the Middle East.*

agree to, agree with   *Agree to* means "consent to," and *agree with* means "be in accord with": *How can they agree to a treaty when they don't agree with each other about the terms?*

ain't   Nonstandard for *am not, isn't,* or *aren't.*

all, all of   Usually *all* is sufficient to modify a noun: *all my loving, all the things you are.* Before a pronoun or proper noun, *all of* is usually appropriate: *all of me, in all of France.*

all ready, already   *All ready* means "completely prepared," and *already* means "by now" or "before now": *We were all ready to go to the movie, but it had already started.*

all right   *All right* is always two words. *Alright* is a common error.

all together, altogether   *All together* means "in unison" or "gathered in one place." *Altogether* means "entirely." *It's not altogether true that our family never spends vacations all together.*

allusion, illusion   An *allusion* is an indirect reference, and an *illusion* is a deceptive appearance: *Paul's constant allusions to Shakespeare created the illusion that he was an intellectual.*

almost, most   *Almost* means "nearly"; *most* means "the greater number (or part) of." In formal writing, *most* should not be used as a substitute for *almost*: *We see each other almost* [not *most*] *every day.*

a lot   *A lot* is always two words, used informally to mean "many." *Alot* is a common misspelling.

among, between   Use *among* for relationships involving more than two people or things. Use *between* for relationships involving only two or for comparing one thing to a group to which it belongs. *The four of them agreed among themselves that the choice was between New York and Los Angeles.*

amongst   Although common in British English, in American English *amongst* is an overrefined substitute for *among.*

amount, number   Use *amount* with a singular noun that names something not countable (a noncount noun): *The amount of food varies.* Use *number* with a plural noun that names more than one of something countable (a plural count noun): *The number of calories must stay the same.*

an, and   *An* is an article (see *a, an*). *And* is a coordinating conjunction.

and etc.   *Et cetera* (*etc.*) means "and the rest"; *and etc.* therefore is redundant. See also *et al., etc.*

and/or   *And/or* indicates three options: one or the other or both (*The decision is made by the mayor and/or the council*). If you mean all three options, *and/or* is appropriate. Otherwise, use *and* if you mean both, *or* if you mean either.

and which, and who   *And which* or *and who* is correct only when used to introduce a second clause beginning with the same relative pronoun: *Jill is my cousin who goes to school here and who calls me constantly.* Otherwise, *and* is not needed: *WCAS is my favorite AM radio station, which* [not *and which*] *I listen to every morning.*

ante-, anti- The prefix *ante-* means "before" (*antedate, antebellum*); the prefix *anti-* means "against" (*antiwar, antinuclear*). Before a capital letter or *i*, *anti-* takes a hyphen: *anti-Freudian, anti-isolationist.*

anxious, eager *Anxious* means "nervous" or "worried" and is usually followed by *about*. *Eager* means "looking forward" and is usually followed by *to*. *I've been anxious about getting blisters. I'm eager* [not *anxious*] *to get new running shoes.*

anybody, any body; anyone, any one *Anybody* and *anyone* are indefinite pronouns; *any body* is a noun modified by *any*; *any one* is a pronoun or adjective modified by *any*. *How can anybody communicate with any body of government? Can anyone help Amy? She has more work than any one person can handle.*

any more, anymore *Any more* means "no more"; *anymore* means "now." Both are used in negative constructions: *He doesn't want any more. She doesn't live here anymore.*

anyplace Colloquial for *anywhere.*

anyways, anywheres Nonstandard for *anyway* and *anywhere.*

apt, liable, likely *Apt* and *likely* are interchangeable. Strictly speaking, though, *apt* means "having a tendency to": *Horace is apt to forget his lunch in the morning. Likely* means "probably going to": *Horace is leaving so early today that he's likely to catch the first bus.*

   Liable normally means "in danger of" and should be confined to situations with undesirable consequences: *Horace is liable to trip over that hose.* Strictly, *liable* means "responsible" or "exposed to": *The owner will be liable for Horace's injuries.*

are, is Use *are* with a plural subject (*books are*), *is* with a singular subject (*book is*).

as *As* may be vague or ambiguous when it substitutes for *because, since,* or *while*: *As the researchers asked more questions, their money ran out.* (Does *as* mean "while" or "because"?) *As* should never be used as a substitute for *whether* or *who*. *I'm not sure whether* [not *as*] *we can make it. That's the man who* [not *as*] *gave me directions.*

as, like See *like, as.*

as, than In comparisons, *as* and *than* precede a subjective-case pronoun when the pronoun is a subject: *I love you more than he* [*loves you*]. *As* and *than* precede an objective-case pronoun when the pronoun is an object: *I love you as much as* [*I love*] *him.* (See also p. 290.)

assure, ensure, insure *Assure* means "to promise": *He assured us that we would miss the traffic. Ensure* and *insure* are often used interchangeably to mean "make certain," but some reserve *insure* for matters of legal and financial protection and use *ensure* for more general meanings: *We left early to ensure that we would miss the traffic. It's expensive to insure yourself against floods.*

as to A stuffy substitute for *about*: *The suspect was questioned about* [not *as to*] *her actions.*

at The use of *at* after *where* is wordy and should be avoided: *Where are you meeting him?* is preferable to *Where are you meeting him at?*

at this point in time   Wordy for *now, at this point,* or *at this time.*

averse, adverse   See *adverse, averse.*

awful, awfully   Strictly speaking, *awful* means "awe-inspiring." As intensifiers meaning "very" or "extremely" (*He tried awfully hard*), *awful* and *awfully* should be avoided in formal speech or writing.

a while, awhile   *Awhile* is an adverb; *a while* is an article and a noun. Thus *awhile* can modify a verb but cannot serve as the object of a preposition, and *a while* is just the opposite: *I will be gone awhile* [not *a while*]. *I will be gone for a while* [not *awhile*].

bad, badly   In formal speech and writing, *bad* should be used only as an adjective; the adverb is *badly. He felt bad because his tooth ached badly.* In *He felt bad,* the verb *felt* is a linking verb and the adjective *bad* is a subject complement. (See also pp. 338–39.)

being as, being that   Colloquial for *because,* the preferable word in formal speech or writing: *Because* [not *Being as*] *the world is round, Columbus never did fall off the edge.*

beside, besides   *Beside* is a preposition meaning "next to." *Besides* is a preposition meaning "except" or "in addition to" as well as an adverb meaning "in addition." *Besides, several other people besides you want to sit beside Dr. Christensen.*

better, had better   *Had better* (meaning "ought to") is a verb modified by an adverb. The verb is necessary and should not be omitted: *You had better* [not just *better*] *go.*

between, among   See *among, between.*

bring, take   Use *bring* only for movement from a farther place to a nearer one and *take* for any other movement. *First, take these books to the library for renewal, then take them to Mr. Daniels. Bring them back to me when he's finished.*

bunch   In formal speech and writing, *bunch* (as a noun) should be used only to refer to clusters of things growing or fastened together, such as bananas and grapes. Its use to mean a group of items or people is colloquial; *crowd* or *group* is preferable.

burst, bursted; bust, busted   *Burst* is a standard verb form meaning "to fly apart suddenly." Its main forms are *burst, burst, burst;* the form *bursted* is nonstandard. The verb *bust* (*busted*) is slang.

but, hardly, scarcely   These words are negative in their own right; using *not* with any of them produces a double negative (see p. 342). *We have but* [not *haven't got but*] *an hour before our plane leaves. I could hardly* [not *couldn't hardly*] *make out her face.*

but, however, yet   Each of these words is adequate to express contrast. Don't combine them. *He had finished, yet* [not *but yet*] *he continued.*

but that, but what   These wordy substitutes for *that* and *what* should be avoided: *I don't doubt that* [not *but that*] *you are right.*

calculate, figure, reckon   As substitutes for *expect* or *imagine* (*I figure I'll go*), these words are colloquial.

can, may   Strictly, *can* indicates capacity or ability, and *may* indicates permission: *If I may talk with you a moment, I believe I can solve your problem. May* also indicates possibility: *You may like what you hear.*

can't help but   This idiom is common but redundant. Either *I can't help wishing* or the more formal *I cannot but wish* is preferable to *I can't help but wish.*

case, instance, line   Expressions such as *in the case of, in the instance of,* and *along the lines of* are usually padding and should be avoided.

censor, censure   To *censor* is to edit or remove from public view on moral or some other grounds; to *censure* is to give a formal scolding. *The lieutenant was censured by Major Taylor for censoring the letters her soldiers wrote home from boot camp.*

center around   *Center on* is more logical than, and preferable to, *center around.*

climatic, climactic   *Climatic* comes from *climate* and refers to weather: *Recent droughts may indicate a climatic change. Climactic* comes from *climax* and refers to a dramatic high point: *During the climactic duel between Hamlet and Laertes, Gertrude drinks poisoned wine.*

complement, compliment   To *complement* something is to add to, complete, or reinforce it: *Her yellow blouse complemented her black hair.* To *compliment* something is to make a flattering remark about it: *He complimented her on her hair. Compliment* also functions as a noun: *She thanked him for the compliment.* The adjective *complimentary* can also mean "free": *complimentary tickets.*

compose, comprise   *Compose* means "to make up": *The parts compose the whole. Comprise* means "to consist of": *The whole comprises the parts.* Thus, *The band comprises* [not *is comprised of*] *twelve musicians. Twelve musicians compose* [not *comprise*] *the band.*

conscience, conscious   *Conscience* is a noun meaning "a sense of right and wrong"; *conscious* is an adjective meaning "aware" or "awake." *Though I was barely conscious, my conscience nagged me.*

contact   Often used imprecisely as a verb instead of a more exact word such as *consult, talk with, telephone,* or *write to.*

continual, continuous   *Continual* means "constantly recurring": *Most movies on television are continually interrupted by commercials. Continuous* means "unceasing": *Some cable channels present movies continuously without commercials.*

convince, persuade   In the strictest sense, to *convince* someone means to change his or her opinion; to *persuade* someone means to move him or her to action. *Convince* is thus properly followed by *of* or *that,* whereas *persuade* is followed by *to: Once he had convinced Othello of Desdemona's infidelity, Iago easily persuaded him to kill her.*

could care less   The expression is *could not* [*couldn't*] *care less. Could care less* indicates some care, the opposite of what is intended.

could of   See *have, of.*

couple of   Used colloquially to mean "a few" or "several."

credible, creditable, credulous   *Credible* means "believable": *It's a strange story, but it seems credible to me. Creditable* means "deserving of credit" or "worthy": *Steve gave a creditable performance. Credulous* means "gullible": *The credulous Claire believed Tim's lies.* See also *incredible, incredulous.*

criteria The plural of *criterion* (meaning "standard for judgment"): *Our criteria are strict. The most important criterion is a sense of humor.*

data The plural of *datum* (meaning "fact"): *Out of all the data generated by these experiments, not one datum supports our hypothesis.* Usually, a more common term such as *fact, result,* or *figure* is preferred to *datum.* Though *data* is often used with a singular verb, many readers prefer the plural verb and it is always correct: *The data fail* [not *fails*] *to support the hypothesis.*

device, devise *Device* is the noun, and *devise* is the verb: *Can you devise some device for getting his attention?*

different from, different than *Different from* is preferred: *His purpose is different from mine.* But *different than* is widely accepted when a construction using *from* would be wordy: *I'm a different person now than I used to be* is preferable to *I'm a different person now from the person I used to be.*

differ from, differ with To *differ from* is to be unlike: *The twins differ from each other only in their hairstyles.* To *differ with* is to disagree with: *I have to differ with you on that point.*

discreet, discrete *Discreet* (noun form *discretion*) means "tactful": *What's a discreet way of telling Maud to be quiet?* *Discrete* (noun form *discreteness*) means "separate and distinct": *Within a computer's memory are millions of discrete bits of information.*

disinterested, uninterested *Disinterested* means "impartial": *We chose Pete, as a disinterested third party, to decide who was right.* *Uninterested* means "bored" or "lacking interest": *Unfortunately, Pete was completely uninterested in the question.*

don't *Don't* is the contraction for *do not,* not for *does not: I don't care, you don't care, and he doesn't* [not *don't*] *care.*

due to *Due* is an adjective or noun; thus *due to* is always acceptable as a subject complement: *His gray hairs were due to age.* Many object to *due to* as a preposition meaning "because of" (*Due to the holiday, class was canceled*). A rule of thumb is that *due to* is always correct after a form of the verb *be* but questionable otherwise.

due to the fact that Wordy for *because.*

each and every Wordy for *each* or *every.* Write *each one of us* or *every one of us,* not *each and every one of us.*

eager, anxious See *anxious, eager.*

effect See *affect, effect.*

elicit, illicit *Elicit* is a verb meaning "bring out" or "call forth." *Illicit* is an adjective meaning "unlawful." *The crime elicited an outcry against illicit drugs.*

emigrate, immigrate *Emigrate* means "to leave one place and move to another" (the Latin prefix *e-* means "out of": "migrate out of"): *The Chus emigrated from Korea.* *Immigrate* means "to move into a place where one was not born" (the Latin prefix *im-* means "into": "migrate into"): *They immigrated to the United States.*

ensure See *assure, ensure, insure.*

enthused   Used colloquially as an adjective meaning "showing enthusiasm." The preferred adjective is *enthusiastic*: *The coach was enthusiastic* [not *enthused*] *about the team's prospects.*

especially, specially   *Especially* means "particularly" or "more than other things"; *specially* means "for a specific reason." *I especially treasure my boots. They were made specially for me.*

et al., etc.   Use *et al.*, the Latin abbreviation for "and other people," only in source citations: *Jones et al.* Avoid *etc.*, the Latin abbreviation for "and other things," in formal writing, and do not use it to refer to people or to substitute for precision, as in *The government provides health care, etc.* See also *and etc.*

everybody, every body; everyone, every one   *Everybody* and *everyone* are indefinite pronouns: *Everybody* [or *Everyone*] *knows Tom steals. Every one* is a pronoun modified by *every*, and *every body* is a noun modified by *every*. Both refer to each thing or person of a specific group and are typically followed by *of*: *The game commissioner has stocked every body of fresh water in the state with fish, and now every one of our rivers is a potential trout stream.*

everyday, every day   *Everyday* is an adjective meaning "used daily" or "common"; *every day* is a noun modified by *every*: *Everyday problems tend to arise every day.*

everywheres   Nonstandard for *everywhere*.

except   See *accept, except.*

except for the fact that   Wordy for *except that*.

explicit, implicit   *Explicit* means "stated outright": *I left explicit instructions. He explicitly consented. Implicit* means "implied, unstated": *We had an implicit understanding. I trust Marcia implicitly.*

farther, further   *Farther* refers to additional distance (*How much farther is it to the beach?*), and *further* refers to additional time, amount, or other abstract matters (*I don't want to discuss this any further*).

feel   Avoid this word in place of *think* or *believe*: *She thinks* [not *feels*] *that the law should be changed.*

fewer, less   *Fewer* refers to individual countable items (a plural count noun), *less* to general amounts (a noncount noun, always singular): *Skim milk has fewer calories than whole milk. We have less milk left than I thought.*

field   The phrase *the field of* is wordy and generally unnecessary: *Margaret plans to specialize in* [not *in the field of*] *family medicine.*

figure   See *calculate, figure, reckon.*

fixing to   Avoid this colloquial substitute for "intend to": *The school intends* [not *is fixing*] *to build a new library.*

flaunt, flout   *Flaunt* means "show off": *If you have style, flaunt it. Flout* means "scorn" or "defy": *Hester Prynne flouted convention and paid the price.*

flunk   A colloquial substitute for *fail*.

former, latter   *Former* refers to the first-named of two things, *latter* to the second-named: *I like both skiing and swimming, the former in the winter* *and the latter all year round*. To refer to the first- or last-named of three or more things, say *first* or *last*: *I like jogging, swimming, and hang gliding, but the last is inconvenient in the city*.

fun As an adjective, *fun* is colloquial and should be avoided in most writing: *It was a pleasurable* [not *fun*] *evening*.

further See *farther, further*.

get This common verb is used in many slang and colloquial expressions: *get lost, that really gets me, getting on*. *Get* is easy to overuse; watch out for it in expressions such as *it's getting better* (substitute *improving*) and *we got done* (substitute *finished*).

go As a substitute for *say* or *reply*, *go* is colloquial: *He says* [not *goes*], *"How do you do, madam?"*

good, well *Good* is an adjective, and *well* is nearly always an adverb: *Larry's a good dancer. He and Linda dance well together. Well* is properly used as an adjective only to refer to health: *You look well*. (*You look good*, in contrast, means "Your appearance is pleasing.")

good and Colloquial for "very": *I was very* [not *good and*] *tired*.

had better See *better, had better*.

had ought The *had* is unnecessary and should be omitted: *He ought* [not *had ought*] *to listen to his mother*.

half Either *half a* or *a half* is appropriate usage, but *a half a* is redundant: *Half a loaf* [not *A half a loaf*] *is better than none. I'd like a half-gallon* [not *a half a gallon*] *of mineral water, please*.

hanged, hung Though both are past-tense forms of *hang*, *hanged* is used to refer to executions and *hung* is used for all other meanings: *Tom Dooley was hanged* [not *hung*] *from a white oak tree. I hung* [not *hanged*] *the picture you gave me*.

hardly See *but, hardly, scarcely*.

have, of Use *have*, not *of*, after helping verbs such as *could, should, would, may, must*, and *might: You should have* [not *should of*] *told me*.

he, she; he/she Convention has allowed the use of *he* to mean "he or she": *After the infant learns to creep, he progresses to crawling*. However, many writers today consider this usage inaccurate and unfair because it seems to exclude females. The construction *he/she*, one substitute for *he*, is awkward and objectionable to most readers. The better choice is to make the pronoun plural, to rephrase, or, sparingly, to use *he or she*. For instance: *After infants learn to creep, they progress to crawling. After learning to creep, the infant progresses to crawling. After the infant learns to creep, he or she progresses to crawling*. (See also pp. 333–34 and 530–31.)

herself, himself See *myself, herself, himself, yourself*.

hisself Nonstandard for *himself*.

hopefully *Hopefully* means "with hope": *Freddy waited hopefully for a glimpse of Eliza*. The use of *hopefully* to mean "it is to be hoped," "I hope," or "let's hope" is now very common; but try to avoid it in writing because many readers continue to object strongly to the usage. *I hope* [not *Hopefully*] *the law will pass*.

idea, ideal An *idea* is a thought or conception. An *ideal* (noun) is a model of perfection or a goal. *Ideal* should not be used in place of *idea*: *The idea* [not *ideal*] *of the play is that our ideals often sustain us.*

if, whether For clarity, use *whether* rather than *if* when you are expressing an alternative: *If I laugh hard, people can't tell whether I'm crying.*

illicit See *elicit, illicit.*

illusion See *allusion, illusion.*

immigrate, emigrate See *emigrate, immigrate.*

impact Both the noun and the verb *impact* connote forceful or even violent collision. Avoid the increasingly common diluted meanings of *impact*: "an effect" (noun) or "to have an effect on" (verb). The diluted verb (*The budget cuts impacted social science research*) is bureaucratic jargon.

implicit See *explicit, implicit.*

imply, infer Writers or speakers *imply*, meaning "suggest": *Jim's letter implies he's having a good time.* Readers or listeners *infer*, meaning "conclude": *From Jim's letter I infer he's having a good time.*

in, into *In* indicates location or condition: *He was in the garage. She was in a coma. Into* indicates movement or a change in condition: *He went into the garage. She fell into a coma.* Generally avoid the slang sense of *into* meaning "interested in" or "involved in": *I am into Zen.*

in . . . A number of phrases beginning with *in* are needlessly wordy and should be avoided: *in the event that* (for *if*); *in the neighborhood of* (for *approximately* or *about*); *in this day and age* (for *now* or *nowadays*); *in spite of the fact that* (for *although* or *even though*); and *in view of the fact that* (for *because* or *considering that*). Certain other *in* phrases are nothing but padding and can be omitted entirely: *in nature, in number, in reality*, and *in a very real sense*. (See also pp. 547–48.)

incredible, incredulous *Incredible* means "unbelievable"; *incredulous* means "unbelieving": *When Nancy heard Dennis's incredible story, she was frankly incredulous.* See also *credible, creditable, credulous.*

individual, person, party *Individual* should refer to a single human being in contrast to a group or should stress uniqueness: *The US Constitution places strong emphasis on the rights of the individual.* For other meanings *person* is preferable: *What person* [not *individual*] *wouldn't want the security promised in that advertisement? Party* means "group" (*Can you seat a party of four for dinner?*) and should not be used to refer to an individual except in legal documents. See also *people, persons.*

infer See *imply, infer.*

in regards to Nonstandard for *in regard to, as regards,* or *regarding*. See also *regarding.*

inside of, outside of The *of* is unnecessary when *inside* and *outside* are used as prepositions: *Stay inside* [not *inside of*] *the house. The decision is outside* [not *outside of*] *my authority. Inside of* may refer colloquially to time, though in formal English *within* is preferred: *The law was passed within* [not *inside of*] *a year.*

instance See *case, instance, line.*

insure   See *assure, ensure, insure.*

irregardless   Nonstandard for *regardless.*

is, are   See *are, is.*

is because   See *reason is because.*

is when, is where   These are faulty constructions in sentences that define: *Adolescence is a stage* [not *is when a person is*] *between childhood and adulthood. Socialism is a system in which* [not *is where*] *government owns the means of production.* (See also p. 393.)

its, it's   *Its* is the pronoun *it* in the possessive case: *That plant is losing its leaves. It's* is a contraction for *it is* or *it has: It's* [*It is*] *likely to die. It's* [*It has*] *got a fungus.* Many people confuse *it's* and *its* because possessives are most often formed with *-'s;* but the possessive *its*, like *his* and *hers*, never takes an apostrophe.

-ize, -wise   The suffix *-ize* changes a noun or an adjective into a verb: *revolutionize, immunize.* The suffix *-wise* changes a noun or adjective into an adverb: *clockwise, otherwise, likewise.* Avoid the two suffixes except in established words: *The two nations are ready to settle on* [not *finalize*] *an agreement. I'm highly sensitive* [not *sensitized*] *to that kind of criticism. Financially* [not *Moneywise*], *it's a good time to buy land.*

kind of, sort of, type of   In formal speech and writing, avoid using *kind of* or *sort of* to mean "somewhat": *He was rather* [not *kind of*] *tall.*

   Kind, sort, and *type* are singular and take singular modifiers and verbs: *This kind of dog is easily trained.* Agreement errors often occur when these singular nouns are combined with the plural adjectives *these* and *those: These kinds* [not *kind*] *of dogs are easily trained. Kind, sort,* and *type* should be followed by *of* but not by *a: I don't know what type of* [not *type* or *type of a*] *dog that is.*

   Use *kind of, sort of,* or *type of* only when the word *kind, sort,* or *type* is important: *That was a strange* [not *strange sort of*] *statement.*

later, latter   *Later* refers to time; *latter* refers to the second-named of two items. See also *former, latter.*

lay, lie   *Lay* means "put" or "place" and takes a direct object: *We could lay the tablecloth in the sun.* Its main forms are *lay, laid, laid. Lie* means "recline" or "be situated" and does not take an object: *I lie awake at night. The town lies east of the river.* Its main forms are *lie, lay, lain.* (See also p. 300.)

leave, let   *Leave* and *let* are interchangeable only when followed by *alone; leave me alone* is the same as *let me alone.* Otherwise, *leave* means "depart" and *let* means "allow": *Julia would not let Susan leave.*

less   See *fewer, less.*

let   See *leave, let.*

liable   See *apt, liable, likely.*

lie, lay   See *lay, lie.*

like, as   In formal speech and writing, *like* should not introduce a full clause (with a subject and a verb) because it is a preposition. The preferred choice is *as* or *as if: The plan succeeded as* [not *like*] *we hoped. It seemed as if* [not *like*] *it might fail. Other plans like it have failed.*

When *as* serves as a preposition, the distinction between *as* and *like* depends on meaning. *As* suggests that the subject is equivalent or identical to the description: *She was hired as an engineer. Like* suggests resemblance but not identity: *People like her do well in such jobs.* See also *like, such as.*

like, such as   Strictly, *such as* precedes an example that represents a larger subject, whereas *like* indicates that two subjects are comparable. *Steve has recordings of many great saxophonists such as Ben Webster and Lee Konitz. Steve wants to be a great jazz saxophonist like Ben Webster and Lee Konitz.*

Many writers prefer to keep *such* and *as* together: *Steve admires saxophonists such as* . . . rather than *Steve admires such saxophonists as.* . . .

likely   See *apt, liable, likely.*

line   See *case, instance, line.*

literally   This word means "actually" or "just as the words say," and it should not be used to qualify or intensify expressions whose words are not to be taken at face value. The sentence *He was literally climbing the walls* describes a person behaving like an insect, not a person who is restless or anxious. For the latter meaning, *literally* should be omitted.

lose, loose   *Lose* means "mislay": *Did you lose a brown glove? Loose* means "unrestrained" or "not tight": *Ann's canary got loose. Loose* can also function as a verb meaning "let loose": *They loose the dogs as soon as they spot the bear.*

lots, lots of   Colloquial substitutes for *very many, a great many,* or *much.* Avoid *lots* and *lots of* in college or business writing. When you use either one informally, be careful to maintain subject-verb agreement: *There are* [not *is*] *lots of fish in the pond.*

may, can   See *can, may.*

may be, maybe   *May be* is a verb, and *maybe* is an adverb meaning "perhaps": *Tuesday may be a legal holiday. Maybe we won't have classes.*

may of   See *have, of.*

media   *Media* is the plural of *medium* and takes a plural verb: *All the news media are increasingly visual.* The singular verb is common, even in the media, but many readers prefer the plural verb and it is always correct.

might of   See *have, of.*

moral, morale   As a noun, *moral* means "ethical conclusion" or "lesson": *The moral of the story escapes me. Morale* means "spirit" or "state of mind": *Victory improved the team's morale.*

most, almost   See *almost, most.*

must of   See *have, of.*

myself, herself, himself, yourself   The *-self* pronouns refer to or intensify another word or words: *Paul helped himself; Jill herself said so.* The *-self* pronouns are often used colloquially in place of personal pronouns, but that use should be avoided in formal speech and writing: *No one except me* [not *myself*] *saw the accident. Our delegates will be Susan and you* [not *yourself*]. See also pp. 287–88 on the unchanging forms of the *-self* pronouns in standard American English.

nohow   Nonstandard for *in no way* or *in any way.*

nothing like, nowhere near   These colloquial substitutes for *not nearly* are best avoided in formal speech and writing: *That program is not nearly* [not *nowhere near*] *as expensive.*

nowheres   Nonstandard for *nowhere.*

number   See *amount, number.*

of, have   See *have, of.*

off of   *Of* is unnecessary. Use *off* or *from* rather than *off of: He jumped off* [or *from,* not *off of*] *the roof.*

OK, O.K., okay   All three spellings are acceptable, but avoid this colloquial term in formal speech and writing.

on, upon   In modern English, *upon* is usually just a stuffy way of saying *on.* Unless you need a formal effect, use *on: We decided on* [not *upon*] *a location for our next meeting.*

on account of   Wordy for *because of.*

on the other hand   This transitional expression of contrast should be preceded by its mate, *on the one hand: On the one hand, we hoped for snow. On the other hand, we worried that it would harm the animals.* However, the two combined can be unwieldy, and a simple *but, however, yet,* or *in contrast* often suffices: *We hoped for snow. Yet we worried that it would harm the animals.*

outside of   See *inside of, outside of.*

owing to the fact that   Wordy for *because.*

party   See *individual, person, party.*

people, persons   In formal usage, *people* refers to a general group: *We the people of the United States. . . . Persons* refers to a collection of individuals: *Will the person or persons who saw the accident please notify. . . .* Except when emphasizing individuals, prefer *people* to *persons.* See also *individual, person, party.*

per   Except in technical writing, an English equivalent is usually preferable to the Latin *per: $10 an* [not *per*] *hour; sent by* [not *per*] *parcel post; requested in* [not *per* or *as per*] *your letter.*

percent (per cent), percentage   Both of these terms refer to fractions of one hundred. *Percent* always follows a number (*40 percent of the voters*), and the word is often used instead of the symbol (%) in nontechnical writing. *Percentage* stands alone (*the percentage of votes*) or follows an adjective (*a high percentage*).

person   See *individual, person, party.*

persons   See *people, persons.*

persuade   See *convince, persuade.*

phenomena   The plural of *phenomenon* (meaning "perceivable fact" or "unusual occurrence"): *Many phenomena are not recorded. One phenomenon is attracting attention.*

plenty   A colloquial substitute for *very: The reaction occurred very* [not *plenty*] *fast.*

plus   *Plus* is standard as a preposition meaning *in addition to: His income plus mine is sufficient.* But *plus* is colloquial as a conjunctive adverb: *Our organization is larger than theirs; moreover* [not *plus*], *we have more money.*

practicable, practical   *Practicable* means "capable of being put into practice"; *practical* means "useful" or "sensible": *We figured out a practical new design for our kitchen, but it was too expensive to be practicable.*

precede, proceed   The verb *precede* means "come before": *My name precedes yours in the alphabet.* The verb *proceed* means "move on": *We were told to proceed to the waiting room.*

prejudice, prejudiced   *Prejudice* is a noun; *prejudiced* is an adjective. Do not drop the *-d* from *prejudiced*: *I knew that my parents were prejudiced* [not *prejudice*].

pretty   Overworked as an adverb meaning "rather" or "somewhat": *He was somewhat* [not *pretty*] *irked at the suggestion.*

previous to, prior to   Wordy for *before.*

principal, principle   *Principal* is an adjective meaning "foremost" or "major," a noun meaning "chief official," or, in finance, a noun meaning "capital sum." *Principle* is a noun only, meaning "rule" or "axiom." *Her principal reasons for confessing were her principles of right and wrong.*

proceed, precede   See *precede, proceed.*

provided, providing   *Provided* may serve as a subordinating conjunction meaning "on the condition (that)"; *providing* may not. *The grocer will begin providing food for the soup kitchen provided* [not *providing*] *we find a suitable space.*

question of whether, question as to whether   Wordy substitutes for *whether.*

raise, rise   *Raise* means "lift" or "bring up" and takes a direct object: *The Kirks raise cattle.* Its main forms are *raise, raised, raised. Rise* means "get up" and does not take an object: *They must rise at dawn.* Its main forms are *rise, rose, risen.* (See also p. 300.)

real, really   In formal speech and writing, *real* should not be used as an adverb; *really* is the adverb and *real* an adjective. *Popular reaction to the announcement was really* [not *real*] *enthusiastic.*

reason is because   Although colloquially common, this expression should be avoided in formal speech and writing. Use a *that* clause after *reason is*: *The reason he is absent is that* [not *is because*] *he is sick.* Or: *He is absent because he is sick.*

reckon   See *calculate, figure, reckon.*

regarding, in regard to, with regard to, relating to, relative to, with respect to, respecting   Stuffy substitutes for *on, about,* or *concerning*: *Mr. McGee spoke about* [not *with regard to*] *the plans for the merger.*

respectful, respective   *Respectful* means "full of (or showing) respect": *Be respectful of other people. Respective* means "separate": *The French and the Germans occupied their respective trenches.*

rise, raise   See *raise, rise.*

scarcely   See *but, hardly, scarcely.*

sensual, sensuous   *Sensual* suggests sexuality; *sensuous* means "pleasing to the senses." *Stirred by the sensuous scent of meadow grass and flowers, Cheryl and Paul found their thoughts growing increasingly sensual.*

set, sit *Set* means "put" or "place" and takes a direct object: *He sets the pitcher down.* Its main forms are *set, set, set. Sit* means "be seated" and does not take an object: *She sits on the sofa.* Its main forms are *sit, sat, sat.* (See also p. 300.)

shall, will *Will* is the future-tense helping verb for all persons: *I will go, you will go, they will go.* The main use of *shall* is for first-person questions requesting an opinion or consent: *Shall I order a pizza? Shall we dance?* (Questions that merely inquire about the future use *will: When will I see you again?*) *Shall* can also be used for the first person when a formal effect is desired (*I shall expect you around three*), and it is occasionally used with the second or third person to express the speaker's determination (*You shall do as I say*).

should, would *Should* expresses obligation: *I should fix dinner. You should set the table. Jack should wash the dishes. Would* expresses a wish or hypothetical condition: *I would do it. Wouldn't you?* When the context is formal, however, *should* is sometimes used instead of *would* in the first person: *We should be delighted to accept.*

should of See *have, of.*

since *Since* mainly relates to time: *I've been waiting since noon.* But *since* is also often used to mean "because": *Since you ask, I'll tell you.* Revise sentences in which the word could have either meaning, such as *Since I studied physics, I have been planning to major in engineering.*

sit, set See *set, sit.*

situation Often unnecessary, as in *The situation is that we have to get some help* (revise to *We have to get some help*) or *The team was faced with a punting situation* (revise to *The team was faced with punting* or *The team had to punt*).

so Avoid using *so* alone as a vague intensifier: *He was so late. So* needs to be followed by *that* and a clause that states a result: *He was so late that I left without him.*

some *Some* is colloquial as an adverb meaning "somewhat" or "to some extent" and as an adjective meaning "remarkable": *We'll have to hurry somewhat* [not *some*] *to get there in time. Those are remarkable* [not *some*] *photographs.*

somebody, some body; someone, some one *Somebody* and *someone* are indefinite pronouns; *some body* is a noun modified by *some*; and *some one* is a pronoun or an adjective modified by *some. Somebody ought to invent a shampoo that will give hair some body. Someone told Janine she should choose some one plan and stick with it.*

someplace Informal for *somewhere.*

sometime, sometimes, some time *Sometime* means "at an indefinite time in the future": *Why don't you come up and see me sometime? Sometimes* means "now and then": *I still see my old friend Joe sometimes. Some time* means "a span of time": *I need some time to make the payments.*

somewheres Nonstandard for *somewhere.*

sort of, sort of a See *kind of, sort of, type of.*

specially See *especially, specially.*

such   Avoid using *such* as a vague intensifier: *It was such a cold winter. Such* should be followed by *that* and a clause that states a result: *It was such a cold winter that Napoleon's troops had to turn back.*

such as   See *like, such as.*

supposed to, used to   In both of these expressions, the *-d* is essential: *I used to* [not *use to*] *think so. He's supposed to* [not *suppose to*] *meet us.*

sure   Colloquial when used as an adverb meaning *surely: James Madison sure was right about the need for the Bill of Rights.* If you merely want to be emphatic, use *certainly: Madison certainly was right.* If your goal is to convince a possibly reluctant reader, use *surely: Madison surely was right. Surely Madison was right.*

sure and, sure to; try and, try to   *Sure to* and *try to* are the correct forms: *Be sure to* [not *sure and*] *vote. Try to* [not *Try and*] *vote early to avoid a line.*

take, bring   See *bring, take.*

than, as   See *as, than.*

than, then   *Than* is a conjunction used in comparisons, *then* an adverb indicating time: *Holmes knew then that Moriarty was wilier than he had thought.*

that, which   *That* always introduces an essential clause: *We should use the lettuce that Susan bought* (*that Susan bought* limits *lettuce* to a particular lettuce). *Which* can introduce both essential and nonessential clauses, but many writers reserve *which* only for nonessential clauses: *The leftover lettuce, which is in the refrigerator, would make a good salad* (*which is in the refrigerator* simply provides more information about the lettuce we already know of). Essential clauses (with *that* or *which*) are not set off by commas; nonessential clauses (with *which*) are. (See also pp. 450–51.)

that, who, which   Use *that* to refer to most animals and to things: *The animals that escaped included a zebra. The rocket that failed cost millions.* Use *who* to refer to people and to animals with names: *Dorothy is the girl who visits Oz. Her dog, Toto, who accompanies her, gives her courage.* Use *which* only to refer to animals and things: *The river, which runs more than a thousand miles, empties into the Indian Ocean.* (See also pp. 372–73.)

their, there, they're   *Their* is the possessive form of *they: Give them their money. There* indicates place (*I saw her standing there*) or functions to postpone the sentence subject (*There is a hole behind you*). *They're* is a contraction for *they are: They're going fast.*

theirselves   Nonstandard for *themselves.*

them   In standard American English, *them* does not serve as an adjective: *Those* [not *Them*] *people want to know.*

then, than   See *than, then.*

these kind, these sort, these type, those kind   See *kind of, sort of, type of.*

this, these   *This* is singular: *this car* or *This is the reason I left. These* is plural: *these cars* or *These are not valid reasons.*

this here, these here, that there, them there   Nonstandard for *this, these, that,* and *those.*

thru A colloquial spelling of *through* that should be avoided in all academic and business writing.

thusly A mistaken form of *thus*.

till, until, 'til *Till* and *until* have the same meaning; either is acceptable. *'Til*, a contraction of *until*, is an old form that has been replaced by *till*.

time period Since a *period* is an interval of time, the expression is redundant: *They did not see each other for a long time* [not *time period*]. *Six accidents occurred in a three-week period* [not *time period*].

to, too, two *To* is a preposition; *too* is an adverb meaning "also" or "excessively"; and *two* is a number. *I too have been to Europe two times.*

too Avoid using *too* as a vague intensifier: *Monkeys are too mean.* When you do use *too*, explain the consequences of the excessive quality: *Monkeys are too mean to make good pets.*

toward, towards Both are acceptable, though *toward* is preferred. Use one or the other consistently.

try and, try to See *sure and, sure to; try and, try to.*

type of See *kind of, sort of, type of.* Don't use *type* without *of*: *It was a family type of* [not *type*] *restaurant.* Or, better: *It was a family restaurant.*

uninterested See *disinterested, uninterested.*

unique *Unique* means "the only one of its kind" and so cannot sensibly be modified with words such as *very* or *most*: *That was a unique* [not *a very unique* or *the most unique*] *movie.*

until See *till, until, 'til.*

upon, on See *on, upon.*

usage, use *Usage* refers to conventions, most often those of a language: *Is "hadn't ought" proper usage? Usage* is often misused in place of the noun *use*: *Wise use* [not *usage*] *of insulation can save fuel.*

use, utilize *Utilize* can be used to mean "make good use of": *Many teachers utilize computers for instruction.* But for all other senses of "place in service" or "employ," prefer *use*.

used to See *supposed to, used to.*

wait for, wait on In formal speech and writing, *wait for* means "await" (*I'm waiting for Paul*), and *wait on* means "serve" (*The owner of the store herself waited on us*).

ways Colloquial as a substitute for *way*: *We have only a little way* [not *ways*] *to go.*

well See *good, well.*

whether, if See *if, whether.*

which, that See *that, which.*

which, who, that See *that, who, which.*

who, whom *Who* is the subject of a sentence or clause (*We don't know who will come*). *Whom* is the object of a verb or preposition (*We do not know whom we invited*). (See also pp. 291–92.)

who's, whose *Who's* is the contraction of *who is* or *who has*: *Who's* [*Who is*] *at the door? Jim is the only one who's* [*who has*] *passed. Whose* is the possessive form of *who*: *Whose book is that?*

will, shall   See *shall, will.*

wise   See *-ize, -wise.*

with regard to, with respect to   See *regarding.*

would   See *should, would.*

would be   Often used instead of *is* or *are* to soften statements need-lessly: *One example is* [not *would be*] *gun-control laws. Would* can com-bine with other verbs for the same unassertive effect: *would ask, would seem, would suggest,* and so on.

would have   Avoid this construction in place of *had* in clauses that begin *if* and state a condition contrary to fact: *If the tree had* [not *would have*] *withstood the fire, it would have been the oldest in the state.* (See also p. 319.)

would of   See *have, of.*

you   In all but very formal writing, *you* is generally appropriate as long as it means "you, the reader." In all writing, avoid indefinite uses of *you,* such as *In one ancient tribe your first loyalty was to your parents.* (See also p. 372.)

your, you're   *Your* is the possessive form of *you: Your dinner is ready. You're* is the contraction of *you are: You're bound to be late.*

yourself   See *myself, herself, himself, yourself.*

Glossary of Terms

This glossary defines terms of grammar, rhetoric, literary analysis, research, and other aspects of writing. Page numbers in parentheses refer you to sections of the text where the terms are explained more fully.

absolute phrase   A phrase consisting of a noun or pronoun plus the *-ing* or *-ed* form of a verb (a participle): *Our accommodations arranged, we set out on our journey. They will hire a local person, other things being equal.* An absolute phrase modifies a whole clause or sentence (rather than a single word), and it is not joined to the rest of the sentence by a connector. (See p. 271.)

abstract and concrete   Two kinds of language. **Abstract** words refer to ideas, qualities, attitudes, and conditions that can't be perceived with the senses: *beauty, guilty, victory.* **Concrete** words refer to objects, persons, places, or conditions that can be perceived with the senses: *Abilene, scratchy, toolbox.* See also *general and specific.* (See p. 871.)

acronym   A pronounceable word formed from the initial letter or letters of each word in an organization's title: for example, NATO (North Atlantic Treaty Organization).

active voice   See *verb voice.*

adjectival   A term sometimes used to describe any word or word group, other than an adjective, that is used to modify a noun. Common adjectivals include nouns (*wagon train, railroad ties*), phrases (*fool on the hill*), and clauses (*the man that I used to be*).

adjective   A word used to modify a noun (*beautiful morning*) or a pronoun (*ordinary one*). (See Chapter 16.) Nouns, some verb forms, phrases, and clauses may also serve as adjectives: *book sale; a used book; sale of old books; the sale, which occurs annually.* (See *clauses, prepositional phrases,* and *verbals and verbal phrases.*)
Adjectives come in several classes:

- A **descriptive adjective** names some quality of a noun: *beautiful morning, dark horse.*
- A **limiting adjective** narrows the scope of a noun. It may be a **possessive** (*my, their*); a **demonstrative adjective** (*this train, these days*); an **interrogative adjective** (*what time? whose body?*); or a number (*two boys*).
- A **proper adjective** is derived from a proper noun: *French language, Machiavellian scheme.*

Adjectives can also be classified according to position:

- An **attributive adjective** appears next to the noun it modifies: *full moon.*
- A **predicate adjective** is connected to its noun by a linking verb: *The moon is full.* See also *complement.*

adjective clause   See *adjective.*

adjective phrase See *adjective.*

adverb A word used to modify a verb (*warmly greet*), an adjective (*only three people*), another adverb (*quite seriously*), or a whole sentence (*Fortunately, she is employed*). (See Chapter 16.) Some verb forms, phrases, and clauses may also serve as adverbs: *easy to stop, drove by a farm, plowed the fields when the earth thawed.* (See *clause, prepositional phrase,* and *verbals and verbal phrases.*)

adverb clause See *adverb.*

adverbial A term sometimes used to describe any word or word group, other than an adverb, that is used to modify a verb, an adjective, another adverb, or a whole sentence. Common adverbials include nouns (*This little piggy stayed home*), phrases (*This little piggy went to market*), and clauses (*This little piggy went wherever he wanted*).

adverbial conjunction See *conjunctive adverb.*

adverb phrase See *adverb.*

agreement The correspondence of one word to another in person, number, or gender. A verb must agree with its subject (*The chef orders egg sandwiches*), a pronoun must agree with its antecedent (*The chef surveys her breakfast*), and a demonstrative adjective must agree with its noun (*She likes these kinds of sandwiches*). (See Chapter 15.)

   Logical agreement requires consistency in number between other related words, usually nouns: *The students brought their books* [not *book*]. (See p. 376.)

analogy A comparison between members of different classes, such as a nursery school and a barnyard or a molecule and a pair of dancers. Usually, the purpose is to explain something unfamiliar to readers through something familiar. (See p. 105.)

analysis The separation of a subject into its elements. Sometimes called **division,** analysis is fundamental to critical thinking, reading, and writing (pp. 155–56, 164–65) and is a useful tool for developing essays (p. 34) and paragraphs (pp. 102–03).

antecedent The word to which a pronoun refers: *Jonah, who is not yet ten, has already chosen the college he will attend* (*Jonah* is the antecedent of the pronouns *who* and *he*). (See pp. 331–35.)

APA style The style of documentation recommended by the American Psychological Association and used in many of the social sciences. (For discussion and examples, see pp. 804–23.)

appeals Attempts to engage and persuade readers. An **emotional appeal** touches readers' feelings, beliefs, and values. An **ethical appeal** presents the writer as competent, sincere, and fair. A **rational appeal** engages readers' powers of reasoning. (See pp. 219–21.)

appositive A word or phrase appearing next to a noun or pronoun that renames or identifies it and is equivalent to it: *My brother Michael, the best horn player in town, won the state competition* (*Michael* identifies which brother is being referred to; *the best horn player in town* renames *Michael*). (See pp. 276–77.)

argument Writing whose primary purpose is to convince readers of an idea or persuade them to act. (See Chapters 8–9.)

article The word *a, an,* or *the.* Articles are sometimes called **determiners** because they always signal that a noun follows. (See pp. 344–46 for when to use *a/an* versus *the.* See p. 845 for when to use *a* versus *an.*)

assertion See *claim.*

assumption A stated or unstated belief or opinion. Uncovering assumptions is part of critical thinking, reading, and writing (see pp. 156, 166–68). In argument, assumptions connect claims and evidence (see pp. 194–95).

audience The intended readers of a piece of writing. Knowledge of the audience's needs and expectations helps a writer shape writing so that it is clear, interesting, and convincing. (See pp. 19–22, 191–92.)

auxiliary verb See *helping verb.*

balanced sentence A sentence consisting of two clauses with parallel constructions: *Do as I say, not as I do. Befriend all animals; exploit none.* Their balance makes such sentences highly emphatic. (See p. 405.)

belief A conviction based on morality, values, or faith. Statements of belief may serve as assumptions or even as evidence, but they are not arguable and so cannot serve as the thesis in an argument. (See p. 189.)

blog A Web site, often created and maintained by a person or small group of people, with regular, dated entries of commentary or descriptions of events.

body In a piece of writing, the large central part where ideas supporting the thesis are presented and developed. See also *conclusion* and *introduction.*

brainstorming A technique for generating ideas about a subject: concentrating on the subject for a fixed time (say, fifteen minutes), you list every idea and detail that comes to mind. (See pp. 31–32.)

cardinal number The type of number that shows amount: *two, sixty, ninety-seven.* Contrast *ordinal number* (such as *second, ninety-seventh*).

case The form of a noun or pronoun that indicates its function in the sentence. Most pronouns have three cases:

- The **subjective case** (*I, she*) for the subject of a verb or for a subject complement.
- The **objective case** (*me, her*) for the object of a verb, verbal, or preposition.
- The **possessive case** to indicate ownership, used either as an adjective (*my, her*) or as a noun (*mine, hers*).

(See p. 287 for a list of the forms of personal and relative pronouns.)
    Nouns use the subjective form (*dog, America*) for all cases except the possessive (*dog's, America's*).

cause-and-effect analysis The determination of why something happened or what its consequences were or will be. (See pp. 35 and 106.)

characters The people in a literary work, including the narrator of a story or the speaker of a poem. (See p. 763.)

Chicago style A style of documentation recommended by *The Chicago Manual of Style* and used in history, art, and some other humanities. (For discussion and examples, see pp. 785–96.)

chronological organization The arrangement of events as they occurred in time, usually from first to last. (See pp. 48–49, 89.)

citation In research writing, the way of acknowledging material borrowed from sources. Most citation systems use a number or brief parenthetical reference in the text to signal that material is borrowed and to direct the reader to information on the source at the end of the work. (See pp. 667–713 for MLA style, pp. 785–96 for Chicago style, pp. 804–23 for APA style, and pp. 834–41 for CSE style.)

claim A positive statement or assertion that requires support. Claims are the backbone of any argument. (See pp. 188–90.)

Terms

classification The sorting of many elements into groups based on their similarities. (See pp. 34 and 103–04.)

clause A group of related words containing a subject and a predicate. A **main (independent) clause** can stand by itself as a sentence. A **subordinate (dependent) clause** serves as a single part of speech and so cannot stand by itself as a sentence.

> Main clause We can go to the movies.
> Subordinate clause We can go if Julie gets back on time.

A subordinate clause may function as an adjective (*The car that hit Fred was speeding*), an adverb (*The car hit Fred when it ran a red light*), or a noun (*Whoever was driving should be arrested*). (See p. 274.)

clichés See *trite expressions.*

climactic organization The arrangement of material in order of increasing drama or interest, leading to a climax. (See pp. 50, 91.)

clustering A technique for generating ideas about a subject: drawing and writing, you branch outward from a center point (the subject) to pursue the implications of ideas. (See pp. 32–33.)

coherence The quality of an effective essay or paragraph that helps readers see relations among ideas and move easily from one idea to the next. (See pp. 50–51, 86–96.)

collaborative learning Students working together in groups to help each other become better writers and readers. (See pp. 75–78.)

collective noun See *noun.*

colloquial language The words and expressions of everyday speech. Colloquial language can enliven informal writing but is generally inappropriate in formal academic or business writing. See also *formal and informal.* (See p. 527.)

comma splice A sentence error in which two main clauses are separated by a comma with no coordinating conjunction. (See Chapter 18.)

> Comma splice The book was long, it contained useful data.
> Revised The book was long; it contained useful data.
> Revised The book was long, and it contained useful data.

common noun See *noun.*

comparative See *comparison.*

comparison The form of an adverb or adjective that shows its degree of quality or amount.

- The **positive degree** is the simple, uncompared form: *gross, shyly.*
- The **comparative degree** compares the thing modified to at least one other thing: *grosser, more shyly.*
- The **superlative degree** indicates that the thing modified exceeds all other things to which it is being compared: *grossest, most shyly.*

The comparative and superlative degrees are formed either with the endings *-er/-est* or with the words *more/most, less/least.* (See pp. 340–41.)

comparison and contrast   The identification of similarities (comparison) and differences (contrast) between two or more subjects. (See pp. 34, 104–05.)

complement   A word or word group that completes the sense of a subject, an object, or a verb. (See pp. 259–61.)

- A **subject complement** follows a linking verb and renames or describes the subject. It may be an adjective, noun, or pronoun. *I am a lion tamer, but I am not yet experienced* (the noun *lion tamer* and the adjective *experienced* complement the subject *I*). Adjective complements are also called **predicate adjectives.** Noun complements are also called **predicate nouns** or **predicate nominatives.**
- An **object complement** follows and modifies or refers to a direct object. The complement may be an adjective or a noun. *If you elect me president, I'll keep the students satisfied* (the noun *president* complements the direct object *me,* and the adjective *satisfied* complements the direct object *students*).
- A **verb complement** is a direct or indirect object of a verb. It may be a noun or pronoun. *Don't give the chimp that peanut* (*chimp* is the indirect object and *peanut* is the direct object of the verb *give;* both objects are verb complements).

complete predicate   See *predicate.*

complete subject   See *subject.*

complex sentence   See *sentence.*

compound construction   Two or more words or word groups serving the same function, such as a **compound subject** (*Harriet and Peter poled their barge down the river*), **compound predicate** (*The scout watched and waited*) or parts of a predicate (*She grew tired and hungry*), and **compound sentence** (*He smiled, and I laughed*). (See p. 278.) **Compound words** include nouns (*featherbrain, strip-mining*) and adjectives (*two-year-old, downtrodden*).

compound-complex sentence   See *sentence.*

compound predicate   See *compound construction.*

compound sentence   See *sentence.*

compound subject   See *compound construction.*

conciseness   Use of the fewest and freshest words to express meaning clearly and achieve the desired effect with readers. (See Chapter 39.)

conclusion   The closing of an essay, tying off the writer's thoughts and leaving readers with a sense of completion. (See pp. 114–15 for suggestions.)

A *conclusion* is also the result of deductive reasoning. See *deductive reasoning* and *syllogism.*

concrete See *abstract and concrete.*

conditional statement A statement expressing a condition contrary to fact and using the subjunctive mood of the verb: *If she <u>were</u> mayor, the unions would cooperate.* See also *mood.*

conjugation A list of the forms of a verb showing tense, voice, mood, person, and number. The conjugation of the verb *know* in present tense, active voice, indicative mood is *I know, you know, he/she/it knows, we know, you know, they know.* (See p. 312 for a fuller conjugation.)

conjunction A word that links and relates parts of a sentence.

- **Coordinating conjunctions** (*and, but, or, nor, for, so, yet*) connect words or word groups of equal grammatical rank: *The lights went out, <u>but</u> the doctors <u>and</u> nurses kept caring for patients.* (See p. 279.)
- **Correlative conjunctions** or correlatives (such as *either . . . or, not only . . . but also*) are two or more connecting words that work together: *He was certain that <u>either</u> his parents <u>or</u> his brother would help him.* (See p. 279.)
- **Subordinating conjunctions** (*after, although, as if, because, if, when,* and so on) begin subordinate clauses and link them to main clauses: *The seven dwarfs whistle <u>while</u> they work.* (See p. 273.)

conjunctive adverb (adverbial conjunction) An adverb (such as *besides, consequently, however, indeed,* or *therefore*) that relates two main clauses in a sentence: *We had hoped to own a house by now; <u>however,</u> housing costs have risen too fast.* (See p. 281.) The error known as a comma splice results when two main clauses related by a conjunctive adverb are separated only by a comma. (See pp. 364–65.)

connector (connective) Any word or phrase that links words, phrases, clauses, or sentences. Common connectors include coordinating, correlative, and subordinating conjunctions; conjunctive adverbs; and prepositions.

connotation An association called up by a word, beyond its dictionary definition. Contrast *denotation.* (See pp. 536–37.)

construction Any group of grammatically related words, such as a phrase, a clause, or a sentence.

contraction A condensation of an expression, with an apostrophe replacing the missing letters: for example, *doesn't* (for *does not*), *we'll* (for *we will*). (See pp. 478–79.)

contrast See *comparison and contrast.*

coordinate adjectives Two or more adjectives that equally modify the same noun or pronoun: *The camera panned the <u>vast, empty</u> desert.* (See pp. 455–56.)

coordinating conjunction See *conjunction.*

coordination The linking of words, phrases, or clauses that are of equal importance, usually with a coordinating conjunction: *He <u>and</u> I laughed, <u>but</u> she was not amused.* Contrast *subordination.* (See pp. 410–12.)

correlative conjunction (correlative) See *conjunction.*

count noun See *noun.*

critical thinking, reading, and writing Looking beneath the surface of words and images to discern meaning and relationships and to build knowledge. (See Chapter 6.)

CSE style Either of two styles of documenting sources recommended by the Council of Science Editors and frequently used in the natural and applied sciences and in mathematics. (For discussion and examples, see pp. 834–41.)

cumulative (loose) sentence A sentence in which modifiers follow the subject and verb: *Ducks waddled by, their tails swaying and their quacks rising to heaven.* Contrast *periodic sentence.* (See p. 403.)

dangling modifier A modifier that does not sensibly describe anything in its sentence. (See pp. 388–89.)

Dangling   Having arrived late, the concert was underway.

Revised   Having arrived late, we found that the concert was underway.

data In argument, a term used for *evidence.* See *evidence.*

database A collection and organization of information (data). A database may be printed, but the term is most often used for electronic sources.

declension A list of the forms of a noun or pronoun, showing inflections for person (for pronouns), number, and case. See p. 287 for a declension of the personal and relative pronouns.

deductive reasoning Applying a generalization to specific circumstances in order to reach a conclusion. See also *syllogism.* Contrast *inductive reasoning.* (See pp. 215–17.)

definition Specifying the characteristics of something to establish what it is and is not. (See pp. 34, 102, 190.)

degree See *comparison.*

demonstrative adjective See *adjective.*

demonstrative pronoun See *pronoun.*

denotation The main or dictionary definition of a word. Contrast *connotation.* (See pp. 536–37.)

dependent clause See *clause.*

derivational suffix See *suffix.*

description Detailing the sensory qualities of a thing, person, place, or feeling. (See pp. 34 and 100.)

descriptive adjective See *adjective.*

descriptor See *keyword(s).*

determiner A word that marks and precedes a noun: for example, *a, an, the, my, your.* See also *article.* (See pp. 344–48 for the uses of determiners before nouns.)

dialect A variety of a language used by a specific group or in a specific region. A dialect may be distinguished by its pronunciation, vocabulary, and grammar. (See pp. 177–79 and 525–26.)

diction The choice and use of words. (See Chapters 37–39.)

dictionary form See *plain form.*

Digital Object Identifier (DOI)   A unique identifier assigned to journal articles, books, and other publications. (See p. 809.)

direct address   A construction in which a word or phrase indicates the person or group spoken to: *Have you finished, John? Farmers, unite.*

direct object   See *object.*

direct question   A sentence asking a question and concluding with a question mark: *Do they know we are watching?* Contrast *indirect question.*

direct quotation (direct discourse)   See *quotation.*

discussion list   A mailing list of subscribers who use e-mail to converse on a particular subject.

Terms

division   See *analysis.*

documentation   In research writing, supplying citations that legitimate the use of borrowed material and support claims about its origins. Contrast *plagiarism.* (See pp. 657–58.)

document design   The control of a document's elements to achieve the flow, spacing, grouping, emphasis, and standardization that are appropriate for the writing situation. (See Chapter 5.)

domain   The part of a Web address (or URL) that gives the organization sponsoring the site.

double negative   A generally nonstandard form consisting of two negative words used in the same construction so that they effectively cancel each other: *I don't have no money.* Rephrase as *I have no money* or *I don't have any money.* (See p. 342.)

double possessive   A possessive using both the ending -'s and the preposition *of*: *That is a favorite expression of Mark's.*

double talk (doublespeak)   Language intended to confuse or to be misunderstood. (See p. 529.)

drafting   The stage of the writing process when ideas are expressed in connected sentences and paragraphs. (See pp. 54–56.)

editing   A distinct step in revising a written work, focusing on clarity, tone, and correctness. Compare *revising.* (See pp. 67–69.)

ellipsis   The omission of a word or words from a quotation, indicated by the three spaced periods of an **ellipsis mark**: *"that all . . . are created equal."*

elliptical clause   A clause omitting a word or words whose meaning is understood from the rest of the clause: *David likes Minneapolis better than [he likes] Chicago.* (See p. 275.)

emotional appeal   See *appeals.*

emphasis   The manipulation of words, sentences, and paragraphs to stress important ideas. (See Chapter 23.)

essay   A nonfiction composition of multiple paragraphs, focused on a single subject and with a central idea or thesis.

essential element   A word or word group that is necessary to the meaning of a sentence because it limits the thing it refers to: removing it would leave the meaning unclear or too general. Also called a **restrictive element,** an essential element is not set off by punctuation: *The keys to the car are on the table. That man who called about the apartment said he'd* *try to call again tonight.* Contrast *nonessential element.* (See pp. 449–53, 463.)

ethical appeal   See *appeals.*

etymology   The history of a word's meanings and forms.

euphemism   A presumably inoffensive word that a writer or speaker substitutes for a word deemed possibly offensive or too blunt—for example, *passed away* for "died." (See pp. 528–29.)

evaluation   A judgment of the quality, value, currency, bias, or other aspects of a work. (See pp. 159–60, 168, 612–25.)

evidence   The facts, examples, expert opinions, and other information that support the claims in an argument. (See pp. 190–94, 218–19.)

expletive   A sentence that postpones the subject by beginning with *there* or *it* and a form of the verb *be*: *It is impossible to get a ticket. There should be more seats available.* (See p. 283.)

exposition   Writing whose primary purpose is to explain something about a subject.

fallacies   Errors in reasoning. Some evade the issue of the argument; others oversimplify the argument. (See pp. 199–204.)

faulty predication   A sentence error in which the meanings of subject and predicate conflict, so that the subject is said to be or do something illogical: *The installation of air bags takes up space in a car's steering wheel and dashboard.* (See pp. 393–94.)

figurative language (figures of speech)   Expressions that suggest meanings different from their literal meanings in order to achieve special effects. (See pp. 542–43.) Some common figures:

- **Hyperbole,** deliberate exaggeration: *The bag weighed a ton.*
- **Metaphor,** an implied comparison between two unlike things: *The wind stabbed through our clothes.*
- **Personification,** the attribution of human qualities to a thing or idea: *The water beckoned seductively.*
- **Simile,** an explicit comparison, using *like* or *as,* between two unlike things: *The sky glowered like an angry parent.*

A **mixed metaphor** is a confusing or ludicrous combination of incompatible figures: *The wind stabbed through our clothes and shook our bones.*

finite verb   Any verb that makes an assertion or expresses a state of being and can stand as the main verb of a sentence or clause: *The moose eats the leaves.* (See pp. 267–68.) Contrast *verbal,* which is formed from a finite verb but is unable to stand alone as the main verb of a sentence: *I saw the moose eating the leaves.*

first person   See *person.*

foil   A character in a literary work who contrasts with another character and thus helps to define that other character. (See p. 777.)

formal and informal   Levels of usage achieved through word choice and sentence structure. More informal writing, as in a letter to an acquaintance or a personal essay, resembles some speech in its colloquial language, contractions, and short, fairly simple sentences. More formal writing, as in academic papers and business reports, avoids these attributes of speech and tends to rely on longer and more complicated sentences.

format   The arrangement and spacing of elements in a document. See also *document design.*

fragment   See *sentence fragment.*

freewriting   A technique for generating ideas: in a fixed amount of time (say, fifteen minutes), you write continuously without stopping to reread. (See pp. 30–31.)

function word   A word, such as an article, conjunction, or preposition, that serves primarily to clarify the roles of and relations between other words in a sentence: *We chased the goat for an hour but finally caught it.* Contrast *lexical word.*

Terms

fused sentence (run-on sentence)   A sentence error in which two main clauses are joined with no punctuation or connecting word between them. (See p. 365.)

> Fused   I heard his lecture it was dull.
>
> Revised   I heard his lecture; it was dull.

future perfect tense   See *tense.*

future tense   See *tense.*

gender   The classification of nouns or pronouns as masculine (*he, boy, handyman*), feminine (*she, woman, actress*), or neuter (*it, typewriter, dog*).

general and specific   Terms designating the relative number of instances or objects included in a group signified by a word. The following list moves from most **general** (including the most objects) to most **specific** (including the fewest objects): *vehicle, four-wheeled vehicle, automobile, sedan, Ford Taurus, blue Ford Taurus, my sister's blue Ford Taurus named Hank.* See also *abstract and concrete.* (See p. 862.)

generalization   A claim inferred from evidence. See also *inductive reasoning.*

generic he   *He* used to mean *he or she.* For ways to avoid *he* when you intend either or both genders, see pp. 333–34 and 531.

generic noun   A noun that refers to a typical member of a group rather than to a specific person or thing: *Any person may come. A student needs good work habits.* A singular generic noun takes a singular pronoun (*he, she,* or *it*). (See pp. 333–35.)

genitive case   Another term for possessive case. See *case.*

genre   A type of writing, such as case study, research report, essay, or poem. (See pp. 23–24 and 172.)

gerund   A verbal that ends in *-ing* and functions as a noun: *Working is all right for killing time* (*working* is the subject of *is; killing* is the object of *for*). See also *verbals and verbal phrases.* (See p. 268.)

gerund phrase   A word group consisting of a gerund plus any modifiers or objects. See also *verbals and verbal phrases.*

grammar   A description of how a language works.

grounds   A term used for *evidence* in argument. See *evidence.*

helping verb (auxiliary verb)   A verb used with another verb to convey time, obligation, and other meanings: *You should write a letter. You have* *written other letters.* The **modals** include *can, could, may, might, must, ought, shall, should, will, would.* The other helping verbs are forms of *be, have,* and *do.* (See pp. 296, 302–06.)

homonyms Words that are pronounced the same but have different spellings and meanings, such as *heard/herd* and *to/too/two.* (See pp. 554–55 for a list.)

hyperbole See *figurative language.*

idiom An expression that is peculiar to a language and that may not make sense if taken literally: for example, *bide your time,* and *by and large.* See pp. 540–41 for a list of idioms involving prepositions, such as *agree with them* and *agree to the contract.*

illustration or support Examples or reasons that develop an idea. (See pp. 34 and 101.)

imagery A word or phrase that draws on the sense of sight, hearing, touch, taste, or smell to describe an object or feeling, as in *she wrapped the shaking child in her spindly arms, thundering waves beat the beach,* or *his smooth skin suggested a life lived indoors.*

imperative See *mood.*

indefinite pronoun See *pronoun.*

independent clause See *clause.*

indicative See *mood.*

indirect object See *object.*

indirect question A sentence reporting a question, usually in a subordinate clause, and ending with a period: *The student asked when the paper was due.* Contrast *direct question.*

indirect quotation (indirect discourse) See *quotation.*

inductive reasoning Inferring a generalization from specific evidence. Contrast *deductive reasoning.* (See pp. 214–15.)

infinitive A verbal formed from the plain form of the verb plus the **infinitive marker** *to: to swim, to write.* Infinitives and infinitive phrases may function as nouns, adjectives, or adverbs. See also *verbals and verbal phrases.* (See p. 269.)

infinitive marker See *infinitive.*

infinitive phrase A word group consisting of an infinitive plus any subject, objects, or modifiers. See also *verbals and verbal phrases.*

inflection The variation in the form of a word that indicates its function in a particular context. See *declension,* the inflection of nouns and pronouns; *conjugation,* the inflection of verbs; and *comparison,* the inflection of adjectives and adverbs.

inflectional suffix See *suffix.*

informal See *formal and informal.*

intensifier A modifier that adds emphasis to the word(s) it modifies: for example, *very slow, so angry.*

intensive pronoun See *pronoun.*

interjection A word standing by itself or inserted in a construction to exclaim or command attention: *Hey! Ouch! What the heck happened?*

interpretation   The determination of meaning or significance—for instance, in a work such as a poem or photograph or in the literature on some issue such as job discrimination. (See pp. 159, 166.)

interrogative   Functioning as or involving a question.

interrogative adjective   See *adjective*.

interrogative pronoun   See *pronoun*.

intransitive verb   A verb that does not take a direct object: *The woman laughed*. (See p. 258.)

introduction   The opening of an essay, a transition for readers between their world and the writer's. The introduction often contains a statement of the writer's thesis. (See pp. 110–13 for suggestions.)

invention   The discovery and exploration of ideas, usually occurring most intensively in the early stages of the writing process. (See pp. 25–35 for invention techniques.)

inversion   A reversal of the usual word order in a sentence, as when a verb precedes its subject or an object precedes its verb: *Down swooped the hawk. Our aims we stated clearly.*

irony   The use of words to suggest a meaning different from what the words say literally: *What a happy face!* (said to someone scowling miserably); *With that kind of planning, prices are sure to go down* (written with the expectation that prices will rise).

irregular verb   A verb that forms its past tense and past participle in some other way than by the addition of -*d* or -*ed* to the plain form: for example, *go, went, gone; give, gave, given*. Contrast *regular verb*. (See pp. 298–99 for a list of irregular verbs.)

jargon   In one sense, jargon is the specialized language of any group, such as doctors or baseball players. In another sense, jargon is vague, pretentious, wordy, and ultimately unclear writing such as that found in some academic, business, and government publications. (See p. 551.)

journal   A personal record of observations, reactions, ideas, and other thoughts. Besides providing a private place to think in writing, a journal is useful for making notes about reading (pp. 146, 151, 161–63, 758–59), discovering ideas for essays (pp. 28–29), and keeping track of research (pp. 571, 758–59, 801, 831).

journalist's questions   A set of questions useful for probing a subject to discover ideas about it. (See p. 33.)

keyword(s)   A word or words that define a subject, used for searching the Web and databases such as periodical indexes. (See pp. 584–87.)

lexical word   A word, such as a noun, verb, or modifier, that carries part of the meaning of language. Contrast *function word*.

linear text   Text such as a conventional printed document that is intended to be read in sequence. Contrast *hypertext*.

linking verb   A verb that relates a subject to its complement: *Julie is a Democrat. He looks harmless. The boy became a man.* Common linking verbs are the forms of *be*; the verbs relating to the senses, such as *look* and *smell*; and the verbs *become, appear,* and *seem*. (See p. 259.)

listserv   See *discussion list*.

Terms

logical agreement   See *agreement.*

logical fallacies   See *fallacies.*

main clause   See *clause.*

main verb   The part of a verb phrase that carries the principal meaning: *had been <u>walking</u>, could <u>happen</u>, was <u>chilled</u>.* See also *verb phrase.*

mass noun   Another term for noncount noun. See *noun.*

mechanics   The use of capital letters, italics or underlining, abbreviations, numbers, and divided words. (See Chapters 33–36.)

metaphor   See *figurative language.*

misplaced modifier   A modifier so far from the term it modifies or so close to another term it could modify that its relation to the rest of the sentence is unclear. (See Chapter 21.)

Misplaced	The boys played with firecrackers that they bought illegally <u>in the field</u>.
Revised	The boys played <u>in the field</u> with firecrackers that they bought illegally.

A squinting modifier could modify the words on either side of it: *The plan we considered <u>seriously</u> worries me.*

mixed construction   A sentence containing two or more parts that do not fit together in grammar or in meaning. (See pp. 391–94.)

mixed metaphor   See *figurative language.*

MLA style   The style of documenting sources recommended by the Modern Language Association and used in many of the humanities, including English. (For explanation and examples, see Chapter 46.)

modal   See *helping verb.*

modifier   Any word or word group that limits or qualifies the meaning of another word or word group. Modifiers include adjectives and adverbs as well as words, phrases, and clauses that act as adjectives and adverbs.

mood   The form of a verb that shows how the speaker or writer views the action. (See pp. 318–19.)

- The **indicative mood,** the most common, is used to make statements or ask questions: *The play <u>will be performed</u> Saturday. Did you <u>get</u> the tickets?*
- The **imperative mood** gives a command: *Please <u>get</u> good seats.*
- The **subjunctive mood** expresses a wish, a condition contrary to fact, a recommendation, or a request: *I wish George <u>were coming</u> with us. Did you suggest that he <u>join</u> us?*

narration   Recounting a sequence of events, usually in the order of their occurrence. (See pp. 34 and 100.) Literary narration tells a story. (See Chapter 49.)

narrator   The speaker in a poem or the voice who tells a story. (See pp. 763, 773, 774.)

neologism   A word coined recently and not in established use. (See p. 528.)

newsgroup   An Internet discussion group with a common site where all postings are recorded. (See p. 604.)

nominal   A noun, a pronoun, or a word or word group used as a noun: *Joan and I talked. The rich owe a debt to the poor* (adjectives acting as subject and object). *Baby-sitting can be exhausting* (gerund acting as subject). *I like to play with children* (infinitive phrase acting as object).

nominative   Another term for subjective case. See *case.*

noncount noun   See *noun.*

nonessential element   A word or word group that does not limit the term or construction it refers to and thus is not essential to the meaning of the sentence. Also called a **nonrestrictive element,** a nonessential element is set off by punctuation, usually commas: *The new apartment building, in shades of tan and gray, will house fifty people* (nonessential adjective phrase). *Sleep, which we all need, occupies a third of our lives* (nonessential adjective clause). *His wife, Patricia, is a chemist* (nonessential appositive). Contrast *essential element.* (See pp. 449–53.)

nonfinite verb   See *verbals and verbal phrases.*

nonrestrictive element   See *nonessential element.*

nonstandard   Words and grammatical forms not conforming to standard American English. (See pp. 525–26.)

noun   A word that names a person, place, thing, quality, or idea: *Maggie, Alabama, clarinet, satisfaction, socialism.* Nouns normally form the possessive case by adding -'s (*Maggie's*) and the plural by adding -s or -es (*clarinets, messes*), although there are exceptions (*men, women, children*). The forms of nouns depend partly on where they fit in certain overlapping groups:

- **Common nouns** name general classes and are not capitalized: *book, government, music.*
- **Proper nouns** name specific people, places, and things and are capitalized: *Susan, Athens, Fenway Park.*
- **Count nouns** name things considered countable in English (they form plurals): *ounce/ounces, camera/cameras, person/people.*
- **Noncount nouns** name things not considered countable in English (they don't form plurals): *chaos, fortitude, silver, earth, information.*
- **Collective nouns** are singular in form but name groups: *team, class, family.*

noun clause   A word group containing a subject and a verb and functioning as a subject, object, or complement: *Everyone wondered how the door opened. Whoever opened it had left.*

number   The form of a noun, pronoun, demonstrative adjective, or verb that indicates whether it is singular or plural: *woman, women; I, we; this, these; runs, run.*

object   A noun, pronoun, or word group that receives the action of or is influenced by a transitive verb, a verbal, or a preposition.

- A **direct object** receives the action of a verb or verbal and frequently follows it in a sentence: *We sat watching the stars. Emily caught whatever it was you had.* (See p. 258.)
- An **indirect object** tells for or to whom something is done: *I lent Stan my car. Reiner bought us all champagne.* (See p. 260.)

Terms

▪ An **object of a preposition** usually follows a preposition and is linked by it to the rest of the sentence: *They are going to Rhode Island for the blues festival.* (See p. 265.)

object complement See *complement.*

objective See *case.*

opinion A conclusion based on facts; an arguable, potentially changeable claim. Claims of opinion form the backbone of any argument. (See p. 188.)

ordinal number The type of number that shows order: *first, eleventh, twenty-fifth.* Contrast *cardinal number* (such as *one, twenty-five*).

paragraph Generally, a group of sentences set off by a beginning indention and developing a single idea. That idea is often stated in a **topic sentence.** (See Chapter 4.)

parallelism Similarity of grammatical form between two or more coordinated elements: *Rising prices and declining incomes left many people in bad debt and worse despair.* (See Chapter 25.)

paraphrase The restatement of source material in one's own words and sentence structures, useful for borrowing the original author's line of reasoning but not his or her exact words. Paraphrases must always be acknowledged in source citations. (See pp. 634–37.)

parenthetical citation In the text of a paper, a brief reference, enclosed in parentheses, indicating that material is borrowed and directing the reader to the source of the material. See also *citation.*

parenthetical expression A word or construction that interrupts a sentence and is not part of its main structure, called *parenthetical* because it could (or does) appear in parentheses: *Childe Hassam (1859–1935) was an American painter. The book, incidentally, is terrible.* (See pp. 494–95.)

participial phrase A word group consisting of a participle plus any objects or modifiers. See also *verbals and verbal phrases.*

participle A verbal showing continuing or completed action, used as an adjective or part of a verb phrase but never as the main verb of a sentence or clause. (See p. 268.)

▪ A **present participle** ends in *-ing*: *My heart is breaking* (part of verb phrase). *I like to watch the rolling waves* (adjective).
▪ A **past participle** most commonly ends in *-d, -ed, -n,* or *-en* (*wished, shown, given*) but sometimes changes the spelling of the verb (*sung, done, slept*): *Jeff has broken his own record* (part of verb phrase). *The closed door beckoned* (adjective).

See also *verbals and verbal phrases.*

particle A preposition or adverb in a two-word verb: *look up, catch on.* (See pp. 309–10.)

parts of speech The classes into which words are commonly grouped according to their form, function, and meaning: nouns, pronouns, verbs, adjectives, adverbs, conjunctions, prepositions, and interjections. See separate entries for each part of speech.

passive voice See *verb voice.*

past participle See *participle.*

past perfect tense   See *tense.*

past tense   See *tense.*

patterns of development   Ways of thinking that can help you develop and organize ideas in essays and paragraphs. (See pp. 34–35 and 99–108.)

perfect tenses   See *tense.*

periodic sentence   A suspenseful sentence in which modifiers precede the main clause, which falls at the end: *Postponing decisions about family while striving to establish themselves in careers, many young adults are falsely accused of greed.* Contrast *cumulative sentence.* (See pp. 403–04.)

person   The form of a verb or pronoun that indicates whether the subject is speaking, spoken to, or spoken about. In English only personal pronouns and verbs change form to indicate difference in person. In the **first person**, the subject is speaking: *I am* [or *We are*] *planning a party.* In the **second person**, the subject is being spoken to: *Are you coming?* In the **third person**, the subject is being spoken about: *She was* [or *They were*] *going.*

personal pronoun   See *pronoun.*

personification   See *figurative language.*

phrase   A group of related words that lacks a subject or a predicate or both and that acts as a single part of speech. See *absolute phrase, prepositional phrase, verbals and verbal phrases,* and *verb phrase.*

plagiarism   The presentation of someone else's ideas or words as if they were one's own. Whether accidental or deliberate, plagiarism is a serious and often punishable offense. (See pp. 648–54.)

plain case   Another term for the subjective case of nouns. See *case.*

plain form   The dictionary form of a verb: *make, run, swivel.* See also *verb forms.*

plot   The pattern of events in a work of literature. (See p. 763.)

plural   More than one. See *number.*

point of view   The perspective or attitude of the narrator or speaker in a work of literature. See also *person.* (See p. 763.)

positive degree   See *comparison.*

possessive   See *case.*

predicate   The part of a sentence that makes an assertion about the subject. A predicate must contain a finite verb and may contain modifiers, objects of the verb, and complements. The **simple predicate** consists of the verb and its helping verbs: *A wiser person would have made a different decision.* The **complete predicate** includes the simple predicate and any modifiers, objects, and complements: *A wiser person would have made a different decision.* See also *intransitive verb, linking verb,* and *transitive verb.* (See pp. 253–54, 258–61.)

predicate adjective   See *complement.*

predicate noun (predicate nominative)   See *complement.*

prefix   A letter or group of letters (such as *sub, in, dis, pre*) that can be added at the beginning of a root or word to create a new word: *sub + marine = submarine; dis + grace = disgrace.* Contrast *suffix.*

premise   Generally, a claim or assumption basic to an argument. In a deductive syllogism, one premise applied to another leads logically to a conclusion. See also *syllogism.* (See pp. 215–17.)

preposition   A word that forms a noun or pronoun (plus any modifiers) into a prepositional phrase: *about* love, *down* the steep stairs. The common prepositions include these as well as *after, before, by, for, from, in, on, to,* and many others. (See p. 264.)

prepositional phrase   A word group consisting of a preposition and its object, plus any modifiers. A prepositional phrase usually functions as an adjective (*The boy in green stood up*) or as an adverb (*He walked to the speaker's platform*). (See pp. 264–65.)

present participle   See *participle.*

present perfect tense   See *tense.*

present tense   See *tense.*

pretentious writing   Writing that is more elaborate than the situation requires, usually full of fancy phrases and showy words. (See pp. 528–29.)

primary source   Firsthand information, such as an eyewitness account of events; a diary, speech, or other historical document; a work of literature or art; a report of a survey or experiment; and one's own interview, observation, or correspondence. Contrast *secondary source.* (See p. 577.)

principal clause   A main or independent clause. See *clause.*

principal parts   The plain form, past-tense form, and past participle of a verb. See *verb forms.* (See pp. 294–96.)

problem-solution organization   The arrangement of material to state and explain a problem and then to propose and explain a solution. (See pp. 50, 90.)

process analysis   The explanation of how something works or how to do something. (See pp. 35, 107.)

progressive tense   See *tense.*

pronoun   A word used in place of a noun. There are eight types of pronouns:

- **Personal pronouns** refer to a specific individual or to individuals: *I, you, he, she, it, we, they.* (See p. 287.)
- **Indefinite pronouns,** such as *everybody* and *some,* do not refer to specific nouns (*Everybody* speaks). (See pp. 327–28.)
- **Relative pronouns**—*who, whoever, which, that*—relate groups of words to nouns or pronouns (*The book that won is a novel*). (See pp. 273, 287.)
- **Interrogative pronouns**—*who, whom, whose, which, what*—introduce questions (*Who will contribute?*).
- **Intensive pronouns**—personal pronouns plus *-self* or *-selves*—emphasize a noun or other pronoun (*He himself asked that question*). (See pp. 287–88, 855.)

- **Reflexive pronouns** have the same form as intensive pronouns. They indicate that the sentence subject also receives the action of the verb (*They injured <u>themselves</u>*). (See pp. 287–88.)
- **Demonstrative pronouns** such as *this*, *that*, and *such* identify or point to nouns (<u>*This*</u> *is the problem*).
- **Reciprocal pronouns**—*each other* and *one another*—are used as objects of verbs when the subjects are plural (*They loved <u>each other</u>*).

proofreading   Reading and correcting a final draft for misspellings, typographical errors, and other mistakes. (See pp. 72–73.)

proper adjective   See *adjective*.

proper noun   See *noun*.

purpose   For a writer, the chief reason for communicating something about a subject to a particular audience. Purposes are both general (usually explanation or persuasion) and specific (taking into account the subject and desired outcome). (See pp. 17–19.)

quotation   Repetition of what someone has written or spoken. In **direct quotation (direct discourse)**, the person's words are duplicated exactly and enclosed in quotation marks: *Polonius told his son, Laertes, "Neither a borrower nor a lender be."* An **indirect quotation (indirect discourse)** reports what someone said or wrote but not in the exact words and not in quotation marks: *Polonius advised his son, Laertes, not to borrow or lend.*

rational appeal   See *appeals*.

reciprocal pronoun   See *pronoun*.

reflexive pronoun   See *pronoun*.

regional language   Expressions common to the people in a particular geographical area. (See p. 527.)

regular verb   A verb that forms its past tense and past participle by adding *-d* or *-ed* to the plain form: *love, loved, loved; open, opened, opened.* Contrast *irregular verb*. (See p. 297.)

relative clause   A subordinate clause beginning with a relative pronoun such as *who* or *that* and functioning as an adjective.

relative pronoun   See *pronoun*.

restrictive element   See *essential element*.

revising   The stage of the writing process in which one considers and improves the meaning and underlying structure of a draft. Compare *editing*. (See pp. 58–64.)

rhetoric   The principles for finding and arranging ideas and for using language in speech or writing to achieve the writer's purpose in addressing his or her audience.

rhetorical question   A question asked for effect, with no answer expected. The person asking the question either intends to provide the answer or assumes it is obvious: *If we let one factory pollute the river, what does that say to other factories that want to dump wastes there?*

run-on sentence   See *fused sentence*.

sans serif   See *serifs*.

Terms

secondary source   A source reporting or analyzing information in other sources, such as a critic's view of a work of art, a historian's report on eyewitness accounts, or a sociologist's summary of others' studies. Contrast *primary source*. (See p. 577.)

second person   See *person*.

sentence   A complete unit of thought, consisting of at least a subject and a predicate that are not introduced by a subordinating word. Sentences can be classed by structure in four ways. A **simple sentence** contains one main clause: *I'm leaving*. A **compound sentence** contains at least two main clauses: *I'd like to stay, but I'm leaving*. A **complex sentence** contains one main clause and at least one subordinate clause: *If you let me go now, you'll be sorry*. A **compound-complex sentence** contains at least two main clauses and at least one subordinate clause: *I'm leaving because you want me to, but I'd rather stay*. (See pp. 284–85.)

sentence fragment   A sentence error in which a group of words is set off as a sentence even though it begins with a subordinating word or lacks a subject or a predicate or both. (See Chapter 17.)

Fragment	She lost the race. Because she was injured. [*Because*, a subordinating conjunction, makes the underlined clause subordinate.]
Revised	She lost the race because she was injured.
Fragment	He could not light a fire. Thus could not warm the room. [The underlined word group lacks a subject.]
Revised	He could not light a fire. Thus he could not warm the room.

sentence modifier   An adverb or a word or word group acting as an adverb that modifies the idea of the whole sentence in which it appears rather than any specific word: *In fact, people will always complain.*

series   A sequence of three or more items of equal importance: *The children are named John, Hallie, and Nancy*. The items in a series are separated with commas. (See p. 455.)

serifs   Small lines on the characters in type fonts, such as those at the bottom of this A. **Sans serif** type, such as Arial, does not have serifs. (See p. 121.)

setting   The place where the action of a literary work happens. (See p. 764.)

sexist language   Language expressing narrow ideas about men's and women's roles, positions, capabilities, or value. (See pp. 529–31.)

signal phrase   Words that indicate who is being quoted: *"In the future," said Andy Warhol, "everyone will be world-famous for fifteen minutes."* (For punctuating signal phrases, see pp. 458–59. For using signal phrases to integrate quotations, see pp. 644–45.)

simile   See *figurative language*.

simple predicate   See *predicate*.

simple sentence   See *sentence*.

simple subject   See *subject*.

simple tense   See *tense*.

singular   One. See *number*.

slang   Expressions used by the members of a group to create bonds and sometimes exclude others. Most slang is too vague, short-lived, and narrowly understood to be used in any but very informal writing. (See pp. 526–27.)

spatial organization   In a description of a person, place, or thing, the arrangement of details as they would be scanned by a viewer—for instance, from top to bottom or near to far. (See pp. 48 and 88–89.)

specific   See *general and specific.*

split infinitive   The often awkward interruption of an infinitive and its marker *to* by an adverb: *Management decided to immediately introduce the new product.* (See pp. 384–85.)

squinting modifier   See *misplaced modifier.*

standard American English   The dialect of English used and expected by educated writers and readers in colleges and universities, businesses, and professions. (See pp. 177–79, 525–26.)

subject   In grammar, the part of a sentence that names something and about which an assertion is made in the predicate. The **simple subject** consists of the noun alone: *The quick brown fox jumps over the lazy dog.* The **complete subject** includes the simple subject and its modifiers: *The quick brown fox jumps over the lazy dog.* (See pp. 253–54.)

subject complement   See *complement.*

subjective   See *case.*

subjunctive   See *mood.*

subordinate clause   See *clause.*

subordinating conjunction   See *conjunction.*

subordination   The use of grammatical constructions to de-emphasize one element in a sentence by making it dependent on rather than equal to another element: *Although I left six messages for him, the doctor failed to call.* Contrast *coordination.* (See pp. 413–18.)

substantive   A word or word group used as a noun.

suffix   A **derivational suffix** is a letter or group of letters that can be added to the end of a root word to make a new word, often a different part of speech: *child, childish; shrewd, shrewdly; visual, visualize.* An **inflectional suffix** adapts a word to different grammatical relations: *boy, boys; fast, faster; tack, tacked.*

summary   A condensation and restatement of source material in one's own words and sentence structures, useful in reading for comprehending the material (see pp. 152–54) and in research writing for presenting the gist of the original author's idea (pp. 633–34). Summaries appearing in a paper must always be acknowledged in source citations.

superlative   See *comparison.*

syllogism   A form of deductive reasoning in which two premises stating generalizations or assumptions together lead to a conclusion. *Premise: Hot stoves can burn me. Premise: This stove is hot. Conclusion: This stove can burn me.* See also *deductive reasoning.* (See pp. 215–17.)

symbolism   The use of a concrete thing to suggest something larger and more abstract, as a red rose may symbolize passion. (See p. 764.)

Terms

synonyms Words with approximately but not exactly the same meanings, such as *snicker, giggle,* and *chortle.* (See p. 534.)

syntax In sentences, the grammatical relations among words and the ways those relations are indicated.

synthesis Drawing one's own conclusions about the elements within a work (such as the images in a poem) or entire works (entire poems). Synthesis is an essential skill in critical thinking and reading (pp. 157–59, 168), in academic writing (pp. 174–75), and in research writing (pp. 626–28).

tag question A question attached to the end of a statement and consisting of a pronoun, a helping verb, and sometimes the word *not*: *It isn't raining, is it? It is sunny, isn't it?*

tense The form of a verb that expresses the time of its action, usually indicated by the verb's inflection and by helping verbs.

- The **simple tenses** are the **present** (*I race, you go*), the **past** (*I raced, you went*), and the **future,** formed with the helping verb *will* (*I will race, you will go*).
- The **perfect tenses,** formed with the helping verbs *have* and *had,* indicate completed action. They are the **present perfect** (*I have raced, you have gone*), the **past perfect** (*I had raced, you had gone*), and the **future perfect** (*I will have raced, you will have gone*).
- The **progressive tenses,** formed with the helping verb *be* plus the present participle, indicate continuing action. They include the **present progressive** (*I am racing, you are going*), the **past progressive** (*I was racing, you were going*), and the **future progressive** (*I will be racing, you will be going*).

(See p. 312 for a list of tenses with examples.)

theme The main idea of a work of literature. (See p. 764.)

thesis The central, controlling idea of an essay, to which all assertions and details relate. (See p. 36.)

thesis statement A sentence or more that asserts the central, controlling idea of an essay and perhaps previews the essay's organization. (See pp. 36–40.)

third person See *person.*

tone The sense of a writer's attitudes toward self, subject, and readers revealed by words and sentence structures as well as by content. (See pp. 22, 195, 220–21, 763.)

topic The subject of an essay or paragraph.

topic sentence See *paragraph.*

transitional expression A word or phrase, such as *thus* or *for example,* that links sentences and shows the relations between them. (See pp. 94–95 for a list.) The error known as a comma splice occurs when two main clauses related by a transitional expression are separated only by a comma. (See pp. 364–65.)

transitive verb A verb that requires a direct object to complete its meaning. (See pp. 258–59.)

trite expressions (clichés)   Stale expressions that make writing dull and suggest that the writer is careless or lazy. (See p. 544.)

two-word verb   A verb plus a preposition or adverb that affects the meaning of the verb: *jump off, put away, help out.* (See pp. 309–10.)

unity   The quality of an effective essay or paragraph in which all parts relate to the central idea and to each other. (See pp. 50 and 82–85.)

URL (uniform resource locator)   An address for a Web site or document.

variety   Among connected sentences, changes in length, structure, and word order that help readers see the importance and complexity of ideas. (See Chapter 26.)

verb   A word or group of words indicating the action or state of being of a subject. The inflection of a verb and the use of helping verbs with it indicate its tense, mood, voice, number, and sometimes person. See separate listings for each aspect and for *predicate.* (See Chapter 14.)

verbals and verbal phrases   **Verbals** are verb forms used as adjectives (*swimming children*), adverbs (*designed to succeed*), or nouns (*addicted to running*). The verbals in the preceding examples are a participle, an infinitive, and a gerund, respectively. (See separate entries for each type.) Verbal phrases consist of verbals plus objects or modifiers: *Swimming fast, the children reached the raft. Willem tried to unlatch the gate. Running in the park is his only recreation.* (See pp. 267–70.)
  A verbal is a **nonfinite verb:** it cannot serve as the only verb in the predicate of a sentence. For that, it requires a helping verb. (See pp. 267–68.)

verb forms   Verbs have five distinctive forms. The first three are the verb's **principal parts:**

- The **plain form** is the dictionary form: *live, swim.*
- The **past-tense form** adds *-d* or *-ed* to the plain form if the verb is regular: *live, lived.* If the verb is irregular, the plain form changes in some other way, such as *swim, swam.*
- The **past participle** is the same as the past-tense form for regular verbs. For irregular verbs, the past participle may differ (*swum*).
- The **present participle** adds *-ing* to the plain form: *living, swimming.*
- The **-s form** adds *-s* or *-es* to the plain form: *lives, swims.*

verb phrase   A verb consisting of a helping verb and a main verb: *has started, will have been invited.* A verb phrase can serve as the predicate of a clause: *The movie has started.*

verb voice   The form of a verb that tells whether the sentence subject performs the action or is acted upon. In the active voice the subject acts: *We made the decision.* In the passive voice the subject is acted upon: *The decision was made by us.* (See pp. 320–21.)

voice   The sense of oneself projected in one's writing through selection of information, role played in relation to readers, and tone. (See pp. 21–22.)

warrant   A term used for *assumption* in argument. See *assumption.*

Web forum   A discussion group on the Web, open to everyone and organized around subjects.

wiki   A Web site that can be contributed to or modified by anyone who registers to use the site.

word order The arrangement of the words in a sentence, which plays a large part in determining the grammatical relation among words in English.

writing process The activities involved in producing a finished piece of writing. The overlapping stages of the process—developing or planning, drafting, and revising—vary among writers and even for the same writer in different writing situations. (See Chapters 1–3.)

writing situation The unique combination of writer, subject, audience, purpose, and other elements that defines an assignment or occasion and helps direct the writer's choices. (See pp. 12–14.)

Credits

Text and Illustrations

Ali, Agha Shahid. "Postcard from Kashmir," *The Veiled Suite: The Collected Poems*. © 2009 by Agha Shahid Ali. Reprinted by permission of Wesleyan University Press.

Bogdanovich, Peter. *Pieces in Time*. Arbor House Publishing Company, 1973.

Britt, Suzanne. "That Lean and Hungry Look." *Newsweek*, October 9, 1978.

Campbell, Neil A., and Jane B. Reece. *Biology*, 7th edition. Glenview: Benjamin Cummings, 2005, p. 47.

Catton, Bruce. "Grant and Lee: A Study in Contrasts" by Bruce Catton, 1956. Copyright © 1956 United States Capitol Historical Society. Reprinted with permission.

Cunningham, John A., and Peter Selby. "Relighting Cigarettes: How Common Is It?" by John A. Cunningham and Peter Selby, *Nicotine and Tobacco Research*, 9 (5), 621–623, 2007, reprinted by permission of Taylor & Francis Ltd., www.tandf.co.uk/journals.

Devoe, Alan. "Nature's Utmost" by Alan Devoe.

Dyson, Freeman J. From *Disturbing the Universe* by Freeman J. Dyson. Copyright © 1979 by Freeman J. Dyson. Reprinted by permission of Basic Books, a member of Perseus Books Group.

Ferris, Timothy. *Coming of Age in the Milky Way*. HarperCollins, 2003.

Friedman, Thomas L. "It's a Flat World, after All," *The New York Times*, April 3, 2005.

Goreau, Angeline. "Hers: Worthy Women Revisited" by Angeline Goreau. Copyright © 1986 by Angeline Goreau. Originally appeared in *The New York Times*, December 11, 1986. Reprinted by permission of Georges Borchardt, Inc., for the author.

Jeffrey, Mac. "Does Rx Spell Rip-Off?" *The New York Times*, April 7, 1978.

Mayer, Lawrence. "The Confounding Enemy of Sleep." *Fortune*, June, 1974.

Ornstein, Robert. From "A Letter to the Director" by Robert Ornstein, *Human Nature*, August 1978. Reprinted by permission of the author.

Ouchi, William G. *Theory Z*.Addison-Wesley, 1981.

Reston, James, Jr. "You Cannot Refine It." *The New Yorker*, 1985.

Rose, Phyllis. "Shopping and Other Spiritual Adventures" from *Never Say Goodbye* by Phyllis Rose. Doubleday, 1986.

Rosen, Ruth. "Search for Yesterday" by Ruth Rosen, from *Watching Television*, edited by Todd Gitlin. Pantheon Books, 1986.

Sale, Kirkpatrick. "The Environmental Crisis Is Not Our Fault" from *The Nation*, April 30, 1990. Reprinted with permission. For subscription information, call 1-800-333-8536. Portions of each week's *Nation* magazine can be accessed at http://www.thenation.com.

Shor, Juliet B. *The Overworked American*. Basic Books, 1992.

Shteir, Rachel. *The Steal: A Cultural History of Shoplifting*. © 2011 by Rachel Shteir. Used by permission of The Penguin Press, a division of Penguin Group (USA) Inc.

Sowell, Thomas. "Student Loans" from *"Is Reality Optional?" and Other Essays* by Thomas Sowell. Copyright © 1993 by Thomas Sowell. Reprinted by permission of Creators Syndicate.

Staples, Brent. Excerpt from "Black Men and Public Space" by Brent Staples, *Harper's*, December 1986. Copyright © 1986 by Brent Staples. Reprinted by permission of the author.

Tuchman, Barbara. "The Decline of Quality" by Barbara Tuchman, *The New York Times*, November 2, 1980. Copyright © 1980 by Barbara Tuchman. Reprinted by the permission of Russell & Volkening as agents for the author.

UNFPA. "AIDS Clock" from the UNFPA Web site, *www.unfpa.org*, 2008. Produced by UNFPA, the United Nations Population Fund, using data provided by UNAIDS. Design by Allysson Lucca. Reprinted by permission.

Wax, Judith. *Starting in the Middle*. Holt, Rinehart, and Winston, 1979.

Wetzsteon, Ross. "Psychochatter" by Ross Wetzsteon, *Channels Magazine*. © Universal Press Syndicate. Reprinted with permission. All rights reserved.

Woodward, Kenneth L. "Life after Death?" by Kenneth L. Woodward. From *Newsweek*, July 12, 1976. © 1976 Newsweek Inc. All rights reserved. Used by permission and protected by the copyright Laws of the United States. The printing, copying, redistribution, or retransmission of the material without express written permission is prohibited.

Woolf, Virginia. *The Waves*. Harcourt, 1931.

Zinsser, William. *The Lunacy Boom*. Harper & Row, 1970.

Photos

Title page, clockwise from top left: David Fischer/Digital Vision/Getty; Stone/Getty; Jamie Grill/Iconica/Getty; The Image Source/Getty; Andersen Ross/Blend Images/Getty. **9:** Image Source/Getty Images. **118:** Universal/ Courtesy Everett Collection. **127:** NASA. **128:** AP Images. **129 left:** Image Courtesy of The Advertising Archives. **129 right:** Photo Courtesy AB Electrolux. **133:** Bill Aron/PhotoEdit. **134:** Cartoon provided by the author. **141 top:** Loren Santow/Getty Images. **141 bottom:** Bill Aron/PhotoEdit. **143:** David Fischer/Getty Images. **162:** *BoostUp.org*. **166:** Steve Simon. **167:** UNFPA, the UN Population Fund. **183:** *BoostUp.org*. **206:** Army materials courtesy of the US government. **210:** Image courtesy of the National Highway Traffic Safety Administration and the Ad Council. **251:** Steve Cole/Getty Images. **351:** Sabah Arar/AFP/Getty Images. **399:** Steven Hunt/Getty Images. **437:** Paul Taylor/Getty Images. **503:** Shinya Sasaki/NeoVision/Getty Images. **523:** Exactostock/SuperStock. **569:** Jeffrey L. Rotman/Corbis. **596, 597:** Reproduced with permission of EBSCO Publishing, Inc. **621 bottom:** Reprinted by permission from Macmillan Publishers Ltd: *Nature Climate Change* 1, 29–31, copyright 2011. **625:** Environmental Defense Fund. **696:** The Lemelson Center. **753:** Todd Warnock/Getty Images.

Index

Index

Index

Index

Index

Index

Index

Index

Index

Index

Index

Index

Index

Index

Index

Index

Index

Index

Index

W

Index

College is confusing.
We're here to help you.

for A grades

www.etipsforagrades.com

Want help budgeting your money, but don't know who to ask?

Need to declare a major, but can't make up your mind?

Searching for career options but don't know where to go?

Welcome to e-tips for A grades, a site created for students, by students. Get the most out of your college experience with tips and advice from current students and recent grads. Let their wisdom and our tools lead you to your own success!

✔ Improve study habits
✔ Choose a major
✔ Navigate your freshman year
✔ Manage your finances
✔ Tackle college papers
✔ Prepare for your first job

Giveaways! Downloads! Free advice!